FROMMER'S

BERMUDA AND THE BAHAMAS

PLUS TURKS AND CAICOS

DARWIN PORTER

Assisted by
Danforth Prince
and
Margaret Foresman

□

1990–1991

Published by Prentice Hall Trade Division
A Division of Simon & Schuster Inc.
Gulf + Western Building
One Gulf + Western Plaza
New York, New York 10023

ISBN 0-13-332628-4
ISSN 1042-8305

Manufactured in the United States of America

Although every effort was made to ensure the accuracy of price information appearing in this book, it should be kept in mind that prices can and do fluctuate in the course of time.

CONTENTS

PART TWO: THE BAHAMAS

PART THREE: TURKS AND CAICOS

MAPS

A DISCLAIMER: I don't have to tell you that whatever the level of inflation, prices do rise. In researching this book, I have made every effort to obtain up-to-the-minute prices, but even the most conscientious researcher cannot keep up with the constantly changing prices of the travel industry. As this guide goes to press, I believe I have obtained the most reliable data possible. Nonetheless, in the lifetime of this edition—particularly in its second year (1991)—the wise traveler will add 15% to the prices quoted throughout these pages.

WHAT THE SYMBOLS MEAN: Travelers to The Bahamas and Bermuda may at first be confused by classifications on rate sheets. I've used these same classifications in this guide. One of the most common rates is **MAP,** meaning "modified American plan." Simply put, that usually means room, breakfast, and dinner, unless the room rate has been quoted separately, and then it means only breakfast and dinner. **CP** means continental plan—that is, room and a light breakfast. **EP** is European plan, which means room only. **AP** (American plan) is the most expensive rate of all, because it includes not only your room but also three meals a day. To make matters even more confusing, travelers to Bermuda often see **BP** (Bermuda plan) rates quoted. That means a room and a full "Bermudian breakfast."

INTRODUCTION

FROMMER'S BERMUDA AND THE BAHAMAS

□ □ □

All the descriptive clichés ever used to describe tropical islands—in either the Atlantic or the Pacific—are applicable to the subjects of this book, Bermuda and The Bahamas. Sun-drenched bits of land where unpolluted waters ranging from pale green to deep turquoise lave clean white or pink sand beaches . . . vines and trees blossoming in a riot of color—white, pale gold, orchid, blue, orange, and bright red . . . smiling faces welcoming you to a touch of paradise. All these await you where the sea waters of the Atlantic are pierced by land.

The brilliance of blooming plants—oleander, hibiscus, bougainvillea, poinciana (flamboyant), and poinsettia, to name a few—complements the homes painted white, light pink, yellow, green, blue, and other pastels. Bananas and oranges and exotic fruits grow in profusion. No frost, no snow are ever seen, and the flow of warm ocean currents together with the gentle trade winds blowing westward make the two island chains called Bermuda and The Bahamas the stuff that dreams are made of for the vacationer.

It doesn't seem possible that these two island countries could be so similar, lying as they do some 800 miles apart, but they are spiritually linked in climate and culture.

The Tropic of Cancer cuts the Bahamian archipelago almost in half, and Bermuda is far north of the tropical latitude, but both have pleasant climatic conditions year-round, with sunshine all but a few days of the year. The chief source of Bermuda's mild climate, matching that of The Bahamas, is the Gulf Stream, that broad belt of warm water formed by equatorial currents, whose northern reaches separate the islands of Bermuda from North America and, with the prevailing northeast winds, temper the wintry blasts that sweep across the Atlantic from west and north.

Both Bermuda and The Bahamas were settled in recent history by people from the British Isles, and certain ties to Britain still exist in both countries. (Today, Bermuda is a self-governing colony of Great Britain, and the Commonwealth of The Bahamas is a member of the Commonwealth of Nations, of which the British monarch is the symbolic head.) The histories of these two island entities reveal striking similarities in their loyalty to Britain at the time of the American Revolution, sympathy with the Confederacy at the time of the American Civil War, which led to involvement in blockade running, and their prosperity from rum-running when Prohibition was supposed to de-alcoholize the United States.

Most early landowners in both Bermuda and The Bahamas were also slave-owners until the government of Great Britain ordered emancipation. The islanders of African racial stock long ago outnumbered the white population, and in fairly recent years have become leaders in their countries.

They're alike, yet the little Bermuda island chain and the big Bahamian archipelago are not really twins. The difference in size makes a visit to one subtly unlike a visit to the other. I find both of them inviting and rewarding in either winter or summer.

Also described in this book are the Turks and Caicos Islands, which lie entirely within the tropics at the southern end of The Bahamas. Considering the distance between The Bahamas and Bermuda, Turks and Caicos are virtually only a stone's throw from the southernmost Bahamian islands, Haiti, and Cuba.

A British Crown Colony, Turks and Caicos are in the process of developing new tourist facilities to supplement those they already possess. If you'd like to see what other of the neighboring islands of The Bahamas and on down in the Caribbean were like some 20 to 25 years ago, I suggest a trip to Turks and Caicos before development proceeds too far.

The political climate of Bermuda, The Bahamas, and Turks and Caicos makes them comfortable for visitors, a claim that cannot be made wholesale for islands to the south in the Caribbean.

Swim in gin-clear waters, lie in the tanning sun on a beach shaded by a row of palm trees, listen to the murmur of the surf, sip a goombay smash, and frolic to the sound of drums. These islands offer the chance to visit a different world only hours away from home.

WHICH ISLAND IS FOR YOU? This question may seem too obvious at first, but it is a legitimate one. A general answer is easy: Bermuda or The Bahamas? The images of both island countries are so fixed in the vacationer's mind that most visitors know at once if they're anxious to enjoy hospitality Bermudian style or in the Bahamian way.

Deep in the heart of winter, if you want good beach weather, your days spent in the sun, your nights in a casino, then it's definitely The Bahamas for you.

But if it's a sunny May day, then all the spring flowers in full bloom may lure you to Bermuda, where you can sail in crystal waters, basking in fresh air and feeling that it was worth the effort to have survived another long, cold winter.

On the other hand, if it's to be Turks and Caicos, that will take more of a hard sell. Few visitors have ever heard of them.

Sunny Bermuda, lying 570 miles east of the Carolina coast, is usually thought of as a single destination, even though it is made up of some 300 islands and islets.

The confusion comes with The Bahamas, that maze is some 700 low coral islands and islets. Here, there is a bewildering variety of islands—each one different—which have hotels, restaurants, flight connections, whatever. Knowing where to go presents a problem, and forms one of the main "reasons why" of this guide.

If you, too, are confused, know that you are in good company. The first European tourist, Christopher Columbus, had the same problem back in 1492. He is said to have made his first footprints in the western hemisphere on a Bahamian island. To Isabella back home in Spain, he wrote in a rapturous letter, "I saw so many islands I could hardly decide which to visit first." As far as decisions go, things haven't changed that much for today's southbound, sun-seeking tourist.

As diverse in mood as they are in number, the islands of The Bahamas are each gifted with a distinctive sparkle and style, even when part of the same nation. The short trip from Nassau to Harbour Island, for example, takes you from a glittering world of cruise ships, casinos, and high-rise hotels to a nostalgic island peopled with "Brilanders," as they call themselves. Here, in a world of pastel-painted clapboard and stone houses, you go back in time, meeting descendants of Loyalists who fled America after the Revolution. Dunmore Town might strike you as some tropical outpost of New England.

Likewise, Turks and Caicos, hidden between Miami and Puerto Rico, is another island colony where you'll need to know where you're going. Grand Turk, for example, is quite different from Salt Cay. And then there's North Caicos, as opposed to South Caicos. You might be torn between Providenciales or Pine Cay.

Wherever you travel—be it Bermuda, The Bahamas, or Turks and Caicos—know that you're not in the Caribbean. Although all three island countries may have similarities in climate and culture to the Caribbean, they are not geographically a part of it.

The question of a specific destination depends largely on who you are and what your vacation goals are—to snorkel and scuba-dive at remote Rum Cay; to attend the annual championship dog shows in Bermuda; to steer a yacht to a secluded cove in some remote out island in the Turks and Caicos; to savor conch stew, herb-flavored shark hash, even cabbage grown out in the backyard of a fisherman's cottage in St. David's Island; to shop in the merchandise-loaded bazaars of Nassau and Freeport/Lucaya; or to play golf on courses designed by Robert Trent Jones on one of the Family Islands.

If deciding on the island or islands to visit seems complicated, selecting a place to live once you get there may be even more perplexing. In both Bermuda and The Bahamas, much less so in Turks and Caicos, a wide range of accommodations awaits your decision: an elegant town house in Nassau that was once owned by royalty and visited by Sir Winston Churchill; an oasis of luxury with gardens on Paradise Island leading to a 12th-century cloister that was imported there by millionaire Huntington Hartford; a simple guesthouse owned by a legendary woman who used to shelter celebrated blacks such as champion Joe Louis (when they weren't allowed in other hotels in Nassau); a masterpiece of nostalgia, a colonial inn complete with gingerbread trim and verandas in New Plymouth; a handsomely restored old Bermudian waterfront villa with a subtropical garden; an appealing private home, built in 1734 in Bermuda, that was once purchased by a pirate as a home for his daughter; or perhaps an inn developed by a 19th-century salt baron in remote South Caicos some 600 miles southeast of Miami.

I've surveyed the widest possible range of accommodations, from deluxe citadels to simply furnished, low-cost cottages near the sea where you can save money by doing your own cookery and housekeeping. There's even a yoga retreat previewed right on Paradise Island with its posh hotels, deluxe restaurants, and casinos.

THE GOALS OF THIS BOOK: In brief, this is a guidebook giving specific, practical details (including prices) about the hotels, restaurants, sightseeing attractions, and nightlife of Bermuda, The Bahamas, and Turks and Caicos. Establishments in *all* price ranges have been documented and described, from the classily elegant Graycliff Hotel and Restaurant in Nassau (where everybody from Winston Churchill to Paul McCartney has stayed) to "mom and pop" locally run informal inns in the remote Family Islands.

In all cases establishments have been judged by the strict yardstick of value. If they "measured up," they were included in this book—regardless of price classification. The uniqueness of this book, I think, lies in the fact that it could be used by everybody from the yachting set to a free-wheeling, adventure-seeking collegian heading for Bermuda for his or her spring vacation.

The major focus of this book is not centered on the impecunious whose sole resources jingle in their pockets, or the affluent whose gold rests in numbered accounts in the Cayman Islands. Rather, my chief concern is the average, middle-income voyager who'd like to patronize some of the less documented hotels of Bermuda, The Bahamas, and Turks and Caicos, those places travel agents are sometimes reluctant to tell you about because the commission is not high.

This guide attempts to lead the reader through the maze of attractions such as Old Nassau, then introduce him or her to a number of less publicized locales such as Cat Island in The Bahamas. Most important, the hours of operation and the prices of admission of attractions have been detailed.

All these specifics are presented against a backdrop of history and culture that has spanned centuries, ever since the Age of Discovery when flagships of every major European power cruised through these blue waters.

On the trail of Columbus followed such other explorers as Ponce de León, who sought the Fountain of Youth. The influence of the colonial powers remains. For example, in Nassau the judges still wear white wigs the way they do in England. But at night in some local club, you hear the drumbeat born in Africa long ago.

I think this guide has struck the proper balance among sightseeing attractions, hotels, and restaurants, as well as fun-time resorts, good shopping buys, the sporting life (such as tennis, golf, scuba, and snorkel holidays), and nighttime diversions.

A TRAVELER'S ADVISORY: "How safe are the islands?" is one of the questions most often asked by the first-time visitor, and in some ways it's one of the most difficult to answer. Can a guidebook writer safely recommend traveling to New York, Miami, or some other major American metropolis? Are you, in fact, free from harm in your own home?

The "attitude toward the visitor" takes on a wide range of meaning depending on whose attitude you are talking about. In this guide, I cover three separate island nations, two of which have broken, at least on paper, from a colonial power—in this case, Britain—that has dominated their cultures for years, and another, Turks and Caicos, which prefers to retain its safe links with the past.

That attitude I mentioned might mean friendliness and hospitality, or it could encompass everything from indifferent service in a hotel dining room to theft and perhaps violence.

The tourist boards of Bermuda and The Bahamas are sensitive to the treatment of visitors, because their nations' fragile economies depend on how many people their islands attract. Rudeness, room burglaries, anything that results in unfavorable publicity can cause damage. As a result, The Bahamas, for example, is taking steps to make its own people more aware of the importance of tourism, and to encourage them to treat and respect their guests as they themselves would want to be treated if traveling in a foreign land.

Of course, many of the problems in the past have come from the tourists themselves. A white person arriving in a predominantly black society such as The Bahamas may feel threatened—or worse, superior—and that can create difficulties. The people of Bermuda, The Bahamas, and Turks and Caicos must be given their respect and dignity. A smile usually wins a smile.

In addition, many of the islanders are deeply religious, and are offended by tourists who wear bikinis on shopping expeditions, such as along Nassau's Bay Street. One Bahamian woman who runs a small guesthouse was shocked to see young American males, under the influence of marijuana, pull off their clothes and run nude up and down the beach. She was yet more horrified when her two teenage daughters witnessed the same scene.

There is less crime in Bermuda than in Nassau and Freeport. Bermuda is about as safe as one of the Family Islands, such as Harbour Island, off the coast of Eleuthera. Turks and Caicos, on the other hand, like The Bahamas, have attracted much drug peddling and smuggling, and it's a destination that requires far more caution than you'd need in Bermuda.

But even in Bermuda only foolish visitors (as happens every year) would leave such valuables as cameras and cash-stuffed purses lying unattended on the beach when they go for a swim. Would you be so careless of your possessions in any town or city in Europe or America? Bahamian tourist officials often warn visitors, "If you've got it, don't flaunt it."

Problems do exist, and tomorrow's headlines in Nassau may speak of an attack on a tourist or violence of some sort. But these are rare events and certainly not the commonplace occurrences they are in Miami, which lies just a short flight away.

Know that most of the people of Bermuda, The Bahamas, and Turks and Caicos are proud, very proper, and most respectable, and if you treat them as such, they will likely treat you in the same way. Others in these islands—certainly the minority, but a visible minority, especially in Nassau and Freeport—are downright antagonistic. Some, in fact, are skunks. But, then, any country on the globe has its share of that type.

Some islands are more hospitable to tourists than others. Your greeting in the Exumas is likely to be friendlier than it is in more jaded destinations such as Paradise Island.

To show how difficult it is to assess the honesty and friendliness of a people, let me cite one example. By accident I left a travel bag containing documents, cash, credit cards, and traveler's checks in the back seat of a taxi. The driver pulled out before the bag could be retrieved. A bartender at the hotel tracked down the driver while he still had the bag on his person. Under threat of calling the police, the bartender forced the driver to turn over the property. Both were citizens of the same country, but in honesty, integrity, and responsibility, they were a world apart—just like the people in your hometown.

TRAVELING IN WINTER: The so-called season in The Bahamas and Turks and Caicos runs roughly from the middle of December to the middle of April. Bermuda, on the other hand, begins its season around Easter, lasting until November. Differing from Bermuda, hotels in The Bahamas and Turks and Caicos charge their highest prices during the peak winter period when visitors fleeing from the cold north winds crowd into the islands. Winter is the dry season in The Bahamas and in Turks and Caicos, and most of the days are invariably sunny.

During the winter months, make reservations two to three months in advance, and if you rely on writing directly to the hotels, know that the mails are often unreliable and take a long time (if your letter gets through at all). At certain hotels in The Bahamas it is virtually impossible to secure reservations at Christmas and during the heavily booked period of February and early March. One hotel in Eleuthera books its rooms in February about a year in advance.

Instead of writing directly to reserve your own room, it's better to book through one of the many Stateside representatives that all major and many minor hotels use, or else to deal directly with a travel agent. If you don't want to do that, you should telephone the hotel of your choice or call the Bahamas reservation service (more about that later). If speaking directly to a hotel, agree on terms, then rush a deposit to hold your room.

Air-conditioned by trade winds, The Bahamas has surprisingly slight temperature variations, ranging between 75° and 85° Fahrenheit in both winter and summer.

It's a different story in Bermuda. Because Bermuda, being farther north in the Atlantic, is much cooler in winter than either The Bahamas or Turks and Caicos, and its slow season begins in December, lasting until around the first of March when business starts to pick up. Many hotels, therefore, quote their low-season rates in winter. During the autumn and winter, many hotels quote some very attractively priced package deals, and you may want to inquire about what is currently being offered at the time of your projected visit. Other hotels, because of lack of business, shut down for a week or two, maybe even a month or two.

20% TO 60% REDUCTIONS: The off-season in The Bahamas and Turks and Caicos—roughly from mid-April to mid-December (although this varies from hotel to hotel)—virtually amounts to a summer sale. Except that summer in this context is eight months long, stretched out to include spring and autumn, often ideal times for travel to these islands.

Bermuda, as mentioned, is a different story: it charges its highest rates in spring, summer, and early fall, then lowers its tariffs attractively during the winter months when the temperature drops (for exact descriptions of the climate of Bermuda, refer to the ABCs in Chapter II).

However, even if the Burmudian off-season comes at a different time of year than the Bahamian, these off-seasons have one important thing in common: in most cases, hotel rates are slashed a startling 20% to 60%, and these rate reductions are emphasized in this guide by being set in *italics*.

It's a bonanza for cost-conscious travelers, especially families who like to go on vacations together. Unbelievable, you say. You need proof.

In the chapters ahead, I'll spell out in specific dollars the amounts hotels charge off-season.

GOOMBAY PACKAGES: Every year several hotels in The Bahamas offer a value-packed Goombay package, which is usually available right up to December 16.

In Nassau/Paradise Island/Cable Beach, the Great Goombay packages are usually for three days and two nights. All rates, incidentally, are per person, based on double occupancy. Air fare is extra.

On Grand Bahama Island, the Goombay are packages for a four-day/three-night stay. And Goombay Getaway packages in the Family Islands are often for four days and three nights.

HOTELS AND RESORTS: One of the most galling experiences you can have in Bermuda or The Bahamas is to run into someone from your hometown and learn that he or she is staying in the same hotel that you are, even enjoying an ocean view as opposed to your "garden view," and paying some $200 to $300 less per week than you are.

That happens more often than you might imagine. A lot of it stems from a zeal among hoteliers, especially during the slow months, to promote business. There are package deals galore, and though they have many disadvantages, they are always cheaper than rack rates. (A rack rate is what an individual pays who literally walks in from the street.) Therefore it's always good to go to a reliable travel agent to find out what, if anything, is available in the way of a land-and-air package before booking into a particular accommodation.

There is no rigid classification of hotel properties in the islands. The word "deluxe" is often used—or misused—when "first class" might have been a more appropriate term. First class itself often isn't. For that and other reasons, I've presented fairly detailed descriptions of the properties, so that you'll get an idea of what to expect once you're there. However, even in the deluxe and first-class resorts and hotels, don't expect top-rate service and efficiency. "Things," as they are called in the islands, don't seem to work as well here as they do in certain fancy resorts of California, Florida, or Europe. Life here has its disadvantages. When you go to turn on the shower, sometimes you get water and sometimes you don't. You may even experience power failures.

Facilities often determine the choice of a hotel. For example, if golf is your passion, you may want to book into a resort hotel in Bermuda, perhaps Castle Harbour. If scuba-diving is your goal, then head, say, for Small Hope Bay Lodge on Andros. Regardless of your particular interest, there is probably a hotel for you. All the big, first-class resort hotels have swimming pools. Usually a beach is nearby if not directly in front of the hotel property. If you want to save money, you can book into one of the more moderate accommodations less desirably located. Then, often for only a small fee, you can use the facilities of the larger and more expensive resorts. However, don't try to "crash" a resort. It's better to be a paying customer. Often if you have lunch or patronize the bar, you can stick around and enjoy the afternoon. Policies vary from resort to resort: some are stricter than others.

In the modern properties of Bermuda and The Bahamas, your hotel room is likely to look like one you had in Florida or California—that is, two standard oversize beds, a private bath, sometimes a TV, and perhaps a balcony or small terrace. The larger hotels are likely to have more than one choice for dining, perhaps a "gourmet" restaurant as well as a coffeeshop. The chain hotels, such as the Princess, are highly reliable.

Some islands, such as Paradise Island, have a deluxe property, for example, the Ocean Club, that is even more luxurious than your typical first-class chain operation. These accommodations are always listed at the top of my recommendations. If economy is one of the major requirements for your holiday, then read the recommendations from the bottom up.

Many Family Islands in The Bahamas, such as the Exumas, Cat Island, Long Island, the Berry Islands, and Andros, have very limited tourist facilities, but many readers prefer to seek out these offbeat retreats. Others, wishing to be in the center of the tourist hustle-bustle, will head to such old reliable meccas as Bermuda, Nassau, Freeport, Cable Beach, and Paradise Island.

THE GUESTHOUSE: An entirely different type of accommodation from the hotels just cited is available at the guesthouse in Bermuda and The Bahamas. The guesthouse is where many Bermudians and Bahamians themselves stay when they're traveling in their own islands. Some of these establishments are quite comfortable, and in fact Bermuda has the finest guesthouses of all when compared with either the Caribbean or The Bahamas. Some are almost luxurious, in addition to giving you a chance to live with a Bermudian family. Some of these guesthouses even have swimming pools, and private bath with each room. You may or may not have air conditioning.

The rooms are sometimes cooled by ceiling fans or trade winds blowing through open windows at night. Of course, don't expect the facilities of a fabulous resort hotel, but for value the guesthouse can't be topped. Staying in a guesthouse, you can journey over to a big beach resort, using its facilities for a small charge.

In the Family Islands of The Bahamas, the guesthouses are not as luxurious for the most part as those of Bermuda. Although bereft of frills in general, the Bahamian guesthouses I've recommended are clean, decent, and safe for families or single women. Many of the cheapest ones are not places you'd like to live in all night and day, because of their simple, modern furnishings (often worn) and other amenities (or lack of them).

However, many of today's new breed of traveler to The Bahamas don't want to spend more than eight hours in their rooms anyway. You'll find them on the beach, snorkeling or going scuba-diving, and at night patronizing the out-of-the-way taverns that serve local food, and just getting to know the people. To this type of traveler a hotel is a mere convenience, a place to go to for sleep after an activity-filled day and a nightlife-packed evening.

Dressing up for dinner and otherwise practicing a routine familiar at American country clubs may not appeal to many of today's more adventurous travelers, who often arrive in The Bahamas with a bikini, a T-shirt, and a pair of jeans.

In Bermuda, The Bahamas, and to a very limited extent in Turks and Caicos, the term "guesthouse" can mean anything. Sometimes so-called guesthouses are really like simple motels built around swimming pools. Others are small individual cottages, with their own kitchenettes, constructed around a main building in which you'll often find a bar and restaurant serving local food.

Giving fair warning, I'll point out that many of these guesthouses are very basic. You must remember that nearly every piece of furniture must be imported, often at outrageous costs to the owner of the establishment. Salt spray on metal or fabric takes a serious toll, and chipped paint is commonplace. Bathrooms can fall in the vintage category, and sometimes the water isn't heated. But when it's 85° to 92° Fahrenheit outside, you don't need hot water.

Guesthouses are rarely built on the best beaches, but sometimes they lie across the street or perhaps a five- to ten-minute stroll from the sands. That's why they can afford to charge such low prices.

Although not said to disappoint, these comments are made to anyone experiencing cultural shock or to a first-time visitor to The Bahamas who may never have encountered such a leisurely, beachcombing life as prevails there.

Having said that, let me add another word about the hospitality and convivial atmosphere often created in these small places, which not only attract locals, but are themselves most often locally owned and run.

Staying in a guesthouse is for the serious tourist who'd like to meet some of the local people as well as fellow visitors with similar interests. Often, spontaneous barbecues are staged, and even in some of the smaller places a steel band is brought in on a Saturday night for a "jump-up."

SELF-CATERING HOLIDAYS: Particularly if you're a family or a congenial group, a housekeeping holiday can be one of the least expensive ways to stay in Bermuda, The Bahamas, or Turks and Caicos. These types of accommodations are now available on all the islands previewed in this guide. Sometimes you can rent individual cottages; others are housed in one building. Some are private homes rented when the owners are away. All have small kitchens or kitchenettes where you can do your home-cooking after shopping for groceries, including freshly caught grouper or some Bahamian lobster. Life this way is easy and pleasant. You can get up anytime you choose and prepare your own breakfast with eggs just as you like them. You can even turn shopping into an adventure, particularly at a local marketplace where you may see fresh vegetables such as christophine (a kind of squash) that you've never tried before. The fruits, such as soursop, are luscious as well.

A housekeeping holiday, however, doesn't always mean you'll have to do maid's work. Most of the self-catering establishments have maid service included in the weekly rental, and you're given a supply of fresh linen as well.

Cooking most of your meals yourself and dining out on occasion, such as when a neighboring big hotel has a beachside barbecue with entertainment, is the surest way of keeping holiday costs at a minimum.

IS THE SUMMER TOO HOT? This question applies to The Bahamas or to Turks and Caicos, not to Bermuda, which is overrun with tourists in summer.

For many travelers, the islands of The Bahamas simply do not exist except when fearsome winds beat around corners and ice and slush pile up on the sidewalks up north. Regrettably, because everybody wants to visit The Bahamas then —"just anyplace warm"—"the season" developed. Knowing that they have a hot item to sell—warm, sandy beaches when much of North America is hit by blizzards—hotel entrepreneurs charge the maximum for their accommodations in winter, the "maximum" meaning all the traffic will bear.

When North America warms up, vacationers head for Bermuda (where hotel owners then up their prices) or to such Stateside destinations as Cape Cod or the beaches of California, forgetting The Bahamas. Some people think The Bahamas are a caldron in summer. Actually, the mid-80s prevail throughout most of this region, and trade winds make for comfortable days and nights, even in cheaper places that don't have air conditioning.

Truth is, you're better off in The Bahamas most of the time than you are suffering through a roaring August heat wave in either Chicago or New York.

Dollar for dollar, you'll save more money by renting a house or self-sufficient unit in The Bahamas than you would on Cape Cod, Fire Island, Laguna Beach, or the coast of Maine.

In essence, because of the trade winds and the Gulf Stream, The Bahamas, unlike Bermuda, is virtually "seasonless."

OTHER OFF-SEASON ADVANTAGES: In addition to price slashes at hotels, there are some other important reasons for visiting The Bahamas (or Turks and Caicos) in spring, summer, and autumn.

□ After the winter hordes have left, a less hurried way of life prevails. You'll have a better chance to appreciate the food, the culture, and the local customs.

□ Because summer business has grown in recent years, resort facilities are often offered at reduced rates. This is likely to include, among other activities, snorkeling, windsurfing, parasailing, boating, and scuba-diving.

□ To survive, resort boutiques often feature summer sales, hoping to clear the merchandise they didn't move in February to make way for the new season. They've ordered stock for the coming winter, and must clean their shelves and clear their racks. Duty-free items in free-port shopping areas are draws all year too.

□ You can often walk in unannounced at a top restaurant and get a seat for dinner, a seat that would have been denied you in winter unless you'd made a reservation far in advance. When the waiters are less hurried, you'll get far better service too.

□ The endless waiting game is over in the off-season. No waiting for a rented car (only to be told none is available). No long tee-up for golf. More immediate access to the tennis courts and water sports.

□ The atmosphere is more cosmopolitan in the off-season than it is in high season, mainly because of the influx of Europeans. You'll no longer feel as if you're at a Canadian or American outpost. Also, the Bermudians and the Bahamians often travel in off-season, and your holiday can become more of a people-to-people experience.

□ Some package-tour fares are as much as 20% cheaper, and individual excursion fares are also reduced between 5% and 10%.

□ All accommodations, including airline seats and hotel rooms, are much easier to obtain.

□ Summer is the time for family travel, which is not possible during the winter season. Or parents can travel while children are away at camp.

□ Finally, the very best of the wintertime attractions remain undiminished —that is, sea, sand, sun, and surf.

FOR SINGLE TRAVELERS: If you've ever read bargain-travel advertisements, you'll sometimes see an asterisk, indicating below (in fine print) that the tempting deal being presented is "based on double occupancy." If you're a lone wolf or without a traveling companion, you'll often get hit with a painful supplement called a surcharge in the industry. That surcharge can be at least 35% and perhaps a lot more. The hotelier in Bermuda or The Bahamas, of course, likes to shelter at least two in a room, and sometimes crowd in three or four. It's the same room, and two or three guests spend a lot more on drinks, water sports, and food.

In addition to the cruises for singles that have gained mass popularity in the past few years, there is another way to keep costs bone-trimmed and take advantage of some of the package tours, cruises, and cut-rate hotel deals. But it means you have to join a club.

One of the most successful groups is **Gramercy's Singleworld,** 401 Theodore Frend Ave., Rye, NY 10580 (tel. 914/967-3334), which for more than 30 years has catered to single and unattached persons—the never-married, the separated, divorced, widowed, and those traveling alone. They have no age limits, although most of their club members are under 35. Certain cruise and tour departures are designated for people of all ages or people under 35.

Anyone who is single or traveling alone is eligible for membership. The membership fee is $20 (nonrefundable). However, it is effective from the date of departure for one full year. Singleworld emphasizes that they are *not* a lonely hearts club, *not* a matrimonial bureau, and do *not* guarantee equal numbers of men and women in their groups.

Because Singleworld has more than 500 departures a year, the prices offered for the cruise and tour departures are at wholesale. In addition, you can avoid the extra expense of a single-room accommodation by sharing a unit with another member. Most cruises are for seven days, although there are some for three or four days.

WHAT TO WEAR: In this day when dress is such a personal statement, I can no longer present checklists of what to pack. Many beachcombers arrive in The Bahamas or Turks and Caicos carrying with them what they have on their backs, perhaps a toothbrush and a bikini.

On the other hand, the dress code in Bermuda is much stricter. It's also much more formal at certain upper-bracket resorts not only on Paradise Island but in the Family Islands. One resort in particular shuns the idea of women appearing in slacks. In the ABCs of each country, I'll try to give more specific guidelines.

In general, however, most travelers are aware of clothing needed in subtropical or tropical climates. You'll want to dress casually to stay cool, and you'll want to select apparel that is easy to clean, of course.

If you're living at deluxe and first-class hotels, women should be prepared with at least an evening cocktail dress. Some restaurants and hotels—and admittedly it's a hopeless battle—still require men to wear a jacket and tie in the evening.

Treading the balance between a personal statement in apparel and concern for others, clothing in Bermuda and The Bahamas becomes a matter of taste. Some resorts still have dress codes—that is, men are required to wear jackets after

6 p.m. Others, in despair, have taken to posting signs suggesting that clients should be "casual but chic." You are allowed to interpret that according to your wishes. I have attempted to give clues in individual writeups when hotels have set particular standards of dress.

Obviously, you should take coordinated clothing so that you can travel lightly.

AN INVITATION TO READERS: Like all Frommer books, *Frommer's Bermuda and The Bahamas* hopes to maintain a continuing dialogue between its author and its readers. All of us share a common goal—to travel as widely and as well as possible, at the best value for our money. And in achieving that, your comments and suggestions can be of tremendous help. Therefore if you've come across a particularly appealing hotel, restaurant, shop, even a sightseeing attraction, please don't keep it to yourself.

Your letters need not apply to new places only, but to hotels and restaurants already recommended in this guide. The fact that a listing appears in this edition doesn't give it squatter's rights in future publications. If its services have deteriorated, its chef grown stale, its prices risen unfairly, whatever, these failings should be known.

Even if you enjoyed every place and found every description on target—that too can cheer many a gray day. Every letter will be read by me personally, although I find it well-nigh impossible to answer each and every one. Send your comments to Darwin Porter, c/o Frommer Books, Prentice Hall Trade Division, Gulf + Western Building, One Gulf + Western Plaza, New York, NY 10023.

TIME OUT FOR A COMMERCIAL: Many visitors erroneously consider The Bahamas, and even sometimes Bermuda, part of the Caribbean. As mentioned before, that isn't the case. One of the world's greatest travel oases, the Caribbean is a world (or worlds) unto itself.

Technically, it begins only 50 miles south of the remotest island covered in this guide. Because it is so vast, and filled with so many countries, including French-, Spanish-, and, naturally, English-speaking ones, the publishers of *Frommer's Bermuda and The Bahamas* since 1980 have also published a big guide to all the countries south of The Bahamas, a chain that stretches to the doorway of South America.

In just a few hours by plane from the North American continent, you're submerged in lands that have absorbed the cultures of other continents, including America, Europe, and Africa. To lead you through the maze of emerging nations and colonial outposts, we have another, much larger guide, called *Frommer's Caribbean,* which is updated annually.

In some ways, these two guides could be called "companions" of each other, because they explore a part of the world that is linked spiritually in climate and culture, even though one describes land bordering and in the Caribbean Sea and the other Bermuda and The Bahamas, Atlantic Ocean nations.

If you develop "island fever" after visiting either Bermuda or The Bahamas, and you want to continue your search for a tropical hideaway, *Frommer's Caribbean* will offer you hundreds of possibilities.

FROMMER'S ™ DOLLARWISE® TRAVEL CLUB—HOW TO SAVE MONEY ON ALL YOUR TRAVELS

In this book we'll be looking at how to get your money's worth in Bermuda and The Bahamas, but there is a "device" for saving money and determining value on *all* your trips. It's the popular, international Frommer's Dollarwise Travel Club, now in its 28th successful year of operation. The club was formed at the urging of numerous readers of the $-A-Day and Frommer Guides, who felt that such an organization could provide continuing travel information and a sense of community to value-minded travelers in all parts of the world. And so it does!

In keeping with the budget concept, the annual membership fee is low and is immediately exceeded by the value of your benefits. Upon receipt of $18 (U.S. residents), or $20 U.S. by check drawn on a U.S. bank or via international postal money order in U.S. funds (Canadian, Mexican, and other foreign residents) to cover one year's membership, we will send all new members the following items:

(1) Any *two* of the following books

Please designate in your letter which two you wish to receive:

Frommer™ $-A-Day® Guides

Europe on $40 a Day
Australia on $30 a Day
Eastern Europe on $25 a Day
England on $40 a Day
Greece on $30 a Day
Hawaii on $50 a Day
India on $25 a Day
Ireland on $35 a Day
Israel on $30 & $35 a Day
Mexico (plus Belize and Guatemala) on $25 a Day
New York on $50 a Day
New Zealand on $40 a Day
Scandinavia on $60 a Day
Scotland and Wales on $40 a Day
South America on $30 a Day
Spain and Morocco (plus the Canary Is.) on $40 a Day
Turkey on $25 a Day
Washington, D.C. & Historic Virginia on $40 a Day

($-A-Day Guides document hundreds of budget accommodations and facilities, helping you get the most for your travel dollars.)

Frommer™ Guides

Australia
Austria and Hungary
Belgium, Holland, & Luxembourg
Bermuda and The Bahamas
Brazil
Canada
Caribbean
Egypt
England and Scotland
France
Germany
Italy
Japan and Hong Kong
Portugal, Madeira, and the Azores
South Pacific
Switzerland and Liechtenstein
Alaska

California and Las Vegas
Florida
Mid-Atlantic States
New England
New York State
Northwest
Skiing USA—East
Skiing USA—West
Southeast and New Orleans
Southeast Asia
Southwest
Texas
USA

(Frommer Guides discuss accommodations and facilities in all price ranges, with emphasis on the medium-priced.)

Frommer™ Touring Guides

Australia
Egypt
Florence
London
Paris
Scotland
Thailand
Venice

(These new, color illustrated guides include walking tours, cultural and historic sites, and other vital travel information.)

Gault Millau

Chicago
France
Italy
London
Los Angeles
New England
New York
San Francisco
Washington, D.C.

(Irreverent, savvy, and comprehensive, each of these renowned guides candidly reviews over 1,000 restaurants, hotels, shops, nightspots, museums, and sights.)

Serious Shopper's Guides

Italy
London
Los Angeles
Paris

(Practical and comprehensive, each of these handsomely illustrated guides lists hundreds of stores, selling everything from antiques to wine, conveniently organized alphabetically by category.)

A Shopper's Guide to the Caribbean

(Two experienced Caribbean hands guide you through this shopper's paradise, offering witty insights and helpful tips on the wares and emporia of more than 25 islands.)

Beat the High Cost of Travel
(This practical guide details how to save money on absolutely all travel items—accommodations, transportation, dining, sightseeing, shopping, taxes, and more. Includes special budget information for seniors, students, singles, and families.)

Bed & Breakfast—North America
(This guide contains a directory of over 150 organizations that offer bed & breakfast referrals and reservations throughout North America. The scenic attractions, and major schools and universities near the homes of each are also listed.)

California with Kids
(A must for parents traveling in California, providing key information on selecting the best accommodations, restaurants, and sightseeing attractions for the particular needs of the family, whether the kids are toddlers, school-age, preteens, or teens.)

Frommer's Belgium
(Arthur Frommer unlocks the treasures of a country overlooked by most travelers to Europe. Discover the medieval charm, modern sophistication, and natural beauty of this quintessentially European county.)

Frommer's Cruises
(This complete guide covers all the basics of cruising—ports of call, costs, fly-cruise package bargains, cabin selection booking, embarkation and debarkation—and describes in detail over 60 or so ships cruising the waters of Alaska, the Caribbean, Mexico, Hawaii, Panama, Canada, and the United States.)

Frommer's Skiing Europe
(Describes top ski resorts in Austria, France, Italy, and Switzerland. Illustrated with maps of each resort area. Includes supplement on Argentinian resorts.)

Guide to Honeymoon Destinations
(A special guide for that most romantic trip of your life, with full details on planning and choosing the destination that will be just right in the U.S. [California, New England, Hawaii, Florida, New York, South Carolina, etc.], Canada, Mexico, and the Caribbean.)

Marilyn Wood's Wonderful Weekends
(This very selective guide covers the best mini-vacation destinations within a 200-mile radius of New York City. It describes special country inns and other accommodations, restaurants, picnic spots, sights, and activities—all the information needed for a two- or three-day stay.)

Manhattan's Outdoor Sculpture
(A total guide, fully illustrated with black and white photos, to more than 300 sculptures and monuments that grace Manhattan's plazas, parks, and other public spaces.)

Motorist's Phrase Book
(A practical phrase book in French, German, and Spanish designed specifically for the English-speaking motorist touring abroad.)

Paris Rendez-Vous
(An amusing and *au courant* guide to the best meeting places in Paris, organized for hour-to-hour use: from power breakfasts and fun brunches, through tea at four or cocktails at five, to romantic dinners and dancing 'til dawn.)

Swap and Go—Home Exchanging Made Easy
(Two veteran home exchangers explain in detail all the money-saving benefits of a home exchange, and then describe precisely how to do it. Also includes information on home rentals and many tips on low-cost travel.)

The Candy Apple: New York for Kids
(A spirited guide to the wonders of the Big Apple by a savvy New York grandmother with a kid's-eye view to fun. Indispensable for visitors and residents alike.)

The New World of Travel
(From America's #1 travel expert, Arthur Frommer, an annual sourcebook with the hottest news and latest trends that's guaranteed to change the way you travel —and save you hundreds of dollars. Jam-packed with alternative new modes of travel that will lead you to vacations that cater to the mind, the spirit, and a sense of thrift.)

Travel Diary and Record Book
(A 96-page diary for personal travel notes plus a section for such vital data as passport and traveler's check numbers, itinerary, postcard list, special people and places to visit, and a reference section with temperature and conversion charts, and world maps with distance zones.)

Where to Stay USA
(By the Council on International Educational Exchange, this extraordinary guide is the first to list accommodations in all 50 states that cost anywhere from $3 to $30 per night.)

(2) Any *one* of the Frommer™ City Guides

Amsterdam
Athens
Atlantic City and Cape May
Boston
Cancún, Cozumel, and the Yucatán
Chicago
Dublin and Ireland
Hawaii
Las Vegas
Lisbon, Madrid, and Costa del Sol
London
Los Angeles
Mexico City and Acapulco
Minneapolis and St. Paul
Montréal and Québec City
New Orleans
New York
Orlando, Disney World, and EPCOT
Paris

Philadelphia
Rio
Rome
San Francisco
Santa Fe, Taos, and Albuquerque
Sydney
Washington, D.C.

(Pocket-size guides to hotels, restaurants, nightspots, and sightseeing attractions covering all price ranges.)

(3) A one-year subscription to *The Dollarwise® Traveler*

This quarterly eight-page tabloid newspaper keeps you up to date on fastbreaking developments in low-cost travel in all parts of the world bringing you the latest money-saving information—the kind of information you'd have to pay $35 a year to obtain elsewhere. This consumer-conscious publication also features columns of special interest to readers: **Hospitality Exchange** (members all over the world who are willing to provide hospitality to other members as they pass through their home cities); **Share-a-Trip** (offers and requests from members for travel companions who can share costs and help avoid the burdensome single supplement); and **Readers Ask . . . Readers Reply** (travel questions from members to which other members reply with authentic firsthand information).

(4) Your personal membership card

Membership entitles you to purchase through the club all Frommer publications for a third to a half off their regular retail prices during the term of your membership.

So why not join this hardy band of international budgeteers and participate in its exchange of travel information and hospitality? Simply send your name and address, together with your annual membership fee of $18 (U.S. residents) or $20 U.S. (Canadian, Mexican, and other foreign residents), by check drawn on a U.S. bank or via international postal money order in U.S. funds to: Frommer's Dollarwise Travel Club, Inc., Gulf + Western Building, One Gulf + Western Plaza, New York, NY 10023. And please remember to specify which *two* of the books in section (1) and which *one* in section (2) you wish to receive in your initial package of members' benefits. Or, if you prefer, use the order form at the end of the book and enclose $18 or $20 in U.S. currency.

Once you are a member, there is no obligation to buy additional books. No books will be mailed to you without your specific order.

PART ONE

BERMUDA

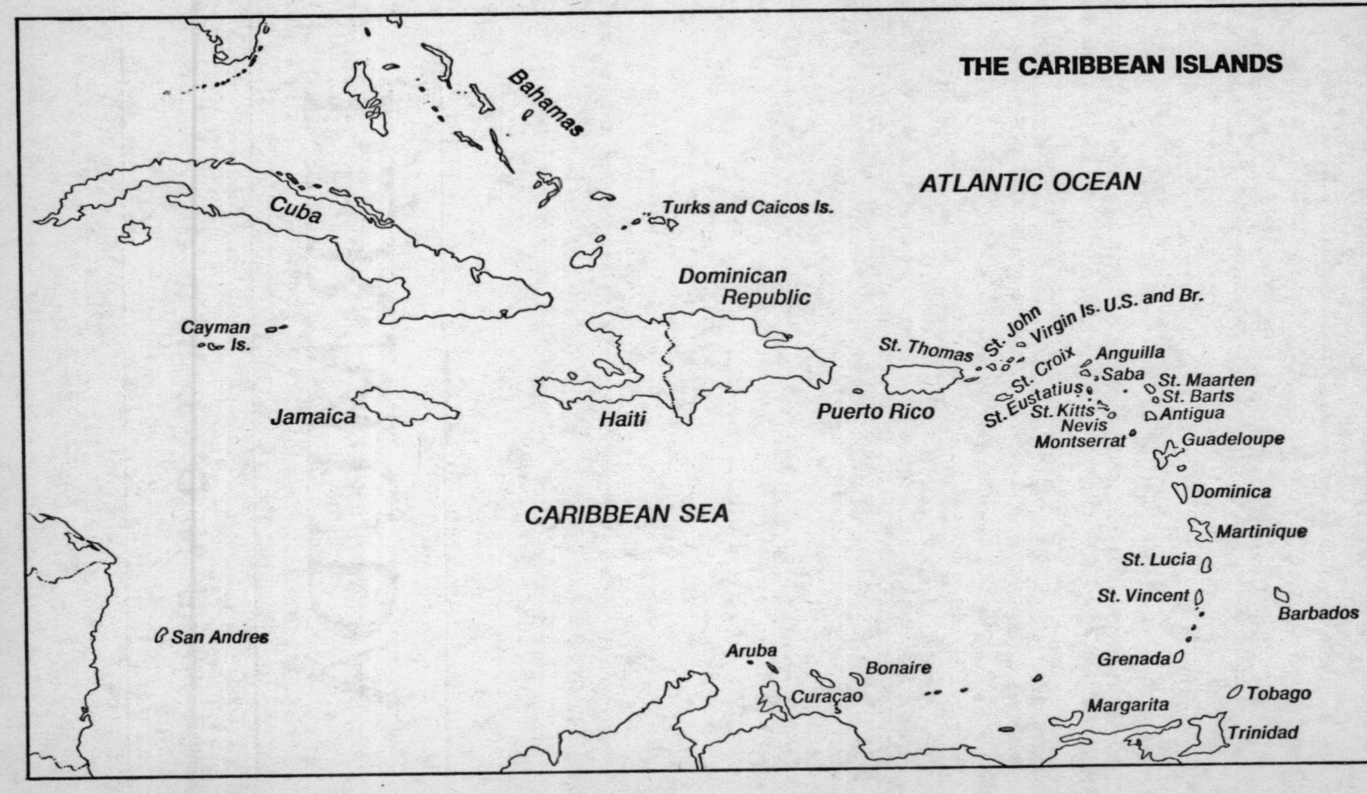
THE CARIBBEAN ISLANDS
Bahamas
ATLANTIC OCEAN
Cuba
Turks and Caicos Is.
Dominican
Republic
Cayman
Is.
St. Thomas
St. John
Virgin Is. U.S. and Br.
Anguilla
St. Croix
Saba
St. Maarten
St. Eustatius
St. Barts
St. Kitts
Antigua
Nevis
Jamaica
Haiti
Puerto Rico
Montserrat
Guadeloupe
Dominica
CARIBBEAN SEA
Martinique
St. Lucia
St. Vincent
Barbados
San Andres
Aruba
Bonaire
Grenada
Curaçao
Tobago
Margarita
Trinidad

CHAPTER I

GETTING TO AND AROUND BERMUDA

□ □ □

Less than two hours from the U.S. coastline, another world unfolds very different from the shores you left behind. Horse-drawn carriages are still seen on the streets of Hamilton (although strictly for tourists), "bobbies" and businessmen go around in Bermuda shorts, judges still wear powdered wigs as they head to Sessions House, and miles and miles of pink sandy beaches await your swimsuit-clad body.

Bermuda has been called one of the "most attractive and civilized places on earth," and it certainly is one of the world's most sophisticated resorts.

Getting to Bermuda has now become easier than ever, thanks to more frequent flights, often direct ones if you live in such key gateway cities as New York, Boston, and Washington, D.C., among many others.

For those who'd like to relive the glamorous days of cruising to Bermuda, several cruise lines sail to Bermuda from spring until late autumn.

In this chapter I'll survey some of the most popular air carriers and their routes from the American mainland, then follow with an overview of going by cruise ship.

Once there, you'll learn about how to get around Bermuda. In Bermuda, transportation is of vital concern to many visitors, because you're forbidden to rent a car and you must use other means of transport: if not the expensive taxi, then a motor-assisted cycle or the old-fashioned pushbike.

In Bermuda, you learn to do things their way, and sometimes that can be part of the fun in going there.

Before I begin with transportation, a slight digression. Seasoned travelers know much about Bermuda, but first-time visitors still persist in thinking that it's a "tropical" island. It isn't. To reach the tropics, you must go much farther south.

Isolated in the Atlantic Ocean, Bermuda enjoys a mild, but not a tropical, climate. The Gulf Stream keeps those polar-bear blasts away from the little island chain. Snow and frost are also avoided. In fact, the term "Bermuda high" has come to mean sunny days and clear skies.

1. FLYING IN

Several airlines fly from the United States into Bermuda, but one that seems particularly committed to the efficient servicing of the island is **American Airlines.** American flies in daily to Bermuda from Boston's Logan Airport and New York's La Guardia. However, in midwinter there are no flights from either city on Tuesday and Wednesday. Otherwise, there's a daily flight from either city.

Most arrivals fly into Bermuda on excursion fares which require no advance bookings and which permit a stopover of between two days and 45 days. For reservations and information, call toll free throughout the United States by dialing 800/433-7300. If you're already in Bermuda and want information about return flights to the mainland, then call 809/293-1420.

American Airlines began its life in 1926 as a St. Louis–based carrier that ferried the mail to and from Chicago. (Charles Lindbergh was one of the airline's first pilots before spearheading, years in advance, the airline's eventual regularly scheduled flights into Paris.) By 1929 the airline had merged with 85 other regional carriers to form the base of what is today one of the world's most respected airlines. American recently emerged in a poll of 30,000 frequent flyers as the top carrier by a Swiss-based consumers' group, and for five consecutive years was judged as the best U.S. domestic carrier by a London-based travel authority.

American is not alone, of course, in flying to Bermuda. Other airlines servicing the area include **Pan American,** which has direct flights from both Boston and New York's JFK Airport. Pan Am was in the vanguard of air service to Bermuda with its celebrated Flying Boats, landing off Darrell's Island.

In 1988, **United Airlines** introduced its first ever service to Bermuda, offering daily nonstop flights from Washington's Dulles Airport. Through the Dulles flight, you can hook up with a series of United Midwest connections which include such cities as Columbus, Cleveland, and Chicago. There is also a connection to Jacksonville, Florida.

British Airways in 1988 began a new service to Bermuda from Tampa, offering nonstop flights on Monday, Wednesday, Thursday, and Saturday, returning in the midafternoon. In addition, BA also offers five flights a week from London.

Eastern Airlines has direct service from New York, Newark, Philadelphia, and Baltimore (although a strike at presstime has disrupted some service).

Delta offers service from Boston and Atlanta. The airline features golf, honeymoon, and tennis packages.

From Canada, **Air Canada** has direct flights from Toronto with connecting services from all of Canada and the New York/Bermuda carriers.

CHARTER FLIGHTS: Charters were once severely restricted in Bermuda. However, a more relaxed situation has led to increased charter traffic to the island chain, which means that many more Canadians and U.S. citizens can now visit Bermuda than in the past. In general, charter flights are not allowed from "gateway" cities such as New York or other points where major international carriers service Bermuda. If the gateway is not serviced by a nonstop flight, then charters can also be permitted. It is an extremely complicated situation that changes yearly or even monthly, and it's best to take your problems to a good travel agent who should know the least expensive and most direct route you can fly from your home to Bermuda.

A long time ago charter flights were extended to the general public. Essentially, they allow visitors to Bermuda to fly at a less expensive fare than on a regu-

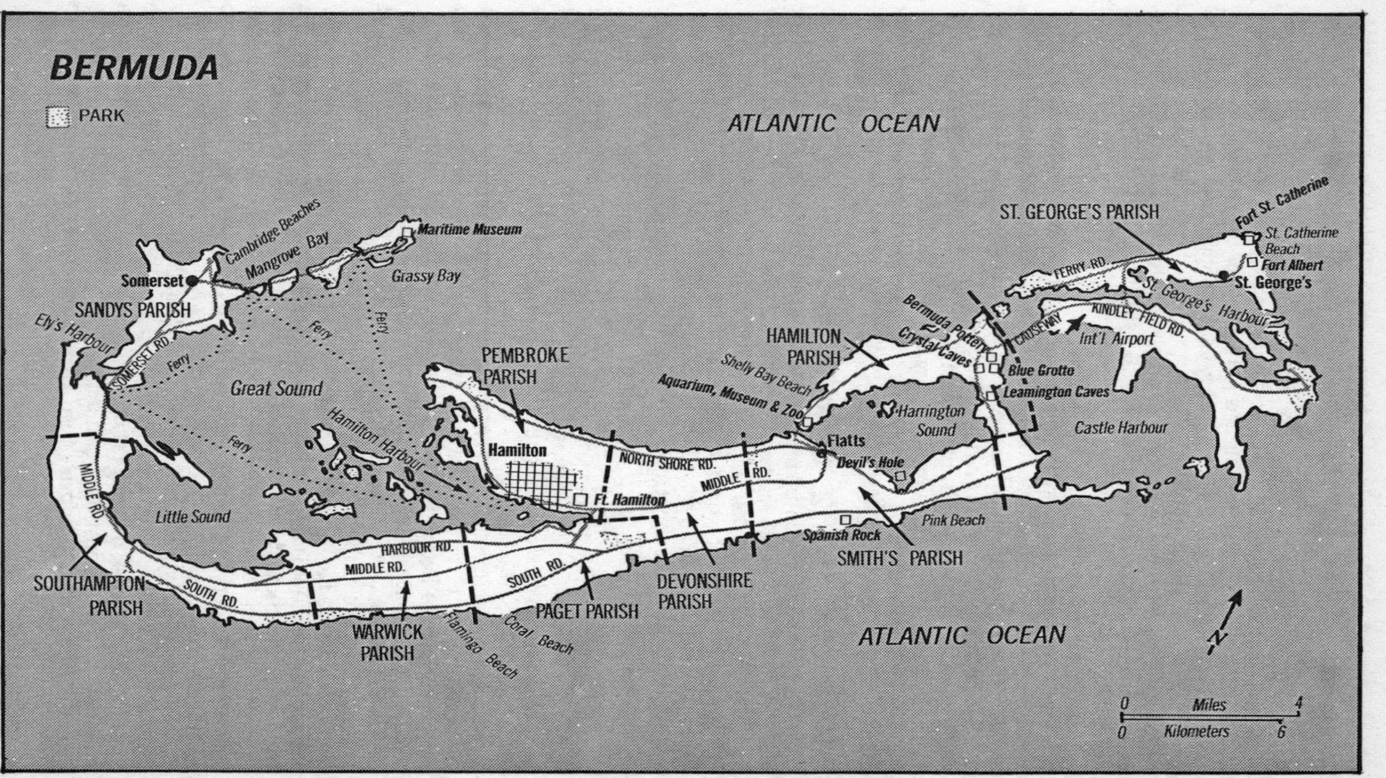
BERMUDA
PARK
ATLANTIC OCEAN
Cambridge Beaches
Mangrove Bay
Maritime Museum
Grassy Bay
Somerset
SANDYS PARISH
Ely's Harbour
SOMERSET RD.
Ferry
Ferry
Ferry
Ferry
Great Sound
Hamilton Harbour
PEMBROKE PARISH
Hamilton
Ft. Hamilton
NORTH SHORE RD.
MIDDLE RD.
MIDDLE RD.
Little Sound
SOUTHAMPTON PARISH
SOUTH RD.
HARBOUR RD.
MIDDLE RD.
SOUTH RD.
WARWICK PARISH
Flamingo Beach
Coral Beach
PAGET PARISH
DEVONSHIRE PARISH
ST. GEORGE'S PARISH
Fort St. Catherine
St. Catherine Beach
Fort Albert
St. George's
FERRY RD.
St. George's Harbour
Bermuda Pottery
Crystal Caves
CAUSEWAY
KINDLEY FIELD RD.
Int'l Airport
HAMILTON PARISH
Shelly Bay Beach
Aquarium, Museum & Zoo
Blue Grotto
Leamington Caves
Harrington Sound
Castle Harbour
Flatts
Devil's Hole
Spanish Rock
Pink Beach
SMITH'S PARISH
ATLANTIC OCEAN
N
0
Miles
4
0
Kilometers
6

larly scheduled flight. In some cases a charter flight is 30% or more cheaper than a regular air fare. But that's only a general rule and can vary considerably from flight to flight.

It's not a completely rosy picture, however, as charter flights have several drawbacks. One is the long advance booking often required. For example, many require that you make reservations and purchase your ticket at least 45 days or more before your actual trip. That certainly takes the spontaneity out of going to Bermuda.

Should you be forced by unforeseen circumstances to cancel your flight, you could lose most of the cash you've advanced. To avoid such a disaster, there is cancellation insurance you can now take out, and you should ask your travel agent about it.

The charter flight always requires that you go to Bermuda and come back on a certain date. Again, this allows for no flexibility in your scheduling.

Some of the charter flights also require that you prebook hotel rooms and pay for what is called certain "ground arrangements."

If nothing is tempting in the charter field after you've talked to a travel agent, ask about APEX fares, meaning advance purchase. These individual inclusive fares include land arrangements along with your excursion fare, and can represent a considerable savings to you.

2. CRUISE SHIPS

Conditions have improved remarkably since that "Innocent Abroad," Mark Twain, used to take a rough sea trip to Bermuda. He considered the place "hell to get to," but thought the charms of Bermuda were worth the tough sea voyage. The American humorist would surely be amazed at the luxurious way today's seagoing passengers can go from East Coast seaports to sunny Bermuda.

Even so, the cruise-ship trip to Bermuda isn't as highly developed or as important as it is to Nassau, which is the big cruise-ship port of this guide.

Cruise ships, because of the island's lack of facilities and other reasons, have been deliberately kept limited in Bermuda. Some Bermudians object to permitting cruise ships to come to their island at all. However, I've never heard any of these objections expressed by the merchants along Front Street in the capital city of Hamilton.

There is an increased movement to divide the cruise-ship business between Hamilton Harbour (the city of Hamilton) and the old capital of St. George's in the eastern part of Bermuda. That way it is hoped that facilities will not be so taxed, and that congestion and other problems can be alleviated.

If your time is severely limited, you may want to fly to Bermuda, as most passengers do, preferring to spend your days on Bermuda's pink sandy beaches rather than days lodged at sea. Cruise ships aren't for many people, and they may not be for you. However, if you'd like to try this method of travel, Bermuda is a good choice for the first-timer because of the short time involved. Since you can sail from the East Coast to Bermuda and back in just a few days, you won't be locked into a long time on the sea, the way you'd be if you took an extended trip to, say, the Caribbean.

Once only the wealthy could afford to sail from New York Harbor to Bermuda, and such a trip in winter enjoyed a high social status in its heyday before World War II. Because of many factors in the travel industry, cruise ships are no longer to be enjoyed just by the affluent. Many package deals and other cost-saving methods in the industry have opened the doors to the cruise ship to today's middle-income voyager.

The cruise-ship season today is from April to November, a reverse of what snobbish New York once viewed as "the season" in Bermuda. As one woman wrote in her memoirs of New York society, "No one thought of going to Bermuda in the summer. It just wasn't done." Now the seasons are reversed, and the spring, summer, and fall are the cruise-ship months for Bermuda. In winter, as one industry spokesman said, "It's quiet."

Once you've decided to go by cruise ship, selecting your line becomes the next big problem. Some cruise-ship operators want their passengers to have a total vacation—one filled with activities from "sunup to sundown." Others see time lodged at sea as a period of tranquillity and relaxation, with less emphasis on "fun, fun" organized activities (which tend to get a little corny anyway).

The reason restaurant owners and others often protest against cruise ships is that passengers don't spend money in their establishments, as they do in the stores, boutiques, and other shops. That's because a cruise ship is a self-contained "floating resort." It offers everything—food, entertainment, a "hotel" room, whatever. The only thing it doesn't contain is the island itself, which can be seen on a sightseeing jaunt once the ship reaches its port of call.

To keep your costs trimmed, you can ask for one of the more cramped, inside cabins, which are considered less desirable and thus are much cheaper. If you plan to be active during most of the day, spending little time in your cabin, this might be ideal for you. In other words, it would be just a place to sleep. In your quarters, you couldn't throw a party for the crew. Most cabins today have a private shower and toilet, regardless of how confined the space is, so you're not reduced to having to use shared facilities. Many readers report that in a midship cabin they are less likely to experience severe rolling and pitching. Modern vessels have more standardized accommodations. It is usually on the older vessels that the cabins come in such widely different sizes, beginning with deluxe stateroom suites, a throwback to the old days of ocean-going transatlantic voyages so beloved in the era of Douglas Fairbanks and Mary Pickford.

Gone too, for the most part, are the "white tie and tails" days of yesterday. However, it's still a good idea for a man to take along a dark suit. Women should also bring along at least one cocktail dress. It's not necessary to dress up every evening on most lines. Men often wear sports coats and slacks with open shirts, and women appear in sports dresses or pant suits.

On cruises to Bermuda you'll usually need a sweater, especially if you're traveling in the spring and autumn. A sun hat or scarf will do nicely for women as well. Once you arrive in Bermuda, dress tends to be more formal than it is in The Bahamas. If you're planning to go out at night, patronizing some of the more elegant restaurants or clubs, men are required to wear a jacket and tie in some places. Otherwise, for actual touring in Bermuda, or participating in the deck activities there and back, men can wear sport shirts, slacks, walking shorts (certainly Bermuda shorts), and a comfortable pair of walking shoes. Women will need sun dresses, blouses, shifts, culottes, and shorts. Walking shoes are preferred for touring the island. Naturally, you should take along a bathing suit or bikini.

Finally, and in some ways unfortunately (considering the investment of your capital), the one ingredient needed for a successful cruise is the hardest to know in advance. That's the list of your fellow passengers. The right crowd can be a lot of fun. A group incompatible with your interests can leave you sulking in your cabin.

Economy tip: You are granted considerable savings on these seven-day cruises by booking early. See a travel agent or call the ship line itself.

In summer the *Queen of Bermuda,* operated by **Bermuda Star Line,** sails weekly on a Saturday from New York to what it calls "the two Bermudas"—that is, both the capital of Hamilton, overlooking Hamilton Harbour, and the former capital and more historic town of St. George's, lying at the far eastern end of the island. It provides regular seven-day service. Carrying as many as 715 passengers, the *Queen of Bermuda* spends two nights in St. George's, followed by one night at Hamilton. A maximum of two children under the age of 8 can stay free with two full-fare passengers per cabin on selected dates.

The 23,500-ton cruise liner, launched in 1957, was formerly known as Holland-America's S.S. *Volendam.* Some 85% of its cabins are outside (with two lower beds), and each unit has a private shower and toilet. The ship has a swimming pool and gym, casino, youth recreation center, beauty salon, and fitness center.

Complimentary four-color brochures may be obtained from travel agents or by writing directly to the Bermuda Star Line Inc., 1086 Teaneck Rd., Teaneck, NJ 07666.

Another popular cruise is aboard the *Nordic Prince,* the handsome 1,038-passenger liner of the **Royal Caribbean Cruise Line.** The ship leaves New York on Sunday, arriving in Bermuda on Tuesday. The departure from Bermuda is on Friday, with New York arrival on Sunday. Docking on Tuesday is at Hamilton. Royal Caribbean Cruise Line's offices are at 903 South America Way, Miami, FL 33132 (tel. 305/379-2601).

Chandris Fantasy Cruises operates two ships on its U.S.-Bermuda schedule. The *Galileo* has a varied schedule of five- and six-night sailings from Baltimore, Boston, Charleston (South Carolina), Philadelphia, and Wilmington (Delaware) to Bermuda. In the summer, the *Galileo* sails every Sunday from New York on five-night sailings to Bermuda. The *Galileo* docks at the new West End Pier. From May to October, the *Amerikanis* sails every Sunday to Bermuda. The six-night itinerary brings the ship into St. George's on Tuesday where it docks. With three days in Bermuda, the *Amerikanis* sails Thursday afternoon for New York, arriving Saturday. This year, Chandris will have in service a new 45,000-ton vessel that will dock in both Hamilton and St. George's. The Chandris office is at 900 Third Ave., New York, NY 10022 (tel. 212/750-0044, or toll free 800/223-0848).

Featuring "breakaway cruises" to Bermuda, the **Royal Viking Star** began service to Bermuda in the spring of 1989. For those who desire shorter vacations, the vessel sails on Saturday from New York to Bermuda. Visitors enjoy four nights at sea and three nights in Hamilton, the capital. The ship, which has a spa and a casino, berths at Front Street, the main shopping drag of the capital. The *Viking Star* heads back to New York on the following Saturday. The ship has a capacity of 900 passengers. For more information, contact **Royal Viking Line,** 750 Battery St., San Francisco, CA 94111 (tel. 415/398-8000 or toll free at 800/422-8000).

3. GETTING AROUND BERMUDA

The national speed limit is 20 mph in Bermuda, 15 mph in busier areas. Cars are limited one to a family—and none at all to visitors. In such a far-off Eden, the most popular form of transportation is the motorized bicycle, called "putt-putts," and the most romantic means of transport is the colorful fringe-topped surrey.

AIRPORT LIMOUSINES: Service is provided by Bermuda Aviation Services Ltd. (tel. 809/293-2500), which has eight-passenger minibuses taking people to the smaller hotels and 26-seater buses serving the larger hotels, with several passenger stops en route. Fares are divided among five zones and are per person one way. Zone 1, from the airport to Grotto Bay, costs $2; zone 2, airport to Flatts,

$4.50; zone 3, airport to Paget, $7; zone 4, airport to Southampton, $8; and zone 5, airport to Ireland Island, $13.

TAXIS: Every cruise ship or incoming flight is met by a fleet of taxis. A typical fare from the airport to, say, a hotel right outside Hamilton costs about $12.50. Taxis are metered and are only allowed to carry a maximum of four passengers.

The meter is set at $1.20 for the first mile or portion thereof when you start your trip. Your driver will wait for you free for the first five minutes, 18¢ per minute thereafter. Light packages and bags can be carried inside the taxi free, but baggage that has to be placed in the trunk or on the roof costs 25¢ per item, maximum $3 per trip. There's a 25% surcharge for taxi travel between midnight and 6 a.m.

The hourly charge for taxis is $16, but if you want to take one on a sightseeing tour, the minimum is three hours. When a taxi driver, man or woman, has a blue flag on the hood of the vehicle (the locals refer to it as the "bonnet"), that means that the driver is qualified to serve as a tour guide. This is the type of driver, checked out and tested by the government, that you should use if you're planning to take the expensive method of touring Bermuda by taxi. "Blue bonnet" drivers charge no more than regular taxi drivers who are not qualified to serve as guides.

Once settled in your hotel, you might want to arrange less expensive means of transport than taxis. Chief among these are—

CYCLES: If you're looking for lots of exercise, you may want to try a pedal bicycle, the old Bermudian way to travel around the island, although some of the hills may be a real challenge to your stamina.

Many people prefer a motor-assisted cycle—moped, motor scooter, whatever—which you can rent on an hourly, daily, or weekly arrangement. The operator of such a vehicle must be at least 16 years of age, although younger persons may be carried as passengers. Some are large enough for two adults. Both driver and passenger are required by law to wear a helmet, which will be furnished by the place from which you rent your machine. Straps must be securely fastened. *Warning:* Visitors on mopeds have a high accident rate, but no one seems to talk about that. Exercise extreme caution.

Don't forget: You must *drive on the left,* as in England.

Astwood Cycles Ltd. (tel. 809/292-2245) has shops where you can rent either mopeds or 50-cc scooters on Front Street in Hamilton, and at Flatts Village, the Princess, the Sonesta Beach, the Belmont, and Horizons. Scooters rent for $36 per day, $66 for two days. A $20 deposit and a $10 one-time insurance payment are required.

Charging comparable prices and also renting either type of vehicle is **Wheels Ltd.,** Trott Road, Hamilton (tel. 809/295-0112, or the Southampton Princess (tel. 809/238-1398).

For motorized vehicles, you can also try **Ray's Cycles Ltd.,** Pompano Road, Southampton West (tel. 809/234-0629), and Lantana Club, Somerset (tel. 809/234-0141). It's open seven days a week from 8 a.m. to 5 p.m. The company rents two kinds of vehicles. A small moped costs $20 for the first day and $33 for two days. A bigger and more powerful Honda motorscooter rents for $36 for one day, $68 for two days. Helmets and locks come with each rental. The insurance charge which is part of each rental is $8 for the moped and $12 for the scooter. This is a one-time charge levied against each rental regardless of how many days you keep the vehicle. There's sometimes a 20% discount in the winter season.

Oleander Cycles Ltd., P.O. Box 114, Valley Road, Paget Parish (tel. 809/236-5235). In season, a single moped rents for $20 per day but it's only $16 per day in winter. However, a Puch Lido scooter will cost $36 daily in summer, $29 in winter. Scooters and mopeds tend to be reliable and well maintained. There is another location on Gorham Road in Hamilton (tel. 809/295-0919). Both locations are open seven days a week.

If you want to use your own "motor" and pedal your way around Bermuda, then try **Bike World,** Reid Street East in Hamilton (tel. 809/295-9972). Most of this well-known company's business comes from the sale of five- and ten-speed bicycles and their components. Visitors to Bermuda, however, can rent a bicycle from them as well. Rates are usually $10 per day for the first day with subsequent reductions.

BUSES: You can't have a car. Taxis are expensive. You may not want or be able to ride a bicycle or a motor bike. What's left for getting around Bermuda? Buses, of course. All major routes are covered by the bus network, but be prepared for waits. There's even a do-it-yourself sightseeing tour by bus and ferry, and regularly scheduled buses go to most of the destinations that tourists find of interest in Bermuda. However, some routes are not operated on Sunday and holidays, so be sure to find out about the trip you want to make.

Bermuda is divided into 14 zones of about two miles each. Fare for adults is $1 for the first three zones, $3.50 for any longer trip. You can save some nickels by purchasing tokens, which are 75¢ for the first three zones you travel, $1.75 for more than three zones. *Note:* You must have the exact fare, either in coins or a token, ready to deposit in the farebox as you board the bus. Drivers do not make change.

You can also purchase tickets at sub-post offices or at the **Central Terminal** on Washington Street in Hamilton where all routes begin and end. It's just off Church Street a few steps east of City Hall. You can get there from Front Street or Reid Street by going along Queen Street or through Walker Arcade and Washington Mall. Tickets are sold in booklets of 15. You pay $9 for a three-zone booklet or $16 for a 14-zone packet. A ticket is also valid for the Somerset Ferry and a one-zone bus ride in Sandys Parish. Children under 13 pay 55¢ in cash for all zones or $4.75 for a 15-ticket booklet. Children under 3 ride free.

A **Mini-Bus Service** also traverses the island. It begins its operation in St. George's at 7 in the morning, continuing late into the evening. From Town Square in St. George's, it branches out to the outlying areas. Fares for this service are $1 for a one-way ride, and you should phone 809/297-8492 for times of departures.

A **do-it-yourself sightseeing tour** might be taken as follows:

Leave Hamilton at 10:15 a.m. on a bus marked "Dockyard," enjoying views of Great Sound en route. At 11:25 a.m. you will arrive at the Maritime Museum, where the driver will drop you off at the entrance on request. After your visit to the museum, you leave the Dockyard main gate at 12:35 p.m. on a bus marked "Hamilton." Ask the driver to point out the Watford Bridge Ferry Dock. At 12:45 p.m. you arrive at Mangrove Bay where you have a choice of restaurants and a pub for lunch and can browse in the local shops. You leave Watford Bridge by ferry at 2:25 p.m., going via Cavello Bay and Somerset Bridge, with views of Somerset homes and harbor islands en route, arriving back at the Hamilton Ferry Terminal at 3:15 p.m.

For more **information** regarding the bus service, telephone 809/292-3854. Nearly all hotels, guesthouses, and restaurants have bus stops close by.

FERRY SERVICE: One of the most interesting methods of transportation is the government-operated ferry service. Ferries crisscross Great Sound between Hamilton and Somerset, charging a $2 fare one way, and they also take the harbor route, going from Hamilton to the parishes of Paget and Warwick where so many hotels are concentrated. From Hamilton to Paget costs only $1. Motorcycles are allowed on the Hamilton to Somerset run (you must pay $2 for your cycle, however). For ferry service **information,** telephone 809/295-4506.

HORSE-DRAWN CARRIAGES: Being romanticists, Bermudians have retained at least some of their horse-drawn carriages. They once were plentiful, but now only about a dozen are left. Drivers congregate on Front Street in Hamilton, adjacent to the No. 1 passenger terminal near the cruise-ship docks. Before 1946 the horse was the principal mode of transport. After that, the first automobiles came to the island. For a tour of the island's midriff, you can book one of these four-wheeled rigs for a chauffeured ride. Rates are $7.50 per half hour for two persons in a single-seat vehicle, $10 for up to four persons in a double-seater. If you want to take a ride lasting more than three hours, the fee is negotiable. Unless you make arrangements for night rides, you aren't likely to find any carriages after 4:30 p.m.

TOURS: The best conducted tours on the island are run by **Penboss Tours,** 66 Front St. (tel. 809/295-3927), using both bus and taxi. Bus tours operate only from March 1 to November 30, and include a five-hour combination of St. George's and Harrington Sound at $32 per person and a three-hour tour covering the points of interest in Hamilton and taking you to Verdmont, a historic mansion, and the Botanical Gardens, costing $19. Tours are narrated by the Bermudian driver-guide.

Taxi tours can be arranged throughout the year from 9 a.m. to 5 p.m. Monday through Saturday, and even on most holidays. Minimum is two people per cab, and children are not entitled to reduced rates. Departure and time are at the client's convenience, and the rates are $22 per person with four in a cab, going up to $38 with only two in the cab. It's customary to try to get someone at your hotel to join you to defray costs. Rates given were for the most popular tour, a three-hour trip around Harrington Sound, visiting everything from the Crystal Caves to the Aquarium.

Penboss also offers a wide choice of water cruises, including two-hour sea garden trips to the reefs, snorkeling expeditions for full or half days, and evening dinner cruises.

SEA EXCURSIONS: From Hamilton Harbour you can strike out in almost any direction on almost any tour. **BDA Water Tours Ltd.,** P.O. Box 1572, Hamilton (tel. 809/295-3727), offers 2-, 3-, 5½-, and 6-hour trips, most of which include the sea gardens where passengers board glass-bottom boats to view the wonders of coral reefs and fish. Also available is a wide variety of water trips, ranging from two-hour sea garden tours to full-day, moonlight, and dinner cruises.

CHAPTER II

A PREVIEW OF BERMUDA

□ □ □

Until the 17th century the islands of Bermuda were known to seafarers as the "Isles of Devils." They probably had contributed to the popular pre-Columbian belief that ships sailing too far west from Europe fell over the edge of the earth into a monster-filled pit. Many ships sailing too close to these remote and uninhabited islands came to grief on the treacherous reefs close to the surface of the turquoise Atlantic. Even Shakespeare was familiar with the reputation of the "Isles of Devils," making "the still-vex't Bermoothes" the setting for *The Tempest.*

The first recorded discovery of the islands was made in 1503 by a Spanish mariner, Juan de Bermudez, for whom they were named. The uncharted islands were a navigational menace to ships following the trade routes of the Atlantic, as Spanish vessels did on voyages from the New World, and Bermuda was looked upon with the same fearful respect as the bubonic plague.

Bermuda's location is at a point in the ocean where galleons from New Spain could easily run into trouble in less than perfect weather, and the eroded wreckage of many ships scattered on the ocean floor amid reefs and shoals bears mute testimony to tragedies, some dating from four or five centuries ago.

This tiny, fishhook-shaped archipelago is made up of some 150 small islands, only 20 of which are inhabited. The chain is about 22 miles long and less than two miles across at the widest point, so that no residents live more than a mile from the sea. The seven largest islands are now joined by causeways and bridges, presenting a connection of land that is known simply as the island of Bermuda.

Bermuda is based on the upper parts of an extinct volcano, which may date from 100 million years ago. Through the millennia, wind and water have brought limestone deposits and formed the islands far from any land mass—the closest is Cape Hatteras, almost 600 miles away. Early residents soon learned that the limestone base of their land made excellent building stone, easily sawed soon after it was quarried but gaining hardness and durability upon exposure to the sun.

1. BERMUDA—THEN AND NOW

A SHORT HISTORY: Although the discovery and naming of the Bermuda islands is attributed to the Spanish, no territorial claim was made by Spain and no settlement established. It was a little more than 100 years after Bermudez wrote about this place that the English staked a claim and began colonization. Spain's archives reveal that during that century some Spaniards survived shipwrecks in the waters off Bermuda, but they devoted their energies to building boats to take them home. It took an English shipwreck to initiate permanent settlement here.

In 1609 the flagship of British Admiral Sir George Somers, the *Sea Venture,* en route to the struggling Jamestown settlement in Virginia with much-needed supplies, was wrecked on Bermuda's reefs. The dauntless Englishmen built two new ships and sailed on to the American colony, but three sailors hid out and stayed on Bermuda. From that point on, the islands have been inhabited.

Just three years after the wreck of the *Sea Venture,* the islands of Bermuda were included in the third British charter of the Virginia Company, and 60 colonists were sent there from England. St. George's Town was quickly founded.

Bermuda's status as a colony dates from 1620, when the first Parliament sat, making it the oldest in the British Empire in continuous operation. It became a Crown Colony in 1684, under King Charles II.

Slaves became a part of life in Bermuda shortly after the official settlement. The majority of these were from Africa, but a few were American Indians. Later, Scots imprisoned for fighting against Cromwell and, in 1651, Irish slaves were brought to the islands. The lot of these bond servants was never so cruel as that of plantation slaves in America and the West Indies, the very nature and size of Bermuda causing them to be used in less strenuous capacities. All slaves were freed by the United Kingdom Emancipation Act of 1834, which provided compensation for the former owners.

After early whaling and tobacco-growing ventures of the islanders failed, the Bermudians turned their attention to shipbuilding, using the cedar trees that grew in abundance on the islands. The expertise gained led to cabinetmaking, and fine furniture was turned out, using the indigenous cedarwood and the skills developed through the building of tight ships.

Although Bermuda is a thousand miles north of the West Indies and more than half that distance from the American mainland, it was inevitable that close links would be maintained in the early colonial days with both those outposts of Great Britain. With their own ships, the islanders set up a thriving mercantile American trade on the eastern seaboard, especially with southern ports, and with all the Bahamian and other West Indian islands. The major commodity sold by Bermuda's merchant ships was salt from Turks Island, which they controlled before losing it to The Bahamas around 1800.

The American Revolution dealt a blow to Bermuda's prospering economy, the rebellious colonies on the mainland being unwilling to trade with their former business associates because of their close link with Britain, despite the fact that many Bermudians and Americans had family connections and close friendships. The seafaring islanders, never much for farming, had depended heavily on America for food and reached a point of near starvation after trade was cut off.

The mainland colonies, meanwhile, had a great need for gunpowder. After certain discreet communications, a powder magazine in St. George's was left carelessly "guarded" one dark night in August 1775, and a number of kegs of gunpowder were stolen. Those kegs next appeared in Boston, where they arrived aboard American ships and were later used to oust the British from that area in early 1776. A large shipment of food arrived in Bermuda shortly thereafter. This little breach of the rules of war did not, however, alter Bermuda's loyalty to England.

With a complement of "wooden ships and iron men," a natural step for some owners or captains of seagoing vessels was to turn their skill to privateering and even to piracy in those "happy days of yore" when those pursuits were flourishing in the Bahamian islands and throughout the Caribbean. Privateering had a certain aura of respectability, as it was legal then to prey on enemy ships. It was an easy sail into piracy, and the lack of speedy communications often persuaded sea captains that all ships were enemies.

The successful revolt of the colonies and establishment of the United States of America forced more of Bermuda's seafarers, now lacking trade routes, to look for economic aid. They found it in privateering, piracy, and wrecking. Wrecking was the name given the business of salvaging goods from wrecked or foundered ships, a highly lucrative venture in these shoal- and reef-filled waters. Unfortunately, if business lagged, some wreckers would lure vessels onto the rocks by placement of beacons, presumably promising safety, in such positions as to doom storm-tossed ships.

Britain's loss of its important American colonial ports on the eastern seaboard led to a naval buildup in Bermuda, beginning with a dockyard from which ships and troops sailed in 1814 to burn Washington, D.C., and the Executive Mansion, renamed the White House after an emergency repainting.

Bermuda got a new lease on a healthy economic life during America's War Between the States, or Civil War. Being sympathetic to the Confederacy, it was perhaps natural that the island business and government, with approval of the government in London, would participate in running the blockade the Union placed on exports, especially of cotton, by the southern states. St. George's harbor was a principal Atlantic base for the lucrative operation of sending manufactured goods into Confederate ports and bringing out cotton and turpentine cargoes.

When the Confederacy fell, so did Bermuda's economy, although on a less permanent basis. Seeing no immediate source of money from the Atlantic in the last quarter of the 19th century, the islanders turned their attention to agriculture and found that the colony's fertile soil and salubrious climate produced excellent vegetables—chief among them, onions. Portuguese people were brought in as farmers, and soon celery, potatoes, and tomatoes were being shipped to the New York market. During this period Bermuda came to be called "The Onion Patch," because of the abundance of big, sweet onions shipped to the United States, which Americans found superior to home-grown products.

(Enterprising Texas farmers learned how to duplicate the island onions through additions to and fertilization of their soil. They registered the name "Bermuda onions" and, aided by a high tariff placed on imported produce, they virtually put Bermuda out of the export farming business.)

Bermudians again profited by problems of the United States during the Prohibition era, from passage of the 18th Amendment in 1919 to its repeal in 1933, when rum-running was a lucrative business. Although the distance from the islands to the mainland was too great to allow a quick crossing in small, booze-laden boats, as was the case from the Bahama islands and Cuba, Bermuda played a part in transporting alcoholic beverages to America.

Bermuda has many connections—historic and present—with the United States. U.S. Air Force and Navy ties date from World War II.

World War II Espionage

Bermuda had an important role in World War II, beginning with the establishment of the "Imperial Censorship Headquarters" at the Hamilton Princess

Hotel in 1940 when Britain, under Churchill, was in the darkest days of World War II.

The story is most dramatically related in *A Man Called Intrepid,* the 1976 bestseller (more than two million copies sold) by William Stevenson about "the secret war" (you may recall the film with Michael York, Barbara Hershey, and David Niven). The book, curiously, although written by William Stevenson, was about Sir William Stephenson (no relation), the master superspy. An aide to Stephenson (alias Intrepid) was Ian Fleming, who later created the James Bond character.

Under the Hamilton Princess, Britain employed men and women to decode Nazi signals picked up by "radio nets." Unknown to the Germans, the British early in the war had broken the Nazi code. The German coding-decoding machine was called "Enigma," and it was vastly complicated, which explained Hitler's reliance on it. (Knowledge of its workings was so valuable to Churchill that he failed to order the evacuation of Coventry—even though he knew it was slated for aerial bombardment. To have evacuated Coventry presumably would have tipped off the Nazis that the British had broken their precious code.)

The commanders of the dreaded U-boats, which were, at least in 1942, efficiently destroying Allied shipping across the Atlantic, relied heavily on radio signals. This proved to be an Achilles' heel. They also believed in the integrity of Enigma, foolishly unaware that their code had been broken. Even when German submarines with their Enigma unharmed were captured by Allied vessels, the Nazi hierarchy did not become overly alarmed. The powers in Berlin believed that the Allies, even with an Enigma sitting in front of them, would be unable to figure out the intricate workings of the coding-machine drums, and how they could be continually altered.

In a different operation, a carefully trained British staff, working in Bermuda in cramped, stifling conditions under the Princess Hotel, intercepted and examined mail between Europe and the United States.

Bermuda was used as a refueling stop between the two continents. While airplane pilots were entertained at the Yacht Club in Bermuda, the mail was taken off the carriers and examined by experts.

An innocent-appearing series of letters from Lisbon, for example, often had messages written in secret ink. These letters were part of a vast German spy network. The British became skilled at opening carefully sealed envelopes, examining the written material, then resealing them, without the person at the other end knowing that his or her mail had been tampered with.

This highly skilled crew was called the "trappers." In his account, William Stevenson wrote: "And by some quirk in the law of averages, the girls who shone in this work had well-turned ankles." The author quotes a medical official as reporting that it was "fairly certain that a girl with unshapely legs would make a bad trapper." Therefore, amazingly, women seeking recruitment in Bermuda as trappers were asked to display what World War II men called their "gams."

These women with shapely ankles discovered the "Duff" method of transporting secret spy messages. This was a reference to a microdot. An important military secret could be hidden under a punctuation dot such as a comma. It was possible to shrink a regularly typed page to so small a size. The British likened these secret messages to a plum duff, a popular English dessert. To author Stevenson, they were "punctuation dots scattered through a letter like raisins in the suet puddings." The nickname, Duff, stuck throughout the war.

J. Edgar Hoover sent his FBI agents to Bermuda to join in these intelligence operations, which continued in Bermuda until 1945.

British officials in Bermuda often took bolder steps than opening the mail. They sometimes confiscated stolen art from Europe. The Nazis—Goebbels, in particular—intended to sell the stolen treasures in New York to help finance the

Nazi war effort. An example cited in *A Man Called Intrepid* concerns the *Excalibur*, an American Export Lines vessel. The captain of the ship refused to allow the authorities to enter a strong room that had been sealed off like a bank vault. Like a safecracker, the British broke into the room, only to discover 270 works by French impressionists. At the end of the war these impressionist paintings were returned to their rightful owner in Paris, who in all probability thought he'd never see his art again.

A Rendezvous for World Leaders

Churchill, taking great risks, flew to Bermuda even during some of the most dangerous aerial and sea bombardment over the North Atlantic in World War II. Perhaps the balmy shores of Bermuda were worth the risk. They were certainly far better than war-torn London.

In 1953 Churchill requested that Bermuda be used as the setting for "the Big Three conference," which brought not only Churchill, but President Eisenhower and Joseph Laniel, the prime minister of France. Eisenhower, who seemed to like Bermuda (especially its golf courses), returned in 1956. This time it was for "the Big Two talks," between Ike and Harold Macmillan, the prime minister of Britain.

In 1961 it was another American president, John F. Kennedy, who met with Harold Macmillan for another "Big Two conference."

Shortly before Christmas in 1971 another "Big Two Summit Conference" was held, this time between President Richard Nixon and Prime Minister Edward Heath.

ECONOMY: The fortunes of Bermuda, as noted, have gone up and down over the centuries since the first settlers arrived. Such enterprises as whaling, shipbuilding, mercantile shipping, privateering (and a little piracy), wrecking, blockade running, and farming have been succeeded by a tremendous economic boom—tourism.

Winter holidays to Bermuda from England came into fashion during Queen Victoria's reign, with VIPs, including royalty, coming to the islands. In the early 1900s steamships brought wealthy visitors seeking a place in the sun during American winters. The industry now accounts for by far the major portion of Bermuda's economy.

If you take many sightseeing tours of Bermuda, especially in the eastern parishes, you'll constantly encounter the name of Thomas Moore (1779–1852). He was, in many ways, the island's most famous first tourist. Moore, of course, was the Irish poet, known for both his *Irish Melodies* and his biography of Byron. Some of his songs include "The Last Rose of Summer" and "The Harp That Once through Tara's Halls."

Moore arrived in St. George's in the winter of 1804, only 24 years old. He was to spend four months in Bermuda, working as a registrar in the Court of the Vice-Admiralty (and in that sense he was not, technically, a tourist). During his stay in Bermuda he wrote a total of 13 odes to Nea. Nea was in fact the wife of William Tucker, then governor of Bermuda. Her real name was Hester, and she was already seven months pregnant when Moore became infatuated with her. (The story will be told many times if you're planning to go on a guided tour of St. George's.) The dashing, romantic poet didn't just confine his attention to Hester. He turned out to be a philanderer, and it is said that many a foolish young girl lost her heart to him.

Moore made several visits to see the Trott family, and their old house is now known as Tom Moore's Tavern (see "Dining in Bermuda," Chapter IV). He wrote under the now-famous calabash tree on the Trott estate. One of his odes was a farewell to Bermuda: "Long may the bloom of the lemon and myrtle its vallies perfume."

Moore didn't find the men of Bermuda "very civilized," but he found in the women "a predisposition to loving."

Since Moore actually had a job in Bermuda, the title of "most famous first tourist" might go to Mark Twain. Unlike Moore, Twain needs no introduction to today's visitors. In spite of his intense dislike of the sea voyage to Bermuda, he felt that once he reached the island it was worth the "hell" in getting there.

Like many of today's tourists, Twain was a repeat visitor, and for Bermuda that was gratifying. Twain spent several winters here, staying in the Pitts Bay area with a well-to-do family of that day. Either walking in his white suit or riding in a donkey cart, the American humorist became a familiar figure on the streets of Hamilton. (Twain was joined by another famous figure in 1908, Woodrow Wilson, in signing a petition against bringing the automobile to Bermuda. Someone, somewhere, must have listened, because it wasn't until 1946 that the automobile was introduced.) Twain's first visit in 1877 on the steamer *Quaker City* was vividly recalled in *Innocents Abroad.*

Finally, and sadly, he left Bermuda in 1910. Already ailing, he was heading back to his home in Connecticut where he was soon to die.

The most flattering thing Twain ever wrote about Bermuda was: "Americans on their way to heaven call at Bermuda and think they have already arrived."

If that weren't enticement enough, the tourist business received a shot in the arm through construction of a major airfield by the United States in World War II and the discovery that you didn't have to be a millionaire to vacation here.

The only agricultural export today is the Bermuda Easter lily. Buds are shipped primarily to the United States and Canada. Other export items are toiletries and loquat liqueurs. A free port exists in the former Royal Navy Dockyard at the western end of the colony.

THE PEOPLE: Some Bermudians can trace their ancestry back to the first settlers of the islands and some to successful privateers and to slaves. Today's 57,000 residents—mostly of African, British, and Portuguese derivation—have a high standard of living, with no personal income tax and virtually no unemployment. The color bar, which was there long after slavery was abolished, has almost disappeared, and blacks have assumed a prominent place in the Bermudian civic and government affairs. Interracial unity among the Bermudians is excellent today, except for pockets of dissidents. There is no illiteracy here, and you won't see any slums or poverty.

You'll be strongly aware of the British influence in Bermuda, what with predominantly English accents, police wearing helmets like those of London bobbies, and cars driving on the left. Americans, however, have made an impact as well (which is more obvious to visitors from the United Kingdom than to us).

Schools here are run along the lines of the English system, providing a high standard of preparatory education. Children 5 to 16 years of age must attend school. The Bermuda College offers academic and technical studies and boasts a renowned hotel and catering program.

GOVERNMENT: Britain's oldest colony is self-governing, its self-determination in the conduct of local affairs having been widened by a new constitution in 1968. It has a two-house Parliament, made up of a House of Assembly and a Senate (the upper house); the cabinet is headed by the premier, who is appointed by the royal governor. The governor, the queen's representative, fills in this and other areas the same function as the monarch.

Judicial responsibility falls to the Supreme Court, headed by a chief justice.

English law is the fundamental guide, and the court wears traditional wigs and robes.

Bermuda could become totally independent in the foreseeable future, but its British ties will probably remain strong.

SPORTS: Bermuda offers excellent golf, fishing, tennis, and sailing facilities. The Bermuda-fitted dinghy is one of the world's most distinctive sailing craft, carrying up to 1,000 square feet of sail. At only 14 feet one inch in length, this dinghy carries more sail for its size than any other craft.

Various resort hotels offer rowboats, motorboats, Sunfish, waterskiing, snorkeling, skin- and scuba-diving, pedal boating, windsurfing, and deep-sea fishing. Many resorts have swimming pools, or you can swim, sun, and relax at the fine, pink-sand beaches of Bermuda. For more particulars on sports in the area, see "The Sporting Life" in Chapter V.

FOR HONEYMOONERS: Bermuda seems to have a special magic for honeymooners, whatever their ages. After a long or short stay here, they go home with a priceless treasure trove of memories, convinced that the song which says "Bermuda is another world" is true.

To help newlyweds or second honeymooners store up a lot of goodies in that treasure chest, hotels here offer honeymoon packages of varying lengths and prices, depending on the time of year and the accommodations provided.

One resort advertises, "If you've got the honey, we've got the moon."

Whether a honeymooning couple is looking for a big resort hotel, a small and quietly secluded one, an apartment, a guesthouse, or a cottage colony, Bermuda has one of the widest range of accommodations to be found in either The Bahamas or the Caribbean. Check with a travel agent for the latest offerings of honeymoon packages.

BERMUDA COLLEGE WEEKS: Beginning March 2 and lasting till April 13, Bermuda College Weeks is an annual spring odyssey for lots of American and Canadian youth. College Weeks is actually run under the auspices of the Bermuda Department of Tourism, although they try to discourage some of the more exuberant excesses of previous years, like putting goats in elevators and bottles of laundry detergent in swimming pools.

Bermuda, as everybody knows, is an upmarket resort. Many hoteliers have told me that the island likes to attract families who make a beginning salary of $40,000 to $50,000 a year. Why then is there such an official endorsement of these hell-raising college weeks? The Bermudians wisely know that if the young people flock to Bermuda while they are still in college, they are likely to return with their emerging families when they establish themselves in careers.

These weeks began in 1933 as Rugby Weeks. Rugby teams from such Ivy League schools as Yale came to compete against British or Bermudian teams. "Where the Boys Are," to borrow the popular song title, led to "Where the Girls Are." A tradition was born.

Complimentary beach parties, boat cruises, and various events are arranged by the Department of Tourism. Those who have a valid college identification card are issued a "College Week Courtesy Card." That has been called a springtime passport to a week of beach parties, lunches, boat cruises, dances, and entertainment. And it's all free, a gift of the Bermudian government.

A big beach bash is always staged at the Elbow Beach Surf Club, one of the most popular student hangouts. There's also a party at Horseshoe Bay, where students enjoy limbo dancers and engage in such events as tugs-of-war.

It is estimated that at least 10,000 students flock here every year for this spring ritual. The dates cited above are based on the vacation schedules of colleges in Bermuda's major market area.

BERMUDA RENDEZVOUS TIME: If you need to escape the cold of winter but feel that you don't fit the Florida scene, Bermuda may be just the place for you. If you are not expecting to bake on the beach but do want to be outside and active, walking, playing tennis or golf, or just reading a book on the lawn, Bermuda is perfect.

As the weather is not always favorable, the government knows that to keep tourists happy, amusements must be provided. Therefore, they created a "Rendezvous Time," November 15 to March 31. During this time, walking tours of the historic towns of Hamilton and St. George's (which is as old as Williamsburg) are sponsored, plus a tour of the Botanical Gardens. Pipe and drum with Scottish dancers, a fashion show and tea, a thriving craft market, and many other special events are offered free to the winter visitor.

During the winter months, the Bermuda calendar is jam-packed with such events as golf and tennis invitationals, an international marathon race, a dog show, open house and garden tours, and, of course, **The Bermuda Festival,** a six-week International Performing Arts Festival in Hamilton, featuring drama, dance, jazz, classical and popular music, and other entertainment. The best of artists come from Europe, England, Canada, and the U.S. Some tickets are reserved until 48 hours before curtain time for visitors.

For details, write Mrs. Lee Davidson, The Bermuda Festival, Box HM 297, Hamilton HM AX, Bermuda (tel. 809/295-1291). Major credit cards are accepted.

HOMES AND GARDENS: Each spring, usually from the end of March to mid-May, the Garden Club of Bermuda lays out the welcome mat at a number of private homes and gardens that are open to view. Admission, payable on the viewing day only, is $10. A different set of houses, conveniently located in the same parish, is open every Wednesday during this springtime viewing.

Normally a total of 20 homes participate in the program, many dating back to the 17th and 18th centuries. One year, a tour included Blackburn Place, a stately home built in 1730, featuring extensive cedarwork throughout and set in acres of lush gardens. Other houses of note were Spanish Grange, once the home of the English playwright Sir Terrence Rattigan, and Inwood, built in 1700 and recently restored to its original splendor. Knapton House (circa 1720), whose first owner was one of Bermuda's early silversmiths, was also included on the tour, but participants vary from year to year.

Bermuda's homes have always had a special character and atmosphere, and these spring tours afford a marvelous glimpse into the history of the island.

GOMBEYS: On certain holidays, such as Boxing Day (December 26) or on Easter Monday, you may count yourself lucky to see the Gombey Dancers (the word in The Bahamas is "goombay"). These colorfully costumed dancers, who wear hideous masks and grotesque dress, have their origins deep in African history. Feather-studded headdresses—sometimes with small mirrors—add to the carnival atmosphere. The gyrations of the Gombeys may be centuries old.

Performed to the sound of African-style drums, the dances often have a meaning, relating some long-ago legend. The slaves shipped in from Africa were said to have brought the Gombey dance with them. The dancers, always men, used to dance barefoot, but in recent years many have taken to wearing something protective on their feet.

2. FOOD AND DRINK

For years Bermuda was not considered the island of the grand cuisine. Food was too often bland, lacking in flavor. However, in the past decade there has been a remarkable change. Bermuda has shared the revived interest in fine cuisine that swept across America beginning in the 1970s. Chefs seem better trained than ever, and many top-notch, albeit expensive, restaurants dot the islands, from Sandys Parish in the west to St. George's Parish in the east.

Italian food currently enjoys much vogue. The Chinese have also landed. Fast food is also available, including Kentucky Fried Chicken.

In recent years some Bermudians have shown an interest in their "roots," and many of the oldtime dishes and recipes have been revived and published in books devoted to Bermudian cookery. One of these books might make an interesting souvenir.

Today Bermuda imports most of its foodstuffs from the United States. Because the island has such a high population density, much farmland has now given way to the construction of private homes. Nevertheless, private gardens are still cultivated, and at one Bermudian home I was amazed at the variety of vegetables grown on just a small plot of land. These plants included sorrel, from which a good-tasting soup was made, along with oyster plants and Jerusalem artichokes.

As related in any history of Bermuda, Admiral Sir George Somers and his 150 castaways arrived on the shores of Bermuda from their ill-fated *Sea Venture.* Within 30 minutes they set about fishing for food. They named the fish they caught "rockfish," and later wrote about how sweet and very fat it was.

These early settlers also found wild hogs roaming the island. These swine were believed to have swum to the shore when some ship (or ships) were wrecked off the coast of Bermuda. The settlers captured these boars and fed them cedarberries. That way, when they didn't want to go fishing or the weather was too choppy, they could roast a pig.

Around the coastline of Bermuda more species of both shore and ocean fish are found than in any other place—that is, if you can believe what any local fisherman is likely to tell you. These include grunt, angel fish, yellowtail, gray snapper, and the ubiquitous rockfish. Rockfish is similar to the Bahamian grouper, and it appears on nearly every menu.

This popular fish weighs anywhere from 15 to 135 pounds (or even more). Steamed, broiled, baked, fried, or grilled, rockfish is a challenge to any chef. There's even a dish known as "rockfish maw," which I understand only the most old-fashioned cooks—a handful still left on St. David's Island—know how to prepare. It's the maw or stomach of a rockfish that has been stuffed with a dressing of forcemeat and simmered slowly on the stove.

The most popular dish on the island is Bermuda fish chowder. It allows the cook to use the heads and fins of a fish, so nothing is wasted. Nearly every waiter will pass around a bottle of sherry peppers and some black rum for you to lace your own soup. This adds a distinctive Bermudian flavor.

Shark used to be more popular than it is today. One oldtime cook confided to me, "The young kids who get married today wouldn't know how to cook shark. I grew up on it." Many traditional dishes are still made from shark, including hash, which I first enjoyed on St. David's Island many long years ago. (Shark oil, extracted from the fish, is still used by a lot of oldtimers to tell the weather. It's said to be more reliable than the weatherperson.)

The Bermudian lobster—or "guinea-chick" as it is known locally—has been called a first cousin of the Maine lobster. It is the same spiny lobster that one encounters in The Bahamas, the Caribbean, or the Florida Keys. Fresh lobster is only in season from September to March. The measure of how much of a delicacy it is locally is in the high price tag that accompanies it.

The conch is not as available or as popular as it is in The Bahamas, the Florida Keys, or the Caribbean. But occasionally you can still get a good conch stew in Bermuda at one of the local restaurants.

Sea scallops, while still available, have become increasingly rare. Mussels are cherished in Bermuda. Often they are steamed, but one of the most popular dishes, and one of the most traditional, is mussel pie Bermuda style.

FRUITS AND VEGETABLES: In the latter part of the 19th century, Bermuda enjoyed good revenue from the fresh vegetables, such as potatoes and onions, that it sold to New York markets during the nongrowing season there. To help till the land, farmers were brought in from the Azores. The Portuguese seemed to have left very little of their cuisine on the island, with one exception. In both restaurants and private homes, Portuguese red-bean soup precedes many a meal.

The Bermuda onion was once so common on the island that people of Bermuda, as pointed out, were called "onions." Although the so-called Bermuda onion is most likely from Texas today, the onion still figures in a lot of Bermudian recipes, including onion pie. Bermuda-onion soup has kept many a family happy on a chilly night in January. It's most often flavored with Outerbridge's Original Sherry Peppers. The old people used to consume this dish around a cedarwood fire before a 1940 blight destroyed those trees.

Bermudians grow more potatoes than any other vegetable, chiefly the red Pontiac and the Kennebec white potato. At some homes in Bermuda, the Sunday breakfast of codfish and banana cooked with potatoes is still served. It is eaten all year by some residents, but it is the most traditional breakfast that can be consumed on Easter Sunday morning.

"Peas and plenty," as it is called, is a Bermudian tradition. It is still consumed at New Year's, but can be eaten on any occasion. It is black-eyed peas cooked in onion and salt pork to which rice can be added. Old-fashioned cooks added dumplings or boiled sweet potatoes to the concoction at the last minute.

The familiar peas 'n' rice dish that is so widely consumed in The Bahamas is called Hoppin' John in Bermuda. Many locals eat this as a main dish. It can also accompany a meat or poultry plate. A pig tail or snout was once commonly used to flavor the dish.

Bermudians and Bahamians share the same tradition of Johnny Bread or johnnycake. This bread dates from the early settlers. It is, basically, a pan-cooked bread made with butter, milk, flour, sugar, salt, and baking powder. (Originally it was called "Journey Cake," which was eventually corrupted to johnnycake.) Fishermen could make this simple bread on the deck of their fishing vessels. They'd build a fire in a box that had been filled with sand to keep the flames from spreading to the craft itself.

The cassava was once more important in Bermuda than it is today. Nowadays it is used chiefly at Christmas to make the traditional cassava pie. Cassava is a major source of tapioca and farina.

Many legends grew up around cassava pie, which, before the advent of modern kitchen equipment, used to be very difficult to make. For example, the root of the cassava takes two years to grow, and its pulp has to be squeezed, as the juice is poisonous. There were other hazards too. Because pork was put into the pie, and in the days before refrigeration that meat could turn quickly, many diners were stricken with ptomaine poisoning at the Christmas festivities.

Another dish that has a festive holiday connection is sweet potato pudding, which was traditionally eaten on Guy Fawkes Day. People ate this pudding as if it were cake, as they'd watch the fireworks on this holiday. Because matters got out of hand, the Bermudian government has banned the use of fireworks on this holiday, but the sweet potato pudding remains.

Bermuda grows many fresh fruits, including strawberries, Surinam cherries, guavas, and avocados, and of course, bananas. Guavas are made into jelly, which in turn is often used to make the famous Bermuda syllabub. Traditionally it is accompanied by johnnycake. Because of the British influence on the island, you'll often see an English trifle on the menu.

The plum-like loquat also grows in Bermuda and can be made into a pie, but most often will find its way into a chutney. Introduced by Governor Reid in the mid-19th century, it was said to have come from Malta, and before that, from Japan.

In the spring, my favorite dessert is a Bermudian cherry pie made with the orange-red Surinam cherry allowed to ripen on the tree. Grenada is considered the source of the Surinam cherry, which eventually found its way to Bermuda.

A seedless navel orange—once used to pay rents on the island—is still grown in Bermuda. One local cook recently combined it with a sweet Bermuda onion to make a delectable and refreshing salad.

The papaya is called pawpaw here, the same as it is in the Caribbean. It is consumed either as a fresh fruit or cooked as a vegetable. The green pawpaw is prepared in ways similar to how the Americans cook squash.

Another favorite dish is pumpkin stew, which is made with many kinds of meat or poultry. Sea captains brought in curry powder, and that was often used to give the stew added flavor.

The banana is the favorite fruit of Bermudians. Recently when I arrived to visit an old friend, I was offered a banana from the tree in the backyard. It was a dwarf Cavendish banana, with a wonderfully sweet taste. The banana is not only eaten raw but used to flavor meat, fish, poultry, and desserts. Everybody has had a slice of banana bread, but what about banana pumpkin pie or banana-flavored meatloaf made with chopped meat?

QUENCHING YOUR THIRST: Tap water is safe in Bermuda, but use it sparingly, as it is scarce. Bermuda does not have springs or rivers to supply fresh water, and there have been shortages. The islanders must rely on rainwater. Each house has a whitewashed roof constructed to channel water into an underground cistern for later use. To cover shortages, Bermuda also has a desalinization plant.

Before bottled drinks, ginger beer—made with green ginger and lemons—was an island favorite. Some people still make it from the citrus grown on the island.

Once Bermudians made their own beer from cedarberries. Nowadays beer is more likely to be "tinned" or bottled.

Many herb-based teas are still made on the island. However, with the coming of modern times these old home remedies don't enjoy the popularity they used to. The flowers or leaves of such plants as Father John, periwinkle, and "Strong Back" have traditionally been used to make herbal teas.

For some 300 years rum has been called "the national drink" of Bermuda. Especially popular is Bacardi rum (they have a headquarters in Bermuda) and Demerara rum (also known as "Black Rum").

A rum swizzle is perhaps the most famous alcoholic drink in Bermuda. One version includes a mixture of Barbados rum and Demerara rum, with a dash of Angostura bitters, some lime juice, sugar, and some falernum (a sugar syrup with an almond taste).

An interesting drink is loquat liqueur, which is now exported. In its simplest form, it is made with loquats, rock candy, and gin. In more elaborate concoctions, the gin gives way to brandy and there are such spices as cinnamon, nutmeg, cloves, and allspice.

Both European and California wines are sold in Bermuda, most often at inflated prices. On the whole, wine costs more than it does in New York. If you're saving money, pick and choose your way carefully across a wine carte.

All the name-brand alcoholic beverages are sold in Bermuda, but prices on such a typical drink as scotch and soda can run as high as $5 in some places. You have to watch where you drink or else you can run up some huge bar tabs if you like more than one libation in the evening.

3. THE ABC'S OF BERMUDA

The aim of this "grab bag" section—dealing with the minutiae of your stay—is to make your adjustment to the Bermudian way of life easier. It is maddening to have your trip marred by an incident that could have been avoided had you been tipped off earlier. To prevent this, I'll try to anticipate the addresses, data, and information that might come in handy on all manner of occasions.

A number of situations, such as a medical emergency, might arise during your vacation, and there are various customs, such as tipping, you'll need to know about. The desk personnel at your hotel are usually reliable dispensers of information. If you're staying at a guesthouse, your host or hostess will probably be able to supply any information you need on the immediate vicinity of your parish.

Even with such help, however, the following summary of pertinent survival data may prove helpful, and I've included some information on topics you just might want to know something about.

AIRPORT: You'll arrive in the western end of Bermuda, and, chances are, your hotel will be east of Hamilton, a long taxi haul. The Civil Air Terminal lies at the Kindley Air Force Base, near the U.S. Naval Air Station. If you're returning to the United States from here, you'll clear U.S. Customs before boarding the plane.

AMERICAN EXPRESS: The representative in Hamilton is **L. P. Gutteridge, Ltd.,** Bermudiana Road, P.O. Box HM 1024 (tel. 809/295-4545). The office provides complete travel service, sightseeing tours, airport transfers, hotel reservations, traveler's checks, and emergency check cashing.

BABYSITTING: Arrangements can often be made at your hotel, but never at the last minute. Always ask as far ahead as possible, and be prepared to be turned down. Each arrangement has to be personally negotiated, but the going rate is about $7 per hour.

BANKS: There are three banks, all with their main offices in Hamilton. All banks and their branches have the same hours, with the exception of the airport branch of the Bank of Bermuda. Hours are: Monday to Thursday from 9:30 a.m. to 3 p.m. and on Friday from 9:30 a.m. to 3 p.m. and 4:30 to 5:30 p.m. (9:30 a.m. to 4:30 p.m. at the Bank of Bermuda). At the Bank of Bermuda airport branch, the hours are Monday to Friday from 11 a.m. to 12:30 p.m. and 1 to 4 p.m. All banks are closed Saturday, Sunday, and on public holidays.

The **Bank of Bermuda Ltd.,** Front Street, Hamilton (tel. 809/295-4000), has branches on Church Street, Hamilton; Par-la-Ville Road, Hamilton; King's Square, St. George's; in Somerset; and at the airport.

The **Bank of N.T. Butterfield Ltd.,** Front and Reid Streets, Hamilton (tel. 809/295-1111), has branches at Church Street West, Hamilton; St. George's; Somerset; and at the Southampton Princess.

The **Bermuda Commercial Bank Ltd.** is at 44 Church St., Hamilton (tel. 809/295-5678).

CLIMATE: Bermuda is a semitropical island, and the Gulf Stream, flowing between it and North America, keeps the climate temperate. There is no rainy season and no normal month of excess rain. Showers may be heavy at times, but the skies clear quickly. Summer temperatures are recorded from May to mid-November, with the warmest weather in July, August, and September. The thermometer rarely rises above 85° Fahrenheit. There's nearly always a cool breeze in the evening, and accommodations that require it are air-conditioned. Spring-like temperatures prevail from mid-December to late March, with an average of from the low 60s to 70°. It's usually warm enough for swimming in December and January. From mid-November to mid-December and from late March through April either spring or summer weather can occur, so visitors should be prepared for both (see "Clothing," below).

Hurricanes do sometimes churn up the Atlantic, bringing high winds to the area, but they do not often actually strike Bermuda. At any rate, the people know how to prepare for a big blow, and they'll see to it that you don't suffer. An efficient warning system gives ample notice of the approach of a storm.

A look at the official chart on temperature and rainfall will show you what to expect during the time you plan to visit Bermuda.

Month	Average Temperature	Average Inches of Rainfall
January	64.8°F (18.3°C)	4.06
February	63.5°F (17.5°C)	5.05
March	64.0°F (17.8°C)	4.63
April	65.4°F (18.5°C)	3.01
May	70.0°F (21.1°C)	3.86
June	75.1°F (24.0°C)	5.17
July	78.6°F (25.9°C)	3.98
August	80.0°F (26.6°C)	5.27
September	78.5°F (25.8°C)	5.25
October	74.8°F (23.8°C)	6.02
November	69.1°F (20.6°C)	4.48
December	65.4°F (18.5°C)	3.82

CLOTHING: A certain British reserve and dignity prevails in the atmosphere of accommodations in Bermuda, no matter what the category or cost. As a rule of thumb, dress conservatively. Bathing suits, abbreviated tops, and short-shorts are not acceptable except at beaches and pools. Beachwear must be covered in public, and bare feet and curlers are sternly frowned on. Joggers may wear standard running shorts and shirts, but it's an offense to ride cycles or appear in public without a shirt or with just a tanktop. Casual sports clothing may be worn in restaurants at lunchtime, but most of them, as well as nightclubs, require men to wear jackets and ties in the evening. It's wise to check on dress requirements when you make your reservations for dinner or for a night on the town, as some places occasionally have casual evenings.

In the warmer months, May to mid-November, even though summer-weight dresses and sportswear are suitable, a light dressy sweater or wrap for evening, a raincoat or light windbreaker, and cocktail outfits are best to take to Bermuda. From December to late March, take light woolens or fall casuals, sweaters, skirts, and slacks, and dressy sweaters or wraps and cocktail clothing, plus a raincoat and warm jacket. Mid-November through December and late March through April, you'll probably need a combination of the two sets of clothing suggested above.

Men will need summer sport clothes in the warmer months, a lightweight suit or sport jacket and tie for evenings, and a raincoat or light windbreaker. The same type of clothing but in heavier materials (light woolens, for instance) will do for the cooler months, and the same combination of sets of clothing advised for women is recommended for the in-between times.

COMMUNICATIONS: There is a worldwide cable and overseas phone service. Charges may be reversed. Direct dialing is possible from Bermuda to the U.S. and Canada. To send a cable, go to the Cable and Wireless office on Church Street in Hamilton, open from 8 a.m. to 7 p.m. Monday to Friday, from 9 a.m. to 5 p.m. on weekends, or else telephone 809/295-1815.

CONSULATE: You'll find the **United States Consulate General** in the Vallis Building, Bermudiana Road in Hamilton (tel. 809/295-1342).

CRIME: There is no need for any particular crime alert for Bermuda. Occasionally every few years racial tensions explode, and there are acts of violence. But for the most part the Bermudians are a peaceful people, whites coexisting harmoniously with blacks, especially now since blacks are taking more and more active roles in politics.

However, don't be lulled into any false security. Crime does exist. Protect your valuables, especially when you're at the beach. Lock your moped each time you come to visit a place. Extreme valuables should be placed in your hotel safe (if your hotel is big enough to have one) and never left carelessly in your room.

It is usually safe to go anywhere in Bermuda, but, here again, caution should be exercised, particularly late at night and especially if you're a woman traveling alone.

CURRENCY: Legal tender is the Bermuda dollar (BD$), which is divided into 100 cents. Prior to 1972, the Bermuda dollar was pegged to pound sterling. Since then, it has been pegged through gold to the U.S. dollar on an equal basis. That is, BD$1 equals U.S. $1. U.S. currency is generally accepted at par in shops, restaurants, and hotels. Currencies from the United Kingdom and all other foreign countries are not accepted. However, such currencies can be exchanged for Bermuda dollars at banks. Canadian, British, and all other currencies are liable to daily fluctuations. Banking and credit-card transactions in all foreign currencies involving currency exchange are subject to exchange rates. U.S. traveler's checks are cashed almost anywhere, and credit cards are accepted in many shops and restaurants and in some, certainly not all, hotels. When booking a room at a hotel, check to see if it accepts credit cards.

CUSTOMS: Visitors may bring into Bermuda duty free all wearing apparel and articles for their personal use, including sports equipment, cameras, 200 cigarettes, one quart of liquor, one quart of wine, and approximately 20 pounds of meat. Other foodstuffs may be dutiable. All imports may be inspected on arrival. Visitors entering Bermuda may claim a duty-free gift allowance.

When you return home, you may take $400 worth of merchandise duty free if you've been outside the United States for 48 hours or more and have not claimed a similar exemption within the past 30 days. Articles valued above the $400 duty-free limit but not over $1,000 will be assessed at a flat duty rate of 10%. Gifts for your personal use, not for business purposes, may be included in the $400 exemption. Gifts sent home may be valued at $50. You are limited to one liter of wine, liqueur, *or* liquor. Five cartons of cigarettes can be brought home duty free. U.S. Customs pre-clearance is available for all scheduled flights. Passengers leaving for the U.S. must fill out written declaration forms before clearing U.S. Customs in Bermuda. The forms are available at hotels, travel agencies, and airlines in Bermuda.

If you're Canadian, you must now make a written declaration on your return home, whether or not you have something to declare. Those who have been outside Canada for 48 hours can claim $100 exemption one time during each quarter of the year beginning January 1. This can include 200 cigarettes and 40 ounces of alcoholic beverages. If you've been gone from home for seven or more days, you can claim a $300 exemption once a year.

DOCUMENTS FOR ENTRY: A U.S. or Canadian citizen does not need a passport to enter Bermuda, although one will serve as your required identification if you have it.

Otherwise, visitors entering from the United States are required by Bermuda Immigration authorities to have in their possession any one of the following items: a birth certificate or certified copy, a U.S. naturalization certificate, a U.S. Alien Registration card, a U.S. reentry permit, or a U.S. voter registration card bearing the signature of the holder.

Visitors entering from Canada who do not have a valid passport in their possession must have a birth certificate or certified copy, a Canadian certificate of citizenship, or a valid passport plus proof of their Landed Immigrant status.

If you stay longer than three weeks from your arrival date, you must apply to the Chief Immigration Officer for an extended stay. You must have a return or onward ticket.

All travelers are taxable under the Passenger Tax Act of 1972. For air and ship passengers, see "Taxes," below.

DRIVING REQUIREMENTS: As to automobile driving, there are no specific requirements for visitors for a very simple reason—there are no car-rental agencies in Bermuda. Even Bermudian households are limited to one car. Motor-assisted cycles are available (see "Getting Around Bermuda" in Chapter I), but they may not be operated by children under 16. All cycle drivers and passengers are required by law to wear safety helmets that are securely fastened.

Driving is on the left side of the road. The speed limit is 20 miles per hour.

DRUGS: Importation of, possession of, or dealing with unlawful drugs, including marijuana, is an offense under Bermuda laws, with heavy penalties levied for infraction. Customs officers, at their discretion, may conduct body searches for drugs or other contraband goods.

ELECTRICAL APPLIANCES: Electricity is 110 volts, 60 cycles, AC. American appliances are compatible.

EMERGENCY NUMBERS: Any of these numbers might come in handy. **Police:** call 292-2222 (emergency only). In Somerset, call 234-1010; in St. George's, 297-1122. To get police headquarters, call 295-0011.

Fire: dial 900.

Ambulance: call 236-2000.

Air-Sea Rescue: 297-1010.

Alcoholics Anonymous: phone 236-8293 in the daytime, 236-4806 after 6:30 p.m.

Hospital: dial 236-2345.

Helpline: call 295-5159.

Lifeline: phone 236-0224 from 9 a.m. to 5 p.m., 236-3770 from 5 p.m. to 9 a.m.

Not emergency numbers but helpful:

Time and Temperature: 909.

Weather: 977.

What's on in Bermuda: 974.

FIREARMS: Bringing in any firearm, part of a firearm, or ammunition is forbidden except under a license granted by the commissioner of police. Such a permit will not usually be granted except to visiting rifle club members attending a sports meeting in Bermuda. Spearguns and a variety of dangerous weapons are treated as firearms, but antique weapons made 100 or more years ago may be imported if you can show that they are antique. Breaches of the firearms import law are punishable by imprisonment or heavy fines.

FLORA AND FAUNA: Decorating the gently rolling Bermudian landscape are oleander, hibiscus, royal poinciana, poinsettia, bougainvillea, morning glory (convolvulus), and other flowering plants, shrubs, and trees. Bananas, grapefruit, lemons, oranges, and limes grow profusely. Among trees, you'll see pines, palms, casuarinas (Australian pines), fiddlewood, and bay grapes. Nearly all the important plants of the islands can be seen in the government's Botanical Gardens in Paget Parish. Indigenous trees are the Bermuda cedar, Bermuda olivewood bark, and the palmetto. Indigenous flowers include the Bermudiana (sometimes called the Bermuda iris), Darrell's fleabane (a plant of the daisy family), and the maidenhair fern.

The animal life found here includes several species of small, harmless lizards and the tiny whistling frogs heard making cricket-like sounds on summer nights. There are no snakes on any of the islands. Cardinals and bluebirds make their home here.

GAMBLING: There are no gambling casinos in Bermuda. For that, refer to Part II of this guide on The Bahamas.

HAIRDRESSERS: Bermuda is well supplied with beauty shops and hairdressers. Nearly all the major hotels, such as the Southampton Princess, have hairdressers and beauty shops on the premises.

If you're a man and looking for a place to get your hair cut, you can always head for the **Bosun's Chair** on Front Street (tel. 809/295-5743) in Hamilton. One of a bevy of English women will clip your locks to your desired length. Open from 9 a.m. to 5:30 p.m. Monday to Saturday, the store is sometimes so busy that an advance appointment is necessary. Call the Front Street shop for an appointment there or at any of the other Bosun's Chair locations: Flatts Village, St. George's, Marriott's Castle Harbour Hotel, Elbow Beach Hotel, or Southampton Princess Hotel (Beauty Salon and Health Club). The company also owns and operates the famous spa at Sonesta Beach Hotel.

Women can head for **BerSalon,** Front Street West (tel. 809/295-4804), for an array of hair and skin treatments guaranteed to make you feel like the belle of whatever ball you're heading toward. Open from 9 a.m. to 6 p.m., it too requests appointments.

HELP FOR THE HANDICAPPED: For advice and assistance, call the Bermuda Physically Handicapped Association (tel. 809/292-5025). Many hotels and guesthouses are equipped to accommodate handicapped guests.

HITCHHIKING: There are no special restrictions that I know of. It's usually a safe thing to do. However, don't expect to get "picked up" too easily. Taxis, of course, will only stop if you pay them. The only people allowed to have cars other than taxi drivers are local residents, and they are limited to one to a household. Because of that restriction, family cars are often filled with friends or relatives. Better count on using public transport in Bermuda instead of your thumb.

HOLIDAYS: The following public holidays are observed in Bermuda (the ones listed without a date change from year to year): New Year's Day (January 1), Good Friday, Easter, Bermuda Day (May 24), the Queen's Birthday (first or second Monday in June), Cup Match Days (cricket; Thursday and Friday preceding first Monday in August), Labour Day (first Monday in September), Christmas Day (December 25), and Boxing Day (December 26). Public holidays that fall on a Saturday or Sunday are usually celebrated on the following Monday.

HOSPITAL: It's reassuring to know that **King Edward VII Memorial Hospital,** Point Finger Road (tel. 809/236-2345) in Paget Parish, has a staff of many nationalities and high qualifications. It has Canadian accreditation.

INSECTS: Bermuda is not the Caribbean, or even the U.S. for that matter, and chances are, you won't be bothered by as many insects as you would in some regions. Still, it's always good to carry along some insect repellent in summer.

LAUNDRY AND DRY CLEANING: If you're staying at a hotel, service will be provided in most cases—but with a very expensive price tag.

If you're saving money, try one of the local laundries, such as the **Quickie Lickie Laundromat,** 74 Serpentine Road in Pembroke (tel. 809/295-6097). It is open seven days a week except holidays from 7 a.m. to 10 p.m. (on Sunday from 8 a.m. to 7 p.m.).

Another convenient laundromat is called **Soaps,** The Market Place, Shelly Bay Plaza (tel. 809/293-2303).

If you're out in Somerset, try **Sandy's Laundromat,** Market Place Plaza (tel. 809/238-9426).

LIBRARY: The Bermuda Library (tel. 809/295-2905) in Hamilton is open Monday through Friday from 9:30 a.m. to 6 p.m. (on Saturday to 5 p.m.). It stands in Par-la-Ville on Queen Street, occupying the former house of the celebrated postmaster, W. B. Perot. There are two branch libraries—one at Somerset (tel. 809/234-1980) and another at St. George's (tel. 809/297-1912). The branches are open on Monday, Wednesday, and Saturday from 10 a.m. to 5 p.m.

MAIL AND POSTAGE: The General Post Office is on Church Street in Hamilton (tel. 809/295-5151), open from 8 a.m. to 5 p.m. Monday to Friday, and 8 a.m. to noon on Saturday. Post office branches and Perot Post Office, Queen Street, Hamilton, are open from 8 a.m. to 5 p.m. Monday to Friday (closed Saturday). Some take a lunch break from 11:30 a.m. to 1 p.m.

Airmail for the U.S. and Canada closes at 9:30 a.m. in Hamilton, leaving daily.

Postage rates are: airmail letters up to half an ounce and postcards cost 50¢ to the U.S. or Canada. Sea mail costs 35¢ for letters up to one ounce and 30¢ for postcards.

NATIONAL TRUST: The Bermuda National Trust administers three museums and some of the most historic houses on the island, as well as several scenic open spaces that have been preserved. For information about any of these properties, you can go to the Bermuda National Trust office at the 18th-century Waterville in Paget Parish, just west of the Foot-of-the-Lane Roundabout. Or contact them at P.O. Box HM 61, Hamilton HM AX, Bermuda (tel. 809/236-6483).

NEWSPAPERS: One daily newspaper is published in Bermuda, the *Royal Gazette.* On Friday, two weekly papers, the *Bermuda Sun* and the *Mid Ocean News,* are issued. Major newspapers from the U.S. and Canada are delivered to Bermuda on the day of publication.

PARISHES: Bermuda is composed of nine parishes: St. George's in the northeast end, Hamilton, Smith's, Pembroke, Devonshire, Paget, Warwick, Southampton, and Sandys, which was named in honor of Sir Edwin Sandys, one of the original Bermuda Company investors in the 17th century.

PETS: If you want to take your pet with you to Bermuda, you'll need a special permit issued by the director of the Department of Agriculture, P.O. Box HM 834, Hamilton HM CX, Bermuda (tel. 809/236-4201). Dogs and cats entering Bermuda from any country other than the United Kingdom, Australia, or New Zealand must have received a vaccination against rabies at least one month and not more than one year before the date of their intended arrival. Some guesthouses and hotels will permit you to bring in small animals, but others will not, so be sure to know about this in advance.

PHARMACIES AND DRUGSTORES: In Hamilton, try **Bermuda Pharmacy,** Church Street West (tel. 809/295-5815). It's in the Russell Eve Building, and is open weekdays from 8:30 a.m. to 5:30 p.m. Under the same ownership is the **Phoenix Drugstore,** 2 Reid St. (tel. 809/295-3838), open from 8 a.m. to 6 p.m. Monday to Saturday and from noon to 6:30 p.m. on Sunday.

In Paget Parish, you can go to **Paget Pharmacy,** 130 South Rd. (tel. 809/236-7275), open weekdays from 8:30 a.m. to 8:30 p.m. (closed Sunday).

The **Somerset Pharmacy** is at Mangrove Bay (tel. 809/234-2484), and is open from 8:15 a.m. to 6 p.m. weekdays (closed Sunday and holidays).

PHOTOGRAPHY: Many hotels, gift shops, camera dealers, and drugstores offer 24-hour service on Kodacolor, Ektachrome, and black-and-white film. Kodacolor 110, 120, 126, 127, and 135 pocket Instamatic film sizes can be developed and printed in Bermuda on Kodak quality-controlled equipment. In most cases, you can get same-day service on color prints (except Saturday, Sunday, and holidays) if you bring in your film before midmorning. Most varieties of film are available in Bermuda.

RADIO AND TV: News is broadcast on the hour and the half hour over ZBM AM 1340, ZFB AM 1230, and VSB AM 1450. FM stations are ZBM 89 and ZFB 95. Tourist-oriented programming, island music, and information on activities and special events are aired over VSB 1160 AM daily from 7 a.m. to noon.

The television channel, ZBM 10, is affiliated with CBS.

RELIGION: Nobody can call this "Isle of Devils" today. It's an archipelago of churches. In this relatively small area, with 57,000 in population, the following religions are represented, several by more than one congregation:

African Methodist Episcopal, Anglican, Apostolic Faith, Baha'i, Baptist, Brethren, Christian Science, Church of God in Christ, Church of Christ, Church of God, Church of God of Prophecy, Church of Jesus Christ of Latter Day Saints, Church of the Nazarene, Ethiopian Orthodox, Evangelical, Jehovah's Witnesses, Jewish, Lutheran, Methodist, Muslim, New Testament Church of God, Pentecostal Assemblies of Canada, Presbyterian, Roman Catholic, Salvation Army, Seventh Day Adventist, Twentieth Century Gospel Crusade, United Holy Churches of America, Unity, and Worldwide Church of God.

REST ROOMS: Hamilton (the city) and St. George's provide public facilities, but only during business hours. In Hamilton, toilets are found at City Hall, in Par-la-Ville Gardens, and at Albouy's Point. In St. George's, they are at Town Hall, Somers Gardens, and Market Wharf. Outside of these towns, you'll find rest rooms at the public beaches, the Botanical Gardens, in several of the forts, at the airport, at service stations, but often you'll have to use the facilities in hotels, restaurants, and whatever else you can find.

SPECIAL EVENTS: Bermuda has some festivities that you may want to consider when planning the time for your vacation. December 1 to March 15, as mentioned, is billed as **Rendezvous Time,** during which such daily activities are planned as a date with history in St. George's, a market day with local artisans, a skirling ceremony, and a treasure hunt. Specific dates for these and other events cited below can be obtained in advance from the offices of the Department of Tourism (see "Tourist Information," below) or from your hotel or guesthouse management or local publications when you are here.

The **Bermuda Festival,** held in January and February, is a seven-week international arts festival featuring world-renowned theatrical performers specializing in classical and modern music, Shakespearean and other plays, ballet, puppetry, and other arts presentations.

Beautiful Bermuda **homes and gardens** are open to visitors every Wednesday afternoon in April and May.

The **Beating of Retreat** ceremony of the Bermuda Regiment and massed pipes and drums is held on the last Wednesday in every month except August, from April through October. This takes place on Front Street in Hamilton at 9 p.m. Periodically it's also held in Somerset and St. George's.

A historic and traditional event takes place in April—the **Peppercorn Ceremony,** when His Excellency the governor collects the annual rent of one peppercorn for use of the island's old State House in St. George's. More about this later.

An **agricultural show** in April comprises a three-day exhibit of Bermuda's best fruits, flowers, vegetables, and livestock, as well as featuring equestrian and other ring events.

May is **Bermuda Heritage Month,** when cultural and sporting activities are held, culminating in **Bermuda Day,** May 24, which is a public holiday.

The **Queen's Birthday** (first or second Monday in June) is celebrated by a parade on Front Street in Hamilton.

A truly festive time is had by all during **Cup Match and Somers Days** (held on Thursday and Friday before the first Monday in August). The spectacular match pits the east and west end of the island in that great traditional English sport, cricket.

If you're here in November, you may want to see the traditional ceremony and military guard of honor connected with the **opening of Parliament** by His Excellency the governor as the queen's personal representative.

On **Remembrance Day,** November 11, a gala parade is held, with Bermudian police, British and U.S. military units, Bermudians, and veterans' organizations taking part.

There are numerous **sports events,** ranging from marathon racing to yacht competition to tennis and golf tournaments. For information on the particular field of your choice, ask at your hotel or at the Department of Tourism.

STORE HOURS: Most stores in Hamilton, St. George's, and Somerset are open six days a week (closed Sunday). Hours are generally 9 a.m. to 5:30 p.m., but several shops open at 9:15 a.m. and close at 5 p.m. A few shops are also open in the evening, but usually only when big cruise ships are in port.

TAXES: Air passengers must pay a passenger tax of $10, collected at Bermuda Airport on departure. For ship passengers, the steamship company collects $30 in advance. Children under 2 are exempt from the tax but children 2 to 11 pay $5.

All room rates, regardless of the category of accommodation or the plan under which you stay, are subject to a 6% Bermuda government tax, to be paid when you check out of your hotel.

TIME: Standard time in Bermuda is Greenwich Mean Time minus four hours (one hour ahead of Eastern Standard Time). Daylight Saving Time is in effect from the first Sunday in April to the last Sunday in October, as it is in the United States. Thus when it's 6 a.m. in New York, it's 7 a.m. in Bermuda.

TIPPING: In most cases a service charge is added to your hotel and/or restaurant bill. In hotels, this is in lieu of tipping the various individuals such as the bellman, maids, and restaurant staff (for meals included in a package or in the daily rate). Otherwise, a 15% tip for service is customary.

TOURIST INFORMATION: For further information on Bermuda, see your travel agent or the **Bermuda Department of Tourism** office nearest you. In the United States, they are located in New York: Suite 201, 310 Madison Ave., New York, NY 10017 (tel. 212/818-9800, or toll free 800/223-6106); Boston: Suite 1010, 44 School St., Boston, MA 02108 (tel. 617/742-0405); Chicago: Suite 1070, Randolph Wacker Building, 150 North Wacker Dr., Chicago, IL 60606 (tel. 312/782-5486); and Atlanta: Suite 2008, 235 Peachtree St. NE, Atlanta, GA 30303 (tel. 404/524-1541).

In Canada, it's at Suite 1004, 1200 Bay St., Toronto, Ontario, Canada M5R 2A5 (tel. 416/923-9600).

For information while you're in Bermuda, the following data will prove helpful: headquarters of the **Bermuda Department of Tourism** is at 113 Front St., Hamilton 5-23 (tel. 809/295-1480), which is open Monday to Friday from 9 a.m. to 4:45 p.m. However, you can get answers to most of your questions at the **Visitors Service Bureaus** at the Ferry Terminal, Hamilton (tel. 809/295-1480, or 809/297-1642 Wednesday to Saturday only from 10:30 a.m. to 4 p.m.); King's Square, St. George's (tel. 809/297-1642); or Somerset (tel. 809/234-1388).

WEATHER: This might be an all-important consideration for your Bermuda plans. In addition to the newspaper and the radio, you can also call 977 at any time of the day or night for the latest forecast covering the next 24-hour period.

WEIGHTS AND MEASURES: Since 1975 Bermuda has been adapting to the metric system, although U.S. and Imperial measures are still used. Speed limits, gasoline pumps, distance signs, even the weather report, have gone over to the metric system, much to the objection of many Bermudians who prefer the old way.

You too may prefer the old way; nevertheless, you will have to use the metric measures to an extent. Below is a list of equivalents for quick reference and formulas if you feel the need to convert.

Length

1 millimeter = 0.04 inches (*or* less than 1⁄16 in)
1 centimeter = 0.39 inches (*or* just under ½ in)
1 meter = 1.09 yards (*or* about 39 inches)
1 kilometer = 0.62 mile (*or* about ⅔ mile)

To convert kilometers to miles, take the number of kilometers and multiply by .62 (for example, 25 km × .62 = 15.5 mi).

To convert miles to kilometers, take the number of miles and multiply by 1.61 (for example, 50 mi × 1.61 = 80.5 km).

Capacity

1 liter = 33.92 ounces
= 1.06 quarts
= 0.26 gallons

To convert liters to gallons, take the number of liters and multiply by .26 (for example, 50 l × .26 = 13 gallons).

To convert gallons to liters, take the number of gallons and multiply by 3.79 (for example, 10 gal × 3.79 = 37.9 l).

Weight

1 gram = 0.04 ounces (*or* about a paperclip's weight)
1 kilogram = 2.2 pounds

To convert kilograms to pounds, take the number of kilos and multiply by 2.2 (for example, 75 kg × 2.2 = 165 pounds).

To convert pounds to kilograms, take the number of pounds and multiply by .45 (for example, 90 lb × .45 = 40.5 kg).

Area

1 hectare (100m²) = 2.47 acres

To convert hectares to acres, take the number of hectares and multiply by 2.47 (for example, 20 ha × 2.47 = 49.4 acres).

To convert acres to hectares, take the number of acres and multiply by .41 (for example, 40 acres × .41 = 16.4 hectares).

Temperature

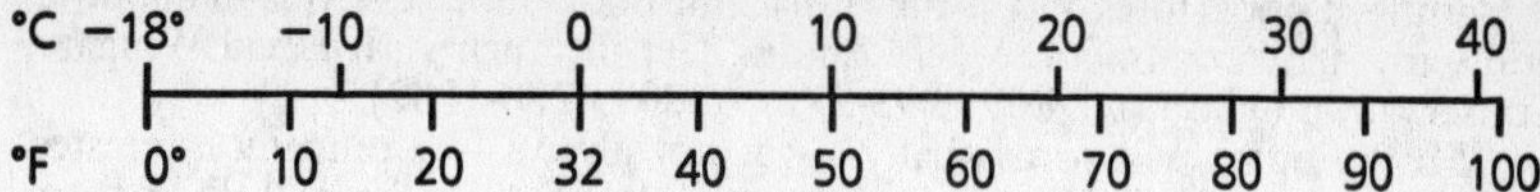

To convert degrees C to degrees F, multiply degrees C by 9, divide by 5, and add 32 (for example $9/5 \times 20°C + 32 = 68°F$).

To convert degrees F to degrees C, subtract 32 from degrees F, then multiply by 5, and divide by 9 (for example, $85°F - 32 \times 5/9 = 29°C$).

4. ALTERNATIVE AND SPECIAL-INTEREST TRAVEL

Mass tourism of the kind that has transported vast numbers of North Americans to points all over the map has created a demand for specialized travel experiences and an increased establishment of organizations that can provide like-minded companions to share and participate in specialized travel plans.

Bermuda is not as affected by alternative travel offers as many other places in the world, because of its size and its lack of mountains, wild rivers, whatever, on which many offerings are based. However, there are still several programs of special interest you might like to explore.

BERMUDA RAILWAY TRAIL: One of the most unusual sightseeing adventures in Bermuda is to walk the Bermuda Railway Trail, which stretches along the old train right-of-way for 21 miles across three of the interconnected islands that make up Bermuda today. The railway is, of course, long deserted. It opened in 1931 but in 1948 was abandoned. The railroad was sold to what was then British Guiana (now Guyana). Before setting out on this trek, arm yourself with a copy of Bermuda Railway Trail Guide, obtainable at the Bermuda Department of Tourism in Hamilton, the Visitors' Service Bureau in Hamilton or in St. George's. With it, you're ready to hit the old trail of the train system which was affectionately called "Rattle and Shake." Once the rail line was the island's main source of transportation, but it gave way to the automobile. The line follows the road between St. George's in the east and Somerset in the west, except for a section stretching for about three miles. That section, where the train whistle was once heard, was lost to roads in and around the capital city of Hamilton.

In some parts the trail connects with main arteries, but for the most part it winds along an automobile-free route left over from the "good old days." Rattle and Shake was considered the most costly rail line, per mile, ever constructed. In many places, the views of Bermuda have not been seen by the general public since the end of World War II. To explore the trail, you face a choice of options: horseback, bike, moped, or your trusty feet. The trail cuts through the five-acre Springfield & Gilbert Nature Reserve (recommended separately under "Exploring Bermuda" in Chapter V). You'll also spot the rare Bermuda cedar which nearly vanished in the blight that struck the island in the early 1940s. Along the trail, you'll take in much greenery and semi-tropical vegetation such as poinsettia, oleander, and hibiscus. At some point you can take time out to visit Fort Scaur, the 1870s fortress.

BIRDWATCHING: There is an active nucleus of birders on Bermuda, but not many organized tours. Visiting birdwatchers are advised to make arrangements directly with the local people involved or find their own way around using the

Check List and Guide to the Birds of Bermuda by David Wingate, which is available at Hamilton bookstores and at the Aquarium Book Shop. Use this in conjunction with standard American field guides. Get in touch with David Wingate, Conservation Officer (tel. 809/293-2727 or 809/238-1282).

Mr. Wingate will occasionally—but not always—accompany interested birdwatchers as part of his conservation work. More frequently, he'll advise them by phone of the island's best retreats, walkways, and hideaways. Eric Amos (tel. 809/236-9056), a professional bird illustrator, is more interested in actually accompanying birdwatchers. A half-day tour, ideally composed of two persons, costs around $25 per person.

STUDYING THE GREENHOUSE EFFECT: Studying a threatening world problem, the **Bermuda Biological Station for Research** has been given a grant to study the "greenhouse effect" by the U.S. National Science Foundation. Some $500,000 will be used every year to study this menace. The greenhouse effect is caused by the destruction of tropical rain forest and by the excessive use of fossil fuels: coal, natural gas, oil, and oil's byproduct, gasoline. Smoke and gases, especially CO_2, produced by burning the forests to clear land for cattle farming and by burning the fossil fuels, build up in the atmosphere and trap heat around our planet. The destroyed forests can no longer absorb the excess CO_2. Our planet starts to heat up like a giant greenhouse. The consequences of the phenomenon include rising global temperatures, expanding deserts, rising sea levels, crop damage, drought, and famine. The greenhouse effect has become so important it has "moved from science to policy" after a meeting of world powers in Toronto in 1988.

The Bermuda Biological Station is best equipped to measure changes in the oceanographic absorption of man-released carbon dioxide, having tracked levels of CO_2 for 35 years 15 miles southeast of Bermuda. The station also has kept extensive data on acid rain for the North American atmosphere.

Now vacationers to Bermuda can learn first-hand what Bermuda-based scientists are studying at the station by taking a free, one-hour guided tour of the station's grounds and laboratory in St. George's. Tour leaders explain what scientific studies are being conducted in Bermuda and how they relate to the overall world environment.

"The tours are a good opportunity for visitors to the island to learn about how the station is contributing to the sphere of science internationally," said Dr. Tony Knapp, director of the Bio Station. "The research we are doing regarding the greenhouse effect and acid rain has helped to position Bermuda as a barometer for global change."

The educational tours on Wednesday at 10 a.m. are conducted by scientists involved in the station's special projects and specially trained volunteers. Visitors should assemble in the Biological Station's main building. Coffee and snacks are served, and participants are asked to give a donation for the refreshments.

Some of the other topics that are discussed on the tour include the island's natural areas, including the coral reefs, protected by strict conservation laws, and how people have caused changes in the fragile ecological environment.

An independent, U.S. non-profit international research facility, the Bermuda Biological Station was established in 1903 through the efforts of scientists from Harvard and New York Universities and the Bermuda Natural History Society. It has been at Ferry Reach, St. George's, since 1932 with funding from both the Bermuda Government and the Rockefeller Foundation. The station is easily accessible by moped, bus, or taxi. It is less than a five-minute drive from the station. For information on the tours, contact the Bermuda Biological Station for Research, 17 Biological Lane, Ferry Reach, St. George's (tel. 809/297-1880).

A SPA: Full-fledged spa facility is available at the Spa, Sonesta Beach Hotel (tel. 809/238-8122), in Southampton. The European-staffed health and beauty spa combines the health and fitness regimes so popular at American spas. Here they offer many exotic and beneficial treatments, one being Ionithermie, the inch-reducing treatment from Europe, as well as deluxe facial care from Paris, ancient forms of therapeutic and relaxing massage such as aromatherapy and reflexology, and Swedish massage. Some people check into the hotel on calorie-controlled four- or seven-day programs. From that moment on, the client's time will be almost totally occupied from 8:30 a.m. to 7 p.m. seven days a week, with aerobics, skin and body care, supervised indoor and outdoor stretching exercises, massages, facials, and beauty regimes.

The facilities can also be used by hotel guests or outsiders who opt for pinpointed treatments rather than the full spa treatments. The up-to-date accoutrements include Universal gym equipment, saunas, steambaths, and massage rooms. The staff directs five-times-a-day exercise classes, which outsiders can join for $6 per lesson. Each procedure is priced separately for nonpackage participants. For example, a 30-minute body massage costs $30, plus tip. For afterworkout pickups, there's a beauty salon adjacent to the health spa for those crowning final touches.

This is recognized as one of the top ten spas in the world.

AN UNDERWATER WALK: The original undersea walk offered by **Bronson Hartley** can be arranged by writing or calling Mr. Hartley at P.O. Box FL 281, Flatts Fl BX, Bermuda (tel. 809/292-4434). Anybody can take part in this adventure, featured twice in *Life* magazine. It's as simple as walking through a garden, and you won't even get your hair wet. A helmet is placed on your shoulders as you stand on the ladder of the boat and begin your guided walk. It is an ideal underwater experience for nonswimmers and those who must wear glasses. Safe and educational, the walk takes you to see the feeding of corals and breathing of sponges, as well as feeding of sea anemones. The skipper and host, Mr. Hartley, personally conducts the tours. His ability to train fish in their natural habitat has been acclaimed in many publications. His 50-foot boat, *Carioca,* leaves Flatts Village at 10 a.m. and 2 p.m. daily. The underwater wonderland walk costs $32 per person.

SENIOR CITIZEN VACATIONS: One of the most dynamic organizations of post-retirement studies for senior citizens is **Elderhostel,** 80 Boylston St., Boston, MA 02116 (tel. 617/426-8056), established in 1975. Elderhostel maintains an array of programs throughout Europe as well as a program in Bermuda, offered frequently. Most courses last for two to three weeks, representing good value considering that air fare, modest accommodations, all meals, and tuition are included. Courses involve no homework, are ungraded, and are mostly concerned with liberal arts. In no way is this to be considered a luxury vacation, but rather an academic fulfillment of a type never possible for senior citizens until several years ago. Participants must be more than 60 years of age. However, if two members go as a couple, only one needs to be over 60. Anyone interested in participating in one of Elderhostel's programs should write for their free newsletter and a list of upcoming courses and destinations.

In Bermuda, the program is at the Bermuda Biological Station, set in 15 acres of parkland at the eastern end near St. George's. Four different topics studied include Atlantic coral reefs, the historic and cultural heritage of the island, Bermuda's delicate balance (people and environment), and flora and fauna. The cost is $400 for a one-week program.

CHAPTER III

WHERE TO STAY IN BERMUDA

□ □ □

Bermuda offers a wide selection of lodgings, ranging from small guesthouses to large luxury hotels. You'll find variations in size and facilities in each category. The Bermuda Hotel Association requires: two nights' deposit within 14 days of confirmation of a reservation; full payment 30 days prior to arrival; and cancellation advice 15 days prior to scheduled arrival or loss of your deposit.

Some smaller hotels and other accommodations levy an energy surcharge. This is a good point to check in advance when you are making your travel arrangements.

All room rates, regardless of what plan you're staying on, are subjected to a 6% Bermuda tax, which is added to your bill. A service charge is added to your room rates in lieu of tips, ranging from 10% to 15%. Service charges do not cover bar tabs. Third-person rates are lower for those occupying a room with two other people, and children's tariffs vary according to their ages.

Generally, there are two major seasons in Bermuda, winter and summer. Bermuda is the reverse of the Bahamian or Caribbean high season, having its major season in spring and summer. Most establishments start to charge their high-season tariffs in March (Easter is the peak period), lowering their rates again around mid-November. A few hotels have all-year rates, and others charge in-between or "shoulder" prices in spring and autumn. If business is slow, many smaller places will shut down in winter.

EMERGENCY ACCOMMODATION: If you haven't time to reserve inexpensive rooms, there is a solution. Throughout the islands are private homes where owners rent out a room or two to earn a few extra dollars. The staff at the **Visitors Service Bureau** of the Chamber of Commerce on Front Street in Hamilton has screened the island to find these hospitality homes where your room rate sometimes includes a Bermudian breakfast. The bath is generally shared, and rooms are adequately furnished, as these selected homes are in pleasant residential areas, each with bus service about a five-minute walk from the door. Some rooms are for single or double occupancy. Other homes offer studio apartments or one- and two-bedroom guest cottages. The rates run $35 to $45 per person per day, based on double occupancy.

This service, at no extra cost to you, is available at the airport, and the tourist office there is open for all flight arrivals. This airport office might be especially helpful. The office is immediately behind the point where newcomers clear customs. Unless someone has a pre-booked hotel reservation and a return airplane ticket, they will not be allowed in Bermuda. Therefore, newcomers without a reservation will be required to have the Visitors Service Bureau book them a room before their passport is returned to them. If you don't want to take a chance, arrangements can be made ahead by writing to the **Visitors Service Bureau,** P.O. Box HM 655, Hamilton HM CX, Bermuda, or calling them at 809/295-1480. Jackie Garcia, who is in charge of the office, must know the exact dates of your arrival and departure, the number of people in your party, the type of accommodation you prefer, and the maximum rate you can pay per person.

1. BIG RESORT HOTELS

The big resort hotels can promise their patrons enough amenities to make it unnecessary to leave the premises, although most visitors tend to want to see what's on the outside. Most of the large hotels have their own beaches or beach clubs and swimming pools. Some have their own golf courses. Most hotels in this category offer luxury resort facilities such as porter and room service, planned activities, sports facilities, shops (including a cycle shop), beauty salons, bars, nightclubs, entertainment, and taxi stands.

Few hotels or guesthouses include taxes and service charges in the prices quoted, so be aware that they will be added to your bill.

Southampton Princess, P.O. Box HM 1379, Hamilton HM FX, Bermuda (tel. 809/238-8000, or toll free 800/223-1818), is, perhaps, *the* most desirable hotel in Bermuda. You receive superlative service and sumptuous accommodations at this 100-acre resort, the biggest and best maintained on the island. It was built on top of a verdant knoll between two views of the sea, at a point where Bermuda narrows to a spit of rock and sand. Since its erection, a team of landscape architects have turned the grounds into the most idyllic large-scale gardens on the island. Guests who check in here are often interested in convention facilities (many international companies hold annual get-togethers here). Other occupants of the resort's 600 rooms are lured to the par-3 executive 18-hole golf course (see "The Sporting Life" in Chapter V).

The hotel's design allows each of the luxurious bedrooms to incorporate a private veranda with a sweeping view of the water. The rooms are arranged around a web-like design that includes three soaring wings, which radiate more or less symmetrically from a central core. These well-furnished accommodations rent for $280 to $420 a day in summer, double occupancy, with breakfast and dinner included. *In winter, rooms, either single or double, range in price from $110 to $165 without meals. The price for meals in winter is $45 extra per person per day.* Meals are taken in one of the hotel's restaurants (see "Dining in Bermuda," Chapter IV). Dining rooms include Windows on the Sound, a three-tiered palace that seems like a happy medley of London's Mayfair of the 1930s and New York's Rainbow Room. Arched windows rising 20 feet look out upon the islands of Great Sound. It's almost a nostalgic re-creation of the grand dining of an earlier era.

The first view many guests get of this rosy-colored palace is as they approach from the flower-bordered access road leading up from the seaside highway. The building towers impressively above a sea of casuarinas, palms, and hibiscus, many planted in evenly spaced rows as foils for both the hotel and the enveloping golf course. The main building is rich in theme restaurants and entertainment facilities (covered separately in this guide). But some of the best parts of this resort are scattered throughout the gardens of the surrounding acreage. The athletic and agile might choose to walk to the 11 outlying tennis courts or to the crystalline sweep of the scenic beach whose private harbor lies within a five-minute walk. The hotel maintains a shuttlebus, which makes almost nonstop runs among the various facilities. Clients who want to sightsee or shop in Hamilton can board one of the hotel's ferryboats, which make runs along Little Sound into the capital. Guests who never want to leave the shelter of the beautifully paneled public rooms enjoy a self-contained village of bars, restaurants, shopping, and athletic facilities. These public rooms, scattered over three plushly carpeted or tile floors, are connected by baronial staircases whose intermediate landings and well-crafted angles provide absorbing vantage points for looking out over the well-dressed clientele. What might be the most dramatic chandelier in Bermuda—a glass, brass, and wrought-iron Spanish-inspired piece especially designed for the space—illuminates three floors of festivities. The array of elegant shops could keep even a compulsive buyer busy for days. The furnishings throughout the hotel are well-upholstered pieces reflecting a restrained kind of 18th-century English dignity. Even the conference rooms are opulent, especially the boardroom, whose decor looks much like what you'd find in an elegant private men's club in London. The polished rosewood walls reflect the ornate chandeliers, fully stocked bar, and concealed movie screen.

As for swimming, the hotel contains both an indoor and an outdoor pool. Although the terrace pool is ideal for a tropical drink in the sunlight, my preferred pool is a re-creation of a Polynesian waterfall, where streams of heated water spill off a man-made limestone cliff, while cascades of flowering vines bloom above the foaming waterjets of the swirling basin. Swimming is possible here even during colder weather because of the greenhouse constructed above. If you crave the salty waters of the sea, the hotel beach is sheltered in a romantically jagged cove, flanked with cliffs and studded with rocky outcroppings lashed by the tides. Bar and restaurant facilities are available on the beach, enabling a guest to remain on the sands for a full day.

The Princess, P.O. Box HM 837, Hamilton HM CX, Bermuda (tel. 809/295-3000, 800/223-1818 toll free in the U.S., or 800/268-7176 toll free in Canada), on the edge of Hamilton Harbour, is a regal pink "wedding cake" landmark. It's graced with a history spanning decades of visits from British aristocrats, Hollywood and European movie stars, and countless discreetly wealthy yachting enthusiasts since it was named after Princess Louise, Queen Victoria's daughter. She stayed here shortly after the hotel opened with international fanfare in 1887. Today it's the flagship hotel of the Princess Hotel chain, and undoubtedly the one with the most glamorous history. When it was initially designed, it was a wintertime palace for the very wealthy. It boasted an all-wood construction to "guarantee against dampness." Before 1932 it had been reconstructed no fewer than four times. By World War II its role as a deciphering center and mail-inspection headquarters for each piece of mail transported from Europe to North America ensured its place in history.

Its elegantly colonial core is flanked with sprawling but well-designed modern wings, each of which is pierced with row upon row of balconied loggias. Depending on who happens to be registered at the time of your visit, several of the loggias might be the scene of this or that cocktail party in honor of whichever yacht team or movie film crew happens to be in Bermuda at the time. One of the hotel's more unusual salons is the gray-and-white Adam Lounge, the central lounge of this prestigious hotel where prewar weekly balls were *the* social event of the colony. The property was designed around a concrete pier extending into the harbor, off of which lies a Japanese-style floating garden, complete with lily ponds, waterfalls, fountains, and towering trees. The theme is repeated in the lobby, where a rivulet of water cascades past rock-climbing orchids near the huge windows.

There are two alluring pools (one heated freshwater pool, another an unheated saltwater pool) set into flagstone terraces. Guests who yearn for tennis, sailing, white sandy beaches, or golf are invited to take one of the frequent ferryboats that the hotel operates between the Hamilton Princess and her younger sister, the Southampton Princess. The hotels lie only an entertainingly scenic boat ride from one another. In addition to the elegantly balustraded terraces on the waterfront (many guests claim that it reminds them of spots on the lakes of northern Italy), the hotel maintains a wide array of drinking and dining facilities. For more information, refer to "Dining in Bermuda" (Chapter IV) and the nightlife section of this guide. Some 40% of the guests are repeat visitors, a fact that proves the allure of this famous hotel.

Management poured $15 million into renovating the tastefully decorated bedrooms and public salons, making a good property even better. Many of the funds were spent on the accommodations, each of which was designed "to create the feeling that you'd choose the same kind of bedroom if you owned a home here." Most of the units have a private balcony, and all of them are air-conditioned. *In winter, between early December and the end of March, single or double accommodations range from $110 to $140 daily, EP.* The rest of the year, single or double rooms range from $155 to $225 daily, also EP.

Marriott's Castle Harbour Resort, Tucker's Town, P.O. Box HM 841, Hamilton, HM CX, Bermuda (tel. 809/293-2040, or toll free 800/268-9250), is on a hilltop overlooking Castle Harbour and Harrington Sound. Originally built of coral blocks in the 1920s, this prestigious property had fallen into disrepair before Marriott poured $60 million into one of the loveliest renovations in Bermuda late in 1986. The renovation added more than 100 bedrooms, landscaped the gardens, and enhanced the public rooms into one of the most strikingly elegant array of spaces of any hotel on the island. The 250 acres of prime real estate surrounding the property are maintained by at least 50 gardeners. From the outside the place looks almost severe, a bit like a modernized version of a Tuscan fortress with abruptly angular outbuildings. One of these is connected to the main building with an elevated concrete catwalk. The most dramatic wing slopes like a modern version of a Mayan pyramid down to the sea.

The 1929 era core was entirely transformed. What might be the most glamorous room in Bermuda is an enormous yet satisfyingly comfortable 18th-century salon, much like what you'd find in an English country house. Filled with copies of Chippendale and Queen Anne furniture, sheathed with mahogany paneling, and glowing with the reflection of rows of soaring windows, it's a showplace for morning coffee, afternoon fish chowder, four o'clock tea, six o'clock hot hors d'oeuvres (accompanied by a live pianist), and after-dinner dance music. Adjacent to it is an elegant dining room where copies of the original Castle Harbour china from the 1920s are part of the meal service. Throughout the property are such refined touches as the Cascade Terrace, stone moongates, and formal garden terraces built around a Bermuda cedar. For sporting diversion, there's a health club as well as a sauna, a golf course, a beach club (accessible by mini-van), a disco, and several restaurants (the Mikado, my favorite, is reviewed separately).

Depending on your tastes, your room might be within one of at least three different buildings on the property. The more than 400 accommodations are either predominantly pink or predominantly yellow and are invariably furnished with a sense of tradition, usually with good copies of English furniture. *In winter, singles or doubles cost $115 to $175 daily; suites, suitable for two persons, begin at*

$240 each. In summer, single or double occupancy is $195 to $295 daily, and suites for two start at $400. MAP is $50 extra per person per day year- round.

Sonesta Beach Hotel & Spa, Southampton Parish, P.O. Box HM 1070, Hamilton HM EX, Bermuda (tel. 809/238-8122), is a long-established luxury resort set on 25 acres of prime seafront property that has benefited from a massive multimillion-dollar restoration. However, its management contract has been sold and during the lifetime of this edition, it will cease to be operated by Sonesta. Therefore, at some point, it may be marketed under a new name. Check with a travel agent before booking in here to see what changes might have been made. Most of the facilities described will probably remain the same for some time into the future. It was built in an even crescent that curves along the spine of a rocky peninsula whose jagged edges provide views of the Bermudian coastline. Benefiting from its status as the only major hotel in Bermuda built directly on the beach, it boasts a trio of sandy beaches, ample lengths of oceanside walkways, and well-trimmed hedges of sea grape, which separate the gardens from the limestone cliffs dropping the short distance to the Atlantic. The property is approached from a winding road that descends the hill from the road above it. A uniformed doorman greets visitors in front of a glass tunnel stretching over a flowering ravine and eventually opening into the tastefully art deco–inspired lobby. With its big windows, blond wood trim, and pastel shades, the lobby is like a 1920s interpretation of the view from a sailboat. In addition to the Greenhouse (see my dining recommendations in Chapter IV), a nightclub, Lilian's, and comfortably panoramic accommodations, the hotel contains a spa facility. Many clients check in on a weight-reduction and muscle-toning regime, which is strictly supervised by the staff.

In addition to the outdoor swimming pool, the hotel contains a complete dive shop for snorkelers and scuba-divers, along with six foliage-concealed tennis courts, each illuminated for night play. There is also a full-time tennis pro, who offers complimentary group lessons twice weekly. The resort also incorporates a favorite beach on the island, Boat Bay, into its facilities. Shaped like an almost-perfect circle and flanked by limestone cliffs and sandy beaches, the bay was used long ago by gunpowder smugglers and later by rum-runners because of its well-camouflaged entrance. From the sea, the rocky coastline almost conceals the narrow inlet that supplies the bay's waters. With its encircling palm-covered cabañas and bars, and soft sandy bottom, the bay looks like a small corner of Polynesia transported onto the buccaneer sands of Bermuda. For cold-weather bathing, there is an indoor pool covered with a symmetrical plastic bubble for a hothouse effect of year-round warmth.

Rates in the sunny accommodations are based solely on the view, since all are basically similar. Each contains a radio alarm, a private terrace, a floral kind of charm, and all the conveniences you'd expect. *Winter rates are $120 to $160 daily in a single and $130 to $170 in a double, BP.* In summer, prices double to $240 to $320 daily in a single, $260 to $340 in a double. For MAP, add another $20 per person daily. MAP clients are served well-prepared evening meals in the Port Royal dining room. Credit is given for meals taken in the Greenhouse Restaurant for those wanting a change of pace. Be sure to ask about the reduced honeymoon packages, if applicable, when you call.

Belmont Hotel, Golf & Country Club, P.O. Box WK 251, Warwick WK BX, Bermuda (tel. 809/236-1301, 416/363-6152 in Toronto, or toll free in the U.S. 800/225-5843), overlooking Hamilton Harbour with views over Great Sound, is an exclusive country-club resort, situated on 110 acres of manicured grounds. Trusthouse Forte, the managing company, poured millions of dollars into creating one of the most desirable properties in Bermuda. Less than a minute's walk from the hotel is the first tee of the Belmont's 18-hole championship golf course, designed by Robert Trent Jones. Tennis is available day and night on three floodlit courts, and the outdoor pool completes the resort's sporting life. There is a pier that serves as the stopping point for the government ferryboat, which goes every 45 minutes to and from Hamilton. Saltwater lovers can catch the hotel shuttle bus, which frequently wends its way to the hotel's facilities at Discovery Bay Beach Club. The full-time social director answers questions and assists with the many planned activities.

The hotel's exterior is a modern interpretation of a Bermuda colonial building. Wide latticed porches flank the entrance portico leading into a formal reception area paneled in Virginia cedar and dotted with Sheraton and Chippendale reproductions. Plushly upholstered English sofas and comfortable wing chairs are illuminated by light streaming through big windows looking out over the lawn and the scattered cays of the Bermuda coast. You'll find a garden with a limestone moongate, plus a handful of outdoor bars. However, my favorite place for a drink is the Harbour Bar, off the main lobby. One of the most elegant modern bars in Bermuda, the decor is of green carpeting, beautifully finished hardwoods, and panoramic views, adding up to a sophisticated ambience.

The 151 luxurious rooms of the hotel feature designer decor and Queen Anne–style furniture. Each unit contains air conditioning, a phone, and TV. Prices in summer are $140 daily in a standard single, $190 to $205 in a superior or deluxe single, with higher rates for suites. Doubles go for $150 to $215, depending on the room's category, and again suites are more expensive. *Winter rates are $105 to $155 daily single or double.* A third person in a room is charged $30 per day. Children under 17 can share their parents' room free. MAP can be arranged for an extra $40 per person per day. MAP guests enjoy their meals in the main dining room, called The Gallery, with a view over the golf course. All the hotel's restaurants offer continental cuisine and Bermudian specialties. The Belmont has a beauty salon and a handful of boutiques.

Elbow Beach Hotel, P.O. Box HM 455, Hamilton HM BX, Bermuda (tel. 809/236-3535), is a self-contained resort set in 34 acres of gardens, with its own quarter-mile pink sandy beach, ten minutes by taxi from downtown Hamilton. On the South Shore, it accommodates up to 600 guests in a choice of well-furnished, air-conditioned rooms, suites, cottages, and family lanais. An array of special package rates is likely to be offered. Otherwise, MAP rates for singles from mid-March to mid-November are $188 daily in a standard room, $294 in a superior accommodation, and $475 in a royal suite. Doubles rent for $111 per person in a standard room, $164 per person in a superior unit, and $254 per person in a royal suite. A third person sharing a double pays $74 daily. *In winter, the charges in a standard single are $130, going to $184 in a superior room and $312 in a royal suite. Doubles cost $81 per person in a standard unit, $108 per person in a superior room, and $172 per person in a royal suite. A third person sharing a double-occupancy accommodation pays $56 daily.* Children under 12 share their parents' room free. Service is included, but taxes are added to the bill. The resort usually attracts a traditional-minded guest, but during the spring college weeks it draws the largest concentration of young students in Bermuda.

At Elbow Beach, you can expect five-course gourmet dinners and American and English breakfasts, with Sunday brunches and barbecues providing a change of pace. Tennis is played on five all-weather courts, and in addition to the beach, there is a large swimming pool with controlled temperatures. In the evening, guests listen to music and dance either at the Surf Club under the stars or the Peacock Club, or perhaps gravitate to the English-style Seahorse Pub where guests are entertained with comedy and song. The Seahorse Grill restaurant is recommended separately.

Grotto Bay Beach Hotel & Tennis Club, 11 Blue Hole Hill, Hamilton Parish CR 04, Bermuda (tel. 809/293-8333, or toll free 800/225-2230, 800/982-4770 in Massachusetts). The only major complaint any guest could have about this top-notch resort is that it's slightly isolated from the rest of the island. The man-made and natural advantages of this place, however, make up for any inconvenience this might cause. The resort is named after the subterranean caves that perforate the 21 acres surrounding it. The organizers have turned these caves into their best advantage, conducting tours, communal swimfests, and spelunking expeditions through them, creating one of the most unusual hotel attractions in Bermuda. One of the caves has been turned into my favorite disco, Prospero's (see the nightlife section in Chapter V). The property is rife with tropical fruit trees, which permit clients to eat loquats, oranges, papayas, and a local kind of kiwi called "locust and wild honey" from one end of the grounds to the other. Nightly live entertainment is provided in the Rum House Lounge. There is a handful of bars on the property and a stylishly lighthearted decor that includes quilted wall hangings and pendulous macramés.

There is a good social program. The swimming pool is blasted out of natural rock and ringed with serpentine edges, much like a grotto in its own right. Under a peaked Bermuda roof, swimmers enjoy the swim-up bar, where a handful of underwater chairs permit guests to "sip and dip." A sandy beach nearby offers a view of an unused series of railroad pylons, leading onto a forested island across the bay. There, what used to be a lighthouse was demolished for one of the explosion scenes in the film *The Deep*. The island, believe it or not, is called Coney Island. Guests are invited to participate in the resort's nature walks, the twice-weekly "cave crawls," and a daily cave swim, plus a complete program for children. There are frequent tennis clinics, daily "Jazzercise" in the Rum House Lounge before breakfast, and such activities as scavenger hunts, communal croquet near the bar, fish feeding, bridge competitions, afternoon tea, a daily happy hour, and organized activities for teenagers.

The 201 accommodations are contained in 11 three-story "lodges" (actually modern buff-colored buildings with prominent balconies and sea views). Several package rates are available for those who remain more than six nights and for families who stay more than four. Scuba, tennis, or golf packages are also available for stays of more than five nights. *In winter, BP rates range from $130 to $150 daily, double occupancy.* In summer, BP doubles cost from $158 to $240 daily. In any season, singles can deduct $15 per day from the tariffs quoted, and MAP costs another $20 per person daily in any season. For an extra $25 per room per day, the hotel can arrange a number of extra amenities, including a color TV, refrigerator, daily newspapers, and other thoughtful touches. The airy public areas, from the sea side, look like a modernized version of a mogul's palace, with big windows, thick white walls, and a trio of peaked roofs with curved eaves.

Inverurie Hotel, P.O. Box HM 1189, Hamilton HM EX, Bermuda (tel. 809/236-1000, or toll free 800/221-1294), on Harbour Road where Paget and Warwick parishes meet, has had a loyal following for more than three-quarters of a century. Named after the Scottish resort town (pronounced In-ver-roor-ee), the resort overlooks Hamilton Harbour, with Hamilton only a ten-minute ride by the frequent ferries. Well-furnished bedrooms, many with their own separate dressing rooms, coffee-makers, and refrigerators, have walls of sliding glass opening onto private terraces or balconies. They are in the midst of landscaped grounds with a large, open-air, temperature-controlled swimming pool.

Golf, honeymoon, and family plans are featured. Otherwise from mid-April to mid-November, MAP rates range from $100 to $150 per person daily for double occupancy, the higher price for suites. For single occupancy, double the rate per person, then deduct $25. *MAP prices in winter are $75 to $112.50 per person daily.* BP rates are also available The main buildings in Bermuda pink have a decorative style set by Dorothy Draper. The recently redecorated rooms include a cocktail lounge, a dining room, a number of the bedrooms, and Le Cabaret, a nightclub. Good food is served in the waterfront Great Sound House, and an English afternoon tea is offered daily. The Marine Terrace features outdoor dining, dancing, and entertainment under a night sky.

Club Med–St. George's Cove Village, P.O. Box GE 59, St. George's GE BX, Bermuda (tel. 809/297-8222, or toll free 800/528-3103), at the extreme eastern end of Bermuda is a five-minute walk from the old town and about ten minutes from the airport. A winding road leads up to this big resort atop its seaside promontory with swimming pools. Set on a 65-acre complex, it rents large double rooms, each air-conditioned with spacious bathrooms (tub and shower combination). Most units have floor-to-ceiling sliding glass doors leading out to a terrace overlooking the ocean or St. George's golf course, which winds around the base of the hotel village, and sea. Designed by Robert Trent Jones, the 18-hole course is available to Club Med members, but at an extra charge. In contrast to some Club Med properties, guests at the Bermuda hotel have locks on their doors. Land arrangements in summer go for $1,000 to $1,400 weekly per person. However, *in the off-season, the cooler months, they are lowered to $750 to $920 per person weekly.*

As at all Club Med properties around the world, meals are included in any or all of its restaurants in this weekly package plan, with unlimited wine and beer at lunch or dinner. There is no tipping, and there are no surcharges. What makes the Bermuda property unique is its choice of restaurants. On the top floor of the hotel village are three small restaurants: Italian, Moroccan, and Chinese, each decorated to make dining a chance to discover not only the cuisine, but something about the art of the people. In addition, there is a large main restaurant, where overflowing buffets are turned out daily for breakfast and lunch. Dinner is served at tables for eight. A patio steakhouse offers dining under the stars on the parade grounds of Fort Albert, one of the two historic forts on the club's property. Noontime buffet lunches are also served at Fort Albert. Fort Victoria, the other fort on the club's grounds, houses a snazzy disco, the Arts & Crafts Workshop (small charge for materials), and a second swimming pool. Daily aerobic classes are frequently held outdoors near the pool. Aside from golf, free sports, with instruction and equipment included in the package, are tennis (a total of nine courts), kayaking, windsurfing, sailing, aerobics, snorkeling, land sports, and archery. Mopeds can be rented at the club, and deep-sea fishing and a full program of excursions around the island are available at an extra charge.

Club Med vacations are open to members only, but membership is available to all. For information on membership and vacations for all Club Med Villages, phone any travel agent or the club's toll free number 800/CLUB-MED, Monday through Saturday.

2. SMALL HOTELS

More informal than the big luxury and first-class hotels are the places in the small hotels category. Many of these establishments have their own good dining rooms and bars, and some feature their own beaches or beach clubs. All of these hotels have their own pools and patios.

Pompano Beach Club, 32 Pompano Beach Rd., Southampton SB 03, Bermuda (tel. 809/234-0222, 617/237-2242 in the Greater Boston area, or toll free 800/343-4155; in Massachusetts and Canada, 508/358-7737 collect), on the southwest shore, is said to be the only hotel in Bermuda wholly owned by Americans. It's also one of the most delightful smaller hotels on the island. Part of its allure is because of its setting on the side of a limestone hill. Years ago it was cut in a stair-shaped series of terraces to accommodate the various buildings of this well-maintained property. Each of these is painted in a shade of rose that local paint merchants call "Pompano Pink," which other homeowners around the island have tried to emulate. Arizona-born David Southworth and his wife, Aimee, are the owners and managers of this attractive property. Many aspects of the interior design were chosen by Aimee herself, including the original design of the carpeting in the dining room. Not satisfied with the patterns that were commercially available, she commissioned a design from a swatch of antique fabric, varying the colors to match the environment created by the dining room's sweep of bay windows. Opposite these are hand-painted murals depicting a Bermudian village on a sunlit seacoast. The result is a pleasingly spacious eating area furnished with difficult-to-obtain Bermudian cedar tables and chairs. Most new construction in Bermuda uses Virginia cedar, which is redder than Bermudian cedar, since local cedar was almost universally afflicted by a blight in 1940.

My favorite place in this establishment, especially at sunset, is in the corner bar of the reception area. There, enormous windows encompass the multihued azures of the shallow coastal waters, which snorkelers and skindivers say are among the best in Bermuda. From the terraced beach below the clubhouse it's possible for water lovers to walk in waist-deep water along a clean sandy bottom for the length of 2½ football fields before finally reaching deep water. The renovated accommodations present this view to its best advantage, offering balconies or terraces from each of the hillside villas scattered over the landscaped property. For guests who prefer to admire the sunlit ocean from the edge of a pool, the resort offers a crescent-shaped freshwater oasis with an adjacent bar, Tea by the Sea, and a mosaic depiction of a pompano, the fish that made these waters famous. There's also an oceanside Jacuzzi.

Year-round, accommodations range from \$220 to \$270 daily, double occupancy, with MAP included. For singles, the price of each unit is reduced by \$20. A third adult can stay in any double for another \$60, MAP. Children under 16 pay another \$60 per day, MAP, if they stay in their parents' room.

Meals in the dining room are both international and successful. Nonresidents can reserve a place for the fixed-price evening meal, which offers a wide selection of courses. Each dish is prepared by a team of five chefs (German, Swiss, Austrian, American, and Malaysian). The price of dinner is \$28 per person. Breads, pastries, and desserts are made fresh daily. Extras provided by this resort include a blazing cold-weather fire (built every evening when needed in one of the stone-trimmed lounges), a honeymoon gate, a tennis court, and easy access to the government-owned Port Royal Golf Course. Designed by Robert Trent Jones, it has a par of 71. Six of its holes lie immediately adjacent to the hotel.

Glencoe, P.O. Box PG 297, Paget PG BX, Bermuda (tel. 809/236-5274, 800/468-1500 direct from U.S., 800/268-0424 in Canada), lies in Salt Kettle on the harbor's edge. During racing season this club-like hotel is likely to be filled to capacity with yachting enthusiasts. It's built at the edge of a cove lined with private houses and filled with boats in any season. The oldest core of this property dates from 1744. When it was still a private residence, it was visited many times by Woodrow Wilson, who stayed here before he became president. The Cooper family, the owners, has expanded it to include pink-walled extensions, containing a total of 40 rooms. Reggie Cooper, who runs it, was the captain of Bermuda's yachting team in the 1964 and 1968 Olympics. Today Reggie and his wife, Margot, who runs a real-estate operation from an office in the main building, welcome nautically minded guests, many of whom reserve the best rooms months in advance.

Each of the public rooms faces a waterfront terrace, where a black ebony tree blooms every year on May 1, according to Reggie. Some of the ceiling beams of the original house are visible below the billiard tables. When it was built, the house was sold to Josiah Darrell for ten shillings, two peppercorns, and three hogsheads of rum. Today the sophisticated decor includes a paneled bar with a working fireplace. There's entertainment nightly from calypso bands or a live pianist. In summer, doubles range from $180 to $250 daily, MAP. Singles pay $15 less per category. A third person staying in any double is charged another $60, MAP. *In winter, each unit, regardless of category, costs $140, MAP.* Each accommodation has a veranda. Tariffs do not include service and taxes. Reggie rebuilt his dock and added a nautically inspired conference room whose windows open onto views of Hamilton Harbour and the Princess Hotel. The government ferryboat makes frequent stops nearby on its way into the capital.

Harmony Club, P.O. Box PG 299, Paget PG BX, Bermuda (tel. 809/296-3500, or toll free 800/225-5843). Early in 1987, Trusthouse Forte transformed a well-furnished and well-landscaped resort into the first all-inclusive couples-only hideaway in Bermuda. Using a touristic format which has been frequently employed in the Caribbean, the package includes all meals, drinks, and diversionary activities, giving participants the advantage of knowing exactly what their vacation will cost in advance. The resort contains only 70 bedrooms, each elegantly furnished with reproductions of Queen Anne furniture. Units are contained in a series of rambling pink-sided wings, which usually encircle formal gardens containing gazebos and well-tended roses. Visitors walk beneath a pink-and-white portico, leading them inside the reception area, where the daily activities are listed.

Only couples are admitted to this hotel. The managers are a couple, French-born Jean-Pierre and Martine Auriol, who help to set the upbeat tone of the place. The cost for all this is $300 per couple per day in summer. *In the off-season the price is reduced to $240 per couple per day.* No children are accepted. Included in the prices are all taxes and gratuities, plus such extra features as champagne, bathrobes, French toiletries, full English tea every afternoon, an array of constantly available snacks, free and open-bar privileges, carefully prepared evening meals served by candlelight on fine china and crystal, and nightly cocktail parties. There is daily entertainment. On the premises is a freshwater pool, along with tennis courts, Jacuzzis, a sauna, a video library, complimentary beach club privileges, and the unlimited use of a double-seat motorscooter (one per couple) during a week's stay. Guests are granted reduced greens fees at the nearby Belmont golf course.

The Reefs, 56 South Rd., Southampton SN 02, Bermuda tel. 809/238-0222, 800/223-1363 toll free in the U.S., 800/268-0424 toll free in Canada), is a lanai colony on Coral Bay, arranged along a low coral ridge. The uncrowded cluster of salmon-pink cottages faces a private beach of pink-flecked sand surrounded by palm trees and jutting rocks. The Reefs offers lanais decorated with rattan furniture and island colors, all with private sundecks and ocean views. The charge for rooms is $238 to $296 daily for two on MAP in summer. *Off-season, two persons can stay here on the Bermuda Plan for $116 to $168 daily.* On a ledge, also with an ocean view, is a kidney-shaped swimming pool, and there are two all-weather tennis courts on the property. The main clubhouse has a beam-ceiling nautical lounge offering entertainment seven nights a week, ranging from calypso to pub-style sing-along favorites. There is a choice of dining in either the plant-filled dining room or al fresco at Coconuts, the popular waterside beach deck between palm trees.

Stonington Beach Hotel, P.O. Box HM 523, Hamilton HM CX, Bermuda (tel. 809/236-5416), or toll free 800/223-1588 in the U.S., 800/268-0424 in Canada), overlooking South Shore in Paget Parish, is set in what used to be a grape arbor. The $6-million structure is owned and operated by the Bermuda Department of Hotel Technology, whose gleaming white classrooms and headquarters lie at the top of a nearby knoll. Most of the employees are students, supervised by professional international staff and trainers. Few deluxe hotel resorts can offer such a high standard of service, and the students are likely to be more helpful than some battle-trained, jaded personnel in the hotel field. A lamplit drive leads visitors through foliage up to the buff-colored façade. A stucco passageway follows a trail to an inner octagonal courtyard where a palm tree grows as a centerpiece. The reception area is high-ceilinged, its dark pine beams alternating with white plaster.

The accommodations are contained in four outlying buildings. Rooms are comfortably spacious, each with a wide balcony or patio, plus a view of the ocean. They are furnished with Drexel-Heritage pieces, ceiling fans, small refrigerators, and love seats that become extra folding beds. In summer, singles cost $145 to $160 daily, while doubles go for $235 to $255. *In winter, singles are charged $88, and doubles pay $112.* A full American breakfast is included in the rates. A third adult in a room pays another $45 daily, and children 5 to 12 are charged $30 per day. MAP rates are also available. Service charges are included in the room tariff. The hotel's sandy beach is reached via steps cut through foliage and limestone. There's also a freshwater pool with an adjacent terrace bar. A library bar with a fireplace is most inviting, as is a very attractive restaurant, the Norwood (see "Dining in Bermuda," Chapter IV). For reservations and information, get in touch with Reservations Systems, Inc., 6 E. 46th St., New York, NY 10017 (tel. 212/661-4540), or call the toll-free numbers above.

Waterloo House, Pitts Bay Road, P.O. Box HM 333, Hamilton HM BX, Bermuda (tel. 809/295-4480, or toll free from U.S. direct 800/468-4100, 800/268-9051 in Canada), on the edge of Hamilton Harbour in Pembroke Parish, is a remake and an extension of a 19th-century house, lying on the outskirts of town center, right at harborside, offering 35 guest rooms. Terraced gardens descend to the water in the style of the Italian Riviera. Behind salmon walls, the gardens are filled with palms, magnolia, poinsettia, urns of ivy, and a splashing fountain, and white iron garden furniture with fringed parasols. Guests can observe the British custom and take afternoon tea at the water's edge on the lawn. There are nooks for drinks and sunbaths. Shade trees stand on the fringe of an open-air, freshwater swimming pool. There is, as well, a private dock, a waterside barbecue area, and a terrace for rum-swizzle parties.

The bedrooms vary in size and decorative treatment, each with its own flair, suggesting a country-house guest room. In summer, singles cost $95 to $135 daily, with doubles ranging from $164 to $240. Cottages and suites for two persons are $214 to $264 daily. All tariffs are for MAP. *In winter, singles are lowered to $82 to $115 daily, with doubles costing from $130 to $196. Cottages and suites for two persons rent for $168 to $196 daily.* Again, all rates are for MAP. The drawing room is furnished with English antiques and decoratively tiled floors. The main dining room, overlooking the terrace and harbor, is dignified with Queen Anne chairs. On the lower terrace level is a bar lounge, with eclectic decorations, Moorish arches, English armchairs, and hand-woven pillows.

Mermaid Beach Club, South Road, P.O. Box WK 250, Warwick WK BX, Bermuda (tel. 809/236-5031, or toll free 800/441-7087, 800/292-9695 in Pennsylvania, 800/544-8478 in Canada). From the street, this holiday village appears like a solid line of yellow-hued façades set side by side along a rock garden. The real allure, however, comes once you enter the embrace of the inner courtyard between the rear of the buildings and the cliffs leading down to the sea. There, a series of limestone-bordered steps descend to a rounded swimming pool and a pleasant sandy cove. There's a dining room on a bluff at one end of the curved complex that's filled at mealtimes with families who prefer this place. Hanging plants fill the big windows, which look out over the surf. There are 85 units encompassing a wide variety of exposures, sizes, and interior fixtures. About one-quarter of the units, the one-bedroom suites, contain private kitchenettes. Each unit has a balcony or veranda, but not all of them look over the ocean. Summer rates in a double range from $216 to $458 daily, MAP. Each extra adult pays $50, also MAP. Children under 16 are charged $44 per day with MAP if they share their parents' room. *Winter rates are $60 to $85 per person daily in a double.* The club attracts visitors with its Old Ship Pub.

Palmetto Hotel & Cottages, P.O. Box FL 54, Flatts FL BX, Bermuda (tel. 809/293-2323, or toll free 800/982-0026 for reservations), in Flatts Village, Smith's Parish, was the ancestral home of the Bermudian Tucker family, whose best known member is Teddy Tucker. He became famous in the 1950s for dredging up treasure from wrecked ships of the 17th century. The walls of the hotel are pink, and there's a cluster of cottages and outbuildings that are also pink. The main building's reception area is paneled in Bermuda cedar. The Inlet Restaurant (see "Dining in Bermuda," Chapter IV) overlooks the moongate, which frames a view of Harrington Sound. Air-conditioned rooms are attractively furnished. In addition to 26 double rooms with bath in the hotel, there are 16 double units with bath in separate cottages, all with a view of the water and private patios. From mid-March to the end of October, EP rates range from $105 in a single and from $130 in a double. Cottages for two to three people rent for $180 daily, EP. *In winter, EP rates in a single range from $55 daily and in a twin from $75. Cottages for two or three guests cost from $110, EP.* The hotel also offers a number of special package plans. Dinner can be taken on an à la carte basis or booked for your entire stay at the rate of $25 per person extra daily.

The Ha'Penny Pub is a darkly intimate hideaway with big windows behind the dark-grained bar. In summer, barbecues are held on the terrace. The location is on the waters of Harrington Sound, about 4½ miles from Hamilton. A raised beach rests on the side of the sound, with access for both swimming and snorkeling to the sandy bottom of the bay. A swimming pool on the grounds also overlooks the water. Complimentary taxis take guests to a beach, five minutes away on the South Shore.

Rosedon, P.O. Box HM 290, Hamilton HM AX, Bermuda (tel. 809/295-1640), on the outskirts of the city of Hamilton in Pembroke Parish, is an old manor house just across the lawn from the Princess Hotel, surrounded by extensive gardens and lawns. Its back modern veranda rooms—called lanai suites—open onto a pool, and there are, as well, fully air-conditioned rooms in the main house. Guests sit on a flagstone terrace under parasol tables around the large, temperature-controlled pool. In the old manor, the formal entry hall is dominated by an open staircase, and a midway landing window. There is a tastefully appointed lounge with a fireplace, plus another lounge. Altogether, 42 individually decorated bedrooms with private baths are rented out. The Bermuda Plan rates include a full breakfast, room service, English afternoon tea, and unlimited tennis and beach use at Elbow Beach, with free, round-trip taxi service (ten minutes). In high season, based on double occupancy, the tariffs are $65 to $75 per person daily, BP. *Off-season (December to April), these rates are reduced to $46 to $69 per person daily, also BP.* The Bermudian staff brings a personalized warmth to a stay here. For information and reservations, write to Jenkins-Gibson, Ltd., P.O. Box 10685, Towson, MD 21285 (tel. 301/321-1219, or toll free 800/225-5567).

Newstead, P.O. Box PG 196, Paget PG BX, Bermuda (tel. 809/236-6060, or toll free 800/468-4111 direct from U.S.), on Harbour Road in Paget Parish, overlooking Hamilton Harbour, is owned by a prominent local family. It is a Bermuda landmark, with a long and colorful history. The original guesthouse accommodated only 12 guests when it opened in 1923, but nowadays there is room for 107 guests in 50 units. Part of the property, Lyndham, was the former home of Sir Richard and Lady Fairey. It was long ago expanded to include adjoining properties, forming a waterfront resort on a flowering hillside overlooking Hamilton Harbour. The ancestral home, painted in three shades of green, has become the hub of social activities. It is popular with the sailing set, and it's impossible to get in here during race week in Bermuda. The setting is traditional, with drawing rooms, a library, and lounges, furnished in part with English antiques, a true country-house flavor, and many informal touches.

Extended from the manor is a sun-pocket swimming pool and a sauna room. Swimming is also possible from two private docks, and the hotel has two tennis courts. At an outdoor terrace, guests enjoy waterside barbecue buffets, rum-swizzle parties, calypso music, and dancing, according to the season. On the extensive grounds are well-designed and furnished bungalows, with either a view of the harbor or of the garden with its flowering hibiscus, coconut palms, and cut-flower beds. *With MAP included, winter rates range from $150 to $190 daily, double occupancy.* In summer, double occupancy, also MAP, costs from $176 to $250 daily. Single residents pay 75% of the double rate, and clients who want EP can deduct $16 per person daily from the above tariffs. Air-conditioned accommodations are in either the main house or the garden bungalows. Dining around is available through the Bermuda Collection, a fraternity of seven different properties. Formal dinners are presented in the main dining room, and coffee is served afterward in the drawing room with its old beamed ceiling and arched wall cupboards. A nine-hole mashie golf course at Horizons is available to guests of Newstead. The privileges of the Coral Beach Tennis Club are also extended to guests of Newstead. From the estate, it's a ten-minute ferry ride to Hamilton.

3. COTTAGE COLONIES

These are considered uniquely Bermudian and feature a main clubhouse with a dining room, lounge, and bar. The cottage units are spread throughout landscaped grounds and offer privacy and often luxury. Most have a kitchenette for beverages and light snacks, but may not be used for full-time cooking. All have their own beach and/or pool.

The St. George's Club, P.O. Box GE 92, St. George's GE BX, Bermuda (tel. 809/297-1200, or toll free 800/268-1332 for reservations), is an all-suites resort, featuring clusters of traditionally designed Bermudian one- and two-bedroom cottages. The luxurious accommodations offer private balconies or patios, comfortable living and dining areas, fully equipped kitchens, baths with sunken tubs and marble vanities, cable TV, and air conditioning. The cottages have a choice of ocean, pool, or golf-course views. In high season, one-bedroom units for two rent for $250 per night, and two-bedroom cottages for four cost $450. *In winter, one-bedroom accommodations for two go for $150 per night, two-bedroom units for four persons being priced at $250.* On 18 acres atop Rose Hill in St. George's, the resort has much to offer. An elegant restaurant called the Margaret Rose, the Sir George Pub, and a convenience store, the Ample Hamper, are in the spacious clubhouse. There are three freshwater swimming pools, one of which is heated, and also a tennis facility. The beach club at Achilles Bay is connected by a short shuttlebus ride. Golfers receive preferential tee times at reduced rates on the adjacent 18-hole Robert Trent Jones–designed golf course.

Lantana Colony Club, P.O. Box SB90, Sandys SB BX, Bermuda (tel. 809/234-0141, or toll free 800/468-3733), is like a private club, where dining is a strong asset. Overlooking the Great Sound, the cottage colony is in a far-out location, attracting those seeking peace more than action (a 25-minute ferry ride to Hamilton). A fashionable colony club, it is spread over 23 acres of cultivated gardens, with both poolside and bay swimming, along with tennis courts. Mr. and

Mrs. Young have guided the destiny of Lantana for more than 40 years. Their son-in-law, Paul Leseur, is managing director. A popular rendezvous point is the clubhouse with its large fireplace. A superb dinner is served in the midst of much greenery and flowers. The chef skillfully prepares a continental cuisine, and the staff is well trained. Placed around the main building are clusters of Bermudian cottages and lanai suites. The emphasis here is on comfort: you'll even find an iron and hairdryers. One cottage has its own private swimming pool. Accommodations are restrained and traditional in decor. On the MAP, a single person pays $225 to $300 nightly in summer, and a double costs $220 to $320. *In the off-season (that is, from November 16 until the end of March), an MAP single rents for $120 to $165 daily, and a double goes for $140 to $245.*

Cambridge Beaches, 26 King's Point, Sandys MA 02, Bermuda (tel. 809/234-0331, or toll free 800/468-7300), on a peninsula overlooking Mangrove Bay in Somerset, has qualities no other cottage colony has, and for that reason heads the desirability list in its category. Its position is one of a kind, occupying the entire western tip of the island, 25 acres of semitropical gardens, lush green lawns, and a choice of five palm-fringed private beaches. As the pioneer of Bermudian cottage colonies, Cambridge Beaches has at its center an old sea captain's house. The main lounges are tastefully furnished with some antiques. With its library and drawing room, a country-estate flavor prevails. One lounge has a beamed pitched ceiling, chintz-covered sofas, and chairs placed around a fireplace. Scattered throughout the gardens are some 78 skillfully furnished, air-conditioned pink-and-white units, some of which are nearly 300 years old, retaining Bermudian architectural features. The furnishings are restrained, color and fabric coordinated. All cottages, several of which were once private homes, have a sun and breakfast terrace, mostly with an unmarred view of the bay and gardens. The MAP charge is $115 to $160 per person per night for rooms. Cottage suites, also on the MAP, rent for $165 per person. *A 20% reduction is granted in winter on all tariffs, except during the Christmas holidays.*

Informal lounges for drinks include the Port O'Call Pub and the residents' piano bar. Calypso and other entertainment are often offered six nights a week. Dining is in the air-conditioned main room or else out on the terrace where barbecues are held. The hotel has three all-weather tennis courts, and a Robert Trent Jones-designed golf course, Port Royal, is seven minutes away, and the resort has its own putting green. Guests swim in a temperature-controlled pool or on the many beaches. Cambridge Beaches has a full marina with Boston whalers and various kinds of sailboats. Water sports include windsurfing with instruction, canoeing, kayaking, snorkeling, and fishing with equipment available. Parasailing, sailing, and snorkeling trips, plus glass-bottom boat excursions and fishing voyages, are offered from the property. Adjacent to the colony are two bonefishing flats. The hotel's ferry will take you directly to Hamilton.

Pink Beach Club & Cottages, P.O. Box HM 1017, Hamilton HM DX, Bermuda (tel. 809/293-1666, or toll free 800/372-1323), on South Road, Smith's Parish, is a luxurious colony of pink cottages surrounding two private South Shore beaches. The largest cottage colony on the island, with 81 units, it enjoys an 18-acre garden setting, filled with bay grape trees and flowering hibiscus bushes. Attracting a loyal list of international habitués, since its inception in 1947, the resort offers a wide range of cottages from a studio (bed-sitting room, bath, and patio) to an individual unit (living room, two bedrooms, two baths, and two private terraces), the latter suitable for four people. In summer, most cottages are in the $255 to $315 daily price range for two persons on the MAP. *Off-season, reductions of 50% are granted.* Executive suites and individual cottages are more expensive, of course. The heart of the colony is the limestone clubhouse painted pink, with its natural-wood dining room where "backyard vegetables" and fresh seafood are served. Every table has a view of the ocean and the South Shore breakers. The drawing room is harmoniously decorated in tones of daisy yellow with mahogany wooden pieces. On extensive landscaped grounds are found a large saltwater pool, a sun terrace, and two tennis courts, one of which is lit for nighttime play. A maid will come around to one of the little kitchenettes located just outside your door and prepare breakfast for you (just as you requested it the night before). The staff is one of the best on the island, including many who have been with Pink Beach since right after World War II.

Horizons and Cottages, South Road, P.O. Box PG 198, Paget PG BX, Bermuda (tel. 809/236-0047, or toll free 800/468-0022), has as its core a converted manor farm (circa 1690) where much of the romantic atmosphere of the past has been retained. A Relais & Châteaux member, it is set on a 25-acre estate with terraced gardens and lawns, on a hilltop overlooking Coral Beach. It has its own nine-hole mashie golf course, an 18-hole putting green, tennis courts, and a heated freshwater swimming pool. The manor house has fine reception rooms, containing old Bermudian architectural details. Throughout are some antiques from England and the continent, and several drawing rooms have open fireplaces. The main dining room serves superb French *cuisine naturelle* using all fresh products, as guests sit on country chairs before an open fireplace. The buffet suppers are popular. Lunch can be served on a terrace furnished with white garden furniture. In the evening that terrace is transformed into an entertainment area, with informal dancing and often calypso music.

The complex was increased with the addition of two junior suites and six bed-sitting room suites just below the main house and now consists of 50 double accommodations in either the cottages or the main building. All are handsomely furnished, with separate dressing areas and private terraces overlooking the ocean, along with ceiling fans, Italian terracotta tile floors, scatter rugs, and traditional tray ceilings. Some units are split level. All accommodations are air-conditioned, whether rooms, bungalows, or suites. MAP rates are $214 to $320 daily for two persons all year. For breakfast only, deduct $20 per day for two persons. Lunches and dinners, by reservation, can be exchanged at Newstead and Waterloo House. Outside reservations for dinner at Horizons and Cottages are limited, so you should book as far in advance as possible.

Ariel Sands Beach Club, South Road, Devonshire, P.O. Box HM 334, Hamilton HM BX, Bermuda (tel. 809/236-1010, toll free from U.S. 800/468-6610, or collect from Canada), is one of the best-established cottage colonies in Bermuda. You'll reach it by driving down a winding lane leading through a park, which eventually deposits you near a lime-green clubhouse with forest-green shutters. The accommodations each have a private entrance, air conditioning, and a simple but attractive decor of white walls, Bermudian flower paintings, and bentwood furniture. Most of them have private porches as well. Each lies adjacent to other units, which can be connected to create units of up to eight rooms, ideal for large families or reunions of old friends. In summer, with MAP included, doubles cost $96 to $129 per person daily, and an extra person in a room pays $48, also MAP. Children under 12, however, need pay only $38 daily for MAP. *In winter, MAP costs are $117 to $148 daily in a single, $92 to $123 per person for a double.*

The grounds are well landscaped with flowering trees and coconut palms, each with a view of the ocean. Water lovers can swim in an oval freshwater pool, a rectangular saltwater pool whose waters are replenished every day by rising tides, or at a sandy beach. One of the most original sculptures on the island is the stainless-steel statue of Ariel who dances like a water sprite on the surf. The statue was made in Princeton, New Jersey, by Seward Johnson. The resort contains three tennis courts, two of them floodlit, plus a series of public rooms where a double-hearth fireplace throws cold-weather light and heat into both a reception lounge and a conservatively attractive bar area designed in cardinal red to look like an English library. The resort is owned and directed by the Dill family. The Sunday-night swizzle party is attended by many of the guests. Those who want to explore Hamilton can take a public bus, which stops nearby. The 2½-mile ride takes about 15 minutes. Mopeds can also be rented for $18 per day, and babysitters can be booked for $6 per hour.

Flamingo Beach Club, South Shore Road, Warwick (mailing address: P.O. Box HM 466, Hamilton, HM BX, Bermuda) (tel. 809/236-3786), is a cottage colony set on a bluff rising above the white sands of its own beach. This well-organized resort includes 16 comfortably furnished accommodations, eight with their own kitchenettes. Clustered around the waters of a Jacuzzi-enhanced swimming pool, its concrete walls are painted in a vivid flamingo pink. Its roofs are designed in traditional Bermudian motifs of coral slabs. Owned and operated by Bermuda-born Juanita Mathias, it contains the also-recommended Jolly Lobster Restaurant. Each room was tastefully designed by Ms. Mathias herself, containing large bathrooms, at least one print or lithograph by a Bermudian artist, summery furniture, and restful shades of pink, coral, and white. Units are set on a lawn rather than directly on the beach, but a steep and curving path leads to the sea. *It is closed in January and February, but charges around $80 daily, EP, for a double from mid-November to December 31 and in March.* In summer, MAP is mandatory, costing $170 to $200 daily in a double. During the season, entertainment is planned, including barbecues and swizzle parties.

4. HOUSEKEEPING UNITS

Housekeeping apartments, Bermuda's efficiency units, vary from modest to superior. Most have kitchens or kitchenettes and minimal daily maid service. Housekeeping cottages all have fully equipped kitchens, are either on or convenient to a beach, and are air-conditioned. The cottages offer privacy and casual living.

Fourways Inn, Middle Road, P.O. Box PG 294, Paget PG BX, Bermuda (tel. 809/236-6517, 800/962-7654 toll free from U.S.). Pink-sided, airy, and stylish, this cluster of Bermudian cottages was added to the garden of one of the best restaurants on the island. Each of the quintet of cottages contains two accommodations, offering views of the harbor or of the Sound, a patio, a private safe, air conditioning, a fully equipped kitchenette, conservatively comfortable furniture, satellite-connected TV, and lots of extra touches. The cottages ring a communal swimming pool and a well-maintained garden. The beaches of the South Shore lie nearby. In summer, single or double occupancy, depending on the accommodation, costs $205 to $275 daily. A two-bedroom cottage, suitable for four people, rents for $480 daily. *In winter, single or double occupancy costs $130 to $180 daily, and a deluxe two-bedroom cottage goes for $310.* Vacationers who want to remain for a week or longer are offered discounts.

Surf Side Beach Club, P.O. Box WK101, Warwick WK BX, Bermuda (tel. 809/236-7100, or toll free 800/553-9990), was terraced into a steeply sloping hillside, which descends, after passing through gardens, to a crescent-shaped sweep of private beachfront. The property was purchased by Norway-born Erling D. Naess and his wife, Elisabeth, who designed the property nearly a quarter of a century ago and who still maintain the varied array of flowering trees and panoramic walkways. The stone masons added several quiet vantage points at various places in the gardens, from which visitors can see grouper and other fish swimming in the distant rocks of the shallow sea.

Accommodations include one-bedroom apartments near the terrace pool. Other lodgings are in hillside buildings. Each of the units is simple and sunny, furnished in bright colors with comfortable accessories. There are also two hillside penthouses, one of which contains a fireplace. Each of the 37 accommodations is self-contained with kitchenettes, air conditioning, and private balcony or patio. Linens and towels are provided. In summer, the apartments rent for $135 to $160, depending on the accommodation, for either one or two guests. Four people can rent an apartment or one of the penthouses for $195 to $270 daily. A third person in a double pays another $20 per day. *In winter, accommodations for one or two persons cost $80 to $96. Apartments or either of the penthouses go for $160 to $180 for four persons.* These tariffs do not include taxes and service. Mr. and Mrs. Naess host Tuesday-night swizzle parties in summer. Also in summer, an à la carte coffeeshop serves breakfast and lunch at open-air tables beside the pool. The staff is pleasant and friendly.

Longtail Cliffs, P.O. Box HM 836, Hamilton HM CX, Bermuda (tel. 809/236-2864), is in a scenic spot in Warwick Parish. Birdwatchers will enjoy the dozens of longtails (a form of seagull) that nest in the cliffs below this establishment. The façade that you'll see from the road might not appear very dramatic, but once you're inside one of the rooms, especially those on the upper floor, you'll be rewarded with lots of space, cathedral-like ceilings, and comfortable accommodations. The Stuttgart-born manager, Doris Joell, keeps the facilities in good working order. Each unit has a kitchen, a phone, a radio, a wall safe, and air conditioning, along with a panoramic view over the sea. A swimming pool is set into a lawn, and a row of hedges signals the beginning of a steep dropoff toward the sea. Beachcombers walk a short distance to one of the neighboring coves. Twelve of the units contain two bedrooms and two baths. In summer, these cost $155 for two people, $215 for three or four. *In winter, the charge is $110 for two occupants, $150 for three or four.* In a separate building is a one-bedroom apartment with a garden setting, renting for $95 double, plus $20 for each additional person in summer. *Winter charges for this unit are $75 double occupancy, plus $15 per additional person.*

Pretty Penny, P.O. Box PG 137, Paget PG BX, Bermuda (tel. 809/236-1194, or toll free 800/541-7426), is a charming home in an excellent neighborhood, where there are nine apartments, each with a kitchenette. Each unit is contained in its own hillside bungalow, with air conditioning and attractive furnishings. The owner and manager of this retreat is a Bermudian citizen, Stephen Martin. You'll be welcomed into a bright and airy living room, his personal residence, for a weekly cocktail party. A fire usually burns in a stone hearth during cooler weather, but in summer, Mr. Martin entertains on an outdoor terrace. A food market is within easy reach so that guests can replenish their supplies. The ferryboat to Hamilton is just a two-minute walk from the front desk. A selection of beaches lie within a ten-minute walk of the premises, and there's a deck-ringed pool right on the grounds. Some of the names of the accommodations evoke a smile: Tuppence, Thruppence, Sixpence, Playpenny, and Sevenpence. One of the units contains a fireplace. Rates in summer range from $44 to $49 per person for double occupancy. Each additional person sharing any double (up to four occupants) pays $35. *In winter, the rates per person, based on double occupancy, range from $35 to $40, depending on the accommodation. Additional guests sharing pay $20 each for up to four.*

Astwood Cove, 49 South Rd., Warwick WK 07, Bermuda (tel. 809/236-0984, or toll free 800/223-5695), has self-contained, fully air-conditioned units. Nigel (Nicky) and Gabrielle (Gaby) Lewin own this homestead, built in 1720, on a dairy farm, and have added apartments in the terraced garden where guests have privacy. From here, the closest large beach, Long Bay, is a quarter of a mile away. However, Astwood's beach and Mermaid beach are only a three-minute stroll from the compound. The cove house has tradition. Three Astwood sisters, Maude, Ada, and Mary, willed the house with the stipulation that it always carry their name. The Lewins have a swimming pool, opening onto the subtropical garden where you can help yourself to papayas, grapefruit, bananas, and oranges, depending on the season. Each of the rental units has a private bath with shower (no tubs), phone (no charge for local calls), radio, ceiling fans, and a terrace or porch, and some of them have sitting rooms as well. They all have compact fully equipped kitchenettes, with English bone china, wine glasses, even salt and pepper shakers. An all-suites building added in 1985 has a communal terrace and pavilion with TV and an exercise cycle. Two people can rent an apartment from April 1 to November 15 at a cost ranging from $84 to $112 daily. Children 15 and under pay $20, that tariff reduced to $15 for those 4 and under. Single occupancy is more expensive. *In the winter months, two people are charged $56 to $80 daily.* The apartment resort enjoys a peaceful setting overlooking lightly wooded meadows and the South Shore, with such extra features as a sauna, pool, and gas-fired barbecue stations.

Somerset Bridge Hotel, P.O. Box SB 149, Sandys SB BX, Bermuda (tel. 809/234-1042, or toll free 800/468-5501 from the U.S.), was skillfully designed to fit into its hillside terrain and is almost completely hidden from the road on which it sits. Consequently, you climb down, rather than up, a flight of avocado-colored steps after registering at the upper-level reception area. Each unit is like an urban studio apartment, complete with kitchenette, private bath, air conditioning, and phone. At night, a pair of Murphy beds (one double and one single) folds down from one of the closets. There's also a double bed contained in one of the foldaway couches. When the beds are folded up and out of sight, the rooms become comfortably furnished living rooms with large glass doors opening onto a private balcony. In summer, MAP rates are $92 per person, based on double occupancy. A single, also on the MAP, pays $132 daily. Additional guests, up to four per unit, are charged another $69.50 per person for MAP. Clients who prefer BP (breakfast only) pay about $25 less per person per day. *In winter, tariffs are reduced about 10%.*

This establishment is owned by the Roberts family, whose head serves in the Bermudian Parliament. The property is managed by the owner's charming daughter, Karen. A swimming pool is set between the hotel and Ely's Bay, where guests can swim. A government ferryboat stops at a nearby wharf five or six times a day on its way to Hamilton. The Blue Foam Restaurant (see Chapter IV, "Dining in Bermuda") is the establishment's dining hideaway, opening onto the water.

Sky-Top Cottages, South Shore Road, P.O. Box PG 227, Paget PG BX, Bermuda (tel. 809/236-7984). Set on a hilltop high above Paget's southern shoreline, this white-walled collection of cottages provide some of the most comfortably isolated accommodations in their price bracket. The 11 units are contained in four cozy, English-style cottages, two dating from early this century, which were assembled into one administrative unit by the English-born wives of two local doctors, Marion Stubbs and Susan Harvey. Each is air-conditioned, containing a tastefully conservative decor of well-chosen furniture, thick carpeting, and in most cases, a small private terrace. Each has a private bathroom, and nine of the units contain fully equipped kitchenettes. In summer, double occupancy costs $65 to $95 daily per unit, depending on the accommodation. *In winter, double occupancy is $55 to $75.* Singles in any season are charged 10% less. Additional guests occupying a double unit pay $20 per night in summer, *$15 in winter.*

The units take their names from some of the flowers in the gardens, so you might find yourself staying in Morning Glory, Pink Coralita, or Allamander. On all sides of the property, emerald-colored lawns encompass shrubs and trees, whose sightlines stretch down to a sweeping view of the sea. Few social activities are planned, except for an occasional rainy-day party to cheer everybody up. Nonetheless, a kind of English-inspired camaraderie sometimes permeates the consciously private accommodations. The sands of Elbow Beach are only five minutes' walk away, and Hamilton can be reached in about ten minutes by cab, bus, or moped.

Paraquet Guest Apartments, P.O. Box PG 173, Paget PG BX, Bermuda (tel. 809/236-5842), is a buff-colored collection of Bermudian houses, attractively landscaped into a gentle knoll a five-minute walk of Elbow Beach. Built in the mid-1970s, they contain 13 apartments, 9 of which have kitchenettes. The Portuguese-born Correia family are the owners. Its focal point is a restaurant and coffeeshop, recommended separately. There's a small swimming pool on the premises. Each unit has a private bath, TV, maid service, air conditioning, and functional but comfortable modern furniture. *In winter, rooms without kitchens rent for $52 daily in a single, rising to $64 in a double. Efficiency apartments with small kitchenettes cost $65 daily in a single and $80 in a double.* In summer, regular singles are charged $65 daily, going up to $75 in a double. Efficiency units cost $75 daily in a single and $95 in a double. A third occupant of any double room pays $19 daily in winter or $21 in summer.

Marley Beach Cottages, P.O. Box PG 278, Paget PG BX, Bermuda (tel. 809/296-8910, or toll free 800/247-2447). Pink-walled, spacious, and beautifully located, these 14 cottages are set in a steep but verdantly landscaped plot of land. Each is attractively airy, with its own sea-view patio and sense of spaciousness. All are air conditioned and have fully equipped kitchens. In summer, units occupied by two guests cost $59 to $84 per person daily, depending on the accommodation. *Expect reductions of 30% in winter.* On the premises is a curved swimming pool and whirlpool, plus a trio of narrow beaches at the bottom of the steep slope leading down to the sea. Each has a name, like Heaven, Next to Heaven, Halfway to Heaven, Bit of Heaven, and Heavens Above.

Rosemont, 41 Rosemont Ave., P.O. Box HM 37, Hamilton HM AX, Bermuda (tel. 809/292-1055, or toll free 800/367-0040), is a gray-walled cottage cluster set on a flowered hillside a short distance from the Princess Hotel. The harbor with its passing ships is visible from the raised terrace beside the small L-shaped swimming pool. Mrs. Karen Cooper Olson, assisted by her sister, Mrs. Lorri Cooper Lewis, is the attractive and vivacious owner. The policy of the hotel is to "keep it quiet" so that the commercial travelers, families, and mature couples who stay here won't be disturbed. In fact, this hotel usually doesn't accept college students or large groups. A grocery store is within a few minutes' walk, and the heart of the city lies only ten pedestrian minutes away. Elbow Beach, a 15-minute ride, provides saltwater swimming, and a motorscooter can be delivered.

Each of the simply furnished rooms has lots of sunlight, a kitchenette, air conditioning, radio/alarm, a full bath, and cable TV. It's possible to connect as many as three rooms together, which some families prefer to do. In summer, either single or double occupancy costs $104 to $110 daily. *In winter, the single or double rate is lowered to $76 to $82.* In summer, a third adult can stay in a double room for $25 per day, while a child under 13 is charged $20. *In winter, the charge for an extra adult is $20; for a child, $12 daily.* These tariffs do not include service and taxes.

Sandpiper Apartments, South Shore, P.O. Box HM 685, Hamilton HM CX, Bermuda (tel. 809/236-7093), built in 1979 and frequently upgraded, is a 14-unit apartment complex. An excellent choice for a budget-conscious vacation, it is within a short walk of several beaches. Nine of the units are studios suitable for single or double occupancy. The studios have a bedroom with two double beds, bath, and fully equipped kitchenette. Five of the units have bedrooms with king-size or twin beds, kitchens, baths, and living/dining areas with two double pull-out sofa beds. All of the apartments have air conditioning, phones, radios, and balconies, plus daily maid service. Year-round, single or double occupancy costs $98 EP daily, with triples priced at $136 and quads at $160. You can relax in the outdoor whirlpool and swimming pool or lounge in the inviting gardens. The Sandpiper is only minutes from restaurants and the supermarket.

5. GUESTHOUSES

Guesthouses are usually comfortable old converted manor houses in garden settings. Some have pools and terraces. The smaller ones have fewer facilities and are much more casual. Most guesthouses serve only breakfast. The guesthouses taking fewer than 12 guests are usually small private homes, some having several housekeeping units, while others provide shared kitchen facilities for the preparation of snacks.

Royal Heights Guest House, Lighthouse Hill, P.O. Box SN 144, Southampton SN BX, Bermuda (tel. 809/238-0043, or toll free in the U.S. 800/247-2447). The strangest part about this amply proportioned guesthouse is that it isn't better known. Set at the top of a steeply inclined driveway near the summit of Lighthouse Hill, it's convenient to the Southampton Princess Hotel and its assorted nightlife and restaurant facilities. This is a modern turquoise-trimmed building whose pair of wings embrace either side of the front entryway. Terraced near the foundation, a sparkling swimming pool encompasses a view of the passing ships of the Great Sound. Guests are welcome to congregate in the stylish modern living room of the owners, Russell Richardson and his wife Jean. Each of their seven, very clean bedrooms has air conditioning, a balcony, and comfortable furniture. Your hosts will suggest activities for you, although guests here tend to be independent types. In summer, with breakfast included, singles and doubles cost $90 daily, and triples go for $130. *In winter, singles and doubles rent for $80 daily, triples for $110.* Children under 12 sharing a room with their parents pay $40 in any season.

Loughlands, 79 South Rd., Paget PG 03, Bermuda (tel. 809/236-1253), is a stately, once-private residence built in 1920 as the home of Mr. Lough, president of the Staten Island Savings Bank in New York. It is now the largest guesthouse on the island with 25 bedrooms. Set on nine acres of landscaped grounds in the center of the island, it is plantation chalkwhite, its entry hall containing a large portrait of Queen Victoria. Loughlands was purchased in 1973 by Mary Pickles, who sold her large country house in Cornwall, England, shipping many of her antiques to Bermuda. The bedrooms at Loughlands are handsomely decorated, some with high-post beds and antique chests. Rates here include a continental breakfast with such Bermudian touches as fresh citrus fruit or bananas and homemade preserves. In summer, a twin rents for $94, *dropping to $60 off-season.* Singles range from $67 daily in summer to *$45 off-season.* Rooms are air-conditioned, with private baths as well. On the grounds is a swimming pool and a tennis court, and bus service to all parts of the island is close by. Elbow Beach is just a short walk away.

Greenbank & Cottages, P.O. Box PG 201, Paget PG BX, Bermuda (tel. 809/236-3615), on the water's edge in Salt Kettle, stand across the bay from Hamilton, reached by a ten-minute ferry ride. It's an old Bermuda home, hidden under pine and palm trees with shady lawns and flower gardens. The owner, Joan Ashton, is one of the most gracious hostesses in Bermuda, extending hospitality to guests and welcoming them to her drawing room with its original floors, fireplace, well-styled couches and chairs, a grand piano, and her antiques collection

The atmosphere is relaxed and personalized. Greenbank offers accommodations with private entrances, baths, and kitchens, either waterside cottages or garden-view apartments. EP rates are $80 to $85 daily for two persons in summer. *Winter prices are $70 to $75 daily for two.* There is maid service daily. Greenbank has a private dock for swimming, plus a boat rental and charter operation on the property, where sailing, snorkeling, motorboats, and sailboats are offered.

Granaway Guest House & Cottages, Longford Hill, Harbour Road, P.O. Box WK 533, Warwick WK BX, Bermuda (tel. 809/236-1805), is an appealing private home built in 1734. The house has had a colorful past, Hezekiah Frith, the pirate, is said to have purchased the home for a daughter, and—much later—the TV tube was invented in the basement. The present owners acquired the house from a Russian prince and princess. The princess was an expert gardener who planted passion flowers, birds of paradise, and citrus trees. Michael and Carol Ashton are your hosts. Michael is a third-generation Bermudian and a psychologist. He met Boston-bred Carol at Hamilton's Hog Penny Pub on her 21st birthday. As part of their hospitality, the Ashtons create bicycle tours of Bermuda for their guests.

All the flavor and style of their old Bermudian home are intact, with wide-plank floors and high ceilings. Some of the rooms overlook the water across Harbour Road. There are four bedrooms, each with private bath, plus one cottage. The yellow room is a particular favorite because of its cedar beams and its central post—in almost the exact center of the room—that supports the ceiling. The most interesting place to stay, however, is the old slave quarters, converted into a charming suite. It has its own private bath and rock garden. Rooms, either single or double occupancy, cost $85 daily in summer, *dropping to $70 in winter.* Breakfast is included. The old slave quarters cost $100 per day for two occupants in summer, *$75 in winter.*

Mrs. Ashton will bring a tray and a smile into your bedroom in the morning, unless you prefer a spot in the garden. The flatware is silver, and the china is imported from Hungary. There's a dock across Harbour Road, with a walled-in sandy area for swimming. Guests come here on balmy evenings for sunset watching. Snorkeling is good in nearby waters (you'll have to provide your own equipment). The sports, restaurant, and nightlife facilities of the Belmont Hotel are a short distance away.

Royal Palms Club Hotel & Restaurant, 24 Rosemont Ave., P.O. Box HM 499, Hamilton HM CX, Bermuda (tel. 809/292-1854, or toll free 800/441-7087 in the U.S.), in Pembroke Parish, is one of the most sought-after guesthouses in the city. Residents of nearby houses often walk by its gardens just to admire the masses of marigolds and zinnias that bloom in the front yard. The property is the domain of Horst E. Finkbeiner, who was born and educated in West Germany and boasts more than 25 years in the hospitality industry, in management positions at a number of major hotels, such as the Princess in Hamilton and the Elbow Beach Hotel. He has also served as honorary consul to Bermuda for the Federal Republic of Germany.

The house is one of the prettiest around, with other-colored walls, gold shutters, and a white roof, plus a wraparound front porch dotted with rocking chairs and sofas. The 12 rooms were converted from living rooms, parlors, and bedrooms of what used to be a very grand private house. Today each of them is spacious, sunny, and comfortably if simply furnished. Ten units are equipped with private bath, air conditioning, and a phone. In summer, accommodations on EP rent for $78 to $90 daily, and doubles go for $106. *EP charges in winter are $72 daily in a single, $82 in a double.* Year-round, MAP is an additional $32 per person daily.

Serenity, 29 St. Michael's Rd., P.O. Box PG 34, Paget PG BX, Bermuda (tel. 809/292-4718), is a small guesthouse. Sun worshippers sometimes regret the trek to the nearest beach, but few other guesthouses offer such reasonable rates and such an intimate view of Bermuda life. Owned and operated by Jamaican-born Mrs. Cecilia Couchman, this buff-colored house sits within a development behind a circular driveway ringed with flowers. Each of the half dozen rooms has a private bathroom, air conditioning, and access to a comfortable guest lounge which is like a Bermudian family's private living room. A few of the units have a veranda and a kitchenette. Depending on the accommodation, *winter rates are $45 to $55 daily in a single, $70 to $80 in a double, and $85 to $100 in a triple.* In summer, singles range from $55 to $65 daily, with doubles going for $80 to $90 and triples for $100 to $115. Children under 4 stay free, and children 4 to 12 pay $25 per person daily.

The Oxford House, Woodbourne Avenue, P.O. Box HN 374, Hamilton HM BX, Bermuda (tel. 809/295-0503, or toll free 800/223-5695), is one of the most centrally located—and one of the best—guesthouses in the city of Hamilton. It lies on a side street leading into Front Street near the Bermudiana Hotel. It was built in 1938 by a doctor and his French wife, who requested that some of the architectural features follow French designs. The white- and cream-colored entrance portico is flanked by Doric columns, corner mullions, and urn-shaped balustrades. Inside, a curved stairwell sweeps upward to the spacious, well-furnished bedrooms, each of which is named after one of Bermuda's parishes. There's even an upstairs sitting room bathed in sunlight. Each accommodation gives the feeling of a private home, containing air conditioning, a direct-dial phone, and a private bath. In summer, singles cost $75 daily, and doubles go for $88, triples for $109, and quads for $128. *In winter, singles are $63 daily; doubles, $76; triples, $92; and quads, $114.* The Bermuda breakfast, included in all rates, has fresh-fruit salad (in season), made with oranges and grapefruit grown in the yard. The gracious manager of the establishment is Ann Smith.

Greene's Guest House, 71 Middle Rd., P.O. Box SN 395, Southampton SN BX, Bermuda (tel. 809/238-0834), overlooks Great Sound. The outside of this place appears well maintained, clean, and unpretentious. A look on the inside reveals a pleasant and conservatively furnished environment that's even better than you might have initially supposed. The entryway is flanked by a pair of lions resting on stone columns. The dining room, which can be closed off from the adjacent kitchen by a curtain, is set with a full formal dinner service throughout the day. Wall-to-wall carpeting covers the floors of the entrance lobby as well as the spacious and well-furnished living room. Guests are free to use this room, as well as the sun-washed terraces in back. A swimming pool is in the back garden. The owners are Walter ("Dickie") Greene and his wife, June. Mr. Greene has been the organizer and promoter of the annual "Miss Queen of Bermuda" contest. A hospitable man, he makes his guests feel at home.

Of the six bedrooms, four contain full baths, ironing boards with iron, coffee makers, video TV, phones, refrigerators, and air conditioning. There's even a cozy bar facing the sea, where guests use the honor system to record their drinks. Year-round rates, with breakfast included, are $100 in a double and $60 in a single. Dinners, upon request, can be prepared. A public bus stops at the front door for runs into Hamilton. The beach and the Port Royal golf course are both about five minutes away.

Edgehill Manor, Rosemont Avenue, P.O. Box HM 1084, Hamilton HM EX, Bermuda (tel. 809/295-7124), outside the Hamilton city limits, in Pembroke Parish, might just become "your little home in Bermuda." It's a small guesthouse with well-lit, airy, and high-ceilinged units, in a quiet residential area that is convenient to restaurants and shopping in Hamilton. Your landlady is British-born Bridget Marshall, who still observes the custom of English tea in the afternoon. Some of her units are cooled by ceiling fans and others have air conditioning. At least two are equipped with kitchenettes. All of the accommodations come with a small balcony or patio. Singles cost $70 daily in summer, and doubles go for $80 to $86. An extra $10 is charged for children under 12 sharing their parents' room. *In winter, prices are $50 in a single, $60 to $68 in a double.* All tariffs are on the CP. If you're interested, ask Bridget Marshall about her special honeymoon rates. The atmosphere is informal and casual, but still with just the right touch of proper reserve and dignity.

Hillcrest Guest House, Nea's Alley, P.O. Box GE 96, St. George's GE BX, Bermuda (tel. 809/297-1630), is a green-and-white early-18th-century home, spread on the rise of a hill off Old Maid's Lane. With its wide verandas, lawns, and trees, it has a home-like look, and the interior is pleasant and comfortable. The small entry hall has Edwardian furnishings, and the bedrooms are on two levels. All accommodations have private bathrooms. The rate is $40 to $45 daily in a single, $60 to $65 in a double. All are air-conditioned and have clock-radios. Tom Moore, the Irish poet, roomed here in 1804 for many weeks. He was quite taken with Hester Tucker next door, and wrote her some romantic verse. Hillcrest also has a moongate on the lawn. Hillcrest is three to five minutes from restaurants, shops, golfing, the bus route, and all points of interest in the historic town of St. George's. Write to Mrs. E. Trew Robinson at the address given above for a reservation.

CHAPTER IV

DINING IN BERMUDA

□ □ □

Wahoo steak, shark hash, mussel pie, fish chowder laced with rum and sherry peppers, Hoppin' John (black-eyed peas and rice), and the succulent spiny Bermuda lobster (called guinea-chicks) are some of the unusual dining experiences awaiting you in Bermuda. Trouble is, you'll have to search hard to find these offbeat dishes. Many hotels and a large number of restaurants serve typical international resort cookery. For a more detailed description of Bermudian cookery, refer to the "Food and Drink" section of Chapter II.

Bermudian food has been much improved in recent years, although dining out is still not the major reason to visit these islands. British dishes such as steak-and-kidney pie are common, as are American ones. Most of the meat has to be imported, so whenever possible it's best to stick to selections from the briny. Fish is generally excellent, especially Bermuda rockfish.

Most restaurants, at least the better ones, insist on a dress code, preferring men to wear a jacket and tie after 6 p.m.

Sunday brunch is a Bermuda tradition. Hot and cold dishes are served buffet style at several restaurants recommended below. My preferred choice for brunch is the Waterlot Inn (see below).

1. THE CITY OF HAMILTON

Romanoff Restaurant lies right in the heart of Hamilton's Church Street, just west of Burnaby (tel. 809/295-0333). In the last few years it has established itself as the most prestigious gourmet restaurant in Bermuda. You get a splendid continental cuisine—not just Russian, as the name implies—along with impeccable service. In an atmosphere evoking the style of Old Vienna, the haute cuisine of the continent is dispensed, after you're greeted by the manager, Antun Duzevic. Some $250,000 in renovations was poured into rejuvenating the site, and all the fine Wedgwood china, Damask linen, brass lamps, and crystal were brought out for your elegant repast, which is likely to cost from $60 per person for dinner. The smoked-glass mirrors deceivingly make you think the burgundy-colored room is larger than it is. Men are asked to wear jackets and ties to dinner.

Appetizers include snails in garlic butter and smoked rainbow trout. The chef prepares crêpes filled with assorted seafood and also makes tempting kettles of soup, including the traditional Russian borscht and also lobster bisque and French onion soup. *Les crustacés* and *les poissons* may lure you to the sea long before you get to the grills and the main meat and poultry dishes. Dover sole is prepared in classic ways, but if you want something fresh from local waters, try either the broiled wahoo filet or the Bermudian lobster. Shashlyk is served Georgian style (that is, flambéed with vodka), and you might also prefer chicken Kiev or duckling à l'orange. However, the chef's pièce de résistance is his tournedos flambé Alexandra, which is beef tenderloin flamed with cognac and served with a superb sauce made at your table. Each night you can also select the chef's creation of the evening from a silver trolley. For dessert, there are marvelous soufflés and crêpes, or perhaps a zabaglione. Lunch is served Monday to Friday from noon to 2:30 p.m., a business repast with six choices going for $10.75. Dinner Monday to Saturday is served from 7 to 10 p.m.; closed Sunday.

Tiara Room, Princess Hotel, Hamilton (tel. 809/295-3000). The gourmet restaurant of this posh hotel, this modernized restaurant focuses its decor around elaborate tiara-shaped chandeliers and the sweeping panoramic view over Hamilton Harbour. Dinner is festive, when the accoutrements are the finest, the illumination enhanced by the dozens of flickering candles that seem to set fire to the crystal and heavy silver. Flambé dishes are a specialty here, each of which adds a touch of theatricality to the decor.

For an appetizer you have a choice of such dishes as terrine du chef or antipasto. Among the soup selections are chilled soup of the day and Bermuda fish soup. The chef is superb at preparing fish dishes and is said to search the eastern seaboard for unique aquatic catches. From this Atlantic bounty, try the scampi provençale or a brochette of scallops broiled with cherry tomatoes and mushrooms. Among the main poultry and meat dishes, you are likely to find such fare as roast quail served with a cherry sauce, roast rack of lamb with herbs of Provence, or filet mignon with a béarnaise sauce. Of course, menus change, but you get the idea of what to expect.

Full meals cost from $50 per person. Dinner is served nightly except Sunday from 6:30 to 10:30. Reservations are necessary, and in such a setting, men are requested to wear jackets and ties.

Tivoli Gardens Restaurant, 37 Reid St. (tel. 809/295-8592), occupies the second floor of what had been the Hamilton armory. In the 1800s the rifle corps of the island used to go through their exercises here. Nowadays its second-floor precincts have been converted into one of the finest dining rendezvous targets in Bermuda. However, it's not one of the waterfront restaurants, but set back a bit.

Those who have traveled to Denmark may delight in Bermuda at last having a restaurant that specializes in Danish food. The Danes, of course, are well known for their culinary expertise, and the Tivoli Restaurant in Hamilton, named after the famous pleasure gardens in Copenhagen, has had success with its lunchtime smörgåsbord. You can help yourself to herring, shrimp, and cold cuts, then come back for a taste of several hot dishes, vegetables, and potatoes—with cheese and dessert to follow—all for $16 per person. Of course, they also offer smørrebrød, those open-faced Danish sandwiches which are ideal for lunch, dinner, or even a

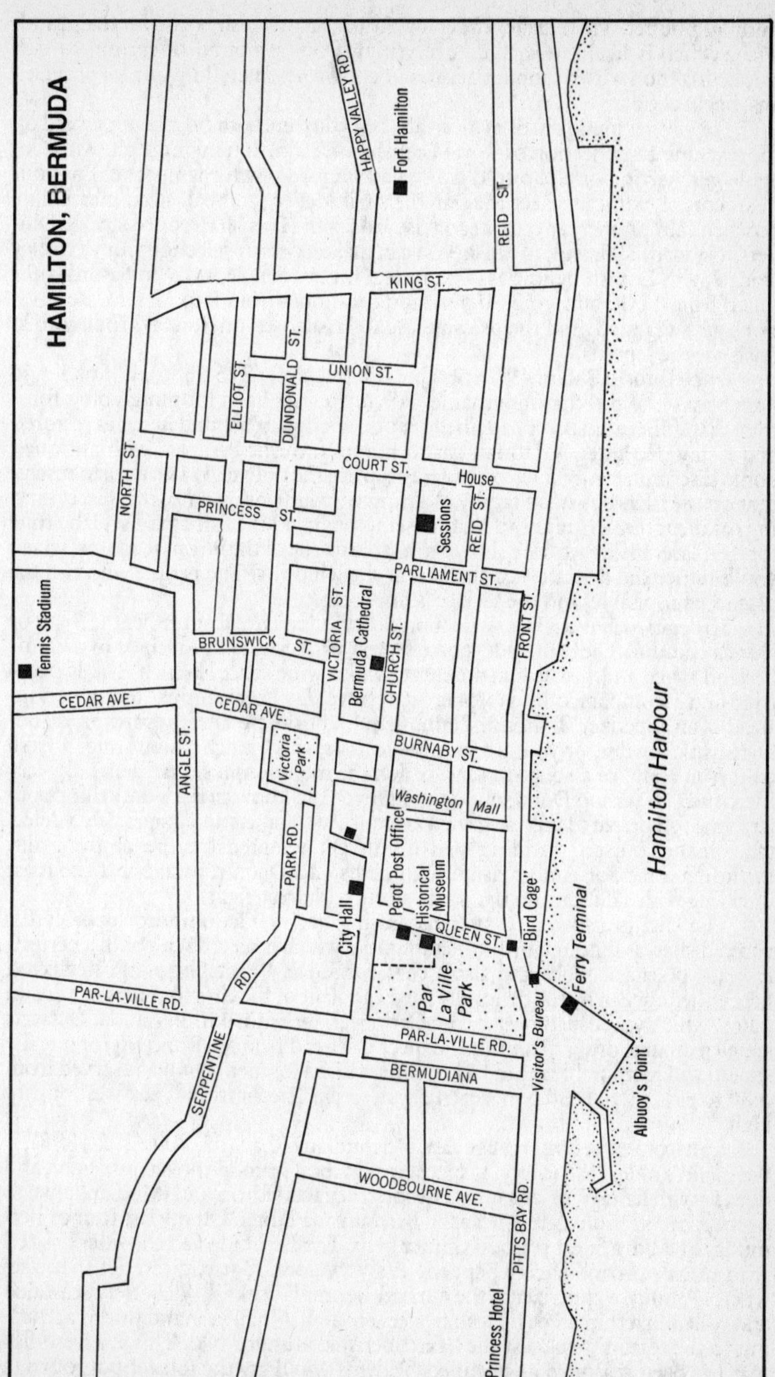
HAMILTON, BERMUDA
HAPPY VALLEY RD.
Fort Hamilton
REID ST.
KING ST.
UNION ST.
ELLIOT ST.
DUNDONALD ST.
NORTH ST.
COURT ST.
House
PRINCESS ST.
Sessions
REID ST.
PARLIAMENT ST.
Tennis Stadium
VICTORIA ST.
Bermuda Cathedral
CHURCH ST.
FRONT ST.
BRUNSWICK ST.
CEDAR AVE.
CEDAR AVE.
ANGLE ST.
Victoria Park
BURNABY ST.
Washington Mall
Hamilton Harbour
PARK RD.
Perot Post Office
Historical Museum
City Hall
QUEEN ST.
"Bird Cage"
Ferry Terminal
Par La Ville Park
PAR-LA-VILLE RD.
RD.
PAR-LA-VILLE RD.
Visitor's Bureau
SERPENTINE
BERMUDIANA
Albuoy's Point
WOODBOURNE AVE.
PITTS BAY RD.
Princess Hotel

midnight buffet. Most Danes order an akvavit or a Danish beer with their sandwich, which is likely to include everything from a mound of shrimp to rich smoked salmon with a topping of caviar. Sandwiches, including one for vegetarians, begin at $5.

The dinner menu changes monthly, but you can count on it being served on the restaurant's collection of Royal Danish porcelain. You might begin with Copenhagen herring or else a cold fruit salad prepared with champagne. For your main course, you can select Margarethe's frikadeller (golf-ball-sized meatballs), poached salmon in a caper sauce, or else hakkebøf (Danish chopped steak). Dinners cost from $25, and, to finish, you can make a dessert selection from a trolley loaded with Danish delicacies. The restaurant is open Monday to Saturday for lunch from 11:45 a.m. to 2:30 p.m. and for dinner from 7 to 10 p.m. Reservations are suggested, and the dress is casual. It is closed on Sunday. Your cordial hosts are the Jensens.

Once Upon a Table, 49 Serpentine Rd. (tel. 809/295-8585). I think I'd go here because of the charming name. Fortunately, it has a lot more going for it than that. If Bermuda ever had a belle époque period, it's found here in a restored and richly decorated Victorian island home, furnished in part with antiques. Some discriminating diners consider this place the only truly Bermudian restaurant on the island. A small family of caring Bermudians operates this place, serving candlelit dinners nightly. An old island buggy in the front yard sets the tone for the place. Inside, you are shown to a table in one of the intimate rooms, where you'll notice the delicate lace curtains at the windows. The people who run the place are hospitable, and the service is impeccable.

To begin, you must face a selection of hors d'oeuvres from either the *froids* or *chauds* column. These include a pâté served with crushed pistachios in a Cumberland sauce and mussels in a delicate white wine sauce. French Brie is deep-fried and accompanied by a raspberry preserve. *Les Potages* might tempt you instead of an appetizer. To honor Bermudian tradition, the chef prepares an island-style fish chowder, or you can go more classic with French onion soup, a fresh cold fruit soup, or a soup du jour, which the menu promises is "generally very inventive." If wahoo Doris sounds strange to you, know that it's only this popular game fish prepared with a white wine sauce with capers and grapes. It's a delectable main course, providing you didn't get tempted by one of the grills, including a rack of lamb roasted with herbs and Dijon mustard and the roast duckling with a delicate orange sauce along with fresh fruits.

The chef is also skilled at transforming beef tenderloin into superbly flavored dishes, as reflected by the filet mignon, which is served with both a perfectly made béarnaise sauce and also a chasseur sauce. Vegetables aren't neglected here either, especially the delicately fried eggplant or the christophines in a cream sauce, which you usually get in the Caribbean more than in Bermuda. Desserts are elegant and often "flaming." Expect to spend from $45 and up for a really superb and memorable meal. Jackets are required for men. Dinner is served from 6:30 to either 9 or 9:30 p.m. seven days a week. The location is just west of City Hall.

Lobster Pot & Boat House Bar, Bermudiana Road (tel. 809/292-6898), is the island's oldest fish eatery. It specializes in local seafood cooked just right, and does so with flair. With its nautical decor, it attracts visitors and 'Mudians alike to its location off Front Street near the Bermudiana Hotel. On my last tour of Bermuda, I had my finest seafood dinner here. The Bermuda fish chowder is laced with black rum and sherry peppers. It's very good, but you can get that elsewhere. A unique appetizer is the curried Bermuda rockfish (delicately seasoned and rolled in a thin crêpe). Fresh oysters are available all year and priced according to the season. I suggest the baked Bermuda fish for two. This is a fresh fish that has been seasoned and stuffed. Perhaps you'll try the lobster potpourri, a mixed fish fry, or the wahoo steak (a game fish). Bermuda lobster, called guinea-chicks, is available in season (that is, from mid-September until the end of March). The typical Bermuda banana fritter is a popular finish to a meal. Expect to pay from $28 for a complete meal.

Lunch, daily, is from 11:30 a.m. to 5 p.m.; dinner, 6 to 11 p.m. Closed Sunday. Dress is casual. This place is extremely popular, and with good reason, so always reserve a table.

The Conch Shell, Emporium Building, 69 Front St. (tel. 809/295-6969), is a sophisticated nighttime rendezvous open for dinner seven nights a week from 6:30 to 10:30. Its most desired tables are outside on a balcony overlooking Hamilton Harbour. The ambience is stylish, with salmon-colored walls, gray-clothed tables, ceiling fans, and aquariums with exquisite fish. The chef specializes in Oriental and Western-style seafood. You might begin with one of the hot appetizers such as crispy egg roll or perhaps shrimp "legs" Nori (raw shelled shrimp with ginger, wine, water chestnuts, and scallions). The most exotic soup is shark's fin, or else you may prefer to begin with a conch salad. For your main course, you can make such selections as fried abalone with oyster sauce, New Orleans–style chicken (that is, with a lemon and orange sauce and chopped almonds) or fresh Bermuda fish seasoned with a touch of Pernod and served papillote style. Prime sirloin steaks are also offered. Full meals cost from $30 per person. Lunch is also served from noon to 3 p.m. daily, offering an array of soups, sandwiches, and salads, costing from $12.

Rum Runners, Front Street (tel. 809/292-4737). Lined with bricks and aged paneling, this warmly decorated restaurant contains a pub which is a popular hangout in its own right. Both establishments lie at the top of a steep flight of steps. Filled with antique rifles and bowsprits, the main dining room, the Nonsuch Room, is open daily from 11:45 a.m. to 4:45 p.m. and 6:30 to 10 p.m. The menu offers standard English, American, and European fare, with beef and veal dishes predominant. You may want to try the prime sirloin steak (ten ounces) or the prime roast rib of beef with Yorkshire pudding, perhaps the chicken Cordon Bleu or the seafood brochette. Full dinners cost from $35, but lunches are less expensive, going for $12 and including sandwiches, salads, fresh fish, crab cakes, burgers, and oysters.

The same menu is served in the nearby pub within view of the harbor. Called the Load of Mischief Pub, it has cedar trim, a beamed tray ceiling, and a somewhat less formal ambience than its neighbor. Meals tend to be less expensive, and no one minds if you order pub grub to supplement your tankard of English ale. Live music is a special event almost every night from 10 p.m. to 1 a.m.

New Harbourfront Restaurant, Front Street (tel. 809/295-4207). In the center of town, across from the ferry station, on the second floor of an old Hamilton building, this spacious restaurant was stylishly renovated with Italian-inspired accents. Formally dressed waiters serve lunch daily from 11:45 a.m. to 3 p.m., dinners from 6:30 to 10:30 p.m. except Sunday. Specialties include such dishes (for two people) as young lamb with an apricot sauce or chateaubriand, as well as poultry and veal dishes. Fresh swordfish in garlic and white wine sauce is a standard, as are veal Oscar, broiled Bermuda lobster (in season), and an array of other seafood dishes. Lunches cost from $15 each, while dinners run from $40. The decor is marine blue and pink. As you dine, melodies from a shiny black piano will accompany your meal and dancing after dinner.

Fisherman's Reef, Burnaby Hill (tel. 809/292-1609), in the heart of Hamilton, lies above the Hog Penny Pub, and is a deserving choice for seafood and typically Bermudian dishes. After a restoration, it offers a nautical setting and a separate bar and cocktail lounge. There is a live lobster tank. For seafood, you can order wahoo, one of Bermuda's most popular game fish dishes. It's cut into steaks and topped with banana and bacon strips. Bermuda rockfish, among the finest caught on the island, is also served. When available, a whole Bermuda fish is seasoned, stuffed, and baked in the island's typical way. Also, Bermuda guinea-chicks—that is, small lobsters—are broiled on the half shell in season. Ask the waiter about the daily catch—snapper, grouper, shark, or yellowtail—which can be pan-fried, broiled, or poached. Most people come here for fish, but the chef is also adept at preparing meat courses. He does an excellent peppersteak flambé and a number of classic veal specials, including Oscar, marsala, and français. Banana fritters laced with black rum is a favorite dessert. Expect to spend from $28 for dinner, $12 for lunch. Dress is informal, and hours are noon to 2:30 p.m. and 6:30 to 10:30 p.m. Reservations may be needed.

Little Venice, Bermudiana Road (tel. 809/295-3503), is definitely Italian, as you might guess. The owner likes to introduce you to his specialties—casseruola di pesce dello chef (a variety of Bermuda lobster, shrimp, fresh fish, mussels, and clams cooked in white wine with herbs and tomatoes) and tournedos Rossini. The pasta dishes are varied, beginning with homemade ravioli filled with spinach and ricotta cheese. Among the soups I'd suggest the fish chowder. The veal dishes featured on my last visit were properly seasoned and prepared. If you have room, you might try the zabaglione. An abbreviated menu is offered at lunch, with meals costing from $18. Dinner, however, is likely to begin at $25. Good Italian, German, and French wines are featured, and wine is also available in carafes. The restaurant is open Monday to Friday for lunch from 11:45 a.m. to 2:30 p.m., seven days a week for dinner from 6:30 to 10:30 p.m. Dress is "smart casual."

Loquats, Bermuda House, 95 Front St. (tel. 809/292-4705). Some visitors to Bermuda immediately claim this as their preferred dining and drinking hangout. It occupies a long and narrow second-story room whose entrance lies off an alleyway a few paces from the main artery of Front Street. You dine beneath a high sloping ceiling whose widely spaced rafters reveal slabs of Bermuda limestone laid in layers as roofing shingles. There's a narrow veranda overlooking the harbor and a long and well-used bar designed a bit like a Victorian antique.

The establishment is open daily except Sunday from 11:30 a.m. to 11 p.m., but mealtimes last from noon to 2 p.m. and 6 to 10 p.m. Lunches cost from $12 and include a large selection of flame-broiled burgers, broiled Bermuda fish, and salads. Dinner from $25 features English-style fish and chips and Bermuda fish papillotte. Spit-roasted specialties include duckling Indonesia with mango slices and green peppercorns, along with a mixed grill from the skewer. Charbroiled main dishes feature everything from veal Dutch-style to meaty pork ribs barbecued. Several dishes are combination platters such as a rack of barbecued baby back ribs with jumbo shrimp. A variety of seasonal fruit and cake desserts is available from the chef's special menu; otherwise, you can settle happily for Apple Brown Betty. Drinks are generously poured, and seem the appropriate accompaniment to the live music featured here on most evenings.

M.R. Onions, Par-le-Ville North (tel. 809/292-5012), is an enormously popular restaurant and bar. The name of the place is a colloquialism. Bermudians are known as onions, and the "M.R." stands for "emare" or "they are." Hence the name means, "They are Bermudians." Designed like an Edwardian-era bar, it's done up with lots of exposed brass, potted palms, leaf-green walls, and miles of oak trim. Many caricatures of Bermudians hang on the walls. A different one is picked each month, first shown at the entrance and then moved into the restaurant. If you go early, have a drink at the large rectangular bar that fills most of the establishment's front room. It's especially popular during happy hour daily from 5 to 7 p.m., when it is a favorite rendezvous for office workers in the neighborhood. The bar is open daily from 11:30 a.m. to 1 a.m.

Well-prepared meals are served in a back room, with specialties including house onion soup, french-fried breaded mushrooms, escargots, barbecued chicken or ribs, shish kebab, steak teriyaki, fish steak of the day, and deep-fried scallops, plus charbroiled fresh Bermuda wahoo and tuna. You can also order an array of burgers and beer by the pitcher or the glass. The dessert specialties are mud pie and cheesecake, or you can choose from the elaborate sweet trolley. There is also a bakery, featuring onion bread and curried onion bread. Lunch is served from noon to 3 p.m. Monday to Friday, costing $4.75 to $15. Dinners, seven days a week from 5:30 to 10 p.m., go for $9.75 to $20. Snacks are available in the bar until 10 p.m.

Harley's, Hamilton Princess, Hamilton (tel. 809/295-3000). Named after the bearded bon vivant who established this hotel a century ago, this is the popular restaurant of this previously recommended landmark hotel. In warm weather, tables are extended outside to the edge of the swimming pool, creating an effect a bit like a flowering terrace on the Italian Riviera. Even in cold weather the establishment is as stylish and lighthearted a place as you'll find anywhere in Hamilton. The restaurant is open daily for breakfast from 7 to 11 a.m., for lunch from noon to 4:30 p.m., and for dinner nightly from 6 to 10 p.m.

Full dinners, costing from $35, include an array of beef, lamb, and poultry dishes. Try the catch of the day, veal marsala, or Asian-style chicken with peppers and teriyaki. Fresh Bermuda chowder, laced with black rum, usually begins most meals. The cuisine is essentially Mediterranean. The chef also prepares a number of fish dishes, including fresh imported Pacific salmon. There is also a selection of familiar pasta dishes such as cannelloni or fettuccine Alfredo. You might want to dine on a two-handed sandwich or one of the fresh-tasting salads at lunch, when full meals cost from $15. Salads include a Greek version of chicken with cashews and oranges, and low-calorie and vegetarian selections are also available.

Hog Penny, Burnaby Hill (tel. 809/292-2534), is Bermuda's most famous pub, built and decorated in the British style with dark paneled rooms and draft beer and ale. Old fishing and farming tools make up part of the decor, along with bentwood chairs and antique mirrors. At lunch you can order pub specials, including shepherd's pie and seafood crêpes, or a tuna salad. The kitchen prepares a number of curries, including chicken and lamb. Fish and chips and steak-and-kidney pie are the perennial favorites, with lunches costing from $15. Dinner, from $25 and up, is more elaborate. You can always order a fresh fish of the day, perhaps Bermuda yellowfin tuna. The Angus beef is excellent, and you may want to precede your meal with Bermuda onion soup. Lunch is from 11:30 a.m. to 5:30 p.m. and dinner from 6 to 11 p.m. Food is served seven days a week. There is nightly entertainment, and dress is casual.

Chopsticks Restaurant, 65 Reid St. East (tel. 809/292-0791), although off the beaten track, offers some of Bermuda's best Chinese cuisine, including spicy soup, tangy pork ribs, and seafood. Mr. Luk, the chef, specializes in Szechuan and Cantonese dishes with an accent on fresh vegetables and delicate sauces. This two-story restaurant, with dining upstairs and downstairs, gives you the best of two worlds. The fine food is served by a Bermudian staff. Dinner for two costs less than $50. Reservations are advised. Meals are served from noon to 2:30 p.m. and 6 to 11 p.m.

The Bombay Bicycle Club, Rego Furniture Building, Reid Street (tel. 809/292-0048), Indian haute cuisine is expertly cooked and served in an upstairs hideaway where you can enjoy lunch or dinner in a relaxed atmosphere. For lunch, they offer A Taste of India buffet, with a different selection daily, costing $8.95. A wide variety of à la carte dishes is on the menu, ranging from mulligatawny soup to chicken, beef, lamb, and seafood either in a choice of sauces, spicy curries, or roasted in the tandoori oven. Indian vegetarian dishes and a continental selection are also available. The place, on the third floor of the building between Court and King Streets, serves lunch from noon to 2:30 p.m. Monday to Friday and dinner from 6:30 to 11 p.m. Monday to Saturday. It's closed Sunday. Dress is smart casual.

The **Pub,** Princess Hotel (tel. 809/295-3000), is a pleasantly informal eatery off the lobby of this famous hotel. It offers temptingly fragrant tropical drinks whose colors include the full spectrum of a sunset. From noon to 2:30 p.m., one of Hamilton's better bargains is the pub's buffet luncheon, whose tempting array of salads and platters draw a busy midday crowd. The price is from $13. Dinners, served from 6:30 to 10 p.m., are à la carte, costing from $25. The roast prime rib of beef is served with the classic Yorkshire pudding and is well flavored. Always ask about the fish du jour if you're interested. The food is good and hearty, also familiar, and that means roast country chicken, English fish and chips, and pork chops. The salads are fresh, and you might begin your meal with a French onion soup. The blue and green plaid carpets and the dark paneling give you a feeling of a Scottish pub.

Primavera, Pitts Bay Road (tel. 809/295-2167), lies in Hamilton West between Front Street and the Princess Hotel. It is one of the finest Italian restaurants in town, often viewed as an alternative to the more traditional fare served in many of the island's restaurants. Here you get classic Italian fare served seven days a week. Lunch is Monday to Friday from 11:45 a.m. to 2:30 p.m. when tabs average around $18. Dinner is seven nights a week from 6:30 to 11. You might begin with a selection of either a hot or cold antipasti, including a cold seafood salad or hot baked clams served in a marinara sauce. You can follow with a soup, perhaps pasta e fagioli in the Venetian style, or a salad, most likely a Caesar. Dinners cost from $30 and beyond and include an array of pasta dishes, featuring ravioli Primavera (the chef's surprise), or chicken breast filled with garlic butter and cheese, or osso buco (the veal shank dish that is a specialty of Milan). Naturally, you'll want to finish such a satisfying meal with either an Italian espresso or a cappuccino.

Portofino, Bermudiana Road (tel. 809/292-2375), is an Italian trattoria near the Bermudiana Hotel. It offers well-prepared and reasonably priced specialties. These include four kinds of spaghetti and all the famous pastas, such as lasagne, ravioli, and cannelloni. There are 13 kinds of nine-inch pizzas offered, along with a classic minestrone. Standard and familiar Italian dishes include Venetian-style liver, veal parmigiana, chicken cacciatore, and beefsteak pizzaiola. Snails are prepared with "a secret recipe." Meals cost from $25. Chianti bottles hang from the ceiling, and the decor is in the typical taverna style. Lunch is served from noon to 3 p.m. and dinner from 6 p.m. to midnight. There is no lunch offered on Saturday and Sunday, however. Otherwise, it is open for lunch and dinner seven days a week.

Red Carpet Bar and Restaurant, Armoury Building, 37 Reid St. (tel. 809/292-6195), serves many Italian dishes even though evocative of an English pub. This place does a thriving lunch business from the many office workers who fill the buildings nearby. Later, after work, its wood-trimmed bar is popular as a place to relax with a beer amid a decor of dark-red carpeting, dim lights, and darkly stained trim. Meals are served daily from 11:30 a.m. to 2:30 p.m. and 6:30 to 10 p.m. Lunches cost from $12 to $15 and include sandwiches, cold platters, and a few hot dishes such as pan-fried fish. Dinners, from $25 to $35, feature a wide selection, including veal scallopine, veal marsala, chicken cacciatore, filet mignon, and New York–strip sirloin.

The **Botanic Garden,** Trimingham's, Front Street (tel. 809/295-1183), is housed on the third floor of the most famous department store in Hamilton. Food is served daily from 9:30 a.m. to 4:30 p.m.; however, if you're going for a hot lunch, the hours are only from 11:30 a.m. to 3 p.m. Naturally the place is filled with shoppers, most of whom know good value when they see it (that's why they're here). The place is informal and self-service, and ideal for morning coffee or a British afternoon tea. There is an array of European sandwiches as well. The luncheon specials are likely to include macaroni and cheese or barbecued chicken, along with a tossed salad and coffee (or tea), all for only $6.50. The pastries, pies, and cakes are excellent, especially the banana bread and the gingerbread. The name of the restaurant suggests the decor.

Royal Palms Club, 24 Rosemont Ave. (tel. 809/292-1854), in the city of Hamilton, is contained in a well-maintained guesthouse with the same name. This restaurant isn't well frequented by tourists, even though it does a thriving business with the local community at lunchtime. It contains a simple bar area where drinks are a bargain at $2 each during the afternoon happy hour from 5 to 7 p.m. Lunch is offered from noon to 2:30 p.m. daily either inside the simple and somewhat old-fashioned interior or on the outdoor terrace. At lunch, you're offered a choice of sandwiches at $6 each. More substantial platters of food, such as chicken Cordon Bleu, are available as well. At dinner, from 6 to 10 p.m., a more elaborate menu has such elegant fare as chicken Kiev, veal scallops with zucchini, U.S. choice sirloin steak, and the catch of the day prepared "the way you like it." Meals cost from $30. Summer barbecues are an island event. Special features of the place are a Wednesday steak and lobster night, costing $26 and a Friday seafood buffet, also $26. It includes shrimp and salmon, among other offerings. For more information about this place, refer to the preceding chapter.

Show Bizz, Reid and King Streets (tel. 809/292-0676), is a small restaurant with a jazzy decor and a pianist who often keeps things lively at night. It is open Monday to Saturday from noon to midnight and on Sunday from 6 p.m. to midnight. There is full bar service until 1 a.m. The kitchen turns out good pasta dishes, salads, hamburgers, seafood, soups, Bermuda fish, sandwiches, and steaks. Look also for their blackboard specials. The char-broiled beef ribs and barbecued ribs are also popular. Dinners cost from $25, with lunches going for around $12.

MacWilliams, 75 Pitts Bay Rd. (tel. 809/295-5759). Set on the waterfront road leading into the most congested part of Hamilton, this informal restaurant is sheathed in light-colored brick and neutral-colored paneling. Clean and bright, and designed in a coffeeshop decor, it serves breakfast, lunch, and dinner, as well as coffee and snacks, daily from 7:30 a.m. to 10:30 p.m. Lunch, costing from $10, includes an array of sandwiches, hamburgers, soups, and salads. Dinners, from $20, feature such dishes as Bermuda fish dinners, fisherman's platter, sirloin steak, liver with onions, spaghetti with meatballs, and barbecued ribs.

Fourways Pastry Shop, Washington Mall, Reid Street (tel. 809/295-3263), lies on the ground floor of a shopping and office complex whose bustling crowds remind visitors of London. Still, its array of very fresh pastries, tartlets, ice creams, petit fours, quiche, and croissant sandwiches evoke a Viennese or Milanese coffeehouse. You can order espresso or cappuccino while waiters dressed in Bermuda shorts bustle to serve the dozens of cramped, tiny tables. Coffee with a pastry costs from $3. The establishment does a thriving business daily except Sunday from 8 a.m. to 5:30 p.m.

2. PAGET PARISH

Fourways Inn, Middle Road (tel. 809/236-6517), is considered by many to be the best restaurant in Bermuda. It was once an 18th-century Georgian house built of coral stone and cedar, which has been tastefully converted into a dining room offering continental specialties and local seafood dishes. The glow of candlelight shines on the old mahogany beams. In the conversion, the traditional Bermudian character was observed. Guests have a choice in season of dining inside or out. On most nights a pianist plays, and the atmosphere is graceful and relaxed, the service good. The popularity of the place makes reservations essential. The old kitchen has been turned into the Peg Leg Bar with a whitewashed fireplace.

Sunday brunch is an elaborate buffet, costing from $27.50. Hours are from 11:30 a.m. to 1:30 p.m. Otherwise, from Monday to Saturday, no lunch is served. At night, a more ambitious menu is featured, beginning with the chef's specialty, cold smoked salmon soup with dill. Main-dish specialties of the chef are tender filet of beef wrapped in light pastry and offered with a truffle and foie gras sauce, filet of lamb in a raspberry-vinegar sauce, and roast prime rib of beef carved to order and served with the traditional Yorkshire pudding. An unusual dish is called le tartare de poissons, which is prepared at your table with fresh raw Bermuda fish. A superb selection is the roast duck in its own gravy accompanied by a fresh pear poached in red wine. For dessert, the chef is known for his soufflés (which should be ordered in advance). Try the black rum soufflé. I find that the most delectable is the chocolate, but you may prefer the strawberry or Grand Marnier. The establishment is one of quality, as reflected by its price scale, which is likely to set you back more than $55 for dinner. The wine cellar is among the finest on the island. Men should wear coats and ties in the evening. In summer, dinner is served nightly from 6:30 to 9:30, but in winter, hours are from 7 to 9 p.m.

Newstead Restaurant, Newstead, Harbour Road (tel. 809/236-6060). Contained in one of the most quietly elegant manor-house hotels in Bermuda, this attractively dignified dining room welcomes nonresidents who telephone for a reservation. Guests dine beneath a beamed tray-style ceiling in a conservative dining room whose chintz-filled decor could have been transported from Britain. As you dine, a view of the lights of Hamilton Harbour slowly emerges as twilight falls. Full dinners are served from 7:30 to 9 every night of the week in low season and every night except Tuesday and Thursday in summer. Between May and October an outdoor barbecue is held every Tuesday and Thursday, accompanied with live dance music and a view of water splashing from a dolphin-shaped fountain above the swimming pool. Regardless of its locale, full fixed-price dinners cost $38 per person without drinks. The chefs offer a frequently changing array of continental inspired food, including roast leg of lamb with mint sauce, grilled sirloin steak with savory butter, and roast chicken Grand-Mère. Introduce yourself to the charming owner, Bermuda-born Brendan Ingham, an avid golfer whose nickname is "Bees."

The **Seahorse Grill,** Elbow Beach Hotel, South Shore, Paget (tel. 809/236-3535), is in a previously recommended hotel that permits a view of the sea and an old-fashioned colonial Bermuda setting. Lunch, daily from 11:30 a.m. to 3 p.m., costs from $8, including such fare as chicken nuggets, pita-bread sandwiches, British fish 'n' chips, and a selection of burgers, pizzas, salads, and ice cream. Dinner, served from 6:30 to 9:30 p.m., costs $12 and up. Menu choices include fettuccine Sarragosa, escargots in crêpes, lobster bisque, Oriental chicken platter, New York–sirloin steak, and different preparations of shrimp and scallops, topped off by such desserts as banana fritters with black rum.

The **Terrace Room,** Elbow Beach Hotel, South Shore, Paget (tel. 809/236-3535). Enormous, stately, and with a view of the sea, this coral-colored dining room is the most formal area in this previously recommended hotel. Only dinner is served in its conservatively decorated confines at two seatings: 6:30 and 8:30 p.m. The establishment offers a fixed-price menu for $35, usually with a choice of five different main dishes. Regular à la carte dinners also cost from $35. Menu choices include a well-selected medley of such continental dishes as roast veal loin with a walnut cream sauce, grilled wahoo sautéed in lemon butter, and Long Island duck with a bing cherry sauce. You might begin with snail in puff pastry with garlic butter or a vegetable soufflé with a raspberry sauce. Desserts tend to be elaborate as reflected by the mint cream parfait, frozen hazelnut soufflé, and traditional English trifle.

Tavern on the Green, set in the beautiful Botanical Gardens in Paget, off Berry Hill or South Shore Road (tel. 809/236-6631), is the ideal al fresco setting for enjoying classic and Bermudian dishes thoughtfully recommended and artfully prepared. The dinner menu features a large selection of fish, veal, and pasta dishes. Specialties include la brochette de scampi et langouste à la sauce d'annis (shrimp and lobster tails served on a skewer sautéed in anise) and Tre Mousquetaire (ravioli, fettuccine, and penne al pesto). Meals cost from $25. There's also a wide variety of dishes available on the luncheon menu. The tavern is open seven days a week. You can have morning coffee (but never on Sunday) from 10 to 11:30 a.m., lunch from 10:30 a.m. to 2:15 p.m., afternoon tea from 2:30 to 5 p.m., and dinner from 6:30 to 10 p.m. Dress is smart casual, with jackets for men requested after 6 p.m.

Paraquet Restaurant, P.O. Box 173 in Paget (tel.809-236-5842). Set near an important traffic junction on the South Shore, this unpretentious restaurant is the center of a previously recommended apartment cluster with the same name. Its decor of lime-colored Formica, tiles, metal chairs, and plants is definitely coffeeshop, but some of the menu specialties include substantial restaurant fare. As you dine, you overlook a circular, formal flower garden which the Portuguese owners created. The establishment is open daily from 9:30 a.m. to 1:30 a.m. without interruption. It has one of the largest sandwich menus on the island, both hot and cold, as well as omelets, homemade soups (which always include a fish chowder), and salads. You can order mixed platters such as turkey breast and crabmeat, or such grilled dishes as T-bone steak, fried liver and onions, and roast chicken. Full meals range from $12 to $30 per person.

Norwood Room, Stonington Beach Hotel, Paget (tel. 809/236-5416), offers stately dining in a large sun-washed room with tartan carpets, spidery iron chandeliers, Spanish-style stucco arches, and fan-shaped windows looking out over the foliage and the water. The restaurant is contained within a state-run hotel training school (see Chapter III, "Where to Stay in Bermuda"). The service and attitude among the youthful employees is most attentive. A piano provides music in the evening, when men should wear jackets and ties.

An à la carte menu is presented, but many guests prefer the $32.50 table d'hôte, whose last order is taken at 8:15 p.m. Dinner is at specific seatings daily at 7, 7:30, and 8 p.m. Appetizers might include scallops in lobster sauce or a cold plate of marinated beef with onions, perhaps mushrooms stuffed with crabmeat or Bermuda fish chowder. Main courses feature fresh fillets of Bermuda fish with prawns and mushrooms, and grilled sirloin with herb butter, the all-time favorite. The cooks have a deft continental flair, as reflected in their veal steak with duxelles of mushrooms and melted cheese and their Hungarian chicken in, naturally, a paprika sauce. The restaurant adjoins the Overplus Bar where you may want to stop for a before-dinner drink. It is also possible to visit here for lunch which is served daily in either the dining room or on the patio from noon to 2 p.m. at a cost of around $15 per person.

3. WARWICK PARISH

The Jolly Lobster, Flamingo Beach Club, South Shore Road, Warwick (tel. 809/236-3786), lies within this previously recommended cottage colony. A popular dining spot in Warwick, it is set within a simply furnished dining room, filled with hanging plants and Windsor chairs. It is graced at one end with a glassed-in porch whose windows overlook the swimming pool. No lunch is served, but dinner is offered nightly except Monday from 6:30 to 10. Diners have a choice of cold and hot appetizers, including octopus cocktail, smoked Scottish salmon, or baked snails Burgundy-style. Or else they may prefer one of the excellent soups, such as South Shore fish chowder laced with black rum and sherry peppers or lobster bisque. Since Bermuda fishermen go out nearly every day, and return with a wide variety of Atlantic fish, the chef might come up with a surprise, everything from shark steak to wahoo, a local favorite. A selection of fish from foreign waters is also featured, including swordfish and salmon. One section of the menu is reserved for the gourmet, including an array of continental dishes such as ocean scallops Mornay and fruits de mer Newburg. Full dinners cost from $30, and the restaurant is closed in January and February.

The **Cedar Room,** White Heron Country Inn, Riddell's Bay, Warwick (tel. 809/238-1655). Guests who find themselves hungry after reveling in the adjacent pub can step into a different ambience by entering the cedar-lined enclaves of this restaurant. The ornate patterned ceiling reflects the highlights and shadows from the hand-carved fireplace. Italian masons labored for weeks on the detailed heraldic carvings of this house, which was built for a private family at the turn of the century. The Virginia cedar that lines the walls is recent. Other architectural details date from the original construction of the house.

You should reserve ahead and make yourself comfortable once you arrive. Menu items include a version of grilled wahoo with béarnaise sauce, or perhaps butterfly wahoo with lemon sauce. Rockfish with lobster butter is usually excellent, or you might try one of the chef's steaks, weighing in at 8, 12, or 16 ounces, depending on how hungry you are. Most diners begin their meal with a Bermuda fish chowder laced with hot peppers and black rum. A full meal costs $25 per person at dinner. The less formal ambience at lunch is conducive to lighter, less expensive fare, costing from $10. Lunch is daily from noon to 3 p.m., and dinner is served from 7 to 10 p.m. No à la carte meals are served on Monday. At that time guests can order fish and chips at $7.50, their portions wrapped in English newspapers in the traditional way.

Miramar, South Shore Road (tel. 809/236-5031), at the Mermaid Beach Cottage Colony, offers a panoramic vista of the water overlooking a private beach. Tenants of nearby cottages come here for good lunches served on the terrace or for fine dinners featuring music several nights a week (often a steel band). A jacket and tie are requested for men at the dinner sitting. At lunch you can order hamburgers and assorted fresh-cut sandwiches. Meals cost from $10. Featured in the evening is a more elaborate menu, which offers such dishes as roast prime ribs with Yorkshire pudding, broiled dolphin, pan-fried Bermuda fish with almonds, and veal piccata. The hors d'oeuvres are excellent and the soups are good, including, on one recent occasion, chilled cucumber. The dinner menu changes nightly, and a table d'hôte costs about $22. The à la carte dinner usually averages $25 per person. Lunch is served daily from noon to 2:45 p.m. and dinner from 7 to 8:30 p.m. You can also order breakfast here from 8 to 9:30 a.m.

Herman's Restaurant, South Shore in Paget (tel. 809/238-9635), could be considered a snackbar, a coffeeshop, or a full-fledged restaurant, depending on your needs and the time of day. Its clientele includes the inhabitants of many of the surrounding guesthouses, as well as a healthy percentage of local residents and their children. Behind a low wall, just off the road, it contains a collection of parasols set on the outside terrace. If you prefer to dine indoors, there's a lunch counter with padded stools, plus an inner room filled with plants and wooden tables and chairs. Sometimes it's so crowded you can't get in.

The polite staff will tell you that the "open menu" allows them to accept orders for breakfast specialties throughout the day, so if you've a fancy for ham and eggs, Herman's will serve them to you day and night. In addition to the early-morning breakfasts, you can get lunches consisting of specialties such as burgers, sandwiches, omelets, "three-alarm" chili, and many kinds of salad, including pasta, at $12 for a full meal. For dinner, you get a bigger choice, and also a bigger price, around $20 and up. You might select fish and chips, or six kinds of pasta, barbecued chicken, or sirloin steak (cooked to order). To begin your meal, try either the red-bean soup or Bermuda fish chowder.

Herman's is open Sunday to Thursday from 9 a.m. to 11 p.m. and on Friday and Saturday from 9 a.m. to midnight.

4. SOUTHAMPTON PARISH

Newport Room, Southampton Princess, Southampton (tel. 809/238-8000). There is no restaurant in Bermuda where the decor is as sumptuously understated as this one. It qualifies as my favorite on the island, mostly for the sheer splendor of its setting. However, its gourmet food rates among the best in Bermuda as well.

None of this elegance comes cheap. Full meals begin at $75 per person, and can easily stretch upward. But if you're interested in yachts, boating, or competitive sailing, the cost will be worth the visual effects that a decorator worked hard to produce. Everything about the place re-creates the expensive interior of a well-maintained yacht. The theme is highlighted by the pair of exact miniature replicas of two of the winning sailing craft in the Newport to Bermuda race, each reportedly costing $15,000. These act as the illuminated centerpieces of a room that is entirely paneled in teak and rosewood and where any of the meticulously appropriate brass accents could grace the sleekest of world racing craft. Large illuminated paintings of the windblown regattas add the only real touch of vibrant color to an otherwise austerely somber yet immensely appealing room. Even the sophisticated overhead lighting was designed to simulate patterns of a starlit sky.

You'll be greeted at the entrance by a formally polite maître d'hôtel, stationed beside a gleaming ship's compass. The plush leather armchairs help you settle comfortably for dinner, which might include gourmet variations of *cuisine moderne.* The finest Wedgwood china and sparkling Waterford crystal appeal to the discriminating diner who selects this restaurant. A wide array of international wines, served in Irish crystal, complement each dinner. The restaurant is open daily only for dinner, beginning at 7 p.m., the last orders accepted at 9:15 p.m. Reservations are suggested, and men are required to wear a jacket and tie.

Waterlot Inn, Middle Road, Southampton (tel. 809/238-0510). Three hundred years ago, merchant sailors unloaded their cargoes directly into the basement of this historic inn and warehouse, which sits within a few feet of the wharves. Today the best way to approach it is still by water, and that's precisely what many Bermudians do, mooring their sailing craft in the sheltered cove that has seen so many dozens of similar boats come and go. At one time the Darrell family owned this house and all the land stretching from Jew's Bay to the Atlantic on the other side of Bermuda. The land was parceled out to subsequent generations of Darrells until its most famous occupant, Claudia Darrell, ran one of the island's best known eateries from the house until she died. She became the subject of international media attention. Over the years the inn has attracted such patrons as James Thurber, Eleanor Roosevelt, Eugene O'Neill, and Mark Twain. After the landmark building was devastated by a gas explosion in 1976, the Southampton Princess had it renovated and today it's one of their gourmet restaurants. Guests are transported from the hotel in a shuttle to this waterside inn.

Diners enjoy a drink in an upstairs bar entertained by the resident classical pianist. After descending a colonial staircase with white balustrades, they sit in one of a trio of conservatively nautical rooms. Each is filled with captain's or Windsor chairs, oil paintings of old clipper ships, and lots of exposed wood. From the outdoor terrace, you can view the movement of pleasure craft to the yacht mooring alongside the dock. Dinner is served nightly from 7 to 10 p.m., when jackets and ties are required for men. The Sunday brunch, from noon to 1:30 p.m., is considered the best on the island, drawing not only hotel guests but lots of Bermudians as well. The cost is from $26. Evening meals range from $50 per person. Main courses are likely to include filet of pan-fried Bermuda rockfish, roast duck with black currant sauce, lamb roasted with herbs and butter, and a pavé of beef with freshly cracked pepper, cognac, and a cream sauce.

Henry VIII, South Shore (tel. 809/238-1977), is a pub restaurant lying between the Southampton Princess and the Sonesta Beach Hotel that has been given the royal treatment. The location is below Gibb's Hill Lighthouse, and it has entertainment in the evening. The pubby atmosphere is enhanced by solid oak furnishings, brass railings, ornaments, and lighting fixtures in keeping with a Tudor flavor. It is red-carpeted throughout. Even if you're just passing through, you might want to drop in at the split-level Oak Room Bar for some English beer on draft.

Hot pub lunches, served from noon to 2:30 p.m. Monday to Saturday, cost from $10 and include such fare as steak-and-kidney pie, mussel pie, and plain old hamburgers. Sandwiches are available from 2:30 to 3:30 p.m. The popular Sunday brunch, costing $16, is served from noon to 3 p.m. In the evening the chef gets more elegant, turning out such whimsically named dishes as "court jester" (broiled combination of seafood) or steak Anne Boleyn (flavored with cognac and simmered in a madeira sauce). The chef also prepares an English mixed grill, peppersteak, and a chateaubriand. Count on spending around $40 for dinner. Reservations are needed at night. There are two seatings for dinner, one at 7 to 7:30 p.m. and another at 8:45 to 9 p.m. The dinner hours are from 7 to 9:30 p.m. seven days a week.

Whaler Inn, Southampton Princess (tel. 809/238-8000), is an eagle's-nest restaurant positioned high above the boulders and jagged outcrops jutting from the soft sands of the beach at this well-known hotel. The multicolored tiles of the restaurant's cliff-bordered terraces sprout with landscaped clusters of sea grape, Norfolk Island pine, and comfortably padded iron armchairs. These offer lookout posts over the sunsets that redden the lapping waves of one of the island's most secluded beaches. If you want to dine on the terrace, someone will bring you a menu shaped, understandably, like a whale. If you prefer indoor dining, the interior's huge windows provide an airy setting where the panoramic view is the main decor. The timeless views of the Atlantic evoke the era when Bermuda's early colonizers complained about being disturbed during their sleep by the whistling of the hundreds of whales that migrated twice a year along the island's coastline.

Dress is casual. Evening meals cost from $35 and include fixed-price items from a three-course table d'hôte menu with a wide selection of choices. To "bait your appetite," you can begin your repast with tiger prawns in a cocktail sauce, shrimp bisque, or oysters on the half shell. The chef's special main courses will be well-seasoned portions of whatever game fish the local fishermen brought in that day, including yellowfin tuna, barracuda, shark, wahoo, or dolphin (the fish). Main courses that are not dependent on the whims of the tides or ocean currents include a kettle of seafood St. David's style, mussels marinière, and a deep-fried fisherman's platter, along with pan-fried local fish with almonds and bananas. Whatever, you'll get a full array of Bermudian fish, either broiled or sautéed in butter. Your "happy ending" could include banana fritters with black rum sauce, and Armagnac ice cream with prunes. The restaurant is closed in January and February. Otherwise, it's open for dinner seven nights a week from 7 to 9:30 p.m.

Greenhouse, Sonesta Beach Hotel (tel. 809/238-8122). The gourmet evening restaurant of this deluxe hotel (see Chapter III) also doubles as a lunchtime value at midday. The evening meal takes on added polish with the addition of a uniformed battalion of staff, yard upon yard of immaculate napery, a host of flickering candles, and meticulously prepared specialties exiting from the modern kitchens. Full evening meals range from $40 per person and might include such specialties as oysters on the half shell (or else Rockefeller), quenelles of sole, oyster and spinach bisque, wahoo steak meunière, or shrimps, scallops, and crabmeat in a puff pastry covered with a Pernod-flavored lobster sauce. The chef also prepares an excellent beef Stroganoff and duckling with muscadet. Dinners are served nightly from 7 to 10:30.

Many guests, however, head for the sun-washed, lattice- and plant-filled locale at lunch for one of the best bargains in Southampton Parish. A fixed-price buffet lunch costs only $12 per person, not including drinks, and it is consumed within view of the Polynesian-style beach at Boat Bay. Lunches are served daily from noon to 3 p.m. If you're not in the mood for a buffet, the restaurant offers summer-style overstuffed sandwiches, luncheon specials, quiches of the day, and freshly baked breads, along with fresh fruits and homemade desserts.

Rib Room Steak House, Southampton Princess, Southampton (tel. 809/238-8000). The moderately priced table d'hôte dinners offered at this sporting-style clubhouse represent one of the island's better values. To get here, you'll have to traverse the far-flung gardens and golf courses of this deluxe hotel. The restaurant sits atop the golf pro shop, near the tee-off point for the first hole. In the midst of panoramic windows and upholstered armchairs, you can enjoy evening meals for about $38. The polite staff will suggest a "Dark and Stormy" (black rum with ginger beer) to get you started. Your drink might be followed by such main courses as baby pork spareribs, several kinds of beef broiled over charcoal, or roast prime rib of beef with Yorkshire pudding. If you don't want beef, you can have a catch of the day as a substitute or one of ten other choices, such as chicken with short ribs or broiled lamb chops. The restaurant is open every night from 7, with the last orders taken at 9 p.m.

5. SANDYS PARISH (SOMERSET)

Lantana Colony Club, Somerset Bridge (tel. 809/234-0141), is the elegant restaurant contained within this exclusive hotel. Guests sometimes prefer a drink near the fireplace of the huge salon before climbing the short flight of steps into the pastel-colored dining room. The decorator probably spent time in Venice before receiving the commission to design the place. The ceiling trusses have been painted a pastel shade of spring green, and the neo-baroque floral stencils were applied between garlands of Italian-style ornamentation. If you prefer a greenhouse effect, a second room has been glassed over with a solarium-style roof and surrounded with plants. A uniformed staff member will usher you to a table where a hibiscus has been placed at each place setting.

The frequently changing menu might on the night of your visit include such specialties as fresh salmon steak with dill sauce, prosciutto with melon, fish terrine, fish soup Lantana, grilled sirloin Delmonico style, breast of chicken with a whisky cream sauce, Bermuda fish meunière, veal Cordon Bleu, and grilled jumbo shrimp, any of which might be accompanied by grilled tomatoes provençale. Meals are served table d'hôte style, with a fixed price of $30 per person. There is a large choice under each heading (appetizers, main courses, desserts, etc.), plus an à la carte listing for possible substitutions. Jackets and ties are required for men. Dinner is served from 7:30 to 9 p.m., and live music is offered for dancing on certain nights of the week.

La Plage, Lantana Colony Club, Somerset Bridge (tel. 809/234-0141). Walking toward this charming restaurant will give you a chance to admire the sculpture scattered throughout the gardens of the most exclusive hotel in Sandys Parish. In many ways, it's the perfect luncheon stopover during a tour of Bermuda's West End. The urn-shaped balustrades that separate the terrace from the cove, fresh flowers, and impeccable service are much like something you might find at the edge of a lake in the north of Italy An endearing statue of an elfin girl gleefully experimenting with her mother's necklaces and lipstick stands guard beside the Roman-style pool where a stone cherub spurts water high into the air. A pier and a dock area a few steps away from the restaurant create the impression that a yacht might pull up for a Bloody Mary at any moment. You'll be able to choose a table near the flowers of the sundeck, or one inside the pink-and-white summertime interior.

The luncheon menu advises that the price of a main course will include a complete meal. You might begin with a Bermuda fish chowder, then follow with an array of dishes, which include items from ordinary sandwiches (peanut butter and bacon) to elaborate fantasies such as salmon mousse, crêpes stuffed with beef and cheese, Bermudian mussel stew, and coquilles St-Jacques. Several salads are offered as well, including a traditional chef's salad or one made with tropical fruit. Lunch is served only from 1 to 2:30 p.m. daily. Full meals range from $12 to $20 apiece. Closed January 4 to March 1.

Il Palio (tel. 809/234-1049) is named after the famous horse race in Siena, Italy. In the center of Somerset in the western end of Bermuda, it lies on the Main Road and near several outstanding attractions which I'll document later. Currently, it's the only restaurant in the western sector specializing in the rich Italian cuisine, and it does so exceedingly well. If you arrive early for your table, you can enjoy a drink in the bar downstairs before going upstairs to your well-set table. The Italian owners serve daily except Monday. Lunch is offered from noon to 2 p.m., and dinner from 6 to 10 p.m. In a cozy, intimate decor, you can order from the menu such specialties as fettuccine Alfredo, named after the famed restaurateur of Rome, or saltimbocca (it literally means "jump in your mouth") alla romana. The latter is a tender veal dish served with ham from Parma in a white wine sauce. You might also try conch with lobster, shrimp, and scallops cooked with mushrooms in a brandy sauce. The chef also does an excellent tender young duckling in a sauce made with green peppercorns. In addition to the fettuccine already mentioned, you are given several other pastas, including cannelloni and lasagne.

The Somerset Country Squire Tavern, Mangrove Bay (tel. 809/234-0105). You'll pass through a moongate arch to reach the raised terrace of this waterside restaurant in the center of town. It's a good choice during your tour of Somerset. If you don't want to eat within the confines of the limestone blocks and hedges that ring the terrace, you can choose the interior dining room downstairs. The restaurant, which can be visited on a trip to the Dockyard on Ireland Island, is open Monday to Saturday from 10 a.m. to 1 a.m. and on Sunday from noon to 1 a.m., if you'd like to drop in for drinks. Lunch, however, is served from noon to 4 p.m. and dinner from 6:30 to 10 p.m. The bill of fare ranges from "pub grub" to fresh fish dishes caught in local seas or else the traditional roast beef with Yorkshire pudding. Local Bermudian favorites include curried mussel pie and fresh Bermuda tuna or wahoo. Look for the specialties of the day, but count on charbroiled and barbecued meals. There is light entertainment six evenings a week.

Village Inn, Watford Bridge (tel. 809/238-9401). What looks like a private vacation house sits a few feet above a boat dock. If you want to dine indoors, you'll have the run of the unpretentious paneled interior. The bar at one end of the room is a good place to share a drink with one of the local residents. Many diners prefer a table, at least for a cocktail, on a series of terraces that have been cut or inserted into the slope of the terrain leading down to the harbor. There, some of the tables have been fashioned from halves of barrels that rest on crisscrossed legs and that are usually sheltered from the sun with a parasol. This restaurant announces that its specialties include both Bermudian and European cuisine, as well as a "native" barbecue. The polite staff will recommend Bermuda seafood, such as fish chowder, rockfish, and when available, lobster. The fine food represents value for money. Dinners range from $25 apiece, and lunches cost from $12. Food is served from noon to 3:30 p.m. and 7 to 10 p.m. The inn is closed on Monday and holidays, and the yearly closing is in January and February.

Loyalty Inn, Somerset (tel. 809/234-0125), is a 250-year-old converted home overlooking Mangrove Bay. A white-painted building, it looks vaguely like a church. The bar, in a separate building, is filled with captain's chairs and a mock fireplace. The restaurant with its decor of cedar paneling and small-paned windows attracts both visitors and locals who prefer its uncluttered atmosphere. The menu of steak, chicken, sandwiches, and seafood is not elaborate, but dishes are well prepared and the portions are generous. The bar is open from 10 a.m. to 1 a.m. daily, and food is served in the restaurant from 11:45 a.m. to 10 p.m. The fish chowder is superb, followed by either the fish plate or tasty scallops and a salad. In the evening, if you have the appetite, you can ask for a seafood dinner. Expect to spend from $25 per head. The restaurant lies about a five-minute walk from the Watford Bridge ferry landing.

Blue Foam Restaurant, Somerset Bridge Hotel, Sandys (tel. 809/238-5501), sits about a hundred yards away from the entrance to the Somerset Bridge Hotel, a short distance down the road. The entrance path, indicated by a sign, winds down the hillside until you reach the pleasantly panoramic restaurant whose view encompasses the bobbing moorings of Ely's Harbour. Lunches are pleasantly informal, with a full array of burgers, salads (including one of pasta and a chef's salad), chicken, fish, or shrimp with chips. Such sandwiches as roast beef with onions and horseradish are offered, and the pizzas are 12 inches wide. Full lunches cost around $12 apiece. At dinner, a more expensive menu is presented. It includes fresh wahoo steak, filet mignon in a mushroom sauce, homemade fish chowder, and other uncomplicated yet savory fare. Full dinners cost from $22. Breakfast is served from 8 to 10 a.m., lunch from 11:30 a.m. to 2:30 p.m., and dinner from 6:30 to 9:30 p.m. seven days a week.

6. ST. GEORGE'S

The Margaret Rose, St. George's Club, Rose Hill, St. George's (tel. 809/297-1200), is stylishly designed, one of the most appealing restaurants in the east end of Bermuda. Named after both Princess Margaret and Rose Hill (on which it sits), the restaurant is decorated fashionably, overlooking the harbor and the old part of town. Lunch is served daily from noon to 2:30 p.m., costing from $15, with dinners from 7 to 9 p.m. going for around $35 per person. At night candlelight adds to the romantic ambience, and reservations are needed. Appetizers and salads include les medallions de homard au fenouil en crouatade (lobster medallions with fennel laced with a light creamy Pernod sauce in puff pastry) or les cailles fumées et paillasson de noix de coco et pommes vertes (smoked quail on a coconut and apple salad). For the main course, you have selections such as le coeur de filet de boeuf grille à l'estragon et moutarde de meaux (broiled filet steak with tarragon flavored mustard sauce) or le poisson des Bermudes à la façon de Picasso (pan-fried Bermuda fish with a mosaic of fresh fruit and ginger). The pastry chef creates scrumptuous concoctions, treats that will tempt even an ardent dieter.

Carriage House, Water Street, Somers Wharf (tel. 809/297-1730), specializing in beef as well as seafood, is housed in an old waterfront storehouse in the same building as the Carriage Museum in St. George's. After careful restoration, it keeps its 18th-century warehouse look with two rows of bare brick arches, the effect softened by hanging baskets of greenery. After placing your order for dinner, you can help yourself at a large salad bar in the rear of the restaurant. But before that, you may want to enjoy an unusually good selection of hot and cold hors d'oeuvres. The chef specializes in prime ribs, the cost depending on the size of your beef, which is always cut to order and served with a ramekin of creamed horseradish in the British tradition. A different soup is offered every day, and a baked Idaho potato, Carriage fries, or rice is included with your main course. Expect to spend $25 each and up for a complete meal. At lunch a large selection of hamburgers is offered. A light luncheon should set you back no more than $13. A choice of excellent desserts is always available.

The Carriage House serves daily, from noon to 2:30 p.m. and 7 to 9:30 p.m. Sunday brunch, buffet style, is also available from noon to 2:30 p.m. Casual dress is accepted.

Wharf Tavern, Somers Wharf (tel. 809/297-1515), is a nautically minded, modern restaurant built on the ground floor of a building with a veranda. It's situated among the cluster of buildings that make up Somers Wharf. Only pedestrians are allowed nearby, which might account for the popularity of the porch, of the window seats, and of the darkly paneled bar area inside. Dinners, which cost from $25 apiece, could include curried mussels, Bermuda fish cakes with peas and rice, pan-fried or broiled rockfish, broiled wahoo, oysters on the half shell, steak-and-kidney pie, both Bermuda and Maine lobsters in season, and steamers (fresh clams in a pot). Lunch, costing about $12, is served from 11:30 a.m. to 2:30 p.m. daily. Dinner is offered from 6 to 10 p.m. The bar stays open throughout the day.

San Giorgio, Water Street (tel. 809/297-1307), is a charming little Italian restaurant that serves only dinner Monday to Saturday from 6:30 to 10:30 p.m. To reach it, guests climb a short flight of steps from a point opposite Somers Wharf. The location is next to the Tucker House Museum. Most guests begin with a selection of antipasto, while others prefer a Caesar salad. Several well-prepared pasta dishes tempt diners, including cannelloni and lasagna. For your main course, you can select such elegant dishes as breast of chicken sautéed with black cherry and rum sauce. The chef also does a good veal marsala. Broiled grouper is also regularly featured on the menu. Dinners cost from $30, and you should call for a reservation.

White Horse Tavern, King's Square (tel. 809/297-1838), is St. George's oldest tavern, a restaurant and cedar bar with a terrace jutting into St. George's Harbour. In fair weather (which is most of the time), guests prefer to sit on this terrace Venetian-style, feeding breadcrumbs to the sparrows. A white building with green shutters, it is one of the most popular taverns in all of Bermuda. First, its location is so central you can't miss it. The most ordered item here is fish and chips which are cooked in the manner of St. David's Island. The Bermuda fish chowder is also good. You can order such dishes as seafood combo, stuffed flounder, and marinated chicken. At lunch a selection of Tavern burgers, fresh salads, and open-faced sandwiches are served. Lunches are from $12, with dinners costing around $25. The tavern is open daily from 10 a.m. to 1 a.m. (on Sunday it doesn't open until noon).

Pub on the Square, King's Square (tel. 809/297-1522), is a British pub with a rustic atmosphere. On a good evening the fun here has been compared to a prewar English music hall. The sing-along can keep St. George's rocking. The pub and restaurant are on two levels. After a mug of beer downstairs, guests can climb a spiral staircase upstairs to the tavern dining room with a veranda bar overlooking the square. Lunch is from noon to 3 p.m. daily, with meals costing from $9 to $15. Dinner is served nightly from 6 to 10 p.m. for around $25. Washed down with draft beer, the fish and chips is the most popular item, and sandwiches are also available. Other good dishes include Bermuda fish chowder laced with rum and sherry peppers and pub-style chicken.

Clyde's Café & Bar, Duke of York Street (tel. 809/297-0158), rarely visited by the cruise-ship crowd, is a secret address known among local residents who come here for some of the best home cooking in the east end. You enter through a bar with a jukebox usually blaring, then head for the family dining room in the rear. If you visit at lunch, you might want to settle for one of their well-stuffed sandwiches served with homemade cole slaw. But you can also order an array of hot dishes at both lunch and dinner. Clyde's is known for its pork chops, Bermuda fish, shrimp, scallops, roast beef, and lobster. Lunches cost from $10, with dinners priced from $18. Service is Monday to Saturday from 11 a.m. to 1 a.m. and on Sunday from noon to 1 a.m. (closed Tuesday). The location is across from Somers Gardens. Clyde's will be on your left.

7. ST. DAVID'S ISLAND

Dennis's Hideaway, Cashew City Road (tel. 809/297-0044). In the easternmost parish of St. George's, Dennis Lamb, a burly St. David's Islander, is one of the treasures of Bermuda. So is his quaint little eatery. As you approach it, you're likely to see Dennis (part Irish, part Mohawk), working in his garden in front (he even grows the cabbage he uses in his coleslaw and the beets for pickling). He'll show you into his fisherman's cottage by one of the island's little coves. Once inside you'll feel you've left Bermuda and are visiting some little pocket-size country with a distinctive personality.

The descendant of whalers and pilots—"wooden ships and iron men"—Dennis and his son will offer you a cuisine that has virtually disappeared in Bermuda's restaurants, practiced only in private homes these days. Dinner from 7 to 10 p.m. daily is the only meal served. For about $25.50, he'll give you "the works," an array of dishes, including conch stew, dolphin (the fish), even herb-flavored shark hash, shrimps, conch fritters—you name it (but please don't order turtle—an endangered species). You bring your own wine. If you don't want to eat so much, request the fish dinner for $15. The fisherman's cottage is accessible by land or sea, and don't dress up. Always call in advance.

This Pa Kettle– ambience is not for everybody, it must be frankly pointed out. Reactions of readers have varied tremendously. Some repeat visitors give it high marks, claiming they've made at least 20 pilgrimages here during their annual visits to Bermuda. Some first-time visitors, however, claim that travel writers who send diners here should be tarred and feathered. So go only if you're a bit adventurous.

Black Horse Tavern (tel. 809/297-1999). If you should land here, in a section of the island that Bermudians call "the country," you won't be disappointed at all. The exterior looks like a dusty-rose-colored version of a private home, complete with green shutters and a rear glassed-in porch that looks over Smith Sound. The bar might be your preferred place here. Hanging above the bar are two stuffed fish, one is a Mako shark, the other a marlin. There's even a section of a whalebone with a rusty knife embedded in it from some long-ago struggle. Your hosts are Gary and Alfreda Lamb. Gary is the cousin of Dennis Lamb, who runs the more famous Dennis's Hideaway, already described. Gary's great-uncle, Belize-born Clarence Borden, is credited with putting Bermudian cookery on the map. Over the years he's been host to many celebrities, including Robert Stigwood, the Australian movie producer. Many of his guests show up in yachts, but others, by far the majority, come from the nearby U.S. naval base, especially on pay day.

You can begin your meal with curried conch stew, shark hash, fish chowder, or curried mussels. This could be followed by one of a choice of sandwiches or burgers, perhaps a platter of fish and chips or chicken and chips. The chef also does a good sirloin steak and will also prepare you a chicken dinner. The house drink, especially if you're in love, is a honeymoon special. It combines rum, apricot brandy, and tequila in one potent drink. The establishment is open Monday to Saturday from 10 a.m. to 1 a.m. Sunday hours are noon to 1 a.m. Lunch costs from $8; dinner, from $20.

8. HAMILTON PARISH

Tom Moore's Tavern, Bailey's Bay (tel. 809/293-8020), is Bermuda's oldest eating house, built in 1652. Once it was a private home, and was visited in 1804 by Tom Moore, the romantic Irish poet who wrote some of his verses here, making reference to a calabash tree that still exists some 200 yards from the tavern. The location is on Walsingham Bay near the Crystal Caves in Hamilton Parish. The tavern is also the most famous dining room in Bermuda, which has known many incarnations. In 1985 two Italians, Bologna-born Bruno Fiocca and his Venetian partner, Franco Bortoli, opened it for dinner, quickly establishing it as one of the most popular upmarket restaurants in Bermuda. Fortunately, they have maintained the old character of this landmark place, with its four fireplaces. A bar and lounge are found upstairs.

The darkened cedar walls are a backdrop for the classical French and Italian cuisine served here. Seafood, impeccably prepared, is the specialty. A lobster tank is found outside during the season for Bermudian lobster (in the off-season months Maine lobster is served). The Bermudian fish from local waters is likely to be tuna, swordfish, rockfish, or yellowtail. The veal dishes are superb, especially those flavored with fresh basil. The setting, the English silver, the general ambience can make for a memorable visit. The cost is about $50 per person for dinner. Dinner is from 7 to 9:15 p.m. seven days a week, with seatings every half hour.

The Plantation, Bailey's Bay (tel. 809/293-1188), is a charming oasis on the site of Leamington Caves along Harrington Sound Road. It is a yellow colonial-style building with steep white roofs and fireplaces. There are three rooms inside, with plush carpeting, ceiling fans, and rattan furniture, making for a warm, inviting ambience. In fair weather, guests dine al fresco in the tropical garden shaded by a giant marquee. The bar with its Bermuda cedar base is ideal for a drink. Christopher and Carol West, your hosts, welcome you for lunch from noon to 2:30 p.m. and for dinner from 7 to 9:30 p.m. daily. Bar service is from 10 a.m., and dinner reservations are suggested. They are closed from mid-December to late February.

Lunches cost from $15 and include an array of sandwiches, such as French dip, and salads, such as an intriguing warm chicken liver and spinach salad. From the charcoal grill comes everything from a jumbo hot dog to a hamburger to the fresh filet of Bermuda fish. Seafood gratin is also offered, along with escargots and French bread. However, the French chef at night shows his excellence in the kitchen by turning out such dishes as a mousseline of Bermuda fish with crabmeat and spinach, a chilled soup of the day, or better yet, one of the appetizers of the day. Each day the chef prepares special hors d'oeuvres, based on the availability of fresh produce. Local fish courses are offered, including one fish filet with bananas and almonds in a local style, another gently coated with Pommery mustard and topped with sliced tomatoes. One of the main specialties of the chef is charcoal-grilled mignon of beef served with homemade Bermuda loquat chutney. In addition, every night the chef prepares a tempting main dish. Dinners cost from $45 per person, including wine and tips.

Mikado, Castle Harbour, Tucker's Town (tel. 809/293-2040). Contained in the lower level of this previously recommended hotel, this is one of the most imaginatively stylish rooms in Bermuda. You pass through lacquered gateways to reach a whimsically art deco version of a Japanese tea garden. An imitation of a reflecting pool, with an arched bridge, allows diners a view of brightly colored fish. An experienced chef is assigned to each group of eight diners. He prepares cuisine much like an actor would prepare theater. Grills are placed as the main distraction near each table, permitting diners a view of whatever is cooking. A fixed-price seven-course Japanese dinner costs $32; à la carte meals go for around $43 each. Rare imported fish is used for the sushi bar, and these are mixed with very fresh Bermudian fish such as wahoo. All the traditional Japanese specialties, along with an aromatic sake, are available. Only dinner is served, nightly, from 6:30 to 10:30 p.m. Reservations are needed. Dress is smart casual.

Swizzle Inn, Blue Hole Hill, Bailey's Bay (tel. 809/293-9300), the home of the Bermuda rum swizzle, lies west of the airport, near the Crystal Caves and the Bermuda Perfume Factory. This is one of the oldest bars in Bermuda, some 300 years old. It's closed Monday in the off-season, but otherwise meals are served continuously during its open hours, 11 a.m. to 1 a.m. The meaty Swizzleburger is most popular. Soups are offered, and fish and chips with coleslaw is a standard. Of course you can have the traditional English bangers and mash. Meals cost from $6.50. The inn can be ideal as a "watering spot" if you're touring the island, wanting a drink or a lunch, even a game of darts. It's customary to plaster your business card on a wall here—then attempt to find it on your next visit to Bermuda.

Bailey's Ice Cream & Food D'Lites Restaurant, on the corner of Wilkinson Avenue and Blue Hole Hill (tel. 809/293-9333), at Bailey's Bay, stands across from the just-recommended Swizzle Inn. For "all-natural" ice cream, there is no comparable place in Bermuda. Forty different flavors are made in the 20-quart ice-cream maker, under the supervision of the owner, Frank T. Powers. The parlor is in a small Bermuda cottage, with a convenient parking lot. You can eat your butterscotch crunch, almond delight, or piña colada ice cream, whatever you choose, at one of the outdoor tables or else take it away. A sandwich nook, which uses fresh-baked breads, is a popular attraction. Also featured are fresh-fruit ices, frozen yogurts, and natural juices. Light meals cost from $6. They're closed in January and February. Otherwise, hours vary depending on the time of year, but in summer, the place is open daily from 11 a.m. to 10 p.m.

The establishment has two other locations: South Road, Smith's Parish at Collector's Hill, between Blue Hole Hill and the City of Hamilton (tel. 809/293-7027); and at 95 Front St., Hamilton (tel. 809/292-3703). The latter features sitdown tables and waiter service, old-fashioned ice-cream-parlor glassware, and exotic creations made from their all-natural ice creams, sherbets, and yogurts. It has a spectacular view of the harbor. Food menus here have been expanded with emphasis on good quality at reasonable prices. A separate section caters to fast take-out ice cream and lunches on the run.

9. SMITH'S PARISH

The **Inlet Restaurant,** Palmetto Hotel and Cottages (tel. 809/293-2323), at Flatts Village, in Smith's Parish. In creating this attractive restaurant, the owners added a slope-roofed modern addition onto what had been a lushly paneled lounge lined with Bermudian cedar. If you choose to dine here, you can select a seat either near the big windows, which look over the moongate, the swimming pool, and the harbor, or you can sit in the darker and more intimate recesses of the back.

Lunches, costing from about $6, are pleasing. You can start with mussels Casino, spinach or Caesar salad, or Bermuda fish chowder. Seafood courses include a platter of shrimp, scallops, fish and chips, seafood Rockefeller (scallops, crab, and other seafood in a cheese sauce on spinach), or perhaps fresh Bermuda fish, broiled or pan-fried. You can also dine on such meat dishes as sirloin steak, Bermuda chicken, or pan-fried liver. Other main courses that might tempt you are steak-and-kidney pie, lasagne, and quiche. There is also a good selection of sandwiches and burgers available for lunch, and light snacks can be taken on the outside patio when the weather is fine. Dinners are more elaborate, with a more detailed menu containing a wider selection of dishes. The price averages around $35 for a repast. Meals are served from noon to 2:30 p.m. and 7 to 10 p.m. daily. Light snacks are served in the pub until 10 p.m

CHAPTER V

BERMUDA—DAY AND NIGHT

□ □ □

1. EXPLORING BERMUDA
2. WHERE TO SHOP
3. THE SPORTING LIFE
4. BERMUDA AFTER DARK

Bermuda is for fun! Even the major attractions are "lightweight," not designed to tax one. Because of the island's small size, it's easy to get to know Bermuda parish by parish on your trusty moped. After 20 miles or so, you'll run into the sea—so don't rush anywhere. At no point on the island are you allowed to go more than 20 miles per hour anyway.

Even though a lot of people have been fitted into a tiny land mass, Bermuda doesn't appear to be as populated as some of the more crowded islands in the Caribbean. Although its population density is higher, it doesn't look that way, mainly because houses have been fitted quite naturally into the landscape. And there are no jarring billboards or neon signs to spoil the countryside. Because there are no car-rental companies, you'll encounter no traffic jams and no polluted air.

Bermuda seems like a perpetual festival, as it has something going on all the time. Sports are always a star attraction, especially golf and tennis. Sailing, horseback riding, and especially the pink sandy beaches are potent lures.

In this chapter we'll go on a guided do-it-yourself tour, taking in Bermuda parish by parish. After that, we'll go on a shopping expedition along Front Street in Hamilton, devoting the next day—and many days thereafter—to sports on the islands.

Our nightlife pickings will be slimmer, but there are some diversions.

1. EXPLORING BERMUDA

From the western tip of Somerset to the eastern end of St. George's there is much to see in Bermuda, either by bike, ferry, bus, or taxi. Just allow plenty of time. You'll need it, as the pace is slow. Chances are, you'll either be on a bicycle, on a motorbike, or in a private taxi. Cars can only travel 15 miles per hour in Hamilton and St. George's, 20 miles per hour outside these towns. This speed limit is rigidly enforced, and penalties for violation are severe.

Bermuda is divided into nine parishes (or counties), including Sandys Parish (in the far western end of the island), Southampton Parish, Warwick Parish,

Paget Parish (center of the greatest concentration of hotels), Pembroke Parish (seat of the government at Hamilton), Devonshire Parish, Smith's Parish, Hamilton Parish (not to be confused with the city of Hamilton), and St. George's Parish (at the far eastern extremity; it also takes in the U.S. naval base and the little seafaring island of St. David's).

In the early days these districts, encompassing 21 square miles, were called "Tribes." By the early 17th century the term "Tribe Road" had come into use to describe the boundaries between the parishes. Pembroke, because it encloses the city of Hamilton, is the largest parish in population, and St. George's has the most land area.

Many local guidebooks are fond of pointing out that "you can't get lost in Bermuda." Don't you believe them. Along narrow, winding roads—originally designed for the horse and carriage—you can get lost, several times, especially if you're looking for an obscure guesthouse along some long-forgotten lane. I've been with taxi drivers of 25 years' experience who have gotten lost in Bermuda.

Fortunately, you won't stay lost for long. Bermuda is so narrow that if you keep going in either an easterly or westerly direction, you'll eventually come to a main road. At its fattest "waistline" Bermuda is only 1½ miles wide. The principal arteries are the North Shore Road, the Middle Road, and the South Shore Road, and with such marvelously descriptive names as those, you'll at least have some indication as to what part of the island you're in.

Sometimes the rain comes almost without warning in Bermuda. Never attempt to stay on your vehicle in drizzly weather. It's better to pull off the road and wait under some shelter. Usually the skies clear rapidly and the road dries quickly, but it's easy to have an accident on Bermuda's slippery roads after a rain, especially if you're not accustomed to using a motor scooter as your principal means of transport.

Gasoline stations—called "petrol" stations by the resident British—appear fairly frequently in Bermuda. But if you "tank up" at the beginning of your run, chances are you'll have plenty of energy to get you to your destination. For example, one tank of gas in a motorbike will take you from Somerset in the west to St. George's in the east.

A THREE-DAY ITINERARY: After you've landed and rested in Bermuda, recuperating by spending a day on its pink sandy beaches, you may be eager to explore the island. For the first three days, I have a suggested itinerary. I hope you'll be around for at least a week so you can break up your sightseeing trips with plenty of time for relaxing, either enjoying the beach, going boating, or engaging in some of the other sports activities offered (see "The Sporting Life," below).

If you've only got one day to devote to sightseeing attractions, I suggest you spend it in the historic capital of **St. George's.** It has everything from a ducking stool to narrow, alleyway-like streets with quaint names: Featherbed Alley, Duke of York Street, Petticoat Lane, Old Maids' Lane, Duke of Kent Street. You can spend a day exploring British pubs, seafood restaurants, shops (several major stores along Front Street in Hamilton have branches here), old forts, museums, and churches. You'll even see stocks and a pillory once used to humiliate wrongdoers. Serious offenses were dealt with more severely of course.

For a second day of sightseeing, I suggest you take the ferry from Hamilton across Great Sound to **Somerset.** Your cycle can be carried on the boat (you'll need it later). You'll be let off at the western end of Somerset Island in Sandys Parish, where you'll find the smallest drawbridge in the world. It's easy to spend an hour walking around Somerset Village. After that, you can head east until you reach a beach on Long Bay along the northern rim of the island. There are several places for lunch in Sandys Parish (see Chapter IV). The Somerset Country Squire, a typical village tavern, is the best of many of them. It's near the Watford Bridge ferry stop at the eastern end of the island.

After lunch you can go across Watford Bridge to Ireland Island, home of the important Maritime Museum. On your return to Somerset Bridge and the ferry back to Hamilton, you might take the turnoff to Fort Scaur. From Scaur Hill you'll have a commanding view of Ely's Harbour. You'll also have an excellent view over Great Sound. Or if you don't want to traverse Somerset again, you can board a ferry at Watford Bridge that will take you back to Hamilton.

Reserve a third day for sightseeing and shopping in **Hamilton.** It's likely you'll be staying in one of the hotels in Paget or Warwick that we've already visited two chapters ago. If so, a ferry from either parish will take you right into Hamilton (the city, not the parish).

In Hamilton, you can always blend sights with shops. For many visitors, the shops are more compelling. Try to time your visit to avoid the arrival of cruise-ship passengers. On those days, facilities in Hamilton can get cramped.

The seat of the government of Bermuda since 1815, Hamilton was once known as "The Show Window of the British Empire." Both Mark Twain and Eugene O'Neill, who lived in places opening onto Hamilton Harbour, cited the beauty of the place. On little islands in the harbor, prisoners-of-war and victims of plagues were held either in prison or in quarantine.

A stroll along Front Street will take you by some of Hamilton's most elegant stores, but you'll want to branch off along the little alleyways to check the shops and boutiques to be found there. If you get tired of walking or shopping (or both), you can also take one of the boats or catamarans waiting to show you the treasures of Little Sound and Great Sound.

On some days you'll be lucky and get to see locals buying their fresh fish—that is, that part of the catch not earmarked for restaurants—right from the fishermen who sell the "catch of the day" at Front Street docks. That catch always seems to turn up more rockfish than any other, although you'll also see snapper, grouper, and many other species. In the 1930s, seaplanes would land passengers right in Hamilton Harbour.

The most famous sight in Hamilton is the policeman in the "bird cage" on Hyle's Corner. From November to May he's in long trousers, but in summer he'll be wearing the famous "Bermuda shorts." These shorts, recently a fad among the preppy crowd, are standard wear in Bermuda.

Most Bermudians consider the winter months too cold to wear the shorts, although you'll see plenty of them. But in May, all the businessmen along Front Street seem to don a pair. The British military introduced these shorts to Bermuda in the early part of the 20th century. By the 1920s and 1930s the garment had become very fashionable. However, they were not worn to dinner parties nor to church services. These shorts were originally worn with a white shirt, a tie, and a jacket, along with knee stockings. It was considered "daring" to wear the shorts five inches above the knee. And to go beyond that and wear Bermuda short-shorts could have gotten you ticketed by the police in the years after World War II. For some, Bermuda shorts, at least at summer cocktail parties, remain *de rigueur*.

ST. GEORGE'S PARISH: Settled in 1612, the town of St. George's was once the capital of Bermuda, before losing that position to Hamilton in 1815. The town was settled three years after Admiral Sir George Somers and his shipwrecked party of English colonists came ashore. A band of settlers, led by Richard Moore, of the newly created Bermuda Company, founded the town, the second English settlement in the New World (Jamestown, Virginia, was the first). The town was named after England's patron saint, and its coat-of-arms depicts St. George and the dragon. Sir George Somers died in Bermuda in 1610, and his heart was buried in the St. George's area.

Almost four centuries of history come alive here, and generations upon generations of sailors have set forth from its sheltered harbor. St. George's even played its role in the American Revolutionary War. Bermuda depended on the American colonies for food. When war came, food ran dangerously short. Loyalties were divided in Bermuda, as many of the people had kinsmen living on the American mainland. A delegation headed by Col. Henry Tucker went to Philadelphia to petition the Continental Congress for food and supplies, for which the Bermudians were willing to trade salt. George Washington had a different idea, however. He needed gunpowder, and a number of kegs of it were stored at St. George's. Without the approval of the British/Bermudian governor, a deal was consummated that resulted in the gunpowder's being trundled aboard American warships waiting in the harbor of Tobacco Bay under cover of darkness. In return the grateful colonies supplied Bermuda with food.

St. George's is about an hour's run from Hamilton. After years of slumber, this community is being restored.

The **Visitors Information Centre** (tel. 809/297-1642) on King's Square will give you a map and any information you need before you set out for exploration on your own, invariably on foot. King's Square is also called Market Square or King's Parade. It is the center of life in St. George's. Opposite the Town Hall, the center is open daily except Sunday from 9 a.m. to 1 p.m. and 2 to 4:45 p.m. in summer. Off-season, it's open only on Wednesday and Saturday.

The square contains two colorful pubs where you may want to stop for a drink after your tour. Also on the square is a pillory and stock where honeymooners like to have themselves photographed. These instruments of humiliation are treated as a joke today, but they were deadly serious at the time. Sometimes victims were placed in the pillory for a certain number of hours—sometimes with one ear nailed to the post! Victims were burnt on the hand or branded, fined in tobacco, nailed to the post, declared "infamous." Often they had their ears cut off or were made to "stand in a sheet on the church porch."

Offenses for which Bermudians were punished in the early days of settlement offer an illuminating glimpse of the social life of the time. Along with such "usual" acts as treason, robbery, arson, murder, and "scandal," records of the Assizes (courts) of the early 1600s include: concealing finds of ambergris, exporting cedarwood, railing against the governor's authority, hiding tobacco, being "notorious cursers and swearers," leading an "uncivil life and calling her neighbor an old Bawd and the like," neglecting to receive Holy Communion, the acting of any stage play of any kind whatsoever, and playing at such unlawful games as dice, cards, ninepins, and "such like."

The **Town Hall,** King's Square (tel. 809/297-1532), stands near the Visitors Information Centre. Headed by a mayor, officers of the Corporation of St. George's meet here. There are three aldermen and five common councillors. It has a collection of Bermuda cedar furnishings, along with photographs of previous mayors. You can go inside Monday to Friday from 9 a.m. to 5 p.m., on Saturday to 4 p.m. A multimedia, audiovisual presentation on the history, culture, and heritage of the colony, *Bermuda Journey,* is presented in the Town Hall several times a day. The half-hour show was produced by the makers of *The New York Experience.* Admission is $3.50 for adults, with a reduction in price for children.

Behind Town Hall, the **Old State House,** Princess Street, is Bermuda's oldest stone building, constructed with turtle oil and lime mortar in 1620. Its masonic lodge members, in a ceremony of pageantry, turn over one peppercorn in rent to the Bermuda government every April. (Peppercorns were sometimes a form of payment in the old days. In the late 18th century, two small islands off King's Square were sold for a peppercorn apiece: in 1782 Henry Tucker bought Ducking Stool Island, and in 1785 Nathaniel Butterfield bought Gallows Island. Several years later Simon Fraser purchased both for 100 peppercorns and built them into one, making what is today Ordnance Island.)

The Old State House, where meetings of the legislative council once took place, was turned over to the Freemasons of St. George's. The government asked the annual rent of one peppercorn, insisting on the right to hold meetings there upon demand.

For the information of those who have never witnessed the 45-minute spectacle, it begins around 11 a.m. with the gathering of the Bermuda Regiment on King's Square and the subsequent arrival of the premier, mayor, and other dignitaries amid the bellowing introductions of the town crier. As soon as all the principals have taken their places, a 17-gun salute is fired, as the governor and his lady make a grand entrance in their open horse-drawn landau. His Excellency inspects a military guard of honor, while the Bermuda Regiment Band plays. The stage is, of course, now set for the center of attention—a peppercorn, which sits on a silver plate atop a velvet cushion. Payment is made in a grand and formal manner, after which the Old State House is immediately used for a meeting of Her Majesty's Council.

The Old State House is open to the public. Visiting is possible only on Wednesday from 10 a.m. to 4 p.m. No admission is charged.

Across from the square and over a bridge, visitors head for Ordnance Island to see ***Deliverance II,*** a full-scale replica of *Deliverance I,* a Bermuda-built pinnace constructed in 1609 by the shipwrecked survivors of *Sea Venture. Deliverance* was the ship that carried these settlers on to Virginia. Admission is $2 for adults and 50¢ for children. There's a tape recording operating to guide visitors through the ship each day, which is open from 10 a.m. to 4 p.m. seven days a week. Alongside *Deliverance* is the **ducking stool,** a replica of a horrible contraption used in 17th-century witch trials. Its use is demonstrated on Wednesday only.

Back on King's Square, head east to the Duke of York Street. Here **St. Peter's Church** (tel. 809/297-8359) is believed to be the oldest Anglican place of worship in the western hemisphere. The original church on this spot, built by the colonists in 1612 almost entirely of cedar with a palmetto-leaf thatch roof, was almost destroyed by a hurricane in 1712. Some of the interior, including the original altar from 1615 (still in daily use) was salvaged, and the church was rebuilt in 1713. It has been restored many times since and provides excellent examples of the architectural work of the 17th to the 20th centuries. The tower was added in 1814. On display in the vestry is a silver communion service given to the church by King William III in 1697. Before the State House was constructed, the colony held public meetings in the church. The first Assize convened in 1616, and the first meeting of Parliament was in 1620. Sunday and weekday services are conducted here. Otherwise, it is open daily from 10 a.m. to 4:30 p.m., and a guide is on hand daily except Sunday. There is no admission charge, but the church always needs donations to help maintain the building.

The **graveyard of St. Peter's** is also an attraction. The entrance is opposite Broad Alley. Some of the tombstones in the graveyard are more than three centuries old. Many tombs mark the graves of slaves. Here you'll find the grave of Midshipman Richard Dale, an American who was the last victim of the War of 1812. The churchyard also contains the tombs of Gov. Sir Richard Sharples and his aide, Capt. Hugh Sayers, who were murdered while walking the grounds of

Government House in 1973. Even the governor's dog, Horsa, was killed. A state of emergency was declared in Bermuda following the assassinations.

The **Confederate Museum,** just off King's Square (tel. 809/297-1423), was once the Globe Hotel, headquarters of Maj. Norman Walker, the Confederate representative in Bermuda, and contains relics from the island's involvement in the U.S. Civil War. St. George's was the port from which ships carrying arms and munitions ran the Union blockade. There is a replica of the Great Seal of the Confederacy fitted to a Victorian press so that visitors can emboss copies as souvenirs. The museum is open Monday to Saturday except holidays from 10 a.m. to 5 p.m. Admission is $1.50 for adults.

Below York Street, on Water Street, is the **Tucker House** (tel. 809/297-0545), honoring the family that has produced important personages in U.S. and British history and some of Bermuda's leaders, including a president of the Council, Henry Tucker, who lived here during the American Revolutionary War and afterward. The old house, filled principally with 18th-century Tucker furniture and portraits, is open daily except Sunday from 10 a.m. to 5 p.m., charging $2 for admission. The house contains a memorial room to Joseph Hayne Rainey, the first black member of the U.S. House of Representatives.

Opposite, **Somers Wharf** has been restored and now contains branches of some of Hamilton's finest shops, including A. S. Cooper & Sons and Trimingham Brothers and the Irish Linen Shop, as well as the Carriage House Restaurant.

Next to the restaurant is the **Carriage Museum,** Water Street (tel. 809/297-1367), which you can inspect for $1 for adults, 50¢ for children. Bermuda allowed only carriages until 1946, when the "automobile age" arrived. But many of these old conveyances were preserved to delight present-day visitors, some of whom go for carriage rides in Hamilton. The site is a renovated old Royal Engineers warehouse. It's open Monday to Saturday from 9 a.m. to 5 p.m.

At **Somers Garden,** on Duke of York Street, the heart of Sir George Somers was buried in 1610. A stone column perpetuates the memory of Bermuda's founder. The garden was opened in 1920 by the Prince of Wales (later King of England, and subsequently Duke of Windsor). It is open daily from 7:30 a.m. to 4:30 p.m.

It's called the **Unfinished Cathedral.** After leaving Somers Garden, head up the steps to the North Gate, opening onto Blockade Alley. This structure is also known as "the folly of St. George's." The plan was that this cathedral, begun in 1874, would replace St. Peter's. But the planners ran into money troubles, a schism developed, and as if that weren't enough, a storm caused more damage.

In Featherbed Alley, **St. George's Historical Society Museum** (tel. 809/297-0423) is housed in a former home built around 1700, containing an original 18th-century Bermuda kitchen complete with utensils from that period. Exhibits include a 300-year-old Bible, a letter from George Washington, and American Indian ax heads. (Some early settlers on St. David's Island were North American Indians, mainly Pequot.) It's open daily except Sunday from 10 a.m. to 4 p.m. for a $1 admission for adults, 50¢ for children.

The **Featherbed Alley Printery** (tel. 809/297-0009) stands on Featherbed Alley. It contains a working press in use for some 350 years. Admission is free, and the shop can be visited daily from 10 a.m. to 4 p.m. except Sunday and holidays. The alley gets its name because featherbeds were placed here for drunks to sleep on until they could sober up.

Petticoat Lane (sometimes called Silk Alley) got its name because two recently emancipated slave girls were said to have paraded up and down the lane, rustling their new and flamboyantly colored silk petticoats

Like Petticoat Lane, **Barber's Lane** is an alley named for a former slave. It honors Joseph Hayne Rainey, mentioned above, a freeman from the Carolinas who fled to Bermuda aboard a blockade runner during the Civil War. He was a barber in Bermuda for the rest of the war. Upon its conclusion he returned to the United States and was elected to Congress, becoming the first black member of the House of Representatives.

At the head of Broad Alley, behind St. Peter's Church, stands the **Old Rectory,** built by a reformed pirate in 1705. A charming old Bermuda cottage, it is administered by the Bermuda National Trust. It was later inhabited by Parson Richardson, who was nicknamed "The Little Bishop." Now a private home, it's open to the public only on Wednesday (unless it falls on a holiday) from 10 a.m. to 5 p.m. Admission is free, but donations are welcomed.

St. George's Library, Aunt Peggy's Lane (tel. 809/297-1912), is in an 18th-century Bermuda home, Stuart Hall. Cedar-beamed rooms and Bermuda furniture provide a cozy atmosphere in this circulation library, a branch of the Bermuda public library. It's open Monday and Wednesday from 10 a.m. to 1 p.m. and 2 to 6 p.m., on Saturday from 10 a.m. to 1 p.m. and 2 to 5 p.m. No admission is charged.

Bridge House Art Gallery is one of the best-known in Bermuda, displaying only works by Bermudian artists, including Alfred Birdsey. Owned by the National Trust, the house was constructed in the very early years of the 18th century. It was home to several of the colony's governors. Perhaps its most colorful owner was Bridger Goodrich, a Loyalist from Virginia, whose privateers once blockaded Chesapeake Bay. So devoted was he to the king that he also sabotaged Bahamian vessels trading with the American colonies. The house is called Bridge because a bridge used to stand over a muddy creek (it's been filled in now). There is also a straw market souvenir shop on the premises, which is open from 9 a.m. to 5 p.m. Monday to Saturday. The art gallery is open from 10 a.m. to 5 p.m. in summer, only on Wednesday and Saturday in winter.

From its earliest days St. George's has been fortified, and although it never saw much military action, the reminders of those former days are interesting to explore. On the outskirts of the town, the sights are reached by Circular Drive.

The first is **Gates Fort,** built by Sir Thomas Gates, one of the original band of settlers on the *Sea Venture.* The fort dates from 1609. Gates was governor-designate for the Colony of Virginia. Nearby, along the coast, is **Building's Bay,** where the shipwrecked victims of the *Sea Venture* built their vessels, including the *Deliverance* in 1610.

Towering above the beach where the shipwrecked crew of the *Sea Venture* landed in 1609 is **Fort St. Catherine,** Barry Road (tel. 809/297-1920), first completed in 1614 and named for the patron saint of wheelwrights and carpenters. The fortifications were upgraded over the years, the last major reconstruction being undertaken from 1865 to 1878, so that the fort's appearance today is largely the result of work done in the 19th century. Now a museum, visitors begin their visits by seeing a series of dioramas, "Highlights in Bermuda's History." Museum figures are used to show various activities taking place in the Magazine of the fort, restored and refurnished as it was in the 1880s. Large Victorian muzzle-loading cannon can be seen on their original carriages. In the Keep, which served as the living quarters of the fort, you can see information on local and overseas regiments that served in Bermuda, a fine small-arms exhibit, a cooking-area display, and an exhibition of replicas of the crown jewels of England. A short audiovisual show on the St. George's defense systems and the fortsof St. George's can be seen here. Fort St. Catherine is open daily except Christmas Day from 10 a.m. to 4:30 p.m. Admission is $2.50 for adults, free for children under 12.

HAMILTON PARISH: Around Harrington Sound, the sights differ greatly from those of St. George's—more action, less history. A public bus from Hamilton goes here in about an hour. Hamilton Parish is bordered on the east by St. George's and on the southwest by Smith's Parish. The parish encloses **Harrington Sound,** a landlocked, saltwater lake that is 1½ miles at its most expansive width and 2⅛ miles long. It was named for John, first Lord Harrington of Rutland, England.

Some experts believe that in unrecorded times Harrington Sound was a cave that fell in. Its gateway to the ocean is through an inlet at Flatts. However, it is believed that there are underwater gateways as well. Several deep-sea fish have been caught in the sound.

At **Bermuda Pottery,** Blue Hole Hill (tel. 809/293-2234), you can see the studio workshop center of locally made pottery, where lead-free glazes are used, reflecting the Bermuda colors of sea green, sky blue, leaf green, and yellow. The pottery is open daily from 8:30 a.m. to 5:30 p.m.

Also at Blue Hole Hill is one of the best dolphin shows in the world, **Blue Grotto Dolphins** (tel. 809/293-0864), next to the causeway leading to the airport. The dolphins perform five shows a day, in season, in a natural setting. Tricks include surfing, diving for coins, basketball playing, and acrobatics. The dolphins are trained to voice commands. Shows are given at 11 a.m., noon, and 2, 3, and 4 p.m. (only at noon and 2 and 3 p.m. from mid-November to mid-January). Admission is $3.50 for adults, $1.50 for children 4 to 12, free for children under 4.

The **Bermuda Perfumery,** 212 North Shore Rd., Bailey's Bay (tel. 809/293-0627), is where Lili Perfumes are made. Visitors are given guided tours showing the perfume-making process, including the old method of extracting scents from native flowers. Among the fragrances produced are passion flower, Bermuda Easter lily, oleander jasmine, and sweet pea. A small botanic garden with a seating area and walkways provides an attractive resting place. You can also visit the orchid house, with more than 500 orchids, and the nature trail that passes through a large area of the property planted with tropical flowers, shrubs, and trees. The perfumery has a gift shop, the Cobweb. The perfumery is open from 9 a.m. to 5 p.m. Monday to Saturday, and admission is free.

Across Flatts Bridge, the **Bermuda Aquarium, Museum, and Zoo,** North Shore Road (tel. 809/293-2727), is home to an amazing collection of tropical fish, Galápagos turtles, and other forms of marine life. Many people consider this aquarium one of the finest in the world. In the museum you can see exhibits tracing the geological development of the Bermuda islands. The complex also has a zoo with turtles, alligators, and monkeys, along with an outstanding collection of birds, including parrots and flamingos. It's open daily from 9 a.m. to 5 p.m., charging $4 for adults, $1 for children 7 to 16 (those under 7 are admitted free). You can bring a picnic lunch or choose from one of several restaurants in Flatts Village. There is parking for cycles and cars across the street from the aquarium. To reach it by public transport, take bus 3, 10, or 11 running from Hamilton, or bus 10 or 11 from St. George's. All these lines stop at the complex.

Crystal Caves, 8 Crystal Caves Rd., Bailey's Bay (tel. 809/293-0640), is composed of translucent formations of stalagmites and stalactites, a fairyland setting including the crystal-clear Cahow Lake. Discovered in 1907, the cave is reached by a gently sloping path and a few steps. At the bottom, 120 feet below the surface, is a floating causeway that follows the winding cavern, where hidden lights illuminate the glistening interior. All tours through Crystal Caves are guided. Hours are daily from 9:30 a.m. to 4:30 p.m. Admission is $2.50 for adults, $1 for children 5 to 11.

Another grotto, this one attached to the Plantation Club, is **Leamington Caves** at Bailey's Bay (tel. 809/293-1188). This grotto has stunning crystal formations and underground lakes. It too was first discovered by a young boy, who noticed a small opening on the rocky hillside that he and his father were clearing for plowing in 1908. He slipped through the hole with a rope and candles and found a wonderland of natural cave splendors some 1½ million years old. It's open daily from 9:30 a.m. to 4 p.m. for an adult admission of $3, $1 for children 4 to 12 (under 4 free). Guided tours take you along lighted walkways with hand rails, through the high-vaulted, amber-tinted grotto.

Also at Bailey's Bay, **Tom Moore's Jungle** consists of wild woods. The poet Tom Moore is said to have spent many hours writing poetry under a still-standing calabash tree. Since the jungle is held in private trust, permission has to be obtained to enter it. However, it's much easier to pay your respects to the romantic poet by calling at the **Tom Moore Tavern** (see Chapter IV).

Devil's Hole, on the Harrington Sound Road (tel. 809/293-2072), is a former cave. The pool is fed by the sea through half a mile of subterranean passages. Used as a natural aquarium since 1847, it's stocked with some 400 individual fish, including moray eels, sharks, giant groupers, and massive green turtles. Visitors can tempt the pond's inhabitants with baited but hookless lines. The place is open Monday to Saturday (except Christmas, Good Friday, and the month of January) from 9:30 a.m. to 5 p.m., 10 a.m. to 5 p.m. on Sunday and holidays. Admission is $3 for adults, $1.50 for children 6 to 12, 50¢ for tots under 5.

For the best sightseeing view of the parish, visitors head for **Crawl Hill,** right before they come to Bailey's Bay. At this point, the highest place in Hamilton Parish, you can enjoy a view of the north shore. Crawl is a corruption of the word "kraal," where turtles were kept before slaughter. Shelly Bay, named for one of the passengers of the *Sea Venture,* is the longest beach along the north shore.

The **Hamilton Parish Church** can be reached by going down Trinity Church Road. It stands on Church Bay and dates from 1623 when it was just a one-room structure. Much work and many alterations have gone into it in just over 3½ centuries.

SMITH'S PARISH: Smith's Parish, named for Sir Thomas Smith, a member of the Bermuda Company, faces the open sea on both its northern and southern borders. To the east is Harrington Sound, and to the west, bucolic Devonshire Parish.

The parish takes in **Flatts Village,** one of the most charming little parish towns of Bermuda. This was a smugglers' port for about 200 years. The origin of the name is lost to history. Once it was the center of power for a coterie of successful "planter politicians" and landowners. Their government ranked in importance only to St. George's, then the capital. People gathered at the rickety Flatts Bridge to "enjoy" such public entertainment as a hanging on the gallows. A so-called blasphemer in 1718 had his tongue bored through with a fire-hot poker. If the offense were serious enough, victims were drawn and quartered here.

From Flatts Village you'll have good views of both the inlet and Harrington Sound.

At the top of McGall's Hill (which you can visit after seeing Verdmont House) is **St. Mark's Church.** Another church once stood near the site of St. Mark's. Constructed in 1746, when it became unsafe, a local family, the Trotts, donated land for the construction of St. Mark's, on which construction began in 1846. It is reported that the first services were conducted here on Easter Sunday in 1848. However, work on the church had not been completed, and subsequent additions, such as the chancel, were made. Work continued until the closing years of the 19th century. St. Mark's Church was based on the same designs as the old Devonshire Parish Church.

Verdmont, Collector's Hill Road (tel. 809/236-7369), is an 18th-century Bermuda mansion, which holds a special significance to U.S. citizens interested in colonial and Revolutionary War history. It stands on property owned in the 17th century by William Sayle, who left Bermuda to found South Carolina on the American mainland, becoming its first governor. The house was built before 1710 by John Dickinson, a prosperous shipowner who was also Speaker of the House of Assembly in Bermuda from 1707 to 1710. Verdmont passed to Mr. Dickinson's granddaughter, Elizabeth, who married the Hon. Thomas Smith, collector of customs, whose oldest daughter, Mary, married Judge John Green, a Loyalist who came to Bermuda in 1765 from Philadelphia. During and after the American Revolution, Green was judge of the Vice-Admiralty Court, who had the final say on prizes brought in by privateers. Needless to say, many American shipowners lost their vessels through his decisions. The house is now administered by the National Trust. It contains many antiques, china, and portraits, along with the finest cedar stair balustrade in Bermuda. Admission is $2, and hours are Monday to Saturday from 10 a.m. to 5 p.m.

On the South Shore Road, turn right for **Spittal Pond,** Bermuda's largest wildlife sanctuary. The most important of the National Trust's open spaces, it is 60 acres in extent, containing about 25 species of waterfowl, which can be seen annually from November to May. Visitors are asked to keep to the scenic trails and footpaths provided. Birdwatchers, in particular, visit in January when as many as 500 different species of birds can be observed wintering on the pond. In general, migrating birds can be spotted anytime from November to April.

Spittal Pond also shelters **Spanish Rock,** on a cliff facing the sea. It contains a cipher dating 1543, probably carved by an Iberian mariner who may have been shipwrecked here. Historians still debate if it was placed here by a Portuguese or a Spanish seafarer.

At the western end of Mangrove Lake, just across the road from Pink Beach, is **North Nature Reserve,** an area of living mangroves growing in a brackish pond. The pond is of interest to students of water fauna and flora. It attracts several species of birds. The reserve is open daily, free.

DEVONSHIRE PARISH: This is one of my favorite parishes in Bermuda. As you wander its narrow lanes, with some imagination you can picture yourself in the original Devon in England. The parish takes its name from the first Earl of Devonshire. It is a lush, hilly parish, rarely spoiled by commercial intrusions.

Devonshire is not rich in accommodations, but it has some (see "Where to Stay in Bermuda," Chapter III). It also has one of the most popular and typically Bermudian nightclubs on the island, Clay House Inn, lying along the North Shore Road (see "Bermuda After Dark," coming up).

Also along the North Shore Road, you reach Devonshire Dock, long a seafarer's haven. It's near the border to Pembroke Parish. Fishermen still bring in such catches as grouper and rockfish here. You can shop for dinner if you've been fortunate enough to get a nearby cottage with a kitchen. British soldiers in the War of 1812 came here to be entertained by local women.

On Middle Road stands the **Old Devonshire Parish Church** (tel. 809/292-1348). A house of worship is said to have been built on the site in 1624, although the present foundation is from 1716. An explosion virtually destroyed the church on Easter 1970, and it was reconstructed. It is very tiny, looking almost more like a vicarage than a church. Some of the church relics survived the blast, including church silver from 1590, said to be the oldest on the island. Old Devonshire Church stands northeast of the "new" Devonshire Church, which dates from 1846. It's built of limestone, with a high-pitched roof, constructed in the early English–style. It was designed by Sir George Grove.

At the **Arboretum** on Middle Road, you'll discover one of the most tranquil oases in Bermuda, an open space with a wide range of some of the island's plant and tree life. It was created by the Department of Agriculture and Fisheries.

Along the South Shore Road, you can visit the **Edmund Gibbons Nature Reserve,** west of the junction with Collector's Hill. This portion of marshland, owned by the National Trust, provides living space for a number of birds and rare species of Bermuda flora. It's open daily at no charge. Visitors must keep out of the marshy area.

Also along the South Shore Road, heading to Hamilton, you'll come to **Palm Grove,** a private estate. It admits visitors free, and has some stunning flower gardens, opening onto a view of the ocean. A map outline of Bermuda is set into a spacious pond. The place is open Monday to Thursday from 8 a.m. to 5 p.m.

PEMBROKE PARISH: The City of Hamilton is not in Hamilton Parish but in Pembroke Parish, which is a peninsula, opening on its northern rim onto the vast Atlantic Ocean and on its southern side onto the beautiful Hamilton Harbour. Its western border edges Great Sound.

The parish is named after the third Earl of Pembroke, who was a power in the Bermuda Company of 1616. Nearly one-fourth of Bermuda's population lives in Pembroke Parish, most of them in the capital of Hamilton (coming up).

The ideal way to see Hamilton or the parish itself for the first time is to sail in through Hamilton Harbour, past the offshore cays. You'll be joining everything and everybody from fishermen to the yachting set to cruise ships.

Earlier we've paid our respects to the Irish poet Tom Moore, and to the American humorist Mark Twain, for publicizing the glories of Bermuda. But for the British at least, the woman who put Bermuda on the tourist map was Princess Louise. The daughter of Queen Victoria, she spent several months in Bermuda in 1883. Her husband was the governor-general of Canada, and he allowed her to spend some time in Bermuda to escape the fierce cold up north.

Although in the 20th century Bermuda was to play host to a string of royal visitors, including Queen Elizabeth II, Princess Louise was the first royal personage to set foot in the colony. And set foot she did, turning up all over the island, visiting and chatting with its friendly people and winning their respect and admiration.

Upon reaching Canada, she told reporters that she'd found the Shangri-La of tourist destinations.

In the beginning, guests could stay only at the Hamilton Hotel on Church Street, which was destroyed by fire in 1955 long after it had been turned into government offices.

The Princess Hotel, still in existence and named in honor of Princess Louise, opened in 1884. Over the years it had a colorful history, none more dramatic than when it was taken over by Allied agents in World War II.

If Princess Louise or her equivalent were to visit today, she would most likely be housed at **Government House,** which stands on North Shore Road and Langton Hill. Not open to the public, it is the magnificent residence of the queen-appointed governor of the island. The large and beautiful grounds may be viewed on request to the governor's aide-de-camp. A Victorian residence, it has sheltered many notable guests, including Queen Elizabeth II and her husband, Prince Philip, as well as Prince Charles, Sir Winston Churchill, and President John F. Kennedy. The saddest moment for Government House was in 1973 when Gov. Sir Richard Sharples and his aide, Capt. Hugh Sayers, along with the governor's dog, Horsa, were assassinated while walking on the grounds. This led to a state of emergency in Bermuda.

While touring Pembroke Parish, visitors are fond of looking at **Black Watch Well.** Excavated by a detachment of the Black Watch Regiment, the well was ordered dug in 1894 when Bermudians suffered through a long drought.

After skirting the environs, it's time to zero in on the capital itself.

City of Hamilton

Since 1815 Hamilton has been the capital of Bermuda. Most people go here to shop, but the city also contains a number of sightseeing attractions. Named for a former governor, Henry Hamilton, it was incorporated as a town in 1793, and in 1815, because of its central location and its large, protected harbor, it was chosen as the Bermuda capital, which was moved from St. George's. It occupies only 182 acres of land in its entirety, so it is most often explored on foot.

Today Hamilton is the hub of the island's economy, but long before it got such fancy labels as "showcase of the Atlantic" it was a modest outlet for the export of Bermuda cedar and fresh vegetables.

Hamilton boasts the largest number of eating and drinking establishments in Bermuda, especially on or near Front Street. These restaurants charge a wide range of prices, and there are many English pubs if you'd like to go on a pub crawl. Although there is a huge conglomeration of bars, religion isn't neglected—there are 12 churches within the city limits, one or two of which merit a sightseeing visit.

Hamilton should be seen not only on land but also from the water, and there are frequent boating tours of the harbor and its coral reefs. If you're visiting from other parishes, the ferry will let you off at the western end of Front Street, which is ideal if you'd like to pay a call to the **Visitors Service Bureau** and pick up a map. The location is near the Ferry Terminal. The staff here also provides information and helpful brochures. Hours are 9 a.m. to 5 p.m. daily (closed Sunday).

To return to the parishes of Paget, Warwick, and Sandys, ferries leave between 6:50 a.m. and 11:20 p.m. On weekends, the schedule is reduced.

Opposite the Visitors Service Bureau stands the much-photographed policeman (or woman) in the **"Bird Cage,"** directing traffic. Visitors have wondered for years if this is for real or for show.

Nearby is **Albuoy's Point,** site of the Royal Bermuda Yacht Club, founded in 1844. The point, named after a 17th-century professor of "physick," is a public park, overlooking Hamilton Harbour.

After leaving the harbor, proceed up Queen Street to the Public Library and **Bermuda Historical Society Museum,** Par-le-Ville, 13 Queen St. (tel. 809/295-2487), which has a collection of old cedar furniture, antique silver, early Bermuda coins (hog pennies), and costumes, plus the sea chest and navigating lodestone of Sir George Sommers, whose shipwrecked crew colonized Bermuda. You'll find portraits of Sir George and Lady Sommers, as well as models of the ill-fated *Sea Venture,* along with the *Deliverance* and *Patience,* other vessels important in the Bermuda colonization. The museum is open daily except Wednesday and Sunday from 9:30 a.m. to 12:30 p.m. and 1:45 to 4:30 p.m. Admission is free.

The library and museum lie in **Par-la-Ville Park** on Queen Street, which still dwells in the 19th century. It was designed by William Bennett Perot, Hamilton's first postmaster, and an eccentric one at that. He was also the most unforgettable character. As he delivered mail around the town, he is said to have placed letters in the crown of his top hat, so as to preserve his dignity. You enter by the landmark rubber tree, planted in 1847.

The **Perot Post Office,** on Queen Street at the park entrance (tel.

809/295-5651), is a landmark building where Bermuda's first stamp was printed. Beloved by collectors from all over the world, the stamps, signed by Perot, are considered priceless. It is said that Perot and his friend, Heyl, who ran an apothecary shop, conceived of the idea of the first postage stamp to protect the post office from cheaters. People used to stop off at the post office and leave letters but not enough pennies to send them. The postage stamp was conceived to make them honest. Of French Huguenot ancestry, Perot held his post from 1818 to 1862. The postage stamps were printed in either black or carmine.

In this same post office, philatelists can purchase Bermuda stamps of today. For its 375th anniversary Bermuda issued stamps honoring its 1609 discovery. One stamp portrays the admiral of the fleet, Sir George Somers, along with Sir Thomas Gates, the captain of the *Sea Venture.* Another depicts a building in the settlement of Jamestown, Virginia, which was on the verge of extinction when Sir George and the survivors of the Bermuda shipwreck finally arrived with supplies in late 1610. A third shows the *Sea Venture* stranded on the coral reefs of Bermuda. Yet another shows the entire fleet, originally bound for Jamestown, leaving Plymouth, England, on June 2, 1609. The old post office is open Monday to Friday from 9 a.m. to 5 p.m.

Hamilton City Hall, Church Street (tel. 809/292-1234), is an imposing white structure with a giant weather vane and wind clock to tell maritime-minded Bermudians which way the wind is blowing. Completed in 1960, the building is headquarters for Hamilton's municipal government. The theater on the first floor is the scene for stage, music, and dance productions throughout the year, as well as being the site of Bermuda's annual Festival of the Performing Arts. It's open Monday to Friday from 9 a.m. to 5 p.m., with no charge for admission.

An art gallery upstairs in City Hall (tel. 809/292-3824) is where the **Bermuda Society of Arts** holds rotating exhibits of both Bermudian and foreign artists, much of whose work can be purchased. The gallery is open Monday to Saturday from 10 a.m. to 4 p.m. April to November and for limited hours on Saturday from December to March. Admission is free. The Bermuda Society of Arts boasts a membership of 500, including many of the island's foremost amateur and professional artists. It is concerned with the promotion of all the visual arts. Besides exhibits, activities include slide shows, workshops, and dinner/film show evenings. For information about coming shows contact the Curator, Bermuda Society of Arts, P.O. Box HM 1202, Hamilton HM FX, Bermuda.

A short distance away, the **Bermuda cathedral** on Church Street (tel. 809/292-4033) is the seat of the Anglican church of Bermuda. It was consecrated in 1894 on the site of Holy Trinity Church, which was destroyed by an arsonist in 1844. The cathedral is in the Gothic style, and inside it contains an interesting reredos.

The **Sessions House,** opening onto Parliament Street (tel. 809/292-7408), built in the 1820s, is an Italian Renaissance-style structure with the **Jubilee Clock Tower,** built in the jubilee year of Queen Victoria. The House of Assembly meets on the second floor. Visitors are allowed in the gallery (you can call to learn the time of assemblies). On the lower floor, the chief justice presides over the Supreme Court. Again there is a visitors' gallery. For times of court, telephone 809/292-1350.

The **Cabinet Building,** occupying the block of Front Street between Court and Parliament Streets (tel. 809/292-5501), is a Hamilton landmark, fronted by the **Cenotaph,** a memorial to Bermuda's dead in the two world wars. The Cabinet Building houses the Cabinet Office that includes the office of the premier. Parliament convenes here every fall. Visitors are allowed into the Senate Chamber where Bermuda's upper house meets every Wednesday at 10 a.m. except during summer recess. The handsome oak throne dates from 1642. The building is open for free visits Monday to Friday from 9 a.m. to 5 p.m.

On the outskirts of Hamilton on Cedar Avenue stands **St. Theresa's** (tel. 809/292-0607), the Roman Catholic cathedral in Bermuda. Unlike the other parish churches of Bermuda, the architecture of St. Theresa's is in the Spanish Mission style. The church dates from 1927, and contains a chalice left by Pope Paul VI when he visited Hamilton in 1968.

Fort Hamilton, a massive Victorian fortification on Happy Valley Road overlooking Hamilton and its harbor, was ordered built in the 19th century by the Duke of Wellington, who had grand plans to turn Bermuda into the Gibraltar of the West. However, the fort was never called into active duty to defend Hamilton. It was allowed to fall into ruins, but is now restored and visitors can wander through its ancient passages and labyrinths. The dry moat is filled with plants and shrubbery, and there is a tea shop. The admission-free fort is open from 9:30 a.m. to 5 p.m. Monday to Friday. From the fort there is a panoramic view of Hamilton and its harbor, and also of Great Sound. It is reached by Victoria and King Streets and Happy Valley Road.

PAGET PARISH: Chances are good that your hotel will be in this desirable residential section, across from Hamilton Harbour. It is a virtual "bedroom" of the city of Hamilton. Visitors flock here not so much for its many sightseeing attractions, but for its beautiful South Shore beaches, among the most beautiful on the chain of islands. Named after the fourth Lord Paget, the parish has a lot of historic homes and gardens, but most of them are not open to public view, except on special occasions. During the springtime College Weeks, Elbow Beach Hotel is the center of most activities.

Most visitors who stay here in one of the section's many hotels use the ferry service, with landing docks at Salt Kettle, Hodson's, and Lower Ferry. It's also possible to "commute" to Warwick or Sandys Parishes to the west.

The Bermuda National Trust, which works to maintain the charm of the parish and its natural settings, is housed at **Waterville,** an 18th-century building (see "National Trust" in the ABCs section of Chapter II).

Paget Parish is also the setting of **Chelston,** on Grape Bay Drive, the official residence of the U.S. consul-general (which is only open during the Garden Club of Bermuda's open houses and gardens program in the spring). It stands on 14½ acres of landscaped grounds overlooking South Shore.

Bermuda Botanical Gardens, at Point Finger and South Shore Roads (main entrance on Berry Hill Road; tel. 809/236-4201), contains hundreds of flowers, shrubs, and trees, all clearly identified. Guided tours leave from the Tavern on the Green parking lot at 10:30 a.m. on Tuesday, Wednesday, and Friday (only Tuesday and Friday in winter).

Paget Marsh, on Middle Road, is 18 acres of unspoiled woods and marshland, with vegetation of ecological interest. It can be visited only when special arrangements are made with the National Trust (tel. 809/236-6483) from 9 a.m. to 5 p.m. Monday to Friday.

One of Bermuda's best-known painters, Alfred Birdsey, invites visitors to his gallery, the **Birdsey Studio,** Stowe Hill (tel. 809/236-6658). His son-in-law, Tony Davis, will probably be there to answer questions and quote prices for original works in watercolor and oils by the painter who has exhibited around the world. Birdsey is known for sun-washed versions of land- and seascapes, with Bermuda settings. The cost of watercolors, all 20 by 26 inches, is from $40 to $200. Oil paintings range from $70 to $1,500, depending on the size. You can also purchase foldover postcards of Birdsey's island scenes at $8 for a packet of

20. The shop is open from 9 a.m. to 4 p.m. weekdays. Birdsey's daughter, Antoinette, exhibits some of her flower paintings, while another daughter, Joanne, displays whimsical and amusing versions of animals for children.

WARWICK PARISH: Famed for its two golf courses, this western parish of Bermuda was named after the second Earl of Warwick, a shareholder in the Bermuda Company of 1610.

It is quite likely that you will stay in this parish, as it boasts a number of hotels and housekeeping cottages, including the Belmont Hotel and Golf Club, the Mermaid Beach Club, Surf Side Beach Club, and the White Heron Inn.

Warwick Long Bay, on the South Shore, with public conveniences, is one of the finest beaches of Bermuda, and forms the major attraction of the parish.

In the vicinity, you can go inside **Christ Church,** across from the Belmont Hotel on Middle Road, from 9 a.m. to 4 p.m. Built in 1719, it is one of the oldest Scottish Presbyterian churches in the New World.

If you're in the parish on a Sunday morning, it seems that nearly everyone heads for Herman's, a popular restaurant serving local Bermudian food (see "Dining in Bermuda," Chapter IV).

SOUTHAMPTON PARISH: This parish is a narrow strip of land opening on its northern rim onto Little Sound and on its southern shore onto the wide Atlantic Ocean. It is bordered by Warwick Parish in the east and Sandys Parish in the west. A U.S. Naval Air Station is here, and you'll sometimes see red flags hoisted in the area, warning of aerial firing—so take care.

Celebrated for its beaches, the parish was named after the third Earl of Southampton. It is the setting for two of Bermuda's poshest resort hotels, the Southampton Princess and the Sonesta, both previewed in Chapter III.

The main attraction of this parish is the **Gibbs Hill Lighthouse,** Lighthouse Road between South Shore and Middle Road (tel. 809/238-0524), built in 1846, the oldest cast-iron lighthouse in the world. The magnificent view of the Bermuda islands and the sweeping shoreline from the lookout balcony at the top is worth the 185-step climb. The workings of the machinery are explained by the lighthouse keeper. In spring, visitors may see migrating whales beyond the South Shore reefs. The climb costs $1.50. You can see a collection of artifacts from shipwrecks recovered by Teddy Tucker, free. The lighthouse is open daily except Christmas from 9 a.m. to 4:30 p.m.

Also in the parish, **Horseshoe Bay** is one of Bermuda's most attractive public beaches, with changing rooms, a snackbar, and space for parking.

SANDYS PARISH: There are those who visit Bermuda by flying into the airport and then heading directly for Sandys Parish, which they never leave until it's time to go home. For many, the far-western tip of Bermuda is that special, with its rolling hills, its lush countryside, and its pleasant bays. The parish is actually made up of a group of islands, and was named in honor of Sir Edwin Sandys, one of the shareholders of the original Somers Island (Bermuda) Company, as well as a director of the Virginia Company and the East India Company.

Somerset Island, the largest of the Sandys group, where the village of Somerset lies, was named to pay tribute to Sir George Somers of *Sea Venture* fame. The parish is often called Somerset. Somehow it has always stood apart from the rest of Bermuda. For example, during the U.S. Civil War, when most of Bermuda sympathized with the Confederate cause, Sandys Parish stood firmly in the Union camp.

To explore this western end, the tip of the fishhook of Bermuda, it is best to take a ferry (fare of $2) plying Great Sound, a 45-minute run from Hamilton to Watford Bridge. Bikes can be taken aboard the ferry (motor-assisted cycles are assessed $2). Ferries also stop at Cavello Bay, Somerset, and the Dockyard. The **Visitors Service Bureau** is on the main road near St. James' Church (tel. 809/234-1388).

Fort Scaur, Somerset Road (tel. 809/234-0908), was part of a ring of fortifications constructed in the 19th century during the troubled relations between Britain and the United States. Built as a last-ditch defense line for H.M. Dockyard, the fort stands on the highest hill on Somerset Island and is skillfully constructed to take advantage of the land contours so that it's well camouflaged from the sea. There are subterranean passages and a dry moat that stretches across the land from Ely's Harbour to the Great Sound. Fort Scaur was opened to visitors in 1957 and has become one of Somerset's most popular tourist attractions. The fort offers breathtaking views of Ely's Harbour and the Great Sound, and points as far away as St. David's Lighthouse and Fort St. Catherine can be seen with the free telescope. Picnic tables, benches, and rest rooms are provided in the fort. Surrounding the fort are 22 acres of parkland filled with interesting trails, picnic areas, a rocky shoreline for fishing, and a public dock for access from the sea. Fort Scaur is open every day of the year except Christmas, from 9:30 a.m. to 4:30 p.m. Admission is free, and visitors are welcome to picnic and photograph the many scenic views it offers.

After leaving the fort, you can continue on the **Somerset Bridge,** the world's smallest drawbridge. When open for marine traffic, the space between the spans is a mere 22 inches at road level. Much photographed, it is just big enough to allow the mast of a sailboat to pass through. The bridge dates from the early 17th century.

In the center of the island is the **Springfield and Gilbert Nature Reserve,** Main Road, Somerset. In it stands **Springfield,** an old plantation home restored by the National Trust that today houses Somerset Library (tel. 809/234-1980), a branch of the Bermuda Public Library. No admission is charged for either the Nature Reserve (open during daylight), the home (the branch library), or the outbuildings (used as a nursery school). The library is open Monday, Wednesday, and Saturday from 9 a.m. to 1 p.m. and 2 to 5 p.m. The nature reserve consists of five acres of unspoiled woodland, and bears the name of the family who owned the property from the beginning of the 18th century until it was acquired by the Bermuda National Trust in conjunction with the Bermuda Audubon Society in 1973.

On Somerset Road is the **Scaur Lodge Property,** an open area that includes the site of Scaur Lodge, a Bermuda cottage that was severely damaged by a waterspout, which moved up on land, turning into a tornado and driving across this neck of Somerset Island. The typical Bermuda steep-shoreline hillside is open daily at no charge.

Sandys Parish has areas of great natural beauty, including **Somerset Long Bay,** a public beach, which the Bermuda Audubon Society is developing into a nature preserve, and **Mangrove Bay,** a protected beach right in the heart of **Somerset Village.** From the public wharf, you can take pictures. If time remains, try to walk around the old village, as it's filled with typically Bermudian houses and contains some interesting shops.

St. James' Anglican Church in the village was built on the site of a structure that was destroyed by a hurricane in 1780. The present church was built nine years later, although the north and south aisles were added in 1836, the entrance gates in 1872, and the spire and chancel in 1880. The church was struck by lightning in 1939 but has been restored.

IRELAND ISLAND: The ferry stops at Ireland Island, a former Royal Navy dockyard, lying in the extreme west end of Bermuda. A multi-million-dollar cruise ship dock and tourist village has grown up here in this historic area which was used by the British navy until 1951. The site also shelters the Bermuda Maritime Museum, a theater, a crafts market, and the Bermuda Arts Centre.

The dockyard has been transformed into a park, with Victorian street lighting and a Terrace Pavilion and bandstand for concerts. Vendors can be found pushing carts filled with food, dry goods, and local crafts. A full service marina with floating docks is in operation along with a marina clubhouse and showers.

In a large 19th-century fortress, the **Bermuda Maritime Museum,** Dockyard, Ireland Island (tel. 809/234-1333), is open from 10 a.m. to 4:30 p.m. daily, costing $5 for adults and $1 for children under 12. The museum continues to improve exhibits about Bermuda's nautical heritage. Its most famous exhibit is in the Treasure House which was opened in 1979. The first gunpowder magazine in the Keep, the building was constructed in 1837. It is devoted to various exhibits, including artifacts such as gold bars, pottery, jewelry, silver coins, and other items recovered from 16th- and 17th-century shipwrecks, including the *Sea Venture.* But most visitors come here to gaze at the Tucker Treasure.

A well-known local diver, Teddy Tucker is credited with making the most significant marine archaeological find of this century when, in 1955, he uncovered one of the richest caches of underwater wealth in the western hemisphere. He discovered the wreck of the *San Antonio,* a Spanish vessel which went down off the coast of Bermuda in a violent storm in 1621. The Spanish tried unsuccessfully to prevent British parties from looting this treasure, but their protests were to no avail. One of the great treasures of this find, the Pectoral Cross, was stolen only minutes before Queen Elizabeth II opened the museum in 1975. The priceless original cross had been replaced by a fake. To this day, the original cross has never been recovered, and its mysterious disappearance is still the subject of much discussion.

After visiting the museum, you're free to explore the dockyard which was begun in 1809. It was built of local hard stone by convicts from England, many of whom died of yellow fever.

In the Cooperage Building, opposite the Maritime Museum entrance, is "The Attack on Washington," an audiovisual presentation about Bermuda's unusual role in the War of 1812 between Great Britain and the United States. The film graphically re-creates the burning of the Executive Mansion (repainted white after the smoke cleared), and the eventual British defeat at Fort McHenry. Admission is $2.50 for adults and $1.50 for children and senior citizens. There are continuous shows daily every half hour from 10 a.m. until the last show at 4 p.m. Call 809/238-0432 for more information.

The Crafts Market, also in The Cooperage, is the place to watch local artists at work and to buy their wares. It is open from 10:30 a.m. to 4 p.m. daily, and admission here is free.

The Bermuda Arts Centre, next to The Cooperage, features works and lectures by local and international artists. New exhibits are installed every month. Admission is $1 for adults and 50¢ for children under 12 years. For more information, call 809/234-2809.

Tucker also discovered the wreck of the *San Pedro,* part of a Tierra Firme Armada, sunk in 1595. Artifacts from this Spanish vessel are also displayed.

As you enter the Parade Ground, you'll notice a 10-foot-high figure of King Neptune. This is a figurehead from the HMS *Irresistible,* recovered when the ship was broken up in 1891. The Queen's Exhibition Hall houses general maritime exhibits, including those on navigation, whaling, cable & wireless, and "Bermuda in Five Hours," the latter a reference to the advertisements touting Pan American's early "flying boats." Under a vaulted brick ceiling (the bricks came from

England), the building was constructed in 1850 for the storage of 4,860 barrels of gunpowder.

The Forster Cooper Building from 1852 illustrates the history of the Royal Navy in Bermuda, including the Bromby Bottle Collection. This exhibit was opened in 1984 by Princess Margaret. The Boatloft houses part of the museum's boat collections, including the century-old fitted dinghy *Victory,* the 17-foot *Spirit of Bermuda,* and the *Rambler,* the only surviving Bermuda pilot gig. The original dockyard clock is a working exhibit on the upper floor, and chimes the quarters and the hours.

On a historical note, when this dockyard, which had been British Admiralty land, was sold in 1953 to the Bermuda government, it marked the end of British naval might in the Western Atlantic.

SIGHTSEEING AT SEA: One of the most popular sightseeing attractions in Bermuda is a ride aboard one of the **Looking Glass Cruises,** Ferry Dock, Hamilton (tel. 809/236-8000 from 8 a.m. to 10 p.m. seven days a week). One of the most interesting is the Reef & Wreck Adventure, lasting two hours and costing $20. Departures are seven days a week at 10 a.m. and 1:30 p.m. Passengers can see the wreck of the H.M.S. *Vixen,* observing reef fish and coral formations. Guests can see 50 islands of the West End, and are provided with a lively commentary. Unlimited complimentary bar is included. The Cruise of Lights is also popular. It lasts 1¾ hours, costing $22.50 per person, and departs Monday to Saturday at 10:30 p.m., with a special cruise on Monday at 8:30 p.m. Honeymooners are especially fond of this one.

The vessel goes through the islands of the Great Sound, as a nocturnal world unfolds, complete with the coral reef and a sunken wreck. The glass-bottom boat is specially lit for the best viewing. Music is also played, and the commentary includes talk of the constellations of the zodiac. The Sea Garden Dinner Cruise takes four hours, costs $47.50 per person, and departs at 6 p.m. Tuesday to Sunday. Providing unlimited complimentary drinks, it takes guests along 50 islands, with good views of the sea gardens. A four-course meal of Bermudian dishes is included at the waterside terrace of the Somerset Village Inn. A calypso guitarist adds to the amusement.

If you'd like a little touch of Jules Verne in your holiday, you can board the submarine *Enterprise* for a look at life below the water line. Built in Scotland, the *Enterprise* is a real submarine which can go to a depth of 250 feet. The submarine dives for one hour, and another 45 minutes is spent traveling to and from the *Enterprise* on a 60-foot motor yacht. The submarine takes 44 passengers past offshore reefs, including an airplane wreck and schools of brightly colored fish. Departures are from the Town Square at St. George's. In summer, there may be two or more cruises per day. You have to confirm this when you call for a reservation. In low season, there is usually one cruise daily. The cost is $50 per person. Children 4 to 12 pay half price, and senior citizens are granted a 20% discount. For more information and reservations, call 809/236-8000.

2. WHERE TO SHOP

Most of Bermuda's best shops are along Front Street in Hamilton. Shopping is relaxed and casual here, no hysterical hustling to sell you merchandise the way you'll experience in many lands to the south. The best buys are usually in imports from Great Britain and Ireland. For example, Shetland and cashmere sweaters cost less in Hamilton than in Britain, certainly less than in the States. You're likely to find good buys in Harris tweed jackets, all kinds of Scottish woolen goods, tartan kilts, as well as fine china and crystal.

Other good buys are the quality merchandise known as "Bermudiana," items either made here or produced exclusively for local stores. These include

Bermuda cedar gifts, original Bermuda carriage bells, 375th-anniversary coins, Bermuda flower plates by Spode, pewter tankerds, handcrafted gold jewelry, traditional-lines handbags with cedar or mahogany handles, miniature Bermuda cottages made in ceramics or Bermuda limestone, Bermuda sharks' teeth hand-polished and mounted in 14-karat gold, decorative kitchen items, Bermuda shorts, and silk scarves, as well as watches with a Bermuda map or Longtail faces.

Liquor is also a good buy. You're allowed one quart duty free. But even with U.S. tax and duty, you can save between 35% and 50%, depending on the brand. Liqueurs offer the largest savings.

Stores in Hamilton, as well as those in St. George's and Somerset, are generally open Monday to Saturday from 9 a.m. to 5:30 p.m. When large liners are in port, stores often open in the evening.

HAMILTON: In Hamilton, the leading shops include—

Trimingham's, Front Street (tel. 809/295-1183), family owned since 1842, specializes in fine European imports at up to 40% and more savings on U.S. prices. Spode, Aynsley, and Royal Worcester china are featured with Waterford and Galway crystal. The cashmere, lambswool, and specialty knitwear collection is unrivaled in Bermuda, and Trimingham's own label men's and women's wear are famous for their quality. French perfumes and European accessories are best buys here, as are fine jewelry, paintings, and gifts. Trimingham's Hamilton store is open daily. Branch shops are to be found throughout the island and at major hotels.

H. A. & E. Smith Ltd., 35 Front St. (tel. 809/295-2288), has been selling top-quality merchandise since 1889, at substantial savings over U.S. prices. Smith's comprehensive stock includes sweaters for men and women in cashmere, lambswool, and Shetland, plus cottons as well as superb British sportswear. Lladro porcelain, and English bone china from Royal Crown Derby, Royal Doulton, Royal Worcester, and Aynsley are featured along with sparkling crystal from Waterford, Thomas Webb, Baccarat, and Swarovski. The perfume room features an outstanding collection from the top French parfumers, as well as cosmetics. Smith's is also noted for an excellent selection of handbags, gloves, fabrics by the yard, and children's clothing. At Smith's you will find Rosenthal china, Burberry raincoats and accessories, Church's shoes, Christian Dior handbags and jewelry, and Alan Paine knitwear.

A.S. Cooper's, Front Street (tel. 809/295-3961), sells all fine lines of china and crystal. Also available are men's and women's fashions and sportswear, as well as children's clothes. The Balcony Restaurant overlooking Front Street is open from 10 a.m. to 4 p.m. Morning coffee and tea are also available.

Archie Brown & Son, Front Street (tel. 809/295-2928), is the Pringle shop of Hamilton, featuring sweaters for men and women in cashmere, lambswool, and Shetland. For women, there are matching skirts as well. From neutrals to spectaculars, the color scope is wide. This shop has been in business for more than half a century.

Cécile, Front Street West (tel. 809/295-1311), lies near the Visitors Service Bureau and the ferry dock. Its small frontage is misleading. Actually, it's well stocked with merchandise and is a center for high fashion in Bermuda. Cécile's claims that a visit to the shop is like a visit to the fashion capitals of the world—from France, Tiktiner; from West Germany, Mondi; from Hong Kong, Ciao and Ciaosport; from Israel, swimwear from Gottex. Its sweater and accessory boutique is outstanding as well, with many hand-detailed and hand-embroidered styles. Prices are sometimes 35% less than you'd pay in the States. Cécile has branches at the Southampton Princess, Marriott Castle Harbour, and Sonesta Beach hotels.

The English Sports Shop, 49 Front St. (tel. 809/295-2672), was established in 1918 and is credited as one of the leading retailers of quality classic and fashionable items for men, women, and children on the island, with branch shops in major hotels.

Scottish Wool Shop, Queen Street (tel. 809/295-0967), has quality Shetland, cashmere, and lambswool sweaters for the whole family, in classic and fashionable designs at up to 50% less than regular U.S. prices. See the extensive collection of tartan kilts, slacks, and other Scottish merchandise.

Calypso, Front Street (tel. 809/295-2112), has the largest and most comprehensive selection of beachwear in Bermuda. The shop is the exclusive Bermuda retailer of Louis Vuitton luggage and accessories, and it is the only store on the island that manufactures its own fashions. Exclusive and exotic designs by Polly Hornburg are available in a variety of internationally collected fabrics. There are branches at both Princess Hotels and the Coral Beach and Tennis Club.

The **Irish Linen Shop,** 31 Front St. (tel. 809/295-4089), stands at Heyl's Corner, near the "Bird Cage" policeman or woman. The shop stocks not only table fabrics of pure linen from Ireland, but a wide-ranging selection of other merchandise from Europe, everything from quilted placemats to men's shirts in French cotton from Souleiado of Provence. European linens purchased in Bermuda can often realize you as much as 50% in savings over American prices. The owners go over to Europe twice a year to bring back imports, including Madeira hand-embroidery and Belgian lace. The shop has other branches at Somers Wharf in St. George's and on Cambridge Road, Mangrove Bay, at Somerset.

Constable's of Bermuda, "Emporium," 69 Front St. (tel. 809/295-3311). Stepping into this spacious and well-carpeted store has induced culture shock in the hardiest travelers. Everything inside was hand-woven or -knitted in Iceland. The inventory ranges from thick woolly blankets to patterned sweaters, both cardigan and pullover, for men and women. If you think you might need a pair of mittens or a wool cap during your vacation in the sun, Constable's will have them, although probably you'll prefer to have them packaged to take back for a cold winter back home. Sweaters are usually priced from $60 to $120, and coats cost from $180.

Pegasus, Pitts Bay Road (tel. 809/295-2900), is where to go if you're looking for antique prints, engravings, or magazine illustrations. You'll find no better anywhere in Bermuda. The inventory is varied, with old maps of many different regions of the world and more than 3,000 medical and legal caricatures from *Vanity Fair,* published between 1869 and 1914. These cost $10 to $100, depending on the subject. The hand-colored engravings of birds, fruit, and flowers are worth framing and sometimes cost as little as $25 each. Owner Bob Lee and his wife, Barbara, scour the print shops of the British Isles to stock this unusual store. Most prints range from the late 1700s to the late 1800s and are carefully grouped according to subject. The authenticity of whatever you buy is guaranteed in writing. They also offer ceramic house signs, costing from $40 each, made at a small pottery in England. Each is unique, based on any design a buyer chooses, then hand-painted together with the house name or a number and street. The shop also has a wide range of English greeting cards, many with botanical designs. Everything purchased here is duty free and will not affect your take-home quota. The shop is across the street from the Hamilton Princess Hotel. Hours are from 10 a.m. to 5 p.m. Monday to Saturday.

For your liquor purchases, I recommend **Burrows, Lightbourn Ltd.,** whose main store is at 87 Front St. (tel. 809/295-0176). The people here have been in business since 1808. You can make your own combination of liquors by asking for a "Select-a-Pac," consisting of any five fifths or two half-gallons. Orders must be placed 24 hours prior to departure, except on Sunday when 48 hours before departure is required. The store will deliver your liquor packages to the airport or else aboard ship. There are actually three stores in Hamilton, one in St. George's, one in Flatts Village, yet another in Paget, and one in Somerset.

Bluck's, Front Street West (tel. 809/295-5367), established in 1844, is well known for some of the finest names in china and crystal. Their wide selection includes Royal Worcester, Spode, Anysley, Royal Doulton, and Herend porcelain from Hungary, to name just a few. The choice in crystal is equally impressive: Waterford, Baccarat, Daum, and of course, Lalique, exclusive with Bluck's. Upstairs, you'll find a superb Antique Room filled with fine English furniture, antique Bermuda maps, and an impressive array of old English silver. Bluck's has branch shops on Water Street in St. George's and in the Southampton Princess and Sonesta Beach hotels.

Tolaram's, Front Street West, opposite the Bank of Bermuda (tel. 809/295-2826), truly is, as it claims, the "treasure house of the East." They have Oriental carved jade, ivory, and soapstone, Chinese cloisonné, gold and silver jewelry, Chinese porcelain, Indian brassware, and a host of other Oriental objects. You can also purchase Seiko and Pulsar watches here at considerable savings over U.S. prices. Another Tolaram shop is at St. George's on Duke of York Street.

Bananas, Front Street West, opposite the Bank of Bermuda (tel. 809/295-1106), offers "Bermuda signature" items that are of good quality and colorful. You'll find T-shirts, jackets, beach bags, and beach umbrellas to take back home and let your friends know where you've been. The store has several other branches in Bermuda.

27th Century Boutique, Chancery Lane (tel. 809/292-2628), has long been known as a stylish and trend-setting boutique in the heart of Hamilton on one of the most charming shopping streets. It offers a fashionable selection of designer clothing, as well as shoes and accessories, for both women and men.

Crisson Jewellers, Queen Street (tel. 809/295-2351), sells such top-name Swiss watches as Ebel, Rolex, Piaget, Baume & Mercier, Longines, and Corum, plus Les Must de Cartier selection of watches, jewelry, and accessories. You'll also be able to purchase gold and silver jewelry for either men or women, as well as Bermuda charms. Crisson has branches at two places in St. George's: at Duke of York and Kent Streets and on Water Street.

Astwood Dickinson Jewellers, Front Street (tel. 809/292-5805), has a treasure trove of famous-name watches, including Patek Philippe, Concord, Tissot, Omega, Chopard, and Movado, plus designer jewelry, all at prices generally below U.S. retail. From their original Bermuda collection, you can select a gold memento of Bermuda to purchase. Other Astwood Dickinson shops are in the Walker Arcade and at the Sonesta Beach Hotel, the Hamilton Princess Hotel, and the Southampton Princess.

For fine luggage and leather goods, try **The Harbourmaster,** Washington Mall, Reid Street (tel. 809/295-5333), where you'll find lightweight, rugged Land pieces, the Gucci accessory collection, and nylon and canvas tote bags. The shop also carries finely crafted leather brooches of Bermuda flowers.

The Knit Shop, Reid Street (tel. 809/295-6722), is the place to go if you knit, embroider, or sew. They have a good choice of needlepoint patterns with Bermuda themes, which are available in kits.

Otto Wurz Co., Vallis Building, Front Street (tel. 809/295-1247), has Bermuda's largest collection of gold and sterling-silver charms and bracelets, along with Staffordshire bone china, silver and enamel thimbles, and English flatware.

Vera P. Card, Front Street (tel. 809/295-1729), is known for its superb offerings of "gifts from around the world." These include the island's largest collection of ship's clocks, mantleclocks, and table clocks. Famous name watches include Nivada, Girard Perregaux, and Michel Herbelin. The dinnerware collection features such famous names as Rosenthal, and the crystal department offers works also by Rosenthal among others. Hummel and Lladro figurines are also on sale. Look for Coalport English bone china, and also for a collection of jewelry in exquisite designs.

Bermuda Book Store (Baxters) Ltd., Queen Street (tel. 809/295-3698), stocks everything that is in print about Bermuda. Some books are only available through this store. There are Bermuda books on gardening, flowers, local characters, and poets, among other subjects. They also have many English publications not easily obtainable in the U.S., as well as a fine selection of children's books. You can also buy maps and prints here. The store has an extensive stationery department.

St. Michael (Bermuda) Ltd., the brand name of Marks & Spencer, Reid Street (tel. 809/295-0031), brings you reliable quality merchandise from Marks & Spencer in England. You'll find men's, women's, and children's fashions in everything from resortwear to sleepwear, including lingerie. There are also well-tailored dresses and suits, dress shirts, blazers, and British-tailored trousers, as well as swimwear, toiletries, and English sweets and biscuits.

The Perfume Shop, 23 Front St. West (tel. 809/295-5535), opposite the Ferry Terminal, carries almost all of the world's most popular perfumes, and you may learn something about the art of choosing and wearing perfume you didn't know from the shop's helpful "fragrance specialists."

E. R. Aubrey, Jeweller, Front Street West (tel. 809/295-3826), also opposite the Ferry Terminal, has a rich collection of gold chains, rings with precious and semiprecious stones, and charms, including the Bermuda longtail.

Bermuda Jewellery Centre, Church Street (tel. 809/292-4199), opposite City Hall, carries a good selection of gold and silver jewelry, and they're also the authorized dealers of Citizen watches. The Ana-Digi-Temp will even tell you the temperature as well as the time.

Philatelists and numismatists will enjoy the **Bermuda Coin & Stamp Co. Ltd.,** Walker Arcade, Front Street (tel. 809/295-5503), where they can browse among stamps and coins, some of them real treasures, including commemorative groupings.

W. J. Boyle & Son Ltd., Queen Street (tel. 809/295-1887), is a family-owned and -operated shoe store which is a longtime Bermuda favorite. They offer good value and fine quality in shoes from England, Spain, Italy, and France.

At **Timeless Antiques,** Church Street (tel. 809/295-5008), opposite the bus terminal, you go down terracotta tile steps to spacious display rooms where you can look over carved early English oak tables, chests, and chairs, clocks of all types and ages, icons, candelabra, pictures, what have you. They also have expert clock repair and restoration services. Packing and shipping of larger items is arranged for you.

Windjammer Gallery, corner of Reid and King Streets (tel. 809/292-7861), housed in a charming yellow cottage, exhibits paintings and bronze sculptures by local and international artists. They also have an extensive selection of cards, prints, and limited editions, including photographs and signed silk-screen prints by Graeme Outerbridge.

Heritage House, Front Street West (tel. 809/295-2615), sells nautical prints, English antiques, old maps, modern porcelain, and the largest collection of fine art on the island. There's also a collection of greeting cards, printed in Bermuda, by local artists, plus top-of-the-line gifts.

Camera Store, Queen Street (tel. 809/295-0303), is Hamilton's leading camera store and has been for quite a while. Here you can find the source of your photographic needs. Kodak and Fuji films come in all formats (including disk), and such name brands are for sale as Konica, Nikon, and Hasselblad. They also sell a complete range of binoculars, and offer fast-film developing and printing. The staff will even repair your camera.

Sail on Bermuda, Old Cellar, Front Street (tel. 809/295-0808), is in the old cellar lane that runs beside the English Sports Shop. You'll find boardsailing goods, but the shop also offers active wear for leisure-minded people. The clothes are unique in Bermuda, colorful, and exclusive to this shop. Everything is here from the "little pink cottage Bermuda earrings" to hats to bathing suits. They also have clothes for evening wear. The establishment has arguably the best T-shirts in Bermuda, designed at the shop. Reorders from the States indicate that the Famous Onions and Bermuda Road Toads shirts are the most popular. The merchandise in this shop comes from around the world.

Ocean Moose, Chancery Lane, Front Street (tel. 809/295-1884), is in the building that runs between British Airways and Rum Runners. The shop has an assemblage of tropical gifts and food from around the world, as well as colorful beachwear and resortwear. The mascot, a huge moosehead, overlooks wooden shelves laden with Moose-wear slippers, bandanas, and clothing. All the T-shirts are designed by Sail On Bermuda, its sister shop.

AROUND THE ISLAND: As you leave Hamilton and tour the island, you may want to continue your shopping expedition, especially for typical Bermudian items, at one of the following addresses:

Art House, South Shore Road, Paget (tel. 809/236-6746), specializes in original Bermuda paintings and hand-signed lithographs by artist Joan Forbes. The store also carries a range of selected handmade Bermuda crafts. It is open daily except Sunday from 10 a.m. to 4 p.m.

The Chameleon, South Shore Road, Paget (tel. 809/236-8675), with branches at major hotels, is the exclusive agent in Bermuda for Iceland's oldest knitwear manufacturer, Alafoss. They have both traditional styles and new fashion colors in Alafoss Icewool.

The **Old Market,** Mangrove Bay (tel. 809/234-0744), in the village of Somerset, occupies premises dating from 1827 when it was a private home. For 65 years, however, it was a meat market, and the original chopping blocks can be seen. This unusual shop offers everything from antiques to curios from Africa, along with woodcarvings, china, crystal, sweaters, and sportswear.

Ye Village Corner, Mangrove Bay (tel. 809/234-1682), in Somerset, sells fine modern and metallic art from around the world, as well as brass ornaments and gift items from Europe. The shop also offers a selection of Bermuda artwork.

Bridge House Straw Market, King's Square, St. George's (tel. 809/297-1853), has a wide array of straw products such as hats, bags, and calypso dolls. Bermuda pottery and cedar items, T-shirts, charms, and other costume jewelry are also offered.

Globe Gift Shop, King's Square, St. George's (tel. 809/297-1670), in a historic old building, offers a good selection of items for souvenirs and gifts. You'll find T-shirts, charms, Bermuda cedar objects, and straw bags. They also sell stamps, bus tokens, cigarettes, ice cream, sodas, and candy. The shop is open daily from 9 a.m. to 11 p.m. Like the Bridge House Straw Market, it is owned by Ronald L. Panchaud.

3. THE SPORTING LIFE

Twenty-one square miles of year-round action: that's what the outdoor sports enthusiast finds in and around Bermuda. A wide array of water sports is pursued here, with plenty of equipment, instructors, and facilities offered. You can go boating, windsurfing, sailing, waterskiing, and shore, reef, or deep-sea fishing on top of the water. If you prefer to disport yourself underwater, you have a choice of helmet diving, scuba-diving, or snorkeling. Or you can just swim around, in the sea or in a pool.

Not a water buff? Then you may want to play tennis on one of the more than 90 courts in Bermuda, or perhaps you'd like to golf on one of the eight fine courses, which support the claim that Bermuda has more golf per square mile than any island on earth. Pedal cycling, bowling, walking, and jogging are engaged in by many Bermudians and visitors alike.

If you'd rather be a viewer than a doer, you'll find a wide variety of spectator sports too. These include such traditional British games as cricket, rugby, and soccer, plus lacrosse, field hockey, softball, cycle scrambling, and track and field events, among other pursuits.

Most of the large hotels have their own water-sports facilities and equipment for the use of hotel guests, which may also be available to guests of other hotels on request. Ask at your hotel.

SPECIAL SPORTS EVENTS: Besides the day-to-day sports activities you can engage in, there's always something going on in Bermuda or its surrounding waters that will be of interest to many sports enthusiasts. The annual **Bermuda Game Fishing Tournament** is held from May 1 to November 30, with special prizes for top catches of 17 species of game fish. All amateur anglers are eligible. You'll learn all about it if you go around any of the docks from which fishing boats depart, or any of the marinas.

Yachtsmen from the U.S., U.K., Canada, and other countries compete with Bermudians in a week of races in April or May. This is called **Invitational International Week.** Other boat-racing events take place in alternate years. The **Blue Water Cruising Race** from Marion, Massachusetts, to Bermuda is held in June in odd-numbered years, as is the **Multi-Hull Ocean Yacht Race** from Newport, Rhode Island, to Bermuda. In June of even-numbered years, some 180 of the world's finest yachts compete in the **Bermuda Race,** from Newport, Rhode Island, to Bermuda.

Invitation Tennis Weeks are held in November, when more than 100 visiting players vie with Bermudians in two weeks of matches.

In December, a week of golfing activity is held. The **Bermuda Goodwill Tournament** attracts 70 to 80 pro/amateur foursomes from international golf clubs to play over 72 holes on four of Bermuda's eight courses.

Bermuda International Marathon and Ten Kilometre Race, with international and local runners participating, is held in January.

Two **international dog shows** are held here, one in March, and the other in November. A **regional bridge tournament,** in January or February, may not be might not know it to watch the ferocity with which some people participate.

GOLF: Since the first course was laid out in Bermuda in 1922, golf has become one of its most popular sports. It can be played year-round, and early spring, winter, and fall offer near-perfect seaside golf conditions. At the eight courses, it is necessary to arrange your starting time in advance through the management of your guesthouse or hotel. Women's and men's clubs, either right- or left-handed, are available at each course, and most leading stores in Bermuda sell golf balls.

Tournaments are held throughout the year, with top players participating. For information, get in touch with the **Bermuda Golf Association,** P.O. Box HM 433, Hamilton HM BX, Bermuda, or the Bermuda Department of Tourism (see "Tourist Information" in the ABCs section of Chapter II).

The Castle Harbour Hotel golf course is considered one of the most scenic courses on the island, while the Port Royal, designed by Robert Trent Jones, is a challenge to your golfing expertise. Two famous courses, the Mid Ocean Club at Tucker's Town and the Riddells Bay Golf and Country Club, are private, requiring introduction by members before you can play there. One of the most photographed golf courses in Bermuda is at the Southampton Princess Hotel, where rolling hills and flowering shrubs add to a player's enjoyment.

The golf courses listed below that are part of a hotel complex also allow nonguests to use their facilities:

Belmont Hotel, Golf & Country Club, Warwick Parish (tel. 809/236-1301): 18 holes, par 70, 5,777 yards; greens fees, $20 for hotel guests, $25 for others; full set of golf clubs, $10; gas golf carts, $25; handcarts, $4. This can also be played as a 9-hole course.

Port Royal Golf Course, Southampton Parish, public course (tel. 809/234-0974): 18 holes, par 71, 6,425 yards; greens fees, $22 (reduced rates after 4 p.m.); no caddies; full set of clubs, $10; gas golf carts, $20; handcarts, $4. The clubhouse overlooks the ocean and the 9th and 18th greens. It boasts a bar and a restaurant, serving breakfast and lunch.

Southampton Princess Golf Club, Southampton Parish (tel. 809/238-0446): 18 holes (2,684 yards of 9 holes each), par 54; greens fees for either hotel guests or visitors, $16 daily for however many holes you play; no caddies; rental of clubs, $7 per 18 holes; gas golf carts, $14.

Castle Harbour Golf Club, Hamilton Parish (tel. 809/293-2040, ext. 6670): 18 holes, par 71, 6,415 yards; greens fees, $60 for 18 holes; no caddies; full set of clubs, $17; gas golf carts, $28 for 18 holes (mandatory use of golf carts); shoe rental, $5.

Queen's Park Golf Course, Ocean View Golf and Country Club, Inc., Devonshire Parish (tel. 809/236-6758): 9 holes, par 35, 2,956 yards; greens fees, $15 (for 9 holes or the course played for 18 holes); no caddies; full set of clubs, $10; gas golf carts, $10 for 9 holes, $20 for 18 holes; handcarts, $3 for 9 or 18 holes.

St. George's Golf Club, St. George's Parish (tel. 809/297-8067): 18 holes, par 64, 4,502 yards; greens fees, 9 or 18 holes, $15 (reduced rate after 4 p.m.); no caddies; full set of clubs, $12; gas golf carts, $17; handcarts, $4.

All of these golf courses have pros, and you can take lessons if you wish.

TENNIS: Nearly all the big hotels, and many of the smaller ones, have courts, which are usually lit for night playing. It's best to come to Bermuda with your own tennis clothing and sneakers, as such an outfit may be required to play the game. Colored tennis togs, so popular in America, have now arrived in Bermuda. Before that, tennis clothing was restricted to white.

There are six clay and two asphalt courts at the **Government Tennis Stadium,** Cedar Avenue, Pembroke Parish (tel. 809/292-0105 for court reservations and to arrange lessons). There are six clay courts and two of asphalt. Charges for clay: $4 for adults, $2.50 for juniors; for asphalt, $3 for adults, $1.50 for juniors. An extra $5 is charged for lit play at night. Tennis attire is mandatory. Rackets rent for $4 per hour, balls for $6 per can. Hours are Monday to Friday from 8 a.m. to 10 p.m., and on Saturday and Sunday from 8 a.m. to 7 p.m.

The previously mentioned **Port Royal Golf Course** also has tennis courts in Southampton Parish (tel. 809/234-0974). The four Plexipave courts cost $5 in daytime, $7 at night.

Elbow Beach Hotel, Paget Parish (tel. 809/236-3535), has five LayKold courts (one only for lessons). Hotel guests are charged $5 (others pay $12) to play here. Two of the courts are lit for night play, when hotel guests pay an extra $3 while other visitors pay $2.

Southampton Princess Hotel, Southampton Parish (tel. 809/238-1005), has the largest tennis court layout on the island, with 11 True-Flex courts, three of them lit for night play. Hotel guests pay $10 per hour, and outsiders are charged $12 per court hour, with a $2 surcharge for lights. Rackets rent for $5 per hour, and balls cost $6 per can.

Each of the facilities described above has a tennis pro on duty, and lessons can be arranged. In case you didn't come prepared, you can rent rackets and buy balls at each place.

SWIMMING AND BEACHES: Bermuda is one of the world's leading beach resorts, with its miles of pink sandy shoreline, broken now and then by cliffs that form sheltered coves. Many stretches have shallow water for some distance out and sandy bottoms, making them safe for children and even nonswimmers. Hotels and private clubs often have their own private beaches, but there is no shortage of public facilities in Bermuda, under the supervision of the Parks Division of the Department for Agriculture and Fisheries.

At most of the public beaches you'll find public rest rooms and usually a place nearby for drinks or snacks. **Shelly Bay,** North Shore, Hamilton Parish, for instance, even has a beach house, with changing rooms, towels, lounging and snorkeling equipment for rent, and a shop where you can buy souvenirs and film. There's a place also to have a hot lunch or a cold drink. The **Shelly Bay Beach House** (tel. 809/293-1327) is open daily from 10 a.m. to 7 p.m. Take a no. 10 or 11 bus from Hamilton.

Other good beaches are: **John Smith's Bay,** South Shore, Smith's Parish, where there are a lunchwagon and rest rooms; **Tobacco Bay** beach, North Shore, St. George's Parish, which has changing rooms and refreshments; **Church Bay and West Whale Bay** beaches, both on the South Shore in Southampton Parish, which have rest rooms; and **Warwick Long Bay,** South Shore, Warwick Parish, with rest rooms.

Bermuda's most famous beach is the one at **Horseshoe Bay,** South Shore, Southampton Parish, where the Beach House (tel. 809/238-2651), contains lockers, changing rooms, toilets, and showers, as well as food and drink and rental equipment for the beach or water. You can also buy magazines, suntan lotion, and other sundries you may need for a relaxed day at the beach in the Bermuda sunshine.

DEEP-SEA FISHING: In these waters are wahoo, amberjack, blue marlin, white marlin, dolphin, tuna, and more. One of the world's finest fishing centers, Bermuda offers a wealth of equipment. Fishing is considered best from May through November. The **Bermuda Department of Tourism,** P.O. Box HM 465, Hamilton (tel. 809/292-0023), can assist with general inquiries about fishing.

Bermuda Sportsfishing, Creek View House, 8 Tulo Lane, Pembroke, HM 02, Bermuda (tel. 809/292-5535), is run by the De Silva family who has been in business for many years. They charge $450 for a half day of fishing and from $550 to $600 for a full day. If given enough notice, the family can compose groups of fishermen into units of six. If so, the charge then is only $75 per person for a half day of fishing and $100 per person for a full day. All equipment and a picnic lunch is included in the price. Boats include a 50-foot all-wood vessel with two bathrooms, a kitchenette, three "fighting chairs," and space for up to 20 persons. There is also a 36-foot sportsfishing boat available.

BOATING: Bermuda is one of the world's sailing capitals. Sail-yourself boats are available on a half-day (four hours) or full-day (eight hours) basis. **Salt Kettle**

Boat Rentals Ltd., P.O. Box PG 201, Paget PG BX, Bermuda (tel. 809/236-4863), rents craft such as Sunfish, daysailers, and motorboats. Boats without skippers cost from $45 to $70 per half day, from $70 to $110 per full day. For private charter yachts with skippers, the half-day cost ranges from $215 to $300, and the full-day charge is $435 to $650. You can join their half-day snorkeling parties for $26 per person or a half-day sailing party for $22 per person. The owner, David Ashton, also supplies fishing and snorkeling gear and gives lessons in sailing.

Bermuda Water Sports, Grotto Bay Hotel, Hamilton Parish (tel. 809/293-2640), has Sunfish-type Phantoms renting for $12 per hour, $40 for a half day, or $60 for a full day (eight hours), a boardsailer costing the same rates. Water bikes rent for $12 per hour and yak boards for $6.

UNDERWATER SPORTS: Bermuda's waters are considered the clearest in the western Atlantic. Hence it's ideal for scuba-diving and snorkeling as well as helmet diving. Many of the hotels, as mentioned, have their own water-sports equipment. If not, there are several independent establishments that rent equipment.

Bermuda's oldest and largest full-service scuba-diving operation, **Blue Water Divers Co. Ltd.,** at Somerset Bridge, Sandys Parish, P.O. Box 5N 165, Southampton SN BX, Bermuda (tel. 809/234-1034), offers introductory lessons and dives at $65 for a half-day experience from March to December. Daily one- and two-tank dive trips cost $50 and $70 each, respectively, with a $15 reduction if you have equipment. Snorkeling trips are $22 per half day. Full certification courses are available through PADI, NAUI, and SSI. All equipment is provided. Reservations are necessary.

South Side Scuba Ltd., Sonesta Beach Hotel, Southampton, P.O. Box HM 1070, Hamilton HM EX, Bermuda (tel. 809/238-1833), and the Grotto Bay Hotel, 11 Blue Hole Hill, Hamilton Parish CR 04, Bermuda (tel. 809/293-2915), is known for its daily two-tank wreck and reef dives, costing $65. A Resort Course lesson and dive is $70. A single-tank dive goes for $45, and you can snorkel off the boat for $20. There is a $10 reduction if you have your own diving gear, except for Resort Courses. Otherwise, the rates include all equipment. The company has two fully equipped, custom-built fiberglass dive boats, with the latest approved safety gear. It is owned by Robert Limes.

Bermuda Water Sports, Grotto Bay Hotel, Hamilton Parish (tel. 809/293-2640), makes snorkeling and glass-bottom-boat cruises from 9 a.m. to 5 p.m. daily, costing $25 per person. All snorkel gear and buoyancy aids are provided. The cruise, lasting three hours, takes its passengers to shallow, sandy water where instructions are given in water they can stand up in, before taking them where more underwater wonders can be seen. Service is from May to November.

Bermuda Cruises, P.O. Box HM 1572, Hamilton (tel. 809/295-3727), picks up passengers from Albuoy's Point, the Princess Hotel dock, and Darrell's Wharf, taking them aboard the 55-foot powerboat *Big Dipper,* for a 3½-hour snorkeling experience, costing $28 per person. Masks, flippers, snorkels, floats, and bouyancy aids are provided. The boat operates from 9 a.m. from May to mid-November.

Note: Spearfishing is not allowed within one mile of any shore, and spearguns are not permitted in Bermuda.

WINDSURFING: For this exciting sport, **Windsurfing Bermuda** operates at Old Cellar, Front Street, Hamilton HM 11 (tel. 809/295-0808). This is the finest windsurfing school in Bermuda. There's also a rental shop. Hugh Watlington taught himself to windsurf and brought the sport to the island in 1977. He competed in the 1984 Olympics. He operates seasonally, weather permitting, daily from 8 a.m. until sunset. He makes a promise to pupils: they'll have the knack after a single 1½-hour lesson at $35. That lesson is conducted on both land and water.

WATERSKIING: You can waterski in the protected waters of Hamilton Harbour, Great Sound, Castle Harbour, Mangrove Bay, Spanish Point, Ferry Reach, Ely's Harbour, Riddells Bay, and Harrington Sound. May through September is the best time for this sport. Bermuda law requires that waterskiers be taken out by a licensed skipper. Only a few boat operators participate in this sport, and charges fluctuate with fuel costs. Rates include the boat, skis, safety belts, and usually an instructor. Hotels and guesthouses can assist with arrangements.

Bermuda Water Sports, Grotto Bay Hotel, Hamilton Parish (tel. 809/293-2640), operates March to November, weather permitting, from 9 a.m. to 5 p.m. Up to three persons are taken for skiing on board a Ski Nautique. You pay $25 for 15 minutes, $40 per half hour.

Bermuda Waterski Centre, East Shore Lane, Sandys MA 02 (tel. 809/234-3354), operates from 8 a.m. to 7:30 p.m. daily from April to the end of October (periodically the rest of the year). Up to four people can go waterskiing with a Mastercraft especially designed for waterskiing. Lessons are available. The charge is $35 for a half hour, $65 for one hour of skiing per person.

PARASAILING: Enthusiasts can find this sport at **Skyrider Bermuda Ltd.,** Robinson's Marina, Somerset Bridge (tel. 809/234-1034), going to the sheltered waters off the Little Sound from 9 a.m. to 7:30 p.m. daily ten months of the year. The charge per flight is $30 per person.

HORSEBACK RIDING: You'll find at the **Spicelands Riding Centre,** Middle Road, Warwick Parish (tel. 809/238-8212), trail rides at $20 per person for one hour. The popular early-morning breakfast ride, a two-hour jaunt with a full breakfast following, costs $35 per person. From May to September, weekly evening rides and lunch rides (costing $25) are offered.

Lee Bow Riding Stables, Tribe Road 1 in Devonshire (tel. 809/292-4181), is especially for children up to the age of 18. Lessons and trail rides are given for $25 per hour.

4. BERMUDA AFTER DARK

Nightlife has never been the primary reason that visitors flocked to Bermuda. However, there is a surprising lot of it. Trouble is, it seems to float from hotel to hotel. Among the independents, it's hard to predict which pub or nightspot will have the best steel drum band, calypso, whatever. Many of the local pubs feature sing-alongs at the piano bar, a popular form of entertainment in Bermuda. Most of the big hotels offer shows after dinner, with combos filling in between shows for couples who like to dance.

Among the clubs, an outstanding choice is **Forty Thieves,** Front Street in Hamilton (tel. 809/292-4040). Who knows what the entertainment here will be on any given night? Count on West Indian steel drum bands, home-grown calypso acts, and limbo. The cover charge is likely to range from $15 to $25, with two drinks included. The price of admission depends on the acts booked. The night spot is open from 9 p.m. to 3 a.m. daily except Sunday.

Oasis Club, Emporium Building, 69 Front St. (tel. 809/292-3379). Acknowledged as the leading disco on the island, it requires that guests ride a glass-cased elevator to the second floor of a stylishly angular commercial building in the center of Hamilton. Although there's a restaurant within its chic interior, the establishment is better known for its dancing facilities upstairs. You can drink at a black lacquer bar amid a high-tech decor. The establishment is thoughtfully designed to permit normal conversation in one area, while a high-volume acoustical system emits some of the best sounds of Bermuda in another part. The club is divided into two sections, one called The Lounge and the other The Disco. One admission entitles guests to enter both precincts. Hours are nightly from 9 p.m. to 3 a.m. The cover charge ranges from $9 to $10. From October to January that admission price includes one drink. However, in season no drinks are included and are priced separately, beginning at $4.50.

For sheer glitter and glamor, the **Empire Room** in the Southampton Princess Hotel (tel. 809/238-8000) is the only establishment of its kind in Bermuda. The tone is set in the boudoir-like entrance vestibule, where realistic mannequins, clad only in spangles and sequins, pose against scarlet-covered niches. A second vestibule is adorned with come-hither photos of the casts of past extravaganzas. At 7 p.m. Monday to Saturday, a dinner show is presented, with a fixed-price menu costing $40 per person. At 10 p.m. the doors reopen for a Broadway-style show, costing from $29 per person. The price includes two drinks. Shows start at 10:30. The carefully choreographed shows are presented on a revolving stage in an amphitheater where the predominant color is red and where the exhibitions are tastefully provocative. Greg Thompson is the Seattle-based choreographer, who combines humor with feathers, long-limbed beauties of both sexes, and lots of flash for the hottest (legal) show in Bermuda. You'll find all this in the lower lobby of the hotel.

Touch Club, Southampton Princess Hotel (tel. 809/238-8000), is the most elegant disco on the western side of the island. On the lower lobby of the Southampton Princess, the spacious room is decorated like a warmly colored version of a London club, filled with what might be tortoiseshell alternating with black and shades of tan. You'll find dozens of intimate corners in which to create your own party, each softly illuminated, with plushly upholstered English sofas. Each conversation area has its own shaded candle, although if you're looking for more of an electronic thrill, the octagonal dance floor is ringed with batteries of colored lights that flash in synchronized patterns with the music. There's a cover charge of $10 on Friday and Saturday, which includes two drinks. The rest of the week there's no cover charge, and drinks cost $5 each. The club is open daily at 9 p.m., closing at 1 a.m., except on Friday and Saturday when it shuts down at 3 a.m.

At **Prospero's,** Grotto Bay Beach Hotel, Hamilton Parish (tel. 809/293-8333), few guests are really prepared for what they'll find once they pass the ancient calabash tree that flanks the entrance. Even if you brought your couture silks to Bermuda, don't wear them here, since dripping water might dampen your outfit even more than your spirits. The entrance leads you down a flight of narrow stone steps to a dimly illuminated concrete walkway that carries you over Bermuda's version of the River Styx, out of which rises a single enormous stalagmite whose base was formed before the grotto was ever flooded with sea water. The cave is said to be 500,000 years old, although the electronic rhythms reverberating around the rock formations are unmistakably 20th century. Musical styles run the gamut of selections from between 1940 and today.

There's no cover charge and no minimum for eerily intimate evenings that begin at 7 and finish around 1 a.m. Drinks cost from $4. You can chat on the bridge, eying newcomers looking furtively for Cerberus, stand at the bar, dance under stalactite spears, or select one of several table groupings spread under a plastic Napoleonic tent. The occasional dripping from the ceiling is hardly noticed by the crowd, which has been known to become gregariously rowdy during college weeks. If you're transported to the point where a jump in the deep subterranean lake seems to be in order (you won't be the first to do so), remember that if the waters haven't been disturbed for a while, there's a layer of freshwater about five inches thick floating on top of a saltwater base.

Rum House Lounge, Grotto Bay Beach Hotel, Hamilton Parish (tel. 809/293-8333), offers a varied program of live entertainment every night, beginning at 9:30. At the time of your visit, the act might include limbo dancers, show bands, dance bands, and an occasional fire-eater or British vaudevillean. There's no cover charge and no minimum at this cabaret nightclub on the grounds of this beach hotel (see "Where to Stay in Bermuda," Chapter III). Drinks cost from $4 each.

Gazebo Lounge, the Princess Hotel (tel. 809/295-3000), in Hamilton, is one of the most stylish nightclubs in the capital. This beautiful lounge with a magnificent view over the harbor presents acts of international and local renown. During the summer months, an international show created by the noted Greg Thompson performs nightly except Sunday, preceded by an hour of Bermudian entertainment. The cover charge of $29 includes two drinks. Doors open nightly (except Sunday) at 9. A local show begins at 9:30, followed by the Greg Thompson revue at 10:30. The club is open Monday to Saturday but only from mid-March to around mid-November.

Lillian's, Sonesta Hotel, Southampton (tel. 809/238-8122), is the most glamorous dining and dancing spot in this previously recommended hotel. Large, ringed with windows and potted palms, and filled with soft shades of mauve and pink, the establishment is done up like an art nouveau fantasy. No lunch is served since the place only shines in the evening. Every night of the week from 7 to 11, a small musical combo plays highly danceable melodies while waiters serve a series of stylish dishes concocted from fish, veal, and beef (many of them grilled) in combinations of new American cuisine. Temptingly caloric desserts are served from a wheeled trolley which inevitably finds its way to your table at the end of a meal. Full dinners cost from $45 per person, and reservations are suggested.

For the most authentic show on the island, I recommend **Clay House Inn,** North Shore Road, Devonshire (for reservations, telephone 809/292-3193). There's a $15 cover charge, and it's well worth that, as you're likely to be entertained by folklore dancers, a "real-thing" steel band, limbo dancers, and calypso artists. In all, it's a package of island entertainment. Show time is nightly at 10:30 p.m.

The Club, Bermudiana Road (tel. 809/295-6693), is the most sophisticated place in Hamilton for late-night viewing of the island's nighttime elite. It's above the Little Venice Restaurant, behind a discreetly understated mirrored entrance that reflects the four stone lions at the portals of the adjacent restaurant. Jackets are required for men. Dancing is from 10 p.m. to 3 a.m. Nonmembers pay a cover charge of $8, after which drinks cost extra. The Club is open seven days a week. Complimentary admission is granted after you dine at the Little Venice, the Harbour front, Tavern on the Green, or La Trattoria restaurants.

White Heron Country Inn, Riddells Bay, Warwick (tel. 809/238-1655). Years ago, a Scottish nanny, whose home was a few yards from Dewar's distillery in Perth, visited Bermuda as an *au pair* childsitter. Shortly after her arrival she met a handsome Bermudian, got married, and helped establish one of the most amusing restaurants and pubs on the island. It's in what used to be one of the most opulent private homes in the parish, built by a Pennsylvania industrialist at the turn of the century. Today this all-purpose social center offers ten bedrooms, a charming restaurant, and a pub. When the fire in the restaurant is blazing, it's one of my favorite places in Bermuda (see "Dining in Bermuda," Chapter IV).

During college week the place jumps with partying students from Virginia and North Carolina. The rest of the year as many as 400 people at a time come to the weekly special events held beside the backyard pool. It's open seven nights a week. Sundays are especially popular, with a jam session drawing live musicians (and an occasional bagpiper from Canada). They perform from 5 to 8 p.m. The place is fun, informal, and worth a visit. Phone ahead for any special events that might be going on while you're in Bermuda. The place even serves "pub grub" for around $8 for a greasy but succulent meal of steak-and-kidney pie, fish and chips, or conch fritters.

Ye Olde Cock and Feather, 29-31 Front Street, Hamilton (tel. 809/295-2263). Local wits sometimes debate whether it's more painful to climb up to this pub at the beginning of a long evening or to fall down the stairs after a few drinks. The steps leading up from the street, like much of the rest of the establishment, are flanked with cedar paneling. This multiroom hideaway offers seating on the streetside balcony with a view over carriages lining up under a shade tree, or at the long bar where a worker will pull you a draft beer from the old English taps.

If you want a meal, you can sit in one of a duo of dark-paneled rooms, one of which lies under the soaring eaves, with a view of the exposed structural elements of the limestone roof. At midday, meals include hamburgers, sandwiches, deep-fried Bermuda fish, steak-and-kidney pie, "bangers and mash," and salads. Evening meals are more formal, featuring any of the above items, as well as curried seafood Madras style, prime sirloin, and Wiener schnitzel. Lunch is served daily from 11 a.m. to 5:30 p.m., after which you can order dinner. The house's special drink is a blend of secret ingredients with orange juice and coconut milk called a Cock-a-doodle-doo. This might whet your appetite for lunch, which costs from $12, or dinner, from $25. There's a dartboard for competition in the pub, and live music is presented every evening from 9 until 1 a.m. You can also watch sports events on large-screen TV via satellite.

PART TWO

THE BAHAMAS

CHAPTER VI

GETTING TO AND AROUND THE BAHAMAS

□ □ □

The Bahamas, as a country, is completely different from the United States. You are indeed "going abroad." But unlike a trip from the U.S. mainland to Europe, you can be in The Bahamas after only a 35-minute jet-hop, providing you use Miami as your gateway. Even if you live in New York, it's easy to wing your way south to The Bahamas. In just a matter of hours you can flee the north winds and be lying on the beach, sipping a goombay smash.

Travel agents who keep up-to-the-minute schedules and rates can inform you about the latest package deals if you're contemplating either a summer or winter holiday. Fortunately, many of these package deals aren't offered just in the slow season, the summer, but appear frequently throughout the winter, except during the heavily booked Christmas period.

1. FLYING TO THE BAHAMAS

More than a dozen international airlines fly into Nassau International Airport from the United States. (Freeport is another important gateway to The Bahamas from the United States.)

Flights are available from New York, Chicago, and Atlanta. But Florida, because of its proximity, has the most flights, leaving from such cities as Miami, Fort Lauderdale, Tampa, and Palm Beach. If you're coming from such major American cities as Dallas, Los Angeles, Houston, or wherever, Miami is still your best gateway, because of its elaborate air links with the rest of the mainland. Most foreigners who visit from abroad come through Miami as well, unless they can get on a direct flight, such as ones offered by Air Canada or British Airways.

Of course neither Nassau nor Freeport may be your final destination in The

Bahamas. If you're headed for one of the Family Islands (formerly known as the "Out Islands") refer to the "Getting There" section, which appears at the beginning of my review of each island chain.

You face a choice of booking a seat on a regularly scheduled flight or a charter plane, the latter being cheaper of course. On a regular flight you can cancel your ticket without penalty. On a charter you do not have such leeway.

WINGING TO NASSAU: From the U.S. mainland, about a half dozen international carriers fly nonstop to Nassau International Airport. Experienced travelers know that when an itinerary involves an airplane change at the midway point, it's more convenient to remain booked on the same airline for each segment of the trip.

Of the many carriers flying from North America to Nassau, one that has pleased the travel community with its scope, scale, and power is **Delta.** This airline maintains excellent nonstop flights daily from three U.S. gateways into Nassau or Freeport. These connections include New York's La Guardia, Atlanta, and Fort Lauderdale. Good connections are also available daily from New York's JFK Airport and from Dallas via Fort Lauderdale.

Each of Delta's hubs connects with cities through North America, Europe, and the Far East. The acquisition of dozens of new routes for Delta was the result of a corporate reorganization of the airline in the mid-1980s which added the routes of Western Airlines to its own. In addition, Delta has pursued an aggressive policy of acquiring new routes in the past several years, a policy which has added Delta flights to eight cities in Europe and three capitals of the Far East. Most of these depart from Delta's headquarters in Atlanta.

In the past several years, residents of such far-flung U.S. cities as Las Vegas, as well as the major cities of California and the Pacific Northwest, a rich selection of cities in the American Southeast, the Grain Belt, and such Sun Belt cities as Tucson, Phoenix, Lubbock (Texas), El Paso, Amarillo, Dallas, and Houston can remain on one carrier from their home-towns into Nassau, usually with just one change of airplane. Tickets are usually less expensive in terms of mileage covered.

For reservations and information, call a travel agent or else Delta (toll free at 800/221-1212) with your preferred dates of departure. An agent will work out the best deal, including the most economical air fares. Try to have alternate dates in mind in case less expensive tickets might be available for different days of departure.

Of course, Delta is not alone in flying to Nassau. Five times a week, **Trans World Airlines** goes nonstop from New York to Nassau and Grand Bahama Island (Freeport/Lucaya). It also has service from St. Louis to Nassau. **Eastern Airlines** is another popular carrier, offering nonstop service daily from Philadelphia and Newark (New Jersey) to Nassau.

A more recent routing is on **Midway Airlines** (its first international run), with service from Chicago's Midway Airport to Nassau. There is a stopover in Fort Lauderdale. Following a merger with USAir, **Piedmont** now features daily nonstop service from Baltimore and Charlotte (North Carolina) to Nassau. Another division, the **Piedmont Shuttle** also advertises daily nonstop service from Washington, D.C., and Chicago to Nassau. Orlando (Florida) is also emerging as a gateway to Nassau. Service is provided by **Braniff Airlines** from Orlando to Nassau.

Pan Am flies from New York's JFK Airport to Nassau daily, and it also flies to Freeport from Miami daily.

Finally, any second-time visitor to The Bahamas is fully aware of **Bahamasair**'s routes between Nassau and the Family Islands (a lot more about those later). Bahamasair, however, also plays a pivotal role in bringing crowds of sun-seekers into The Bahamas from such North American cities as Miami, Tampa/Orlando, Newark, and Washington D.C.'s Dulles International Airport. Flights leave Miami for Nassau as frequently as seven times a day (from Dulles, four times a week). For reservations and information, and for data about connections in the Family Islands, call toll free at 800/222-4262.

Aero Coach offers more than 70 scheduled flights a day to Grand Bahama and the Family Islands. The island destinations serviced from three Florida gateways—West Palm Beach, Fort Lauderdale, and Miami—are Bimini, Georgetown in the Exumas, North Eleuthera, Rock Sound and Governor's Harbour on Eleuthera, Freeport and West End on Grand Bahama, and both Treasure Cay and Marsh Harbour in the Abacos. For tickets and reservation information, call in Fort Lauderdale 305/359-1600, or toll free 800/327-0010. The airline promises not to overbook and has been servicing the islands for more than eight years. Aero Coach International's address is P.O. Box 21604, Fort Lauderdale, FL 33335.

Piedmont/Henson (tel. 800/251-5720) flies from Fort Lauderdale, Florida, to several Bahamian destinations. Flights are available between Fort Lauderdale and Treasure Cay and Marsh Harbour in the Abacos; North Eleuthera; Governor's Harbour; Rock Sound; and Nassau. There is also service between West Palm Beach and Freeport, Grand Bahama.

CHARTER FLIGHTS: Now open to the general public, charter flights allow visitors to The Bahamas to travel at rates cheaper than on regularly scheduled flights. Many of the major carriers offer charter flights to The Bahamas at rates that are sometimes 30% (or more) off the regular fare.

There are some drawbacks to charter flights that you need to consider. Advance booking, for example, of up to 45 days or more may be required. You could lose most of the money you've advanced if an emergency should force you to cancel a flight. However, it is now possible to take out cancellation insurance against such an eventuality.

Unfortunately, on the charter flight you are forced to depart and return on a scheduled date. It will do no good to call the airline and tell them you're in the hospital with yellow fever! If you're not on the plane, you can kiss your money good-bye.

Since charter flights are so complicated, it's best to go to a good travel agent and ask him or her to explain to you the problems and advantages. Sometimes charters require ground arrangements, such as the prebooking of hotel rooms.

While there, ask about APEX fares, meaning advance purchase. These individual inclusive fares include land arrangements along with your excursion fare, and can represent a considerable savings to you.

The major agent for booking charter flights to The Bahamas is a rapidly emerging company called **Bahamas Express.** It doesn't actually own any aircraft of its own, but often partially fills seats on both Bahamasair and Continental Airlines flights. These flights depart from Newark, New Jersey, and go either to Freeport or Nassau. Departures are frequent. They require an advance reservation and pre-payment, and are becoming increasingly popular as a way of reaching The Bahamas from North America. These flights are booked with hotel package rates which offer substantial discounts, especially for stays of three days or longer in both New Providence and the Family Islands. For information and reservations about these charter arrangements, call toll free at 800/722-4262.

PRIVATE PILOTS: Many private pilots fly to The Bahamas from the U.S. mainland, especially from Florida. Of the dozens of airports and airstrips, many in private hands, 20 are designated as official ports of entry by the Bahamian government. This means that someone from the Bahamian government, representing Customs and Immigration, will be there to process you. Many other airstrips, of course, are used illegally by drug smugglers.

However, legitimate private pilots coming for a holiday can write the nearest Bahamas tourist office (see the ABCs section of Chapter VII) for a fact-filled "flight planner and air navigation chart," or in the U.S. call the Pilot Hotline toll free at 800/327-3853.

FLYING FROM FLORIDA ON CHALK'S: Chalk's International Airlines, a subsidiary of Resorts International, Inc., flies from Florida to Paradise Island.

Founded in 1919 by World War I pilot Arthur Burns (Pappy) Chalk, the airline stakes its claim as the oldest in the world in continuous service. Its seaplanes have carried a distinguished array of celebrities, such as Judy Garland, Errol Flynn, and the elusive Howard Hughes (who lived at the Britannia Towers on Paradise Island). To this day many celebrities use the airline to avoid the attention they attract at the large Miami International Airport.

From its Watson Island Terminal in downtown Miami and from Fort Lauderdale International Airport, Chalk's services Paradise Island/Nassau with regular flights. Chalk's terminal on Paradise Island is just minutes from all the island's hotels, which eliminates the cost of the half-hour ride to and from Nassau International Airport. Travelers can leave Miami or Fort Lauderdale and be in their Bahamas hotel rooms in a little more than an hour.

In addition, Chalk's has service between Miami and Fort Lauderdale to Bimini. It also offers daily service between Miami and the privately held Cat Cay, south of Bimini.

For more information, call Chalk's toll free (except in Florida) at 800/327-2521. The phone numbers in Florida are: Miami, 305/895-1223; Broward County (Fort Lauderdale), 305/467-7233; other locations in Florida, toll free 800/432-8807. Or write to Chalk's International Airlines, 1550 S.W. 43rd St., Fort Lauderdale, FL 33315.

2. TOURING BY CRUISE SHIP

If you'd like to sail The Bahamas, having a home with an ocean view, a cruise ship might be for you. It's slow and easy, and it's no longer to be enjoyed only by the idle rich who have months to spend away from home. Most cruises today appeal to the middle-income voyager who probably has no more than one week (or two at the most) to spend cruising at sea. Some 300 passenger ships sail the Caribbean and The Bahamas all year, and in January and February that figure may go up another hundred or so.

Most cruise-ship operators suggest the concept of a "total vacation." Some promote activities "from sunup to sundown" while others suggest the possibility of "having absolutely nothing to do but lounge." Cruise ships are self-contained resorts, offering everything on board but actual sightseeing once you arrive in a port of call.

If you don't want to spend all your time at sea, some lines offer a fly-and-cruise vacation. Terms vary widely under this arrangement. You spend a week cruising, another week staying at an interesting hotel at reduced prices. These total packages cost less (or should!) than if you'd purchased the cruise and air portions separately.

On yet another interpretation of "fly and cruise," you fly to meet the cruise and to leave it. Although multifarious in nature, most plans offer a package deal from the principal airport closest to your residence to the nearest major airport to the cruise departure point. Otherwise, you can purchase your air ticket on your own—say, from Kansas City to Fort Lauderdale—and book your cruise ticket separately as well, but you'll save money by combining the fares in a package deal.

Miami is the "cruise capital of the world," and vessels also leave from New York, Port Everglades, Los Angeles, and other points of embarkation as well.

As in a hotel, if you're keeping costs at a minimum, ask for one of the smaller, inside cabins when booking space on a cruise ship. If you're the type who likes to be active all day and for most of the night, spending little time in your cabin except to sleep or whatever, you need not pay the extra money, which can be considerable, to rent luxurious suites aboard these seagoing vessels. Nearly all cabins rented today have a shower and a toilet, regardless of how cramped and confining it is. If you get a midship cabin, you are less likely to experience severe rolling and pitching. Most of the modern vessels have standardized accommodations, and the older vessels offer cabins of widely varying sizes, ranging from deluxe stateroom suites to "steerage."

Dress is more casual on cruise ships than it used to be in the "white tie and tails" days. Men still can use a dark suit occasionally, and women should have at least one cocktail dress. Most passengers on cruise ships don't dress up every evening, and some don't dress up at all. Men often wear sport coats and slacks with open shirts; women, pant suits or sport dresses.

Some evenings may be cool and you'll need a sweater. For women, a sun hat or scarf will do nicely. Plenty of casual, comfortable clothes are suggested for the day. For actual touring in the islands, or participating in the deck activities, men wear sports shirts, walking shorts, slacks, and a comfortable pair of walking shoes. Women will need sun dresses, skirts, blouses, shifts, culottes, and shorts. Walking shoes are preferred to city footwear.

Naturally, you'll need a bathing suit or a bikini. For women, even that kooky dress may be worn too, as Bahamian cruises lend themselves to masquerades.

Most of the cruise ships prefer to do their traveling at night, arriving the next morning at the day's port of call, as anyone who has ever been trampled underfoot in Nassau's Straw Market will testify. In port, passengers can go ashore for sightseeing and shopping. It's also possible to have lunch at a local restaurant of your choice to sample some of the island specialties and break the monotony of taking every meal aboard ship.

Prices vary so widely that I cannot possibly document them here. Sometimes the same route, stopping at the identical ports of call, will carry different fares.

Unfortunately, the one ingredient needed for a successful cruise is the hardest to know in advance—and that's the list of your fellow passengers. The right crowd can be a lot of fun. A group incompatible with your interests can leave you sulking in your cabin.

If you've never taken an ocean cruise before, you may find the Miami-to-Nassau cruise, lasting three to four days, a good and proper introduction to cruising. Not only that, it's far kinder to your pocketbook than the more extended cruises to the Caribbean.

If you like action and "fun, fun," try one of the **Carnival Cruise Lines** year-round three- and four-day cruises from Miami to The Bahamas, which they launched in 1984 and 1986. The *Mardi Gras* departs from Fort Lauderdale every Thursday on three-day cruises to Nassau and every Sunday on four-day cruises to Nassau and Freeport. The *Carnivale* departs from Miami every Friday and Monday for the same itinerary. All cruises include a fun-filled day at sea with a complete program of entertainment and activity (and they mean it!). These two ships have the largest casinos of any ships cruising The Bahamas. The 48,000-ton *Jubilee,* carrying 1,486 passengers, was launched in 1986, with three outdoor pools, a casino, and a health spa with whirlpools. Year-round it makes seven-night jaunts which leave Miami on Sunday, calling at Nassau before going on to Puerto Rico's San Juan and Charlotte Amalie (capital of St. Thomas in the U.S. Virgins).

When it was launched in 1962, today's *Mardi Gras* (refurbished in 1985), was known as the *Empress of Canada*. Today, this 27,250-ton vessel carries nearly a thousand passengers who enjoy its two outdoor pools (one indoor pool), and its international casino. It features three-night cruises that leave Fort Lauderdale on Thursday year-round, calling at Nassau. In addition, four-night cruises leave Fort Lauderdale on Sunday, calling at both Freeport (Grand Bahama Island) and Nassau. You can contact Carnival Cruise Lines at 5225 N.W. 87th Ave., Miami, FL 33178 (tel. 305/599-2600). Around the U.S., call toll free 800/327-7373; in Florida but outside Miami, toll free 800/325-1214. The line is popular with singles and honeymooners.

Norwegian Cruise Line, 2 Alhambra Plaza, Coral Gables, FL 33134 (tel. 305/445-0866, or toll free 800/327-7030), operates popular three- and four-day cruises out of Miami, stopping first at Nassau, then at a private Family Island, then Freeport, before its eventual return to Miami. It sails every Friday and Monday from Miami year-round. The line carries more passengers than any other cruise line in North America. Its "Bahamarama cruises," as they are called, are among the most popular in the industry. Passengers sail from Miami to Nassau aboard the *M/S Sunward II,* a white 14,100-ton cruise ship. Their Family Island stopover is at Great Stirrup Cay in the relatively uninhabited Berry Islands, which we'll visit in Chapter XI. Departures are from Miami at 4:30 p.m. on Monday or Friday. Passengers arrive in Nassau the next morning. The four-day cruise adds Freeport to the ports of call. Three-day cruises cost $395 to $860, depending on the accommodations, while four-day voyages go for $525 to $1,015.

Other cruises are offered by **American Canadian Caribbean Line, Inc.,** P.O. Box 368, Warren, RI 02885 (tel. 401/247-0955 in Rhode Island, or toll free 800/556-7450 outside Rhode Island). In winter, it offers 7- and 12-day cruises from Cancún, Belize, The Bahamas, St. Martin, Antigua, Grenada, and the complete Virgin Islands. Weekly prices range from $575 to $1,095 per person. For the 12-day voyages, prices are from $1,049 to $2,150 per person for top cabins. The ambience is informal. For example, the chef prepares food for only one sitting. The line is proud of its bow ramp, which enables the ship to land on out-of-the-way places such as the Exumas that are not visited by cruise lines. Passengers can disembark right on the beach itself. The repeat business is a whopping 65%, so they must be doing something right.

Premier Cruise Lines, 101 George King Blvd., Cape Canaveral, FL 32920 (tel. 407/783-5061), takes pride in its *Star/Ship Royale,* which carries 1,100 passengers, and has been called "part playground, part palace." The vessel was formerly the *Federico C* of the Costa Cruise Lines, built in 1958 for deluxe transatlantic service between Italy and South America. She was later massively overhauled. This 21,000-ton vessel, with an outdoor pool and casino, year-round makes four-night cruises. They leave Monday from Port Canaveral, calling at Nassau and Salt Cay. Three-night cruises depart on Friday from Port Canaveral, calling at Nassau and Salt Cay. The *Star/Ship Atlantic,* with a capacity of 1,600 passengers, complete with an indoor pool with a sliding Magrodome roof and an outdoor pool, was launched as the *Atlantic* in 1982, but was refitted in 1988. It sails year-round on three-night cruises departing on Friday from Port Canaveral, with calls at Nassau and Salt Cay. Four-night cruises depart on Monday from Port Canaveral, and these also call at Nassau and Salt Cay. Launched in 1965 as the *Oceanic,* but refitted in 1986, the *Star/Ship Oceanic* carries 1,500 passengers who use its casino and pair of indoor and pair of outdoor pools (with a sliding Magrodome roof). It offers four-night cruises year-round. They leave Monday from Port Canaveral, calling, like their sister ships, at Nassau and Salt Cay.

Sun-Line Cruises offers transatlantic cruises that stop at Nassau. The 20-day westbound and 22-day eastbound cruises are on the five-star Sun Line flagship, the *Stella Solaris.* Information can be obtained from Sun Line's office, 1 Rockefeller Plaza, Suite 315, New York, NY 10020 (tel. toll free 800/872-6400, or 212/397-6400).

Chandris Fantasy Cruises, 900 Third Ave., New York, NY 10022 (tel. 212/750-0044 or call toll free at 800/621-3446 outside New York State), sends its *Galileo,* with 1,100 passengers on two-night cruises in winter. These depart on Friday from Miami, calling on Nassau. This 29,000-ton vessel, launched in 1963, was overhauled in 1986.

Dolphin Cruise Line, 1007 North America Way, Miami, FL (tel. 305/358-2111 or toll free at 800/999-4299 for information only; reservations at 800/222-1003), sails the *Dolphin IV,* which was refurbished in 1988. It was launched in 1956 as the *Zion.* This small 588-passenger vessel, with an outdoor pool and casino, makes four-night cruises year-round to The Bahamas. They depart on Monday from Miami, with calls at Freeport, Nassau, and "Blue Lagoon Island." They also offer three-night cruises year-round which leave Miami on Friday, calling at Nassau and Blue Lagoon Island.

One of the most affordable cruises is offered by **Admiral Cruises,** 1220 Biscayne Blvd., Miami, FL 33101 (tel. 305/374-1611). Said to be the oldest cruise line operating out of Miami, it operates the *Emerald Seas,* which was a World War II troop transport ship, once known as the *General W. P. Richardson* and later the *President Roosevelt.* The line makes much of its stopover in one of the Family Islands in The Bahamas, Little Stirrup Cay (see Chapter XI, which previews the sparsley settled Berry Islands). The line offers three- and four-night cruises to Nassau.

These are only some of the many, many lines in service between the U.S. mainland and The Bahamas. A travel agent will fill you in on the other possibilities.

3. TOURING BY CHARTERED BOAT

For those who can afford it (or else who know friends who can), this is one of the most luxurious ways to arrive in The Bahamas. On your private boat, you can island-hop at your convenience. Well-equipped marinas are on every major island and many cays. There are designated ports of entry at Abaco, Andros, the Berry Islands, Bimini, Cat Cay, Eleuthera, Exuma, Grand Bahama Island (Freeport/Lucaya), Inagua, New Providence (Nassau), Ragged Island, and San Salvador.

Vessels must check with Customs at the first port of entry and receive a cruising clearance permit to The Bahamas. Carry it with you and return it at the official port of departure.

You should also buy *The Yachtsman's Guide to The Bahamas,* which is available from Tropic Isle Publishers, P.O. Box 610935, North Miami, FL 33161 (tel. 305/893-4277). The cost is $18.95 postpaid in the U.S. (add $4 postage and handling on orders outside the U.S.).

Experienced sailors and navigators, with a sea-wise crew, can charter "bareboat," a term meaning a rental with a fully equipped boat but with no captain or crew. You're on your own, and you'll have to prove you can handle it before you're allowed to take out such craft. Even if you're your own skipper, you may want to take along an experienced yachtsman familiar with local waters, which may be tricky in some places. (The company that insures the craft will definitely want to know that the vessel in question is in safe hands.)

Four to six people, maybe more, often charter yachts varying from 50 to more than 100 feet, and split the cost among them. Often a dozen people will pitch in to finance the sail.

The Bahamas, as will be pointed out many times, offers among the most beautiful and romantic cruising grounds in the world, especially around such island chains as the Exumas, the Abacos, and Eleuthera.

Most yachts are rented on a weekly basis, with a fully stocked bar, plus equipment for fishing and water sports. More and more bareboat charters are learning that they can save money and select menus more suited to their tastes by doing their own provisioning, rather than relying on the yacht company that rented them the vessel.

4. PACKAGE TOURS

If you want everything done for you, plus you want to save money as well, consider traveling to The Bahamas on a package tour. General tours appealing to the average voyager are commonly offered, but many of the tours are very specific —tennis packages, golf packages, scuba and snorkeling packages, and, only for those who qualify, honeymooner specials.

Economy and convenience are the chief advantage of a package tour in that the cost of transportation (usually an airplane fare), a hotel room, food (sometimes), and sightseeing (sometimes) are combined in one package, neatly tied up with a single price tag.

There are extras, of course. There are *always* extras, but in general you'll know roughly what the cost of your vacation will be in advance, and can budget accordingly.

If you booked your flight separately, likewise your hotel, you could not come out as cheaply as on a package tour—hence their immense and increasing appeal. There are disadvantages too. You may find yourself in a hotel you dislike immensely, yet you are virtually trapped there, as you've already paid for it.

Everybody from Idaho potato growers to birdwatchers of Alcatraz seemingly offers package tours to The Bahamas. Choosing the right one can be a bit of a problem. Your travel agent may offer one. Certainly all the major airline carriers will. It's best to go to a travel agent, tell him or her what island (or islands) you'd like to visit, and see what's currently offered.

These packages are available because tour operators can mass-book hotels and make volume purchases. Another disadvantage—you generally have to pay the cost of the total package in advance. Transfers between your hotel and the airport are often included, and this is more of a financial break than it sounds at first, as some airports are situated a $20 taxi ride from a resort. In one case in The Bahamas, a $100 taxi ride!

Many packages carry several options, including the possibility of low-cost car rentals.

The single traveler, regrettably, usually suffers, as nearly all tour packages are based on double occupancy.

Personally, I find one of the biggest drawbacks to taking a package tour to The Bahamas to be the hotel selected. I am especially fond of local inns—small, family-run places—and you don't get those on package tours. Rather, tour operators who have to deal in block bookings can get discounts only at the larger, more impersonal resorts.

Also, I find that many package deals to The Bahamas contain more hidden extras than they should. The list of "free" offerings sometimes sounds better than it is. Forget about that free rum punch at the manager's cocktail party and peruse the fine print to see if your deal includes meals and other costly items.

5. GETTING AROUND THE BAHAMAS

If your final destination is Paradise Island, Freeport, or Nassau (Cable Beach), and you plan to go there by air, you'll have little trouble in reaching your destination.

However, if you're heading for one of the Family Islands, you face more exotic choices, not only of airplanes, but of other means of transport, including a mailboat, the traditional connecting link among the old "Out Islands" in days of yore.

As mentioned, each section on one of the Family Island chains in the Bahamian archipelago will have a specific breakdown of transportation, but in the meantime I'll give you a general overview, beginning with—

FLYING TO THE FAMILY ISLANDS: The national airline of The Bahamas, **Bahamasair,** provides service to the major Family Islands, and other smaller carriers provide service off the eastern Florida coast. At present, the airline uses Miami, Tampa, Orlando, Dulles (Washington, D.C.), Hartford, and Newark.

Most of the Family Islands have either airports, airstrips, or are within a short ferry ride's distance of one of the above.

Besides carrying passengers, as a government-owned airline Bahamasair has another responsibility—to serve the people of The Bahamas by providing transportation of medical supplies, food, and cargo of all kinds to remote areas such as Cat Island and Long Island.

To verify schedules and make reservations, call toll free 800/222-4262 nationwide.

MAILBOATS: Before the advent of better airline connections, the traditional way of exploring the Family Islands—in fact, about the only way of getting to them unless you had your own boat—was by mailboat. This 125-year-old service is still available, but it's recommended only for those who have unlimited time and a sense of adventure—and who don't mind sharing a seat with an odd assortment of cargo headed out to the islands. You may ride with cases of rum and/or beer, oil drums, crawfish pots, live chickens, even an occasional piano.

The boats, 19 of them comprising the "Post Office Navy," under the direction of the Bahamian Chief of Transportation, are often fancifully colored, high-sided, and somewhat clumsy in appearance, but the little motor vessels chug along, serving the 29 inhabited islands of The Bahamas. Schedules can be thrown off by weather and other causes, but most morning mailboats depart from Potter's Cay (under the Paradise Island Bridge in Nassau) or from Prince George Wharf. The voyages last from 4½ hours to most of a day, sometimes even overnight. It's advisable to check the schedule of the particular boat you wish to travel on with the skipper at the dock in Nassau.

Tariffs charged on the mailboats are considerably less than air travel (more about this later). Many of the boats offer two classes of passenger accommodations, first and second. In first class you get a bunk bed and in second you may only be entitled to deck space. The bunk beds are actually usually reserved for the seasick, but first-class passengers sit in a fairly comfortable, enclosed cabin, at least on the larger boats.

For information about mailboats to the Family Islands, get in touch with the Dockmasters Office, under the Paradise Island Bridge (tel. 809/323-1064).

RENTING A CAR: Some judicious research may reveal that renting a car is less expensive than you may have thought, especially if you consider the high cost of transportation by taxi or the inconvenience of traveling by bus. Blithe spirits will also appreciate the freedom afforded only by a car for reaching that out-of-the-way beach or a secluded cove. Many visitors rent cars just to circumnavigate their island, with no particular destination in mind, wishing only to sightsee, to take in the landscape and the sunshine, interrupting the transit only for lunch or a tropical drink.

Of all the locations in The Bahamas, the airports at Nassau (New Providence

Island) and Freeport (Grand Bahama Island) are the most hotly contested as sales territories by North America's car-rental companies. Of course, they compete with a handful of local car-rental companies, some of which may charge a few dollars less.

Most Dollarwise readers, however, when faced with a choice, prefer to do business with one of the major firms. This is because they offer toll-free reservations services, and because the maintenance level of the vehicles, while never perfect, tends to be better than those of most local outfits. From personal experience, there's nothing so depressing as a mechanical breakdown on a lonely road in the tropics.

Reserving a car in Nassau or Freeport is just a matter of making a toll-free phone call from wherever you live in the United States or Canada. Renting a car in the Family Islands, however, may be more difficult. If you plan to remain near your hotel, limiting your excursions to an offshore reef in a scuba or snorkeling outfit, you'll probably be better off relying on one of the dozens of unmetered taxis that await the arrival of incoming airplanes. Of course, one of the major car-rental companies may have opened a branch on one of the Family Islands by the time you go, but at the time of this writing, none of them offered anything outside of Nassau and Freeport.

At the time of my latest inquiry, each of the major firms quoted an unlimited-mileage rate, which varied slightly with the time of year. Each company's system was slightly different, although after the first week the per-day rate was usually less expensive than the daily rate for rentals of less than a week. Of course, there are extra charges, which the fine print of a rental contract will reveal. These sometimes include a small refueling service charge, which applies if the renter returns the car with less fuel than when he or she originally rented it. More important, a renter is able to arrange additional insurance in the form of a collision damage waiver. The average cost in Nassau is around $7 to $8 per day. Without the waiver, depending on the company, a renter is liable for the first several hundred dollars worth of damage to the car in the event of an accident. If the waiver is purchased, the driver waives all financial responsibility in the event of an accident. The amount of liability varies from company to company. If in doubt, I suggest you purchase the waiver.

As for driving requirements, each company has a different age limit for its drivers. All require a minimum age of between 21 and 25, and some won't rent a car to anyone over 70. This varies with the company. Underage drivers can sometimes rent from one or another of the agencies upon payment of a substantial cash (not credit card) deposit. Of course, a valid driver's license must be presented when the rental contract is issued.

For more information about rentals in Nassau or Freeport, you can call the international departments of **Budget Rent-a-Car** toll free at 800/527-0700, **Hertz** at 800/654-3001, **Avis** at 800/331-2112, and **National** at 800/328-4567.

DRIVING REQUIREMENTS: A visitor may drive on his or her home driver's license for up to three months. Longer stays require a Bahamian driver's license. Insurance against injury or death liability is compulsory. Applicants for Bahamian driver's licenses must be at least 17 years old. The cost is $15 and the license is valid for one year. Visitors may also apply for an international driver's license, which costs $25 for one year.

A word of warning: British tradition lives on in The Bahamas. *You must drive on the left!*

GASOLINE: "Petrol" is easily available in Nassau or Freeport. In the Family Islands, where the cost of gasoline is likely to vary from island to island, you should plan your itinerary based on information as to where you'll be able to get fuel. Usually the major towns of the islands have service stations. You should have no problems on New Providence or Grand Bahama unless you start out with a nearly empty tank.

TAXIS: Taxis are plentiful in the Nassau/Cable Beach/Paradise Island area and in the Freeport/Lucaya area on Grand Bahama Island. These cabs, for the most part, are metered. See "Getting Around" in the section on each island.

In the Family Islands, however, you will not be so richly blessed. In general, taxi service is available at all air terminals, at least if those air terminals are of the status of "port of entry" terminals. They are also available in the vicinity of most marinas.

Taxis are usually shared, often with the local residents. Family Island taxis aren't metered, so you must negotiate the fare before you get in. Cars are often old and badly maintained, so be prepared for a bumpy ride over some rough roads if you've selected a particularly remote hotel.

HITCHHIKING: This is a commonplace method of travel, particularly in the Family Islands where it's often depended on as a mode of transportation because of the scarcity of vehicles. It's a less desirable practice in Nassau, Cable Beach, and Freeport/Lucaya, and it's unheard of on Paradise Island.

6. ALTERNATIVE AND SPECIAL-INTEREST TRAVEL

A few suggestions as to something you can do that may present a new challenge and a chance to learn more about The Bahamas than might be possible through regular sightseeing jaunts or staying in a regular, even though deluxe, hotel could make your trip a new adventure.

PEOPLE-TO-PEOPLE: Visitors to Nassau and Freeport/Lucaya on Grand Bahama Island are in for a unique happening. A promotional idea called People-to-People, thought up by the Bahamas Ministry of Tourism, gives visitors a chance to sample some "real" Bahamian culture. If you want to participate in the program, you can get a form in advance of your visit by writing to the Ministry of Tourism, P.O. Box N-3701, Nassau, The Bahamas. If you're already in Nassau, go to one of the Tourist Information Centres, which are at the airport, at Prince George Dock, and at Rawson Square, or telephone 809/326-5371. If you are planning to go to Freeport/Lucaya, the form can be mailed to the Ministry of Tourism, P.O. Box F-251, Freeport/Lucaya, The Bahamas. In Freeport/Lucaya, you can fill out the form at the Tourist Information Centre at the International Bazaar or phone 809/352-8044.

It's a program meant to bring people together and make your stay more meaningful and enjoyable. You will be introduced to a Bahamian family or couple, and they will show you how they live, take you to their churches and social functions, introduce you to their special cuisine, such as soursop ice cream (a real taste sensation), as well as give you a chance for some good conversation. The staff tries to match you up with a host or hostess who might have interests similar to yours. The program works, from all reports, and I suggest that you try it for an unusual and pleasurable experience. Not to mention adding a few friends to your list.

The Bahamians participating in the program represent a cross-section of the community. They volunteer for the program because they enjoy meeting people from other countries and are glad to show visitors a closer view of their life in The Bahamas. Expenses are borne by the individual Bahamians.

To coordinate a People-to-People visit often takes several days, so visitors or their travel agents are encouraged to request the adventure before arrival. However, arrangements can also be made through the hotel where you are staying.

INTERNATIONAL UNDERSTANDING: Many of the world's travelers hold a concern for the future of less wealthy societies whose borders are invaded annually by floods of big-spending tourists. One highly reputable organization, the **Center for Responsible Tourism,** 2 Kensington Rd., San Anselmo, CA 94960 (tel. 415/258-6594), tries to raise the consciousness of travelers as to the unhappy effects which cultural conflicts can bring to fragile third-world societies. Although it doesn't actually sponsor tours into The Bahamas, its newsletter and the schedules of its meetings might be of interest to visitors who are motivated by humanitarian feelings of concern for less developed societies. This group, in its own words, "exists to change the attitudes and practices of North American travelers and to persuade North Americans to be part of the struggle for justice in tourism in the Third World." The organization thrives on contributions and for a small fee will send new members its newsletter and information about upcoming seminars.

A YOGA RETREAT: On New Providence, unusual for Paradise Island is **Sivananda Ashram Yoga Retreat,** P.O. Box N-7550, Paradise Island, The Bahamas (tel. 809/326-2902). One of the island's most extraordinary establishments is made even more extraordinary because of its location near some of the most glitteringly expensive real estate anywhere in The Bahamas. Its organizers call it the "last outpost" on a hectic tourist island and stress that it is the only ashram in The Bahamas or the Caribbean that practices authentic Indian yoga. It was established when a wealthy benefactor willed the land in a 99-year trust to the Swami Vishnu Devananda in gratitude for his having assisted her daughter during withdrawal from a drug dependency. Today the spirit and soul of this place is very distant from that of other resorts on the island. Unless the road leading to the retreat has been repaired by the time of your visit, the only access is either by ferry from the docks at Nassau or on foot over an almost-endless expanse of beachfront. If you're not feeling close to nature by the time you begin your trek from the parking lot of the Holiday Inn, you certainly will by the time you arrive at the retreat.

The central core here is a clapboard building that used to be a private beach house. It contains dormitories, the kitchen, and the roughly constructed al fresco dining area, with long rows of communal sinks where guests are expected to wash their own dishes after the simple vegetarian meals. Some of the accommodations are in a series of redwood huts built on stilts above the sands of the beach. Some of the huts are whimsically capped with onion domes and Oriental-style gingerbread, but other than that they are quite spartan. Many guests sleep in their own tents set up under the trees of the "cathedral of palms," whose walkways are lined by pools of water and leafy vegetation.

The schedule of activities includes mandatory participation by all guests of the ashram. Communal meditation every day at 6 a.m. takes place either on the beach or on a harborside barge. Guests are expected to attend 8 a.m. and 4 p.m. yoga classes. Breakfast at 10 a.m. is followed by free time until 4 p.m., when additional yoga lessons are held. Dinner is unfashionably early, 6 p.m., and is followed by an evening of meditation or an inspirational film. About 75% of the guests here are North Americans, many of whom check in for one of the specialized clinics or workshops whose publicity is handled by ad agencies in Montréal and Florida. These workshops include fasting clinics and four-week yoga seminars, which offer all levels of instruction. No smoking, drinking, or drugs are allowed here, since one of the major goals is the detoxification of the guests within a strongly developed support system. Rates here are the cheapest on the island. In any season, rooms for double occupancy in beach huts cost $55 per person daily, with meals and classes included. Shared rooms holding up to six persons rent for $40 to $45 per person daily for bed, meals, and classes. If you bring your own tent, you are charged $30 per day, again with meals and classes. There are almost no single rooms available at the retreat. In high season (November to Easter in April), all units are usually booked, and since the policy of the retreat is to give as many individuals as possible the opportunity to participate in the yoga program, they prefer occupancy by two or more persons. In summer, there is more chance to obtain a single room. If you phone the ashram upon your arrival in Nassau, someone will pick you up at the Mermaid Dock there.

WILDLIFE PRESERVES: The Bahamas National Trust has under its protection several areas of the islands. Its aims are to conserve wildlife and aesthetic values, while maintaining recreation facilities and educating people in the need to protect and encourage the life on land and in water.

The **Exuma Cays Land and Sea Park,** a 176-square-mile preserve, is some 40 nautical miles from New Providence Island. Here you'll find good anchorages among the small islands, which are dedicated to boating, snorkeling, walking, and looking at the flora and fauna of the land and sea. More than 40 species of birds indigenous to The Bahamas and many migratory birds have been reported in the park. Strict laws allow fishing, with limitations on the number of conchs, crayfish, and other sea creatures that may be brought in.

The National Trust is also in charge of **Inagua Park,** which encompasses some 300 square miles of nesting area of flamingos; Peterson Cay off Grand Bahama; and Abaco's Pelican Cays. The breeding ground of an endangered species, the Bahamian parrot, is protected in a woodland area of Abaco. A stop-off for migratory birds and a breeding ground for turtles is maintained near Rum Cay, at Conception Island.

The Ministry of Agriculture, Fisheries and Local Government is also in the business of protecting certain sites on land and at sea.

A TRAVEL COMPANION: A recent American census showed that 77 million Americans over 15 years of age are single. However, the travel industry is far better geared for double occupancy of hotel rooms. One company that has made heroic efforts to match single travelers with like-minded companions is now the largest and best such company in the United States. Jens Jurgen, the German-born founder, charges $29 to $66 for a six-month listing in his well-publicized records. New applicants desiring a travel companion fill out a form stating their preferences and needs. They then receive a mini-listing of the kinds of potential partners who might be suitable for travel. Companions of the same or opposite sex can be requested. Because of the large number of listings, success is often a reality. For an application and more information, write to Jens Jurgen, **Travel Companion,** Box P-833 Amityville, NY 11701 (tel. 516/454-0880).

CHAPTER VII

A PREVIEW OF THE BAHAMAS

□ □ □

After George Washington visited the Bahama Islands, he wrote that they were the "Isles of Perpetual June," and I can't improve on that capsule comment by the first president of the United States.

Today the 760-mile-long chain of islands, cays, and reefs collectively called The Bahamas, is designated by many as the playground of the Western world and "the South Sea Islands of the Atlantic." The chain stretches from Grand Bahama Island, whose western point is almost due east of Palm Beach, Florida, about 75 miles away, and Great Inagua, southernmost of The Bahamas, lying some 60 miles northeast of Cuba and less than 100 miles north of Haiti. (The self-proclaimed Haitian king, Henri Christophe, is believed to have built a summer palace here in the early 19th century.)

There are 700 of these islands, many of which bear the name *cay,* pronounced *key.* (*Cay* is the Spanish word for small island.) Some, such as Andros, Grand Bahama, Abaco, Eleuthera, Cat Island, and Long Island, are fairly large, while others are tiny enough to seem crowded if more than two persons visit at a time.

Rising out of the Bahama Banks, a 70,000-square-mile area of shoals and broad elevations of the sea floor where the water is relatively shallow, The Bahamas are flat, low-lying islands. Some are no more than 10 feet above sea level at the highest point, with Mount Alvernia on Cat Island holding the height record at just over 200 feet. In most places the warm, shallow water is so clear as to allow an easy view of the bottom, although cuts and channels are deep. The Tongue of the Ocean between Andros and the Exumas, for example, has depths of many thousands of feet.

1. THE BAHAMAS—THEN AND NOW

A SHORT HISTORY: The shallow waters of the Bahama Banks are believed to be the basis of the name of the island chain. After Columbus made his first landfall in the New World somewhere in The Bahamas, subsequently visiting elsewhere in the archipelago in his futile hunt for the Indies and China, Ponce de León voyaged here looking for the legendary Fountain of Youth. This journey, incidentally, led to the European discovery of Florida and the Gulf Stream but not the magic fountain. The historian for Ponce de León described the waters of the Little Bahama Bank—just north of Grand Bahama—as *bajamar* (pronounced bahamar) Spanish for shallow water. This seems a reasonable source of the name Bahamas.

It was Columbus, landing on October 12, 1492, who met the island residents, Arawak Indians called Lucayans. He renamed the island, which its inhabitants called Guanahani, declaring it to be San Salvador. Over the years there has been much dispute as to just which island this was. Long ago, it was decided that the discoverer's first landfall in the New World was a place known as Watling Island, supposedly after one of the buccaneers of the freebooters' era, and the name of that spot of land was changed (back?) to San Salvador in 1926. Recent obviously well-founded claims, however, place the first landing on Samana Cay, 65 miles southeast of San Salvador. In 1986, *National Geographic* propounded and supported this island as the true Columbus landfall, calling it "a small outrider to the sea lying in haunting isolation in the far eastern Bahamas."

The Lucayans who lived in the archipelago are believed to have emigrated here in about the 8th century A.D. from the Greater Antilles (but originally from South America), seeking refuge from the savage Carib Indians then living in the Lesser Antilles. The Lucayans were peaceful people. They welcomed the Spaniards and taught them a skill soon shared with the entire seagoing world—the making of hammocks from heavy cotton cloth. Sailors adapted the swings to shipboard use as beds.

The Spanish who claimed the Bahamian islands for their king and queen did not repay the Lucayans kindly. They did not even establish any settlements on the verdant cays surrounded by clear, warm waters. Finding neither gold nor silver mines nor fertile soil, the conquistadors simply cleared the islands of the Indians, taking some 40,000 doomed Lucayans to other islands in New Spain to work mines or dive for pearls. References to the islands first discovered by Columbus are almost nil after that time for about the next 135 years. They appear somewhat sketchily on maps, but the only actual written mention of the area is when King Ferdinand sent Ponce de León in the early 16th century "to find and settle the island of Bimini," where Indian legend placed a fountain of perpetual youth.

England formally claimed The Bahamas, by then destitute of population, in 1629, beginning with a succession of grants by Charles I and Charles II to territories in America and "Bahama and all other Isles and Islands lying southerly there or nearer upon the foresayd continent." Until 1717 the islands were governed by appointees of the lord proprietors given the king's grants. No settlement took place, however, until the 1640s, and it resulted from religious disputes that arose in Bermuda as in England. A group called the Company of Eleutherian Adventurers was formed in London "for the Plantation of the Islands of Eleutheria, formerly called Buhama in America, and the Adjacent Islands."

English and Bermudan settlers sailed to an island called Cigatoo, changed the name to Eleuthera (from the Greek word for freedom), and launched a tough battle for survival. Many became discouraged and went back to Bermuda, but a few hardy souls hung on, living on the products of the sea—fish, ambergris, shipwreck salvage, and whaling.

Other people from Bermuda and England followed the Eleutherian Adventurers, and New Providence Island (first named Sayle's Island for the Eleutherians' leader) was settled in 1656. Crops of cotton, tobacco, and sugarcane were soon being grown, with Charles Towne, honoring Charles II, being established at the harbor. The promising agricultural economy was short-lived. Several governors of The Bahamas of that era were corrupt, and soon the islands became a refuge for buccaneers. These were English, Dutch, and French seafaring

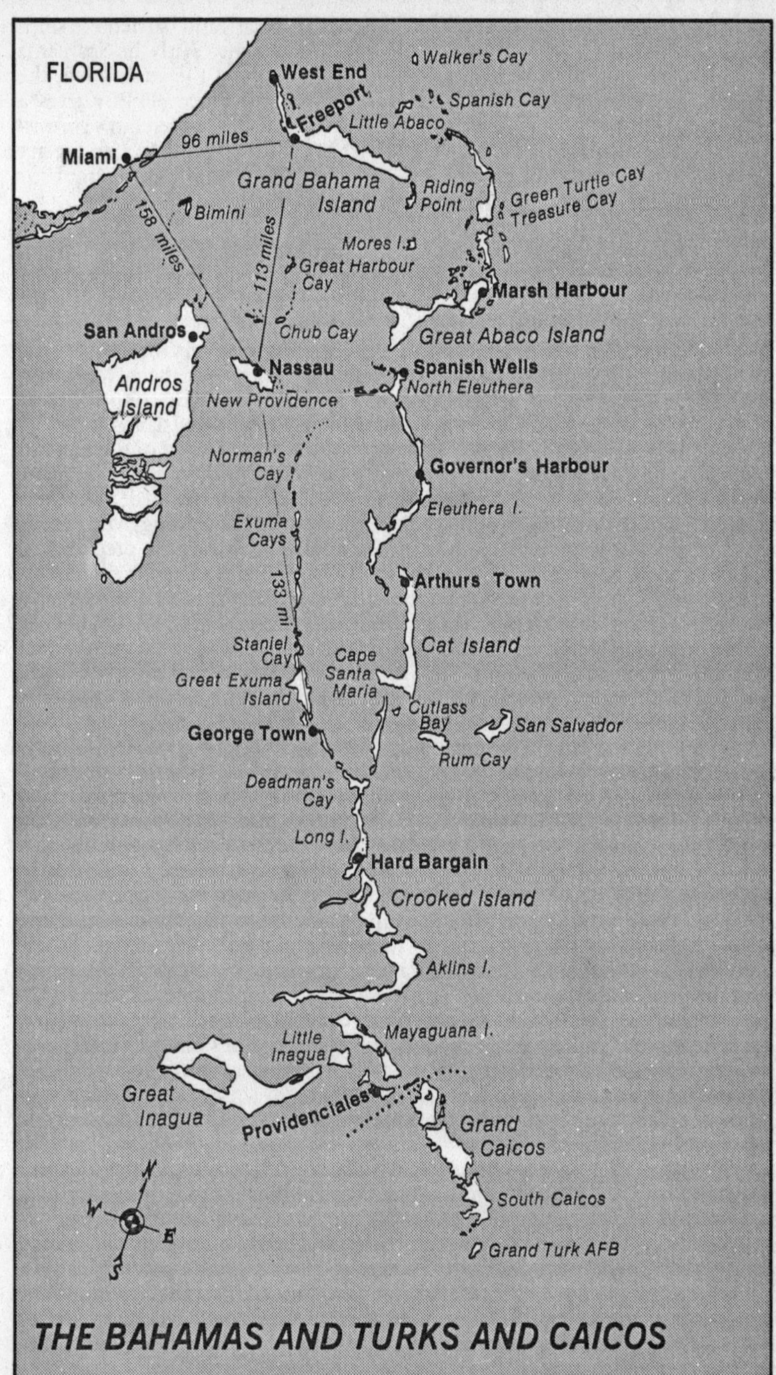
FLORIDA
Miami
96 miles
158 miles
113 miles
133 mi
West End
Freeport
Walker's Cay
Spanish Cay
Little Abaco
Grand Bahama Island
Riding Point
Green Turtle Cay
Treasure Cay
Bimini
Mores I.
Great Harbour Cay
Marsh Harbour
Chub Cay
Great Abaco Island
San Andros
Andros Island
Nassau
New Providence
Spanish Wells
North Eleuthera
Norman's Cay
Governor's Harbour
Eleuthera I.
Exuma Cays
Arthurs Town
Cat Island
Staniel Cay
Great Exuma Island
Cape Santa Maria
Cutlass Bay
George Town
San Salvador
Rum Cay
Deadman's Cay
Long I.
Hard Bargain
Crooked Island
Aklins I.
Little Inagua
Mayaguana I.
Great Inagua
Providenciales
Grand Caicos
South Caicos
Grand Turk AFB
N
W
E
S
THE BAHAMAS AND TURKS AND CAICOS

adventurers who organized as the "Brethren of the Coast" and harried the ships of Spain, which thought it controlled the seas at that time. With the Spaniards repeatedly ravaging New Providence for revenge, many of the settlers left, the remainder apparently finding the pirates a good source of income. Privateers, a slightly more respectable type of freebooters (they had their sovereign's permission to prey on enemy ships), also found the many islets, tricky shoals, and secret harbors of the Bahama Islands to be good hiding places from which to stage their forays on ships sailing between the New and Old Worlds.

Late in the 17th century the name of Charles Towne was changed to Nassau at the instigation of the governor and inhabitants, to honor King William III, then on the British throne, who also had the title of Prince of Nassau (a former German province). But the name change didn't ease the troubled capital, as some 1,000 pirates still called New Providence their home base.

Finally the appeals of merchants and law-abiding islanders for Crown control was heard, and in 1717 the lord proprietors turned over the government, both civil and military, of The Bahamas to King George I, who commissioned Capt. Woodes Rogers as the first royal governor of the Bahama Islands.

Rogers got rid of the pirates. A former privateer in the War of the Spanish Succession, he dealt harshly with the lawless marauders of the sea, seizing many hundreds. Some were sent to England to be tried. Eight were hanged, and others received the king's pardon, promising thereafter to lead law-abiding lives. Rogers was later given authority to set up a representative assembly, the precursor of today's Parliament of the Commonwealth of The Bahamas. Despite such interruptions as the capture of Nassau by the fledgling U.S. Navy in 1776 (over in a few days) and the surrender of the Crown Colony to Spain in 1782 (of almost a year's duration), the government of The Bahamas since Rogers's time has been conducted in an orderly fashion. The Spanish matter was settled in early 1783 in the Peace of Versailles, when Spain permanently ceded The Bahamas to Britain, ending some 300 years of disputed ownership.

Following the American Revolution, several thousand Loyalists from the former colonies emigrated to The Bahamas. Some of these, especially southerners, brought their black slaves with them and tried their luck at planting sea island cotton in the Out Islands, as the land masses other than New Providence were called. Cotton growing was not a lasting success as the plants fell prey to the chenille bug, but by then the former Deep South planters had learned to fish, grow vegetables, and by other means provide for their families and servants.

The first white settlers of The Bahamas had also brought slaves with them, and the early years of the 19th century saw dissension as to the treatment of those in bondage, ending in the United Kingdom Emancipation Act in 1834, which freed the slaves and provided for the government to compensate the former owners for their property loss. A fairly peaceful transition was achieved, although it was many years before any real equality of blacks and whites was discernible.

For a number of years wrecking was a profitable industry in The Bahamas—its unmarked shoals and reefs became graves for many ships. But the erection of lighthouses along major shipping lanes and the issuance of accurate charts made this unprofitable after the 1860s.

The War Between the States, or Civil War, in America brought a transient prosperity to The Bahamas through blockade running. Nassau became a vital base for the Confederacy, with shallow-draft vessels taking manufactured goods to Charleston, S.C., and Wilmington, N.C., and bringing out cotton. Union ships were banned from island harbors, even to take on drinking water. The victory of the Union ended blockade running and plunged Nassau into economic depression. Some Americans who had supported the Confederacy emigrated to The Bahamas after their cause was lost, many bringing their slaves with them, even though they were forced to make the blacks free on arrival.

The next real boom enjoyed by the islands through troubles of their American neighbor was that engendered by U.S. Prohibition. As with the blockade runners—but this time with faster boats and more of them—rum-runners churned the waters between The Bahamas and the southeastern United States. From passage of the 18th Amendment in 1919 to repeal of that law in 1933, Nassau, Bimini, and Grand Bahama were used as bases for running contraband alcoholic beverages across the Gulf Stream to assuage the thirst of Americans. The Coast Guard and the new generation of freebooters battled ceaselessly over the years and the seas. Repeal saw another shattering blow to the Bahamian economy.

World War II healed the wounds of the bootlegging days, as The Bahamas served as an air and sea way-station in the Atlantic. From this, they inherited two airports built for U.S. Air Force use during hostilities with the Germans. The islands were of strategic importance when Nazi submarines intruded into the Atlantic coastal and Caribbean waters. Today U.S. missile-tracking stations exist on some of the outlying islands.

In recent years a new and sinister problem has arisen for the United States through its proximity to The Bahamas—drug smuggling. The same shoal waters, narrow inlets, and small, uninhabited islands that provided safe havens for pirates, blockade runners, and rum-runners are now used for drug transport, with modern, small airfields compounding the problem. The U.S. Coast Guard is diligently pursuing the almost-impossible goal of ending this menace. Unfortunately the Bahamian government has neither the manpower nor the money to police the 70,000 square miles of its domain, so this is an ongoing trouble.

ECONOMY: Despite many efforts over the decades since the Eleutherian Adventurers first settled in The Bahamas, it has only been in this century that a seemingly lasting and lucrative economic base has been discovered—tourism. Earlier entrepreneurs had a vision of this possibility, and the first positive step was taken in 1860 when the Royal Victoria Hotel was built in Nassau for winter visitors. The early years of this hostelry's existence, however, saw it filled with blockade runners and their cohorts, who made its corridors ring with their spirited high jinks and then left it to silence and empty rooms when the Civil War ended. Henry Flagler, who was so successful with his posh hotels and his railroad construction to transport guests to them in Florida, tried to establish a steamer link with Nassau, built a hotel here, and failed. A few wealthy Canadians and Americans found their way to what they enjoyed as a winter paradise, but they weren't much interested in seeing The Bahamas become a lure for just anybody who could afford to come.

After World War II, tourism in The Bahamas really began to catch on. Since that time it has grown fantastically, not just in Nassau but throughout the archipelago, with nearly three million visitors coming here annually. United States and Canadian residents top the list, but thousands come from England, Germany, France, wherever, to this year-round tourist mecca. Sunshine, soft breezes, casino gambling, water sports—these and more draw visitors. The capital of the Commonwealth, Nassau, is a city of old charm and modern resorts, and the second major tourist destination is Freeport/Lucaya, with its casino and plush resorts on Grand Bahama Island. Many North Americans flock to both places in summer or winter, as they lie less than an hour's flight from the United States.

Only a few Bahamian products are suitable for export, such as salt, frozen crawfish (Florida lobster), pulpwood, and vegetables. There is a favorable banking structure, which has proved attractive to investors.

THE PEOPLE: No descendants of the early inhabitants of The Bahamas, the Lucayans (Arawak Indians), survive A few of today's Bahamians can trace their ancestry back to the Eleutherian Adventurers, others to Loyalists of American Revolution times and to southern Americans who fled after the Civil War, all of which brought slaves to the islands. Some Bahamians of today can claim descent from pirates and privateers. Of the overall population of some 200,000 people, blacks are in the great majority, holding positions of leadership in all areas.

The language of The Bahamas is English. Bahamians speak it with a lilt and with more British Isles influence than American. There are some words left from the Arawak Indian tongue (like *cassava* and *guava*), and African words and phrases add to the colorful speech patterns.

THE FAMILY ISLANDS: These are islands scattered like pearls in the Atlantic, that part of the long Bahamian archipelago which has only gradually been awakening from a long somnolence in the subtropical and tropical sun and begun to play a part in the drama of tourism developing throughout their country.

For centuries these bits of land lying varying distances away from New Providence and the Bahamian capital were called the Out Islands. However, in recent years, perhaps with the aim of making them feel more a part of what is now a nation, The Bahamas, the government has changed the appellation to Family Islands. With modern transportation methods—airplanes, helicopters, and speedier boats—and with modern communications systems, the former Out Islands no longer seem so far out of the mainstream of everyday life in The Bahamas.

Many of these areas have already become the homes of modern resorts. Airstrips provide lifelines once supplied only by the infrequent mailboat runs from Nassau. All the major island chains are now serviced by regularly scheduled airplane flights, some from Nassau and Freeport/Lucaya, others from such Florida cities as Miami, Fort Lauderdale, and West Palm Beach. Of course, if you're of a mind to flip back the calendar, you can still take the mailboat or one of the inter-island passenger ferries. (See "Getting Around The Bahamas" in ChapterVI.)

The islands come in every conceivable shape and size. Often they're fringed with sandy beaches and coral reefs, and hundreds of them are deserted or have no permanent residents. Swimming, boating, snorkeling, diving, and fishing here are considered by many to be the best in the world.

Many of the characteristics associated with The Bahamas of old are still preserved in the Family Islands, with their sleepy villages of pastel and whitewashed clapboard houses, a number of which were built by Loyalists who fled here during and just after the American Revolution. People move more slowly in the Family Islands, and you can soon realize that they're right when they ask what there is to be in a hurry about.

Relaxation is the keynote, and it is this, plus the boon of sunny days, waters teeming with sea life, and languid moonlight nights cooled by the trade winds, that has drawn the attention of more and more tourists to the Family Islands.

Each island or small chain has its own character, ranging from the oldtime boatbuilding centers of the Abacos to the flaming-red flamingos of remote Inagua. Therefore it's necessary to read the descriptions of the resorts referred to to find one compatible with your interests. Often you'll find yourself in almost a "house party" situation or in an isolated outpost, so it's important to seek out places where you're likely to fit in with the crowd—or be pleased with the lack of crowds.

An important consideration for any visitor planning to tour the Family Islands is the welcome he or she can expect from the local inhabitants. Hospitality is part of the lifestyle in these islands, and the reception here is almost sure to be far more open and charming than what you can expect in Nassau or Freeport/ Lucaya. The Family Islanders in general are a warm people.

In further chapters in this guide, I will review the inhabited Family Islands and give you a selection of vacation possibilities, ranging from lively resorts complete with nightlife and organized activities, to comfortable but simple guesthouses and cottages in out-of-the-way places.

GOVERNMENT: The Commonwealth of The Bahamas came into being in 1973, becoming the world's 143rd sovereign state, with a ministerial form of government and a bicameral legislature. The end to some 250 years of colonial rule was signaled in 1964 when The Bahamas was granted internal self-government pending drafting of a constitution, adopted in 1969. By choice, the island nation did not completely sever its ties with Great Britain, preferring to remain in the Commonwealth of Nations with the British monarch as its head of state. The queen appoints a Bahamian governor-general to represent the Crown.

In the British tradition, The Bahamas has a two-house Parliament, a ministerial cabinet headed by a prime minister, and an independent judiciary.

SPORTS: The 700 islands in the Bahamian archipelago—fewer than 30 of them inhabited—are surrounded by gin-clear waters, ideal for fishing, sailing, and scuba-diving holidays.

Fishing begins at Bimini, about 50 miles from Miami, Florida, and goes all the way to Great Inagua, southernmost Bahamian island on the northern edge of the Caribbean. You can try your hand at fly fishing, deep-sea fishing, and shore fishing, with all the variations of each. If you are skillful enough, you may want to participate in the fishing tournaments that abound.

Among the catches, large and small, that you can hook into there are tuna, bonefish, marlin, grouper, dolphin(the fish), sailfish, kingfish, amberjack, barracuda, and even the lowly grunt. Charter boats and guides are available at most of the resort islands.

Boating in The Bahamas, whether you bring your own craft or charter one, is great. Getting out on the water—by motor or sail—is a way of life here. Good marinas and yacht clubs are found all over. You can usually rent boats to travel around the islands. Motorboats, sloops, speedy catamarans, even rowboats are available at most docks and waterfront resorts.

Parasailing and **waterskiing** are enjoyed at many places in the Bahamian Islands.

Deep or shallow **diving** in the unpolluted, warm waters is an experience most visitors find memorable. Snorkeling and scuba-diving open up a beautiful new world of undersea life, along coral reefs or amid the remnants of wrecked ships. Equipment for these activities and expert training are offered at dive centers, clubs, shops, hotels, and marinas.

Swimming is available in many hotel pools, although most visitors prefer the warm waters off sun-drenched, sandy beaches.

Golf facilities range from 9- to 18-hole courses and are found from Grand Bahama and New Providence to the Family Islands where resorts have been built. You can play year-round.

Some of the best **tennis** in the world is found in The Bahamas. Almost all those islands that have tourist facilities have tennis courts connected with one hotel or more. Many are lit for night playing.

FESTIVALS: Bahamians believe in having a good time, and they have a variety of holidays during which great festivities are carried on. (See a complete listing under "Holidays" in the ABCs section, below.) The outstanding national celebration is **Junkanoo,** held on Boxing Day, December 26, and New Year's Day.

Junkanoo begins two or three hours before dawn on both days, when the goatskin drums begin to throb, with shak-shak gourds, cowbells, lignum vitae sticks, horns, and whistles adding to the beat of African rhythms. A carnival of cavorting, crêpe-paper-costumed figures prances through the Nassau streets, the Freeport/Lucaya bazaars, and on the Family Islands beaches and narrow lanes. Elaborate headdresses and imaginative, fringed masquerade apparel are worn by throngs of men, women, and children.

Junkanoo is believed to have come down through the centuries from West Africa and the Ivory and Gold Coasts where free people celebrated their festivals. In slavery, they kept the tradition alive for a long time, although changes crept in. The observance, attacked by Christian clergymen and missionaries, died out among American and Caribbean slaves, but Bahamian blacks have preserved the custom.

Authorities differ on the origin of the name Junkanoo, but the general belief is that it derives from John Canoe, a West African folk hero reputed to have presided over tribal rituals as master of the revels. He is supposed to have worn wild costumes and masks at the festivals, while fellow tribesmen danced around him and made loud noises.

Whatever the truth is, the Junkanoos of The Bahamas celebrate the African heritage in music, dancing, and costumes. Visitors and townspeople alike share in this holiday fun. Mini-Junkanoos in which visitors can participate are regular events.

The **Goombay Summer Festival** incorporates the sounds of Junkanoo and the rhythm of Goombay in a round-the-clock celebration for the enjoyment of summer visitors. Goombay is a word derived from the Bantu language of the Kongo people of the lower Congo River. Their *nkumbi* ceremonial drum gave the Bahamians the word, which is now applied to calypso music as it developed in the islands. The date of the Goombay Festival varies, so check with the Bahamas Tourist Office nearest you (see "Tourist Information" in the ABCs section, below) or with your travel agent.

Independence week is marked throughout the islands by festivities, parades, and fireworks in July to celebrate the independence of the Commonwealth of The Bahamas, with the focal point being **Independence Day,** July 10.

Emancipation Day is a public holiday on the first Monday in August, when the freeing of the slaves is commemorated in all The Bahamas. But there's another emancipation celebration, **Fox Hill Day,** observed in Nassau. Because of their isolation from the day-to-day life of Bay Street to its west, the people of Fox Hill, now the east section of Nassau, didn't get the word that they were free until some days after the official date. Therefore Fox Hill Day is celebrated on the second Tuesday of August.

October 12 is the date the history of the New World began with the landing of Christopher Columbus on an island the Arawak Indian residents called Guanahani, which the explorer renamed San Salvador. This date is marked annually throughout The Bahamas as **Discovery Day.** San Salvador has a parade on that day.

Other festive events are an **Easter Egg hunt** in Nassau and **Guy Fawkes Day** on or around November 5. Nighttime parades through the streets are held on many of the islands, culminating in the hanging and burning of the Guy, an effigy of the British malefactor who was involved in the Gunpowder Plot of 1605 in London. The effigy is hauled through the streets in a wheelbarrow or carried by festival participants for a long parade before being taken to the funeral pyre prepared for him earlier.

FLORA AND FAUNA: In this gentle climate, a staggering number of plants abound. At least 34 vegetables grow here, ranging from potatoes, corn, beans, and broccoli to more exotic-sounding produce such as eddoe, cho-cho, and breadfruit. To read a list of the flora found in the islands is like dipping into a botany textbook on tropical and subtropical plants. It would be impossible to name them all in this guide. Suffice it to say that among the more common are 53 trees, 29 shrubs, 21 climbers and vines, 3 grasses, 3 lilies, 1 tuberous plant, 2 succulents, 43 fruit trees, 4 fruit vines, and 6 herbs, in addition to the array of vegetables. At least those are the ones I was able to identify. If you count more—or less—I won't argue. Note that most of these plants are not indigenous to The Bahamas. My count paled into insignificance when I was told there are 950 naturalized and native flowering plants and ferns in the islands, plus 7 indigenous palm trees.

The Bahamas are deficient in mammals, most having been exterminated early in the islands' history. Hutia, a rat-like rodent found only on Atwood Cay, is the only native mammal found today. It was once thought to be extinct. There are donkeys, hogs, and horses in Abaco and cattle in Inagua, and bats are common throughout the archipelago.

Special mention should be made of the Bahamian iguana, which is considered rare or endangered. One of the reasons for this is that since the days of the Lucayan Indians until modern times, the iguana was considered a food delicacy. However, David Blair, founder of Cyclura Research Center, which is dedicated to the conservation and captive propagation of West Indian rock iguanas, states, "The reason for their drastic decline in recent years is, in part, due to habitat loss, the introduction of domestic animals, and the attitude that anything that moves is fair game for food or just target practice."

Today the Bahamian iguana is protected by law. It is forbidden to capture or kill an iguana. Upon conviction, the penalty is a fine of up to $300 and/or imprisonment for a term not exceeding six months. Mr. Blair states that the three species of Bahamian iguanas belong to the genus Cyclura, and that some species of Cyclura are considered to be perhaps the rarest lizards on earth. His research has shown that virtually all iguanas on inhabited islands in The Bahamas have been exterminated and those few remaining are restricted to small uninhabited cays difficult to reach by private boat. He considers the iguana of San Salvador to be the most endangered, and states that the population there is believed to number less than 100 iguanas.

Of course, a vast amount of fish and other sea life thrives in Bahamian waters. A wealth of sports fish (many of them also edible) draws anglers to these islands, so that season limitations have been placed on some. Fishermen seek out tuna—Allison, blackfin, and bluefin or giant. Other coveted denizens of the deep or not-so-deep waters around The Bahamas are white marlin, wahoo, bonefish, dolphin(the fish), tarpon, sailfish, barracuda, amberjack, blue marlin, kingfish, and grouper. Strict prohibitions control the taking of sponges and turtles from Bahamian waters. A close eye is kept by the Ministry of Agriculture, Fisheries and Local Government on catches of crayfish (spiny lobster), and export of conch meat is prohibited. Stone crab cannot be caught within two miles off Bimini or Grand Bahama.

Birds come to The Bahamas from the United States, Cuba, and the Caribbean, but there are also a few indigenous species, such as the Bahamian swallow, the Bahamian parrot, and the woodstar hummingbird. Inagua National Park is a 287-square-mile bird sanctuary, where the flamingo breeding ground has a population of up to 40,000 birds, including reddish egrets and roseate spoonbills. The mangrove swamps of The Bahamas are visited by cattle egrets and various species of herons, which are among migrants from America. You may also see the magnificent (that's part of its name) frigate bird from the tropics and the Caribbean, which sometimes soars as high as 8,000 feet.

Other birds you may observe in The Bahamas, some of which may be hunted in open season, are bobwhite quail, ring-necked pheasant, white-crowned pigeon, wood dove, mourning dove, whistling ducks, Bahama ducks, ruddy ducks, white jaw ducks, jack snipe, coot, chuckar partridge, Wilson's snipe, guinea fowl, and night herons, both black-crowned and yellow-crowned, as well as other migratory ducks and geese.

Among the less-desirable classes of animals, insects have their representatives. Mosquitos are normally bothersome only on the less-populated islands, but you might run into the pesky "no-seeum," a tiny insect that takes a big bite. However, you don't have to worry about poisonous snakes, because there aren't any.

2. FOOD AND DRINK

You're sitting in a plush restaurant reading a menu, and you spot radicchio di treviso alla Cesare listed. If any lettuce today could be called "chic," it is this red endive-like delight. You read on, taking in such gastronomic wonders as tagliatelle alla vodka, osso buco alla milanese, saltimbocca alla romana. Have you been suddenly transplanted from the sunny Bahamas to sunny Italy?

No, you're on Paradise Island, where escargots forestières and strip sirloin of beef Café de Paris are familiar fare in the deluxe restaurants and hotel dining spots.

Suddenly, on this same menu your eyes focus on Bahamian conch chowder. It rests somewhere between the printed lines touting lobster bisque and chilled cream of avocado soup "with a hint of nutmeg."

You realize there is a Bahamian cuisine after all. But except for this continental-inspired chef's one concession to his native cuisine, you will sometimes have to leave the deluxe hostelries of Freeport/Lucaya, New Providence (Nassau and Cable Beach), or Paradise Island to find it. Once you reach the Family Islands, it's a different story. Of course, they too have continental chefs, along with their beef Wellington and crêpes Suzette, but in many places, especially at the little local restaurants previewed in this guide, you get to eat what the Bahamians eat.

To put it bluntly, the Bahamian cook is a thief. By that, I mean the local cooks not only borrowed from the Caribbean cultures to the south (to which their cuisine has a similarity), but they have also taken whatever "tasted good" from the kitchens of the United States, Great Britain and other European countries, and Africa. The Bahamian imagination came into play when they couldn't get hard-to-obtain items that were prevalent in the countries where the recipes originated.

Therefore the Bahamian cooks had to adapt these recipes to what was available locally, and in so doing they developed their own natural talents and ingenuity. The end result is what is called "Bahamian flavor."

THE UBIQUITOUS CONCH: In Nassau, as well as in Freeport, there are many small, local places serving a Bahamian cuisine that is very similar to the fare offered in the Family Islands. In honor of the nation's cookery skills, I have lifted forks on many occasions in the best of these, and perhaps you will too. Economy is just one of the reasons. That $50 dinner on Paradise Island becomes only $15 at the Bahamian Kitchen once you traverse the bridge, heading back to Nassau.

Conch (pronounced konk) is the national food of The Bahamas. The firm white meat of this mollusk—called "the snail of the sea"—is enjoyed throughout the islands. Actually, its taste is somewhat bland, but not when Bahamian chefs finish with it. Locals eat it as a snack (usually served at happy hour in taverns and bars), as a main dish, as a salad, or as an hors d'oeuvre. So far, to my knowledge, it hasn't been made into a dessert.

The Pacific coast resident will look upon it as having the taste of abalone. The conch does not have a fishy taste, like halibut, and it has a chewy consistency, which means that a chef must pound it to tenderize it, the way one might pound Wiener schnitzel.

Every cook has a different recipe, or so it would seem, for making conch chowder. A popular version includes tomatoes, potatoes, sweet peppers, onions, carrots, salt pork or bacon, bay leaf, thyme, and of course, salt and pepper. One local woman cook in Eleuthera revealed to me her secret for conch chowder. She uses a bit of barbecue sauce and poultry seasoning instead of the usual spices.

Conch fritters, shaped like balls, are served with hot sauce, and are made with finely minced sweet peppers, onions, and tomato paste, among other ingredients. Like most fritters, they are deep-fried in oil.

Conch salad is another local favorite, and again it has many variations. Essentially, it is uncooked conch that has been marinated in "Old Sour" to break down its tissues and to add extra flavor. It is served with diced small red (or green) peppers, along with chopped onion. The taste is tangy.

Cracked conch (or fried conch, as the oldtimers used to call it) is like a breaded veal cutlet in preparation. Pounded hard and dipped in batter, it is then sautéed. Conch is also served steamed, in a Créole sauce, curried, "scorched," creamed on toast, and stewed. Instead of conch chowder, you might get conch soup. You'll also see "conchburgers" listed on menus, including that of the Palms Restaurant in Nassau.

Even after you've eaten conch, there are two more advantages to the mollusk: its chewy meat is said to have aphrodisiac powers, and if not that, then you can take along the delicate pink-lined shell as a souvenir of your stay in The Bahamas.

The shell of the conch also makes a fine piece of jewelry, as you'll see as you stroll through the shops along Bay Street in Nassau. Even the Queen of England has been photographed wearing her matching set of conch pearl earrings and a necklace from The Bahamas.

MORE FROM THE SOUP KETTLE: Ranking next to conch chowder in popularity is Bahamian fish chowder. Again, this tasty soup can be prepared in any number of ways. Oldtime Bahamian chefs tell me that it's best when made with grouper. To that they add celery, onions, tomatoes, and an array of flavorings that might include A-1 sauce (or Worcestershire, or both), along with thyme, cooking sherry, a bit of dark rum, and lime juice. To thicken the soup, one chef I know uses a layer of Crown Pilot chowder crackers, which he puts along with sliced potatoes at the bottom of his stew kettle. Hot pepper is added to taste.

Increasingly rare these days, turtle soup was for years a mainstay of the Family Islands (called "Out Islands" back then). Turtle soup and other turtle dishes still appear on some local menus. However, if you have alternatives, it would be better to choose another dish. Turtles are considered an endangered species by environmentalists.

They are rare and endangered precisely because they are a favorite food of islanders and tourists. Add the pressures of habitat destruction and it becomes clear why turtles are in trouble. We of the industrialized West have such a variety of foods from which to choose that we can afford to pass up some items. If we can also work to preserve natural habitat, we might save an ancient, important, and interesting animal.

OTHER FRUITS OF THE SEA: The most expensive item you'll see on nearly any menu in The Bahamas is the spiny local lobster. A tropical cousin of the Maine lobster, it is also called crayfish or "rock lobster." Only the tail is eaten, however. You get fresh lobster only when it's in season, from the first of April until the end of August. Otherwise it's frozen.

Bahamian lobster, in spite of its cost, is not always prepared well. Sometimes a cook leaves it in the oven for too long, and the meat becomes tough and chewy. But when prepared right, such as is done by the famed Graycliff Restaurant in Nassau, it is perfection and worth the exorbitant cost.

The Bahamian lobster lends itself to any international recipe for lobster, including Newburg or Thermidor. It can also be served in a typical local style: curried with lime juice and fresh coconut, among other ingredients.

After conch, grouper is the second most consumed fish in The Bahamas. It's served in a number of ways, often batter-dipped, sautéed, and called "fingers" because of the way it's sliced.

At Family Island inns, you sometimes must decide by noon what you'll want for dinner, since supplies are limited. I've been asked several times "How do you want your grouper done?" It was just assumed that I'd be ordering grouper.

The fish is often steamed and served in a spicy Créole sauce. Sometimes it comes dressed in a sauce of dry white wine, mushrooms, onions, and such seasonings as thyme. Because the fish has a mild taste, the extra flavor of the other ingredients is needed.

Baked bonefish is also common, and it's very simple to prepare. The bonefish is split in half and seasoned with a hot pepper sauce, "Old Sour," and salt, then popped into the oven to bake until ready.

Baked crab is one of the best-known dishes of The Bahamas. A chef mixes the eggs and meat of both land or sea crabs with seasonings and breadcrumbs. The crabs are then replaced in their shells and baked.

You'll also encounter yellowtail, "goggle eyes," jacks, snapper, grunts, and margot, plus many more sea creatures.

PEAS 'N' RICE AND JOHNNYCAKE: If mashed potatoes are still the "national starch" of America, then peas 'n' rice perform that role in The Bahamas. Peas 'n' rice, like mashed potatoes themselves, can be prepared in a number of ways. A popular method is cooking pigeon peas, which grow on pods on small trees (or else black-eyed peas) with salt pork, tomatoes, celery, uncooked rice, thyme, green pepper, onion, salt, pepper, and whatever special touch a chef wants to add. When served as a side dish, Bahamians most often sprinkle hot sauce over the concoction.

Johnnycake, another famed part of the Bahamian table, dates from the early settlers, who most often were simple folk and usually poor. They existed mainly on a diet of fish and rice, supplemented by johnnycake. This is a pan-cooked bread made with butter, milk, flour, sugar, salt, and baking powder. (Originally it was called "Journey Cake," which was eventually corrupted to johnnycake.) Fishermen could make this simple bread on the decks of their fishing vessels. They'd build a fire in a box that had been filled with sand to keep the flames from spreading to the craft.

BIRDS AND BOARS AND WHATEVER: Chicken is grown locally in The Bahamas, especially in Eleuthera. A popular method of cooking it is to make "chicken souse." This is a dish made with chicken, onion, sweet peppers, bay leaves, allspice, and other ingredients left up to a cook's imagination. It's simmered in a pot for about an hour, then lime juice is added and it's simmered a little longer. Pig's feet souse is also a favorite dish. Naturally, the souse in whatever variety of meat or fowl is served with johnnycake.

Goats and sheep are also raised in the Family Islands. Somehow either meat on a menu appears as "mutton," and it's often curried.

Wild boar is caught on some of the Family Islands, and game birds such as ducks and pigeons are shot. Raccoon stew is also eaten.

Most meats, including pork, veal, and beef, are imported. However, even with these dishes, Bahamian cooks show their ingenuity by giving these meats interesting variations. For example, at a Family Island inn, I recently enjoyed pork that had been marinated with vinegar, garlic, onion, celery tops, cloves, mustard, and Worcestershire sauce, then baked and served with gravy. Even a simple baked ham is given a Bahamian touch with the addition of fresh pineapple, coconut milk, and coconut flakes, along with mustard, honey, and brown sugar.

Many vegetables are grown in The Bahamas; others are imported. If it's a cucumber, you can be almost certain it's from one of Edison Key's farms in North Abaco. They not only supply cucumbers to their own country, but it's estimated that they have captured about 5% of the Stateside market for that vegetable as well.

Bahamians also grow their own sweet potatoes, corn, cassava, along with okra and peppers (both sweet and hot), among other produce.

GUAVA DUFF: Guava duff is the dessert specialty of The Bahamas, although one woman cook confided to me, "It takes too long, and we don't like to make it anymore unless there's a special call for it."

The dessert, resembling a jelly-roll, is made with guava pulp that has been run through a food mill or sieve. Nobody seems to agree on the best method of cooking it. One way is to cream sugar and butter and add eggs and such spices as cinnamon and cloves, or nutmeg. The flour is made into a stiff dough and mixed with the guava pulp, which is then placed in the top of a double boiler and cooked over boiling water for hours. It can also be boiled or steamed, and there are those who insist it should be baked. The guava duff is served with hard sauce.

In addition to guava duff, there is a large array of other tasty desserts and breads, including coconut tarts, coconut jimmie, benne seed cakes, and potato bread.

TROPICAL FRUITS: Bahamians are especially fond of fruits, and they make inventive dishes out of them, including soursop ice cream or sapodilla pudding. Guavas are used to make their famous guava duff, which has already been previewed as a dessert. They also grow and enjoy their melons, pineapples, passion fruit, mangoes, and other varieties.

Perhaps their best-known fruit is the papaya, which is called pawpaw or "melon tree." It's made into a dessert or a chutney, or else eaten for breakfast in its natural state.

It's also used in many luncheon or dinner recipes. An old Bahamian custom of using papaya as a meat tenderizer has, at least since the '70s, invaded the nouvelle cuisine kitchens of North America.

Papaya is also used to make fruity tropical drinks such as a Bahama Mama shake.

And if you see it for sale in a local food store, take home some "Goombay" marmalade, made with papaya, pineapple, and green ginger.

THAT OL' DEBBIL RUM: Rum was known to the ancient Romans, even the ancient Chinese as far as that goes. But it is today mostly associated with the islands in the sun, stretching from The Bahamas to the Caribbean.

It's traced back to Columbus. From the Canary Islands, he brought sugarcane cuttings, which his men planted in Jamaica in 1494. These plantings took to Jamaican soil the way a fish does to water. It is said that slaves on plantations were the first to distill the molasses that led to the production of rum.

Although rum came north from Cuba and Jamaica, the people of The Bahamas quickly adopted it as their national alcoholic beverage. And using their imagination, they "invented" several local drinks, including the Yellow Bird, the Bahama Mama, and the Goombay Smash.

The Yellow Bird is made with crème de banana liqueur, Vat 19 rum, orange juice, pineapple juice, apricot brandy, and Galliano; whereas a Bahama Mama is made with Vat 19, citrus juice (perhaps pineapple as well), Bitters, a dash of nutmeg, Crème de Cassis, and a hint of Grenadine.

A favorite—and potent—libation, well suited to the tropical and subtropical climate of The Bahamas, is the Goombay Smash. I don't know the precise origin of this drink, but its fame seems to have spread from the Blue Bee Bar at New Plymouth, Green Turtle Cay, where "Miss Emily" for years concocted the tasty combination of rums and other ingredients. Miss Emily's version has three kinds of rum, and she was always reticent to say what all else. However, throughout the islands it is usually made with coconut rum, pineapple juice, lemon juice, Triple Sec, Vat 19, and a dash of simple syrup. Try it that way, and then go see if you like Miss Emily's better.

Nearly every bartender in the islands has his or her own version of a planter's punch. A classic recipe is to make it with lime juice, sugar, Vat 19, plus a dash of Bitters. It's usually served with a cherry and an orange slice. Bartenders in The Bahamas are also skilled at making daiquiris, especially the banana and strawberry varieties. The piña colada is firmly entrenched here, just as much as it is in the Caribbean.

In addition to these special rum and fruit-juice concoctions, the old standbys such as scotch, bourbon, gin, and vodka are also sold. Drinks in the Nassau and Freeport/Lucaya area tend to be expensive, however.

If you want a typically Bahamian liqueur, try Nassau Royale. Nassau Royale is used to make an increasingly famous drink, the C. C. Rider, which won an international contest in 1983. Other ingredients in this prize-winning drink include Canadian Club, apricot brandy, and pineapple juice, served with crushed ice.

Curiously enough, Bahamians are especially fond of ending a dinner with a small glass of Scotland's Drambuie. After the bottle is emptied, they retain it for use as a container for tropical flowers, because they like the bottle it comes in.

DRINKING WATER: The Bahamians don't need to post "Please Don't Drink the Water" signs, although in some outlying areas it might be in short supply. New Providence and Grand Bahama have ample pure water, filtered and chlorinated. In other islands, only Marsh Harbour on Abaco has chlorinated and piped water, but you will find potable water at all resorts. In addition, bottled water is available at all tourist facilities and at stores and supermarkets.

On many of the Family Islands, ever since the first settlers arrived, rainfall has been a main source of water for drinking and other household uses. This is caught and kept in the cisterns that most houses have. The roofs are white or very light in color. The drainpipe systems are such that the first of a rainfall washes off the roof impurities that may have gathered and runs off to the ground. After that cleansing, the remaining rain is piped into the cisterns. In this land of no factories and no polluted air, you can be sure it's safe to drink the water.

3. THE ABC'S OF THE BAHAMAS

The aim of this "grab bag" section—dealing with the minutiae of your stay—is to make your adjustment to the Bahamian way of life easier. It is maddening to have your trip marred by an incident that could have been avoided had you been tipped off earlier. To prevent this, I'll try to anticipate the addresses, data, and information that might come in handy on all manner of occasions.

A number of situations, such as a medical emergency, might arise during your vacation, and there are various customs, such as tipping, you'll need to know about. The desk personnel at your hotel are usually reliable dispensers of information. If you are staying at a guesthouse, especially on one of the smaller outlying islands, your host or hostess will probably be able to supply any information you need on that immediate vicinity.

Even with such help, however, the following summary of pertinent survival data may prove helpful, and I've included some information on topics you just might want to know something about.

Note: ABC-type data pertaining only to Nassau or to the Grand Bahama–Freeport/Lucaya area will be listed as "Practical Facts" under those entries in this book.

ACCOMMODATIONS: The Bahamas offers a wide selection of accommodations, ranging from small, private guesthouses where only lodging is available, to large luxury resorts, cottage colonies, housekeeping units, apartment hotels, and apartment cottage units. The subject of the Bahamian guesthouses, which are operated in several forms, has been explored in the introduction to this book.

Hotels vary in size and facilities, from deluxe (offering room service, planned activities, sports, shops, beauty salons, swimming pools, entertainment, even private beaches, golf courses, and tennis courts) to fairly simple hostelries (which still may have swimming pools, a restaurant, a bar, and sports activities). Apartments, either in a hotel format or as cottages, may have kitchens and sometimes maid service, but many do not have restaurant and bar facilities. Cottage colonies range from luxury type, surrounding a main clubhouse with a bar, lounge, and dining room, plus a private beach and/or swimming pool and sports facilities. These are designed to offer maximum privacy.

If you live in the United States or Canada, it's not recommended that you call one of the hotels in the Family Islands to confirm a hotel reservation. Service is spotty, and numbers are sometimes vague if they exist at all. In some cases you communicate with an island by use of a walkie-talkie. If you're not using a travel agent, then dial a toll-free number in Coral Gables, Florida, to reach the **Bahamas Reservation Service.** Dial from anywhere in the U.S. by calling 800/327-0787. If you live in Miami, dial 443-3821. Canadians should dial ZE9-9110. The service is a fully computerized reservation system that provides instant confirmation and confirmed reservation vouchers for all hotels throughout The Bahamas. Call anytime from 9 a.m. to 7 p.m. weekdays, from 9:30 a.m. to 2:30 p.m. on Saturday, Eastern Time.

AMERICAN EXPRESS: Representing American Express in The Bahamas are **Playtours,** Shirley Street, Nassau (tel. 809/322-2931), and **Mundytours,** Block 4 Regent Centre, Suite 20, Freeport (tel. 809/352-4444). At either of these offices you can receive assistance with all American Express services including customer services, cardmember personal check cashing, traveler's check sales and refunds, emergency card replacement, and all travel and tour arrangements. Hours are 9 a.m. to 5 p.m. Monday to Friday. Traveler's checks are issued upon presentation of a personal check and an American Express card.

BABYSITTERS: At the larger resort hotels and in Nassau, Cable Beach, and Freeport/Lucaya, your hotel desk will help you arrange for the services of a reliable person to stay with your child or children while you are absent. At practically every accommodation in the Family Islands, you'll find it easy to secure someone for this purpose by simply asking your host or hostess, or inquiring at a store or post office on the island.

BANKS: For Nassau, Cable Beach, and Freeport/Lucaya, commercial banking hours are Monday to Thursday from 9:30 a.m. to 3 p.m., to 5 p.m. on Friday. Hours are likely to vary widely in the Family Islands. Ask at your hotel.

CHURCHES: You'll find many houses of worship in The Bahamas, with denominations including Anglican, Assembly of God, Baptist, Christian Science, Church of God, Church of God of Prophecy, Greek Orthodox, Jewish, Jehovah's Witnesses, Lutheran, Methodist, Presbyterian, Roman Catholic, Seventh-Day Adventist, and several smaller sects.

CLIMATE: The Tropic of Cancer crosses the Bahamian archipelago at about the halfway mark, passing through Exuma and the northern part of Long Island. Thus there is some variation between the mean temperatures in the northernmost and southernmost of the islands, but the climate overall is mild. The Gulf Stream sweeps along the western shores with its clear, warm waters, and the prevailing trade winds blow steadily in from the southeast. As a result, temperatures seldom drop below 60° Fahrenheit, even in the islands farthest north, nor rise above 90°.

A look at the official government chart on temperatures and rainfall will let you know what to expect during the time you plan to visit The Bahamas.

Month	Average Temperature	Average Inches of Rainfall
January	70°F (21°C)	1.9
February	70°F (21°C)	1.6
March	72°F (22°C)	1.4
April	75°F (24°C)	1.9
May	77°F (25°C)	4.8
June	80°F (27°C)	9.2
July	81°F (27°C)	6.1
August	82°F (28°C)	6.3
September	81°F (27°C)	7.5
October	78°F (26°C)	8.3
November	74°F (23°C)	2.3
December	71°F (22°C)	1.5

The Bahamas can be affected by hurricanes and tropical storms between June and November, but an efficient warning system gives ample notice for necessary precautions to be taken.

CLOTHING: Wear casual, informal, comfortable—but decent—clothing in The Bahamas. You'll probably spend most of your days in a swimsuit, shorts, slacks, or jeans. You may well want to dress up a bit for dinner and evening pursuits, depending on your choice of place. You can even appear in formal clothes in the casinos or at the more luxurious nightclubs or restaurants, although that is not required. Generally, a man should wear a jacket and tie in the evening at deluxe hotels. In fact such garb is required at some resort hotels and at Nassau, Cable Beach, and Freeport/Lucaya restaurants. However, a tie is not always *de* *rigueur.* In many cases a sport jacket over a short-sleeve shirt with slacks will be perfectly acceptable.

A lightweight dress or chic pantsuit is appropriate for women to wear in the evening. It's advisable to take along a wrap, stole, or evening sweater for cool evenings too. Bikinis are worn on the beaches, not to the shops. It's best to have a beach jacket to wear from your room to the water.

CRIME: When going to Nassau (New Providence), Cable Beach, or Paradise Island, exercise the kind of caution you would if visiting an American metropolis such as Miami. Whatever you do, if you're approached by people peddling drugs, view them as if they had the bubonic plague. Americans have gotten into much trouble in The Bahamas by purchasing illegal drugs.

Women, especially, should take caution if walking alone on the streets of Nassau after dark, especially if those streets *appear* to be deserted. Pickpockets (often foreigners) work the crowded casino floors of both Paradise Beach and Cable Beach. See that your wallet or money, or whatever, is secured.

If you're driving a rented car, always make sure your car door is locked, the same way you'd do in Los Angeles or New York City. If you have valuables with you, don't leave them unguarded in hotel rooms. That most definitely includes jewelry. Many of the bigger hotels will provide safes.

Nowadays the advice given for Nassau, Cable Beach, and Paradise Island also applies to Freeport/Lucaya.

You're less likely to get mugged in the Family Islands, where life is generally more peaceful. There are some resort hotels that—even today—don't have locks on the doors (never a good policy, in my opinion).

However, there can easily be trouble in paradise. Drug dealers frequent many of the Family Islands, especially Bimini, because of its proximity to Miami. Take special care if you plan to vacation there. Transporting illegal drugs between Bimini and the Florida coastline is so commonplace that the boating set every day sees bales of marijuana floating on the water as they make the crossing. The marijuana is dumped when vessels are spotted by the Coast Guard as they approach American territorial waters.

CURRENCY: The legal tender is the Bahamian dollar (B$1), which is on a par with the U.S. dollar. Both U.S. and Bahamian dollars are accepted on an equal basis throughout The Bahamas. There is no restriction on the amount of foreign currency brought into the country by a tourist. Currency transfers must be handled through banks as there are no provisions for "Western Union" type money cabling. If you wish to send home for funds, you can do so by telephoning, cabling, or writing to your Stateside bank with the request that a specified sum be transmitted to a bank in The Bahamas. Traveler's checks are accepted by most large hotels and stores, but you may have trouble getting a personal check honored.

CUSTOMS: Customs requires only an oral baggage declaration, unless you're bringing in something on which duty must be paid. However, your baggage is subject to Customs inspection. Each adult visitor coming to The Bahamas is allowed 50 cigars, 200 cigarettes, or one pound of tobacco; one quart of spirits; and personal effects, articles that have been in the possession and use of the visitor before arrival. These include personal jewelry, two still cameras with a reasonable quantity of film, one pair of binoculars, one portable musical instrument, one portable phonograph with a reasonable quantity of records, one portable radio and television, portable sound-recording apparatus, a portable typewriter, a baby carriage, personal sports equipment (including a bicycle, surfboards, Sunfish, a moped, and fishing rods), an iron, a clock, and a hair dryer. Firearms may not be brought into The Bahamas without a Bahamian gun license (see "Firearms," below).

When you return home, you may take $400 worth of merchandise duty free if you've been outside the U.S. for 48 hours or more and have not claimed an exemption in the past 30 days. Articles valued in excess of $1,000 will be assessed at a flat duty rate of 10%. Gifts for your personal use, not for business purposes, may be included in the $400 exemption. Gifts sent home may be valued at $50. You are limited to one liter of wine, liqueur, or liquor. Five cartons of cigarettes can be brought home duty free.

DOCUMENTS FOR ENTRY: To enter The Bahamas, citizens of the United States coming in as bona fide visitors for a period not to exceed eight months need only proof of citizenship, such as a passport or a birth certificate. Canadian citizens entering The Bahamas as visitors for a period not exceeding three weeks must present the same proof of citizenship.

On entry to The Bahamas, you'll be given an Immigration Card to complete and sign. The card has a carbon copy that you must keep until departure, at which time it must be turned in. Also, a departure tax is levied before you can exit the country (see "Taxes," below).

Visitors leaving Nassau or Freeport/Lucaya for most U.S. destinations clear U.S. Customs and Immigration before leaving The Bahamas. Charter companies can make special arrangements with the Nassau or Freeport flight services and U.S. Customs and Immigration for preclearance. No further formalities are required upon arrival in the U.S. once the preclearance has taken place in Nassau or Freeport.

DRUGS: The Bahamaian government has enacted strict laws regarding possession of dangerous drugs and firearms. The Dangerous Drugs Act makes it illegal for any person (other than a qualified individual) to import, export, or be in possession of marijuana, LSD, morphine, cocaine, or opium in the Bahama islands. A qualified person is one who has special permission to have such drugs for medical or scientific purposes (for instance, a licensed pharmacist, medical practitioner, dentist, or veterinary surgeon). Penalties for infractions of this act are severe.

ELECTRICAL APPLIANCES: Electricity is normally 120 volts, 60 cycles, AC. American appliances are compatible.

EMBASSIES AND CONSULATES: The **U.S. Embassy** is on Queen Street (P.O. Box N-8197), Nassau (tel. 809/322-4753); and the **Canadian Consulate** is on the ground floor of the Out Island Traders Building, East Bay Street (tel. 809/323-2123), near the foot of the Paradise Island Bridge.

FILM: This is not a major concern for travelers to The Bahamas, as film of various kinds is readily available at major points. However, it might be well to stock up if you're going to some of the remote Family Islands and need a special kind of film.

FIREARMS: Licenses are required for all firearms in The Bahamas. The Firearms Act cites three categories of licenses: revolvers, rifles and other firearms and ammunition, and guns (smooth bore, such as shotguns with barrels 20 inches or more long). If you wish to bring a firearm with you, to The Bahamas inquire in person at the office of the police commissioner on New Providence or the district commissioner of any of the Family Islands before bringing in the firearm . Special authorization is necessary.

GAMBLING: Casino gambling is legal in The Bahamas for visitors. Bahamians and Bahamas residents are prohibited from gambling, although they can enter the casinos in the company of friends from elsewhere. Games offered are dice, roulette, blackjack, baccarat, wheel of fortune, and slot machines. There is a casino at Cable Beach on New Providence, one on Paradise Island, and two at Freeport/Lucaya on Grand Bahama Island.

HAIRDRESSERS AND BARBERS: The major resorts, Nassau, Cable Beach, and Freeport/Lucaya have beauty salons and barbershops that are easy to find. Just ask at your hotel desk. However, in some of the Family Islands you may have to inquire around a bit, perhaps settle for someone to take care of such services in his or her own home.

HELP FOR THE HANDICAPPED: Some 30 hotels and resorts have facilities for the physically handicapped, which allow full or limited use of the accommodations and facilities. Many of these have been built or restored so that free access to the public rooms and some or all of the bedrooms is within the capacities of handicapped persons. This includes bathroom access, as well as easy use of the dining rooms, nightclubs, pool areas, and the like.

Such accommodations can be found in Nassau, Cable Beach, and on Paradise Island, Grand Bahama, Abaco, Andros, Cat Island, Eleuthera, Inagua, Long Island, and Spanish Wells, according to a survey conducted by The Bahamas Paraplegic Association in Nassau.

Some other small hotels, guesthouses, and cottages have also made provisions for comfortable stays by the physically handicapped. Ask your travel agent or inquire about Family Islands accommodations at the Bahamas Reservation Service (tel. toll free 800/327-0787 in the U.S., 443-3821 in Miami, or ZE9-9110 in Toronto or Montréal).

HOLIDAYS: Public holidays observed in The Bahamas are: New Year's Day, Good Friday, Easter Monday, Whit Monday (seven weeks after Easter), Labour Day (the first Friday in June), Independence Day (July 10), Emancipation Day (the first Monday in August), Discovery Day (October 12), Christmas Day, and Boxing Day (the day after Christmas). When a holiday falls on Saturday or Sunday, it is usually marked on the following Monday by the closing of stores and offices.

INSECTS: In The Bahamas, they are called "no-see-'ums." But they're for real all right. Bites by insects can cause skin irritation, itching, or whatever. Carry insect repellent with you, and don't become dinner for a colony of mosquitoes. It's commonplace to have insects invade your room—and that goes for the deluxe establishments as well as the beachside bungalows. Carry along some insect spray—it might come in handy. If you've booked that secluded cottage in one of the remote Family Islands, remember that you are retreating from civilization, not from nature.

LAUNDRY AND DRY CLEANING: These matters present no problem in Nassau, Cable Beach, Freeport/Lucaya, or at the large resorts, where such service is part of the amenities. You could face difficulties on some of the smaller, remote islands, but usually, just by asking around, you can find someone who is willing to do your laundry.

MAIL AND POSTAGE RATES: Only Bahamian postage stamps are acceptable for the payment of postage from The Bahamas. To send that postcard back home to the U.S. or Canada by airmail will cost 25¢. Airmail letters cost 45¢ per half ounce.

From the U.S., mail to the Family Islands is sometimes slow. Airmail may go by air to Nassau and by boat to its final destination. If a resort has a U.S. or Nassau address, it is preferable to use it.

MARRIAGE/DIVORCE: Want to have a romantic Bahamas wedding? If non-residents wish to tie the knot here, one member of the couple must spend 15 days in the country and submit proof of presence. A waiver may be granted if one of the couple has been in The Bahamas at least three days. If either party has been divorced, proof of divorce must be produced. Applications for marriage licenses cost $20 and are obtainable on New Providence at the Registrar General's Office, East Hill Street (P.O. Box N-532). No blood test is required. Minimum age without parental consent is 21. Minors may be married with the consent of all parents. Nothing special is required of widows or widowers; the Registry will take your word for it that your spouse is dead.

Regardless of nationality, couples can get a divorce in The Bahamas if the husband is a bona fide resident, but it's not easy. Don't think you can fly in, get a decree, and fly right home. Better consult a Bahamian attorney if you're eligible and if you really want to take this route. Otherwise, do it at home.

MEDICAL SERVICES: Medical facilities in The Bahamas are considered excellent for an island group so small in population and so diverse in distribution. Physicians and surgeons in private practice are readily available in Nassau, Cable Beach, and Freeport/Lucaya. In the Family Islands, there are 13 Health Centres. Satellite clinics are held periodically in small settlements by health personnel, plus 36 other clinics, making a total of 49 health facilities throughout the outlying islands. Where intensive or urgent care is required, patients are brought by Emergency Flight Service to Princess Margaret Hospital in Nassau.

There is a government-operated hospital, Rand Memorial, in Freeport, plus government-operated clinics on Grand Bahama Island. Nassau and Freeport/Lucaya also have private hospitals.

Dentists are plentiful in Nassau, somewhat less so on Grand Bahama. You'll find two dentists on Abaco, one at Marsh Harbour and another at Treasure Cay, and there's one in Eleuthera.

Some of the big resort hotels have in-house physicians or can quickly secure one for you. Staffs are also knowledgeable as to where to go for dental care.

NATIONAL SYMBOLS: The Bahamian flag is a black, equilateral triangle on a background of three equal horizontal colored stripes, the center one gold flanked by two of aquamarine. The national tree is the lignum vitae or tree of life, the national flower is the yellow elder, and the national bird is the flamingo.

NEWSPAPERS: Two newspapers are published in Nassau and circulated there and in Freeport: the *Nassau Guardian,* a morning paper, and the *Tribune,* printed in the afternoon. Both publish Monday through Saturday. Circulation in the Family Islands is limited and likely to be slow. The *Freeport News* is published Monday through Friday.

You can find the *New York Times,* the *Wall Street Journal,* the *Miami Herald, The Times* of London, and the *Daily Telegraph* at newsstands in your hotel and elsewhere in Nassau, usually the day after they are published but sometimes later.

PETS: A valid import permit is required to import any animal into the Commonwealth of The Bahamas. Application for such a permit must be made in writing, accompanied by a $10 processing fee, to the Director of Agriculture, Department of Agriculture, P.O. Box N-3028, Nassau, The Bahamas (tel. 809/325-

7502), a minimum of three weeks in advance. The application must give the name and address of the person wishing to bring in the animal(s), the type and number of animals the applicant wishes to import, the country of export and origin, the purpose for importing the animal(s), plus the anticipated date of arrival and the destination in The Bahamas. Dogs and cats over the age of six months arriving from the U.S. and Canada must be accompanied by a rabies vaccination certificate issued a minimum of 30 days and a maximum of one year prior to arrival. The animal must be inspected by a qualified veterinarian within 24 hours after the arrival of the animal. Dogs and cats under less than six months of age require a Veterinary Health Certificate only. The conditions for the importation of animals were under review at press time, and may be subject to change. It is best to follow the directions on an import permit if issued.

RADIO AND TV: Government-owned Radio Bahamas is run by the Broadcasting Corporation of The Bahamas and supported by advertising. ZNS-1, the most powerful of the three, is located in Nassau but can be heard throughout the country. ZNS-2 also operates out of Nassau, and ZNS-3 is Freeport based. ZNS-1 broadcasts 24 hours a day.

The ZNS TV transmits on Channel 13 in full color, for six hours a day Monday through Friday. On Saturday it transmits for 16 hours, on Sunday for 12. The Bahamas Broadcasting Company handles all programming. Most large hotels have cable television and can receive U.S. telecasts via Miami from all major networks. Islands nearest the U.S. receive TV without cable.

REST ROOMS: Adequate toilet facilities are found at hotels, restaurants, and air terminals in The Bahamas that are frequented by the public, although they may turn out to be in short supply at some of the points of interest you may go to see. Also, if you're in some of the more remote Family Islands not well supplied with public places, you may have difficulty finding a comfort station. Well . . . there's always a clump of trees or a sand hill to shelter you.

SHOPPING: Plan your shopping sprees for Nassau, Cable Beach, and Freeport/Lucaya if you can. You'll also find boutiques and gift shops at the major resorts, but in smaller places not much is offered. For data on the best places to shop, see the chapters on Nassau, Cable Beach, and Freeport/Lucaya in this book. In the Abacos, both Marsh Harbour and Treasure Cay have fully equipped shopping centers, while most of the resorts have gift shops for their guests. On Andros there's a shopping center at Nicholl's Town and additional shops at other towns on the island. You'll be able to purchase food on practically all the Family Islands, and you can find T-shirts all over.

STORE HOURS: These vary from island to island, so don't count on anything until you check with your hotel desk or go see for yourself. Particularly in the smaller Family Islands, you may have to roust the storekeeper out from his or her nearby home to open the door for you, but they are usually pleasant.

TAXES: Departure tax is $5 for travelers over 12 years of age, $2.50 for those from 2 to 12, and free for travelers under 2. International airline and steamship tickets issued in The Bahamas are subject to a $2 government tax. Hotel tax of 6%, based on the European Plan rate, is collected by all hotels in The Bahamas. There is no sales tax in this country.

TELECOMMUNICATIONS: Communications via telephone and cable to resorts in The Bahamas have improved recently, although some of the Family Islands are difficult to reach because of distance and equipment. The Bahamas Telecommunications Corporation operates phone, cable, teletype, and leased circuits, as well as mobile-phone service. It's also in charge of licensing marine radio and other private radio-phone stations. Service between Florida, Nassau, Freeport, and some of the major resort islands is available 24 hours a day. Other radiotelephone systems link the Family Islands to Nassau and through Nassau to the world. Not all radio-phone stations in the outlying areas are connected to telephones in homes and offices. In such cases it is necessary to call the operator at the nearest radio station to the person being called and arrange to have him or her summoned to the station to complete the call. Such stations close at 9 p.m. and are on an emergency basis during the night.

Direct Distance Dialing between North America and Nassau, Grand Bahama, Abaco, Andros, Berry Islands, Bimini, Eleuthera, Harbour Island, Spanish Wells, Exuma, and Stella Maris on Long Island is available. The **area code** for The Bahamas is 809. Cables to The Bahamas are usually delivered by phone or by citizens' band radio. Urgent telegrams are charged at double the full rate, although no urgent-rate messages to the United States mainland are accepted.

TIME: Eastern Standard Time is used throughout The Bahamas. In recent years, Eastern Daylight Time has been adopted during the summer to avoid confusion in scheduling transportation to and from the United States. April to October, EDT; October to April, EST.

TIPPING: Many establishments add a service charge, but it's customary to leave something extra if service has been especially fine. If you're not sure whether service has been included in your bill, ask. Unfortunately, in most places you have to pay the 15% service charge even if an incompetent waiter has spilled soup on you.

Bellboys and porters, at least in the upper-bracket hotels, have come to expect a tip of $1 per bag. It's also customary to tip your chambermaid at least $1 per day—more if she has performed special services such as getting a shirt or blouse laundered. Most service personnel, including taxi drivers, waiters, and the like, expect 15% (perhaps 20% in deluxe restaurants).

TOURIST INFORMATION: For further information on The Bahamas, see your travel agent or **The Bahamas Tourist Office** nearest you. In the United States, offices are found in: **New York,** 150 E. 52nd St., 28th Floor N, New York, NY 10022 (tel. 212/758-2777); **Atlanta:** 1950 Century Blvd. NE, Suite 26, Atlanta, GA 30345 (tel. 404/633-1793); **Boston:** 1027 Statler Office Bldg., Boston, MA 02116 (tel. 617/426-3144); **Chicago:** 875 N. Michigan Ave., Suite 1816, Chicago, IL 60611 (tel. 312/787-8203); **Dallas:** World Trade Center, Suite 186, 2050 Stemmons Frwy., P.O. Box 581408, Dallas, TX 75259-1408 (tel. 214/742-1886); **Houston:** 5177 Richmond Ave., Suite 755, Houston, TX 77056 (tel. 713/626-1566); **Detroit:** 26400 Lahser Rd., Suite 112A, Southfield, MI 48034 (tel. 313/357-2940); **Los Angeles:** 3450 Wilshire Blvd., Suite 208, Los Angeles, CA 90010 (tel. 213/385-0033); **San Francisco:** 44 Montgomery Center, Suite 503, San Francisco, CA 94104 (tel. 415/398-5502); **Washington, D.C.:** 1730 Rhode Island Ave. NW, Washington, DC 20036 (tel. 202/659-9135); **Miami:**255 Alhambra Circle, Suite 425, Coral Gables, FL 33134 (tel. 305/442-4860).

In Canada, you can write or call: **Montréal:** 1255 Phillips Square, Montréal, Québec H3B 3G1 (tel. 514/861-6797); **Toronto:** 85 Richmond St. West, Toronto, Ontario M5H 2C9 (tel. 416/363-4441).

WEIGHTS AND MEASURES: Like Bermuda, The Bahamas uses the metric system. See Chapter II for equivalents and conversion factors to the old system.

CHAPTER VIII

NEW PROVIDENCE (NASSAU/CABLE BEACH)

□ □ □

The capital of the Bahamas, the historic city of Nassau, stands on the island of New Providence, less than an hour's flight from the United States and a favorite cruise-ship port of call. It offers the charm of an antique, and has a tropical indolence, yet it boasts up-to-date tourist facilities and modern hotels. Nassau lies on the north side of New Providence, which is 21 miles long and 7 miles wide at its greatest point.

Horse-drawn surreys still wind down narrow streets, and faded pastel-colored homes look out onto the sea. The waterfront, too, still looks much the same as it did when Winslow Homer painted it. The major difference now is that an arched bridge joins Nassau with Paradise Island (described in the next chapter), with its hotels, continental-style restaurants, and gambling casino.

Before getting involved in city life, it's customary to purchase a straw hat at the market on Rawson Square and then begin your journey of discovery.

Much has changed in this Bahamian capital, once the haunt of pirates and rum-soaked sailors. Whitewashed and latticed houses evoke memories of a colonial past. But today's Nassau is alive and bustling, forging its own destiny as a contemporary resort city.

Once it was known as a mecca for the rich and socially secure of the world, particularly when the Duke and Duchess of Windsor were in residence. (He was governor of The Bahamas from 1940 to 1945, living at Government House.) As a honeymoon haven, it rivaled (and rivals) Bermuda. However, today's visitors are more broad-based in lifestyles and pocketbooks, ranging from yachting people to underwater explorers on a budget. The rich are still very much in evidence, discreetly so. Because of its tax advantages, Nassau is such a center of international banking that some refer to it as the Switzerland of The Bahamas.

Nassau is the heart of The Bahamas, the hub from which sea and air roads fan outward. Unless Freeport is your gateway, chances are you'll be stopping here even if your ultimate destination is the Family Islands. You may want to linger long enough to get to know it.

1. SETTLING IN

After you land at the Nassau International Airport, you immediately face the problem of transportation to your hotel. If you're renting a car, you can drive there. If not, you'll find no inexpensive bus service waiting for you, and must take a taxi instead, unless you're being met by a special van. (Nassau taxi drivers years ago blocked the major traffic arteries of New Providence when the government attempted to inaugurate bus service from the airport to the hotels of Cable Beach, downtown Nassau, and Paradise Island.)

After an overview on local transportation, I'll highlight some practical facts to ease your adjustment into the Bahamian capital.

GETTING AROUND: The elegant, traditional way to see Nassau was in a **horse-drawn surrey**—the kind with the fringe on top and a wilted hibiscus stuck in the straw hat shielding the horse from the sun. But these aren't as plentiful anymore, and when available, are usually too expensive for the average visitor. (Before you get in, you should negotiate with the driver and agree on the price. The average price is $8 to $10 for one or two people for a 30-minute ride.) The maximum load is three adults plus one or two children under the age of 12. The surreys are generally available seven days a week from 9 a.m. to 4:30 p.m., except when horses are rested, from 1 to 3 p.m., from May to October and from 1 to 2 p.m. from November to April. If you want to go on a short trip, you'll find the surreys at Rawson Square, off Bay Street.

Taxis are more practical, at least for longer island trips, as their rates for New Providence, including Nassau, are set by the government. When you get in, you should find a working meter, as this is a requirement. For the first one-quarter mile, one or two passengers are charged $1.20, and 20¢ for each additional one-quarter mile. Each additional passenger is assessed another $1.50. Typical fares are $8 from the airport to Cable Beach, $10 to downtown Nassau, and $18 (plus the $2 bridge toll) to Paradise Island. Taxis can also be hired on the hourly rate of $12 to $20 for a five-passenger cab. Luggage is carried at a cost of 30¢ per piece. The radio taxi call number is 809/323-4555.

The least expensive means of transport is by **jitney,** really VW minibuses, which leave from the downtown Nassau area to outposts on New Providence, costing from 50¢ to $1 per ride. They operate daily from 6:30 a.m. to 7:30 p.m. Some hotels on Paradise Island and Cable Beach run their own jitney service free. However, jitneys and buses are not allowed to operate from the airport to Cable Beach, Nassau, or Paradise Island (the taxi union saw to that).

Water taxis operate daily from 8:30 a.m. to 6 p.m. at 20-minute intervals between Paradise Island and Prince George Wharf at a round-trip cost of $3 per person.

There is also **ferry** service from the end of Casuarina Drive on Paradise Island across the harbor to Rawson Square for a round-trip fare of $2 per person. The ferry operates daily from 9:30 a.m. to 4:15 p.m., with departures every half hour from both sides of the harbor.

Motor scooters have become a favorite mode of transportation among tourists. The little mopeds with their identifying white license tag and helmeted riders scoot all over New Providence. Unless you're an experienced moped rider, it's wise for you to stay on quiet roads until you feel at ease with your vehicle.

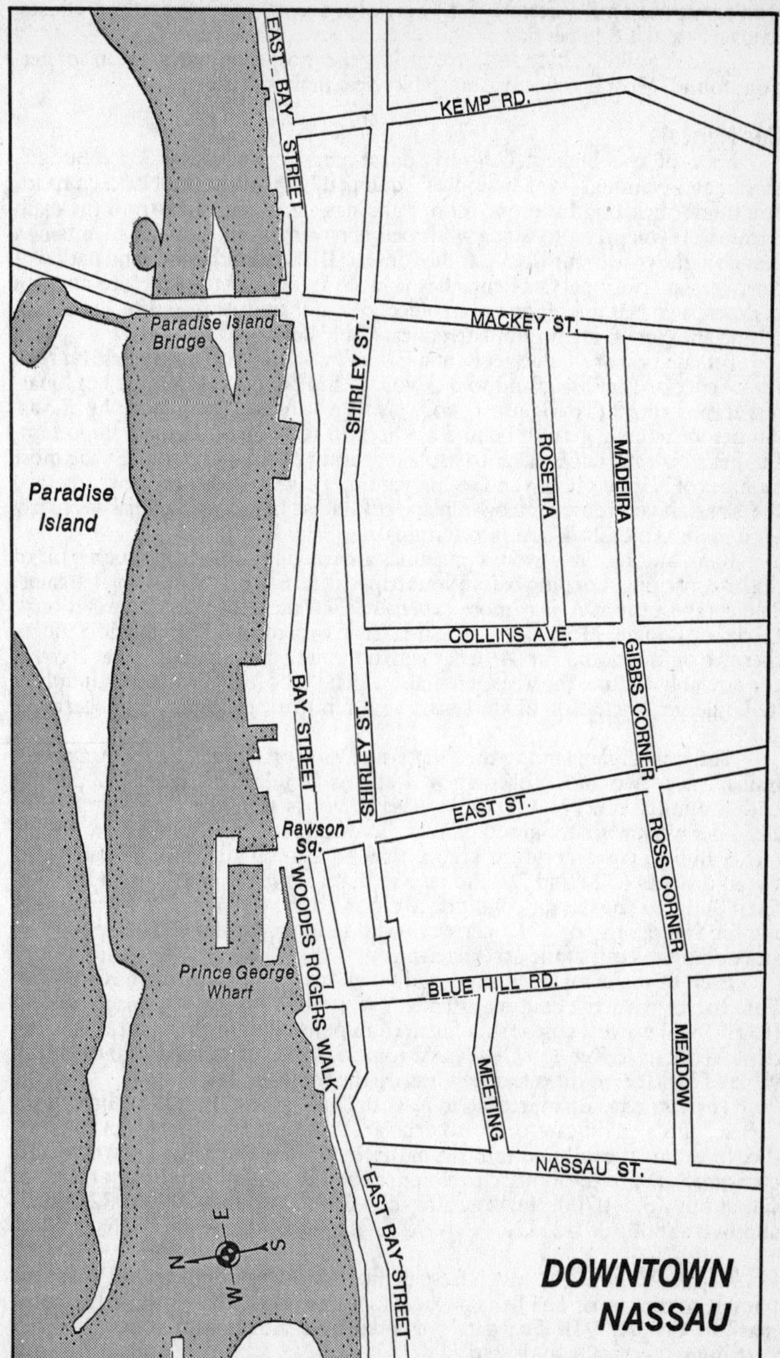

EAST BAY STREET
KEMP RD.
MACKEY ST.
Paradise Island Bridge
SHIRLEY ST.
ROSETTA
MADEIRA
Paradise Island
COLLINS AVE.
GIBBS CORNER
BAY STREET
SHIRLEY ST.
EAST ST.
Rawson Sq.
ROSS CORNER
WOODES ROGERS WALK
Prince George Wharf
BLUE HILL RD.
MEETING
MEADOW
NASSAU ST.
EAST BAY STREET
E
S
N
W
DOWNTOWN NASSAU

Don't start out on Bay Street. Many hotels have rental vehicles on the premises. Average rental is $28 per day.

Besides walking, **bicycles** are certainly the most economical means of getting around. Most hotels can arrange bicycle rentals for you.

Car Rentals

Four of the biggest U.S.-based car-rental companies—Avis, Budget, Hertz, and National—maintain well-equipped branches at the Nassau airport. You'll find their booths in one-room buildings across the street from the main terminal. If you prefer to wait a while before renting a car, Avis also maintains a branch at the cruise-ship docks, at the Paradise Island Holiday Inn, and in downtown Nassau. National Car Rental has a branch at the Cable Beach Hotel and one in downtown Nassau. Hertz has an office at Wyndham's Ambassador Beach Hotel and another on Hampshire Street near Cable Beach.

Perhaps best of all, Budget Rent-a-Car will send a driver to anywhere on New Providence or Paradise Island to pick you up and deliver you to their headquarters at the airport. (This is also a good way to get a feel for the geography of Nassau before actually getting behind a wheel on your own.) Equally important, Budget's Nassau staff is eager to explain routing instructions to even the most far-flung of Nassau's hotels and seems genuinely eager to welcome newcomers to the island. If you're arriving by seaplane at Paradise Island, Budget has a recently built kiosk at the Chalk's Airline Terminal.

Rates among the various companies are roughly similar, although a bit of dollar-conscious shopping before your trip may reveal some surprising bargains. The cheapest car at Avis is more expensive than the cheapest one at National, Hertz, or Budget. Hertz offers a Honda Civic with manual transmission and either two or four doors, for $49 a day with unlimited mileage. The rate at Hertz is considerably cheaper for weekly rentals, which cost $295 per week with unlimited mileage. A selection of Hertz cars with automatic transmission is also available.

The real bargain among the "Big Four," however, is at Budget. A manual-transmission two-door Volkswagen Beetle or Honda Civic costs $42 per day with unlimited mileage. Of course, weekly rentals represent better bargains at $252 per week with unlimited mileage. To qualify for the less expensive weekly rate, a Budget customer must keep a car for a five-day minimum rental, be between the ages of 21 and 70, and reserve the car at least seven days in advance. Even Budget's rates for air-conditioned cars (a Toyota Corolla with air conditioning for $54 per day or $312 per week with unlimited mileage) is cheaper than air-conditioned cars at the other agencies.

Each of the companies offers additional insurance for $8 to $10 per day. Purchase of what the counter attendant will call a "collision damage waiver" (CDW) will waive a customer's financial responsibility in the event of an accident. Without arranging a CDW, a customer is liable for from $1,500 to the full value of damages to the car, depending on the company.

There's no tax on car rentals in Nassau. Drivers must present a valid driver's license, plus a credit card or a cash deposit. These and other details can be handled by calling the toll-free numbers of the four major North American car-rental companies. For reservations, current prices, and availability, call **Budget Rent-a-Car** at 800/527-0700, **Hertz** at 800/654-3001, **National** at 800/328-4567, and **Avis** at 800/331-2112.

PRACTICAL FACTS: Much factual information regarding Nassau is also applicable to the rest of The Bahamas and appears under "The ABCs of The Bahamas" in Chapter VII. The data presented here should help you on matters pertaining specifically to the capital.

Churches: Bahamians tend to be religious people, with a history of religious tolerance. The number and variety of **houses of worship** around Nassau may surprise you. Of the major faiths, the following churches are established here: **Anglican**—Christ Church Cathedral, King and George Streets (tel. 809/322-4186); St. Matthews, Shirley Street and Church Lane (tel. 809/325-2191). **Baptist**—Zion, East and Shirley Streets (tel. 809/325-3556). **Roman Catholic**—St. Francis Xavier's Cathedral, West and West Hill Streets (tel. 809/323-3802); Sacred Heart Church, East Shirley Street (tel. 809/326-6274). **Methodist**—Trinity, Fredrick Street (tel. 809/325-2552); Ebenezer, East Shirley Street (tel. 809/323-2936). **Presbyterian**—St. Andrew's Kirk, Princes Street (tel. 809/322-4085). **Lutheran**—Lutheran Church of Nassau, John F. Kennedy Drive (tel. 809/323-4107).

Credit cards: Major credit cards are generally accepted throughout the city. Some local offices for major cards are: **American Express,** Playtours travel agency, Shirley Street (tel. 809/322-2931); **VISA,** Barclays Bank, Bay Street (tel. 809/322-4921); and **MasterCard,** Bank of New Providence, Shirley and Charlotte Streets (tel. 809/322-8134).

Drugs: The strict drug law of The Bahamas was cited in the ABCs in the preceding chapter, but a warning bears repeating. The authorities do not smile on visitors possessing or selling marijuana or other narcotics, and offenders are speedily and severely punished. A normal lapse of three days between arrest and sentencing can be expected. Penalties are harsh.

Emergencies: Some phone numbers you may need in case of emergency are **police,** 919; **fire department,** 919 (other than emergency, 809/322-4444); **ambulance,** 809/322-2221 (if busy, an alternate number is 809/322-2861).

Medical and dental care: If you need a **doctor,** Nassau has a large number of qualified persons, ranging from general practitioners to specialists in obstetrics and gynecology, surgery, psychiatry, ophthamology, orthopedics, psychology, dermatology, pediatrics, internal medicine, and radiology.

In medical facilities, **Princess Margaret Hospital** on Shirley Street (tel. 809/322-2861) is the leading hospital in The Bahamas. Its bed capacity is 455, and it has departments with well-qualified staffs in medicine, surgery, maternity, pediatrics, intensive care, eye, and chest, as well as an emergency ward, a dialysis unit, a laboratory with a blood bank, X-ray facilities, and a pharmacy. It is a government-operated hospital. The privately owned doctors' **Rassin Hospital,** with 26 beds, is at the corner of Shirley Street and Collins Avenue, P.O. Box N-972 (tel. 809/322-8411).

There are also numerous **dentists** in Nassau, a half dozen or so connected with the dental department of the Princess Margaret Hospital.

Tourist information: Assistance is available at a booth at the Nassau International Airport. Otherwise, you'll find an **Information Booth** at Prince George Dock (tel. 809/325-9155) and at Rawson Square (tel. 809/325-9171).

Weather: New Providence, which is fairly centrally located in The Bahamas, has temperatures in winter that vary from about 60° to 75° Fahrenheit daily. Summer variations are 78° to the high 80s.

2. STAYING AND DINING IN OLD NASSAU

Many visitors prefer to find lodgings or to dine in historic downtown Nassau. Accommodations generally tend to be more reasonably priced in this area, and there are many good places to eat, whether you're in the mood for elegance or just for a quick meal to stave off hunger. First, I'll recommend a number of places to stay and follow with my dining selections.

WHERE TO STAY: Many old properties, such as the Sheraton British Colonial Hotel downtown, have been considerably revamped and refurbished. The legendary Royal Victoria couldn't keep up and was gutted. The accommodation picture is brighter than ever, as new managements have pumped fresh energy into tired properties.

If you're economizing, I suggest a moderate- or budget-priced hotel, or even better, a guesthouse in Nassau. You'll find moderate, and in some cases bargain, price tags, but you'll have to "commute" to the beaches on Paradise Island or Cable Beach.

Incidentally, the hotels of The Bahamas are known for quoting package rates that are sometimes amazing cut-rate discounts. These change frequently, so I've therefore given only regular room tariffs, called "rack rates" in the travel industry. In booking, however, always inquire about honeymoon specials, golf packages, summer weeks, whatever.

In many cases, hotels and restaurants add government tax and service charge to your bills, rather than including them with the quoted prices. Ask about this ahead to save yourself what might be nasty surprises.

A Touch of Elegance

Graycliff, West Hill Street, P.O. Box N-10246, Nassau, The Bahamas (tel. 809/322-2796), stands deep in the heart of Old Nassau, an exceptionally well-preserved colonial villa across the street from Government House. It's the only Relais & Châteaux hotel in The Bahamas. The main house of Graycliff is some 250 years old, built by Capt. John Howard Graysmith, a pirate who was noted for his exploits against Spanish shipping and who was commander of the notorious *Graywolf,* which was scuttled off New Providence in 1726. Captain Graysmith settled in Nassau and used some of his riches to build Graycliff. There is no written history on the use to which this fine example of Georgian colonial architecture was put after the captain's death in 1734, but it may once have housed the British West Indies Regiment. It is believed that the cellars, with their low thick walls and bars, may indicate that a garrison occupied the house. By 1844 Graycliff was a hotel for "gentlefolk and invalids."

Over the years since then, when the house was sometimes a hotel, sometimes a private residence, a handsome swimming pool was added and extensive additions and renovations made to the property while keeping the main house intact. Both as hotel and home, the house has hosted the rich and famous. The Duke and Duchess of Windsor often visited here while he served as governor of The Bahamas and lived across the street. Sir Winston Churchill used to enjoy the swimming pool, paddling around with a cigar in his mouth. Lord Mountbatten, Aristotle Onassis, even the Beatles were guests at Graycliff at one time or another. In 1966 the Earl and Countess Dudley of Staffordshire purchased the house and occupied it as a winter home. Since that time it has been sold and changed again to a 14-room hotel. It is furnished with exceptional and luxuriously styled antiques. Here you're likely to run into Paul Newman, Perry Como, Michael Caine, Brooke Shields, or Kenny Rogers, among the celebrities who come to relax in this gracious ambience. A pool cottage for two is the most expensive accommodation, costing $240 to $300 a day all year. Other rooms range from $120 to $140 in a single, $190 to $240 in a double daily with a full breakfast.

The present owner, Enrico Garzaroli, brings his own aristocratic ways and tastes to this chic oasis. Graycliff is also one of the finest restaurants in Nassau, certainly the most elegant (see my recommendations for dining out). Always reserve well in advance.

A Traditional Favorite

The British Colonial Hotel, 1 Bay St., P.O. Box N-7148, Nassau, The Bahamas (tel. 809/322-3301), is in the heart of Nassau, just steps away from the shopping area of Bay Street on eight tropical acres. It is a regenerated queen of

Nassau's bayfront. Nevertheless, whether or not you like this place may depend on your room assignment. The hotel is a monument to resort living, spread out along the shore. You won't need to go off the premises, as you have everything here, including an Olympic-size swimming pool and 325 large rooms. In winter, per-person rates range from $114 to $210 daily, the former price charged for the cheapest accommodation (a standard city-view unit), the latter the tariff for a one-bedroom suite with an ocean view. *In summer, the per-person rates range from $89 to $169 daily.* A third or fourth adult in each accommodation is charged another $25, and children age 17 or under are allowed to stay free on the EP when sharing an adult's room. When booking, ask if they're featuring special Goombay package deals. For breakfast and dinner, add $35 per person daily in addition to the tariffs quoted.

The British Colonial is the only major hotel in the downtown area. The facilities include Blackbeard's Forge, Bayside Restaurant, and Wharf Café, three championship tennis courts lit for night play, and a private beach. Deep-sea fishing, skindiving, and snorkeling can be arranged. Some of the hotel's dining and bar facilities are recommended separately.

On Silver Cay

Coral World Villas, P.O. Box N-7797, Nassau, The Bahamas (tel. 809/328-1036), lies isolated on the private island of Silver Cay (site of the underwater attraction, Coral World, reviewed later), midway between downtown Nassau and Cable Beach. It promotes secluded luxuries in this 22-villa property, which opened in 1988, making Silver Cay the 21st of the inhabited islands of the archipelago. You can cross a small bridge to the "mainland" (New Providence), but many guests find this little world sufficient unto itself. They can roam about the private island, which becomes quite tranquil after the Coral World sightseeing crowds have departed.

These villas, furnished in a light Caribbean motif with wicker furniture and tropical accents, come with a private swimming pool for each villa. All of them open onto ocean views. Decorator designed, each villa has a king-size bed and a pull-out queen-size sleeping sofa, ideal if the unit is shared with children. The villas also contain their own kitchens, complete with microwaves, and a bar. A complimentary continental breakfast will be delivered to your private pool patio. The bathrooms are sheathed in marble, and from your oval bathtub you can take in a view of the waves through a picture window as you make your own waves. Amenities include remote control color cable TV and phones. Year-round these villas rent for $195 a night for two persons, with a third or fourth party paying another $15 each. However, there is no charge for children 12 years or younger sharing with an adult (a maximum of two children per room).

Guests can dine at the Conch Club terrace restaurant at the hotel or else lunch at Coral World's oceanfront Clipper Restaurant. Call toll free 800/221-0203 to make reservations (in New York City, call 212/541-7420).

A Sailor's Favorite

The Pilot House, East Bay Street, P.O. Box N-4941, Nassau, The Bahamas (tel. 809/322-8431), is built on the site of a 150-year-old pilot house. It has half of its life indoors, the other centering around the swimming-pool garden with banana and palm trees. Its location is a five-minute walk from Paradise Island Bridge, two miles from the center of town and 15 miles from the airport. The bedrooms, for the most part, have balconies or patios overlooking the garden. Housekeeping, as several readers have noted, is definitely casual. In winter, a room rents for $95 to $115 per day, either single or double occupancy. Children under 12 years of age who share a room with an adult are accepted free. *In summer, single or double charges are $70 to $90.* For breakfast and dinner, add $24 per person daily to the rates quoted. Many guests come to Pilot House just to dine. The Three Ladies and the Regatta Room are recommended separately. You can enjoy drinks in the Captain's Lounge, which has a nautical decor, or at the Windward Mark in the tower building. The marina, where you can rent boats and get equipment for scuba-diving and snorkeling, is across the street. A private ferry will take you free to downtown Nassau or Paradise Beach.

Small Budget Hotels

The Orchard, Village Road, P.O. Box N-1514, Nassau, The Bahamas (tel. 809/323-1297), only 500 yards from Montagu Beach, is an apartment/hotel complex offering individual cottage facilities grouped around a central swimming pool in a semitropical garden of two acres. The cottages are in a residential part of Nassau, within 800 yards of a large supermarket and a five-minute drive to tennis and squash courts and several island restaurants. There are 10 efficiencies and 12 pink cottages. All units are air-conditioned, with fully equipped kitchens, baths, balconies, and daily maid service. Year-round rates are $32 per person daily, based on double occupancy in one of the efficiencies, and $36 per person daily for one of the cottages. Sometimes costs are split among three or four people occupying one cottage. Taxes and service are extra. Guests can take a bus, which stops near the hotel, if they want to go shopping in downtown Nassau (the bus service also runs to Paradise Island). Later, economy-minded vacationers share stories at the convivial Tree Frog Bar, on the premises.

The New Olympia Hotel, West Bay Street, P.O. Box N-984, Nassau, The Bahamas (tel. 809/322-4971), is a three-story hostelry whose blue and white façade reflects the national colors of Greece, a bow to their heritage by owners Kate Kiriaze and her brother, John Constantakis, although they were born in The Bahamas. Their hotel is across from the community beach in the heart of Nassau, just a short walk from West Beach and the shopping along Bay Street. The pleasantly decorated, sunny rooms, 48 in all, are accessible via long hallways. The oceanside accommodations have views of the water and private balconies. Each room contains two beds, air conditioning, a private bath, color TV, and a phone. Many have been recently refurbished with wallpaper and paint. In winter, singles and doubles range from $72 to $80, while triples cost $90 and quads run $105. *In summer, the charge for singles and doubles is $55 to $65, while triples cost $74 and quads are $86.* After a refreshing dip in the ocean, you can head for the garden patio or Sonny's Pizzeria & Sports Pub, outfitted with antique decorations from Europe and the Orient. Menu offerings have been expanded. The pub is definitely the hotel's social center, offering satellite TV and cold drinks. A lobbyside drugstore and boutique make shopping for sundries especially easy.

Parthenon Hotel, West Bay Street, P.O. Box N-4930, Nassau, The Bahamas (tel. 809/322-2643), is a small hotel only three minutes from Bay Street and the beaches. Although modern, it's styled in the old Bahamian way with continuous covered balconies overlooking a well-tended garden. The 18 rooms are simple, with a basic, restrained decor, air conditioning, and private baths. In winter, singles or doubles begin at $50, a triple at $56. *Reductions are granted in summer, ranging from $42 in a single or double, and $48 in a triple.* Rates quoted are on the EP. Fishing, golfing, tennis, and water sports can be arranged.

Ocean Spray Hotel, West Bay Street, P.O. Box N-3035, Nassau, The Bahamas (tel. 809/322-8032), is a modestly modern 30-room corner hotel, a short stroll from the shopping district and across the street from the beach. Bedrooms are conservative, with twin beds, air conditioning, private baths, phones, and wall-to-wall carpeting. Best known for its Restaurant-Bar Europe, the hotel serves good imported wines and continental, Bahamian, German, and American specialties. It has an informal atmosphere. In winter, singles rent for $60 daily, with doubles costing $73. *Prices are lowered in summer to $50 daily in a single and $60 in a double.* Ocean Spray offers guests both beach and town, a winning combination in Nassau.

El Greco Hotel, West Bay Street, P.O. Box N-4187, Nassau, The Bahamas (tel. 809/325-1121), stands across the street from Lighthouse Beach, within a five-minute walk from the shops and restaurants of Bay Street. Its design has a Spanish flavor. Rounded archways accent its façade, and black-painted iron chandeliers are found inside the reception area. The owners direct a staff who seem to care about the well-being of guests. The rooms are clustered around a tiny central swimming pool set between the vine-covered and hedge-trimmed confines of an Iberian-style courtyard. Many of the 26 accommodations have separate sitting rooms, while each has a tile bath, air conditioning, and furniture such as you might find in Spain. In winter, singles cost $75 daily, while doubles rent for $85. *In summer, singles cost $55 daily, and doubles go for $65.* The hotel restaurant, Del Prado, is covered below in the section on dining.

A Guesthouse

Pearl Cox Guest House, Augusta Street, P.O. Box N-1268, Nassau, The Bahamas (tel. 809/325-2627). A Bahamian woman, Pearl Cox is a local legend. She's been around for quite a while, and she's seen a lot of changes in Nassau. She'll tell you about how she first got into the business of taking in paying guests in the first place. Black visitors, even prominent ones, were once not allowed to stay in the major hotels of Nassau. Joe Louis, the boxing champion, planned a visit, and Mrs. Cox was asked not only to meet him at the airport in her new car, but to offer him shelter. Apparently they got along fabulously. When he returned to the States, he spread the word, and over the years a host of black celebrities have made their way to the door of Mrs. Cox. And she's got mementos of some of their visits. Those long-ago discriminatory policies have been abandoned of course, but the world (in all colors) still comes to Mrs. Cox's door, where they know they'll receive old-fashioned Bahamian hospitality. To caution you, know that everything is simple around here in her half dozen or so rooms, and there's only one accommodation with its own private bath and air conditioning. For that, guests pay $25 a night, double occupancy year-round. Doubles without bath rent for $16 to $20 a night, and singles are charged only $12. Guests have use of a separate kitchen, and store their food in an icebox, dining on the patio. Dozens of Germans, Swiss, and Dutch visitors have discovered this place as a budget-conscious alternative to the astronomical prices of Nassau. The house, painted white, is inviting with its vines and flowery plants. It's in a residential section, within walking distance of the shops of Bay Street.

DINING IN NASSAU: I'll recommend a range of places offering good food in downtown Nassau, where you'll find hotel restaurants serving American and continental specialties, as well as a number of Bahamian restaurants, where you can enjoy crab fat and dumplings, peas 'n' rice, cracked conch (also conch chowder, conch fritters, and conch salad), grouper (in every way known), and red snapper in anchovy sauce (see "Food and Drink" in Chapter VII). Most meat is imported frozen, and it's better, in general, to rely on the tasty local fresh fish and seafood.

Leading Restaurants in Old Nassau

Graycliff, West Hill Street (tel. 809/322-2796), is the elegant and aristocratic dining choice of Nassau (see my hotel recommendations). In an antique-filled colonial mansion, opposite Government House, Graycliff was once the home of the Earl and Countess Dudley of Staffordshire. Its present owner, Enrico Garzaroli, has hired an exciting young Bahamian chef, Phillip Bethel, who produces food of culinary excellence, served in a restrained, polite setting of charm and grace, surrounded by lush gardens.

The menu opens with caviar and gourmet terrines, including foie gras with truffles and a pâté of hare with pine kernels, perhaps young wild Abaco boar pâté with walnuts. The soups and pastas are outstanding, including chilled cream of cucumber or fettuccine Enrico (made with a mixture of white truffles if you're willing to pay extra). The chef is a master at the charcoal grill and spit, as my recently sampled spit-roasted duckling flambé with apple brandy showed. Such classic main courses are offered as a roast rack of lamb with herbs and chateaubriand with a perfectly made béarnaise sauce. The seafood pasta is another favorite order. The fish selection in general is outstanding, including grilled spiny lobster, grouper in a cream and Dijon mustard sauce, and Dover sole meunière. All main dishes are cooked *à la minute.*

If, after all that, you have still survived, you'll find a masterful array of Italian desserts, including a cassata, a chilled zabaglione, and/or a selection from the master pastry chef. Expect to spend at least $75 for dinner, plus wine and service. The table settings are opulent, and the wine list is the best in The Bahamas, with more than 1,000 selections, some often stunning vintages priced at thousands of dollars. Before dinner, try the charming balcony bar. Lunch is served Monday to Friday from noon to 3 p.m.; dinner, from 7 to 10 p.m. A reservation is essential, and men should wear jackets.

Buena Vista, Delancy and Meeting Streets (tel. 809/322-2811), is a 200-year-old colonial mansion set on five acres of tropical foliage, a dining choice of traditional elegance and fine eating. The house has had a long and colorful history and was once owned by a Presbyterian minister. Perhaps Rhett Butler types stayed here during the Civil War, loading schooners to run through the North's blockade. Today, it's a favorite of the local banking and business community. When the weather's right, which is most of the time, tables are set out on the garden patio, surrounded by flowers and palms. A menu of daily specialties is featured, including a set dinner for $35. Otherwise, you can order from the regular à la carte menu costing from $40 per person, which features a number of main dishes for two, such as a roast rack of lamb in the style of Provence. The chef also prepares excellent beef and veal dishes. Many guests like to begin their meal with the daily pasta. One of the chef's specialties is cream of garlic soup, a novelty dish. Desserts include cherries jubilee or orange crêpes au Grand Marnier. Buena Vista is open for dinner only, from 7 to 10 p.m., and it's necessary to make a reservation. In addition to haute cuisine under the direction of Stan Bocus, the host, the restaurant turns out a number of nouvelle cuisine dishes. Service is deft and efficient, but also polite. Delancy Street is opposite the cathedral close of St. Francis Xavier, only a short distance from Bay Street.

The **Regatta Room,** Pilot House Hotel, East Bay Street (tel. 809/322-8431), is popular with the yachting set. It's a five-minute walk from Paradise Island Bridge in a previously recommended hotel, across the street from a marina. Offering meals costing $30 and up, it's open only in the evening from 7 to 11. It adjoins the Three Ladies, a less expensive restaurant operated by the same hotel. Against a backdrop of a nautically inspired decor, you might begin with gazpacho or perhaps oysters Rockefeller. The chef makes an excellent Bahamian conch salad. Main courses include Bahamian lobster tails, spaghetti in fish stock with baby clams, filet of grouper with mussels, sirloin steak, or roast chicken with rosemary. You can also order a chateaubriand or roast rack of lamb. Service is polite and efficient.

Sun and . . . ,Lake View Road, off Shirley Street (tel. 809/323-1205), is one of the oldest restaurants in Nassau. Everybody has dined here from Sir Winston Churchill to the Gabors, even Queen Elizabeth and Prince Philip. The place became a bit of a local legend when it was run by Pete Gardner, a former Battle of Britain "ace" who'd originally come to Nassau when he was an aide to the then governor, Lord Ranfurly. Nowadays its present owners, Ronnie and Esther Deryckere, maintain the same high standards.

You pass over a drawbridge between two pools, going into a Spanish-style courtyard of a fine old Bahamian home, complete with fountains. You can order drinks in the patio bar, followed by dinner either inside or al fresco around the rock pool. The pool, incidentally, is the oldest private swimming pool in Nassau. As a historical note, the rock removed from it was used to build the house. You might begin with conch chowder and then follow with any number of main dishes, reflecting both a Stateside and a continental cuisine. Main dishes are likely to include braised duckling in lemon sauce, sweetbreads and kidneys in mustard sauce, spiny Caribbean lobster with a corn and pimiento sauce, or roast grouper with scallop mousse and a light lobster sauce. The dessert specialty is a coconut soufflé. The restaurant shuts down every year from the first of August until the first of October. Otherwise it is open daily except Monday from 6:30 to 9:30 p.m. You should make a reservation. Your tab will run around $50 or more.

The flavor and cuisine of an authentic French restaurant has been re-created in Nassau at **Del Prado Restaurant,** West Bay Street (tel. 809/325-0324), just west of town. Stained glass windows complement the contemporary decor while fine bone china, crystal, silver, and candlelight complete the ambience. The creator of the cuisine is a talented chef and restaurant manager, Dave McCorquodale. For drinks to desserts, Del Prado chefs combine classic flavors with local fresh fruits, fish, vegetables and liqueurs. A local seafood coquille, conch chowder, and lobster bisque are additions to the more traditional appetizers of pâté, escargot, and sautéed squid. Local fish and chicken creations swell the list of main dishes that include steaks, lamb, veal, and duckling, some in the most well-flavored sauces. Try le magret de canard senteurs d'Orient or the medallions de veau a l'orange.

Presentation and service are important, too, at Del Prado. It all adds up to one of the better restaurants in town. Full meals range upward from $50 per person, although a "Sundowner" five-course dinner special is offered for $26.25 every day from 6 to 9 p.m., with a glass of wine included. Reservations are suggested, and jackets are preferred. Only dinner is served, from 6 to 11 p.m. seven days a week.

Nassau's Moderately Priced Restaurants

The **Green Shutters Restaurant,** 48 Parliament St. (tel. 809/325-5702), is about as close as Nassau comes to having an authentic English country pub, which features five imported British beers and serves steak-and-kidney pie. After being gutted by fire in 1971, this charming 190-year-old colonial house was completely restored. The place is large, offering dining in the pub section with the regulars or in the mahogany-paneled restaurant. Francis Goodwin-Davies, known as the "Gov," uses only Bahamian cooks. His menu is varied, offering the best from The Bahamas, with fresh seafood complemented by traditional British fare: bangers and mash, shepherd's pie, and "chip butty." For dinner, roast prime rib with Yorkshire pudding and fresh key lime pie for dessert is a winner. Some Bahamian specialties such as grouper and conch salad are also featured. Vichyssoise, called "tater soup" here, and escargots with fresh spinach salad may tempt you. The sandwiches at lunch are particularly good and well stuffed, including the triple-decker club. Courage beer is on tap, and the bartender also offers fresh frozen sugar apple-banana daiquiris. Count on spending $12 for lunch and $22 for dinner. Lunch is served from 11:30 a.m. to 4 p.m. and dinner from 6 to 10:30 p.m. The place has live music five nights a week.

Liz's Restaurant, Elizabeth Avenue (tel. 809/322-4780), just off Bay Street, is one of the most popular restaurants in Nassau, serving good, tender steaks such as T-bone and sirloin, sizzling from the grill, along with a selection of seafood, including lobster Thermidor, Bahamian red snapper in lemon butter, and a conch fritter boat. You might also prefer grouper royal with bananas and chutney. Set behind a West Indian louvered façade, the restaurant offers good-tasting meals for around $40. Dinner begins at 6:30 p.m., lasting "until the wee hours," or when the crowd goes home.

Blackbeard's Forge, Sheraton-British Colonial Hotel, 1 Bay St. (tel. 809-322-3301), is a far cry from the rough-and-ready pirate days in Nassau, with its rich red velvet, good food, and courteous service. It does, however, boast a modern "pirates' decor" of wood and chrome tables, each with a box-shaped smoke vent above to catch the smoke from its individual grill. Rope coils surround the columns. Nautical touches, such as old prints and maps, and the huge bay window shaped like the stern of a sailing vessel remind diners of the days when Nassau was a pirates' haven. You can feast on Bahamian conch chowder or onion soup, sirloin steak, jumbo shrimp kebab, lobster tail, grouper filets, surf and turf, or breast of chicken, topped with coconut-cream layer cake or walnut cake. Expect to pay from $18. Blackbeard's is open daily from 6 to 11 p.m. Reservations are advised.

Europe, Ocean Spray Hotel, West Bay Street (tel. 809/322-8032), offers the best German specialties in Nassau, along with a sampling of continental dishes. Attached to a moderately priced hotel already recommended, the Europe restaurant is appropriately named. It is attracting more and more German visitors who are "discovering" The Bahamas, but it also draws a good patronage among locals as well as North Americans. If you're driving you'll find parking in the rear of the restaurant.

You might begin with such fare as a hearty soup, perhaps lima bean and sausage. You can then go on to bratwurst, a Wiener schnitzel, perhaps peppersteak cognac. Sauerbraten is an eternal favorite, and the chef also prepares two kinds of fondue, both bourguignonne and cheese. Everybody's favorite dessert is German chocolate cake. Meals cost $10 to $25. Hours are from 8 a.m. to 1 a.m. Monday to Saturday, from 5 p.m. to 1:30 a.m. Sunday.

Mai Tai Chinese-Polynesian Restaurant, Waterloo Lodge, East Bay Street (tel. 809/326-5088), near Fort Montagu, is a family-run establishment hailed as the leading Oriental eating place in Nassau. Peter Wong and his family provide dinners with everything from exotic drinks to Polynesian, Szechuan, and Cantonese dishes, with some Hawaiian influences evident. Before settling down to lunch or dinner in this old Bahamian mansion, try one of the drinks the place offers to complement the Oriental theme: Volcanic Flame (served with flaming rum), Lover's Paradise, or perhaps a Fog Cutter.

Appetizers may vary from a pupu platter with ingredients heated over a flaming brazier to tidbits served on wooden platters. In the Polynesian mood? You might choose chow samsee, deviled Bahamian lobster, Mandarin orange duck, or sizzling Mai Tai steak. Szechuan dishes include, among many others, hot shredded spiced beef, kung pao chicken ding, or such chef's specials as chu ka fook (happy family) or lemon chicken. Cantonese selections are lengthy, with chicken almond ding and moo goo gai pan competing for my preference with the sweet-and-sour chicken or pork. The list of excellent Chinese-Polynesian dishes makes it hard to decide what to select, but of course you can go with a party and follow tradition by having everybody order something different so you get a taste of a lot of delectable dishes. Also the place has take-out service. Mai Tai is open daily for lunch from 11:30 a.m. to 3 p.m. and for dinner from 5:30 to 11 p.m. A complete dinner is likely to cost from $35 per person, and you get a lot of good food and polite service for that.

Roselawn Café, Bank Lane, off Bay Street (tel. 809/325-1018), operated by the previously recommended Buena Vista restaurant, is one of the most delightful places for dining in downtown Nassau. You'll forget the bargain-seeking cruise-ship crowds, as you wander into its private courtyard. At this old Bahamian house you can select a table inside or one on the patio, in a setting of potted plants and statues. I go here mainly for the superb homemade pastas, including creamy lasagne and spaghetti cooked al dente. They even have a pizza oven, turning out familiar favorites, including a house special made with olives and anchovies. There is a selection of antipasti, and also an array of fresh Bahamian seafood, including spiny lobster. The chef also prepares an excellent minestrone, which might be a fine beginning to your meal. Desserts are luscious as well. In the evening, there is live entertainment. Lunches cost about $10; dinners, $15 to $20. The restaurant is open for lunch from 11:30 a.m. to 2:30 p.m. and for dinner from 6:30 to 10 p.m. Look for the daily specials. The place is also open from 10 p.m. to 6 a.m. for drinks and supper, such as pizzas and pastas.

The **Parliament Terrace Café,** 18 Parliament St. (tel. 809/322-2836), is set in the palm-studded tropical garden of Nassau's oldest operating hotel, in the Parliament. Casually dressed diners go here for Bahamian seafood specialties and native entertainment in the evening, anytime from 6 to 10. Bahamian calypsos are heard here, making the Parliament one of the few places left in Nassau where you can hear this type of music. It's run by the husband-and-wife team of Graham and Anne Bruce. Their chef is "Pappy" Sam Smith, who knows how to produce an onion soup that is said to have come from Farouk, former king of Egypt.

Appetizers include conch salad or snails in garlic butter. The fish dishes are excellent, especially the house special, grouper florentine. Try also cracked conch or conch curry. The dessert special is Graham's own English trifle. Dinners cost from $18. The regular luncheon buffet, costing $8, usually lets you choose a hot dish with vegetables and rice as well as making a trip to the salad bar. The café is open daily from 7:30 to 10 a.m., 11:30 a.m. to 4 p.m., and 6 to 10 p.m. Closed Sunday at lunch. There is, as well, a large tropical drink menu, featuring frozen fruit daiquiris. With a view of the Supreme Court Building, the café stands in downtown Nassau.

The Three Ladies, Pilot House Hotel, East Bay Street (tel. 809/322-8431), was named after a trio of experts on Bahamian cookery. It is separated from the inner courtyard's pool of this hotel with low lattice balustrades and awnings. It's al fresco dining, and there is a large floral mural against the wall. It offers American, continental, and Bahamian dishes, meals costing from $20. Among the latter offerings are steamed Andros conch, native curried lamb, barbecued short ribs, and fish chowder Eleuthera style. The setting, drawing the boating crowd, is especially pleasant in the evening. Hours are 7:30 to 10:30 a.m. for breakfast, noon to 2:30 p.m. for lunch, and 7 to 10 p.m. for dinner. At happy hour here, you get conch fritters and two drinks for the price of one (that is, every day but Thursday).

The Poop Deck, East Bay Street (tel. 809/322-8175), is a favorite with the yachting set, who find a perch on the second-floor open-air terrace, overlooking the harbor. Across from the Pilot House, the deck opens not only onto the yachts in the harbor, but fronts Paradise Island as well. The outside tables are reserved for lunch and dinner service, and there's an inside bar as well if you're dropping in only for a drink. The bar, incidentally, opens at 11:30 a.m. Food is served all day, seven days a week. Lunch is from noon to 5 p.m.; dinner, from 5 to 10:30 p.m. At lunch, you can order conch chowder, followed by beefburgers. In the evening, native grouper fingers are served with peas 'n' rice, or you might prefer Rosie's special chicken or Bahamian broiled crayfish. Stuffed deviled crab is another specialty, and the chef does a homemade lasagne with crisp garlic bread. Your check should come to $12 at lunch, $25 at dinner.

The **Cellar and Garden Patio,** 11 Charlotte St. (tel. 809/322-8877), lies half a block from Bay Street in the downtown section, near the Straw Market and Rawson Square. It makes for a pleasant dining choice, not only because of its good food but because its garden patio setting creates an oasis of greenery. Midday meals are served from a countertop in the outermost room, near the entrance. In an ambience midway between a Mediterranean cellar and an English pub, you can lunch on specials, salads, and sandwiches for $12 per person, served daily from 11 a.m. to 4 p.m. During dinner the setting moves to the lattice-rimmed courtyard where glass-topped tables are set under cascading vines. Many diners, however, prefer the formal dining room in an old cottage at the far end of the courtyard. When it was built, it was a simple clapboard out-building with a large fireplace at the far end. Today the napery, candlelight, and well-prepared food make the rustic setting even more charming. Since only eight tables can be served here without cramping, dinner reservations are important.

Specialties include chicken gumbo Cajun style, steamed filet of grouper in a piquant sauce, shrimp Créole (or shrimp jambalaya), filet of pork in a lemon sauce flavored with coriander, steak-and-mushroom pie cooked in Guinness, and lamb cutlets in an orange-and-ginger sauce. Several main dishes have the vegetarian in mind. There is always a homemade soup of the day, and the chef also prepares delectable appetizers (and not just conch fritters). Dinner is served from 6 to 10 p.m. daily except Sunday. Full dinners cost from $25. Owners Lila and Allan Pinder hire live steel drum bands to perform nightly on the patio from 6:30 to 10 Monday to Saturday.

The **Bayside Buffet Restaurant,** Sheraton-British Colonial Hotel, 1 Bay St. (tel. 809/322-7479), is worth visiting almost as much for its view as for its good and reasonably priced food. The tall, 100-foot-long windows front on the entrance to Nassau's harbor, allowing a panoramic view of cruise ships, yachts, and other boats around Prince George Wharf. Lunch is offered for $10 and dinner for $15 and up, with such selections as prime rib, steamed shrimp, ham, turkey, roast pork loin, fish, homemade pasta salads, and crabmeat salad, as well as salads of greens, fresh vegetables, and other ingredients. The salad bar is arguably the best in town. You can have breakfast here from 7 to 11:30 a.m., with other meals served until 11 p.m. If you don't want to choose from the buffet, you might like to have lunch or dinner à la carte at the Wharf Café, next to the Bayside's buffet area. Omelets, seafood salad, chef's salad, and desserts are offered. A meal costs around $10.

For Low-Cost Bahamian Food

The **Bahamian Kitchen,** Trinity Place, off Market Street (tel. 809/325-0702), next to Trinity Church, is one of the best places for good Bahamian cookery at modest prices. Specialties include lobster Bahamian style, fried red snapper, conch salad, stewed fish, steamed mutton, okra soup, and pea soup and dumplings. Most dishes are served with peas 'n' rice. For dessert, the guava duff is my preference, but I'm also tempted by the coconut pie, the rum cake, and the banana pudding. Lunch runs from $12, and dinner costs from $18. Breakfast, costing from $6, is an event here, including such old-fashioned Bahamian fare as stewed fish and corned beef and grits, all served with johnnycake. Of course, you can order ham and eggs as well. There is a takeout service. The place, open daily from 8 a.m. to 11 p.m., is honest, decent, and upright.

Palm Restaurant, Bay Street (tel. 809/323-7444). At first glance you might think this place is just a coffeeshop, but the menu reveals a varied selection. Decorated like a tropical version of a Stateside cafeteria, it has ceiling fans, fern-patterned wallpaper, and waitress service. It's a sure bet as a place where you can get an early dinner or even a midafternoon snack after browsing in the shops that line the sidewalks on either side. Conchburgers are an unusual adaptation of the familiar favorite shellfish, or you can order Bahamian fried chicken, barbecued spareribs, black-bean soup, several veal dishes, crab thermidor, or an array of salads and sandwiches. For dessert, you can select from an array of ice-cream flavors, including rum raisin, guava, and soursop. Full meals range from around $18, although lighter orders will cost less. The location is opposite John Bull. Hours are 7:30 a.m. to 9:30 p.m. daily except Sunday.

Coco's Café, West Bay Street (tel. 809/323-8778), stands across from the Sheraton British Colonial Hotel. A casual, informal café, decorated in a modern art deco style with neon, it is a good all-around choice for either breakfast (7:30 to 11 a.m.), lunch (11:30 a.m. to 5 p.m.), or dinner (5 to 11 p.m.). It is also open seven days a week. You might begin by perusing their drink menu, including every concoction from Bahama Mama to Goombay Smash. The menu is quite extensive, including hot and cold sandwiches, along with such prepared dishes as crab thermidor or cracked conch. You can order that old budgeteer's favorite, grouper fingers, or perhaps a seafood lasagne. There is also a long list of burgers, or perhaps you'd prefer a generous Caesar salad. Cheesecake comes with a choice of toppings, or else you might prefer one of their rich, moist cakes, perhaps chocolate or carrot. Meals cost from $12 and up. At breakfast, you could come here for that typically Bahamian favorite, boiled fish and grits, should you desire. But the kitchen will also prepare eggs any way you want them, along with pancakes and French toast.

Pirate's Tavern, East Street (tel. 809/322-1550), lies right off Bay Street near Rawson Square. Centrally perched in the heart of downtown Nassau, it's a subterranean tavern open from 11 a.m. till midnight Monday through Saturday, serving a limited but well-selected menu, not only some good local dishes but tropical drinks as well. Andros crab soup vies for prominence with Exuma conch chowder, or perhaps the Cat Island lobster salad will tempt you as an appetizer instead of the soup. Main courses, including grouper, are served with a vegetable and a side order of your choice. Count on spending about $15 each. Service is extra. You head down one flight of stairs into a nautically decorated setting.

Natural Foods in Nassau

Choosy Foods, Market Street (tel. 809/326-5232), is housed in a colonial-style building one block from the Straw Market. The floor space is divided between a health-food store and a "natural foods" restaurant. You can browse through the inventory of books, herbal teas, and macrobiotic supplies after enjoying a wholesome meal that might include vegetable soup, quiche, freshly squeezed juice, and vegetarian specials. The lobster lasagne is a gourmet treat you may not want to miss. There's also a salad bar and an array of deli-style sandwiches. Of course, conch is the featured salad, although a full range of others can be ordered as well. A full meal costs from $12. Lunch is served from 11 a.m. to 5 p.m. and dinner from 5 to 9:30 p.m., Monday to Saturday. Only regular beer, non-alcoholic beer, and wine are served.

Dining Oriental on a Budget

The **Oriental Express Restaurant,** on Bay Street opposite the Straw Market (tel. 809/326-7127), one level below the street, is a budget Oriental eatery. Chinese food is served cafeteria style, with large helpings, in a dining room decorated with Oriental fittings and a mirrored ceiling that lends an airy feel. A meal of standard Chinese dishes, such as sweet-and-sour ribs, pork, shrimp, or chicken, barbecued ribs, and pineapple chicken or beef, costs from $12. The restaurant is open from 11:30 a.m. to 9 p.m. Monday to Saturday.

At Saunders Beach

Tony Roma's, West Bay Street (tel. 809/325-2022), on the main road between Nassau and Cable Beach, at Saunders Beach, is one of my favorite places on New Providence for rib-sticking portions and good value. The stone-trimmed modern building offers views of Saunders Beach from the tables of its open-air veranda. Inside, the decor includes exposed paneling, spindle-backed captain's chairs, and ceiling fans.

The establishment advertises itself as "the place for ribs," and if you order them, you'll discover that they are a good choice for the house specialty. Barbecued in a special sauce, they come in small (lunchtime) or large orders. They can be accompanied by barbecued chicken as part of the same platter. Juicy sandwiches made from barbecued beef or London broil, about the best hamburgers on the island, Bahamian conch chowder, chef's or green salads, and pan-fried grouper are also offered. Every weekday there's a daily special, such as Eleuthera chicken curry, roast turkey with giblet gravy, or Exuma steamed conch. I always begin my meal with an order of the succulent onion rings, which are served in a steaming loaf to be eaten with a spicy sauce. Beer on tap can accompany any meal, and there is also an array of tropical drinks, such as the bananaroma float. Open daily from 11 a.m. to midnight (to 2 a.m. on Friday and Saturday), the restaurant charges $15 to $20 for full meals. Special Monday to Friday lunches can cost as little as $6.50 with dinner specials priced at only $10.95.

3. CABLE BEACH LODGING AND DINING

Cable Beach is regarded by many as the ultimate island resort area, with broad stretches of beachfront, a wide array of activity and entertainment, and hotel facilities that offer an ideal blend of modern convenience with tropical charm. The range is from a deluxe penthouse suite to a simple housekeeping unit in an apartment hotel.

Sports facilities abound on both land and water. For example, the tennis facility at the Cable Beach Hotel offers ten courts, five of them lit, plus a stadium for tournament and exhibition play. Adjacent is an indoor complex featuring three courts each for squash and racquetball, while an 18-hole championship golf course is just across the street.

Along the beachfront, craft and equipment are available for all manner of water sports, often including private instruction. Sailing and waterskiing are the traditional activities, but windsurfing and parasailing are the rage with contemporary travelers.

The shoreline west of the city of Nassau was named for the telegraph cable laid in 1892 from Jupiter, Florida, to The Bahamas, making it possible for the first time to send messages directly to the United States and England.

For many years horse racing was the main attraction at Cable Beach. The 104-acre Hobby Horse Hall Race Course was mentioned in newspaper accounts as early as 1809. Racing continued throughout the 19th century, carried on mainly by officers of the British West India Regiment stationed in Nassau. After a hiatus during World War I, horse racing resumed in 1933, marking the beginning of an annual season that continued until the track closed in 1975.

Much of Cable Beach was once devoted to the cultivation of pineapple the J.S. Johnson Company, which exported to the United States. In the 1920s, according to the historian Michael Craton, the area "became dotted with the stucco palaces of American nouveaux riches."

HOTELS OF CABLE BEACH: After World War II Nassau's first luxury beach resorts were built on Cable Beach. The 213-room Emerald Beach Hotel, opened in 1954, was the first to feature air conditioning. The 145-room Balmoral Beach Hotel was built in 1946 as a private club and opened as a resort in 1967. The 410-room Nassau Beach Hotel was built in the late '60s by the Crothers family of Canada and acquired in 1969 by Trusthouse Forte. The 400-room Ambassador Beach Hotel, built by Sonesta Hotels, opened in 1971.

In 1974 the government bought the Emerald Beach, Balmoral Beach, and Ambassador Beach Hotels for a total of $20 million, and the Hotel Corporation of The Bahamas was set up to run them.

Of all these hotels, the Balmoral was a special case. It was created by the British developer Sir Oliver Simmonds, who began work on its construction almost immediately following the close of World War II. For years he'd been aware that the wealthy, the powerful—world leaders, royalty, and the most famous stage, screen, opera, ballet, and concert stars—were constantly searching for closed little corners of the world where they could find peace and privacy, along with the best accommodations available.

Simmonds spread the word that his Balmoral Beach Club was so ultra-exclusive that it would operate as a private club and would be absolutely restricted only to members and their approved guests. As a result, Simmonds found himself besieged with requests for membership and reservations from all corners of the world. The Balmoral became an immediate success worldwide. After 16 years of this, Simmonds decided on semi-retirement and leased the property to the Hotel Corporation of America. Beginning in 1962 and for 22 years thereafter, the Balmoral underwent constant changes in physical structure and in management.

When the Beatles were being mobbed from New York City to Hong Kong and could find no place where they could escape from their fame, they were accepted by the Balmoral. The lads from Liverpool were awed by the fact that they could walk the byways of the compound, sun at the poolside, walk through the dining room, and roam the beaches of Balmoral Island seemingly unrecognized.

The Duke and Duchess of Windsor frequently journeyed to The Bahamas, where the former King of England and governor of The Bahamas enjoyed the blessings of being just another Balmoral guest. Another frequent visitor was Richard Nixon, who also appreciated the anonymity afforded by the hotel. He used to arrive unexpectedly, sometimes by boat. The Gabors visited to become simple, unadored, and unadorned—but only for so long.

Changes in management continued until 1974 when Simmonds resumed control of the property, but only long enough to sell it outright to the Hotel Corporation of The Bahamas. In 1984 the corporation decided on a major multi-million-dollar restoration of the historic property, and Wyndham Hotels, a subsidiary of the Trammell Crow Hotel Company, was named to operate and manage the property.

One of the first steps was to change the name from the Balmoral Beach Club to the Royal Bahamian and begin a $7-million remodeling program to restore the resort to its niche among luxury retreats. The transformation was completed, and the resort reopened in December 1984. In the previous year, the 700-room Cable Beach Hotel had opened, making Cable Beach a glittering beachfront strip in its new incarnation. It has now been taken over by the French-owned Le Meridien. Its latest and most dazzling property is Carnival's Crystal Palace Resort & Casino.

All of these hotels are previewed below.

The Big Resort Hotels

Carnival's Crystal Palace Resort & Casino, P.O. Box N-8306, Nassau, The Bahamas (tel. 809/327-6200 or toll free at 800/453-5301), is the largest and most spectacular hotel in The Bahamas, a 900,000-square-foot resort and casino complex costing in the tens of millions. Flamboyantly painted in colors of purple, pink, lilac, and mauve, it has made such an impact on Cable Beach that the name was changed to the "Bahamian Riviera." This resort, which has unfolded in the heart of this new Riviera, was a joint undertaking of Carnival Cruise Lines and the Continental Companies of Miami, a hotel management and development firm. Set on its own beach, the hotel was designed by Joe Farcus, known for his innovative work on Carnival's three superliners.

The Crystal Palace consists of five towers, the last of which opened in 1989. All 867 rooms are decorated in the same color theme evocative of the interior, a medley of violets and mauves, along with accents in aqua and turquoise. Each accommodation has its own balcony, and most open onto sea views. The deluxe accommodations are called "premium player" suites, occupying the top three floors of the Casino Tower.

In winter, single or double occupancy ranges from $140 to $215 nightly, *with 20% reductions granted in summer.* A family plan grants two children under the age of 18 a free stay when sharing the same accommodation with their parents, using existing bedding. Suites costs a lot, lot more. For example, corner suites for two begin at $300 daily, but can climb to $1,500 a night for two in one of the specialty theme suites. If none of the above is lavish enough to please you, the Crystal Palace has designed the ultimate suite, not only in The Bahamas, but in all the Caribbean. At $25,000 a night (you heard right), it is called Galactic Fantasy. In white and silver, it is a taste of the 21st century today. You're even attended by a friendly robot who explains the functions of all the high-tech "toys" at your command. You get, among other things, thunder and lightning at the touch of a button should that be your desire. This is just one of six fanciful penthouse suites created for the Casino Tower. Other such suites include a sultry Casablanca, a Hemingway bit of grandeur (called Kilimanjaro), even a Japanese Kyoto and a French Versailles.

The resort also features a number of restaurants, including the unique Chan and Schwartz, which is an informal half-Chinese, half–New York deli offering everything from lobster cantonese to a pastrami on rye with lots of mustard. The Sole Mare, a gourmet Italian restaurant, is the premier dining room of the resort. At Le Grille, you can select your steak during the day and return that evening to have it prepared to your specification. Regardless of when you want to eat, there's an around-the-clock big buffet always laid out. To top it off, a sushi bar overlooks the ocean. Recreational facilities are vast, including eight tennis courts (clay and hard), squash courts, an 18-hole golf course nearby, a gym, sauna, steam room, aerobics classes, a body-surfing ramp, a 20-foot spiral water slide, and two whirlpools. Before entering a two-level swimming pool, with a waterfall, you can change into your swimming suit in a $1 million re-created "ship" on the beach which was made of concrete and teak. As for service, this vast complex employs more staff than any other organization in The Bahamas with the exception of the government.

Cable Beach Hotel, P.O. Box N-4914, Nassau, The Bahamas (tel. 809/329-6000, or toll free 800/822-4200), stands next door to Carnival's Crystal Palace Resort & Casino, which purchased it for $82.5 million and might even be marketing it under a different banner by the time you read this. Expect major changes to happen here during the lifetime of this edition, so check with a travel agent before booking a room. With an Aztec-inspired collection of sharp angles and buff-color surfaces, it evokes thoughts of Las Vegas, with the rows of fountains in front seeming to point to the arcade leading to the adjacent casino. This hotel is an excellent choice for anyone who never wants to run out of things to do. With 693 bedrooms the place is big enough to get lost in, but it's easy to find plenty of intimate retreats. A bevy of social hostesses arranges daily activities in and out of the water, and there is literally always something happening, so much so that many guests call this establishment the greatest never-ending show on the island. During the day the party establishes itself around the well-landscaped core of the hotel, near the beach. There, an imaginative series of man-made rock formations channels splashing cascades of recirculating waterfalls down their jagged sides. The water splashes into jungle-style lagoons that serve as reflecting pools, children's wading pools, Jacuzzis, and play areas for frolicsome guests. There's also a more conventional rectangular pool, as well as a complicated series of terraces dotted with tropical bars, chaises longues, and shingle-roofed umbrellas, which stretch along the sugar-white beachfront.

The comfortable rooms are contained in nine floors in an air-conditioned, modern design. Each benefits from an ocean view, attractive furnishings, and a private bath. Singles or doubles range from \$160 to \$220 daily in winter, \$110 to \$170 in summer. The hotel embraces its beach facilities in a vast, U-shaped sweep of symmetrical wings. Its four-story lobby is sheathed in glass and ringed with facilities that include a cabaña bar with live music, an array of boutiques, and dozens of comfortable banquettes bathed in natural light. There are five dining facilities inside. For a description of the complete water-sports program of this resort giant, refer to "The Sporting Life," coming up. There are also ten tennis courts and facilities for squash and racquetball, as well as a fully equipped health club.

Le Meridien Royal Bahamian, P.O. Box N-10422, Nassau, The Bahamas (tel. 809/325-6400, or toll free 800/543-4300), is an elegant and lavishly refurbished hotel acquired by this French chain. Built as a private club in 1946 to shelter the rich and the famous from prying eyes and outsiders, it became a hotel in 1967, the Balmoral Beach. The hostelry still exudes a kind of undated colonial charm. A sweeping canopy shelters guests on their way to the entrance portico, where smartly tailored female concièrges welcome newcomers with offers of assistance. Many old British customs are observed here, including the serving of tea at 4 p.m. in one of the lavishly decorated public rooms. These have been furnished with Chippendale reproductions, brass chandeliers, marble and carpeted floors, comfortable French settees, and, along the curved walls of one of the rose-colored salons, about a dozen bandy-legged desks for letter writing.

The central core of the property, the Manor House, has a courtyard where a stork fountain spits water at what may remind you of the façade of a Corinthian temple. Manor House living is not the only option for guests, as the resort contains ten spacious and imaginatively decorated villas, each done in warm-weather opulence. The largest will accommodate six to eight occupants. Some have Jacuzzis and private pools, and some of the bathrooms are as spacious as many big-city apartments. A well-trained and discreet staff add the final cachet to a fine hotel. The bedrooms have cove moldings, formal English furniture, satellite TV, air conditioning, and baths loaded with such amenities as bathrobes, perfumed soaps, and cosmetics. The ocean-view rooms offer small curved terraces with ornate iron railings and views of Balmoral Island. In winter, the 145 rooms rent for \$145 to \$220 per night, single or double occupancy; suites, of course, cost more. *In summer, single or double rooms range from \$95 to \$140 per day.* Its restaurants are previewed separately.

There's a complete spa facility on the premises, equipped with many kinds of massage, exercise, and health-inducing regimes. The establishment also offers a complete array of water sports, racquet sports, and golf. Some of these are conducted at the nearby Cable Beach Hotel, which is connected to the Royal Bahamian with frequent free transportation. There's a long stretch of sandy beach, an hourglass-shaped pool, and one of my favorite bars in The Bahamas, the Palm Bar, where you can listen to the evening pianist. Waiters serve your drinks as you're seated in low-slung French armchairs. The entrance to the bar is guarded by a pair of life-size porcelain English setters, and the lamps in the room have porcelain bases shaped like retrievers.

Nassau Beach Hotel, P.O. Box N-7756, Nassau, The Bahamas (tel. 809/327-7711, 212/686-7537 in New York City, or toll free 800/223-5672, 800/268-9761 in Canada), was built in a dignified gray-and-white, twin-towered design with neo-Georgian accents. It has three wings. This 411-room resort is now better than ever, following an $8.5-million renovation program. It's managed by Trusthouse Forte properties, which also handles such illustrious addresses as the Grosvenor House in London and the Plaza Athenée in Paris. As you enter, the lobby sets the tone. The tile floors and marble are enhanced by a Bahamian ambience that includes ceiling paddle fans and upholstered wicker furniture. After you check in, you are shown to one of the guest rooms or suites. The rooms are not only attractively furnished, but they contain marble baths and dressing areas. Units also have hairdryers and color TVs. The Nassau Beach was the first major resort in The Bahamas to include daily taxes and service in its tariffs. In winter, a single or double on the EP ranges in price from $145 to $210 daily. *In summer, rates in a single or a double are $125 to $175 daily.* Suites and the oceanfront two-bedroom penthouse cost far more, of course. There's even a presidential suite.

The hotel also has an entry into the popular, all-inclusive market, the Palm Club. Included in all four-, five-, and eight-day packages are a chilled bottle of champagne on arrival, deluxe accommodations in a reserved wing of the Nassau Beach Hotel with views of the Atlantic or the resort's gardens, chauffeur-driven limousine transfers, a private concierge suite, cocktails, complete recreation including unlimited greens fees at the Cable Beach Golf Club, taxes and tips, and special amenities including a full-time club director. Vacationers at the Palm Club may choose from among the hotel's restaurants to eat breakfast, lunch, and dinner, with complimentary wine. Entertainment is a day-long affair, whether it's by a live band on the all-day boat excursions to Rose Island or a casino revue. *Off-season, prices at the Palm Club per person are $499 for double or triple occupancy for four days, $799 as a single. For five days, the charge is $599 for doubles or triples, $899 single. The eight-day package rent is $1,099 double or triple, $1,499 single.* In winter, per-person rates are $599 double or triple, $849 single. A five-day stay is priced at $699 double or triple, $949 single, with an eight-day package costing $1,199 double or triple, $1,599 single.

In spite of its size, this hotel somehow manages to avoid the impersonal sprawling look. Instead of a dining room three square miles in size, it has wisely chosen to break up its facilities into several theme restaurants. For example, if you want gourmet fare, you can patronize Pineapple Place. For yet another dining experience, you can grill your own steak in the Beef Cellar. There's even an American Café if you're with kids and/or economizing. The most elegant dining spot is Frilsham House. The Out Island Bar, for drinks and dancing in the evening, is one of the major after-dark attractions along Cable Beach. Several of these facilities will be recommended separately, since the Nassau Beach Hotel attracts many nonresidents to its entertainment and restaurant facilities. Thursday night is festive here: the hotel stages a Junkanoo, where visitors get to sample such Bahamian foods as conch fritters, grouper fingers, peas 'n' rice, and rum pies.

The resort is also one of the most sports-oriented along Cable Beach. It opens onto a 3,000-foot white sand beach and has a tennis complex of six all-weather courts lit for night games. A teaching pro is on hand, and there are health spa facilities as well. The hotel is home to the Bahamas International Windsurfing Regatta, the richest Pro-Am boardsailing event in the North Atlantic. For reservations or more information, contact any travel agent or the Nassau Beach Hotel, 500 Deer Run, Miami, FL 33166 (tel. 305/871-1830), or Trusthouse Forte Hotels (tel. toll free 800/225-5843 in the U.S.).

Wyndham Ambassador Beach Hotel, P.O. Box N-3026, Nassau, The Bahamas (tel. 809/327-8231, or toll free 800/822-4200, 800/631-4200 in Canada), is a resort and convention hotel, which, although owned by the Commonwealth of The Bahamas, is operated and staffed by the Wyndham Hotel Corp. of Dallas, Texas. The inner courtyard formed by the hotel's U-shaped design embraces a leafy collection of palms, a freshwater swimming pool, and a sugar-white stretch of fine-sand beach. The property combines both modern and colonial style in an informally attractive collection of restaurants, bars, and public rooms, which are upholstered and sheathed in decorator colors of dusty rose, peach, and mauve, whose tones are highlighted with paneling painted either in white enamel or in natural-grain finishes.

Winter rates for single or double rooms range from $120 to $165 per night, plus service and taxes. A third person can share an accommodation for an additional $35 per night. *In summer, single or double units cost $95 to $100 per night.* MAP can be arranged for an additional $31 per person per day. On the premises are the Palm Court Bar and a game room with wide-screen satellite TV. A full array of water sports can be arranged, as well as day or night tennis, squash, and racquetball.

Housekeeping Units

Cable Beach Manor, P.O. Box N-8333, Nassau, The Bahamas (tel. 809/327-7785), is on an excellent sandy beach in the Cable Beach area five miles west of Nassau and caters to those seeking self-sufficient accommodations. A tastefully designed group of carnation-pink and white apartments, where guests have all the comforts of home, it's built like a Santa Barbara hacienda, with long encircling covered verandas, all overlooking a swimming pool and gardens. Under tall palms and umbrella trees are shady spots with adjoining sunbathing areas. The location is about 15 minutes from the airport, the same distance into downtown Nassau. Around the corner is a supermarket, a liquor store, and a bus stop.

Studio apartments have a combination living room and bedroom (with two beds, a full-size kitchen, and a bath). *In summer, single occupancy of a studio ranges from $65 to $75 daily, with double occupancy costing $70 to $80. A one-bedroom unit for two goes from $90 to $105, with a two-bedroom accommodation for four costing from $125 to $150.* In winter, a single in a studio ranges from $110 to $130 daily. The most expensive units open onto an oceanview, while the least expensive front the pool. Double occupancy in a studio goes from $120 to $140 daily, a one-bedroom apartment for two costing from $150 to $170, and a two-bedroom apartment for four priced from $200 to $230. Daily maid service is included and, if required, help for babysitting and cooking can be had. Each apartment is decorated in Nordic modern, all harmoniously brought together in matching tones. There's a lounge with books, TV, and free video movies.

Casuarinas of Cable Beach, Wester Road, P.O. Box N-4016, Nassau, The Bahamas (tel. 809/327-7921), just grew and grew, until it now takes up both sides of the street, offering two restaurants (see my dining recommendations) along with two swimming pools and a lobby/piano lounge. This family-run apartment-hotel complex is the creation of Nettie Symonette, a tall, statuesque woman who was the former general manager of the old Balmoral Beach Hotel before acquiring her own place. In her former post she became the first native-born Bahamian general manager of a major hotel, and the first woman to hold such a position in The Bahamas. Over the years she has welcomed an array of international guests, including everybody from Sen. Bob Graham of Florida to Stevie Wonder.

At a location five miles from the airport, you have a choice of accommodations. The establishment's less expensive accommodations are clustered across the road from the beach around their own swimming pool. The more expensive accommodations are nearer the beach, and they also have their own swimming pool as well. Ms. Symonette rents out a total of 90 units. In winter, standard single or double rooms range from $85 to $100 daily, with a studio apartment for two costing from $105 and a one-bedroom apartment for two renting for $120. A two-bedroom apartment, suitable for four, costs $180. *In summer, standard single or double rooms range from $55 to $70 daily, with studio apartments for two costing $75, one-bedroom apartments for two pegged at $90, and two-bedroom apartments for four priced at $125.*

Henrea Carlette Apartment Hotel, P.O. Box N-4227, Cable Beach, Nassau, The Bahamas (tel. 809/327-7801), opened for business in 1979—named for the infant daughter of the then owner—and it hoped to attract Canadian and European business, as those clients tend to stay longer than does the average visitor from the States. In that, it succeeded. However, more and more Americans have discovered this little colony of 22 self-catering units, finding it one of the bargains of Cable Beach. It also now houses one of the finest restaurants along the "Bahamian Riviera," Androsia, which is recommended separately. Each apartment is furnished in a light, airy motif, and opens onto a large freshwater swimming pool which is on view from your own private balcony. Each of the units has a kitchenette, a tile bath, and a phone. In winter, a two-bedroom apartment for four persons rents for $120 daily, *the price going down in summer to $99.* A one-bedroom apartment for three persons costs $99 daily in winter, *but only $82.50 in summer.* A studio apartment for two persons is priced at $82 daily in winter, *the price lowered to $68 daily in summer.* Children under 12 stay free. The location is just two blocks from a Shopping Center and one block to a tennis court. It lies about a ten-minute walk from Carnival Cruise Line's new casino. Rental cars and scooters are available on the premises, and such watersports as skin diving, snorkeling, sailing, and fishing can be arranged.

RESTAURANTS: That long stretch of beachfront property, Cable Beach, or the Bahamian Riviera, now competes successfully with Paradise Island in top-quality restaurants, many of which are found in the deluxe and first-class hotels.

We'll pick up our forks for a survey of the best of Cable Beach restaurants in all price ranges.

Frilsham House, Nassau Beach Hotel, Cable Beach (tel. 809/327-7639), claims that dining here is "the way it used to be!" There's a lot to the claim, as even the house itself evokes the more glamorous high society heyday of Nassau in the 1940s and 1950s. The Nassau Beach Hotel owns and operates Frilsham House which was the restored oceanfront colonial home of a British lord. Its construction included durable Abaco pine (extinct now for more than 30 years), walls of cypress and fir, and floors of classic Bahamian hand-painted tiles. Before Lord Forte of Trusthouse Forte (owner of the Nassau Beach Hotel), took over the property, it had once belonged to Lord Edward Nauger Iliffe, a newspaper publisher from Birmingham, England.

Diners face a choice of four rooms, each furnished in Chippendale. It is also possible to dine on an air-conditioned veranda overlooking the beachfront gardens and the Atlantic. Service is nightly from 6:30 to 10:30, and reservations are necessary. Dinners, at which men should wear a jacket and tie, cost from $50 per person.

The cuisine was created by Vaughan Archer, who for five years was executive chef at the prestigious Ninety Park Lane at the Trusthouse Forte London landmark, Grosvenor House on Park Lane. His job was to blend a classic French repertoire with the fresh ingredients of The Bahamas. The maître d' is Renzo Negri, who served for more than a dozen years as the personal assistant to Lord Forte. Mr. Negri says he likes the service to appear effortless, yet regal at the same time (he's catered functions for the British royal family). The chef is prepared to tempt you with such dishes as veal loin seasoned with coconut, sirloin steak in burgundy sauce, baby lamb cutlets, or lobster soufflé, each prepared with flair. Fresh fish comes from "today's market." Breast of duck is panfried with Bahamian spices and glazed turnips, and a whole grouper is re-created in butter pastry. Hot soufflés may be ordered for dessert.

The **Baccarat,** Le Meridien Royal Bahamian Hotel (tel. 809/327-6400), is the most elegant restaurant in this previously recommended hotel. Guests are treated to a view of the richly furnished hotel (see "Where to Stay," above) on their way to dinner in the blue-and-white formal dining room. The restaurant includes gilt-and-crystal chandeliers (made, of course, by France's Baccarat factories), mirrors, and big windows looking out over the poolside terrace. Reservations, as well as jackets and ties for men, are suggested.

The restaurant serves only dinner. It's open nightly from 6 to 11 and offers such dishes as mosaic of grouper with fines herbes, suprême of pheasant marinated in vintage port, a gâteau of conch and scallops with saffron, chilled duck soup with beluga caviar, bisque of wild mushrooms with sherry, and petit marmite fisherman's style with leeks. The fresh salads are Belgian endive Baccarat, baby asparagus tips with truffles, and a delectable combination of tomatoes, leeks, and wild mushrooms, among other preparations. Main courses include Dover sole filets with smoked mousse, prime rib, veal medallions, braised duckling, and rack of lamb with herbs. No one here should skip dessert, when you can choose from such specialties as guava duff with a rum sabayon sauce, white-chocolate mousse, and black-and-white soufflé harlequin. Full meals cost from $60 per person.

Androsia Restaurant, Henrea Carlette Hotel, Cable Beach (tel. 809/327-7801), is housed in an unpretentious apartment hotel but sets one of the finest tables on the island, featuring fresh seafood cooked to order among other dishes. At a location west of Cable Beach Hotel, "mein host" Siegfried von Hamm holds forth. He has elegantly fed everybody from Sean Connery and Michael Caine to ordinary folk. The decor of his restaurant is inviting with light fabrics, artwork, and captain's chairs and banquettes upholstered in red. A nautical effect is achieved with such artifacts as fishnets, harpoons from old whaling vessels, and fenders from long-gone ships. Broiled local lobster is one of his most popular dishes or else you can order it thermidor style. Nassau-style grouper is perhaps the most ordinary dish, but you can also ask for a seafood platter and such international fare as a perfectly flavored coq au vin. Filet mignon is another well-chosen dish. Dinner is served nightly from 6 p.m. to midnight Monday to Saturday. After one of the daily dessert specials, you can finish with one of Von Hamm's "coffee adventures." A meal costs $35 and up.

The Lobster Pot, Nassau Beach Hotel (tel. 809/327-7711), is an indoor-outdoor affair. Right in the heart of Cable Beach, at this famed landmark hotel, diners feast not only on seafood but on succulent meats as well. The most popular opener is the bouillabaisse, served in an individual bucket. After that, many diners order the spiny Caribbean lobster. If not that, then perhaps a prime rib carved at your table will be a temptation. Other selections include roast rack of lamb or pork chops in Pommery mustard. There is invariably a "fisherman's choice" featured, which is the local catch of the day, most often grouper. You can also order fresh rock oysters, mussels that have been steamed in white wine and herbs, as well as a Spanish-style paella studded with bits of seafood such as lobster. The house specialty, in addition to its namesake lobster, is red snapper Monte Carlo. This fish is baked in the oven in a crust of salt, in the style of the Spanish Costa del Sol. It is then flamed with Pernod and served in a butter sauce flavored with saffron. Meals cost from $25. The restaurant is open from 6:30 to 10 p.m. The nautical decor is part of the fun, including hatch-cover tables, fishnets, boat rows, ship lanterns, and lobster pots—everything kept cool by ceiling fans.

The Beef Cellar, Nassau Beach Hotel (tel. 809/327-7711). This intimate and cozy hotel restaurant lets you grill your own steak at tableside. The atmosphere is inviting, as guests settle comfortably into a leather-covered booth, surrounded by walls of Bahamian coral. They are first tempted by appetizers, soups, or salads before getting down to meatier choices on the menu. For most people it's a T-bone steak. Whether it's rare, medium rare, or well done is strictly up to each individual diner. You're not limited just to T-bone either. One of the chef's specialties is to offer two mignons of beef with herb butter, including soup and salad, baked potato with chive cream, and a French pastry to finish off with. You might also prefer three French-trimmed lamb cutlets with anchovy butter. Pork chops are juicy and cooked just right, as are the jumbo prawns Oriental, if you want seafood. Count on spending around $25 per head. Reservations are essential. The cellar is open from 6 p.m. to midnight.

Pineapple Place, Nassau Beach Hotel (tel. 809/327-7711). Nestled amid the sheltering wings of this previously recommended hotel, the restaurant's design evokes a Bahamian plantation house in the early 19th century. The views from its interior encompass a sheltered garden-style courtyard with formal plantings and a cedar-shingled gazebo. The backs of the wicker chairs are inspired by the shape of a pineapple, while ornamental pineapple-shaped finials adorn the tops of the decorative walls near the entryways. A buffet breakfast is served every morning here from 8 to 10:30 a.m., costing $12 per person. At lunch, from noon to 2:30 p.m., a menu of salads, sandwiches, and locally caught fish costs from $15 per person. Dinner by candlelight is a festive and gracious event at $45 per person. Two seatings are held every night of the week except Thursday, one from 6:30 to 7 p.m. and another from 8:30 to 9 p.m. Dishes are likely to include escargots, smoked duckling salad, snail soup with herb butter, oven-roasted rack of lamb, breast of duckling, prime rib of beef, filet mignon, and Dover sole meunière. For dessert, try the key lime mousse or the cherries jubilee. Reservations in advance are suggested at dinner.

Café Royale, Le Meridien Royal Bahamian Hotel (tel. 809/327-6400). The hotel is unsurpassed in offering the most sophisticated buffets on Cable Beach. You dine using crisp napery with silver and crystal accessories, in Louis XVI–style armchairs, under fan-topped windows overlooking a manicured courtyard. Lunch, from $18 per person, is served daily from 11:30 a.m. to 3 p.m. Dinner costs from $30 per person, and is served daily from 6 to 11 p.m. Reservations are not essential, but it's advised to dress well.

Round House Restaurant, Casuarinas of Cable Beach, Wester Road (tel. 809/327-7921), Nettie Symonette's restaurant, is reached by an entrance leading through foliage into a room with muted lighting and soft-grained paneling. It's a family affair, serving some of the best Bahamian cuisine on the island. The waiter will bring you a generous drink from the alcove bar if you wish, after which you can enjoy a choice of steak, seafood, or other specialties. These might include New York strip, Eleuthera chicken, and shrimp Créole, plus lobster and conch prepared in various ways. For dessert, try Nettie's guava duff. On Friday a "get-together" family feast costing only $12 is served from 6:30 to 8:30 p.m. At a barbecue in the same time period on Wednesday you can eat all you want for $12. Otherwise, full dinners cost from $30 per person, and regular hours are 6 to 9:30 p.m. daily except Tuesday.

ELSEWHERE ON NEW PROVIDENCE: There are two other spots on the island that must be mentioned. They fulfill the highest expectations of what a Bahamian visit should provide in accommodations, in the first selection, and dining, in the second.

Remotely situated on the southwestern shore of New Providence, **Divi Bahamas Beach Resort and Country Club,** P.O. Box N-8191, Nassau, The Bahamas (tel. 809/326-4391, or toll free 800/367-2484), covers more than 180 acres, including a 1,500-foot white sand beach and an 18-hole golf course. Like other Divi resorts, this complex offers a casual yet sophisticated "barefoot elegance," with personalized attention to your needs. Delightfully secluded, the 120 air-conditioned guestrooms all have one king-size or two double beds and all but eight have private terraces or balconies. Each unit has a phone, TV and VCR, safe-deposit box, and complete bath. *In summer, rooms rent for $90 to $100 daily* single or double occupancy. In winter, depending on the month, the charge is $160 to $180 daily, single or double occupancy. MAP can be arranged for an additional $42 per person per day. Fresh flowers are placed in rooms every day, and there is nightly turn-down service.

Besides the PGA-rated golf course, Divi Bahamas also has a freshwater swimming pool and a full water sports facility that includes a Hi-Fly windsurfing school and a Peter Hughes scuba-diving operation. Four lit tennis courts, volleyball facilities on the beach, and illuminated shuffleboard courts complete the recreational pleasure picture. You can dine in the restaurant and enjoy snacks and drinks at the bars. Guests who want to go shopping can take one of the public buses that frequently head for downtown Nassau.

Traveller's Restaurant, West Bay Street, near Gambier (tel. 809/327-7633), has long been a Bahamian culinary tradition. It's the best bet for dining if you're heading out to West Bay Street in the exclusive Lyford Cay area. Set in a grove of sea grape and palm trees, the place is completely down to earth, serving routine Bahamian fare. But that hasn't stopped the world, including many celebrities, from beating a path to its door. Mick Jagger once came here every day for a week before anyone figured out who he was. Other famous visitors have included Julio Iglesias, Donald Sutherland, and Sidney Poitier.

You can dine outside on wooden tables placed under a portico or else on the terrace. If it's rainy (highly unlikely), you can go inside the tavern with its small bar and decor of local paintings and sea shell art. Many diners bring their swimsuits and use the white sandy beach across from the restaurant; others arrive in their own boats. In this casual laid-back atmosphere, you can feast on grouper-fingers, barbecue ribs, steamed (or curried) conch, and minced crawfish, finishing perhaps with bread pudding. Whatever is being served that day is hand lettered on a blackboard. Count on spending from $22 for a big meal. Hours are daily from noon to 10 p.m., and nobody makes a reservation. You just show up at this stucco building which lies about nine miles west of the center of Nassau.

4. TOURING THE ISLAND

IN AND AROUND NASSAU: Most of Nassau can be covered on foot, beginning at Rawson Square in the center where the stalls of the **Straw Market** are found. I also enjoy the **native market** on the waterfront, a short walk through the Straw Market. Here is where Bahamian fishermen (including two hardy women on my last visit) unload the variety of fish and produce—crates of mangoes, oranges, tomatoes, and limes—eaten by the people of Nassau (lots of crimson-lipped conch), and where you can behold the giant turtles.

Facing Rawson Square is a colonial-style structure, housing Parliament, the Law Courts (where wigged judges dispense standards of British justice), and the Senate. In the center is a statue of Victoria as a young queen.

At the top of George Street, **Government House** is the most imposing building of New Providence. It's the residence of the governor-general of The Bahamas. The Duke and Duchess of Windsor lived here during the war years when he was governor. At the main entrance stands a much photographed 12-foot statue of Columbus, who landed at San Salvador (in The Bahamas) in 1492. Every visitor in town likes to attend the Changing of the Guard ceremony on alternate Saturdays at 10 a.m.

At Elizabeth Avenue, turn right (away from the water) and walk uphill to the **Queen's Staircase,** 65 steps leading to Fort Fincastle. These steps, hand-hewn by slaves, were carved out of solid limestone in the 18th century to allow troops stationed at the fort to escape in case of danger.

At the top, turn right until you see the imposing 126-foot **Water Tower.** After an elevator ride to the top, you can walk on the observation floor, enjoying a view of the harbor.

Nearby, **Fort Fincastle,** built in 1793 like a paddle-wheel steamer, is of little interest except for the view.

Another fort, **Fort Charlotte,** begun in 1787 and built with plenty of dungeons, is worth a trip. The largest of Nassau's three major defenses, it used to command the western harbor. Named after King George III's consort, it has large cannons facing the sea. Treasure galleons caught the trade winds under these same cannons. Built by Governor Lord Dunmore, the last royal governor of New York and Virginia, this fort with its 42 cannons never fired a shot, at least not at an invader (Lord Dunmore was fond of building unnecessary forts). Within the complex are underground passages and a waxworks, which can be viewed on free tours.

Another fort to visit, **Fort Montagu** was built in 1741 and stands guard at the eastern entrance to the harbor of Nassau. It's the oldest fort on the island. The Americans captured this fort in 1776 during the War of Independence.

Another historic mossy ruin, **Blackbeard's Tower,** stands five miles east of Fort Montagu. These crumbling remains of a watchtower are said to have been used by the infamous pirate Edward Teach in the 17th century.

Next door, the **Seafloor Aquarium,** (tel. 809/323-6896), exhibits marine life found in Bahamian seas, including sharks, turtles, dolphins, sea lions, and reef fish—and their feeding. Hours are 9 a.m. to 5:30 p.m. Monday to Saturday. At 10:30 a.m. and 12:30, 2:30, and 4:30 p.m., sea lion-porpoise shows are staged. Admission is $7.50 for adults, $3.50 for children.

Nearby are the **Botanical Gardens** (tel. 809/323-5975), on 16 acres of grounds. More than 600 species of tropical flora are found here, and the curator will answer your questions. The gardens are open from 8 a.m. to 4:30 p.m. Monday to Friday, from 9 a.m. to 4 p.m. on Saturday and Sunday, charging adults $1 for admission, 50¢ for children.

Ardastra Gardens

In almost five acres of lush tropical planting, about a mile west of downtown Nassau and almost in the shadow of Fort Charlotte, are the Ardastra Gardens (tel. 809/323-5806), where the main attraction is the parading flock of pink flamingoes. The Caribbean flamingo, national bird of The Bahamas, had almost disappeared in the early 1940s but was brought back to

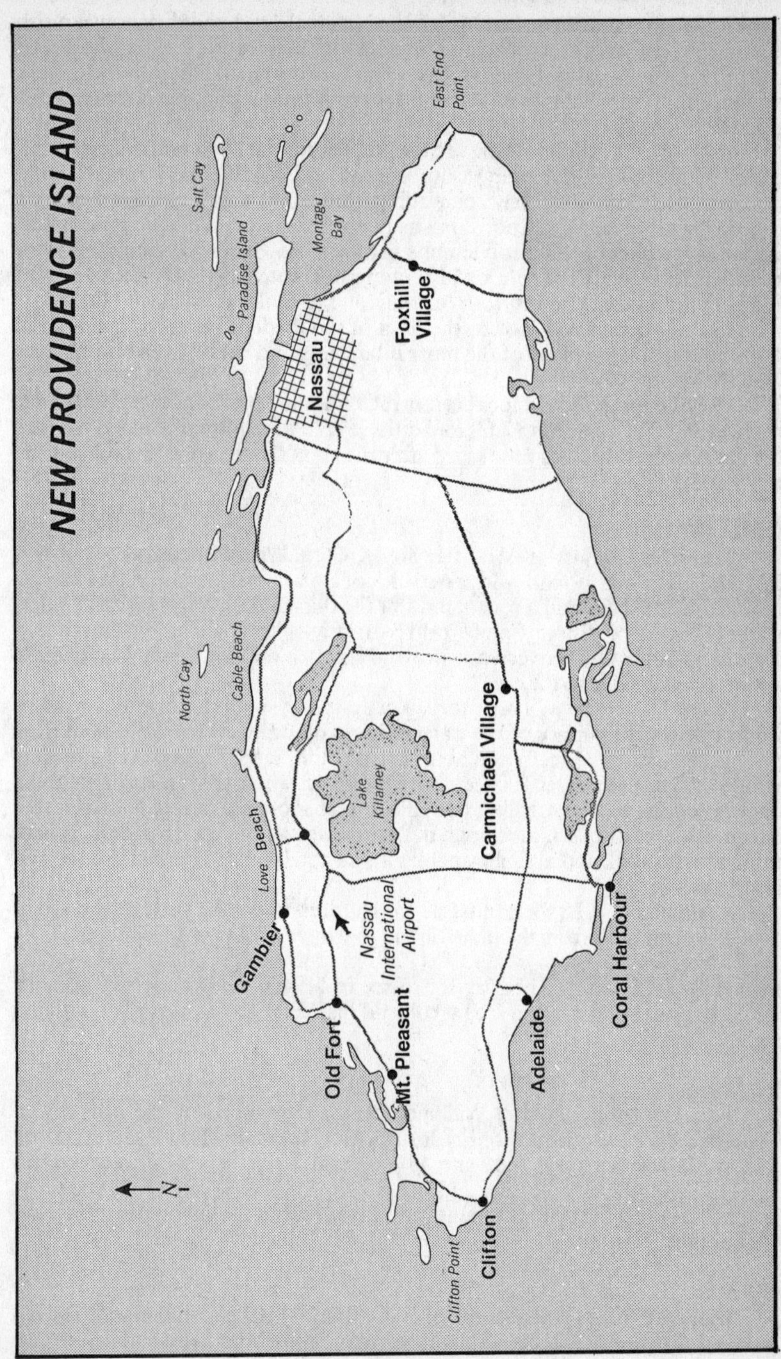
NEW PROVIDENCE ISLAND
N
Salt Cay
Paradise Island
Montagu Bay
East End Point
Nassau
Foxhill Village
North Cay
Cable Beach
Lake Killarney
Carmichael Village
Love Beach
Gambier
Nassau International Airport
Old Fort
Mt. Pleasant
Adelaide
Coral Harbour
Clifton
Clifton Point

significant numbers through efforts of the National Trust and they now flourish in the rookery on Great Inagua. The flock of these exotic tropical feathered creatures at the Ardastra Gardens, has been trained to march in drill formation, responding to the drillmaster's oral orders with long-legged precision and discipline.

Other exotic wildlife to be seen at the gardens are boa constrictors (very tame), kinkajous (honey bears) from Central and South America, green-wing macaws, peacocks and peahens, blue and gold macaws, and Capuchin monkeys, together with iguanas, raccoons, hutias (a rat-like animal indigenous to the islands), ringtail lemurs, red-ruff lemurs, margays, brown-headed tamarins (monkeys), and a crocodile. There are also numerous waterfowl to be seen in Swan Lake, including black swans from Australia and several species of wild ducks.

You can get a good look at the flora of the gardens by walking along the signposted paths, as many of the more interesting and exotic trees bear plaques with their names.

The Marching Flamingoes perform at 11 a.m., 2 p.m., and 4 p.m. Monday to Saturday. The charge is $7.50 for adults, $3.75 for children. Guided tours of the gardens and the aviary are given after the shows, one at 10:15 a.m. and the other at 3:15 p.m.

Coral World

On Silver Cay just off West Bay Street, **Coral World Bahamas** (tel. 809/328-1036) is a marine park with a network of aquariums, landscaped park areas, lounges, a gift shop, and a restaurant, but the outstanding feature is the Underwater Observation Tower. Coral World is directly off the main harbor entrance to Nassau on Silver Cay between downtown Nassau and Cable Beach. Visitors take a tram over a bridge to the cay.

At the Underwater Observatory, you descend a spiral staircase to a depth of 20 feet below the surface of the water, where you can view tropical fish in their natural habitat, coral reefs, and abundant sea life, seen through 24 large clear windows. The tower rises 100 feet above the water, with two viewing decks plus a bar where you can have a drink while enjoying a panoramic view of Nassau, Cable Beach, and Paradise Island. Among the marine attractions are a reef tank, a shark tank, a turtle pool, and a stingray pool, plus 24 aquariums under one roof as well as tidal pools.

Admission is $12 for adults, $8 for children under 12 years of age. Coral World is open daily from 9 a.m. to 6 p.m. in winter, to 7 p.m. in summer.

GROUND TOURS: There's a lot to see in Nassau, and tours have been arranged to suit your tastes in seeing colorful historical Nassau as well as outlying sights of interest.

Walking

Free **Goombay Guided Walking Tours** are arranged by the Ministry of Tourism, leaving from the Tourist Information Booth on Prince George Dock and at Rawson Square at 9:30 and 11 a.m. and 3 p.m. There is no walk from Prince George Dock on Friday and none from Rawson Square on Sunday. The guides show you the historical buildings and tell about the history, customs, and traditions of Nassau.

By Bus

Majestic Tours, Hillside Manor (P.O. Box N-1401), Cumberland, The Bahamas (tel. 809/322-2606), offers a number of trips, both night and day, to take you to many points of interest.

A two-hour city and country tour leaves at 2:30 p.m. daily, going to all points of interest in Nassau, including the forts, the Queen's Staircase, the water tower, the Straw Market, and other sights. It costs $11 per person.

An extended city and country tour, also leaving daily at 2:30 p.m., includes the Ardastra Gardens in its route, the charge being $18 per person. If the Seafloor Aquarium is also included, the cost is $19 per person.

A combination tour, departing at 10 a.m. on Tuesday, Wednesday, and Thursday, is just that—a combination of all the things you see on the first tour listed above, plus the Seafloor Aquarium, the Botanical Gardens, and lunch, at a cost of $25 per person.

Majestic has a native nightclub tour every night except Saturday and Sunday. They take you to one of Nassau's leading nightclubs to see an exotic floor show consisting of limbo, fire-dancing, and other entertainment. Transportation to and from your hotel is included in the prices. The tour without dinner goes for $20 per person; with dinner included, $40 per person.

For information about these tours, as well as for reservations and tickets, many hotels have a Majestic Tours Hospitality Desk in the lobby, and others can supply you with brochures and information as to where to sign up. Ask at the hotel activities desk.

SATELLITE ISLANDS AND CAYS: A short boat trip will take you to several small islands lying off the north coast of New Providence. One of these, **Blue Lagoon Island,** just three miles north of the Narrows at the eastern end of Paradise Island, has seven beaches. Nassau Cruises (see "Boat Trips" in "The Sporting Life" section, below) will take you there to see the pirate's stone watchtower, to relax in a hammock under swaying palms, to party and dance at a pavilion, or just to stroll along narrow pathways edging the sea.

Discovery Island, renamed in honor of the 1992 Quincentennial of Columbus' discovery of The Bahamas, used to be known as Balmoral Island. For years, it was the private stomping ground of the now defunct Balmoral Club. But all that has long ago changed at this island which is visible offshore from the hotels strung along Cable Beach. It is a haven for picnickers and sun worshippers, most of whom consider it a blissful eyrie remote from the civilized world. The island is ringed by a superb beach, with a network of paths connected to the dock. There's even a lookout for sundowners, as well as a bar and barbecue along with toilets and changing rooms. Shuttle boats going from the water sports kiosk at Cable Beach Hotel take you to the casuarina-dotted sands of Discovery Island. The small sandy cay requires a 5- to 10-minute boat ride to reach it, a round-trip ticket costing $5 per person. Boats depart every half hour on the half hour from 9:30 a.m. to 4 p.m. daily. For more information, call the Crystal Palace/Cable Beach Hotel at 809/327-6000. Recreational facilities include windsurfing, parasailing, snorkeling, waterskiing, and volleyball.

Athol Island and **Rose Island** are slivers of land poking up out of the sea northeast of the Prince George waterfront docks of Nassau. Shelling is one of the lures of these little islands. Do-it-yourself skippers can make the trip in motorboats.

You don't have to go to sea to reach **Potters Cay.** It's to be found under the Paradise Island Bridge, linked by causeway to Nassau, so you can walk to it. The attraction here is a fish and vegetable market. If you want to, you can sample some raw conch fresh from its shell.

5. WHERE TO SHOP

You can find an astonishing variety of bargains in Nassau. Here, you can buy Swiss watches, Japanese cameras, French perfumes, Irish crystal and linens, and British china, usually at prices below those charged in stores in the United States. Goods imported from Europe and elsewhere are subject to Bahamian duty, but are often 30% to 40% lower in price than at home. The main shopping area is a stretch of the main street of town, **Bay Street,** and its side streets downtown, as well as the shops in the arcades of hotels.

Bahamian shops offer so many bargains you may be tempted beyond what you are allowed to take home duty free (see "Customs" in the ABCs section of Chapter VII), but sometimes you'll find the prices lower than back home even if you have to pay duty. And lots of times, especially for such articles as cashmeres, liquor, and the goods mentioned above, the quality will be better too.

A must is a visit to the **Straw Market** in Straw Market Plaza on Bay Street, where you can watch the Bahamian craftswomen weave and plait straw hats, handbags, dolls, placemats, and other items, including straw shopping bags for you to carry your purchases in. You can buy items readymade or order special articles, perhaps bearing your initials, and you can have fun bargaining to get the stated prices reduced.

Don't try to bargain with the salespeople in Nassau stores as you can at the Straw Market. The price asked in the shops is the price you must pay, but you won't be pressed to make a purchase. The salespeople here are courteous and helpful in most cases.

You're likely to find yourself mingling with passengers from the cruise ships docked in the harbor, but there always seems to be a laid-back feeling, perhaps nurtured by the beaming sun and the equally beaming faces of the people of Nassau.

Store hours are 9 a.m. to 5 p.m. Monday through Saturday at most shops in Nassau. The Nassau Shop closes at noon on Thursday, and a few other places lock their doors at noon on Friday. No stores are open on Sunday, although the Straw Market does business seven days a week. You can have purchases mailed to wherever from many stores.

The stores along Bay Street and its tributaries are often in buildings that were constructed in colonial days, and some of them are family-run concerns that have been in business for generations. The merchants are often referred to as "the Bay Street Boys," an appellation given them when their word was pretty much law in civic and government affairs of the town. Independence has made changes in that rule of iron, but many of the store owners still take a keen interest in the present and future of The Bahamas.

A sample of some of the leading Nassau stores follows, and there are lots more, which you may discover for yourself as you go window shopping.

Treasure Traders, P.O. Box N-635, Bay Street (tel. 809/322-8521), offers the biggest selection of gifts made of silver, china, and crystal in The Bahamas. For example, all the big names in China are here, including Royal Doulton and Royal Copenhagen. Georg Jensen is among the prestigious names in silver, and counters contain crystal by Waterford, Lalique, Orrefors, and Royal Brierley. There is a multitude of designs, and the store sells not only traditional designs, but modern sculptured glass as well.

Ambrosine, Marlborough Street (tel. 809/322-4205), near the Sheraton-British Colonial Hotel, is the leading boutique of Nassau, occupying an attractive white gable-roofed building that contains a selection of outstanding European designs for both men and women, from formal to beachwear.

The Scottish Shop, P.O. Box N-422, Charlotte Street (tel. 809/322-4720), just off Bay Street, lives up to its name, offering an array of merchandise from Scotland, including tartan material, kilts for women and children, Shetland wool, lambswool and cashmere sweaters and cardigans, Celtic and clan jewelry, Perthshire paperweights, Edinburgh crystal, Buchan thistle pottery, and much more. You'll also find English-made Kangol hats, heraldic plaques, and Peggy Nisbet dolls. You are welcomed by Mr. and Mrs. Colin G. Honess.

Coin and stamp collectors head to the **Coin of the Realm,** P.O. Box N-4845, on Charlotte Street, just off Bay Street (tel. 809/322-4497). A family-run concern, managed by W. Philip Brown, the shop lies in a lovely building more than two centuries old that was hewn out of solid limestone. The building has been designated as a historic site in Nassau. But that's not why it's visited by the public. It offers not only fine jewelry, but mint and used Bahamian and British postage stamps, as well as rare and not-so-rare Bahamian silver and gold coins. It also sells old and modern paper currency of the Bahamas. Used packages of stamps range from $5 and up, and "mini coin" sets sell from $3.50 to $135. Bahama pennies, the rare ones minted in 1806 and 1807, begin at $150 and range upward.

The **Nassau Shop,** P.O. Box N-3946, Bay Street between Parliament Square and the British Colonial Hotel (tel. 809/322-8405), has long been one of my favorite shopping grounds, as it is one of the largest department stores in the Bahamas, with lots of good buys if you shop and pick carefully. Perfume is good value here, including Hermès. Piaget watches are for sale, as are Shetland pullovers and cardigans, for both men and women.

John Bull, Bay Street, P.O. Box N-3737 (tel. 809/322-3329), acclaimed for its excellence, carries the world's most renowned selection of watches (Cartier and Rolex), jewelry, cameras (Nikon), and accessories. Founded in 1929, the firm recently renovated the Bay Street store, adding to it a wide selection of perfumes and cosmetics (Chanel and Yves Saint Laurent) and a designer boutique featuring accessories from Nina Ricci, Gucci, and many others. For convenience, John Bull also has branches on Paradise Island and in Palmdale. Another store under the same ownership is **Old Nassau,** Bay Street (tel. 809/322-2057), a block east of John Bull.

Pipe of Peace, Bay Street (tel. 809/325-2022), is called "the world's most complete tobacconist," and here you can buy Cuban and Jamaican cigars. For the smoker, the collection is amazing. The shop is really a gift center, selling such name-brand watches as Seiko and Girard-Perregaux, along with cameras, stereos, Dunhill (and other) lighters, and calculators from such firms as Sharp and Casio. Other locations are at the East Bay Shopping Centre (tel. 809/323-2815) and the Paradise Island Shopping Centre (tel. 809/326-2904). There's a third branch on Paradise Island at Loew's Harbour Cove Hotel (tel. 809/326-2488).

The **Treasure Box,** Bay Street, on the corner of Market Street and in the Sunley Shopping Mall (tel. 809/322-1662), offers "gifts from the sea"—that is, conch shell and coral jewelry, including earrings, necklaces, and pillboxes.

Brass and Leather Shop, P.O. Box N-1688, with two shops on Charlotte Street, between Bay and Shirley Streets (tel. 809/322-3806), offers English brass and copper reproductions, Land luggage, briefcases and attachés, and personal accessories. Shop No. 2 has handbags, belts, scarves, and small leather goods from such famous Italian designers as Bottega Veneta, Braccialini, Desmo Fendi, and others.

Leather Masters, Bank Lane, P.O. Box N-3871 (tel. 809/222-7597), and Cable Beach Hotel (tel. 809/327-6770), carries internationally known leather bags and accessories by Gucci (plus Gucci perfumes), Fendi, "I Santi," Lanvin, and Pierre Cardin. There is also an imaginative range of leather wallets and small gift items by Royce. Luggage by Tula of England and Tavera of Colombia is also found at these fine stores.

Bernard's China & Gifts Ltd., Bay Street and 5th Terrace, P.O. Box N-4817, Centreville (tel. 809/322-2841), has a wide selection of Wedgwood, Coalport, Royal Copenhagen, Royal Crown Derby, Royal Worcester, and Crown

Staffordshire china; Baccarat, Lalique, Daum, and Schott Zwiesel crystal; and Ernest Borel and Seiko watches among the merchandise it stocks. You can also find jewelry and gift items here.

Spectrum, a fine art gallery at Charbay Plaza, Charlotte Street North, P.O. Box N-10796 (tel. 809/325-7492), has an elegant yet affordable display of art. Original oil paintings, pastels, watercolors, and prints of Bahamian landscapes, seascapes, and people are to be found here. It's between Bay Street and Woodes Rogers Walk on Charlotte Street.

Cole's of Nassau, Parliament Street, near Bay Street (tel. 809/322-8393), was established in 1956 by an old Bahamian family. In its downtown location, it has been going strong ever since, offering an array of designer fashions and accessories for women. The owner, Marion Cole, provides not only sportswear and separates but sundresses and regular dresses as well. She has an excellent collection of beachwear, along with shoes and handbags, designer costume jewelry (also sterling), and lingerie and hosiery. To find this tasteful collection of boutique items, right off Rawson Square, head up Parliament Street to the Bayparl Building, the first building you reach after leaving the famous Bay Street.

If you're looking for something really special, go to **Sunshine Fashions** in the British Colonial Hotel Mall, where you can get Bahamian sun dresses made for you in just 24 hours for only $10. They also have batik fabrics, wall hangings, caftans, skirts, scarves, and bikinis.

The **Linen Shop,** Bay Street, P.O. Box N-1013 (tel. 809/322-4266), carries such select items as Irish handkerchiefs, hand-embroidered women's blouses, tablecloths, and infant wear, as well as Oriental happy coats, kimonos, and children's pajamas.

Greenfire Emeralds Ltd., Bay Street, west of Parliament Street (tel. 809/326-6564), has a rare collection of pure, deep-green stones from Colombia, which produces gems of high quality. You can purchase emeralds and have them set in jewelry of your choice, or select from the shop's array of rings, earrings, and pendants.

Little Switzerland, Bay Street, P.O. Box N-3218 (tel. 809/322-8324), offers a wide variety of jewelry, watches, china, perfume, crystal, and leather in top brands. For many years this store has sold to Bahamians and visitors world-famous Swiss watches including Ebel, Rado, Omega, Baume & Mercier, Tag-Heuer, Audemars Piguet, Bertolucci, and Gucci, plus such scents as Oscar de la Renta, Dior, Chloë, and Giorgio. Figurines from Royal Doulton and Lladro, Bing & Grondahl, as well as crystal by Schott Zwiesel and, of course, Waterford will please your eye and your pocketbook.

National Hand Prints, corner of Machey and Shirley Streets, P.O. Box SS-6416 (tel. 809/323-1974), welcomes visitors to its display room and workshop to watch fabrics being screen printed and processed. You can buy goods by the yard or made up into ready-to-wear items for men, women, and children, including shirts, shorts, dresses, shirts, and tops. Placemats, tea towels, wall hangings, aprons, and pillow covers make good gifts to take home.

Good savings on world-famous perfumes are offered at the **Perfume Shop,** corner of Bay and Fredrick Streets, P.O. Box N-431 (tel. 809/322-2375). Please yourself or someone important to you with a flacon of Joy, Shalimar, Fidji, Magie Noire, Lys Bleu, L'Air du Temps, or Anaïs Anaïs. Those are just a few of the heavenly scents usually associated with women. For men, there are Tabac and Versailles.

The **Nassau International Bazaar** consists of some 30 shops selling international goods in a new arcade, pleasant for strolling and browsing at leisure. The $1.8-million complex sells goods from around the globe, including shopping items from South America, Spain, Mexico, and Greece. The bazaar runs from

Bay Street down to the waterfront (near the Prince George Wharf where cruise liners berth, unloading passengers who go on shopping sprees). At the bazaar, alleyways have been cobbled and storefronts are garreted, evoking the villages of old Europe.

Guccini, International Bazaar, P.O. Box N-871 (tel. 809/325-7774), is the exclusive agent for Gucci watches and also has handsome timepieces by Citizen, Genieve, and Cartier, as well as 14-karat and 18-karat gold jewelry.

Prince George Plaza (P.O. Box N-871 or telephone 809/325-7774 for information) is the latest venture of George and Cally Papageorge who developed the just-previewed International Bazaar. Their new shopping plaza, which is popular with cruise-ship passengers, has a Mediterranean feeling, perhaps as befits their Greek background. Many fine shops selling quality merchandise such as Gucci are found here. Not only that, but you can patronize an open-air rooftop restaurant overlooking Bay Street and another fast-food place offering not only hamburgers but also shish kebabs.

Bahama Sponge Exporters, West Bay Street, P.O. Box SS-6091 (tel. 809/323-8525). Stopping here offers a visitor more local color than it does variety of merchandise. The turn-of-the-century warehouse has dusty beams supporting its high ceiling and small windows, which dimly illuminate the thousands of sponges brought from the Bahamian ocean waters into various grades. No prices are marked; ask and someone will tell you. Natural sponges, their value eclipsed for a long time by plastic substitutes, have been making a comeback in recent years as good for use in the shower and as household servants. Grass sponges are the least expensive, priced from 50¢ up. The most costly items are wool sponges, costing from $1 up.

Stamp fanciers can find the beautiful Bahamian stamps at the **Bahamas Post Office Philatelic Bureau,** in the General Post Office at the top of Parliament Street on East Hill Street, P.O. Box N-8302 (tel. 809/322-3344). Destined to become collector's items is a series of stamps, printed in lithography, and issued to commemorate the discovery of the New World. Called "Discovery stamps," they were first released on February 24, 1988. In all, there are four stamps, the first of a number of issues culminating in 1992. One stamp depicts Ferdinand and Isabella, another shows Columbus before the Talavera Committee (convened to examine his claims).

Balmain Antiques, Bay Street, P.O. Box N-9562 (tel. 809/323-7421). Its merits become visible after you probe and search the contents of its voluminous but hidden inventories. There's probably no other store in The Bahamas with as wide and varied an assortment of 19th-century etchings, engravings, and maps, many of them antique and all of them reasonable in price. Jonathan Ramsey, the owner, scours Britain for stock. It's usually best to discuss your interests with Mr. Ramsey before you begin your hunt, so he can direct you to the proper drawers. Prices begin as low as $10, but stretch up to the hundreds. The location is on the second floor of a building two doors east of Charlotte Street.

6. THE SPORTING LIFE

One of the great sports centers of the world, Nassau is for swimming and sunning, snorkeling and scuba-diving, boating, waterskiing, and deep-sea fishing, as well as tennis and golf.

At last count, there are 32 different sports in The Bahamas. You can find out about any of them by calling a toll-free number for **The Bahamas Sports and Aviation Information Center:** 800/32-SPORT, from anywhere in the continental U.S. It's staffed by experts who can answer questions about anything from skeet shooting to motorbiking. Call anytime weekdays from 9 a.m. to 5 p.m., EST. Or write them at 255 Alhambra Circle, Suite 412, Coral Gables, FL 33134.

They also give briefings to pilots of private aircraft about flying conditions in The Bahamas, including the locations of airports, conditions of landing strips, and a general overall briefing. They will send a flight planning chart if you request it. They do NOT, however, give weather briefings.

BEACHES: On New Providence, the hotels at Cable Beach have their own stretches of sand, as do the hotels on Paradise Island. Of course, everyone wants to head for the famed **Paradise Beach,** especially those occupants of downtown Nassau hotels. The beach can be reached by boat from the Prince George Wharf, costing $3 per person for a round-trip ticket. However, you must pay a separate $3 for admission to the beach, but this fee includes the use of a shower and locker. An extra $10 deposit is required for the safe return of towels. If you're traveling with children under 12, you pay $1 admission each for them. It's also possible to drive to the beach across the Paradise Island Bridge for a toll of $2, 25¢ to walk.

A HEALTH CLUB: A coeducational gym, the **Health Club** is at the Nassau Beach Hotel (tel. 809/327-7711, ext. 1233). If you miss your hometown gym or just want to work out the kinks you may have developed while working on your suntan, head for this place every day between 9 a.m. and 7 p.m. On the premises are facilities for sauna, heat treatments, facials, and massage, as well as hourly exercise classes.

SPORTS AT THE CABLE BEACH HOTEL: Some of the most complete water-sports facilities in New Providence can be visited in a beachfront cabaña near the Cable Beach Hotel (tel. 809/327-6000, ext. 6265). Most participants in the various offerings are registered at the hotel, although no one minds if outsiders use the facilities. The offerings are so varied that determining how you want to begin might present a challenge.

A Hobie Cat rents for $30 for the first hour and $20 for each additional hour. Sunfish rent for $15 for the first hour, $10 for each additional hour. An aquabike costs $12 for the first half hour, $24 for a full hour. Windsurfers are available at $12 for the first hour, $8 for each additional hour. Snorkeling equipment costs $8 for one hour, $3 for each additional one. Management requires a $50 deposit on each boat in advance, except for Hobie Cats, for which the deposit required is $75.

You can go parasailing even if you don't know how to waterski, according to the staff. The price is $25 for the first three to five minutes aloft. A two-tank scuba trip costs $50 per half day, and only certified divers need apply. However, beginners can avail themselves of a resort course for $70, for lessons and two tanks. The water-sports center is open seven days a week from 9 a.m. to 5 p.m.

Finally, clients in neighboring hotels who are looking for one of the most popular beaches of the area can come for a day beside the bars, refreshment stands, artificial waterfalls, and man-made lagoons of the Cable Beach Hotel. The sports center also is in charge of maintenance on the ten hotel tennis courts, the three indoor racquetball courts, and the three squash courts.

SCUBA DIVING: You'll find good service at **Peter Hughes Dive South Ocean,** P.O. Box N-8191, Divi Bahamas Beach Resort & Country Club (tel. 809/326-4391). It is a five-star training facility, the largest and most complete diving facility on New Providence. The shop is open from 8 a.m. to 5 p.m. daily. A resort course begins in the pool, and a one-tank shallow dive in water 35 to 45 feet deep. All gear is included, and the center accepts children 12 and up. The cost is $70 for the course, including one hour in the pool. A one-tank dive for already certified divers costs $35, including weight belts and tanks. If all equipment is included, the price goes up to $53.

Runaway, much publicized in skin-diving magazines, is one popular dive site in the neighborhood. Big stingrays come up to feed and to be cleaned by a host of smaller fish who remove parasites from their bodies. Divers explore "the James Bond wreck," a 90-foot freighter, called the Tears of Allah, which was sunk for the filming of a 1969 Bond movie. Soft coral and feeding fish now glide through the steel infrastructure of a mockup Vulcan Fighter plane, also used in the film. Weather permitting, you can go eight miles southwest of Divi Beach Hotel to razorback reef and playground reef which teem with marine life, including thousands of fish and eels. A two-tank dive, including a deep dive and also a shallow dive, costs $50 if you have your own gear or $68 if you need equipment.

Bahama Divers, Pilot House Hotel, East Bay Street, P.O. Box N-5004 (tel. 809/326-5644). There isn't much in the large spartan headquarters of this dive operation except a staff and a scattered inventory of diving equipment. Their true value becomes more obvious at one of the many dive sites that their instructors know about. Some of their packages include a half day of snorkeling to offshore reefs, costing $20 per person, and a half-day scuba trip with preliminary pool instruction for beginners, costing $50. Half-day excursions for experienced divers to offshore coral reefs with a depth of 25 feet go for $35, and half-day scuba trips for certified divers to deeper outlying reefs, dropoffs, and blue holes cost $50 and offer two tanks as part of the experience. Participants in this establishment's excursions receive free transportation from their hotel to the boats.

Nassau Undersea Adventures, P.O. Box CB-11697 (tel. 809/326-4171), in Lyford Cay, is about ten minutes from top dive sites such as the coral reefs, wrecks, and an airplane structure underwater, used in filming James Bond in his 007 mode in *Never Say Never Again, Thunderball, For Your Eyes Only,* and other thrillers. There are also the Porpoise Pen Reefs named for *Flipper* and steep sea walls on the diving agenda. An introductory scuba program costs $65, with morning two-tank dives priced at $50, and one-tank dives (morning, afternoon, or night) going for $35. All boat dives include tanks, backpacks, weights, and belts. An open-water certification course starts at $350. Escorted boat snorkeling trips cost $25.

UNDERSEA WALKS: An educational and exciting experience is offered by the **Hartleys,** P.O. Box SS-5244 (tel. 809/393-7569), who take you out from Nassau Yacht Haven aboard the yacht *Pied Piper.* On the 3½-hour cruise, you're submerged for about 20 minutes, making a shallow-water descent to a point where you walk along the ocean bottom through a "garden" of tropical fish, sponges, and other undersea life. You'll be guided through the underwater world wearing a helmet that allows you to breathe with ease and to see. Entire families can make this walk, costing $35 per person in groups of five. You don't even have to be able to swim to make this safe adventure.

PARASAILING: This increasingly popular sport, which allows you to zoom up to 200 feet in the air, parachute style, is offered at **Sea Sports,** P.O. Box CB-11818, Nassau Beach Hotel, Cable Beach (tel. 809/327-6058). Parasailing costs $30 for seven minutes or $45 for 12 minutes.

WINDSURFING: Your best bet for this sport is **Sea Sports,** P.O. Box CB-11818, Nassau Beach Hotel (tel. 809/327-6058). Windsurfing equipment rents for $20 for the first hour and $15 for each additional hour. If you rent a board for four hours, the total cost is $40. Lessons cost $45 for one hour of instruction.

DEEP-SEA FISHING: Many sportsmen come to Nassau just to fish, and they know the seasons too. May through September produces the oceanic bonita and the blackfin tuna, June and July are the best months for blue marlin, and the amberjack is best found in reefy areas November through May. The list seems endless. This is, of course, a costly sport. Arrangements can be made at big hotels.

GOLF: Some of the best golfing in The Bahamas is found in Nassau. The **Cable Beach/Crystal Palace Golf Course,** Cable Beach, P.O. Box N-4914 (tel. 809/327-6200), has a spectacular 18-hole, par 72 championship golf course. Greens fees for 18 holes are $20 in summer, $25 in winter. Electric golf carts rent for $25 for 18 holes, and golf clubs rent for $10 for 18 holes.

Divi Bahama Beach Resort & Country Club, P.O. Box N-8191 (tel. 809/326-4391), is one of the finest golf courses in The Bahamas, a 30-minute drive from Nassau on the southwest edge of the island. The course has palm-fringed greens and fairways. Overlooking the ocean, the 6,706-yard beauty has some first-rate holes with a backdrop of trees, shrubs, ravines, and undulating hills. The 18-hole, USPGA-sanctioned course, has a par of 72. Players are charged $37.50 for greens fees, the price including a golf cart. It's best to phone ahead in case there's a golf tournament scheduled for the day you had planned to play.

TENNIS: Courts are available at most hotels. Guests usually play free or for a nominal fee, while visitors are charged from $5 per hour at hotels and clubs.

Carnival's Crystal Palace Resort & Casino (tel. 809/327-6200) has eight new courts. **Cable Beach Hotel** (tel. 809/327-6000) has five clay and five all-weather courts. The **Ambassador Beach Hotel** (tel. 809/327-8231), with eight asphalt courts lit for night play, has lessons available.

Others are: **Nassau Beach Hotel** (tel. 809/327-7711), nine Flexipave courts, lit; **Nassau Squash and Racquet Club** (tel. 809/322-3882), eight Har-Tru courts, open seven days; **Sheraton-British Colonial Hotel** (tel. 809/322-3301), three hard-surface, lit courts; and **Divi Bahamas Beach Resort & Country Club** (tel. 809/326-4391), four asphalt courts, lit.

HORSEBACK RIDING: At Coral Harbour, on the southwest shore, **Happy Trails Stables,** P.O. Box N-7992 (tel. 809/326-1820), offers a one-hour horseback trail ride for $25 per person. This includes free transportation to and from your hotel. Weight limit is 200 pounds.

BOAT TRIPS: Cruises from the harbors around New Providence Island are offered by a number of operators, with trips ranging from daytime voyages for diving, picnicking, sunning, and swimming to sunset and night cruises mainly for leisure activity.

Wild Harp Cruises, P.O. Box 1914 (tel. 809/322-1149 days, 809/324-7445 nights), operates trips aboard the 56-foot, two-masted schooner *Wild Harp,* to deserted Rose Island where you can swim, snorkel, or just relax in the sun on the sand. Lunch and snorkeling gear are included in the $30-per-person price. A sunset dinner cruise costs $35 per person. A full-course Bahamian dinner is served, with complimentary Wild Harp punch and a glass of wine, all accompanied by music and a fun crew. Morning departures are at 10 from The Bahamas Agricultural Corporation Dock, off Bay Street, in downtown Nassau. The dinner cruise departs at 5 p.m. The boat then stops at either 10:15 a.m. or 5:15 p.m. at the Loews Harbour Dock on Paradise Island to take on more passengers. If you make arrangements in advance, the *Wild Harp* staff will arrange to have you picked up in a mini-van at your hotel in time to reach one of the two departure points.

Nautilus Ltd., P.O. Box N-7061 (tel. 809/325-2871), is the place to arrange for various boat trips. The 97-foot *Nautilus,* a glass-bottom showboat, leaves from the New Mermaid Marina, at the corner of Bay and Deveaux Streets, daily at 1:30 and 3:30 p.m., trips costing $20 per person. The vessel takes passengers to the *Mahoney* shipwreck and over the teeming reefs offshore. Each cruise lasts 1 hour and 45 minutes. Morning departures aren't recommended, as they are almost always fully booked with cruise ship passengers in Nassau just for the day.

Majestic Tours Ltd., Hillside Manor, P.O. Box N-1401 (tel. 809/322-2606), will book three-hour cruises on two of the biggest catamarans in the Atlantic, offering you views of the water, sun, sand, and outlying reefs. *Yellow Bird* is suitable for up to 250 passengers, and *Tropic Bird* carries up to 170 passengers. They depart from either Prince George's Dock or Woodes Rogers Walk near the British Colonial Hotel, depending on the day of the week. Ask for the departure point when you make your reservation. There's a 9:45 a.m. departure every day except Sunday and Monday and a 1 p.m. departure on Saturday followed by a 2 p.m. departure on Sunday. The cruises include a one-hour stop on a relatively isolated portion of Paradise Island's Cabbage Beach. The cost is $15 per adult, with children under 12 paying $7.50 on either cruise.

Another offering which you can book through Majestic Tours (see above) is a **Robinson Crusoe tour,** departing every Monday through Friday from Loews Harbour Cove Dock at 10 a.m. and returning at 4:30 p.m. Majestic Tours will send a minivan or bus to your hotel any time from 9 to 9:30 a.m. Tours depart on an 85-foot catamaran suitable for carrying 300 passengers for an all-day picnic. The catamaran is called *Majestic Lady.* The cost of $35 per person includes a buffet lunch and snorkeling gear. Much of the time is spent on an offshore sandy cay allowing for maximum beach exposure.

Nassau Cruises Ltd., P.O. Box N-8209 (tel. 809/326-3577), offers dinner cruises on the *Calypso I* and *Calypso II,* leaving Paradise Island at 8 p.m. and returning at 11 p.m. Tickets, costing $35 per person, include a steak and grouper dinner and a glass of wine. The dinner cruises take place on Monday, Wednesday, and Saturday, and reservations are required. Daytime trips are also offered, *Calypso I* going to secluded Blue Lagoon Island and *Calypso II* taking passengers to Blue Lagoon West, where a party pavilion is the center of the fun. A complete buffet lunch is included, and complimentary snorkeling is available. The six-hour day cruises cost $35 per person.

El Galleon II/El Buccanero II, P.O. Box N-4941 (tel. 809/328-7772), which bears a double name, docks behind Victor's Department Store off Bay Street. Suitable for up to 300 passengers, this is a 93-foot replica of an 18th-century Spanish galleon. Daytime cruises depart at 10:30 a.m., returning to the dock at 4 p.m. daily except Monday and Wednesday. This tour includes a buffet lunch, free snorkeling equipment, unlimited punch, and at least three hours on an offshore cay called Discovery Island. The cost is $35. Nighttime cruises last from 7:30 to 10:30 every Monday, Thursday, Friday, and Saturday at a cost of $35 per person. Included in the price is a buffet dinner along with unlimited punch. Reservations are a good idea.

Treasure Island Cruises Ltd., P.O. Box N-1461 (tel. 809/326-5818), offers one-day excursions to Treasure Island Tuesday to Sunday, leaving Nassau Harbour Club at 9:45 a.m. and Loews Harbour Cove Dock at 10 a.m., returning at 4 p.m. The cost of $35 per adult and $17.50 for children 12 and under includes white wine with lunch, use of the island and all facilities including snorkel gear, hammocks, and beach umbrellas. Bar service is available. Depending on conditions, an alternate island might be visited. The cruises are aboard the 50-foot *Sandy Cay*.

7. AFTER DARK

Gone are the days of such famous native nightclubs as The Yellow Bird and The Big Bamboo, where tuxedo-clad gentlemen with their elegantly gowned ladies drank and danced the night away. Life is much more democratic now. You still get dancing, along with limbo and calypso. But for most visitors, the major attraction is a rendezvous with Lady Luck. First, that rendezvous.

CASINO AND HOTEL DIVERSIONS: The dazzling new casino of The Bahamas is **Carnival's Crystal Palace Casino** (P.O. Box N-8360) (tel. 809/327-6200), part of Carnival's Crystal Palace Resort & Casino on the Bahamian Riviera. It's a joint undertaking of Carnival Cruise Lines and the Continental Companies of Miami (the resort was already previewed). The casino complex is a spectacular addition to the island's night life, and it is open daily from 9 a.m. to 4 a.m., charging no admission. In hues of purple, pink, and mauve, the 30,000-square-foot casino is filled with flashing lights. The gaming room features 750 slot machines in true Las Vegas style, along with 51 blackjack tables, seven crap tables, nine roulette wheels, a baccarat table, and one big six. An oval-shaped casino bar extends onto the gambling floor, and the Casino Lounge, with its bar and bandstand (offering live entertainment) overlooks the gaming floor.

A two-story disco was designed to rock the senses with a ceiling-to-floor ocean view, electronic light from above and below, and fluorescent hand-painted designs, along with a super sound system. The disco has an exploding mobilized sculpture that looks like a spiral staircase accented by spotlights. It rotates and creates special effects and unusual patterns. The 800-seat Palace Theater is one of the major nightlife attractions of The Bahamas. With simulated giant palm trees on each side, it is the setting for Las Vegas–type extravaganzas (what management calls "sophisticated adult entertainment" is presented in a separate 2,200-square-foot show lounge).

Dinner and show cost $35 per person, but you can attend just for the spectacle, paying $25 per head. Dinner times vary, as do showtimes. Dinner is 7:30 p.m. on Sunday, 5:30 p.m. on Tuesday, 6:30 p.m. on Wednesday, 7:30 p.m. on Thursday, 6:30 p.m. on Friday, and 5:30 p.m. on Saturday. Showtime is 7:30 and 9:30 p.m. on Sunday, 7:15, 9:30, and 11:45 p.m. on Tuesday, 8:30 and 10:45 p.m. on Friday, and 7:15, 9:30, and 11:45 p.m. on Saturday. Closed Monday. Note: the Tuesday and Saturday shows are usually heavily committed to cruise ship passengers. The dinner menu is international, including such dishes as antipasto, chicken Calvados, Nassau grouper with almonds, and prime ribs of beef.

A good rendezvous is the **Palm Patio Bar** of the British Colonial, 1 Bay St. (tel. 809/322-3301). Many scenes from the James Bond movie *Never Say Never Again* were shot here and on the grounds. It opens every day at 6 p.m., staying open until 2 a.m. There is live music every Friday, Saturday, and Sunday from 8:30 p.m. to 1 a.m. At those times, there is a two-drink minimum. Gin and tonic, for example, costs $3 before 8:30 or $4 thereafter.

Out Island Bar, Nassau Beach Hotel (tel. 809/327-7711), is nostalgically named after the former label of today's so-called Family Islands. Although set in a modern hotel, it often plays music heard on the island for many years. It's open daily from 7 p.m. to 2 a.m. A band plays only Wednesday through Sunday. Drinks cost from $3.50, half price during happy hour 5 to 7 p.m.

NATIVE NIGHTCLUBS: Peanuts Taylor's **Drumbeat Club,** West Bay Street, P.O. Box N-1435 (tel. 809/322-4233). Known as the "King of Drums," Peanuts Taylor is famous locally. His Afro-Bahamian Review has been seen by thousands of visitors, all of whom are invited to bring their cameras. Peanuts usually provides the rhythms for the limbo artists, the dancers of the African fire ritual, and the array of male and female vocalists and comedians. If you precede the show with dinner, the combined tab will be $30 per person. Visitors who prefer just to see the show pay $10 each. There is a two-drink minimum if you don't order dinner. Gin and tonic, for example, costs $4 per drink. Most nights, show times are at 8:30 and 10:30 p.m., but on Tuesday and Saturday, the show begins at 8 or 10 p.m. There is no performance on Sunday.

At some point in Nassau, you'll hear the islanders say it's time to "go over the hill." That's a reference to the **local clubs** that lie in the native quarter beyond Bay Street. Roughly, the border is on a parallel with Gregory Arch, stretching some two miles inland. From downtown Nassau, "over the hill" leads to Grant's Town, where freed slaves settled in 1838. Most of Nassau's native population lives there today in houses often shaded by lacy casuarinas and royal poincianas. If you'd like to check it out, chances are someone at your hotel will inform you of the latest hot spot.

For information on a native nightclub tour, see "Ground Tours" in "Touring the Island," above. Also, for information on nighttime boat party cruises, see under "Boat Trips" in "The Sporting Life" section.

DISCO: There's nonstop dancing until the wee hours at **Club Waterloo,** East Bay Street (tel. 809/323-1108), housed in a former Nassau mansion, is one of the most frequented clubs in town. It is open Monday through Saturday from 11 a.m. to 4 a.m., so you can drop in almost anytime. However, live music is offered only Wednesday through Saturday nights. During the day people take their beer around the pool or in the satellite lounge, with most drinks costing from $3. The club has an ever-changing array of activities (who knows what it will be when you go?). There might be an Oldies Night or even a pool party (bring your swimsuit). It stands next to the Mai Tai Restaurant.

City Limits, Independence Drive (tel. 809/393-4706), is a popular Nassau disco, offering recorded music, all the latest hits, along with rock 'n' roll nightly except Monday from 9 p.m. to 4 a.m. Drinks cost from $3.

Confetti's, Bay and Deveaux Streets (tel. 809/323-8426), is yet another Nassau hot spot with nightly entertainment by good bands. This seaside-bordering club, with its patio bar, jumps from 9 p.m. to 4 a.m. nightly except Monday. Drinks cost from $3.

CHAPTER IX

PARADISE ISLAND

□ □ □

- 1. WHERE TO STAY
- 2. WHERE TO DINE
- 3. SHOPPING NOTES
- 4. THE SPORTING LIFE
- 5. AFTER DARK

The choicest real estate in The Bahamas was once known as "Hog Island," serving as the farm for Nassau. Purchased for $294 by William Sayle in the 17th century, it was to become the fiefdom of the A&P grocery chain heir, Huntington Hartford, in 1960, although he eventually sold out his interests. After paying out $11 million, he decided to rename it "Paradise."

With dreams of Versailles, he spent many more millions of dollars, turning the four-mile-long sliver of land, just 600 feet off the north shore of Nassau, into a resort. In front of the Ocean Club, a 14th-century cloister built by Augustinian monks in France was reassembled in The Bahamas stone by stone. The gardens, extending over the rise to Nassau Harbour, are filled with tropical flowers and classic statuary. No admission is charged to visit them. The A&P heir purchased the cloister from the estate of William Randolph Hearst at San Simeon in California. Regrettably, when the newspaper czar originally purchased the cloister, it had been dismantled in France for shipment to America. The parts were not numbered. Arriving unlabeled on Paradise Island, the cloister baffled the experts until artist and sculptor Jean Castre-Manne set about to reassemble it piece by piece. It took him two years, and what you see today, presumably, bears some similarity to the original.

Celebrated for its white sandy beach, the island also has beautiful foliage, including brilliant red hibiscus and a grove of casuarina trees sweeping down to form a tropical arcade. It has become one of the favorite vacation areas in the western hemisphere.

The Paradise Island Resort & Casino, which is comprised of the Britannia Towers, the Paradise Towers, the Paradise Club, and the Paradise Island Casino (my recommendations coming up), all operate under one facility. Extending over several acres, it is considered the world's most complete island resort and casino. There's nothing in Europe, not even on the Riviera, and certainly nothing in the Caribbean, to match it.

FROM HOG TO PARADISE: Little is known of the early history of Hog Island, although the Lucayan Indians knew it, as proved by discovery of their relics here. In the 1700s the island was a favorite watering hole for pirates, many of whom made Nassau their home port, going out to prey on ships in the trade routes of the Atlantic and scurrying back to the comparative safety of Bahamian waters. It isn't known if Edward Teach (popularly called "Blackbeard") came here, but this and New Providence Island were for a long time a haven for freebooters, especially those of British origin.

During the American Civil War, munitions and medical supplies were sometimes stored here, hidden away from Yankee spies infiltrating the hierarchy of Nassau—supplies awaiting shipment to the South by Confederate blockade runners. Later, bootleggers stashed alcoholic beverages on what is now Paradise Island—liquor to be delivered at night across the Gulf Stream to Florida during the Prohibition era.

The island is experiencing a massive building boom, and its old Bahamian charm is now gone forever, as high-rises, condos, and second homes of the wintering wealthy, plus casino gambling, take over. It has long been a retreat for millionaires.

How did this extravaganza begin (forgetting the Indians, the pirates, and the rum-runners)?

Before it developed worldwide publicity in the 1960s, Hog Island was the home of a couple of multimillionaires. One was Joseph Lynch, who has become part of the vocabulary of the stockbroker's world, as he was a partner in the brokerage firm of Merrill, Lynch, Pierce, Fenner, and Smith. He lived on the island in the 1930s.

Shortly, he was followed by Dr. Axel Wenner-Gren, a Swedish industrialist and real estate tycoon (now deceased). Wenner-Gren became friends with the Duke and Duchess of Windsor, when the former king was the wartime governor of The Bahamas. The duke found much poverty and unemployment in the islands, and he persuaded Wenner-Gren to construct a canal system and make other improvements on Hog Island to provide employment to many Bahamians, some of whom had not had a full-time job since Prohibition days. A horde of Bahamian men constructed a rock-bottom lake on Hog Island at a cost of $50,000. Each of the hard-working laborers was paid a dollar a week for his efforts.

Dr. Wenner-Gren sold his share of Hog Island to the A&P heir, Hartford, and it was with that purchase that the little strip of land began to make world headlines. Hartford not only bought Wenner-Gren's huge portion of the island, he also purchased more property from other individual owners who had constructed houses there. Realizing that the name Hog Island wouldn't be likely to attract the jet set, Hartford, seeking a complete switch of imagery, renamed it Paradise Island.

Dr. Wenner-Gren's guesthouse, which was on the shore of the man-made Paradise Lake, was eventually turned into the Café Martinique (which we'll visit when we explore the restaurants of Paradise Island). The Ocean Club, which had been Dr. Wenner-Gren's winter home, was converted into Hartford's winter retreat.

In 1966 Hartford, disenchanted because the Bahamian government would not grant him gambling-casino rights, sold Paradise Island to Paradise Island Ltd., a Bahamian-franchised firm owned by Mary Carter, the famed Florida-based paint company. It was under this organization that Paradise Island really started to grow. The company purchased the Ocean Club and the Café Martinique, and by 1969 it had opened the Britannia Beach Hotel.

Billionaire recluse Howard Hughes for a while retreated to Paradise Island, occupying suites at the Britannia Towers and earning more fame for what was increasingly becoming a favorite haven for winter vacationers, cutting heavily into the Caribbean business. More and more hotels and cheaper package deals began to change the image of Paradise Island. It was no longer the exclusive retreat of the wintering wealthy, and it was connected by a bridge to Nassau.

It became so popular that its owners went out of the paint business (selling the name "Mary Carter," of course), going whole hog, so to speak, into the Hog/Paradise Island resort industry. The company then became known as Resorts International, Inc., which runs the choice real estate to this day.

By 1980 Resorts had opened a 352-room addition to what was then the Britannia Beach Hotel and Casino. In 1982 it also took over operation of the Paradise Island Hotel, and the two were incorporated into the Paradise Island Resort & Casino, which combination makes it the most complete offshore resort/casino in the world. By 1984 it had purchased the 100-room Paradise Beach Inn, which lies on nine acres of the west end of the island and opens onto Paradise Beach. The inn was renamed Paradise Paradise (see below). In a $900-million deal in 1988, television impresario Merv Griffin concluded a real estate deal with tycoon Donald Trump and became the owner of Resorts International's properties. As he admitted to the press, the deal with Mr. Trump included some "rough spots."

To prevent guests from getting bored from "just going to the beach," most of the big hotels here have activity-packed calendars, especially for that occasional windy, rainy day that comes in winter. Hordes of Americans can be seen taking group lessons such as how to play backgammon or how to cook native style. They are even taught how to mix such tropical drinks as a Goombay Smash or a Yellow Bird. There are also lessons in how to play whist and tennis, even to dance Bahamian style.

At some point during the day everyone likes to stop by and watch Brit and Tanya, pet performing dolphins who swim in a private tank at the Paradise Island Resort. There are two free shows daily, at noon and at 4 p.m. Cameras are out en masse when the dolphins perform. Hotel waiters are fond of pointing out that the dolphin offered on the menu is "quite a different kettle of fish" from Brit and Tanya (who are really mammals, not fish). In other words, Flipper isn't being served for dinner.

As of this writing (with new projects planned), Resorts International now owns Britannia Towers, Paradise Towers, Ocean Club, Paradise Paradise, Paradise Island Golf Club, Café Martinique, the Boathouse Restaurant, and Le Cabaret Theatre, as well as operating the Paradise Island Casino and owning Chalk's International Airlines. All of these properties will be described in detail.

TRANSPORTATION: The most popular way to reach Paradise Island is to drive or walk across the $2-million **toll bridge** that connects "P.I.," as it is called by its wealthy residents, with Nassau. A car costs $2 going over (nothing on the return), and you can walk across for just 25¢. The bridge opened in 1967.

If you're without a car and don't want to take a taxi, you can go to Nassau by **a ferry service.** If you're already on Paradise Island, you may want to take a shopping stroll along Bay Street. If so, the ferry to Nassau leaves from behind the Café Martinique (recommended below). It runs every half hour on the hour, the ten-minute ride costing $2 round-trip. Quicker and easier than a taxi, the ferry deposits you right at Bay Street. Service is from 9:30 a.m. to 4:15 p.m.

If you arrive at the Nassau International Airport, there is no airline bus waiting to take you to Paradise Island unless you're on a package deal that includes transfers. If so, then your hotel may have made arrangements to have you met and your luggage transferred.

Unless you're renting a car, you'll need to take a **taxi.** Taxis in Nassau are metered. It will usually cost you $18 to go by cab from the airport to your hotel on Paradise Island. The driver will also ask you to pay the bridge toll. Luggage is carried at the cost of 50¢ per piece.

If you want to leave Paradise Island and tour New Providence by taxi, you can make arrangements. Taxis wait at the entrances to all the major hotels. The going hourly rate is about $12 to $20, depending on the size of the vehicle.

Water taxis also operate daily from 8:30 a.m. to 6 p.m. at 20-minute intervals between Paradise Island and Prince George Wharf in Nassau. A round-trip fare is $3 per person.

You can also go by **jitney** from Nassau to Paradise Island at a cost of 50¢ to $1 per ride. Buses operate daily from 8 a.m. to 1 a.m., every half hour. They make regular stops at all hotels on Paradise Island. After 6 p.m. the bus stops only at the entrance to the casino. Some hotels on Paradise Island run their own jitney service.

If you are a guest of one of the properties of Paradise Island Resort & Casino, you can take a complimentary tour of the island, leaving daily at 10 and 11 a.m. and at 2 p.m. There is no tour on Tuesday, however.

A free bus service is offered daily to Rawson Square in Nassau for Paradise Island Resort & Casino guests. The bus departs from the Paradise Towers. Tickets can be obtained from the bell captain's desk.

Access to Paradise Island was facilitated in 1989 with the opening of a $2.5-million, 3,000-foot "stolport" on the eastern side of the island, accommodating aircraft with short takeoff and landing capabilities. It's just a two-minute drive from all island hotels. The stolport handles Resorts International's 48-passenger De Havilland Dash-7 aircraft, offering flights from South Florida. Now operating from two gateways, Miami and Fort Lauderdale, the company plans to increase the number of daily flights.

The island is also serviced by **Chalk's International Airlines** (see Chapter VI, "Getting to and Around the Bahamas"). The airline is a subsidiary of Resorts International. Chalk's offers daily direct seaplane service to Paradise Island from Watson Island in Miami and from Fort Lauderdale and Palm Beach, Florida. The Chalk's Terminal on Paradise Island is a two-minute drive from the Paradise Island Resort & Casino.

1. WHERE TO STAY

You're faced with your most spectacular choice of lodgings in all The Bahamas, and they come in a wide range of prices, from the deluxe and exclusive Ocean Club to the more moderately priced Paradise Paradise. You can stay at an expensive Club Med or a very modestly priced (and rather incongruously located) Yoga Retreat. As a final alternative for lodgings, some condo developments will also rent you space when their owners aren't in residence.

If you're contemplating a visit during the busy winter season, always nail down a reservation far in advance.

THE TOP RESORTS: A bastion of the good life, the **Paradise Island Resort & Casino,** P.O. Box N-4777, Paradise Island, The Bahamas (tel. 809/326-3000; 305/891-3888 in Dade County, Florida; 305/462-8555 in Broward County, Florida; or toll free 800/321-3000), is a world unto itself. It's filled with so many entertainment and dining facilities that many visitors are not even tempted to leave the compound. Run by Resorts International, the property is the unquestioned focal point of Paradise Island. It lies between three miles of beachfront and a saltwater lagoon and consists of the **Paradise Island Casino,** (see "After Dark," below), the **Britannia Towers,** and the **Paradise Towers.**

Although both hotels were initially constructed as separate units, Resorts

International combined them architecturally and administratively into one consolidated resort. Today the hotels are linked to the casino and to one another by a complicated series of covered passageways containing a few of the restaurants (12 in all) and nightlife facilities that are scattered throughout. The accommodations cater to a wide array of price ranges and budgets. Top-of-the-line opulence is created within the upper four floors of the north wing of the Britannia Towers, where the **Paradise Club** operates as a superluxurious hotel within a hotel. It recently added a new oceanfront wing containing the most luxurious rooms of all. There, uniformed concierges serve continental breakfasts in a panoramic lounge with a view of the sea. Accommodations here are better, more spacious, more opulent, and more glamorous than those throughout the rest of the hotel. The battalion of attractively uniformed staffers is well trained to perform dozens of personal services not available on the lower floors. These could include a personalized speedy check-in or, if requested, the arrangements for a seven-course dinner in the parlor of your suite. Recent publicity-conscious guests who have stayed here, and of whom you might catch a glimpse during cocktails or breakfast, include Sean Connery, Julio Iglesias, members of Duran Duran, Patrick O'Neal, and an array of Spanish-speaking TV stars. Single or double wintertime accommodations cost $330 per night. *In summer, the rates go down to $245 per night.*

Accommodations throughout the rest of the Britannia Towers (where Howard Hughes once lived in a one-bedroom suite) and the adjacent Paradise Towers are only slightly less opulent, and certainly they confer enough luxury to make practically any visitor feel pampered. A recent addition to the Britannia Towers added another 352 rooms, with the ratio of staff to guest rooms an astonishing three to one. Each of the resort's 1,200 units has been completely redecorated and has a refrigerator, color TV with satellite and U.S. network programming, a balcony with water view, and 24-hour room service (a rarity in The Bahamas). Each accommodation contains either two queen-size or one king-size bed and dozens of amenities. Rates in both buildings for single or double occupancy begin at $175 daily in winter, *$125 in summer.*

Facilities of this complete resort could entertain a guest for many weeks (many are covered in subsequent sections of this chapter). These include 12 gourmet and specialty restaurants, a dozen bars and lounges, a full array of discos and nightlife possibilities, 12 tennis courts illuminated for night play, a health club and sauna, a jogging path, an array of shops, all water sports, a menagerie of trained porpoises, an 18-hole golf course, and three miles of pure white beachfront. There are in fact so many options for entertainment here that a guest literally never runs out of things to do.

Ocean Club, P.O. Box N-4777, Paradise Island, The Bahamas (tel. 809/326-2501, or toll free 800/321-3000), is the most discreetly prestigious address on Paradise Island. Guests can revel in the casino and nightlife activities of the other parts of the resort a short distance away, knowing the option always exists for quiet retreats back to the seclusion of this exclusive, small-scale hotel, run by Resorts International. This is one of the best-developed tennis resorts in The Bahamas and includes nine well-maintained courts and a full-time tennis pro within sight of a lattice-covered colonial-style clubhouse. The appointments of the accommodations are plushly comfortable, imbued with a kind of stately contemporary dignity, having air conditioning, satellite TV, refrigerators, spacious tile baths, and tasteful colors and fabrics. In winter, single or double rooms range from $160 to $385, while suites and private villas for two to four people can run as high as $795 per day. *In summer, a twin or single rents for $115 to $195 daily; a villa, suitable for two to four people, for $340.*

Despite the plushness of the bedrooms, the real heart and soul of the resort lies in the surrounding gardens and landscapes, which were designed by the island's former owner, Huntington Hartford, mentioned earlier. During his residency here, all of Paradise Island was almost a private fiefdom for this affluent landowner and his glamorous houseguests. The ornamentation includes formally panoramic gardens whose focal point is a reconstructed French cloister set on 35 acres of manicured lawns. Today the rhythmically graceful 12th-century carvings are visible at the crest of a hill, across a stretch of terraced waterfalls, fountains, a stone gazebo, and rose gardens in a vista that is one of the sights of The Bahamas. The bigger-than-life statues that dot the vine-covered niches on either side of this landscaped extravaganza include quirky reflections of Mr. Hartford's taste—FDR and Dr. Livingstone, the Scottish missionary and explorer in Africa, as well as reclining Renaissance nudes and depictions of Hercules. If you're visiting these gardens, you should begin your promenade at the large swimming pool whose waters initiate the series of reflecting pools stretching out toward the cloister.

The beach that lies adjacent to the colonial-style sweep of the hotel is a white stretch of sand, arguably the best beach in the Nassau/Paradise Island area. The access routes to the accommodations run down the verandas, which ring one of the garden courtyards on the island. One of my favorite dining spots anywhere is the Courtyard Terrace (see "Where to Dine"), which at night is filled with glittering light from a pair of illuminated fountains. The repeat business at this posh resort runs to a high 65%, a fact partially attributable to the skill of the England-born manager, Steve Sawyer.

Sheraton Grand Hotel, Casino Drive, P.O. Box SS-6307, Paradise Island, The Bahamas (tel. 809/326-2011, or toll free 800/325-3535), is dramatically opulent. Its strikingly angled 14-story exterior incorporates spacious balconies and sweeping water views from each of the 360 plushly furnished bedrooms, in which sunlight and breezes from the uncluttered three-mile stretch of beach combine with an eagle-eye view of the surrounding landscape. The architects chose to build this palace on the sands of the ocean, so that guests leaving the shelter of the poolside terrace could settle almost immediately onto one of the waterside chaises longues. The Grand is within walking distance of the casino, restaurants, and nightlife facilities of the Resorts International properties.

If you arrive by car, the smartly uniformed doorman will take charge of your vehicle, giving you a receipt that you'll later use to reclaim it. Welcoming drinks are served while you relax on comfortable chairs near the waterfall of the soaring reception area, as sunlight glitters off the surface of the plant-rimmed lagoon in the wood-trimmed lobby. The hotel is big enough that its frequent conventions hardly make a ripple in the smooth tenor of operations carried out by the staff. A full array of restaurant and entertainment facilities is on the premises. The premier restaurant of the Grand is the Rôtisserie, serving a haute cuisine nightly from 6:30 to 9:30. Other dining choices include the multilevel Verandah Restaurant and its adjoining terrace, where you can order breakfast, lunch, and dinner within view of the sea. Sunbathers in need of a poolside drink will be served at their chaises longues by waiters, and burgers as well as lobster or chicken salads are available all day at the Grand Bar and Grille. After dark, the most elegant disco on Paradise Island, Le Paon (see "After Dark"), is open for dancing the night away. The disco has a computerized sound system where 57 speakers focus the music onto the dance floor, leaving the banquettes free for conversation.

All the accommodations here are deluxe, with tastefully mixed pastels united with gentle angles for a maximum of comfort. Those in the Sheraton Towers, the 12th and 14th floors, are really grand. There, continental breakfast is served in a panoramic, private breakfast room, complete with silver tureens and fine porcelain. You can also have five-o'clock tea in this room, where fresh conch salad and delicately flavored soups are dispensed by a concierge.

Regardless of the category, each of the rooms of this hotel also has air conditioning, satellite color TV with broadcasts of U.S. programs, and direct-dial phone. A range of wintertime packages is offered for stays of more than three nights, many covering use of the hotel's sports facilities, an almost bewildering array, including four tennis courts and a fleet of boats for various water pursuits. EP rates for single or double occupancy not part of a package deal are $155 to $285 daily in winter. *In summer, single or double rooms go for $120 to $150 per night.*

OTHER TOP HOTELS: Set on the bay, **Loews Harbour Cove Hotel,** P.O. Box SS-6249, Paradise Island, The Bahamas (tel. 809/326-2562, or toll free 800/223-0888, 800/522-5455 in New York State), faces the narrow strip of water between Paradise Island and Nassau. It's in a peacefully isolated position, its 250 well-appointed rooms looking out over the water or onto tropical gardens that surround the estate. The hotel operates a ferry to Nassau's Bay Street four times a day, except on Sunday and Wednesday, and a shuttlebus arrives every 45 minutes to take guests to Cabbage Beach or other Paradise Island attractions, including the casino. There's an L-shaped freshwater pool on the bayside terrace with a swim-up bar, as well as tennis courts and a sandy bathing area descending into the bay. Accommodations are air-conditioned and spacious, and some have private balconies. Winter rates that are not part of a package begin at $125 and go as high as $165 for double or single occupancy. *Summer rates for single or double occupancy range from $90 to $125 per day.* Many special discounts are offered by Loews for stays of at least three nights, any of which can be discussed with a Loews phone representative.

Evenings here are lively, with calypso music, Goombay Smash parties, Bloody Mary parties on Sunday morning, pig roasts, and barbecues. The hotel's regular restaurant service is suspended every Tuesday and Saturday night when buffets are held. Dinner is served from 7:30 to 8:30, and then from 8:30 to 10 the place jumps with fire dances, calypso music, whatever. Cost of these buffet shows is $24 per person. Loews spent some $2½ million to renovate the hotel lobby into a wide-open tropical format of flowering plants and expanded spaces. Off it is the Cove Bar. Although it isn't on one of the island's best beaches, many guests prefer its quiet location a short walk from the hustle and bustle of Paradise Island's casino and the busiest nightlife centers. The sweeping sands of superlative beaches lie within a five-minute walk, but many visitors prefer swimming in the nearby channel.

Club Méditerranée, P.O. Box N-7137, Paradise Island, The Bahamas (tel. 809/326-2640, or toll free 800/CLUB-MED), is made up of pastel bungalows curving above the three-mile beach. Accommodations are in two wings. In between stands a Georgian-style mansion housing the intimate restaurant (both indoor and outdoor dining), a midnight disco, and the beach bar. Behind the mansion, guests frolic in a large swimming pool. A walk through the garden brings members to harborside and the main restaurant. Adjoining is an open-air theater/dance floor/bar complex. The village occupies 21 acres. In winter, tours from New York include round-trip air fares, transfers, seven nights' accommodation, three full meals a day (including free unlimited wine at lunch and dinner), all sports activities and facilities, including equipment and qualified instruction, picnics, glass-bottom-boat rides, and live entertainment nightly.

Accommodations are twin-bedded rooms, small but comfortably furnished, each with a private bath. Units are arranged in three-story clusters above the beach, and are decorated with rattan furniture. *In off-season, the per-person rate is about $830 a week, land arrangements only.* In winter, the highest prices are charged at Christmas and New Year's, when the weekly land arrangement can be $980 to $1,250 per person. Otherwise, the winter price hovers around the $830 mark, the same as the summer and autumn rate. However, booking tends to fall off after New Year's, and the price is often reduced to $780 per person weekly, even lower than the off-season tariff. Of course, that figure is always subject to change, and you should call Club Med to verify it before planning a trip. Winter rates are the highest in February. The cheapest rooms cost from $830 per person weekly (the same as the off-season rate), but they could run as high as $980. Special holiday package rates are also quoted, including Fourth of July weekend jaunts and Thanksgiving trips. Everybody here seems to play tennis—there are 20 courts, 8 of which are lit at night.

Pirate's Cove Holiday Inn, P.O. Box SS-6241, Paradise Island, The Bahamas (tel. 809/326-2101). Many guests consider the pool of this 600-room hotel as their favorite splash area in The Bahamas. It stretches sinuously around the cabaña-style bar on the island in its center. Guests who prefer not to undress can reach it via a footbridge here and there, but many guests swim over for their afternoon cocktails. The hotel rises 17 floors in a massive rectangle above a forest of pine trees a few steps from a wide stretch of Pirate's Cove Beach. The comfortable accommodations usually have views of the sea and are decorated in pastel shades of what the staff calls "Goombay colors." In winter singles rent for $125 to $185 per day, with doubles costing from $135 to $195. *In summer, tariffs are reduced to $88 to $125 per day, with doubles paying $98 to $134.* MAP can be arranged for another $39 per person per day.

There are several restaurants here from which to choose, including Matilda's poolside snackbar, where the best cheeseburgers in the area are served with cold beer and tropical drinks. Then there's the garden-style Beachcomber restaurant, where lunches and breakfasts are breezy. Dinner is a gourmet affair at Neptune's Table, where wood paneling combines with seafood and beef specialties for memorable dinners. This is a complete holiday resort, having tennis courts with a full-time pro and all water sports, including parasailing, crab races, and other organized games and contests, plus weekly buffets and poolside parties. The lobby is often the site for daytime lectures on subjects, which might include native crafts, tips on buying mother-of-pearl, and ornamental napkin folding. Later in theday, the spacious lobby resounds to the playing of a musical group, which provides dance tunes every night until 1 a.m.

Paradise Paradise, P.O. Box SS-6259, Paradise Island, The Bahamas (tel. 809/326-2541, or toll free 800/321-3000), is a pleasantly unpretentious hotel run by Resorts International. It's a rambling, veranda-lined building set on sandy soil within an encircling copse of pines. Half the accommodations offer direct access to the beach, which lies on the far side of a stand of trees. In many ways, being here is like living in a forest. The hotel restaurant is a short distance away, in a teepee-shaped building directly on the beach. The hotel also offers free transportation by shuttlebus to the casino and its adjacent bars and restaurants. Each of the 100 rooms was redecorated, with carpeting, draperies, and accessories, to the tune of $1 million. Single or double units range in winter from $130 to $195 per night; *summer rates are around 20% less.* Included free is a variety of water sports: sailing, snorkeling, windsurfing, and waterskiing. Guests are not locked into any meal plan.

HOUSEKEEPING HOLIDAYS: A handsomely landscaped condominium complex, **Bay View Village,** P.O. Box SS-6308, Paradise Island, The Bahamas (tel. 809/326-2555, or toll free 800/327-0787), has verdant and flowery surroundings that occupy the full-time efforts of six gardeners. Although it is near the geographic center of Paradise Island, it's only a short walk to either the sands of Cabbage Beach or the harbor. There are reputedly more than 20 kinds of hibiscus and many varieties of bougainvillea, which screen accommodations from one another. Three pools are scattered around the premises, along with a tennis court.

Vacationers can rent 54 of the units that provide a suitable setup for visitors who prefer independent living. Each of the accommodations is air conditioned and has its own kitchen, TV, and patio or balcony, plus daily maid service. The villas and townhouses have dishwashers, and some have views of the harbor. A full-time maid or personal cook can be arranged on request. The units come in a wide variety of sizes and can hold up to six occupants. Rates are slightly less for weekly rentals, but otherwise, winter tariffs range from $145 daily for two persons to $360 daily for up to six. *In summer, the range is from $100 daily for two occupants to $250 for six persons.* A mini-market and two coin-operated laundry rooms are on the property. The nightlife, casino, and sports facilities of the Paradise Island Resort & Casino are only a few minutes away.

Club Land' Or, P.O. Box SS-6429, Paradise Island, The Bahamas (tel. 809/326-2400, or toll free 800/446-3850, 800/552-2839 in Virginia), lies across the saltwater canal from the outbuildings of the Paradise Island Resort. A series of self-sufficient apartments are in white concrete buildings set in a landscaped garden dotted with shrubs and reflecting pools. Although the club isn't located on the bay, the beach is a short drive away, and there's a small freshwater swimming pool as well as a promenade beside the canal for guests interested in sniffing the salt air. If you wish to visit the casino, you must drive along winding pine-hedged roads to get there. The reception area contains plants and a fountain below the staircase leading up to the Oasis lounge and the Blue Lagoon Restaurant (see "Where to Dine"). This place is for guests interested in a maximum of independence, their own cooking facilities, and something approaching apartment living with dining and bar amenities in easy reach. The management hosts some of the most energetic activities programs on the island, sometimes broadcasting its daily agenda over a public address system.

Each of the 70 accommodations includes a separate bedroom, a patio or balcony, a fully equipped kitchenette, and a living room. Depending on the view (garden or water), apartments rent for $175 to $199 per day for two people in winter, *$120 to $140 in summer.* For reservations and information, get in touch with the club's executive offices: P.O. Box 100, Ladysmith, VA 22501 (tel. 804/448-3500, or the toll free numbers given above).

2. WHERE TO DINE

RESORTS INTERNATIONAL'S DINING PLANS: Available only to guests of Resorts International's Paradise Island hotels are two dining plans, providing interesting culinary experiences, not tied in solely to the hotel where you stay. A minimum of two days' residence is required for either of the plans.

For $52 per person per day, you can sign up for the Gourmet Dining Plan, featuring full breakfasts and a complete choice of dinner menus at all Resorts International's gourmet and specialty restaurants. For $35 per person per day, the Paradise Dining Plan provides for breakfasts and dinners at eight of the specialty restaurants in the Resorts International complex: the Grill Room, Coyaba, Spices, the Terrace Grill, Café Casino, Seagrapes, Paradise Pavilion, and Le Cabaret Theatre. Added dining adventures provided by the Gourmet Plan are at Café

Martinique, the Gulfstream Restaurant, the Courtyard Terrace at the Ocean Club, the Bahamian Club, and the Boat House.

DINING AROUND: Paradise Island also has several other restaurants, especially those at Loews and the Holiday Inn. It even has a few (very few) budget restaurants (see below). Most of the restaurants below are clustered along the famous Bird Cage Walk at the Paradise Island Casino. Door to door to each other, these restaurants tempt you with their international cuisine.

The Upper Bracket

Café Martinique (tel. 809/326-6300), across from the Britannia Towers, is one of the chicest restaurants in The Bahamas, serving everything from beef Wellington to cherries jubilee, at a cost that is likely to zoom to more than $60 per person. James Bond, in front of millions of movie-goers, dined here in *Thunderball,* from a perch overlooking the Paradise Lagoon. Patrons select tables inside or else outdoors under a starry sky. The best French and continental food on Paradise Island is served here, backed up by a well-stocked cellar. When you sit down, enjoying the fin-de-siècle decor, you are presented almost immediately with a list of dessert soufflés. The chef is justifiably proud of these delicacies, and he wants you to consider them when ordering your meal. Because of the time and preparation involved, the soufflés can't be ordered at the last minute (unless you're prepared to wait), and therefore many people order (but don't eat) the dessert first, especially the soufflé Grand Marnier and the soufflé au chocolat.

Then it's on to a dazzling menu, with an appealing list of hors d'oeuvres likely to include everything from escargots bourguignonne to foie gras with truffles. For those to whom money is no object, the kitchen will produce beluga caviar served with a glass of Stolichnaya vodka. There's even conch chowder on the menu (how did it get there?). Fish dishes are limited, but select, including fresh Bahamian grouper with fennel and Noilly Pratt sauce or sautéed with sliced almonds, and Bahamian lobster with spices served in its shell (or broiled with melted butter). For a main course, you might like the grenadin de veau au Calvados, which is prepared perfectly here, or chateaubriand with béarnaise sauce, or perhaps a rack of lamb roasted with herbs in the style of Provence. Café Bahamien would be a nice finish to just a repast. The French-style decor suggests the Moulin Rouge of Paris. Diners once glided in here by boat, but nowadays they cross the bridge. Reservations are absolutely imperative. Dinner seatings are nightly at 7 or 9:30. Jackets are required for men.

The café serves a deluxe Sunday brunch from 11:30 a.m. to 2:30 p.m., costing $22 per person. Enticing arrays of fresh fruits, salads, cold meats, smoked fish, and cheeses are laid out, with hot dishes and a tempting dessert selection. A complimentary glass of champagne or a mimosa is served with the brunch. Reservations are requested.

Villa d'Este, Bird Cage Walk (tel. 809/326-6300), is Nassau's most elegant Italian restaurant, with classic dishes of the repertoire of Rome, Florence, and Venice, prepared with skill and served with flair. Italian murals decorate the walls. The restaurant takes its name from the world-famed hotel on Lake Como. Its viands are outstanding, and the word gets around. Freshly made fettuccine Alfredo can be served as a first course or as a main dish. This Roman dish is prepared here nigh to perfection, although without the golden spoons, which are still in the Eternal City. A good-tasting Florentine version of minestrone is served. Main dishes include several most acceptable chicken and veal dishes, including chicken breasts in a curried herb sauce, scaloppine alla parmigiana, and of course osso buco, prepared the way the Lombards like it in Milan. Diners always seem to like the rice pilaf with "fruits of the sea," including lobster and shrimp. Desserts feature a selection of pastries from the trolley. You are likely to spend around $60 or more for a meal. Not only is the chef Italian, but you also get Italian guitar playing and singing. It's necessary to reserve a table. Only dinner is served, from 6:30 to 11:30 nightly.

The Rôtisserie, Sheraton Grand Hotel (tel. 809/326-2011), is the premier restaurant of this deluxe hotel, lying a short walk from the main lobby. The decor is deliberately understated, with oversize rattan chairs and exposed stone. You'll sit at one of the tables enjoying what might be the thickest cuts of steak and prime rib in The Bahamas. From behind a glass window, a team of uniformed chefs prepares the grills to your specifications. You can also order such beef dishes as blackened Cajun steak or a filet mignon. Should you want seafood, they'll tempt you with Bahamian grouper or perhaps swordfish steak. They'll also prepare several international dishes, including honey glaze duck. Dining is nightly except Tuesday from 6:30 to 10, when a strolling guitarist is featured. Jackets are required.

Courtyard Terrace, Ocean Club (tel. 809/326-2501). When the moon is right, an evening meal here can be the closest thing to paradise on the island. You dine amid palms and flowering shrubs, at tables on the well-scrubbed flagstones of the island's most exclusive hotel. The courtyard is surrounded with colonial verandas flanked by symmetrical fountains whose waters spurt upward in circular patterns. A musical group on one of the upper verandas sends music wafting down onto the patio below. This isn't the most glittering dining room on the island, but in many ways it is the most sophisticated. Much will depend on the weather, but regardless of climate, men are requested to wear jackets and ties, and women should bring some kind of evening wrap in case it becomes chilly. Menu specials include beefsteak tartare, prime sirloin, lobster quiche, chateaubriand, French onion soup, Nassau grouper, shrimp provençale, roast rack of lamb, and calves' liver lyonnaise. Reservations for either of the two evening sittings are requested. Full meals cost from $60. The place is open nightly from 7 to 10:30 seven days a week.

Bahamian Club, Bird Cage Walk (tel. 809/326-3000), was a well-established restaurant and gambling club in Nassau until the developers of Paradise Island offered its management a new home in Bird Cage Walk. Today it's known both for its Caesar salads and its prime ribs and thick steaks. The Georgian colonial-style dining room offers spacious vistas over dark-grained half columns, white walls, tall mirrors, leather-back chairs, and dozens of candles. The prime rib is served from a trolley with a carver to be sure you are satisfied, and it's accompanied by Yorkshire pudding and fresh horseradish. Other specialties include veal Cordon Bleu, calves' liver lyonnaise, duckling à l'orange with wild rice, tournedos Rossini, steak tartare, and a limited selection of Bahamian seafood, such as lobster and grouper. There are some excellent appetizers, such as snow crab claws and fettuccine verde with lobster, shrimps, and scallops. For dessert, try the cherries jubilee or the peach flambé. Full meals cost from $60. Dinner seatings nightly except Tuesday are at 6:30 and 9 p.m. Music and dancing accompany the dinner hours. Jackets are required for men.

Grill Room, Paradise Island Resort & Casino (tel. 809/326-3000), is a spacious and comfortable restaurant that carries a sense of European elegance. Its dignified decor is brightened with patterns of bird of paradise juxtaposed with the palms and the uniformed staff. The establishment is known for its well-prepared steaks, which can be flambéed at your table or charcoal-broiled, as can be fish specialties, depending on your order. Filet mignon sauce choron, strip sirloin Café de Paris, brochette of chicken with peanut sauce, and well-seasoned beef brochettes with Oriental rice are just a few of the meat dishes. There are also many Bahamian seafood specialties, such as fresh Bimini swordfish with pistachio butter and lime-flavored butter, surf and turf on a skewer, tuna marinated in soy and ginger, and of course, lobster, grouper, and snapper. Long Island duckling capped with kiwi fruit and Grand Marnier sauce is a particular favorite. Full meals cost from $50 each and should be preceded by a reservation. The restaurant is behind the reception lobby of the Paradise Towers. Dinner is served every night except Monday from 6:30 to 11.

Gulfstream Restaurant, Paradise Island Resort & Casino (tel. 809/326-3000), is separated from the main lobby of the Paradise Towers by a trio of etched-glass panels depicting three of the nine muses. Once you're inside, a formally dressed waiter will usher you to a seat near walls of exposed stone whose angles are softened with masses of plants, flowers, and candles. This is a seafood restaurant, but if you prefer steak, chicken, or veal, these are also on the menu. Specialties include such appetizers as fresh cherrystone clams, smoked salmon, seafood fettuccine, and stone crab claws with mustard sauce. Soups are lobster bisque and conch chowder prepared either traditionally or in a local adaptation of creamy New England clam chowder. As a main course you might enjoy Bahamian lobster thermidor, Maine lobster (imported live and priced according to the market), shrimp curry Bombay, red snapper, Nassau-style grouper, or scallops diable. Full meals cost from $45 per person. Dinner is served nightly at two seatings, one at 6:30 for early birds and another at the more fashionable hour of 9. You dine to piano music.

The Moderate Range

Boat House, Paradise Island Resort & Casino (tel. 809/326-3000). A group of friends might find this the most appealing restaurant on the island, especially if they don't feel like dressing up. It's next to the canal near the Café Martinique, behind a well-finished nautical façade. Inside, the richly polished leather and hardwood as well as the warm color scheme contribute to a clubhouse ambience that you would expect to find at a marina on one of the most remote Family Islands. You cook your own dinner on the charcoal grill that's the focal point of each group of diners. Suspended above each table is a rectangular copper hood with a powerful suction fan to whisk the smoke away from the conversation and good food. The ambience can be fun, especially if you enjoy participating in the preparation of a meal. The bartender serves generous drinks to accompany the top-quality meats, which are the house specialty.

The menu is limited to a choice of four main courses, each of which is priced as part of a full meal at from $40 per person. Choices, as you'd expect, include a well-marbleized New York sirloin, prime filet mignon, sea and steer (filet mignon with half a Bahamian lobster tail), or gulf shrimp kebab marinated in a special sauce. Each main course is accompanied with Bahamian conch chowder to which a generous splash of sherry is added at your table. Also offered are a crisp Boat House salad and a baked potato or rice. Cheesecake, raisin fudge, and coffee are also included as part of the meal. Reservations are suggested. The restaurant is open only for dinner, seven days a week in winter, closed Sunday in summer. Seatings are at 6:30 and 9 p.m.

Coyaba, Bird Cage Walk (tel. 809/326-3000), offers an Oriental setting and features Szechuan, Cantonese, and Polynesian specialties in a casual and relaxed atmosphere. Many people come here just for a drink, but if you want to eat you'll be faced with an appetizing choice of starters such as curried conch Coyaba (conch, duck liver, barbecued pork, and scallions in a curry sauce), or a two-person pupu bowl (a flaming hibachi on your table with baby back ribs, eggrolls, chicken wings, shrimp tempura, and wontons with an array of succulent spices). These could be followed by three kinds of Chinese soups, ginger or curried salads, or a full range of Chinese main courses. These include twice-barbecued pork (there's an intermediate wok-steaming between the barbecue stages for added tenderness), deboned Polynesian duck, Coyaba duck imperial (cooked with 12 spices for a full three hours), eight treasures of Buddha (eight vegetables cooked quickly in a wok), spicy Paradise chicken, Szechuan shrimp, and a selection of dishes for the less adventuresome. Full meals cost $40 and can be accompanied by tea or one of several deceptively potent tropical drinks. Open nightly from 6:30 to 11.

Restaurant Blue Lagoon, Club Land' Or (tel. 809/326-2400), is a pleasant environment lying across the lagoon from the Paradise Island Resort & Casino. It's two floors above the reception of the Club Land' Or. On your ascent, you can stop in the Oasis bar before climbing the second set of stairs to the restaurant. Your view will encompass the horizon of either the harbor or Paradise Lake. The musical accompaniment of a pianist will complement your meal served by candlelight as well as the light coming through the stained-glass ceiling dome. The decor is unabashedly nautical, with polished railings and lots of full-grain hardwood. À la carte dinners come to around $35. Seafood is the specialty. Menu items are stone crab claws in cocktail sauce, Nassau conch salad, Caesar salad for two, broiled grouper amandine, seafood brochette, grouper (stuffed with chopped shrimp, lobster, and scallops and covered with mornay sauce), almond-fried shrimp, shrimp sautéed in mushroom and garlic butter and served with Créole rice, and other dishes. Meat specialties include steak au poivre with brandy sauce, duck à l'orange, and chicken chasseur. Dessert might include crêpes Suzette for two or a Tía Maria parfait. Dinner is served from 6 to 10 nightly.

Spices, Britannia Towers (tel. 809/326-3000). Since the design of this garden restaurant includes both natural pine and forest-green walls, the look is a lot like the effect you'd get in a tree house. The impression is heightened by the tables clustered together on raised platforms under a skylight admitting the sunshine. The appetizing specialties served here include Out Island conch salad, a basket of deep-fried zucchini, snails in mushroom caps, pasta primavera, and four kinds of soup—breadfruit vichyssoise, gazpacho, soup of the day, and conch chowder. These could be followed by an avocado and grapefruit salad or main courses such as minced lobster Bahamian-style, cracked island conch, and a fish stew. Meat courses include pork tenderloin calypso with fried plantains, medallion of veal with shrimp, and Out Island chicken curry. Finally, if you missed your favorite tropical drink before dinner, you can end your meal with a super-moist slice of piña colada cake. This restaurant is open daily except Thursday for breakfast from 8 to 11 a.m. and dinner from 6:30 to 10 p.m. Complete dinners cost from $25 per person, and breakfasts from $12.

The Captain's Table, Loews Harbour Cove (tel. 809/326-2562). Some of the most succulent seafood on the island is served in a dining room which is fortunately located away from the hordes of diners flocking to the better-known eateries of Paradise Island. Set in the lobby level of the previously recommended Loews Hotel, it serves temptingly flavorful à la carte dinners nightly except Monday and Wednesday from 7 to 10 p.m. Full meals are reasonably priced at $30 each, including an award-winning version of barbecued ribs Junkanoo, three different preparations of grouper (including one which is stuffed and served with a delicate herb sauce), lobster thermidor, cracked conch, and an array of juicy steaks, often brought with a pepper or cognac sauce sizzling to your table. There's usually musical entertainment as part of your dinner. Every Tuesday the restaurant features a sumptuous buffet where a roast suckling pig is the savory and dramatic highlight. Other tempters include barbecued chicken, different preparations of grouper, and roast beef. Saturday is shipwreck night, where steaks, ribs, chicken, and snapper are barbecued and served in copious portions to the sound of a calypso band. Hours for both buffets are 7:30 to 9 p.m., and the price for both nights is $24.

Budget Dining

Paradise Pavilion, Paradise Paradise Hotel (tel. 809/326-2541), with its beachfront location and barbecue specialties, is a good choice for those who want a casual ambience with ocean views, good value, and good food. The restaurant is in an indoor/outdoor thatch-roofed pavilion directly on the beach. The menu includes steaks, barbecued chicken, Bahamian lobster tails, succulent ribs, and a variety of appetizers, soups, salads, and desserts. You might try the Paradise mud pie or key lime pie. Meals cost from $15. You can enjoy a sundowner before dinner if you arrive early at the pavilion, where serving is from 6 to 10 p.m. seven days a week.

Swank's Pizza Restaurant (tel. 809/326-2765), lies at the beginning of the driveway leading to the casino and its nearby hotels. This restaurant is the most conspicuous building in the brick-walled shopping center that surrounds it. Open daily for breakfast at 8 a.m., it remains open throughout the day and evening, closing at 2 a.m. Simple breakfasts cost $5, while pizzas, whose varieties include a Bahamian one, with conch, range from $7.50. Spaghetti and meatballs and lasagne each cost $9. Salads, such as conch or chicken, are available, as is cheesecake for dessert. The place is informal, and no one minds if you only want a snack.

Seagrapes Restaurant, Paradise Towers (tel. 809/326-2431), is off the lobby of the towers, a pleasantly decorated, tropical restaurant serving breakfast from 7 to 11 a.m., a buffet lunch from 12:30 to 3 p.m., and a fixed-price buffet dinner, costing $18, from 6 to 10:30 p.m. Access to the salad bar is $9 per person, plus service, and some patrons consider this to be a full meal. Each day a different specialty is served, such as barbecued ribs, shrimp Créole, beef Stroganoff, and desserts like apple pie and pineapple upside-down cake.

Café Casino, Paradise Island Casino (tel. 809/326-3000). If you want a late-night snack or a break from the activity of the gaming tables, you only have to walk to the far end of the casino to find this rattan-decorated coffeeshop. Its menu includes well-stuffed sandwiches—corned beef, pastrami, and reubens—as well as many kinds of salad. Soup-and-sandwich meals cost around $13, although full dinners, which might include Wiener schnitzel, prime rib, catch of the day, or beef brochette with rice, cost from $20. In addition to the regular dishes, the chef offers a pasta of the day. Dinner is served from 6 to 11 p.m., although you can always get a snack or sandwich until the casino closes at 3 a.m., at 4 a.m. Saturday and Sunday.

3. SHOPPING NOTES

For really serious shopping, you'll want to cross over the Paradise Island Bridge into Nassau (see the preceding chapter). However, many of Nassau's major stores, as previewed below, also have shopping outlets on Paradise Island. There are also a number of fashionable boutiques in the major hotels, which come and go with the seasons.

For chic women's clothing in both Bahamian and foreign styling, **Mademoiselle** is an excellent place to shop. You can find branches of this charming store at Britannia Towers (tel. 809/326-2701); at Holiday Inn (tel. 809/326-3154); at Loews Harbour Cove (tel. 809/326-3747); and at Paradise Village (tel. 809/326-3102). There's yet another branch at Paradise Towers (tel. 809/326-2483). This place specializes in women's sportswear up to size 14. Designs are usually in brightly colored cottons. For this category of clothing, it's a good choice.

John Bull, known for its Bay Street store and as a pioneer of watches throughout The Bahamas, has two branches on Paradise Island, at the Paradise Island Resort & Casino (tel. 809/326-2652) and the Paradise Island Shopping Centre (tel. 809/323-7114), selling watches, cameras, jewelry, and designer accessories.

The **Pipe of Peace** offers its fine selection of watches, cameras, stereos, lighters, and calculators on Paradise Island as it does on Bay Street. The shop here is at the Paradise Village (tel. 809/326-2904). Many choice gift items are on display here.

For a rich collection of emeralds and jewelry from Colombia, as well as other precious and semiprecious stones and pearls from around the world, you can't go wrong by shopping at **Greenfire Emeralds Ltd.,** also agents for Seiko watches. They have a store at the Paradise Towers Hotel (tel. 809/326-2748).

The riches of **Solomon's Mines** are offered to shoppers at the Britannia Towers Hotel (tel. 809/326-3667). Here you'll find good buys in crystal, porcelain figurines, china, perfumes, and gifts—something to suit almost everybody.

Original designs in coral and natural pearls are spread out before you at **Jewels of the Sea** (tel. 809/326-3420) at the Holiday Inn. You can buy gold jewelry set with gemstones at this boutique beside the water.

4. THE SPORTING LIFE

Visitors interested in something more than lazing on the beaches have only to ask hotel personnel to lay on the necessary arrangements. Guests at the Paradise Island Resort & Casino (tel. 809/326-3000), for example, can have a surprising catalog of diversions without so much as leaving the hotel property. They can splash in private pools (one with a swim-up bar), play tennis, Ping-Pong, and shuffleboard, ride the waves, snorkel, and boat from the beach nearby.

Anyone in search of more ambitious water sports can sign up through the hotel for powerboat sightseeing, catamaran sailing, or diving in the waters farther out. Experienced crews run guests four or five miles out to reefs where they strap on snorkel masks or scuba gear.

Sports anglers can fish for grouper, dolphin, red snapper, crabs, even lobster close to shore. Farther out, in first-class fishing boats fitted with outriggers and fighting chairs, they troll for billfish or the giant marlin that Hemingway used to pursue regularly in The Bahamas.

GOLF: The superb **Paradise Island Golf Club** (tel. 809/326-3925), basks in the sunshine at the north end of Paradise Island. This 18-hole championship course, designed by Dick Wilson, has a fully stocked pro shop. Greens fees are $30 for 18 holes, $15 for 9 holes. An electric cart will cost you $30 for 18 holes. Golfers, who have included Jack Nicklaus, Gary Player, and other stars, face the challenge of shooting a ball through the twirling blades of a small windmill, through a waterpipe, over or around a lion's den, and other such obstacles.

The 14th hole of the par-72, 6,562-yard course has the world's largest sand trap: the entire left side of the hole is white sand beach.

TENNIS: Many visitors come to Paradise Island just for the tennis, which can be played day or night on the nine Har-Tru courts near the **Ocean Club** (tel. 809/326-2501). Guests booked into the cabañas and villas of the club can practically roll out of bed onto the courts. Although beginners and intermediate players are welcome, the courts are often filled with first-class competitors. Two major tennis championships a year are played at the Ocean Club courts, drawing players from the world's top 20.

Other hotels with courts are: **Britannia Towers** (tel. 809/326-3000), nine hard-surface courts; **Holiday Inn** (tel. 809/326-2101), four asphalt courts, lit; **Loews Harbour Cove Hotel** (tel. 809/326-2561), two asphalt courts, lit; lessons and equipment to rent are available; the **Sheraton Grand Hotel** (tel. 809/326-2011), four Har-Tru courts, lit; lessons offered. Nonguests usually are charged $3 per hour more for night play.

PARASAILING: For a sport combining the gliding power of a seagull with the aquatic skill of an osprey, try parasailing. It's sometimes the highlight of a vacation here—for daredevils. After donning waterskis, you're connected to a powerboat, which circles around in the shallow, offshore waters, so that a modified parachute takes you aloft.

Paradise Para-Sail, operating from Britannia Towers (tel. 809/326-3000, ext. 6123), can arrange a sail for you. A six- to eight-minute ride costs $25 per person.

HORSEBACK RIDING: Open daily, the **Harbourside Riding Stable Ltd.** (tel. 809/326-3733) offers rides leaving on each hour from 9 a.m. until 4 p.m. The ride along the golf course and beaches costs $25 per person. No previous riding experience is required, and either English or western saddles are available. It's best to make reservations.

HEALTH CLUBS AND BEAUTY SALONS: If you miss your hometown gym or just want to test the newest kinds of exercise equipment, head for the **Britannia Towers Health Spa** (tel. 809/326-3000, ext. 6536), where you can use Universal machines, as well as a sauna and Jacuzzi. There are massage facilities available, although an advance appointment is necessary for this service.

If you're mainly interested in a facial, sauna, or massage, the female staff can take care of you at the **Paradise Island Health Studio,** Paradise Towers (tel. 809/326-2431, ext. 4070). Appointments are necessary.

For fishing or scuba-diving, refer to "The Sporting Life" in Nassau, in Chapter VIII.

5. AFTER DARK

Among all the islands of The Bahamas, nightlife reaches its zenith on Paradise Island. There is no other spot with the diversity of attractions, especially after dark, that this self-contained playground can offer. A few of the choices include—

A CASINO AND THEATER: All roads on the island eventually lead to the focal point of the nightlife: the extravagantly decorated **Paradise Island Casino** (tel. 809/326-3000), run by Resorts International. It's a pleasure palace in the truest sense of the term. No visit to Nassau would be complete without a promenade through the Bird Cage Walk, where assorted restaurants, bars, and cabaret facilities make this one of the single most visited attractions anywhere outside the United States. For sheer gloss, glitter, and show-biz-oriented extravagance, these 30,000 square feet of casino space, with adjacent attractions, is *the* place to go.

The gaming tables provide the main attraction in the sanctum sanctorum of the enormous room, where Doric columns and a kind of modernized British colonial classicism vie with batteries of lights, a mirrored ceiling, and a color scheme of pastel greens and corals. The $50,000 chandelier under the dome of the entrance vestibule is fashioned from clusters of palm leaves crafted from brass, whose motif is repeated in the wall sconces throughout the inner rooms. Some 1,000 whirring and clanging slot machines operate 24 hours a day.

From 10 a.m. until early the following morning, the 60 blackjack tables, the ten roulette wheels, and the 12 tables for craps, three for baccarat, and one for Big Six are seriously busy with the exchange of large sums of money. The casino, of course, benefits from the $25 million recently spent on extension and redecoration to make it even more luxurious.

The boutiques that line the corridors leading to the adjacent hotels offer additional temptations. If you've ever lusted for the flashing glint of a Colombian emerald, a discreetly luxurious Swiss watch, or a complete set of silver dinnerware, you'll find these and other posh articles in the shops near the casino.

The old, and best, days of vaudeville, coupled with battalions of attractive male and female dancers, are extravagantly brought back in the $2-million production. It's presented twice every evening except Sunday in the red and gold **Cabaret Theatre** of the Paradise Island Casino (tel. 809/326-3000). Visitors usually purchase tickets in advance at the booth adjacent to the casino. The line-up before curtain call sends spectators in well-organized waves into the curved seating areas where you sit elbow to elbow with your neighbors.

The show employs an army of magicians, acrobats, jugglers, and comedians, as well as five complete theater sets, one with a skating rink. There's also a trio of "felines": a lion, a panther, and a tiger. Certainly not the least of all, a carefully choreographed set of routines is performed, sometimes with a trapeze, by a bevy of showgirls culled from auditions in New York, Las Vegas, Atlantic City, and of course The Bahamas. Each long-legged beauty is clad in what representatives of the hotel told me is $4,000 worth of feathers and $5,000 worth of body jewelry, sometimes presented in both stage and cinematic versions at the same time. There's even a black-light dance where only the costumes seem to fly through the air.

Some of the magic acts, especially where showgirls are levitated by an impresario, seem to defy explanation. One of my favorite moments in the show involves birds of a different feather, when 50 white doves fly through with a rush of fluttering wings. The cost for the cocktail show is $25, which provides two drinks. If you opt for the dinner show, the charge is $38 per person. Le Cabaret offers the dinner show six days a week featuring a complete dinner: an appetizer; soup; a choice of beef sirloin, filet mignon, or grouper; dessert; and coffee. Dinner is served in the show theater at 5:30 p.m. on Tuesday and Saturday, at 6:15 p.m. on Monday, Wednesday, and Friday, and at 7:30 p.m. on Thursday. After the dinner hour, show time is 7:15 p.m. on Tuesday and Saturday, 8:15 p.m. on Monday, Wednesday, and Friday, and 9:30 p.m. on Thursday. On Tuesday and Saturday, there's a cocktail show at 9:30 p.m. followed by a late show at 11:30 p.m. In other words, Tuesday and Saturday are the big nights. There's no show or dinner ever on a Sunday.

DISCO DANCING: In the Sheraton Grand Hotel, **Le Paon** (The Peacock) (tel. 809/326-2011) is a spacious multilevel disco in the back of the hotel's main lobby. It's decorated in a graceful series of illuminated curved lines and surfaces, and painted in night shades of purple and black. If you're with a group of friends, you may want to establish your nighttime headquarters in the conspicuously isolated circular banquette in the middle of the floor, close to the dancing area. The bar is long, providing views of the ocean. Happy hour is from 5 to 9 p.m., and regular disco takes over from then until the club closes at 2 a.m. There's a two-drink minimum every night, costing around $10 per person. The place is closed on Monday and Tuesday.

Club Pastiche, Paradise Island Casino (tel. 809/326-3000). If you want to dance close to the confines of the casino, you can head for this darkly intimate disco where the sound is broadcast over 116 speakers. The sounds and lights are among the best on the island, although if you just want a drink, soft illumination in the bar area is a lot like that in a tropical jungle at twilight. The club is separated from the blackjack tables of the casino by a low balustrade. Disco music begins at 10 p.m. There's no cover charge except on Friday, Saturday, and Sunday night, when there's a two-drink minimum of $12. Other nights, the two-drink minimum is $10. The club is open from 8 p.m. to 4 a.m. every day of the week.

Tradewinds Lounge, Paradise Towers (tel. 809/326-3000). Crowded, noisy, and deliberately underlit, this is one of the busiest nightclubs on Paradise Island. It's said to have one of the best-engineered sound systems. Hosts of candles turn the pulsating crowd into an intriguing mass of moving shadows. On Tuesday, Friday, Saturday, and Sunday, it is open from 8:30 p.m. to 3 a.m. On those nights, there is a show from 9 to 11 p.m. On Wednesday, hours are from 7:30 p.m. to 3 a.m., with a show that lasts from 8:30 to 10 p.m. On other nights, the club usually closes at midnight. A series of live bands alternate with disco—live music usually begins after 9 p.m. After that time, two drinks are included in the Friday- and Saturday-night cover of $10 per person.

THE BAR SCENE: There are so many different nightspots at the Paradise Island Resort that a visit to each of them could occupy an entire evening for anyone who wanted to "discover" the perfect tropical libation. Drinks in each of these places usually cost $4 each.

One of the best vantage points for a view of both the entrance of the casino and the pedestrian traffic on the Bird Cage Walk is the intimately cozy **Gallery Bar** in Paradise Towers. Set up within a view of a bronze statue of a laughing child, it offers seating in low-slung, comfortable chairs and an English-club atmosphere perfect for watching yet not becoming too intimately involved with the action. Hours are from 11 a.m. to 4 p.m. daily.

If you're looking for a taste of Polynesia, head for the bar in the **Coyaba Restaurant,** recommended in the restaurant section, off the casino's arcade, where fruited cocktails exude a hint of the Pacific.

Daytime drinkers can swim and enjoy a drink at the **swim-up bar** in the pool of the Britannia Towers, before moving on to the **View Bar,** whose scope encompasses the floor of the casino. Also on the properties are a thatched hut beside the pool, which dispenses waterside drinks, as well as a **Beach Bar** at the Britannia Towers.

Buccaneer Lounge, Loews Harbour Cove (tel. 809/326-2561), is a good bet for a convivial crowd, jazzy music, and two-fisted drinks. The lounge is open from 9:30 p.m. to 1 a.m. every day except Monday and Wednesday. A cover charge of $10 includes two drinks. Live calypso bands usually alternate with disco music.

CHAPTER X

GRAND BAHAMA (FREEPORT/LUCAYA)

□ □ □

On Grand Bahama Island, Freeport/Lucaya was once just a dream, some lonely coral and pine stands that almost overnight turned into one of the world's major resorts. The resort was the dream of Wallace Groves, a Virginia-born financier who saw the prospects of developing the island into a miniature Miami Beach/Las Vegas extravaganza. Today, with El Casino, the International Bazaar, high-rise hotels, golf courses, marinas, and a bevy of continental restaurants, that dream has been realized.

Originally, Freeport was developed as an industrial free zone in 1956. Groves wanted to attract international financiers who could appreciate the fact that Grand Bahama was less than 80 miles from Florida and only three hours by air from New York. The package was comfortably lined with tax incentives and Customs exemptions. Billionaire financier D. K. Ludwig built a deep-water harbor to accommodate freight and passenger vessels.

The Lucaya district was born eight years later, as a resort center along the coast. It has evolved into a comfortable blend of residential and tourist facilities. As the two communities grew, their identities became almost indistinguishable.

Grand Bahama Island is the northernmost and fourth-largest land mass in The Bahamas. Nearly everything here is new, including the people. Before the boomtown development, the population numbered only 4,000 souls, some of whom made their living working in a lumber camp that had been in existence since 1929. Historically, not much had happened since Ponce de León is believed to have landed here searching for the Fountain of Youth. Grand Bahama, lying 76 miles east of Palm Beach, is 73 miles long and 4 to 8 miles wide.

In West End, a town 25 miles to the east of Freeport, are skeleton warehouses and half-sunk piers, all reminders of that village's heyday in bootlegging times. Because of its proximity to the Florida coast, in the 1920s the fishing village was a reservoir for liquor to be smuggled into the United States by rum-runners.

Freeport is the downtown, the commercial, and the industrial city, and Lucaya is called the garden city, the resort and residential area with fine sandy beaches.

Freeport/Lucaya is a major sports center. There are six championship golf courses on the island, plus a nine-hole executive layout. Because of the plentiful supply of fresh water, the greens and fairways are in top condition year-round, but the asset that golfers prize most is the fact that there's seldom a wait for starting time. Water sports—skiing, skindiving, swimming, fishing, sailing—abound. With some 40 tennis courts on the island, there's plenty of opportunity to hit the ball. There are also riding stables and jogging tracks.

FLYING TO FREEPORT: For a general discussion of traveling to The Bahamas, refer to Chapter VI.

A number of airlines fly to Freeport from points within the continental United States. Flights between Florida and Freeport can be connected with flights from throughout the United States. Frequent flights between Freeport and the United States are scheduled by Bahamasair, Eastern, Eastern Express, Pan Am, TWA, Comair (the Delta connection), and Aero Coach. In addition, a number of travel tour operators—including Princess Casino Vacations, Flying Vacations, GVW, and Bahamas Express—offer charter service to the island. Air Canada provides the Canadian link.

CRUISE LINKS TO GRAND BAHAMA: Operating nine cruises to Freeport every week, *SeaEscape* sails from both Miami and Fort Lauderdale. The 1,100-passenger *Discovery I* also makes the Fort Lauderdale–Freeport run four times weekly. In addition, Crown Cruise Lines (tel. 800/841-7447) offers cruises to Freeport from the Port of Palm Beach five times weekly. The crossing takes about five hours. *Viking Express* (tel. 305/760-4550) operates a 312-passenger high-speed twin-hulled catamaran between Fort Lauderdale and Freeport daily. This trip takes less than three hours. All cruise passengers have the option to stay over. In addition, some of the major cruise lines, such as **Carnival** (tel. 305/599-2600) and **Norwegian Cruise Lines** (tel. 305/445-0866) regularly make Grand Bahama a port-of-call.

GETTING AROUND: The government sets the **taxi** rates, which are the same for Freeport/Lucaya as in Nassau. The cabs are metered. Taxis are often big U.S. cars.

There is also a public **bus** service from the International Bazaar to downtown Freeport and from the Pub on The Mall to the Lucaya area.

Bicycles and **motorscooters** are good means of transport here. Try **Curtis Enterprises Ltd.,** P.O. Box F-2511, Queens Hwy. (tel. 809/352-7035). Gas is supplied, and there's no charge for mileage. A 10-speed bike requires a deposit of $50 and costs $20 a day, and a one-speed bike takes a $40 deposit and costs $15 a day. A double-seater motorscooter requires a $100 deposit, costing $40 a day, and single-seater motorscooters require a $50 deposit, costing $28 a day. The establishment is open daily from 9 a.m. to 5 p.m. The rental agency also supplies helmets for drivers and passengers, which are required by law. The operator of the vehicle must also have a valid driver's license.

You can charter a plane for flying around Grand Bahama or to other islands at **Taino Air Service** at the Freeport International Airport, P.O. Box F-4006, Freeport, The Bahamas (tel. 809/352-8885). An airborne excursion over the lagoons, golf courses, and outlying reefs of Grand Bahama, suitable for one to five people, costs $225 per hour. The only regularly scheduled flights are from Freeport to the Abacos and Bimini. One-way passage to Marsh Harbour is $49, and flights leave daily except Tuesday and Thursday. Passage to Bimini is daily except Tuesday and Thursday, and the cost is $39 one way. A chartered plane from Freeport to Nassau, a five seater, costs $385.

Car Rentals

Your need for a car will be less intense on Grand Bahama than in Nassau, because of the self-contained nature of many of the island's major hotels. Still, if you want to explore, and if you're looking for self-drive transportation, you can try **Avis, Hertz,** or **National,** each of which maintains offices in small bungalows outside the exit from the Freeport International Airport.

Each of these companies charges a daily or weekly rate, with unlimited mileage included. The arithmetic usually works out that the per-day rate is reduced for rentals of a week or more. You get the cheapest tariff by reserving a car several days in advance. At presstime, Avis offered the least expensive winter charges, a manual transmission Suzuki Fronte without air conditioning costing $270 per week with unlimited mileage. Among cars with air conditioning (which you might appreciate in the summer months), an air-conditioned Suzuki Forza at Hertz rents for $325 per week unlimited mileage.

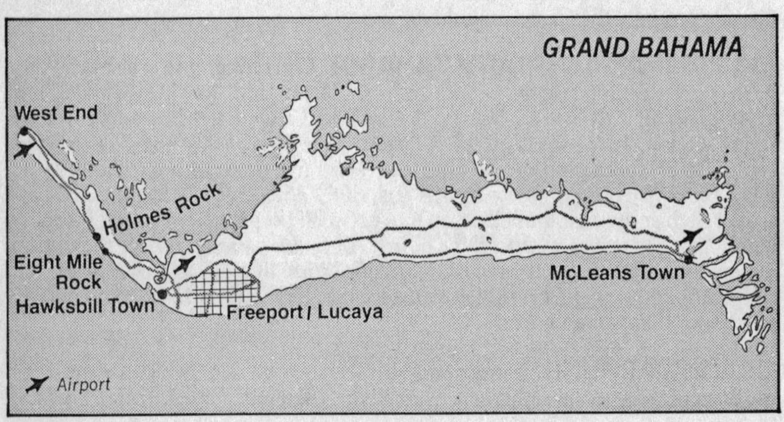

Regardless of the company you select, take the $7-per-day collision damage waiver. It's expensive, but unless you have it you'll be liable for the first $1,500 in damages in case of an accident.

For more information and up-to-the-minute rates (all of which will have changed somewhat by the time you read this), call in the U.S. the following toll-free numbers: Hertz at 800/654-3001, National at 800/328-4567, and Avis at 800/331-2112.

PRACTICAL FACTS: Much factual information regarding Freeport/Lucaya is also applicable to the rest of The Bahamas and appears in "The ABCs of The Bahamas" in Chapter VII. The data presented here should help you on matters pertaining specifically to the Grand Bahama area.

Banks: As in New Providence, the banking hours on Grand Bahama are Monday to Thursday from 9:30 a.m. to 3 p.m., on Friday to 5 p.m. There is no weekend service. U.S., Canadian, and British banks maintain branches in Freeport and Eight Mile Rock. Both Chase Manhattan and Barclays Bank International Ltd. have banks here, among several others. Chase Manhattan is on The Mall and Pioneer's Way, P.O. Box F-876 (tel. 809/352-9792). You'll find Barclays' main branch also on The Mall and Pioneer's Way, P.O. Box F-2404 (tel. 809/352-8391).

Churches: Grand Bahama has a large number of houses of worship. Of the major faiths, the following are established in Freeport/Lucaya: **Anglican:** Christ the King, P.O. Box F-87, East Atlantic Drive and Pioneer's Way (tel. 809/352-5402). **Baptist:** First Baptist Church, Columbus Drive and Nansen Avenue (tel. 809/352-9224); St. John's Native Baptist, Ponce de León and Coral Road (tel. 809/352-2276); **Lutheran:** Our Saviour Lutheran Church, East Sunrise Hwy. (tel. 809/373-3500). **Methodist:** St. Paul's Methodist Church, East Sunrise Hwy. and Beachway Drive (tel. 809/373-1888). **Presbyterian:** Lucaya Presbyterian Kirk, West Beach Road and Kirkwood Place, Lucaya (tel. 809/373-2568). **Roman Catholic:** Mary Star of the Sea, East Sunrise Hwy. and West Beach Road (tel. 809/373-3300).

Drugstore: For prescriptions and other pharmaceutical needs, go to L.M.R. Mini Mall, where you'll find **L.M.R. Prescription Drugs** (tel. 809/352-7327), next door to Burger King. Hours are 8:30 a.m. to 6 p.m.; closed Sunday.

Emergencies: In case of an emergency, some phone numbers you may find helpful are **police,** 911; **fire,** 809/352-8888; **ambulance,** 809/352-2689 or 809/352-6735; **air-sea rescue,** 809/352-2628 or 911.

Medical care: If you have a medical emergency, get in touch with **Rand Memorial Hospital,** P.O. Box F-71, on East Atlantic Drive (tel. 809/352-6735; emergency, 809/352-2639). This is a government-operated, 78-bed hospital, with departments of medicine, surgery, obstetrics and gynecology, pediatrics, and an emergency ward. It also has an outpatient clinic and clinical laboratories. Hospital fees are moderate.

Newspapers: The *Freeport News* is an afternoon daily newspaper published in Freeport Monday through Saturday except holidays. The two dailies published in Nassau, the *Tribune* and the *Nassau Guardian,* are also available here, as are some New York and Miami papers, especially the *Miami Herald,* usually on the date of publication. The cost of these is increased by air freight charges.

Post office: The main post office is on Explorers Way in Freeport, P.O. Box FO (tel. 809/352-9371). Airmail is delivered daily; surface mail, weekly.

Service calls: In Freeport/Lucaya, phone 809/352-8111 for time of day, 809/352-6675 for weather information.

Telephone: It is important to know that the extended area service calls may be made to West End, Eight Mile Rock, and most other local areas of Grand Bahama Island by dialing the full seven-digit number. If you dial "1" plus the seven-digit number, you will be charged for a long-distance call.

Television: Cable TV is received on Grand Bahama, with good reception. Some seven TV stations are relayed.

Tourist information: Assistance and information are available at the **Ministry of Tourism** at the International Bazaar, P.O. Box F-251 (tel. 809/352-8044).

1. WHERE TO STAY

Your choice is between hotels in the Freeport area, near El Casino and the International Shopping Bazaar, or else at Lucaya, closer to the beach. Always inquire about package plans when making reservations, as some very low-cost ones are offered periodically, especially to excursionists coming over from Florida. Sometimes the cost of the room is thrown in for practically nothing. The hotel managements of the major resorts apparently think that once they get you on the premises, money can be made off you in the bars, nightclubs, and restaurants.

Don't expect to find any cheap guesthouses in Freeport, as you will in Nassau. However, some of the smaller hotels at the bottom of my list are so inexpensive they charge "guesthouse prices."

Remember: In most cases, taxes and a service charge will be added to your final bill. Be prepared.

IN FREEPORT: Queen of Freeport's resort hotels, **Bahamas Princess Resort and Casino,** P.O. Box F-2623, The Mall at Sunrise Highway, Freeport, Grand Bahama, The Bahamas, is a multi-million-dollar resort/golf/convention complex set into 2,500 acres of tropical grounds. There are in fact two "Princesses," the Princess Country Club (tel. 809/352-6721) and the Princess Tower (tel. 809/352-9661). Combined, they offer a total of 965 rooms, which, with no contest, make it the largest resort in the Freeport/Lucaya area. Ten minutes from the airport, near the International Bazaar, the resort also takes in the casino and includes two 18-hole championship golf courses, 12 tennis courts, two pools, a Jacuzzi, a beach club, and a full complement of restaurants (some of which will be recommended separately), cocktail lounges and bars, plus a disco (which will be recommended in the "After Dark" section). First, the *Princess Country Club.* The hotel's design is not unlike an enormous wagon wheel, with a Disneyland-style mini-mountain at its core, surrounded by an extravagant swimming pool with cascading waterfalls. There's an arched bridge allowing guests to pass over the water between the rocks. The hotel is so spread out that guests often complain jokingly that they need ground transport to reach their bedrooms, a total of 565. Nine wings radiate from the pool, sheltering buildings that are only two or three stories high (some are sold as time-share units with kitchenettes). Accommodations come in several classifications. However, even the standard rooms are well equipped, with two comfortable double beds, dressing areas, tile baths, and color TV sets. In winter, room rates—and these same tariffs are in effect at the Princess Tower—are classified as standard, deluxe, and "winners circle," the latter available only in the tower. In winter, single or double occupancy costs $125 to $145 daily, or, if you prefer the winners circle, $175, again either single or double occupancy. *In summer, regular single or double rooms rent for $85 to $105 daily, going up to $135 for two persons in the winners circle. MAP is another $35 per person daily.* Many accommodations can also be rented as triples and quads. Both the Country Club and the Tower also rent out a number of lavishly furnished—and expensive—suites, one the "royal suite," the "presidential suite," and get this, "the monarch suite." There is no charge for children under 12 years old when sharing a room with their parents; however, the management limits that to two children.

Daytime dress is casual. In the evening, men are requested to wear a jacket in the Rib Room, but there are several other more informal dining spots. The Rib Room is the most deluxe establishment at the Country Club. There is also dining at Guanahani's, which offers smoked ribs and other dishes in a setting overlooking the waterfall. Only dinner is served. Guests can also order three meals a day, and that means breakfast too, in The Patio, which also has a view over the pool. John B offers lunch, dinner, and late-night snacks, such as hamburgers and quiche. It has an open-air setting.

The *Princess Tower,* lying across the Mall from its larger sister, is smaller, containing 400 luxuriously furnished units, large and airy bedrooms, adjoining the Princess Casino and the International Bazaar. Each unit comes with two double beds. Moorish in theme, the tower rises ten floors, standing on 7½ acres of landscaped grounds. Swimming is in fresh water in an Olympic-size pool, and there is a mile-long sandy beach at the nearby Princess Beach Club. A full program of water sports is available, including arrangements for deep-sea fishing. Three professional-caliber tennis courts are lit for night play, and there are two 18-hole golf courses nearby. The Arabic motif, set by the Moorish-style tower, with turrets, arches, and a white dome, is continued through the octagon-shaped lobby, with its Portuguese hand-painted emerald-green and royal-blue glazed ceramic tile floor, plus a colonnade of white Arabesque arches. Guest rooms are designed in both "tropical and traditional," as they say here, each containing cable TV and individual climate control.

At the Princess Tower you're faced with a choice of different restaurants. Two of the best, Morgan's Bluff and Trattoria, are recommended separately. You can select either the Lemon Peel or the outdoor veranda, La Terraza, which in season has a breakfast buffet spread out. The Lemon Peel reopens for lunch and continues to serve dinner until 11 p.m. The Princess Tower also shelters one of the most popular discos on the island, the Sultan's Tent (more about that later).

For reservations and information, phone Princess Hotels International toll free at 800/223-1818; in New York State, toll free 800/442-8418; in New York City, 212/582-8100; in Ontario and Québec, toll free 800/268-7140; and in other Canadian provinces, toll free 800/268-7176.

Xanadu Beach and Marina Resort, P.O. Box F-2438, Freeport, Grand Bahama, The Bahamas (tel. 809/352-6782). Originally built as condominiums, and later inhabited by the reclusive millionaire Howard Hughes, this symmetrical tower reopened in 1986 after months of costly renovations. It sits amid a complicated series of marinas and peninsulas, a few steps from a wide sandy beach. The hotel, just ten minutes from the international airport, was inspired by the line from Coleridge: "In Xanadu did Kubla Khan a stately pleasure dome decree." In 1969, when it opened, it was an exclusive private club and you were likely to see Sammy Davis, Jr., and Frank Sinatra walking through the lobby. No one saw Mr. Hughes, but he was safely tucked away in the penthouse. When it was his retreat, the hotel appeared frequently on TV. Today an intimate and darkly masculine library, with a flattering portrait, still honors his memory.

Carefully balanced with evenly spaced rows of curved balconies, the hotel combines the kind of pyramid-shaped roof you'd expect on a Tibetan monastery with a certain kind of Space Age theatricality. Inside, amid a decor of heavily geometric dark paneling, is a large stone fireplace, along with oases of deep and plushly upholstered sofas, restaurants, and a disco. Tennis courts, an oval swimming pool, and easily booked water sports are on the premises. There's also a dignified cocktail lounge with live piano music. A golf course is nearby. Rooms are attractively and comfortably furnished, among the finest at the resort. In winter, superior rooms (contained within the three-story pool wing) cost $130 daily, single or double occupancy. Deluxe rooms in the tower rent for $145 daily for two, and junior suites, also for two, cost $190, with one-bedroom suites, again for two, priced at $250. A third party in any room pays another $30 extra per night. *In summer, superior rooms, single or double, in the three-story pool wing rent for $98 daily, rising to $110 in the tower. Junior suites for two cost $140 daily, with one-bedroom suites for two priced at $145.*

Freeport Inn, The Mall, P.O. Box 200, Freeport, Grand Bahama, The Bahamas (tel. 809/352-6648), is composed of a cluster of buildings built Bahamian style with white balustraded covered balconies. In all, 170 well-furnished and air-conditioned rooms overlook a large swimming pool area with an extensive sun terrace, and a snackbar is provided at poolside. Most rooms contain two double beds, and many have dressing areas. Bedrooms have standard American-style, built-in units with traditional design. The accommodations are some of the least expensively priced on the island. *Off-season, singles or doubles range in price from $59 to $74 daily. Triple accommodations cost $69 to $84 daily.* In winter, either single or double occupancy costs $69 to $89 daily, and triples are charged $82 to $104. Add another $12 for a fourth or fifth person sharing a room. For breakfast and dinner, add yet another $25 per person daily. Children under 12 sharing a room with their parents stay free. Some units have kitchenettes. There is courtesy transportation to the beach, ten minutes away. Food served in the Scotch and Sirloin and the Safari Lounge includes steaks and prime ribs. The inn is one mile from El Casino and the International Bazaar.

Caravel Beach Resort, P.O. Box F-3038, Freeport, Grand Bahama, The Bahamas (tel. 809/352-6390), stands across a canal from the famous Xanadu Hotel directly on the beach. It is a 12-unit mini-resort lying within its own garden. Each apartment was designed in a two-story duplex formula reminiscent of a townhouse, with its own kitchenette, color TV, and air conditioning, as well as two bedrooms and one-and-a-half baths. In winter, single or double occupancy costs $125 daily, going up to $165 in a triple and $200 for four. *Expect reductions of 20% in summer.* Deep-sea fishing, tennis, and golf are available nearby. On the premises is the Windsurfer Restaurant and Lounge.

Castaways Resort, P.O. Box F-2629, Freeport, Grand Bahama, The Bahamas (tel. 809/352-6682), is a long hotel with Oriental styling at the International Bazaar and Princess Casino. Each of its floors has pagoda roofing and an indoor and an outdoor Oriental garden lobby, and the hotel is surrounded by well-kept gardens. There is a swimming pool area with a wide terrace. Accommodations have air conditioning with a king-size or two double beds, and all rooms have cable TV. The bedrooms are decorated in cool greens or blues and whites. In the lobby, you'll find a gift shop, a clothing shop that carries both men's and women's apparel, and a game room. Tony Roma's Restaurant is also on the premises, featuring continental and American specialties. The disco Yellow Bird stays open until 6 a.m. *Off-season, one or two guests pay $54 to $76 per day in a room.* These tariffs (either single or double) increase in price in winter to $65 to $85 per day. There is continuous free transportation to Xanadu Beach, five minutes away. The manager's cocktail party, a complimentary feature, is held on Monday.

Sun Club Resort, P.O. Box F-1808, Freeport, Grand Bahama, The Bahamas (tel. 809/352-3462). Clean, well maintained, and relatively economical, this small-scale resort sits at the edge of a busy traffic intersection. White, with shutters, it hides its best section in the rear of the building. There, behind a vine-covered entrance arbor, is a quiet enclave of greenery, encompassing a tennis court, a pool, and a clubhouse with a bar. The establishment contains only 42 rooms, often completely booked. Each has a kitchenette, air conditioning, TV hookup, and a private bath, plus strong colors and simple furniture. In winter, daily rates are $78 in a single, $82 in a double, and $96 in a triple. *In summer, daily rates are reduced to $55 daily in a single, $58 in a double, and $72 in a triple.* A complimentary bus takes residents every hour to the beach, providing service most of the day.

Lakeview Manor Club, P.O. Box F-2699, Freeport, Grand Bahama, The Bahamas (tel. 809/352-9789), was originally built as private apartments and today is classified as a time-sharing project. Offering 25 luxurious one-bedroom and studio apartments, the club overlooks the fifth hole of the PGA-approved Ruby Golf Course. It stands away from the beach, but is ideal for golfers or for anyone to whom a sea view isn't important. The hotel maintains a five-times-per-day shuttle bus taking guests to the dining, drinking, and shopping facilities of the International Bazaar. There is no bar or restaurant on the premises. However, the resort features tennis courts, a swimming pool, free use of bicycles, reduced greens fees, and other extras. This place offers bargain headquarters for those seeking tranquility. Each unit has not only a private balcony, but a bar and kitchen. Rates are the same throughout the year: $75 per night or $450 weekly for two persons in a studio apartment or $100 per night for two or $600 weekly in a one-bedroom apartment. Each unit has well-chosen furnishings and air conditioning. Views are either of the resort's pool and tennis courts or of the golf course. The hotel is closed for one week each November.

IN LUCAYA: Set on a spit of land midway between the open sea and a protected inlet, **Lucayan Beach Resort & Casino,** P.O. Box F-336, Lucaya, Grand Bahama, The Bahamas (tel. 809/373-7777, or toll free 800/772-1227), is the newest incarnation of a well-known hotel which originally opened in the mid-1960s. The result of a complicated cooperation between the Bahamian government and a Malaysia-based hotel corporation, Genting International, it benefited from a lavish outlay of funds as part of a recent renovation. Often heavily booked in winter, it has one of the island's two casinos within its walls, a collection of popular restaurants, a dazzling cabaret act, a sweeping expanse of beachfront, a pool, and a host of water-related activities. There are also tennis, golf, and an array of boutiques. The hotel's gourmet restaurant, Les Oursins, and the cabaret act are reviewed separately.

The nearly 250 accommodations are contained in two wings which stretch toward either edge of a curved garden filled with tropical trees and croton. Each room has air conditioning, a veranda, satellite-transmitted color TV, and all the comforts you'd expect from a major international hotel. In winter, units cost $125 to $180 daily for a single or double room, $150 to $210 in a triple. *In summer, single or double rooms rent for $100 to $165 daily, and triples go for $125 to $190.* MAP can be arranged in any season for another $35 per person daily. The hotel's sister establishment, the Lucayan Marina Hotel, is reviewed separately.

Holiday Inn, P.O. Box F-2496, Lucaya, Grand Bahama, The Bahamas (tel. 809/373-1333, or toll free 800/HOLIDAY), is a large luxury hotel with few surprises, but it is a resort hotel that's far superior to many of its chain sisters. There are 505 rooms, each with its own bath. It is directly on Lucaya Beach, with an entrance portico that seems to envelop arriving visitors in a well-designed sweep of soaring concrete. There is a swimming pool ringed with palm trees, as well as four all-weather tennis courts, which cost $3 per hour. Live entertainment is featured nightly in the lounge. In winter, single rooms range from $85 to $124 per day, and doubles cost $93 to $138. *These tariffs drop to $65 to $88 daily for a single in summer, $74 to $97 in a double.* For breakfast and dinner, add another $38 per person daily to the prices quoted. Children are specially catered to here. If they are under 12, there is no charge for them when sharing a room with an adult. Room service is available here for guests wishing to dine in their rooms on many of the specialties offered in the restaurants. There is an emphasis on sports programs, including water sports, tennis, and golf. Deep-sea fishing trips can be arranged.

Atlantik Beach Hotel, P.O. Box F-531, Lucaya, Grand Bahama, The Bahamas (tel. 809/373-1444), a Swiss International Hotel, is better than ever, following a $5-million renovation. It combines European flair with tropical style. A high-rise opening onto a palm-shaded beach, it stands near the Holiday Inn, about six miles from Freeport. The hotel owns the Lucaya Park Golf and Country Club, a par-72, 18-hole course, and is well equipped for other sports as well, including boating, deep-sea fishing, and tennis. It has a large rectangular pool for those who don't want to go to the adjoining beach. Special features of the hotel include a shopping arcade, with a Swiss chocolate and pastry shop and an espresso bar where some visitors like to take their breakfast. There are several places to dine, including the Butterfly Brasserie coffeeshop where most guests enjoy breakfast along with German jellies, and there is gourmet fare in the second-floor Spanish Main. The Yellow Elder Bar/Lounge, also on the second floor, was named for the Bahamian national flower. Buffets are presented on the lattice-top patio, and there is often entertainment at night. In winter, singles begin at $90 daily, $110 for a suite for a single. Doubles are priced at $115 to $200. *In summer, singles are charged $75 to $95 daily, and doubles pay $85 to $105.*

Lucayan Marina Hotel, P.O. Box F-336, Lucaya, Grand Bahama, The Bahamas (tel. 809/373-8888 or toll free at 800/772-1227), stands on Lucayan Bay, across from the already previewed Lucayan Beach Resort & Casino. Both hotels are jointly owned by the Hotel Corporation of The Bahamas and Genting Berhad, one of the largest corporations of Malaysia, and are managed by Genting International Resorts and Casinos which operates properties throughout the Far East and Australia. The Marina Hotel is a separate hotel unit comprised of 18 villa-type buildings with 142 guest rooms as well as slips for 150 boats. The marina features a swimming pool, a whirlpool spa, and laundry facilities, and a water taxi provides free shuttle service between both hotels at every half hour. Complimentary mini-bus service is also available. Guests staying at either the Lucayan Beach Resort & Casino or the Lucayan Marina Hotel have reciprocal privileges of all facilities at both properties. *In summer, well-furnished single or double units rent for only $60 a day, with triples costing $75.* In winter, singles or doubles cost $70 daily, with triples priced at $90. MAP can be arranged for another $35 per person daily. The main dining facility is Hemingway's After Deck Restaurant & Bar, featuring Bahamian specialties and a selection of American and Italian dishes. There is also a bar offering wine and drinks in a casual setting with a hand-hewn wood bar as its focal point.

Silver Sands Sea Lodge, Royal Palm Way, P.O. Box F-2385, Lucaya, Grand Bahama, The Bahamas (tel. 809/373-5700), consists of three buildings clustered around two swimming pools. There are 144 modern studio apartments, plus 20 one-bedroom first-class suites, all with a view of the ocean, pool area, marina, or garden. The location is 100 yards from a white sand beach, seven miles from the airport at Freeport. All units are air-conditioned, and contain TV, phone, and full maid service. Units are spacious, complete with private bath, balcony, wall-to-wall carpeting, a fully equipped kitchen, and bar. The lodge contains one of the best restaurants in the Freeport/Lucaya area, La Phoenix, recommended separately. In winter, singles or doubles rent for $80 to $100 daily, while a one-bedroom suite for two costs from $110 to $120. *In summer, asingle or double costs only $52 to $72 daily, and a one-bedroom suite rents for $80 a night.* Water sports available include sailing, paddleboating, windsurfing, spearfishing, snorkeling, and scuba-diving. The lodge also has two hard-surface tennis courts (free to guests, $10 per hour for outsiders), two paddleball courts, and two shuffleboard courts. The poolside snackbar, La Conch, is open for breakfast. At Mama Russell's Straw Boutique, you can see her weave straw bags, hats, and other gift items.

Coral Beach, P.O. Box F-2468, Lucaya, Grand Bahama, The Bahamas (tel. 809/373-2468). Built in 1965 as an upscale collection of privately owned condominiums, this peacefully isolated property sits amid groves of casuarinas in a well-heeled residential neighborhood. Only a handful of apartments and rooms are rented to vacationers. The gardens are well maintained, and the units each have air conditioning, TV, and a private bath. Some contain verandas, but not all have kitchenettes. Studio units with verandas and kitchenettes cost $69 daily in a single and $79 in a double in winter, with studio units without kitchens or porches going for $55 single and $65 double. *In summer, studio units with verandas and kitchenettes rent for $55 daily in a single and $60 in a double, whereas units* *without kitchenettes and porches cost $45 daily in a single and $55 in a double.* The private community aura of the place makes it a high-quality hideaway for the discerning. On the premises is a sandy and well-maintained beach, as well as a swimming pool. Even if you're not staying there, the public can visit **Chicago's** (tel. 809/373-6600), featuring U.S. prime beef, or **Juliat Lin's Chinese Restaurant** (tel. 809/373-8061), which is open for lunch and dinner from noon to 9:30 p.m., serving an array of Mandarin and Szechuan food.

Channel House, P.O. Box F-1337, Lucaya, Grand Bahama, The Bahamas (tel. 809/373-5405), is owned and managed by Mike Bass, a former defensive back with the Super Bowl Washington Redskins. Built in the late 1960s before the massive Port Lucaya complex came into being, it lies across the road from one of the island's finest beaches. It is within walking distance of the Lucayan Beach Casino and the scuba diving at Underwater Explorers Society. Considered an inexpensive mini-resort in its own right, it has a swimming pool, two tennis courts, a bar, and a pool bar where choices are limited to hamburgers, salads, and steak sandwiches. There is no formal restaurant on the premises, but many excellent choices are a short walk away. Each well-furnished and spacious unit has a full kitchen, queen-size bed, a love seat which unfolds into a bed, a veranda or patio, air conditioning, and TV. In winter, single or double occupancy costs $85 daily, with triples priced at $97. *In summer, single or double rooms rent for only $65 a day, with triples costing $77.*

2. WHERE TO DINE

In The Bahamas, Freeport/Lucaya is second only to Nassau and Paradise Island in the nature and scope of its international restaurants. Many are centered around the big resort hotels, but there are a few native places as well. My choices follow.

THE LEADING INDEPENDENTS: A popular dining nook on Grand Bahama is the **Stoned Crab,** at Taino Beach, Lucaya (tel. 809/373-1442), great if you don't mind the cab fare from downtown Freeport to its waterside perch. A pleasant oceanfront restaurant right on the beach, the restaurant vaguely evokes an alpine chalet, the type built in France. Guests can dine inside or on the beach patio. Reservations are necessary, as this place fills up at night, not only with visitors, but with local residents as well who know of the large portions and the fine seafood.

To get you going, try the conch chowder. The snow crab claws are sweet and delicate. You might also like the stone crab claws. In honor of its namesake, the restaurant specializes in a number of crab dishes, including crab Andrew and a crab-and-avocado cocktail. Dolphin is regularly featured, as is the game fish, wahoo. Accompaniments include a salad bowl, as well as the Crab's own home-baked raisin bread. Fresh, not frozen, fish are used whenever possible. You might like to cap your meal with Irish coffee. That meal could easily top the $35 mark. The drinks are overscale, and if you've managed to finish your before-dinner libation you might not be too waterlogged to order a carafe of the house wine. The Crab also has a very nice burgundy bottled under its own label in France. The bartender's special is a "Stoned Crab" drink based on various liqueurs, fruit juices, and rum. At night, taxis are usually lined up outside to hustle you back to Princess Casino. The restaurant serves dinner only, from 5 to 11:30 nightly.

Captain's Charthouse Restaurant, P.O. Box 449, East Sunrise Hwy. and Beach Drive ("five minutes from anywhere"; tel. 809/373-3900), is open seven days a week. In a relaxed, treetop-level dining room, guests can select from an international menu that features such specialties as prime rib of beef, teriyaki steak, chateaubriand for two, lobster thermidor, the catch of the day, surf and turf, Bahamian lobster, grouper filet, and other seafood selections, along with the chef's homemade bread and "do-it-yourself" salad bar. You can also have a Caesar salad for two, prepared at your table. Portions are large, but if you still have an appetite you can choose from a list of homemade desserts, including a coconut tart and key lime pie. The tab is likely to be around $25. A happy hour is held in the Mates Lounge from 5 to 7 p.m., offering complimentary hors d'oeuvres. An early-bird special meal from 5 to 6:30 p.m. costs from $7. Dinner is from 5 to 11 p.m., and entertainment is also presented nightly. The atmosphere is nautical, vaguely Polynesian, and the service is deft.

Ruby Swiss Restaurant, West Sunrise Hwy. at West Atlantic Avenue (tel. 809/352-8507). Airy, open, and imaginative, this Swiss-owned restaurant occupies a building capped with a quintet of steeply pointed roofs. The design creates an unexpected spaciousness which is appreciated by the professional organizations that arrange to meet here. Inside are two bars (one, rescued from a Victorian building, is an antique), an inviting dining room, and a less formal eating area for snacks and drinks. There are three different menus listing the food items offered during the establishment's long service hours. Lunch, from 11 a.m. to 5 p.m., includes pâté maison, seafood or Caesar salads, burgers, and reuben or club sandwiches. The cost ranges from $11 to $20. Dinner, served from 6 to 10:30 p.m., costs $35 to $45 and might include lobster cocktail, seafood platter, scampi with garlic, catch of the day, Créole-style shrimp, filet Stroganoff, fondue bourguignonne, and filet Richelieu with hollandaise sauce. Viennese strudel is a dessert specialty. Late-night snacks, often served to diners taking a break from the gambling casino, are offered from 11 p.m. to 5 a.m. Platters of food such as omelets, scrambled eggs, sandwiches, conch chowder, and burgers cost from $5. The restaurant is open every day.

Mai-Tai, Emerald Country Club (tel. 809/352-7637). The stone-trimmed entrance to this Chinese and Polynesian restaurant is flanked by a pair of Easter Island–type heads. This sets the tone for the decor of this isolated restaurant, which lies near a golf course about a half mile from the casino. In fact, golfers from the nearby links may drop in for a midday cocktail, while other guests include members of the local business community.

The interior contains hanging buoys, palm-frond ceilings, and big windows through which the iron grill can be observed during the preparation of your dinner. Meals are served daily at lunch and dinner, and include both Polynesian and Szechuan specialties. Flaming appetizers feature a pupu platter, fried wontons, Mai-Tai sardar beef (barbecued beef on bamboo sticks), lobster chicken ball, deviled native lobster, Szechuan shrimp with green peas, and tempura shrimps and vegetables. There are also dishes from the Cantonese repertoire, as well as American dishes and a wide range of sandwiches at lunchtime. Full dinners begin at $30, with light lunches costing from $15. The house drink, of course, is the mai tai, although the Maui Maui sour is also popular, as is the Volcanic Flame, which someone will ignite before it arrives at your table. Open Monday to Saturday from 11 a.m. to 10 p.m., on Sunday from 5:30 to 10 p.m.

Marcella's, The Mall (tel. 809/352-5085), is the way Italian restaurants used to be. It's been around since 1963, and has seen competitors come and go. Decorated somewhat like a New York trattoria, with a bar and TV screen, it serves Monday to Friday from 11:45 a.m. to 2:30 p.m. and 5:45 to 10:30 p.m. On Saturday and Sunday it is open only from 5:45 to 11 p.m. You might begin with an antipasto or else pasta and bean soup, certainly a minestrone. The menu is large, with all the classic Italian dishes, including a fisherman's risotto, chicken cacciatore, saltimbocca, Venetian liver, and scaloppine Marsala. You can, in addition, order a zuppa di pesce (fisherman's soup) or calamari (squid) fritti. Full meals are reasonably priced at $20 per person.

Lucayan Lobster & Steak House, Midshipman Road, P.O. Box F-2798 (tel. 809/373-5101), near the Britannia Pub, is large and popular, drawing a lot of local residents as well as visitors. The prices are right, with meals costing around $13, and the food is hearty, familiar fare, well cooked and pleasantly served. It's a surf-and-turf kind of place, except, as an unusual variation, it mixes a plate of cracked conch and lobster tail on one order. Conch chowder is the usual opener, together with a lobster or conch salad, followed by the catch of the day. That might be Bahamian baked grouper. The chef also does good prime rib, and you might like a side order of onion rings. Early-bird specials, costing around $9, are offered from 4 to 6:30 p.m. The restaurant is open daily from 4 p.m. until midnight. Diners often precede their meal with a libation near the front entrance (the bartender makes a powerful drink).

THE BEST HOTEL DINING: In the Princess Casino, the **Crown Room** (tel. 809/352-7811) is for those who prefer casino dining. It serves nightly from 6:30 to midnight, offering an international menu. It's like the chicest dining room on an art deco ocean liner, with green-and-red fern-patterned carpeting and pink marble accents, along with brass-trimmed walls and rose-colored mirrors. The armchairs are Eastlake inspired, and the chandeliers are sophisticated clusters of etched-glass leaves gathered into illuminated sheaves. You have to walk through a section of the casino to reach this restaurant. Dinners cost around $40, and reservations are recommended. The restaurant features eight hot and cold hors d'oeuvres, ranging from liver pâté to shrimp deJonge, from oysters to fresh wild mushrooms. Soups include conch bisque, onion, matzoh ball, and vichyssoise. The salads are "the house" and Caesar. Among the 14 fish and meat main dishes are lobster, grouper, jumbo shrimps, fettuccine, duckling, rack of lamb, filet mignon, roast prime rib of beef, medallions of veal, and chicken. Desserts range from crêpes Casino to selections from the pastry trolley. The restaurant, which has a candlelit setting, can seat 100, whether they're gamblers or otherwise.

Among the "gourmet" dining rooms in the big hotels, I'm fond of the **Rib Room** at the Princess Country Club (tel. 809/352-6721), which serves dinner only, from 6 to 11 nightly. At this seafood and beef specialty restaurant, you'll be delighted with the traditional British-pub decor and service. You can select from broiled Bahamian lobster, native grouper, succulent shrimps, steak au poivre, steak Diane, or rack of lamb for two. Selected blue-ribbon prime rib of beef with Yorkshire pudding is also served. Your meal might begin with one of a goodly selection of "soups from the kettle," including vichyssoise, French onion, conch chowder, and lobster bisque, all international favorites. The final bill is around $30 per person. There is an excellent wine list to complement your meal. The Rib Room stands in the Queen's Walk area at the Country Club. Reservations are necessary, as patrons at the hotel can quickly fill up the limited number of seats, and jackets are required for men.

Guanahani's Restaurant, Princess Country Club, on the Mall (tel. 809/352-6721), is an attractive place that's easy to find, as it lies within the circular poolside arcade of this previously recommended hotel. To enter, you cross over a small drawbridge before passing through louvered doors. The decor is country-style tropical with massive brass chandeliers, lots of exposed wood, and bentwood chairs. The restaurant is named after the designation the Arawak Indians gave to San Salvador, the island on which Columbus first landed in the New World. The establishment prepares island roasts and barbecues by marinating top-quality meats and then roasting them for hours in specially constructed barbecue ovens. The house specialty is hickory-smoked ribs. Other choices include scampi, sirloin steak, beef brisket, fried conch with red sauce and fresh limes, and a Bahamian lobster and fish pot. Full meals cost $35 and are served only at dinner, daily from 5:30 to 10:30 p.m.

Les Oursins (Sea Urchins), Lucayan Beach Hotel (tel. 809/373-7777), lies a few steps from the entrance to the busy Lucayan Casino. It is the most elegant—and most expensive—restaurant in the previously recommended Lucayan Beach Hotel. Its minimalist decor includes a gray and white collection of tables, some of which are set on daises, and framed silk scarves in brilliant tones of aquamarine and rose. A uniformed staff caters to your needs during full dinners served nightly from 6 to 11 Sunday to Thursday, from 6 to midnight on Friday and Saturday; closed Tuesday in summer. Full meals cost from $50 and include an array of sophisticated European dishes, perhaps a creamy lobster bisque with dumplings, fresh goose liver terrine with black truffles, many different preparations of lobster, bay scallops with garlic and provençal herbs, and several beef, veal, and chicken dishes. Dessert might be a baked alaska or a Sachertorte. Reservations are suggested.

Morgan's Bluff, Princess Tower (tel. 809/352-9661). Near the reception desk of the previously recommended Princess Tower, this interesting restaurant looks a bit like a hi-tech version of a pirate's lair. Painted an enticing shade of coral, and accented with a duet of huge tropical murals, it serves full meals for $25. It's open only for dinner, from 6 to 11 p.m., offering such seafood specialties as lobster thermidor, a captain's platter of mixed seafood, cracked conch, Bahamian lobster tail, lobster bisque, seafood crêpes, and clams Benedict. Closed Monday and Tuesday.

La Trattoria, Princess Tower (tel. 809/352-9661). The focused spotlights aimed at the open parasols near the entrance imitate the Mediterranean sunlight glaring down a café terrace you might find in Capri. A few steps later, you find yourself among the stucco arches of what looks a lot like a thick-walled cellar. Some of the most interesting photographs in Freeport, depicting the workaday poses of some of Italy's least pretentious citizens, line the walls. The restaurant is open nightly except Thursday from 5:30 to 10:30. Budgeteers are encouraged to dine before 6:30 p.m. when a fixed-price bargain is offered for $12, plus service. After that, regular à la carte meals are served for $25 per person, including five versions of pizza and nine kinds of pastas such as fettuccine Alfredo and spaghetti carbonara. You can follow any of these with a Caesar salad, saltimbocca, and veal milanese, finished off with either a cappuccino or espresso.

The Phoenix, Silver Sands, Royal Palm Way (tel. 809/373-5700). Amusing, witty, and nautically inspired, this highly recommendable restaurant sits above the reception area of a previously endorsed hotel. Diners climb a broad flight of exterior stairs to reach it. An eclectic decor of driftwood paneling, Bahamian paintings, plants, and intimate table groupings usually provides for evenings which sometimes verge on fun. A huge iron chandelier, hanging in the center of it all, almost fills the room. The restaurant serves only dinner every night of the week. From 6:30 to 11 p.m., à la carte dinners range from $18 to $25. Specialties include fresh grouper Phoenix style, seafood stew, seafood kebab, cracked conch, fresh lobster kebab, sirloin kebab, and chicken Kiev, climaxed by either Nassau or Irish coffee. Reservations are a good idea.

PUB DINING: Britannia Pub, King's Road on Bell Channel (tel. 809/373-5919), is a mock-Tudor structure that is one of the most convivial bars on the island if you're doing a pub crawl of Grand Bahama. Men gather at the bar to watch sports on TV, and English beer is available on draft. The pub is also a restaurant, serving both a Bahamian and a Greek cuisine. Meals, costing from $22, might include lobster tails, the invariable "catch of the day," grouper meunière, and cracked conch. The chef will also prepare barbecued ribs or a Greek shish kebab. You might begin with stuffed crab served as an appetizer, or a Greek salad. There are also a few beef dishes. Hours are from 11 a.m. to 5 p.m. daily.

Sir Winston Churchill, East Mall, next to the Straw Market and the International Bazaar (tel. 809/352-8866), is a pub and restaurant, offering not only a beer garden out back, but meals, a happy hour, even entertainment. Short-time visitors to Freeport have been known to adopt it quickly as their local watering spot. From 11 a.m. to 2 a.m., the pub swings with activity. At lunch you can order the open hot sandwiches or pizzas, followed by homemade apple pie. The Chartwell Room in back of the pub features a complete menu, including cracked conch, fish platters, T-bone steaks, and prime rib of beef. Lunch can cost as little as $12 or less, and dinner averages around $25 per person. Some readers have found it better for drinking than dining.

The Pub on the Mall, Ranfurly Circus (P.O. Box F-395), opposite the International Bazaar (tel. 809/352-5110), gives you several types of rooms in which to eat, including an Italian restaurant. The pub and two other rooms have a British flavor. In the pub at lunchtime, you can order an English-style shepherd's pie, and fish and chips. The Baron's Hall Grill Room, decorated in a medieval fashion, serves a well-selected menu including certified Angus beef, fish, and fowl. Prime rib is a specialty of the house. English imported draft beer is served, and the chef does some Bahamian specialties. The Prince of Wales Lounge is an area where both locals and tourists eat lunch and dinner. This opens at 11:30 a.m. and remains so until 4 a.m. Monday through Saturday. Another room, Silvano's Italian Restaurant, offers Italian dishes and fresh pasta, serving dinner from 5:30 to 11 p.m. All the rooms are fully air-conditioned. Lunch begins at around $6 if you're eating light, but expect to pay from $15 for dinner.

THE BEST BAHAMIAN RESTAURANT: An unpretentious local restaurant, **Freddie's Native Restaurant,** P.O. Box 1281, Hunters (tel. 809/352-3250), well scrubbed and welcoming, offers an unusual alternative to the many foreign-owned restaurants filling the more commercial neighborhoods of the casino districts. It sits on a flat sandy plot of land in Hunters, said to be the site of one of the Grand Bahama's oldest settlements. From the outside it's little more than a painted concrete house. Inside, carefully installed pinewood planks add warmth. The owner, Freddie Russell, with some help, did most of the carpentry. His wife, Janet, does an excellent Bahamian cuisine. Full meals are served daily except Sunday. Lunch, from 11 a.m. to 3 p.m., costs $6. Dinner, from 5 to 11 p.m., is priced at $15 to $20 and includes lobster salad, conch salad, cracked conch, grouper, pork chops, shrimp, seafood platters, steak, and several different preparations of chicken. A wine list accompanies your meal.

DINING IN THE INTERNATIONAL BAZAAR: Within this shopping complex, you can also travel to many lands by dining out, sampling the cuisine of several countries.

Japanese Steak House (tel. 809/352-9521) is my favorite, a touch of the Orient in the tropics. Kimono-clad waitresses serve a complete hibachi steak and chicken dinner. The house specialties are sukiyaki steak and tappanyaki steak. Both are cooked on a hibachi in front of you. The restaurant's most expensive dish—and a favorite—is hibachi steak, including New York strip steak and a lobster tail. Dinners cost from $25 to $30 per person. The owners welcome you, offering, in addition to the Japanese steak dinner, Oriental food and Occidental drinks, such as "Playgirl." You can, in addition, ask for sake and plum wine. Most dinners include soup, salad, and five different vegetables as well as rice. Meals are served until 10:30 nightly except Sunday. However, if you want to save money, go for dinner from 5 to 8:30 p.m. when an "early bird special" is presented, costing only $13.95. Lunch is also served daily except Sunday from 11:30 a.m. to 2:30 p.m. Representing one of the best noontime bargains in town, it costs only $6.95. You have unlimited access to a buffet arrangement of vegetables and salads. A main dish is brought to your table. Choices include Japanese peppersteak, teriyaki pork loin, tempura don (that is, tempura shrimp and vegetables), and Japanese-style fried rice.

Café Valencia, Spanish section (tel. 809/352-8717), is sheltered under a tile-roofed building. On several occasions I have come here to sample their paella, but the chef prepares an array of other specialties as well, including Spanish, Italian, Bahamian, and American dishes. You might begin with a chowder or onion soup or a lobster salad if you're visiting for lunch, that costs $15 to $20. Dinner, at $25 to $30, features such pasta dishes as lasagne and fettuccine. You might also like the Bahamian grouper cutlet or the yellowtail. The stuffed lobster is also good, as is the stuffed chicken breast. Spence Cooper, the owner, will welcome you to this place, which has a relaxed mood at night created by soft lights. Dinner reservations are suggested. For regular dining, it's open from 11 a.m. to 11 p.m. Monday to Saturday and 5 to 11 p.m. on Sunday. A late-night menu is in effect from 11:30 p.m. to 4 a.m.

Michel's, French section (tel. 809/352-2191), is an open-air place, which has an adjoining popular bar, where guests prefer a café table placed under an umbrella. Breakfast is served from 9 a.m. to 11:30 a.m. and lunch from 11:30 a.m. to 5 p.m. Dinner, prepared by European chefs, is served from 6 to 9 p.m. Lunch, costing from $15, always features a plat du jour, along with such standard favorites as prime rib, fresh broiled grouper, broiled lobster, and seafood platter. At dinner, costing $25 and up, continental specialties predominate. The café is closed on Sunday.

China Temple, Hong Kong Street (tel. 809/352-5610), offers Chinese food daily from 10:30 a.m. to 10:30 p.m. Monday to Saturday, from 11 a.m. to 4:30 p.m. Sunday. A restaurant that also does takeout orders, the China Temple has outside café tables, or you can retreat inside. It's the bargain dining spot of the Bazaar, offering lunchtime specialties from $5.50. It's the typically classic Chinese "chop suey menu," with all the standard items such as sweet-and-sour fish. A three-course set dinner costs $11.75.

Bavarian Beer Garden (tel. 809/352-5050) is a hearty choice for food and drink anytime from 10:30 a.m. to 7 p.m. daily. Try for an outside table located beneath the Moorish-style arches of the Bazaar. Happy hour is from 5 to 7 p.m., when highballs cost $1. You get such German fare here as knockwurst, bauernwurst, sauerkraut, and snacks, along with bottled German beer or Budweiser on tap. Meals cost from $10 to $15.

DINING AT PORT LUCAYA: A unique place to eat, **Pusser's Co. Store & Pub** (tel. 809/373-8450) is the most popular place to hang out at this new shopping and dining complex in the Lucaya area. While a robot piano player hammers out golden oldies, you can dine indoors in air-conditioned comfort among memorabilia or else outside at a table overlooking the yachts in the marina. You dine at pinewood tables while seated on reproductions of antique pine chairs, amid plank floors covered with sawdust. There's an open grill turning out your favorite foods, and plenty of stained glass, polished brass, and pub artifacts.

It is open Monday to Saturday from 11 a.m. to 1 a.m. and on Sunday from noon to 1 a.m. For lunch most guests select either a New York sandwich, such as a reuben or hot pastrami, or else an English pie ranging from shepherd's to fisherman's. You can also order fish and chips. Meals cost from $10. Dinners are more elaborate, including a wide list of appetizers ranging from potato skins with Bahamian seasonings to lobster bisque. English pies include steak and ale along with chicken asparagus. For the main course, you can order the catch of the day, calves' liver, or double-cut lamb chops or center-cut pork chops. For dessert, try either Pusser's pecan pie or key lime pie. Dinners cost from $20, maybe less.

Luciano's (tel. 809/373-9100) brings continental chic and a refined cuisine to Port Lucaya. It is, in fact, the finest and most sophisticated Italian restaurant in Grand Bahama. Although it is found upstairs from a Pizza Hut, all thoughts of mass market fast food are abandoned as you enter its rarefied precincts, decorated in a monochromatic gray and pink color scheme. Luciano is Italian-born Luciano Guindani, but the chef, Francis Marque, is from Toulouse. You can go early and enjoy an apéritif in the little bar inside or else on the wooden deck overlooking the marina.

Food is freshly prepared from high quality ingredients and beautifully served. You might begin with everything from oysters Rockefeller to smoked salmon, then go on to one of the soups, perhaps a thick, rich fish soup made of mussels, fish, and lobster. One of the potages is based on the chef's culinary inspiration for that day. Fish and shellfish are regularly featured, and imaginatively prepared in such dishes as filet of merou Bercy poached in a white wine and cream sauce or bay scallops simmered in a delicate sauce made with shallots and parsley. Steak Diane is one of Luciano's classics, or else the chef will prepare a rack of baby lamb in the style of Provence. Veal Luciano's is the finest milk-fed veal sautéed with shrimp and plump pieces of lobster. Meals cost from $50, and there is also an impressive wine list. The restaurant is open nightly except Sunday for dinner from 6 to 11 p.m.

Fatman's Nephew (tel. 809/373-8520) serves some of the best Bahamian regional cuisine in the Lucaya area. It lies on the second floor above Pusser's Co. Store & Pub, overlooking the marina at Port Lucaya. Guests can enjoy drinks or meals inside a well-decorated main dining room; but, if the weather is right (and it is most of the time), diners prefer to eat on a large deck where they can survey the action in the harbor. Service is Monday to Saturday from noon to 11 p.m. and on Sunday from 5 p.m. to midnight. Reservations are rarely needed. As you climb the steps, you'll see "today's catch" posted on blackboard menus. Dishes are likely to include the game fish, wahoo. Cajun blackened fish is also served. I suggest you begin your meal with either a freshly made conch salad or conch chowder. If you don't want fish, you can order such selections as curried chicken. For those who want something simpler, the chef prepares the usual array of tuna fish sandwiches and hamburgers at lunch. Lunch costs around $10, with dinners going for $25.

Big Buddha (tel. 809/373-8499) is a Japanese restaurant overlooking the yachts in the harbor along the waterfront of this shopping complex. Decorated in a restrained style, it offers both inside and outside dining. Its hours are daily from 11 a.m. to 3 p.m. for lunch and 5 to 10:30 p.m. for dinner. However, no lunch is served on Sunday. Specials are offered from 5 to 7:30 p.m. daily, with light meals costing from about $15. A full dinner will run about $20 later in the evening. You might want to visit the sushi bar, or select from an à la carte menu. Several versions of tempura are offered, but you may prefer the salmon teriyaki or the broiled snapper. Lobster fried rice is another favorite, and the chef also offers prime rib of beef.

Mr. Conch (tel. 809/373-8532) is an intimate and charming little cottage-like place next door to the Bahama Mama lounge. Conch obviously is king here, and management urges you to indulge in more than one of their many conch offerings. To make it appetizing, they'll prepare it in a chowder or as fritters, curried or steamed with vegetables and spices. You can also order souse conch or cracked conch (the latter is like a mollusk Wiener schnitzel). Even the wallpaper is conch patterned. Should you, heaven forbid, not like conch, you'll be able to order the usual pork chops, fried chicken, or spare ribs. If you drop in for breakfast, you can ask for pigs' feet souse (or sheep tongue souse), along with johnnycake and grits. Service is daily from 8 a.m. to 11 p.m. There's a marvelous lack of pretension about this place. It may be in a multi-million development, but it steadfastly offers the cuisine that many Bahamians were reared on.

3. THE SIGHTS OF GRAND BAHAMA

SEEING THE SIGHTS: Except for the coral rock and pines, there isn't much on Grand Bahama that's very old, unless you count some of the Lucayan Indian artifacts. However, the efforts toward beautification have paid off in interesting botanical gardens and parks where you can see tropical plants in their glory in the right seasons. Also, plant preservation has become important here.

Garden of the Groves

The prime attraction of the island is this garden, honoring the founder, Wallace Groves, and his wife, Georgette. It's an 11-acre botanical garden seven miles east of the International Bazaar. This scenic preserve of waterfalls and flowering shrubs has some 10,000 trees. Tropical birds flock here, making this a lure for birdwatchers and ornithologists. There are free-form lakes, footbridges, ornamental borders, lawns, and flowers. A small chapel, open to visitors, looks down on the garden from a hill. The nondenominational chapel is a miniature of an old church that once served the now-defunct community of Pine Ridge, where Wallace and Georgette Groves pioneered the lumber industry on Grand Bahama Island. The Grand Bahama Museum (tel. 809/373-5668) traces the history of Grand Bahama for four centuries, up to the development since 1955. There are displays of Arawak (Lucayan) Indian sites. Admission to the museum is $2 for adults, $1 for children under 15, while there is no charge to visit the garden, which is open daily except Monday.

Lucaya National Park

This 40-acre park consists of unspoiled growths of mangroves, pine, and palm trees, plus one of the loveliest, most secluded beaches on Grand Bahama. The long, wide, dune-covered stretch of sandy beach is found by following a wooden path winding through the trees. As you wander through the park, you'll cross Gold Rock Creek fed by a spring from what is said to be the world's largest underground freshwater cavern system. Two of the caves can be seen, exposed when a portion of ground collapsed. The pools there are composed of six feet of fresh water atop a heavier layer of salt water. Spiral wooden steps have been built down to the pools. There are 36,000 passages in the cavern system, some of which may have been opened to scuba-diving by the time of your visit.

The freshwater springs once lured Lucayan Indians, those Arawak-connected tribes who lived on the island and depended on fishing for their livelihood. They would come inland to get fresh water for their habitats on the beach. Lucayan bones and artifacts, such as pottery, have been found in the caves, as well as on the beaches.

Rand Memorial Nature Centre

Another attraction for nature lovers is the 100-acre site of this nature center, on East Settlers Way (tel. 809/352-5438), about five minutes from downtown Freeport. Charging visitors $2, it offers a naturalist-guided nature walk at 10:30 a.m. and 2 and 3 p.m. Monday to Friday and at 2 and 3 p.m. on Sunday. The center is closed on Saturday. The gates open half an hour before the nature walks begin. Children under 8 years of age are not admitted. Named after James Rand, founder of Remington Rand and one of the pioneer developers of the island, the memorial is the only Bahamian nature center, a site of unspoiled forest and trails where 5,000 birds have banded together, including rare olive-capped warblers and striped-headed tanagers, as well as West Indian flamingos.

Hydroflora Garden

On East Beach at Sunrise Highway, a man-made botanical wonder is the Hydroflora Garden (tel. 809/352-6052), where you can see 154 specimens of plants that grow in The Bahamas. A special section is devoted to bush medicine, widely practiced by Bahamians who have been using herbs and other plants to cure everything from sunburn to insomnia since the Lucayan Indians were here centuries ago. The garden is open daily except Sunday from 9 a.m. to 5:30 p.m. Admission is $1 for adults, 50¢ for children. Guided tours cost $2 per person.

ORGANIZED TOURS: Several informative tours of Grand Bahama are offered. One company is Super Combination Tour, Executive Tours, P.O. Box 2509, Freeport, The Bahamas (tel. 809/352-8858). Tours depart daily except Sunday at 10 a.m., lasting three hours. They take in some of the island's most interesting sights and provide opportunities for shopping. Included are visits to the Garden of the Groves, drives past residential sections, visits to open fish and vegetable markets, a view of one of the West End's distilleries, and a drive by the late Count Basie's home, terminating at the International Bazaar for shopping. The cost is $16 per adult or $12 for children under 12.

4. A SHOPPING EXPEDITION

There's no place in the world for shopping quite like the International Bazaar, where the goods of the world come together for you to browse among. In the 93 fascinating shops, you're bound to find something that is both a discovery and a bargain. Here are displayed African handcrafts, French perfumes, Chinese jade, British china, Spanish silver and leather, Swiss watches, Irish linens, and Colombian emeralds—and that's just for starters. The price tags on goods you find here will probably be from 10% to 40% below those on the same merchandise at home.

At the Straw Market are items with a special Bahamian touch—colorful baskets, hats, handbags, and placemats—all of which make good gifts and souvenirs of your trip. The Straw Market is beside the International Bazaar.

Keep your eyes open as you stroll through downtown Freeport or explore the smaller settlements of the island. You'll often find special items at bargain prices.

Shopping hours in Freeport/Lucaya are 9:30 a.m. to 3 p.m. Monday through Thursday, to 5 p.m. on Friday. Many shops are closed on Saturday and Sunday. However, in the International Bazaar hours vary widely. Most places there are open Monday through Saturday, closing only on Sunday. Some begin business at 9:30 a.m. daily, others not opening until 10 a.m. Closing time ranges from 5:30 to 6 p.m. The Discount Bazaar (see below) closes at 10 p.m.

SHOPPING AT THE INTERNATIONAL BAZAAR: One of the world's most unusual shopping marts, the International Bazaar covers ten acres. Built at a cost of more than $4 million, it was designed by Charles Perrin, a Hollywood special-effects artist. Visitors walk through the much-photographed Torii Gate, a Japanese symbol of welcome, into a miniature world's fair setting. Continental cafés and dozens of shops loaded with merchandise await visitors. The bazaar blends architecture and cultures from some 25 countries. The place was re-created with worn cobblestones, narrow alleys, and authentically reproduced architecture.

On a street patterned after the Ginza in Tokyo, just inside the entrance to the bazaar, is the Oriental section. A rich collection of merchandise from the Far East is here for your scrutiny and purchase, including cameras, handmade teak furniture, fine silken goods, and even places where you can have clothing custom made. If browsing among the jade figurines and kimonos makes you think of Japanese food, drop in at the Japanese Steak House, previously recommended, for sushi or other Oriental delicacies.

To the left you'll find the Left Bank of Paris, or a reasonable facsimile, with sidewalk cafés where you can enjoy a café au lait and perhaps a pastry under shade trees.

In the Continental Pavillion, there are offerings of leather goods, jewelry, lingerie, and gifts at shops with names such as Love Boutique.

A narrow alley leads you from the French section to East India, where shops sell such exotic goods as taxi horns and silk saris. Moving on from the India House, past Kon Tiki, you arrive in Africa, where you can purchase carvings from the dark continent or a colorful dashiki, the loose-fitting African robe worn from Cape Horn to the Mediterranean.

For a taste of Latin America and Iberia, make your way to the Spanish section, where serapes and piñatas hang from the cast-iron railings. Imports are displayed along the cobblestone walks. Besides browsing through the shops, you may enjoy stopping in Hispanic restaurants such as Café Valencia.

Many items sold in the shops here are said to be about 40% less costly than if you bought them in the U.S. You can have purchases sent anywhere you wish (you'll pay the charges, of course). In case a shop is not able to fill your order from the warehouse stock, many of them will have your purchase sent to you directly from the manufacturer, especially in the case of European makers.

Far East Traders, Chinese section (tel. 809/352-4756)—linens, exotic gifts, decorative ornaments, silk happy coats, hand-embroidered dresses and blouses, coral jewelry, freshwater pearls.

Casa Simpatica, Spanish section (tel. 809/352-6425)—gold, silver, gemstone jewelry, semiprecious beads, coral, Swiss and Japanese watches; warehouse-style shopping; some items discounted up to 50%.

Casablanca Perfumes, Moroccan section (tel. 809/352-5380)—a wide range of perfumes (the latest from Paris), Lancôme cosmetics, skin-care products.

Parfum de Paris, old French section (tel. 809/352-8164)—practically all existing French perfumes and colognes; up to 40% less than in U.S. (There's another branch at the Holiday Inn.)

Colombian Emeralds International, South American section (tel. 809/352-5464)—emeralds, of course, and gold and silver jewelry, prestige watches from Japan and Switzerland; Gem Mine housing unmounted gemstones; Jewellery Factory where local craftsmen set gemstones in jewelry while explaining the process; authorized agents for Ebel, Omega, Seiko, Citizen, Tissot, Heuer, Audemars Piguet, and other well-known watches.

Garden Gallery, Arcade (tel. 809/352-9755)—paintings and prints by local Bahamian and international artists, Bahamian art and craft souvenirs; art is duty free.

Flovin Gallery, Arcade (tel. 809/352-7564)—original Bahamian and international art, oil paintings, frames, lithographs, prints, posters, and pottery.

Gemini I, Scandia section (tel. 809/352-4809)—a shoe boutique with a wide range of designer shoes, leather bags, costume jewelry.

El Galleon, Spanish section (tel. 809/352-5380)—Spanish antiques and gift items, watches by Courrèges and Michel Herbelin, international jewelry.

Pipe of Peace, International section (tel. 809/352-7704)—pipes, tobacco, cigars, cigarettes, lighters, watches, figurines, cameras, jewelry, souvenirs.

La Sandale, old French section (tel. 809/352-5380)—fine women's footwear, Michel Herbelin and Courrèges watches.

London Pacesetter Boutique (tel. 809/352-2929)—stylish sportswear, Pringle and Braemar cashmere sweaters, Gottex swimwear, assorted European fashions. London Pacesetter Boutique also has a shop in Regent Centre (tel. 809/352-2844).

Penny Lane, P.O. Box F-2569 (tel. 809/352-3654)—women's boutique with good selection of casual wear, swimwear, cocktail dresses, and accessories.

Ginza, Far East section (tel. 809/352-7515)—14-karat and 18-karat gold chains, Mikimoto pearls, bracelets and rings, some with gemstones; watches from Baume & Mercier, Pulsar, Seiko, Rolex, Raymond Weil; Cartier leather collection; top-brand cameras.

Solomon's Mines, Arcade (tel. 809/352-7273)—crystal by Waterford; figurines by Lladro; top line of English china such as Royal Doulton and Wedgwood.

Leather and Things (tel. 809/352-5491)—leather goods from Italy and South America including belts, handbags, wallets, briefcases, Whiting and Davis evening bags, Land luggage; accessories from Dior, Halston, Pandora; Oscar de la Renta scarves; Samsonite luggage; gift items.

The Sweater Shop, Indian section (tel. 809/352-7863)—men's and women's sweaters in lambswool, cashmere, and cotton from such diverse countries as Scotland and Italy. Cotton sweaters, made in Italy, were especially created for The Bahamas market.

The **Old Curiosity Shop,** P.O. Box F-2060 (tel. 809/352-8008)—specializes in antique English bric-a-brac, including original and reproduction items: Victorian dinner rings and cameos, antique engagement rings, English lithographs, old and new silver and porcelain, and brass candlesticks and trivets.

Midnight Sun (tel. 809/352-9510)—sculptures of European porcelain, high-quality dinnerware from several well-known manufacturers displayed in twin boutiques.

Gemini II (tel. 809/353-2377)—funny and irreverent, with a European-inspired collection of female accessories, including women's suits, sweaters, and purses arranged boutique fashion.

Androsia of Lucaya (tel. 809/352-9865)—made-in-the-Bahamas bright cotton in both men's and women's clothing, cloth silkscreened on Andros Island with bird and shell motifs.

Island Galleria, P.O. Box F-697 (tel. 809/352-8194)—china, sometimes cheaper than in Europe, by Wedgwood, Rosenthal, and Aynsley, and crystal by Waterford. Bahamian paintings are in the art gallery in the back room.

Bahamas Coin and Stamp Ltd. (tel. 809/352-8989)—stamps, coins, commemorative medallions, and uncirculated coin sets; Bahamian and Grenadian stamps; $100 gold coins; British half-sovereigns; gold jewelry.

PORT LUCAYA MARKETPLACE: The first of its kind in The Bahamas, Port Lucaya was named after the original settlers of Grand Bahama. This is a shopping and dining complex set in Lucaya on six acres near the Lucayan Beach Resort & Casino, Holiday Inn, and Atlantik Beach Resort. Free entertainment, such as steel drum bands, strolling musicians, jugglers, mimes, and magicians, add to a festival atmosphere. The architecture and pastel colors of the buildings were influenced by the design of traditional island homes, but the marketplace was modeled along the lines of Miami Bayside or Faneuil Hall in Boston.

The new complex rose on the site of a former Bahamian straw market, but the good ladies and their straw products are back in full force after being temporarily dislodged.

Full advantage is taken of the waterfront location. Many of the restaurants and shops overlook a 50-slip marina, home of a "fantasy" pirate ship featuring lunch and dinner/dancing cruises. Glass-bottom boats, deep-sea fishing boats, catamarans, and a variety of charter vessels are also based at the Port Lucaya Marina. Dockage at the marina is available to visitors coming to shop or dine by boat.

A boardwalk along the water makes it an easy stroll to watch the frolicking dolphins at the Underwater Explorers Society (UNEXSO). Visitors can swim with the dolphins or book passage on one of the UNEXSO boats for a scuba or snorkeling adventure on the coral reef.

Merchandise in the shops of Port Lucaya ranges from linens to leather and lingerie to jeweled watches to wind chimes. Traditional and contemporary fashions are featured for men, women, and children. Shoppers will also discover perfumes, Colombian emeralds, imported china and crystal, hand-embroidered items, as well as an international selection of liquors.

Many of the shops represented here have already been cited in the general description of the International Bazaar at Freeport. Some of the more important ones maintain branches at Port Lucaya.

However, one is exceptional. It's **Pusser's Co. Store & Pub,** Port Lucaya (tel. 809/373-8450), which in addition to its pub and restaurant (described later) is also part nautical museum, part general store. It's a shopping adventure, with Pusser's own line of travel and sports clothing in classical design, along with fine ship models, antiques, and other nauticalia. You'll also find unusual gift items, flags, and pennants, along with rum ceramic flagons, decanters, and hip flasks.

Coconits by Androsia (tel. 809/373-8387) is yet another outlet of this famous batik house, whose designs and colors capture "the spirit of The Bahamas." Fabrics are handmade on Andros Island, and the store sells quality resort wear and fabric of 100% cotton knit. A new line offers air-brushed cotton knits in simple skirts, tops, and jackets for women. This industry was created by Rosi Birch who is often at this store.

ON THE GLAMOUR TRAIL: One of the best places for beauty and grooming service is the **Modalena Beauty Salon,** Princess Tower (tel. 809/352-2829). It combines its services in two large rooms. Open from 9 a.m. to 5 p.m. Monday to Saturday, from 10 a.m. to 2 p.m. Sunday, it prefers that clients call ahead for an appointment.

A SHOP FOR CHILDREN: Living up to its labels, **Precious Kids,** Churchill Square (tel. 809/352-6692), is the cutest little store in town. You can find beautiful clothes for children imported from around the world, plus slippers, shoes, soft toys, and gift items. You'll see such brands as Petite Bateau, Absorba, Sylvia White, Lemon Drop, and Hang Ten.

MADE IN THE BAHAMAS: An island experience, **Bahamian Tings,** P.O. Box F-2103, 15B Poplar Crescent, Pestco Building (tel. 809/352-9550), offers Bahamian-made products—jewelry, perfume, clothing, arts and crafts, and Androsia fabrics. With the unusual selection of items here, you have a chance to"take home a little bit of our islands" that is different.

PERFUMES OF THE ISLANDS: Near Eight Mile Rock, **Fragrance of The Bahamas Ltd.,** (tel. 809/352-9391), is a perfume factory in Hepburn

Town, a native settlement about 15 miles from Freeport. The founder, a retired executive from the United States, began this enterprise with a scent called Island Promises, created by a top-grade perfumer. This is sold today as cologne, perfume, and after-shave lotion. Later products have been Paradise, a cologne and perfume, and Sand, a top-selling cologne and after-shave lotion, as well as aloe lotion, Carib-Tan suntan lotion, and T-shirts emblazoned with the names of the fragrances. The perfumery is in two early-19th-century buildings that once housed the first Baptist church and the first school in the area. You can take a tour of the factory and see Bahamians at work producing the sweet fragrances.

If you buy a bottle of Sand, the citrus-based after-shave lotion, you'll take a little of The Bahamas home with you: a small quantity of pure white, sterilized Bahamian sand is placed at the bottom of the bottle. Sand also comes in colognes, after-shave lotion and balm, and a body moisturizer. A sister product, Pink Pearl, has conch pearls in the bottles.

5. THE SPORTING LIFE

A wide variety of sports activities abounds on Grand Bahama Island. Miles of white sand beaches, some of the finest golf courses anywhere in the islands, and lighted tennis courts are easily accessible. The blue-green waters are also enticing for swimmers.

Other sports popular with visitors are fishing, scuba-diving, snorkeling, and horseback riding.

SNORKELING AND SCUBA: Next to the Lucayan Bay Hotel, the **Underwater Explorers Society (UNEXSO),** P.O. Box F-2433 (tel. 809/373-1244), has top instructors and facilities for snorkeling and scuba-diving. It is the largest dive operation in The Bahamas, and one of the most complete even when stacked up against the Caribbean. *Skin Diver* magazine called it "one of the most modern dive resorts in the world." More than 50,000 people have learned to dive here, from 12-year-old children to adults in their 60s. There are three dive trips daily, as well as night dives to offshore reefs. Multidive discounts are granted. A guided reef dive is $29; a three-dive package, $75. A seven-day unlimited pass (up to three dives per day) goes for $295. A three-hour "learn to dive" course costs $79. The following morning, students dive with their instructor on the shallow ocean reef. Daily snorkeling trips go for $15, all equipment included, and a half hour snorkeling lesson is $10. Facilities include a pro shop and boutique.

A museum on the premises attracts both divers and nondivers. It displays a wide variety of artifacts recovered from shipwrecks, including cannon balls, barshot and pottery, brass spikes, and urns. Many of the items were from the wreck of the *Matanceros,* a blockade runner during the war between Spain and England, which ran aground on a reef in 1741. Other exhibits are of sea shells, fossils, and a giant crab claw.

You can also contact them in the U.S.: P.O. Box 5608, Fort Lauderdale, FL 33310 (tel. toll free 800/992-DIVE; in Florida, 305/761-7679).

Paradise Watersports, P.O. Box F-3529 (tel. 809/352-2887), at the Xanadu Beach and Marina Resort, offers snorkeling trips. You cruise to a coral reef on a 28-foot pontoon boat for $10 per person ($7 if you're just along for the ride). Snorkel gear costs $7 per hour. Sunfish are rented for $15 per half hour, $20 per hour. Perhaps you're more the paddleboat type. They rent for $7 for a half hour, $10 per hour. Waterskiing, hydrosliding, and ski biscuit rides are priced at $15 for a 15-minute ride. Windsurfing, at $15 per hour, and other water activities are offered. The buoyant and enthusiastic owners, Toronto-born Colleen Lewis and Bahamas-born Larry Lewis, also offer parasailing at $25 for a seven-minute ride. They have a 46-foot sailboat that takes participants on a sightseeing tour through the canals and waterways of Grand Bahama as far as Port Lucaya. Cost is around $25 per person. In addition, they offer a sunset cruise at $18 per person, including live dance music, unlimited Bahama Mamas (the drink, that is), and cheese and crackers. A glass-bottom boat charges $12 for adults and $6 for children under 12 for a cruise lasting 1½ hours.

PARASAILING: When the weather is rough, which it often is in winter, no one goes parasailing, of course. But during most of the year this is a popular sport. **Sands Watersports** (no phone) offers this activity. Their kiosk is found midway between the Holiday Inn and the Atlantik Beach Hotel. The cost is $30 for a ride lasting three to five minutes. The tour desk at either the Holiday Inn (tel. 809/373-1333) or at the Atlantik (tel. 809/373-1444) will provide information.

WINDSURFING: Courses are offered at the **Atlantik Beach Hotel,** Royal Palm Way (tel. 809/373-1444), for beginners, advanced, and freestyle. Each course is eight hours and costs $150. Windsurfing boards and equipment rent for $15 per hour or $40 per day.

SPORT FISHING: In the waters off Grand Bahama you can fish for barracuda, snapper, grouper, yellowtail, wahoo, and kingfish, along with other denizens of the deep.

Check with **Running Mon Marina,** Bahama Terrace, P.O. Box F-2663 (tel. 809/352-2663). A half day's deep-sea fishing costs $300, a full day going for $600, and it takes six people to make up the party.

Reef Tours Ltd., Port Lucaya, P.O. Box F-2609 (tel. 809/373-5880), offers the least expensive way to go deep-sea fishing around Grand Bahama Island. Adults pay $50 if they fish, $25 if they only go along to watch. Departures for thehalf-day excursion are at 8:30 a.m. and 1 p.m. seven days a week. Included in the cost are bait, tackle, and ice.

THE DOLPHIN EXPERIENCE: A group of bottlenose dolphins are involved in a unique training program at the **Underwater Explorers Society** (tel. 809/373-1250), at the Port Lucaya Marina. When the training is completed, the dolphins will be released daily into the open ocean to swim freely with scuba divers on the coral reef. Whether they return to their playpen at night is anyone's guess. As part of the human-dolphin familiarization process, swimmers and snorkelers are invited to get into the water and swim with the animals for about 20 minutes. Following a seminar and acoustic workshop, swim sessions are conducted in safe waters in the dolphin enclosure. The workshop costs $10 and the swim session is $49. Swim sessions are at 10 a.m. and 2 p.m. Monday to Friday and at 10 a.m., noon, and 2 p.m. on Sunday.

GLASS-BOTTOM BOAT TOURS: Any tour agent can arrange for you to go out on a glass-bottom boat, the *Mermaid Kitty,* which is supposed to be the world's largest twin-diesel-engine glass-bottom boat. You'll get an excellent view of the beautiful underwater marine life that lives off the coast of Grand Bahama. Departures are from the Lucayan Bay Hotel at 10:30 a.m. and 12:30 and 2:30 p.m., lasting 1½ hours. The tour costs $10 for adults, $5 for children. For information or reservations, contact **International Travel & Tours,** P.O. Box F-850 (tel. 809/352-9311).

TENNIS: This game is widely available on Grand Bahama Island.

The **Bahamas Princess Resort and Casino** seems to have the monopoly.

At its Princess Country Club (tel. 809/352-6721), there are six hard-surface courts. Guests and nonguests are charged $5 per hour. Lessons are also available. At the Princess Tower (tel. 809/352-9661), there are three clay and three hard-surface courts, all of which are lit for night play. The charge for both guests and nonguests is $5 ($10 at night).

Holiday Inn (tel. 809/373-1333) has four privately owned hard-surface courts, charging $3 per hour for guests and nonguests alike. There is no night playing.

At the **Lucayan Beach Hotel** (tel. 809/373-6545), there are four hard courts (not illuminated). Free for guests, these courts cost nonresidents $5 per hour.

GOLF: This island boasts more golf links than any other of The Bahamas or the Caribbean. In a week here, you can play on a different course almost every day, taking two days off for rest and relaxation on a white sand beach. Most courses are tight, with heavily wooded areas demanding precision golfing. Most courses are within seven miles of each other, and you'll find no traffic and no waiting to play. Here is a rundown of the major courses in Freeport/Lucaya, plus the one at West End:

Lucayan Park Golf & Country Club, P.O. Box F-333 (tel. 809/373-1066). This is the best-kept and most manicured course on Grand Bahama. Greens are fast, and there are a couple of par fives more than 500 yards long. It totals 6,824 yards from the blue tees and 6,488 from the whites. Par is 72. Greens fees are $27 for 18 holes. Electric carts cost $26, and you can rent clubs for $8.50.

Fortune Hills Golf and Country Club, P.O. Box F-2619 (tel. 809/373-4500). Designed as an 18-hole course, the back 9 were never completed. You can replay the front 9 for 18 holes and a total of 6,916 yards from the blue tees. Par is 72. The club caters to members, many of whom are expatriate executives working for Freeport industry, but the course is open to the public. Greens fees are $8 for 9 holes, $14 for 18. Electric carts cost $14 and $22 for 9 and 18 holes respectively. The nearest hotels are the Atlantik Beach, Holiday Inn, and Lucayan Beach.

Princess Ruby Course, P.O. Box F-207 (tel. 809/352-6721). This is one of two courses owned and operated by the Bahamas Princess Resort & Casino. The championship course was designed by Joe Lee, and it was the former site of the Hoerman Cup Caribbean Championship. Fees are $10 if you are a Princess guest, $18 if you are staying elsewhere. Carts are $32 for 18 holes. It's a total of 6,750 yards if played from the championship blue tees. Under the same management, the **Princess Emerald Course** was designed by Dick Wilson. It was the site of the Bahamas National Open some years back. The course has plenty of trees along fairways, as well as an abundance of water hazards and bunkers. The toughest hole is the ninth, a par five with 545 yards from the blue tees to the hole. Fees are the same as at the Princess Ruby.

Jack Tar Village, West End (tel. 809/346-6211), is a massive, self-contained resort. It is at West End, about 45 miles from Freeport, and has a 27-hole golf course. Greens fees are included if you are a guest here. Otherwise, there's a charge of $22 for 18 holes, $34 for 27 holes. Many holes are oceanfront.

All courses in Grand Bahama are open to the public year-round, and clubs can be rented from all pro shops on the island.

FITNESS CENTER: For complete fitness services, try the **Princess Fitness Centre,** Princess Country Club, Bahamas Princess Resort & Casino (tel. 809/352-6721, ext. 4606). A health club, which you can join even if you're not a guest of the hotel, is open from 10 a.m. to 7 p.m., offering sauna, facials, massages, and use of an exercise room with bodybuilding equipment. Aerobics and dance classes (tel. 809/352-6721, ext. 4656) are available at the Bahamas Dance Theatre of the hotel. Aerobics classes are at 10 a.m. and 6 p.m. Monday through Friday. Ballet is taught at 4 p.m. Monday through Friday and at 11 a.m. (for children 4 to 6 years) on Saturday. Jazz, Monday through Friday, is at 5 p.m., with tap on Saturday at noon. Classes last an hour.

HORSEBACK RIDING: Get back in the saddle again at **Pinetree Stables,** Beachway Drive, P.O. Box F-2915, Freeport, (tel. 809/373-3600), offering trail rides to the beach daily except Monday at 9 a.m., 11 a.m., and 2 p.m. The cost is $25 per person for a ride lasting 1½ hours. Lessons in dressage and jumping are available for $30 for 45 minutes of instruction. English-born Myra Wagener is probably the best equestrienne and operates the best stables in all of The Bahamas. Certified by the American Riding Instructors Program as well as by the British Horse Society, she is well known among the island's expatriate colony.

BOAT CRUISES: Excursions (for adults only) are offered by **Island Time Yachting Excursions,** Britannia Pub, P.O. Box F-246, in Freeport. Telephone 809/352-3575 for more information. Its most popular offering is a luncheon cruise, departing at 11 a.m. (in some seasons it leaves an hour later to profit from the increased daylight). This five-hour cruise costs $35 per person, including transport from your hotel to the dock, a buffet lunch, and hours of snorkeling in the shallow waters of Treasure Reef. Drinks are served after the end of the snorkeling period. The lunch is a Bahamian-inspired barbecue with chicken, rice and peas, and beef. *Island Time* is a 40-foot catamaran. Children under 18 are not included. They also offer two nightly "booze cruises" for sunset watchers, departing at 5 p.m. and again at 7:30 p.m., weather permitting. Drinks are served, including white wine and Bahama Mamas (a form of rum punch). Each cruise lasts two hours and costs $20 per person.

You can also enjoy cruises aboard *El Bucanero,* whose tours can be booked directly through **Executive Tours,** P.O. Box F-2509 in Freeport (tel. 809/373-7863). All big hotels also have tour operators in their lobbies. They offer a once-a-week beach party from 11 a.m. to 6:30 p.m. held every Wednesday or Thursday (check ahead). The cost is $30 per person, and the vessel sails to a point about three miles from its harbor, then drops anchor at a deserted beach. Snorkeling equipment is available for $3 per person, and recorded calypso music is played. A cash bar serves drinks, and a buffet lunch and barbecue is offered, presumably after you're good and hungry, at 4 p.m. A dinner cruise is also held, usually in the winter season. When it goes out, it costs $35 per person, beginning at 7:30 p.m. two nights a week.

6. AFTER DARK

Most of the nightlife in Freeport/Lucaya centers around the glittering **Princess Casino** (tel. 809/352-7811), the giant Moroccan-style palace that's one of the largest casinos in The Bahamas and the Caribbean. Under this Moorish-domed place, visitors play games of chance and attend Las Vegas–type floor shows. They can also dine in the gourmet restaurant, the Crown Room.

Many guests, however, come here to attend the **Casino Royale Showroom** (tel. 809/352-7811), which presents two shows nightly, one at 8:30 and again at 10:45 p.m. (there are no shows on Monday). Shows come and go but there are usually Las Vegas–type revues. Expect more than a dozen performers who cavort in goombay-inspired colors with lots of glitter and a smattering of toplessness.

Back at the Princess Tower, the **Sultan's Tent** continues the theme of Arabian Nights (tel. 809/352-6682 for reservations). You can dance to the latest international records (there are no floor shows, but there are live bands). The cover charge of $10 per person includes your first two drinks. The place is open from 9 p.m. to 3 a.m.

If you're staying at Lucaya, you'll want to attend the **Showcase Theatre,** in the Lucayan Beach Hotel (tel. 809/373-7777). The decor is predictably cabaret oriented, with endless rows of parallel tables. But what makes the place unique is the high quality and professionalism of its Las Vegas-type shows. The revues are among the best in The Bahamas. Shows change all the time, sometimes lasting no more than two weeks. Count on spending from $19.95 per person, including two drinks, but that could go higher, depending on the show offered. Performances are nightly except Monday at 8:30 and 10:30. Because of the popularity of the room, reservations are needed.

Yellow Bird Show Club, P.O. Box 566 (tel. 809/352-6682), in the rear of Howard Johnson's Restaurant, offers an evening of native entertainment, with steel drums, the limbo, conga drums telling stories, the fire dance, and glass-eating. The show even presents its highly stylized version of the Caribbean Queen of Calypso. The charge of $18 covers two drinks and the tip. Doors open at 9 p.m., with show time at 10:30 p.m. except Sunday. You can disco here after the show.

Skipper's Lounge, at the Princess Country Club (tel. 809/352-6721), is a good bet if you want tamer fare. There is no cover, no minimum, and drinks are priced from $3.50. In the east lobby of the hotel a five-piece combo plays good jazz and you get a "little soft shoe." Live music is provided nightly except Thursday from 9 p.m. to 2 a.m.

Panache Disco, Holiday Inn (tel. 809/373-1333), can fill up with 200 frenzied patrons. The management has totally rebuilt the disco and decorated it in red-wine colors. A good sound system enables guests to hold conversations while still listening to the disco beat. A live band performs daily except Monday and Tuesday from 9 p.m. to 3 a.m., and the $10 door charge covers the cost of your first two drinks.

Holiday Inn (tel. 809/373-1333) has "theme" nights, which are very popular in Lucaya, often attracting local residents as well as visitors. Although these are planned mainly for guests staying at the hotel, they are also open to outsiders, providing they've made a reservation and there is enough space. On Tuesday night there's a Bahamian Luau, with a live native show from 6:30 to 9 p.m. Adults pay $23. For that, you get a buffet spread with fresh salads, desserts, and such main courses as sweet-and-sour pork, chicken, roast beef, shrimp chow mein, and barbecued spareribs. From 6 to 9 p.m. on Thursday, Italian nights are presented, with a lavish Italian spread costing $17 per person. On Saturday, the hotel features candlelit dining "under the stars" from 6 to 9 p.m. at a cost of $14.95.

7. WEST END

One of your most refreshing days on Grand Bahama can be spent by escaping from the plush hotels and casinos of Freeport/Lucaya and heading to West End, 28 miles from Freeport. At this old fishing village you'll get glimpses of how things used to be before the development of Freeport and before package-tour groups started arriving on Grand Bahama.

To reach West End, you head north along Queen's Highway, going through Eight Mile Rock and on to the northernmost point of the island. West End has several good restaurants, so you can plan to make a day (or a night) of it.

A lot of the old buildings of the village now stand dilapidated, but a nostalgic air prevails. Many oldtimers remember a better day (at least for them economically), when boats were busy and the docks buzzed with activity day and night. This was during the era from about 1919 to 1933 when Prohibition reigned in the United States—but not with great success. West End was so close to the U.S. mainland that rum-running became a lucrative business, with booze flowing out of West End to be slipped into Florida at night so that the flappers and their beaux of the Roaring '20s would not go thirsty in the speakeasies. Al Capone is reputed to have been a frequent visitor.

Villages along the way to West End have colorful names, such as Hawksbill Creek. For a preview of some local life, try to visit the fish market along the harbor here. You'll pass some thriving harbor areas too, but the vessels you see will be oil tankers, not rum-runners.

Eight Mile Rock is a hamlet of mostly ramshackle houses that stretch along both sides of the road for—you guessed it—eight miles. Near here at tiny **Hepburn Town** is the Fragrance of The Bahamas Ltd. factory (see "A Shopping Expedition," above), which you may want to visit. The names of other little hamlets may intrigue you, places like Bootle Bay, for instance.

At West End, you come to an abrupt stop. Then it's time to visit the weathered old Star (see below). If you stick around till night, you're likely to hear some calypso music nearby.

Harry's American Bar (see below) is the place for a sundowner. You can either enjoy a meal there or at the Buccaneer nearby before heading back to Freeport/Lucaya to catch the last show at the casino.

A COMPLETE RESORT: A world apart, **Jack Tar Village,** West End, Grand Bahama, The Bahamas (tel. 809/348-2030, or toll free 800/527-9299), is remote from the action of Freeport, offering 414 air-conditioned modern rooms. The International Airport lies about a mile from the hotel lobby. Considered the most complete resort in The Bahamas, this self-sufficient club, built in the 1950s, boasts the largest saltwater swimming pool in the western hemisphere. It also has a 27-hole oceanside golf course, with a trio of starting positions. More than 100 yachts can tie up at its marina, and boats leave daily, taking visitors troll or drift fishing. In addition, a glass-bottom paddle-wheeler takes up to 200 passengers on sightseeing trips or rum parties. The Sports Dock is well stocked, with equipment for waterskiing, and scuba- and skindiving; instructors are available. There are also six Rubico tennis courts, just outside the hotel lobby. In all, this hotel complex occupies more than 2,000 acres of subtropical gardens. You can ride along narrow, winding trails of the hotel's botanic gardens, which are sanctuaries for birds and other Bahamian wildlife.

In winter, the cost for one person on AP is $150 per night, based on double occupancy, $160 in a single. Included in the tariffs are drinks, greens fees, tennis, snorkeling, sailing, waterskiing, paddleboating, paddle-wheeler cruises, drift fishing, and scuba demonstrations in the pool. *In summer, charges are $120 per person based on double occupancy, $150 in a single.* On the premises is a modern shopping complex, and in the evening there is dancing and entertainment, as well as a host of activities ranging from luau cookouts to crab races and limbo dancing. In fact, this is said to be the "most fun" of any Jack Tar.

A DINING TREK TO WEST END: Many people head for **Pier One,** Freeport Harbour (tel. 809/352-6674). Because of its location at the edge of the waterway used by the cruise ships which arrive daily from Florida, this is the first Bahamian restaurant many arriving passengers see. Covered with gray-tinged cedar shingles, it rises on stilts above a rocky shoreline a few steps from the water's edge. A wooden footbridge leads into a plank-covered interior loaded with nautical artifacts. Don't overlook the high-ceilinged bar as a place for a round of drinks before your meal. There are several dining rooms, the most desirable of which overlooks schools of fish.

Award-winning chef Uwe Nath is the owner, and he runs a good ship. Lunch is daily except Sunday from 11 a.m. to 4 p.m., costing from $15. The bill of fare includes a delectable version of a cream-based clam chowder, lobster soup, fresh oysters, fresh conch salad, spaghetti with seafood, the fresh fish of the day, and pan-fried grouper. Dinner is daily from 4 to 10 p.m., costing from $30 per person. Specialties include baked stuffed flounder, red snapper filet with Pernod, coconut-flavored shrimp, shrimp curry, and filet of lemon shark with green Madagascar peppercorns and pineapples. Meat dishes include roast prime rib and sirloin. For dessert, you might try Black Forest cake, Italian rum cake, or key lime pie. Reservations are suggested for dinner.

Buccaneer Club, Deadman's Reef (tel. 809/348-3794), is a tropical version of a German beer garden and is one of my favorite places on Grand Bahama. Most of the inspiration for the whimsical decor came from Switzerland-born Heinz Fischbacher who, with his Bahamian wife, Kitty, added as much lighthearted Teutonic flavor as you'll find west of the Rhine. The compound is ringed with stone walls, within which are palm-dotted terraces where foot-stomping alpine music provides lots of fun for the yachting crowd you'll see here. The collection of inner rooms contains mismatched crystal chandeliers, pine trim, oddly shaped pieces of weathered driftwood, and a beerhall ambience that's unique in The Bahamas. Some of the spinning ceiling fans come breathtakingly close to hitting some of the clustered teardrops of the baroque chandeliers, although no one seems to notice, especially when the place is crowded. Many guests of the nearby Jack Tar Village come here.

Three times weekly, the Fischbachers have beach parties, which cost $30 per person. The price includes transportation from hotels, an hour-long open bar, a table-groaning buffet, a beer-drinking contest, spaghetti-eating contests, crab races, limbo dancing, and lively games of musical chairs. The establishment is open daily except Monday. Only dinner is served, from 5 to 10 p.m. If anyone senses romance in the air, he or she might like to know that Heinz first met Kitty on a blind date here when the Buccaneer belonged to someone else. Three years later they returned as a married couple and bought the place.

Harry's American Bar, Deadman's Reef (tel. 809/348-2660), is an isolated rendezvous point on a side lane leading off the only road into the West End. You pass beneath a pair of stone columns marking the entrance and come to a compound dotted with shrubs and trees. On a good day, the seafront terrace, with its frond-covered sun umbrellas and seagrape trees, can be one of the most relaxing places on the island.

Kitty Fischbacher, who is also the part owner of the previously recommended Buccaneer Club (see above), runs the place. Only lunch is served, and it's offered daily except Monday, Wednesday, and Friday from 10 a.m. to 5 p.m. After dark, the party moves to the nearby Buccaneer Club. Lunches, costing from $10, include soup, salads, sandwiches, and cheeseburgers. The house special drink is called a Harry's Hurricane, and is made with coconut- and banana-flavored rums, Bacardi, and fruit juices.

The **Star Club,** Bayshore Road (tel. 809/346-6207). When it was built in the 1940s, this was the first hotel on Grand Bahama. Today it contains the only 24-hour-a-day bar and snackbar on the island, which sometimes encourages people from the casino to motor out here after a night at the tables. At one time the Star was painted white and had accommodations. Today it's only a restaurant, bar, and pool hall with a jukebox and slightly tattered naugahyde furniture. You'll probably be able to strike up a conversation with Austin Henry Grant, Jr., a former Bahamian Senator who owns the place. Mr. Grant knew many of the famous guests who stayed here incognito in the 1940s, when West End enjoyed a cachet that it has since lost to the burgeoning center, Freeport/Lucaya. His daughter, Anne Grant, is likely to be here as well.

A full range of drinks is available as well as simple meals. Menu items include Bahamian chicken in the bag, hamburgers, cheeseburgers, fish and chips, and "fresh sexy" conch prepared as chowder, fritters, or salads. Drinks cost $2.50, while informal meals go for $10.

CHAPTER XI

BIMINI, THE BERRY ISLANDS, AND ANDROS

□ □ □

In this chapter we begin to travel through the Family Islands to a very different world from that found in the major tourist meccas of Nassau, Cable Beach, Paradise Island, and Freeport/Lucaya, which we have considered so far.

To begin our exploration, we have an unusual blend of Bimini, the Berry Islands, and Andros. Bimini is famous and overrun with tourists, particularly in summer, but the typical visitor practically has Andros and the Berry Islands to himself or herself. These islands to the north and west of Nassau might be called the "westerly islands," as they, along with Grand Bahama, lie at the northwestern fringe of The Bahamas. As such, they are the closest islands to the Florida coastline.

Of all three islands, Andros in many ways is the most fascinating. Actually a series of islands, it looks like a mosaic when you fly over it because of all the bodies of water that divide the island. It is laced with creeks and densely forested inlands, once said to have been inhabited by mysterious creatures. It is also considered the bonefishing capital of the world. Two of its major attractions are offshore: the Tongue of the Ocean, 1,000 fathoms deep and 142 miles long, and the Great Barrier Reef, the second-largest underwater coral reef in the world. But more about these later.

First, after takeoff in Miami, our plane will wing its way to Bimini where our trip will begin.

1. BIMINI

Bimini is known as the big-game fishing capital of the world, and fishing is excellent through the year in flats, on the reefs, and in the streams. Ponce de León didn't find the legendary Fountain of Youth on Bimini, but Ernest Hemingway came to write and fish and publicize Bimini around the world in his *Islands in the Stream,* in which he described the artistic self-discipline of a "good painter," Thomas Hudson, on the lush island, once the rum-running capital of the world.

Fifty miles east of Miami, Bimini consists of a number of islands, islets, and cays, including North and South Bimini, the targets of most visitors.

Guided by native fishermen, visitors can go bonefishing or deep-sea fishing. Divers find the reefs laced with conch, lobster, coral, and many tropical fish. Sightseers are allowed to visit the Lerner Marine Laboratory for Marine Research on North Bimini. It was founded by Michael Lerner, an outstanding fisherman.

It's also traditional to pay a visit to the former haunt of the late, controversial congressman Adam Clayton Powell, at the End of the World Bar in Alice Town (see "Bimini After Dark," below).

Off North Bimini, in 30 feet of water, are some big hewn-stone formations. Many people believe them to be from the lost continent of Atlantis.

You'll most often encounter the word "Bimini," but it might be more proper to say the "Biminis." That's because North Bimini and South Bimini are two distinct islands, separated by a narrow ocean passage. There is ferry service between the islands.

Most tourists visit North Bimini, especially Alice Town, its major settlement. Most of the hotels, restaurants, and bars are in Alice Town.

Bimini's location off the Florida coastline is at a point where the Gulf Stream meets the Bahamas Banks. That has made Bimini a favorite cruising ground for America's yachting set, who follow the channel between North and South Bimini into a spacious, sheltered harbor where they can stock up on food, drink, fuel, and supplies at well-equipped marinas.

Hook-shaped North Bimini is 7½ miles long. Combined with South Bimini, it makes up a land mass of only nine square miles. That's why Alice Town looks so crowded, everything squeezed together. Another reason is that a large part of Bimini is privately owned, and in spite of pressure from the Bahamian government, the landholders have not sold their acreage yet—so Bimini can't "spread out" until they do.

At Alice Town, the land is so narrow that you can walk "from sea to shining sea" in just a short time. Most of Bimini's population of some 1,600 people live in Alice Town. Other hamlets include Bailey Town and Porgy Bay.

South Florida visitors flock to Bimini in the summer months; winter, especially the season from mid-December to mid-March, is quieter. In that sense, Bimini is different from the other islands in The Bahamas. Winter months in the rest of the Family Islands, including Nassau, Paradise Island, and Freeport/Lucaya, are the high season.

Fishermen, as mentioned, and divers are attracted to Bimini, and have been for years. But in recent years Bimini is attracting more and more visitors who don't care about sports at all. The reason for this is that many Americans, especially from the Middle West and the Great Lakes states, drive to Florida. Great numbers of these visitors have never set foot outside the United States. Therefore a "foreign country" lying just 50 miles off the coastline of Florida, a "short take-off and land" flight, becomes a potent lure.

If you're not a fisherman or scuba-diver, one of the most interesting experiences in Bimini is to cruise the cays that begin south of South Bimini. Each has its own special interest, beginning with Turtle Rocks and stretching to South Cat Cay. Along the way you'll pass Holm Cay, Gun Cay, and North Cat Cay.

THE MYTHS OF BIMINI: Bimini has long been shrouded in myths, none greater than the one that claims that the lost continent of Atlantis lies off the shores of North Bimini. This legend grew because of the weirdly shaped rock formations that lie submerged in about 30 feet of water near the shoreline. Pilots flying over North Bimini have reported what they envision as a "lost

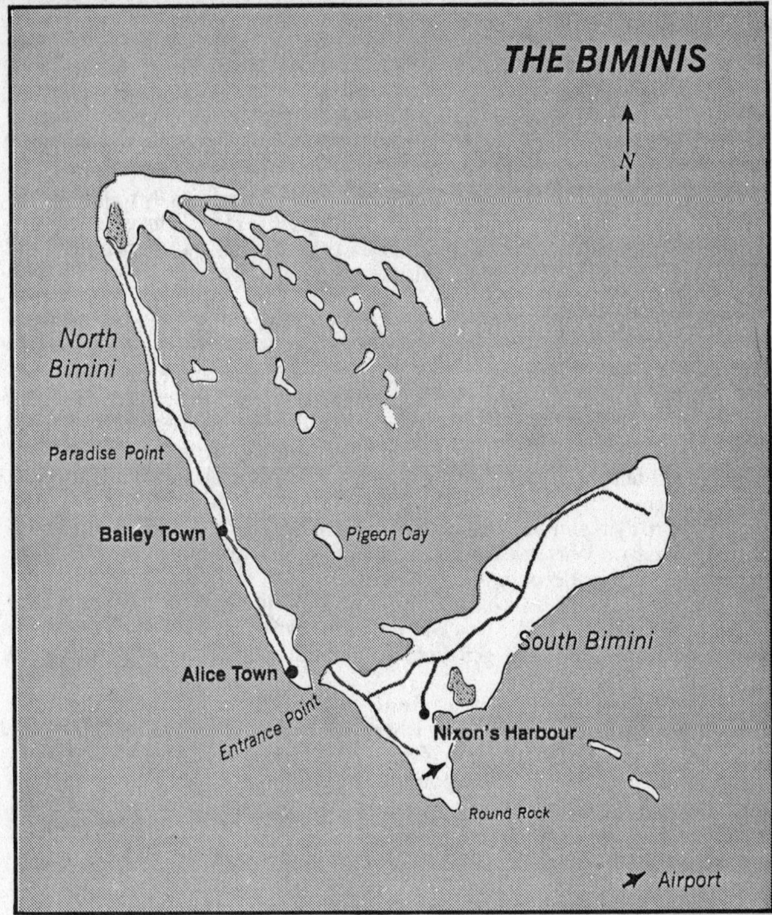

highway" under the sea. This myth continues, and many scuba-divers are attracted to North Bimini to explore these rocks.

Ponce de León came to South Bimini looking for that legendary Fountain of Youth. He never found it, but people still come to South Bimini today in search of it. Near the turn of the century it was reported that a religious sect came here to "take the waters." Supposedly there was a bubbling fountain, or at least a spring, in those days.

If you arrive in South Bimini and seem interested enough, a local guide (for a fee) will be only too happy to show you "the exact spot" where the Fountain of Youth once bubbled. The area around the airport is uninviting and overgrown, and I suggest you'd be better off to skip it.

Long before Ponce de León came this way, much less Hemingway, Arawak Indians had settlements on Bimini. It is also reported that the Seminoles came over from Florida to form settlements as well.

If you go to Bimini, you'll hear a lot of people mention **Cat Cay,** and you may want to go there. Only problem is, you can't without an invitation. This is a privately owned island, attracting titans of industry and such famous families as the Goulds. It is for the exclusive use of Cat Cay Club members and their guests, who enjoy a magnificent golf course, a large marina, white sandy beaches, and club facilities such as restaurants and bars. Many wealthy Americans maintain homes on the island, which has a private airstrip (Chalk's International flies into the cay from Fort Lauderdale and Miami).

Don't confuse Cat Cay with Cat Island, far to the south (see Chapter XV).

FLYING TO BIMINI FROM FLORIDA: Many Americans fly to Bimini, on either a scheduled airline, a charter flight, or in a private plane. There is an airstrip on South Bimini. From South Bimini, guests have to take a ferry to reach the hotels on North Bimini. A general aviation pilot can home in on its paved 5,000-foot runway anytime from dawn to dusk.

From Miami, there is regular service by **Chalk's International Airlines,** owned by Resorts International, which also operates the Paradise Island Resort & Casino. Chalk's has a fleet of amphibious aircraft, so you are transported directly to North Bimini, which is a much faster way of reaching your hotel.

Chalk's seaplanes depart from Watson Island near downtown Miami. Since so many taxi drivers are new and don't even know their way around Miami, you may have to tell them that Watson Island is a seaplane airport lying opposite where the cruise ships dock—that's on the MacArthur Causeway side.

If you're flying into Miami and planning to head directly to Bimini, the seaplane terminal on Watson Island is about a 20-minute drive from the Miami International Airport, depending on traffic of course.

Because the seaplane is likely to be crowded—in both summer and winter—the people at the Chalk's check-in desk ask that you always show up with a confirmed reservation, and get there at least an hour before departure, even though the flight is short.

There is a baggage allowance of only 30 pounds per passenger. But don't worry: there's no place in Bimini where you'll need to dress up. However, if you're carrying heavy travel or fishing gear, you'll be hit with overweight charges (the price is 45¢ per pound). In addition, Chalk's doesn't allow any hand luggage on board. Every piece of your luggage must be checked and weighed in.

Unfortunately, at certain peak periods the plane is fully booked and the passengers have a lot of excess luggage. In that event, your luggage may not accompany you on the flight, but should be on the next plane leaving Miami.

After you've checked in, don't fret about gate or seat numbers (this is a very small operation). After all those regulations and the trouble of getting there, you're airborne only 19 minutes before landing in Alice Town in North Bimini.

Chalk's also has service between Fort Lauderdale and Bimini. The Monday through Saturday hour-long flights depart Fort Lauderdale at 7 a.m. The daily flight from Bimini direct to Fort Lauderdale departs at 5 p.m. These flights are $98 round-trip, or $83 if you're taking only a one-day excursion to Bimini.

In addition, Chalk's also has service between Miami and Cat Cay in The Bahamas.

For more information, call toll free 800/327-2521, except in Florida. In Florida, call 305/895-1223 in Dade County, 305/467-7233 in Broward County, and toll free 800/432-8807 elsewhere in Florida. Or you can write to Chalk's International Airlines, 1550 S.W. 43rd St., Fort Lauderdale, FL 33315.

Aero Coach Aviation International, Inc., P.O. Box 21604, Fort Lauderdale, FL 33335 (tel. 305/359-1600), or toll free 800/327-0010, 800/432-

5034 in Florida), flies to and from Bimini, linking it with Fort Lauderdale and Miami on a daily basis.

ARRIVING BY BOAT: In olden days, long before anyone ever heard of Chalk's Airlines, the traditional way of going from Nassau to Bimini was by a slow-moving boat. That sea trip still exists. You can go by sea on the M/V *Bimini Mack,* leaving from Potter's Cay Dock in Nassau, stopping at Cat Cay and Bimini. The vessel leaves Nassau weekly on Thursday at 4 p.m., returning to Nassau weekly on Monday. For details of sailing (subject to change), write to the Dock Master at Potter's Cay Dock in Nassau (tel. 809/323-1064). One-way fare is $25.

CUSTOMS AND IMMIGRATION: The Chalk's plane from Miami stops right near the office of Customs and Immigration (tel. 809/347-2100) for The Bahamas. For many visiting mainlanders, Bimini will be their gateway to The Bahamas. The small size of this building is a proper introduction to the way things are done in the Family Islands. Outside of Nassau and Freeport, everybody thinks small here. There's only one Immigration officer, plus another Customs official.

In Miami you will have been handed a Bahamian Immigration card, which you should have filled out. You must carry proof of your U.S. (or Canadian, or whatever) citizenship. For U.S. visitors, that most ideally would be a passport, but a voter registration card or a birth certificate will also do. Regrettably, many passengers cross over from Miami with only a driver's license, hoping that it will be sufficient proof of citizenship. *A driver's license will not be accepted by Immigration.*

The officer will ask the nature of your visit, the hotel at which you plan to stay, and the duration of your trip. Customs may or may not examine your baggage, depending on whether or not the officer likes your looks. He will ask you if all items carried by you are for any use other than "personal or sporting."

DRUG WARNING: The rum-runners of the Prohibition era have now given way to a more deadly criminal: the smuggler of illegal drugs into the United States from The Bahamas. Because of its proximity to the U.S. mainland, Bimini, as is no secret to anyone, is now a major dropoff point for drugs, many of which have found their way here from Colombia, South America. If not intercepted by the U.S. Coast Guard, those drugs will find their way to the Florida mainland and eventually to the rest of the United States.

As I pointed out in the introduction to The Bahamas, buying and/or selling illegal drugs such as cocaine and marijuana in The Bahamas is an extremely risky business. You may be approached several times by pushers in Bimini, but make sure you don't get "pushed" into jail. If caught with any illegal drugs in Bimini, or elsewhere in The Bahamas, you will be apprehended and you face immediate imprisonment.

Incidentally, all sorts of undercover agents, particularly U.S. narcotics agents, are likely to be found on Bimini. You can usually spot them because they're disguised like "hippies" from 1967—bearded and wearing cut-off jeans.

GETTING AROUND: Most people, if they've taken my advice and traveled lightly to Bimini, can walk to their hotel from the point where the Chalk's seaplane lands in Alice Town. If not, then a small minibus will transport them there for $3 per person.

Very few visitors need a car on Bimini—in fact, there are no car-rental agencies. Most people walk to where they want to go. The walk is up and down King's Highway, which has no sidewalks. It's so narrow that two automobiles have a tough time squeezing by.

This highway, lined with low-rise buildings, splits Alice Town in North Bimini. If you're a beachcombing type, stick to the side bordering the Gulf Stream. It's here you'll find the best beaches. The harborside at Alice Town contains a handful of inns (many of which are previewed below), along with marinas and docks unloading supplies. You'll see many Floridians arriving on yachts.

Scooters and mopeds are another means of getting about. You'll find some for rent close to the Big Game Fishing Club & Hotel.

PRACTICAL FACTS: Call 919 to report a **fire** or to summon Bimini's limited **police** force.

Banks: For necessary transactions, the **Royal Bank of Canada** has a branch office in Alice Town (tel. 809/347-2031), open from 9 a.m. to 1 p.m. Monday to Friday.

Churches: Houses of worship include the largest congregation, Mount Zion Baptist, P.O. Box 645 (tel. 809/347-2056), and the Anglican Church Rectory, P.O. Box 666 (tel. 809/347-2268).

Clothing: Don't bother with a coat and tie in Bimini. This place is *casual.* No one requires that you wear a jacket; however, if you're going to Bimini in the winter months, you'd better take along a windbreaker for those occasional chilly nights. At night such hotels as the Bimini Big Game Fishing Club & Hotel will not accept dinner guests in bathing suits or without shoes. The most comfortable clothes for relaxing you've got in your wardrobe would fit in just fine in Bimini.

Laundry: Chances are, you won't need any dry cleaning done on Bimini, but you may need some laundry done. Most of the housekeeping staffs of the major hotels, for a fee, will be glad to do your laundry for you.

Mail: If you're sending mail back to the U.S., I suggest you skip the Bahamian postal service entirely and drop your letter off at Chalk's Airlines special basket. You can use U.S. postage stamps, and your mail will reach its mainland target far quicker than by the usual route.

Medical care: There is a doctor, nurses, and a dentist on the island, as well as a **government health clinic** (tel. 809/347-2210). However, for a medical emergency, patients are usually airlifted to either Miami or Nassau. Helicopters can land in the well-lit baseball field in North Bimini.

EXPLORING: At the southern tip of North Bimini, **Alice Town** is all that many visitors ever see of the island. The hotel center of Bimini, it can be thoroughly explored in an hour or two.

If you're traversing the island, you may want to stop off at the Bimini **Straw Market** and speak with some of the Bahamians, perhaps pick up a souvenir or take home an example of one of their crafts.

Nothing is spic and span in Alice Town. First-timers are warned not to judge The Bahamas by Bimini. A yachting guide poses a question: "Would you judge the rest of America if you visited only Miami?"

King's Highway runs through the town and continues north. It's lined with houses, painted in such colors as gold, lime, buttercup yellow, and pink, pastels gleaming in the bright sunshine.

At some point you may notice the ruins of Bimini's first hotel, the Bimini Bay Rod and Gun Club. Built in the early 1920s, it did a flourishing business with 165 rooms and a casino until a hurricane later in that decade wiped it out. It was never rebuilt.

If you want to cross over to **South Bimini,** still, like Ponce de León, hopelessly looking for that Fountain of Youth, you can take a ferry, costing $3 and leaving every 20 minutes from Government Dock. The ferry ride takes about ten minutes or so.

Once you land at South Bimini, you can rent a taxi to see the island's limited attractions for about $12. There's not a lot to see, but you are liable to hear some "tall tales" worth the cab fare.

One of the chief points of interest can only be reached by boat. It's the **Sapona,** which was built by Henry Ford during World War I. This huge concrete ship lies between South Bimini and Cat Cay. It was once a private club and a rum-runner's storehouse in the Roaring '20s. The 1929 hurricane blew it ashore, and in World War II U.S. Navy pilots used it as a practice bomb range. Now spearfishermen are attracted to the ruins, looking for the giant grouper. The dive operations on Bimini include it in their repertoire.

Back in Alice Town, and on the trail of Papa Hemingway, you may want to visit **The Compleat Angler,** P.O. Box 601, Bimini, The Bahamas (tel. 809/347-2122), where its manager, Ossie Brown, presides over a museum of Hemingway memorabilia. The collection of prints and writings describes the times he spent in Bimini, mainly from 1935 to 1937. The prints are posted in the sitting room downstairs. In case you didn't read it, Hemingway devoted nearly a third of his novel *Islands in the Stream* to Bimini; Cuba was one of the other islands. Much of this memorabilia makes interesting browsing. For example, in a page from *My Brother, Ernest Hemingway,* Leicester wrote of a fight he had with Ernest at the Bimini dock. After the fight, Leicester wrote, "Ernest was worried about what he had done. Back in his room at the Compleat Angler, he showered and found that he had ripped off the tops of two toenails on the dock." There is a wide variety of books by Hemingway in the library collection.

WHERE TO STAY: Accommodations in Bimini are extremely limited, and it's almost impossible to get a room during one of the big fishing tournaments unless you've reserved way in advance. Inns are cozy and simple, many often family owned and operated (chances are, your innkeeper's name will be Brown). No one puts on airs here: the dress code, even in the evening, is very simple and relaxed. From where you're staying in Alice Town, it's usually easy to walk to another hotel for dinner or drinks.

Bimini Big Game Fishing Club & Hotel, P.O. Box 699, Bimini, The Bahamas (tel. 809/347-2391, 305/447-7480 in Miami, or toll free 800/327-4149), run by the Bacardi rum people, is the premier place for accommodations in Bimini. Filled with fishermen and the yachting crowd, the hotel is the largest place to stay on the island. It's a self-contained world with 35 well-furnished guest rooms in the main building, surrounded by 12 cottages and four luxurious penthouse apartments, the latter often housing VIPs. The general manager, Michael Kaboth, is the most experienced hotelier on the island, and he will see to your requests and help you ease your adjustment to Bimini, especially if you want to know about fishing in all its many forms. Established in 1946, the hotel places most of its accommodations in its central structure, where each unit is large and equipped with two beds. Everything is clean and comfortable, and the rooms are air-conditioned and have TV. These accommodations have patios or porches opening onto a marina and the club's swimming pool. You can usually spot wet fishing clothes drying out in the hot Bimini sun. Guests can also play tennis.

Many of the sporting guests here prefer one of the ground-floor cottages instead. They are even more spacious than the standard bedrooms and have tiny kitchenettes with refrigerators—but they are not to be used for cooking, which is strictly forbidden. If you want to charcoal-broil your catch of the day, you will have to use one of the outdoor grills. Year-round rates are $120 to $135 daily in a single or double; an extra person pays $22. The charge, again for singles or doubles, is $155 daily in one of the cottages, rising to $295 in a penthouse.

A freshwater swimming pool is set aside for guests so that it won't be overrun with "day trippers." Even if you didn't arrive by yacht, you may want to stroll over to the dockmaster's office and look at those who did. Here is where incoming yachts must clear Bahamian Customs and Immigration. There is a 60-slip marina. The hotel is also the best place to go for food on the island, and it's an entertainment hub as well (more about that later). The best anglers at the big-game fishing tournaments stay here. Then it's next to impossible to get a room without reservations long in advance. The Stateside mailing address is P.O. Box 523238, Miami, FL 33152.

Bimini's Blue Water Ltd., P.O. Box 627, Bimini, The Bahamas (tel. 809/347-2166), at Alice Town, has as its main building a white frame waterfront Bahamian guesthouse. Across the highway are more units opening onto the water. Encircling the upper and lower floors are covered latticework verandas, providing a comfortable area for watching sunsets. Rooms overlook the ocean and beach. Blue Water is essentially a resort complex for sports fishermen. The Anchorage, where Michael Lerner, the noted fisherman, used to live, is a separate guesthouse at the top of the hill, with a dining room and bar from which you can look out onto the ocean. The regular bedrooms contain double beds, wood-paneled walls, and white furniture with some sea-blue touches. Picture window doors lead to private balconies. A swimming pool, buried in a tropical garden, with an adjoining refreshment bar, is also available. Blue Water Marina is one of the finest in The Bahamas, with complete dockside services.

Rates are the same all year. A suite at the Anchorage costs $205 per day, and a single or double room goes for $95.40. A three-bedroom/three-bath Marlin Cottage, with large living room and two porches, rents for $302.10 per day. This cottage, although much altered, was one of Hemingway's retreats in the 1930s. In honor of his memory, the hotel sponsors the Hemingway Billfish Tournament every April.

Diandrea's Inn, Alice Town, Bimini, The Bahamas (tel. 809/347-2334). Set behind a rolling front lawn on King's Highway in the center of town, this hotel fills a 1930-era gabled house with a wide veranda. Despite the fact that its 13 rooms are now for rent, there is much about this place that gives the impression of a private house. The hotel is noted as one of the oldest on Bimini. Each of its bedrooms is plainly furnished, with shag carpeting, private bath, air conditioning, and cable color TV. Room 51, with its large floor space, low ceilings, and dormers, is particularly inviting. In winter, single or double occupancy costs $90 to $110 daily, the price going up to $145 in an outlying cottage. *In summer, single or double occupancy is from $75 to $100 in the main house, from $125 in the outlying cottage.* In hot weather, a small bar and its adjacent platform attract live musicians and large crowds whenever there's a concert.

The Compleat Angler Hotel, P.O. Box 601, Bimini, The Bahamas (tel. 809/347-2122), right on the main street, King's Highway, in the heart of Alice Town, was built in the '30s when big-game fishing was at its peak. The building is designed like an old country house with Bahamian timber. The wood on the face of the building is from rum barrels used during the time of Prohibition. Pictures on the walls depict its history. Ernest Hemingway made the hotel his headquarters on and off from 1935 to 1937, and the room in which he stayed and wrote is still available to guests. He worked on *To Have and Have Not* here. At the bar, Ossie Brown, bartender, host, and manager, will be helpful. This is a very small hotel with only 12 bedrooms, and a single room all year rents for $57.65 a day; doubles cost $57.95 to $74.10. Dress is casual in a relaxed and informal atmosphere. You can swim, dine, shop, or fish right at your doorstep, and fishing charters can be booked at the hotel. If you're writing for a reservation, the quickest way to reach them is to write the Compleat Angler Hotel, c/o Chalk's International Airlines, Watson Island, Miami, FL 33132.

Brown's Hotel, P.O. Box 601, Bimini, The Bahamas (tel. 809/347-2227). Here you encounter the Brown name again. The hotel is run by Neville Brown, son of Harcourt Brown, who spawned a whole generation of Bimini innkeepers. A half block from the Chalk's Airline ramp, Brown's Hotel is a simple motel unit built right along the harbor, with 28 rooms and two apartments, each air-conditioned with a private bath. Accommodations are plain, but you get good value for your money here: $55 in a double, $35 in a single. These rates are in effect year-round. It's a favorite of economy-minded Bimini visitors, but it doesn't accept credit cards. There is a 22-slip marina, and fishing boats are for rent. Bahamian specialties are offered in the dining room, and there's talk of the "catch of the day" in the bar.

Weech's Bimini Dock and Bay View Rooms, P.O. Box 613, Bimini, The Bahamas (tel. 809/347-2028), has double rooms, renting for $50 per day all year double occupancy, as well as efficiency apartments, accommodating five to six persons and costing $100 daily year-round. Dockage is also offered.

WHERE TO DINE: Come here to feast on conch and the famous homemade Bimini bread. Outside the hotels (or even in the hotels) restaurants are simple, with a natural and to-be-expected emphasis on fresh seafood (often caught by the guests themselves). Of course, choice steaks and chops are flown in from the mainland as well. Conch salad and conch fritters are everywhere.

Fisherman's Wharf, Bimini Big Game Fishing Club & Hotel (tel. 809/347-2391), consistently serves the finest food on the island in its curved dining room opening onto the pool. Both breakfast and dinner are offered here. Dining includes many island specialties such as crisp homemade Bimini bread and freshly caught kingfish, along with broiled local lobster and grouper meunière. Instead of french fries, why not go Bahamian and order peas 'n' rice with your meal? You can also make a selection from the buffet salad bar, and if you're tired of fish, the kitchen will usually serve you a steak, roast prime rib of beef, lamb chops, or stuffed Cornish game hen. Meals cost from $30. You don't have to dress up for dinner, but wear something! Sport clothes are fine, but not bathing attire. Breakfast is served from 7:30 to 11 a.m., and dinner from 7 to 10:30 p.m. (there is no lunch). Before dinner, you can come and have a drink in the most sophisticated bar in Bimini.

Bimini's Seafood Haven, Bimini Big Game Fishing Club & Hotel (tel. 809/347-2391), is "the other" restaurant at the club. It is less expensive and almost equally popular. You can order lunch daily from 11:30 a.m. to 4:30 p.m., costing from $8. Conch is a Bahamian delicacy, and you can taste it in conch fritters, conch salad, or conch chowder, even cracked conch which is breaded like veal cutlet milanese. You can also order grouper fingers or barbecued back ribs along with a selection of hamburgers and sandwiches. Check out the daily special. At night the temptation is wider, beginning with, for example, smoked game fish or a Bahamian gumbo, a spicy, chunky soup with conch, salt beef, and fresh vegetables. You can also order crab and callaloo (greens and crabmeat). At the salad bar you can make your own combinations with assorted dressings. From the Gulf Stream comes grilled wahoo or dolphin steak broiled to perfection and served with an herb butter. You can also order native lobster broiled just right or "smothered grouper," which is a Bahamian classic. If not fish, then Bimini roast chicken with a banana stuffing and cognac sauce is tempting, as are the finest American lamb chops which will be grilled for you. Dinners cost from $25 and are served nightly from 7 to 10:30.

Anchorage Dining Room (tel. 807/347-2166), run by Bimini's Blue Water Ltd., overlooks the harbor of Alice Town. At night, if you're seeking atmosphere "at the top of the hill," it has the jump on every other establishment. You can see the ocean through picture windows. Have a before-dinner drink in the bar. The modern, paneled room is filled with captain's chairs and Formica tables. You can visit the place for all three meals a day if that is your desire. You might begin with conch chowder, then follow with one of the tempting seafood dishes, including spiny broiled lobster or perhaps a chewy cracked conch. They also do fried Bahamian chicken and a New York sirloin. Lunch costs from $12 and dinner from $25. The Anchorage serves breakfast from 7 to 10 a.m., lunch from noon to 5 p.m., and dinner from 6 to 9:30 p.m. daily.

Red Lion Pub, King's Highway (tel. 809/347-2259). This centrally located restaurant is far larger and more substantial than its simple russet-colored façade would imply. Its creative force lies in the person of Bimini-born Dolores Saunders, who worked as an employee of the place for 20 years before buying it in 1982.Many guests never venture beyond the cozy enclaves of the pub, whose bar fills the room nearest the front entrance. Above the cash register hangs a photograph of Stephanie Saunders, Dolores's daughter, who won the title of Miss Bimini in 1977. The pub is open nightly except Monday from 5 p.m. to 1 a.m. The dining room is in a large extension of the original pub, overlooking the marina in back. Dinner is served nightly except Monday from 6 to 11 p.m. The well-prepared meals, costing from $20 each, include the local fish of the day, cracked conch, barbecued ribs, baked grouper in foil, followed by either key lime pie or banana cream pie.

Blue Marlin (tel. 809/347-2242), in Alice Town, is a good local restaurant for Bahamian and American food. It has such hearty local fare as cracked conch, steamed grouper, fried Bahamian chicken, broiled Bahamian lobster, boiled or stewed fish, and tasty pork chops, and meals cost from $18. It's open daily from 7 a.m. to 2 a.m. In the rear is a pool room.

Bimini also has a number of little restaurants, all serving virtually the same fare, along with the soft, tender, sweet, and warm Bimini bread (this bread is used for sandwiches that the fishermen take out in boxed lunches). Most of these places don't have a phone, and you don't need a reservation—you just drop in to see what's cooking.

Priscilla's Epicurean Delights, King's Highway (no phone). Its very grand name and its flavorful cuisine were invented by island entrepreneur Priscilla Bain. There's only one Formica-topped table inside for dining, so most visitors call to Ms. Bain through a windowless opening which looks out over the street in front of the Bimini Big Game Fishing Club & Hotel. Many of the yacht owners from the nearby marinas make it a point to enjoy at least one take-away meal prepared here. Every day, food is dispensed from 11:30 a.m. to 6:30 p.m. Most of it is prepared early in the morning at another location, then heated up in the simple cottage that houses Epicurean Delights. Only the conch fritters, said to be the best on the island, are deep-fried to order. Selling for $3 a dozen, they are the main dish of many a meal served on some of the ultra-expensive yachts moored nearby. You can order a complete platter of chicken or pork chops, beef stew, fried fish, or meatloaf for around $6, and any of these can be accompanied with pigeon peas 'n' rice, potato bread, macaroni salad, or potato salad. Cold beer is also available.

Fisherman's Paradise (no phone), another local spot, serves (you guessed it). It has good, tasty Bahamian seafood such as grouper, with meals beginning at $10. It keeps no set hours.

If you're exploring South Bimini, you might drop in at **Janet Cox's Restaurant and Bar** (no phone), which has simple fare, such as fish and chicken. Meals begin at $10. Next to the airstrip, Janet's is open daily from 8 a.m. to 5 p.m.

SHOPPING: You might go to the **Bimini Big Game Fishing Club & Hotel** (tel. 809/347-2391), where you will find two shops on the grounds. The first is the

Butler and Sands Liquor Store, which has some of the best liquor buys in town. At the other, Bubbles of Bimini, you can pick up jewelry, watches, and other gift items at tariffs often 20% to 30% (or even more) lower than Stateside prices. If you're a souvenir collector, ask at the front office (a one-room structure that's also the lobby) for T-shirts, sunglasses, coffee mugs, and Big Game Club hats. A mini-boutique has opened at the hotel with six shops, adding a perfume bar, bait and tackle store, a gift shop, and island fashions to the complex.

THE SPORTING LIFE: There are fishermen and scuba-divers who go nowhere but Bimini, reserving their favorite rooms in local inns every year. Otherwise, except for snorkeling, the people of Bimini don't "muck about" with many other water sports.

Sport Fishing

Bimini is called the "Big Game Fishing Capital of the World," and Ernest Hemingway, above all others, has given fame to the sport practiced here. But Zane Grey came this way too, as did Howard Hughes. Richard Nixon used to fish and then relax docked here aboard the posh cruiser of his friend, Miamian Bebe Rebozo. In the trail of Hemingway, fishermen today still flock to fish in the Gulf Stream and the Bahama Banks.

Of course, everyone's after "the big one," and a lot of world records have been set in this area: marlin, sailfish, swordfish, wahoo, grouper, and tuna. Fishing folk can spincast for panfish, and can boat snapper, yellowtail, and kingfish. Many experts consider stalking the shallow flats for bonefish, long a pursuit of baseball great Ted Williams, to be the toughest challenge in the sport.

Five charter boats are available in Bimini for big-game and little-game fishing, with some center console boats rented for both bottom and reef angling. At least eight bonefishing guides are available, and experienced fishermen who have made repeated visits to Bimini know the particular skills of each of these men who take you for a half or full day of "fishing in the flats," as bonefishing is termed. Most skiffs hold two anglers, and part of the fun in hiring a local guide is to hear their fish stories and other island lore. If they tell you that 16-pound bonefish have turned up, don't think it's invented. Such catches have been documented.

Reef and bottom fishing are easier than bonefishing, and can be more productive of results. There are numerous species of snapper and grouper to be found, as well as amberjack. This is the simplest and least expensive boat fishing, as you need only a local guide, a little boat, tackle, and a lot of bait. Sometimes you can negotiate to go out bottom fishing with a Bahamian, but chances are he'll ask you to pay for the boat fuel for his trouble. That night, back at your Bimini inn, the cook will serve you the red snapper or grouper you caught that day. (At least you'll know it's fresh.)

Most hotel owners will tell you to bring your own fishing gear to Bimini. A couple of small shops sell some items, but you'd better bring major equipment with you. Bait, of course, can be purchased locally.

At the **Bimini Big Game Fishing Club & Hotel** (tel. 809/347-2391), you can charter a 41-foot Hatteras at $600 for a full day, $350 for a half day of fishing. A Bertram, either 31 feet or 28 feet, will cost $400 for a full day, $275 for a half.

Bimini Blue Water Ltd. (tel. 809/347-2166) offers for charter a 28-foot Bertram with tackle and crew for $450 or $350 for a full or half day, respectively.

Brown's Marina (tel. 809/347-2227) has full marina facilities, including a restaurant and bar. Here you can charter boats for deep-sea fishing and reef and shark fishing, costing $350 daily or $225 for a half day.

At **Weech's Bimini Dock** (tel. 809/347-2028), you can arrange for a day of deep-sea fishing. A half-day charter aboard a 23-foot Prowler costs $200 for half a day, $300 for a full day. Boston whalers are rented for $50 per half day, $90 per day.

Snorkeling and Scuba

This has become an increasingly popular sport in the last 20 years. Visitors can snorkel above a wonderworld of black coral gardens and reefs, or go scuba-diving, exploring the wrecks and the blue holes, plus a mystery formation on the bottom of the sea that many people claim is part of the lost continent of Atlantis. A major attraction for snorkelers and divers, not to mention fish, is the *Sapona,* lying hard aground in 15 feet of water ever since it was blown there by a hurricane in 1929. In the heyday of the roaring '20s, it was a ship that was a private club and speakeasy. This rum-runner plied the Bimini coast, often with visitors to the Bimini Bay Rod and Gun Club as passengers, attracted to its casino. *Sapona* became a victim of the hurricane in 1929. A cliff extends 2,000 feet down in Bimini waters—known for a breathtaking dropoff at the rim of the Continental Shelf, an underwater mountain.

The people to see are Bill and Nowdla Keefe at their **Bimini Undersea Adventures,** Alicetown, Bimini, The Bahamas (tel. 809/347-2089). Full-day snorkel trips cost $25. Scuba rates are $35 for one-tank dive, $50 for two, and $60 for three. All-inclusive dive packages are also available. For further information or reservations, the Keefes can be reached through P.O. Box 21766, Ft. Lauderdale, FL 33335 (tel. 305/763-2188, or toll free 800/327-8150).

Tennis

The **Bimini Big Game Fishing Club & Hotel** (tel. 809/347-2391) has hard-surface courts, which are complimentary to hotel guests and members. The courts are lit for night play. You can purchase balls at the club.

AFTER DARK: You can dance to a Goombay beat or try to find some disco music. Most people have a leisurely dinner, drink a lot in one of the local taverns, and go back to their hotel rooms by midnight so they can get up early to continue their pursuit of the elusive "big one" the next morning on some fishing boat. Every bar in Alice Town is likely to claim that it was "Papa's favorite." He did hit quite a few of them, in fact. Most drinks cost from $3, and there's rarely a cover charge anywhere unless some special entertainment is being offered.

One of the almost mandatory requirements, to firmly establish you on Bimini soil, is to have a drink at the **End of the World Bar** in Alice Town, P.O. Box 638 (tel. 809/347-2370). When you get there, you may think you're in the wrong place. The place may be famous, but it isn't the Ritz. It's just a waterfront shack with sawdust on the floor. It was the late congressman from Harlem, Adam Clayton Powell, who put this bar on the map. Between stints in Washington battling Congress and preaching at the Abyssinian Baptist Church in Harlem, the controversial congressman might be found sitting at a table in this bar. The world knew where to find him. (One man who had pressing business with Powell couldn't get an appointment with him in Washington. He found it easier to fly to Bimini, where he found Powell very approachable.) Regardless of what his fellow congressmen thought of Powell, he was a hero locally, and many people of Bimini still remember him. For example, Brown's Hotel to this day still has plaques honoring Powell for his contributions to big-game fishing. Maybe this place doesn't attract the media attention it did in Powell's heyday, when the press swarmed all over the bar, but it's still going strong, still a local favorite, and everybody takes a felt marker and signs his or her name. It's open from 11 a.m. to 3 a.m. daily.

Another nighttime diversion is the **Hi-Star Disco** (tel. 809/347-2381), in

Alice Town, where both locals and visitors enjoy the latest in disco paraphernalia. Dancing is until the wee hours of the morning. On Friday and Saturday nights, a $3 cover charge is assessed. Drinks cost from $3.

If you're a fisherman (or woman), or a groupie of a fishing aficionado, chances are you'll head for the **Harbour Lounge** of the Bimini Big Game Fishing Club & Hotel (tel. 809/347-2391) for your sundowner. In some cases that "sundowning" can last until midnight. If you're a first-time visitor, ask for Mr. Cooper's locally celebrated rum punch. Made with Bacardi rums, it's *the* drink to order here. The outside bar is romantically called "Rum Keg," and beginning at lunchtime it's open throughout the day and evening. Adjacent to the main dining room, the major bar opens at 6 p.m. When are closing hours? Management says the bars are open "until . . ."

The favorite watering hole for every visiting Hemingway buff is **The Compleat Angler Hotel** (tel. 809/347-2122). Ossie Brown, the bartender (he's also the manager), is said to make the best Planter's Punch in The Bahamas. He challenges anyone to make a better planter's punch. "I guarantee it can only be equalled," he says. Occasional entertainment by a native calypso band turns this place into a real island hot spot, featuring Goombay drinks. If you've booked a room here, remember that it's only for night owls. The place, as mentioned, is filled with Hemingway memorabilia, and it's open daily from 11 a.m. "until."

2. THE BERRY ISLANDS

A dangling chain of cays and islets on the eastern edge of the Great Bahama Bank, the unspoiled and serene Berry Islands begin 35 miles northeast of New Providence (Nassau), 150 miles east of Miami. This 30-island archipelago is known to sailors, fishermen, yachtsmen, Sammy Davis, Jr., Jack Nicklaus, and a Rockefeller or two, as well as the beachcombers who explore its uninhabited reaches.

As a center of fishing, the Berry Islands are second only to Bimini. At Chub Cay you can charter boats for fishing trips or just plain cruising. At the tip of "The Tongue of the Ocean," called TOTO, world-record-setting big-game fish are found, plus endless bonefish flats. Scuba-diving is arranged for visitors on the semiprivate island of Chub Cay, and a 250-yard driving range attracts golf buffs. There is a fine sheltered marina for yachts of any size.

In the "Berries" you can find your own tropical paradise islet, enjoying, totally unmolested and sans wardrobe, the white sandy beaches against a palm-fringed shore and a backdrop of green foliage.

Some of the best shell collecting in The Bahamas is on the beaches of the Berry Islands and in their shallow-water flats.

The main islands are, beginning in the north, Great Stirrup Cay, Cistern Cay, Great Harbour Cay, Anderson Cay, Haines Cay, Hoffmans Cay, Bonds Cay, Sandy Cay, Whale Cay, and Chub Cay, the last the only place where accommodations can be recommended as of this writing.

The largest is Great Harbour Cay, extending for 3,800 acres. The development here received a great deal of publicity when Douglas Fairbanks, Jr., was connected with its board. It became a multi-million-dollar resort for jet-setters who occupied waterfront town houses and villas overlooking the golf course or marina. There are 7½ miles of almost solitary beachfront. However, the only guests arriving today are those invited by owners of property there.

During the reign of William IV, that spit of land known as Great Stirrup Cay figured in Bahamian history. The king ordered the building of Williamstown (named after himself, of course). It was to be a resettlement post for homeless slaves. A Custom House was erected, the ruins of which remain today. Obviously, the former slaves sought greener cays, or whatever, elsewhere, because the settlement was later abandoned.

Bond's Cay, a bird sanctuary in the south, and tiny Frazer's Hog Cay (stock is raised here) are both privately owned. An English company used to operate a coconut and sisal plantation on Whale Cay, also near the southern tip. For the most part, this chain of islands appears virtually deserted, except by Americans or Europeans who have winter homes here.

Sponge fishermen and their families inhabit some of the islands. One of the very small cays, lying north of Frazer's Hog Cay and Whale Cay, has, in my opinion, the most unappetizing name in the Bahamian archipelago: Cockroach Cay.

GETTING THERE: The deluxe way to go is on your own private plane, which will land at one of several private airstrips. The emphasis, as you'll find in the Berry Islands, is on the word *private.* That's how many of the landowners would like to keep it. After all, they "discovered" the Berry Islands as a retreat from civilization. However, as the world tourist march continues, the Berry Islands may increasingly gain much attention from visitors.

Through **Bahamasair** (at one of their ticket desks), you can make arrangements to fly a charter service from Nassau to Chub Cay (see below). This should be done as far in advance as possible. If you're not in Nassau, you can go to a travel agent.

If you're contemplating the **mailboat** sea-voyage route, the M/V *Captain Dean* leaves Potter's Cay Dock in Nassau weekly on Tuesday, heading for the Berry Islands. The boat returns to Nassau on Friday. Inquire at the Potter's Cay Dock for an up-to-the-minute report (contact the dockmaster at 809/323-1064). Chub Cay and Great Harbour Cay are both official ports of entry for The Bahamas if you're flying from a foreign territory such as the United States.

If arrangements are made far enough in advance, Chub Cay Club has a licensed charter service from Fort Lauderdale.

CHUB CAY: The southernmost cay in the Berry Island chain, Chub Cay, one of the best diving resorts in The Bahamas, is an exclusive retreat attracting members, although the general public is accepted as well. It was once a strictly private facility, however. When the island was originally purchased, there were no native inhabitants. Fifty-five Bahamians were brought in, and housing had to be provided for them. The island is really a tranquil little sandspit.

There is a liquor store on the island, but you can also bring in one quart of liquor from a duty-free shop before you board the plane. Remember to arrive light: the plane allows approximately 50 pounds of baggage, and that's it!

The water temperature around Chub Cay averages 80° to 85° Fahrenheit year-round at all depths. There is only a small tide change, and there is no swell or current noticeable.

It's important to remember that it is forbidden by Bahamian authorities to bring back coral as souvenirs. It violates local ecological laws to take anything from the sea for purposes other than obtaining food. The government wants to preserve the natural beauty of the reefs of the Berry Islands. But you're allowed to look all you want.

Many divers have waxed enthusiastic over the dive spots of the Berry Islands, including Chub Wall and Mamma Rhoda Rock, as well as the caverns, reefs, caves, and tunnels.

The only place to stay is **Chub Cay Club** (for reservations, write Chub Cay Club, P.O. Box 661067, Miami Springs, FL 33266; tel. 305/445-7830), one of the finest fishing resorts in the world. There is no mail delivery to Chub Cay through The Bahamas. The management has set aside a total of 15 units, called Yacht Club rooms, available for non-members, costing $75 per day year-round, either single or double occupancy. Adjacent to the marina and just a step away from the dining room and lounge, the Yacht Club rooms are tastefully decorated and have TV and air conditioning. They overlook a freshwater swimming pool. The 80-slip marina welcomes nonmember boats. There is a laundromat. The club has the Flying Bridge Restaurant, which you are invited to patronize. The food is excellent, especially the well-prepared Bahamian lobster, along with good steaks from the States. MAP is another $35 daily.

THE SPORTING LIFE: The **Chub Cay Club** is a full dive resort, internationally recognized. Neal Watson, who formerly operated Bimini Undersea Adventures in Bimini and also owns Andros Undersea Adventures on that island (see below), runs the superb dive program, a professional diving staff, a dive shop, and large tri-hull dive boats, in addition to an unmatched variety of dive spots, already referred to. A PADI instructor is on the premises. Also offered are a full-service underwater photography program with strobe and camera rentals available.

You can also make arrangements at the marina to go bonefishing. Many fishermen come here to search for the 300-pound blue marlin that Hemingway wrote about in *Islands in the Stream.* Of course it's also possible to catch a 500-pound blue marlin.

It is said that one of the reasons fishing is so good in the Berry Islands is because bait fish are swept up by TOTO. Their hungry pursuers, including dolphin, mako sharks, and barracudas, along with wahoo, go in after them. Unknown to these big fish, yet another hunter—man—is waiting.

In addition, the club has two all-weather surface courts, lit for night play (free to guests).

For more information about the fishing and boating arrangements, as well as their skin- and scuba-diving, write to the Miami Springs address already given.

3. ANDROS

The largest island in The Bahamas—actually a series of islands separated by channels—Andros is also one of the largest unexplored tracts of land in the western hemisphere. Mostly flat, its 2,300 square miles are riddled with lakes and creeks, and most of the local population, who still indulge in fire dances and go on wild boar hunts on occasion, live along the shore.

One of the most mysterious islands in The Bahamas, Andros is 100 miles long and 40 miles wide. Its interior is a dense, tropical forest, really rugged bush and mangrove country. The marshy and relatively uninhabited west coast is called "The Mud," and the east coast is paralleled for 120 miles by the second-largest underwater barrier reef in the world. The reef drops to over a mile into "The Tongue of the Ocean," or TOTO. On the eastern shore, this "tongue" is 142 miles long and 1,000 fathoms deep.

The fishing at Andros is famous, establishing records for blue marlin caught offshore. Skindivers report that the coral reefs are among the most beautiful in the world.

One of the myths of the island is that aborigines live in the interior. These were thought to be a lost tribe of Arawak Indians—remnants of the archipelago's original inhabitants who were exterminated by the Spanish centuries ago. However, low-flying planes, looking for evidence of human settlements, have not turned up any indication to support this far-fetched assertion. But who can dispute that chickcharnies (red-eyed Bahamian elves with three toes, feathers, and beards) live on the island? The demise of Neville Chamberlain's ill-fated sisal plantation was blamed on these mischievous devils.

The chickcharnie once struck terror into the hearts of superstitious islanders. They were supposed to live in the depths of the Androsian wilderness, making their nests in the tops of two intertwined palm trees. Tales are told of how many a woodsman in the old days endured hardship and misery because he thoughtlessly felled the trees that served as stilts for a chickcharnie nest. Like the leprechauns of Ireland, the chickcharnies belong solely to Andros. They are the Bahamian version of the elves, goblins, fairies, and duppies of other lands. Children may be threatened with them if they fail to behave, and business or domestic calamity is immediately attributed to their malevolent activities.

The origin of the legend is shrouded in mystery. One story has it that the tales began in the late 19th century when a Nassau hunting enthusiast who wanted to protect his duck-hunting grounds in Andros invented the malicious elves to frighten off unwanted interlopers. Another has it that the myth was brought to The Bahamas by bands of Seminole Indians fleeing Florida in the early 1880s to escape the depredations of white settlers. Some of the Indians settled on the northern tip of Andros. But the most probable explanation is one that traces the chickcharnie to a once-living being—an extinct, three-foot-high, flightless barn owl *(Tyto pollens)*—which used to inhabit The Bahamas and West Indies.

According to the Bahamas National Trust, the local conservation authority, such a bird "screeching, hissing and clacking its bills in characteristic barn owl fashion, hopping onto its victims or pouncing on them from low tree limbs would have been a memorable sight. And a frightening one."

The species may have survived here into historical times, and Andros, being the largest Bahamian land mass, was probably able to sustain *Tyto pollens* longer than the smaller islands where the necessary prey species died off as the land area shrank during the present interglacial period. It is probable that the early settlers on Andros encountered such beasts, and it's probable, too, that *Tyto pollens* was the inspiration for the chickcharnie, a poor substitute for the real thing.

Nevertheless, the tales are still told in Andros, and there is no doubt that the chickcharnie will live on as a fascinating component of The Bahamas' diverse cultural legacy.

Lying 170 miles southeast of Miami and 30 miles west of Nassau, Andros, although spoken of as if it were one island, is actually divided into three main land areas: North Andros, Middle Andros, and South Andros. Ferries, operated free by the Bahamian government, ply back and forth over the waters separating Mangrove Cay from South Andros. At the end of the road in North Andros, private arrangements can be made to have a boatman take you over to Mangrove Cay. In spite of its size, Andros is very thinly populated, its local residents numbering around 5,000, although the tourist population swells it a bit. The temperature range here averages from 72° to 81° Fahrenheit.

The Spaniards, who came this way in the 16th century looking for Indian slaves, called the island La Isla del Esperitu Santo or the "Island of the Holy Spirit," but the name didn't catch on, although it came from the belief that the Holy Spirit dwells over water, with which Andros is abundantly supplied. It constantly ships the precious liquid to water-scarce New Providence (Nassau) in barges.

The name used for the island today is believed by some experts to have come from Sir Edmund Andros, a British commander.

You won't find the western side of Andros much written about in yachting guides, as it is almost unapproachable by boat because of the tricky shoals. The east coast, however, is studded with little villages, and hotels have been built here that range from simple guest cottages to dive resorts to fishing camps. "Creeks" (I'd call them rivers) intersect the island at its midpoint. Called "bights," in the main they have three channels. Their width ranges from 5 to 25 miles, and they are dotted with tiny cays and islets. There are miles of unspoiled beach along the eastern shore.

Few people draw comparisons between overly developed Paradise Island and underdeveloped Andros. However, their tourism industry has a common

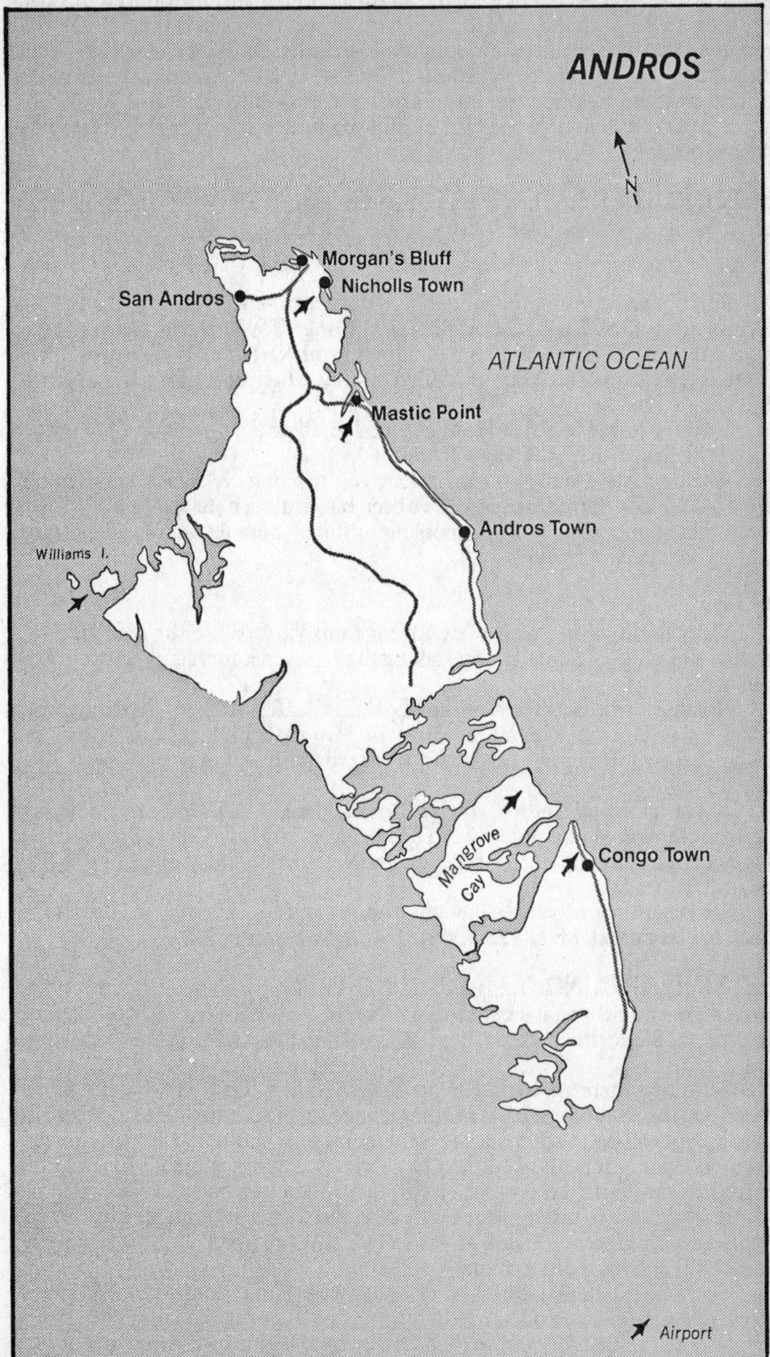
ANDROS
N
Morgan's Bluff
Nicholls Town
San Andros
ATLANTIC OCEAN
Mastic Point
Andros Town
Williams I.
Mangrove Cay
Congo Town
Airport

ancestor, Dr. Axel Wenner-Gren, the Swedish industrialist introduced in Chapter IX on Paradise Island. In addition to investing in what was then Hog Island (renamed Paradise Island by Huntington Hartford), Dr. Wenner-Gren also built the Andros Yacht Club, to the south of Fresh Creek on Andros. That now defunct club began to attract the island's first tourists following World War II.

A word of warning: If you visit Andros, be sure to take along plenty of mosquito repellent.

GETTING THERE: When you arrive somewhere in The Bahamas, you say "Ya reach!"

By Air

Reaching Andros is not that difficult. **Bahamasair** has flights to the airports in Andros: Andros Town, San Andros, and Congo Town (the last terminal is in South Andros). It is only a 15-minute flight from Nassau to, say, Andros Town. There is also a small airstrip on Mangrove Cay. Flight schedules are subject to change.

If you're going to Small Hope Bay Lodge, there is a one-hour flight service from Fort Lauderdale to Andros Town.

Warning: Make sure you know where you're going in Andros. For example, if you land in South Andros and you've been booked in a hotel at Nicholl's Town, you'll find connections nearly impossible at times (both ferryboats and a rough haul across a bad highway).

By Boat

Many locals, along with a few adventurous visitors, use the mailboats as a means of reaching Andros, the trip taking five to seven hours across some beautiful waters.

North Andros is serviced by the M/V *Lisa J. II,* a mailboat departing from Potter's Cay Dock in Nassau, heading for Morgan's Bluff, Mastic Point, and Nicholl's Town. It departs Nassau on Wednesday, returning to Nassau on Tuesday.

To reach Central Andros, you have to take the M/V *Andros Express,* departing from Market Wharf in Nassau. The boat goes to Fresh Creek, Bering Point, Blanket Sound, and Stafford Creek, leaving Nassau on Sunday. It returns to Nassau on Wednesday.

For details about sailing and costs, contact the dockmaster at Potter's Cay Dock in Nassau (tel. 809/323-1064). The one-way fare is $16.

GETTING AROUND: Transportation can be a *big* problem on Andros. If you have to go somewhere, it's better to use one of the local drivers. Most of them have to take some other job, as they find it hard to make a living "just" driving a taxi.

What *cars* there are to rent are in North Andros. These are few and far between, owing to the high costs of shipment of cars to Andros. The weather also takes a great toll on the cars that are brought in, so no car-rental agencies are represented. Your best bet is to ask at your hotel to see what's available. Once you've arrived on the island, expect to spend at least $60 or more per day for a car.

If you'd like to attempt the roads of Andros on a **scooter or bicycle,** call Andros Beach Hotel & Villas, at Nicholl's Town on North Andros (tel. 809/329-2582) and see if one is available for rent.

There are no guided tours as such on Andros. This is do-it-yourself country. If you'd like to look at North Andros by car, it's best to try to put together a party at your hotel, at least four or five to share the costs. If you don't know any of your fellow guests, perhaps the hotel manager will ask around for you or advise you. The reason is simple: a half-day tour is likely to cost in the neighborhood of $180, perhaps more if you have a lot of stopovers. The party will help you share not only the ride, but the huge expense.

On South Andros or Mangrove Cay there will be less to see. You can do the job in 1½ hours by taxi. Again, it's best to share. Prices always have to be negotiated locally.

Taxi drivers—what few there are—know when the planes from Nassau are going to land, and they drive out to the airports, hoping to drum up some business. If two couples, or whatever combination, are heading in the same direction, taxis are most often shared.

PRACTICAL FACTS: Carry traveler's checks and hope that your hotel will be able to cash them for your daily spending money.

Banks: These are rare creatures on Andros. There is one, the Canadian Bank of Commerce (809/368-2071) in Fresh Creek.

Churches: Protestant denominations are represented on the island. If you want to attend, ask at your hotel where the nearest place of worship is. Outsiders are usually warmly welcomed and received in local congregations.

Clothing: Dress is casual, but don't come to Andros expecting to catch up on your dry cleaning. If you need shirts and blouses washed and ironed, ask at your hotel. Even if they don't have a service themselves, they usually know someone in the community who "takes in wash," so to speak.

Hair care: Women should be prepared to do their own hair, unless someone at a hotel tells them about a local woman "who's studying to be a beautician." Men can get a haircut—and that's it.

Mail: The island has no big post office as such, although there is a post-handling office in the Commissioner's Office in Nicholl's Town on North Andros (tel. 809/329-2278). Hotel desks will sell you Bahamian stamps. Make sure you mark cards and letters airmail; otherwise you'll return home before they do, as they're put on a "slow boat to China," in this case the mailboat to Nassau. Each little hamlet in Andros has a store that serves as the post office, just as it was in America of long ago.

Medical care: Government-run clinics are at Mastic Point (tel. 809/329-3055), and at Lowe Sound (tel. 809/329-2055), all on North Andros. On Central Andros, there is a health center at Fresh Creek (tel. 809/368-2038), with a doctor and a nurse. Bring along whatever drugs (legal ones) or medicines you'll need while visiting Andros. Local supplies are very limited.

EXPLORING ANDROS: Andros is vastly unexplored—and with good reason. Getting around takes some doing. Roads—what roads there are—are badly maintained and potholed, except for the main arteries. Sometimes you're a long way between villages or settlements, and if your car breaks down, all you can do is stop and wait, hoping someone will come along and give you a ride to the next settlement, where (you pray) there will be a skilled mechanic. If you're striking out on an exploration, make sure you have a full tank, as service stations are not plentiful.

All of Andros certainly can't be explored by car, although there is a dream that as Andros develops, it will be linked by a road and causeways stretching some 100 miles or more. Most of the driving and exploring is confined to North Andros, and there only along the eastern sector, going by Nicholl's Town, Morgan's Bluff, and San Andros.

If you're driving in Central Andros or South Andros, motorists must stay on the rough Queen's Highway. The road in the south is paved and better than the one in Central Andros, which should be traveled only in an emergency or by a local.

Divers from all over the world come to explore the **Andros barrier reef,** running parallel to the eastern shore of the island. After Australia's Great Barrier Reef, this is the largest in the world, but unlike the one in Australia, some 200 miles off the coast, the barrier reef of Andros is easily accessible, beginning a few hundred yards offshore.

One side of the reef is a peaceful haven for snorkelers and scuba-divers, who report that the fish are tame (often a grouper will eat from your hand, but don't try it with a moray eel). The water here is from 9 to 15 feet deep. On the other side of the reef it's a different story. The water plunges to a depth of a full mile into the awesome TOTO. One diver reported that, as an adventure, diving in the ocean's tongue was tantamount to a flight to the moon.

Much marine life thrives on the reef, and it attracts nature lovers from all over the world. The weirdly shaped coral formations alone are worth the trip. This is a living, breathing garden of the sea, and its caves are often called "cathedral-like."

For many years the U.S. Navy has conducted research at a station on the edge of TOTO. The research center is at Andros Town. It is devoted to oceanographic, underwater weapons, and antisubmarine research. Called AUTEC (Atlantic Undersea Testing and Evaluation Centre), this is a joint U.S. and British undertaking.

When this station first opened, Androsians predicted that the naval researchers would turn up "Lusca." Like the Loch Ness monster, Lusca had been reported as having been sighted by dozens of locals. The sea serpent was accused of sucking both sailors and their vessels into the dangerous "blue holes" around the island's coastline. No one has captured Lusca yet, but the blue holes do exist, including the most famous—made so by Jacques Cousteau—Uncle Charlie's Blue Hole, which is mysterious and fathomless. The other blue holes are almost as incredible. Essentially, these are openings that plunge more than 200 feet down into coral. They are called "blue" because they appear deep blue against the sunlit shadows of Andros.

One of these holes, called Benjamin's Blue Hole, is named after its discoverer, George Benjamin. In 1967 he found stalactites and stalagmites 1,200 feet below sea level. What was remarkable about this discovery is that stalactites and stalagmites are not created underwater. This has led to much speculation that The Bahamas are actually mountaintops, all that remains of a mysterious continent (Atlantis?) that sank beneath the sea in dim, unrecorded times. Although Cousteau came this way to make a film, making the blue holes of Andros internationally famous, most of them, like most of the surface of the island itself, remain unexplored.

Tour boats leaving from Small Hope Bay Lodge (see below) will take you to these holes.

Near the Small Hope Bay Lodge at Andros Town, Rosi Birch has created an industry, and you can visit the workshop where **Androsia batik** is made (that same Androsia batik sold in the shops of Nassau and Paradise Island). This well-known Bahamian batik is also seen now at fashionable resorts around the world. Androsia's artisans create their designs using hot wax on fine cotton and silk fabrics. The fabrics are then made into island-style wear, including blouses, skirts, caftans, dresses, shirts, scarves, bags, and accessories. All hand-painted and hand-signed, the resortwear comes in dazzling reds, blues, purples, greens, and earth browns. Androsia, of course, takes its name from Andros. You can visit the factory, P.O. Box A-931, Andros Town, Andros, The Bahamas (tel. 809/352-2225), Monday to Saturday from 8:30 a.m. to 4 p.m.

Morgan's Bluff lures men and women hoping to strike it rich. Sir Henry Morgan, the pirate, is supposed to have buried a vast treasure here, which remains undiscovered to this day. Many have searched for it, however, using the most scientific of methods.

Typical of discoveries that continue to make Andros mysterious is **Red Bay Village,** where inhabitants were found in recent times living as a tribe. Their leader was "the chief," and old rituals were religiously followed. The passage of time had made little difference to these people. Now the world comes to their door, and changes are inevitable, although the people still follow their longtime customs. The village, it is believed, was settled sometime in the 1840s by Seminoles and blacks fleeing slavery in Florida. Their location is a small community lying off the northwestern coast of Andros. A causeway now connects them to the mainland, and sightseers can visit. Red Bay Village can be reached by road from Nicholl's Town and San Andros. You should be polite and ask permission before indiscriminately photographing these people.

Birdwatchers are attracted to Andros by its varied bird population. In the dense forests, in trees such as lignum vitae, mahogany, madeira, "horseflesh," and pine, lives a huge feathered population: many parrots, doves, and marsh hens. (Ever hear a whistling duck?)

Botanists are also attracted here, because of the wildflowers of Andros. It is said that some 40 to 50 species of wild orchids thrive here, some that are found nowhere else. New discoveries are also being made, as more and more botanists seek out the rich growth of Andros.

One custom in Andros sounds like the Tennessee Williams drama *Suddenly Last Summer.* This is the catching of land crabs, which must leave their safe and protected terrestrial burrows to march relentlessly to the sea to lay their eggs. This annual ritual occurs between May and September. However, many of these hapless crabs will never have offspring. Both visitors and Androsians walk along the beach with baskets, catching the crustaceans as they march to the sea. Later, they clean them, stuff them, and bake them for dinner.

WHERE TO STAY: Chances are, your hotel will be in North Andros, in either Andros Town or Nicholl's Town, unless you're staying at Las Palmas at South Andros.

North Andros is the most developed of the three main Andros islands. Nicholl's Town here is a colorful old settlement with some 600 people and several places serving local foods. Directly to the south is **Mastic Point,** which was founded in 1781. If you ask around, you'll be shown to a couple of concrete dives that offer spareribs and Goombay music. To the north of Nicholl's Town is **Morgan's Bluff,** a Sir Henry Morgan (a pirate later knighted by the British monarch) namesake.

The major hotel at **Nicholl's Town** is the Andros Beach Hotel & Villas. Most visitors come to Nicholl's Town to buy supplies at a shopping complex.

Andros Town, with its abandoned docks, is another hamlet, lying about a 29-mile drive south of Nicholl's Town. Here the major hotel is Small Hope Bay Lodge. On the opposite side of the water is **Coakley Town.** If you're driving, before you get to Andros Town you may want to stop and spend some restful hours on the beach at the hamlet of **Staniard Creek,** another old settlement on Andros. There's a South Seas aura here.

The major reason most visitors come to Andros Town is either to stay at the already-mentioned Small Hope Bay Lodge or to avail themselves of its facilities. The biggest retail industry, Androsia, is in the area too. The scuba-diving—minutes away on the barrier reef—is what lures the world to this tiny place. Many people come here just for the shelling.

Continuing south, **Central Andros** is smaller than either North or South Andros. It's also the least built-up. Queen's Highway runs along the eastern coastline, but the only thing about this road that's regal is its name. In some 4½ miles you can practically travel the island. Talk about sleepy—this place drowses, and for that very reason many people come here to get away from it all.

They don't find much in the way of accommodations. There are a few guesthouses a half mile from the Mangrove Cay Airport. Boating, fishing, scuba-diving, and snorkeling are the popular sports practiced here.

The island is studded with hundreds upon hundreds of palm trees. Another hamlet (don't blink as you pass through or you'll miss it) is **Moxey Town,** where you'll see the fishermen unloading conch.

Finally, **South Andros** takes in the wonderfully named **Congo Town,** location of Las Palmas Hotel. The pace here is that of an escargot on a marathon. The Queen's Highway, lined in part with pink and white conch shells, runs on for about 25 miles or so. The island, as yet undiscovered, has some of the best beaches in The Bahamas, and you can enjoy them almost by yourself.

Andros Town and Fresh Creek

Small Hope Bay Lodge (tel. 809/368-2014; write c/o P.O. Box 21667, Fort Lauderdale, FL 33335), at Fresh Creek, one of the most important underwater centers in The Bahamas, is an intimate and cozy cottage colony on the beach, engulfed by tall coconut palms. Canada-born Richard Birch created the resort, which now is the oldest dive operation on the island. Its name, Small Hope, shouldn't deter you from a vacation here. It comes from a prediction (so far, accurate) from Henry Morgan, the pirate, who claimed there was "small hope" of anyone finding the treasure he's buried on Andros. There is a spacious living and dining room, as opposed to a "lobby." Here guests congregate for conversational get-togethers and to share meals. Andros Town airport is a ten-minute, $12 taxi ride from the lodge. The beach is at the doorstep, and if you want to get a tan all over, you'll be shown a private terrace surrounded by a thatched palm fence. With 20 cabins, a "full house" means only 40 guests at the lodge. Cabins are of coral rock and Andros pine, decorated with batik Androsia fabrics. Honeymooners like to order breakfast served on their waterbed.

The hotel operates on the all-inclusive plan, including three meals a day. Year-round charges for one night are $130 per person daily based on double occupancy, going up to $250 per person for two nights. For guest groups of three or more, the resort has a limited number of family cottages, featuring two separate rooms connected by a single bath. Single travelers have a choice of staying in a family cottage with private accommodations (which is the same as per person double occupancy) or staying in a regular cottage with private bath, to which $50 per person is added nightly.

The bar is an old boat, dubbed *Panacea.* The food is wholesome, plentiful, and good—conch chowder, lobster, hot johnnycake. The chef will even cook your catch for you. Lunch is a buffet; dinner, a choice of seafood and meat every night. Children dine in the games room. A picnic lunch can be prepared for those who request it. Drinks are offered on a rambling patio built out over the sea where conch fritters are served at evening bar time. Nightlife is spontaneous—that is, dancing in the lounge or on the patio; underwater movies and slides are shown. Or you can play the club's guitar yourself. Definitely don't wear a tie at dinner—the owners have been known to snip it off if you do.

When you're making a reservation, inquire about special dive packages. This is the lodge's specialty (see "The Sporting Life," below). The owners have been diving for three decades, and they have sufficient equipment, divers, boats, and flexibility to give a guest any diving he or she wants, whether it be shallow or deep. The lodge closes from Labor Day to mid-November. For reservations, write the address above, direct dial (phone given above), or call toll free 800/223-6961 in the U.S.

Landmark Hotel & Restaurant, Andros Town, Andros, The Bahamas (tel. 809/328-2082), offers 15 of the most comfortable rooms in Andros Town. Each is sheathed in glowing planks of pinewood, complete with carefully crafted cove moldings, modern windows, big closets, private bath, a balcony, color TV, phone, and air conditioning. All of the finish work on the property was executed by the outgoing owner, Wendall (Skinny) Moxie, who takes an entrepreneurial pride in his property. Each of his rooms costs from $80 per night, single or double occupancy, throughout the year. Calabash Bay Beach is within a five-minute walk of the hotel, and guests rarely lack for companionship because of the lively bar on the premises. It's one of the most popular nightlife spots on the island. Some of the nightclubbing students are from the island's branch of the marine biology studies center. Typical Bahamian meals are served here as well.

Chickcharnie Hotel, Fresh Creek, Andros Town, Andros, The Bahamas (tel. 809/368-2025), is charmingly named after those Bahamian elves with three toes, feathers, and beards, all mischievous red-eyed devils. The location is three miles east of the Andros Town airport. A simple inn, often attracting fishermen and an occasional business traveler, this is a concrete structure, containing eight rooms. Four of the units have air conditioning, private bath, and TV with satellite hookup; these rent for $45 per person. The other four rooms have sinks with hot and cold water, access to a bathroom off the hallway, and ceiling fans; they rent for $45 per person. A third person in any room pays an additional $10. Rates are good all year.

Island-born brothers, Henry and Charles Gay, the owners, maintain a grocery store on the ground floor of the building. A few steps away, in the hotel's spartan dining room, meals are served every day of the week. Breakfast and lunch are offered from 9 a.m. to 2 p.m., while dinner is served from 7 to 10 p.m. Fish, chicken, lobster, or conch dinners cost from $10 to $15.

Nicholl's Town

Andros Beach Hotel, Nicholl's Town, Andros, The Bahamas (tel. 809/329-2582, or toll free 800/327-8150 except in Florida), is a pleasantly informal establishment with a stylish low-rise façade where the 24 air-conditioned accommodations lie beneath coconut palms at the edge of a beach. Many visitors choose only to remain in the sun-dappled shade by the sugar-white beach. The resort is very sports oriented, catering to the needs of visitors who want to go scuba-diving. The hotel has its own pool and dock. Occasional live entertainment is provided after Bahamian dinners in the oceanfront dining room or on the garden-style terrace. Each unit of the hotel has a private patio, two double beds, and a private bath. Rates for the accommodations stay the same throughout the year: single or double rooms cost $75, and cottages range from $90 for two.

Tradewind Villas, P.O. Box 4465, Nicholl's Town, Andros, The Bahamas (tel. 809/329-2040), owned and operated by the Friedmann family, rents out 16 private air-conditioned units, consisting of two bedrooms, a living room, a fully equipped kitchen, and a patio. The site opens onto two miles of beach. Nearby is a mini-market. Dress is very informal. At night, if you don't want to cook, there is a restaurant nearby, or you can go to the Andros Beach Hotel. The barrier reef is 200 yards offshore, and the place has its own freshwater pool. Year-round rates are from $70 daily for two persons, EP. Sailboats and complete scuba and snorkeling equipment (as well as instruction) are available.

Lowe Sound

Kevin's Guest House, Lone Sound, Nicholl's Town, Andros, The Bahamas (tel. 809/329-2517). Built in 1986, and connected by the same management to

Big Josh Seafood Restaurant & Lounge a few steps away, this is one of the most recently built motels on the island. Josh Bootle is one of the best bonefishermen guides in Andros, so that speaks a lot for the clientele. The hotel contains only half a dozen windowless rooms, each simply furnished (including a queen-size bed), but with air conditioning and satellite-connected TV. Single or double rooms cost from $65 a day. The hotel is named after one of the Bootle sons. Naturally, you take your meals in the nearby restaurant (see below).

Behring Point

Nottages Cottages, Fresh Creek, Behring Point, Andros, The Bahamas (tel. 809/329-4293). Set on a knoll above the waterway separating North Andros and Mangrove Cay, this clean and stylish guesthouse is fronted with a garden of croton and hibiscus. A favorite with bonefishermen, it has as its social center a blue-and-white dining room where West Bahamian food is served to guests and visiting nonresidents. You can stay in one of ten well-furnished motel-like rooms whose glass windows face the sea, or in an outlying cottage equipped with a kitchenette. Year-round rates based on double occupancy are from $100 per person, including all meals. Four people can rent the cottage from $165 daily without meals. Daisy Nottage is the owner.

Charlie's Haven, Behring Point, Andros, The Bahamas (tel. 809/329-5261) lies about 25 miles from Andros Town Airport near what are said to be some of the best bonefishing banks in the world. This is a remote outpost for fishermen who like the rustic but comfortable hospitality. Many anglers who check in here have tried other fishing spots throughout The Bahamas, ultimately finding this place and returning again and again. It is the very isolation and rather rawboned qualities that appeal to many patrons, most of whom are men, although families of fishermen sometimes come too. As you can imagine, many tall tales of fish that got away are swapped over the informal meals served here. There's occasionally live entertainment following the evening meal, as well as a separate bar area.

The unpainted concrete building sits on the edge of the sound separating North Andros from Mangrove Cay. There are only seven bedrooms, all with air conditioning, ceiling fans, simple white walls, a minimum of furniture, and plenty of space to store fishing rods and tackle. With all meals included, singles rent from $85 daily and doubles go for $140, throughout the year. Most visitors invest in one of the establishment's packages that include fishing, hotel, and restaurant costs. Three days of fishing with four nights of accommodation, for example, cost $675 per person, double occupancy, or $1,150 for a single. Charles Smith, assisted by Prescott, one of his many sons, is the owner and probably Andros Island's leading and most respected bonefish guide.

Mangrove Cay

In Central Andros you'll find a cluster of guesthouses and cottages that offer not only the cheapest living in Andros, but some of the least expensive accommodations in The Bahamas. However, it should be pointed out that this is strictly "no-frills" living. Rooms during the day are often hot and stuffy, and the basic physical plants, meager as they are, aren't always in mint condition. But for those who want to rough it, the way many Bahamians do themselves when they visit Andros for the weekend from Nassau, here are some rawbone selections. You may or may not have a private bath. In addition, forget about a phone in your room.

Bannister Guest House, Lisbon Creek, Mangrove Cay, Andros, The Bahamas (tel. 809/329-4188), is a cluster of modern stone bungalows, where life is most informal. The place is simple, for independent and self-sufficient travelers only. *The price of a room in summer either single or double occupancy is $35 per person* *daily, with three meals included.* The winter rate, single or double, is $45 per person daily. The complex, with only a handful of rooms (one with air conditioning), lies eight miles from the Mangrove Cay airstrip. Ever since a yachting guide to The Bahamas praised the Bahamian cookery of Sylvia Bannister, yachtsmen have been turning up at their door for a good-tasting meal of local specialties, including lots of fresh seafood. Leroy's Harbour Bar is *the* place to congregate in the village. He also has a pool at his club that is filled with hawksbill turtles, conch, and several other kind of fish. He can also arrange for fishing, scuba-diving, and rental boats, along with cars and bicycles.

Longley Guest House, Lisbon Creek, Mangrove Cay, Andros, The Bahamas (tel. 809/329-4311). Bernard Longley is one of the best-known men on Mangrove Cay. He says that if you like "swimming, snorkeling, fishing, beautiful sandy beaches," then come visit his place. His rock house, shaded by awnings, is a basic structure, lying seven miles from the airport. He rents out five bedrooms, charging $20 per day year-round per person for double occupancy, $25 single. They charge $15 for three meals per day. There is a private beach, and bicycles can also be rented. Everything is casual here.

South Andros

Las Palmas Beach Hotel, P.O. Box 800, The Bluff, Andros, The Bahamas (tel. 809/329-4661). Staying here is a lot like staying at a beachside ranch. The hotel has only 20 modest accommodations, which are set on five miles of beachfront on an island containing 10,000 palm trees. The hotel is informally casual—a place to get away from urban life for a sojourn on a white sand beach. No one minds if you wear jeans or a bikini all day long. Guests are treated like members of the family.

There are a freshwater swimming pool, a tennis court, and shuffleboard, scattered over the palm-studded property. The cocktail lounge offers live musical entertainment, and there's sometimes a live native show. The dining room features Bahamian seafood, including broiled lobster and grouper prepared in the local style. Outdoor steak barbecues and seafood buffets are sometimes held. Rooms are large, and some are air-conditioned, and situated directly on the sands of the beach. Year-round rates for single or double accommodations are $45 to $65.

South Bight marina is 1½ miles away, serving as a yacht anchorage for anyone who wants to arrive by boat. The hotel is two miles from the Congo Town airport. You can rent a car, or there are bicycles available if you wish.

WHERE TO DINE: Andros follows the rest of The Bahamas in its cuisine. Conch, in all its many variations, is the staple of most diets, along with heaping peas 'n' rice and johnnycake, pig souse, or chicken souse.

The best places to dine are at the major hotels, including those previously recommended: the **Chickcharnie Hotel,** Fresh Creek, near Andros Town (tel. 809/328-3025); and if you're in South Andros, **Las Palmas,** outside Congo Town (tel. 809/329-4661). Most guests book into these hotels on the modified American plan, which frees them to shop around for lunch. At any of these hotels a dinner will run around $25, maybe less. Sometimes, if business has been slow, you might drop in and find nothing on the stove. You take your chance.

If you're touring the island during the day, you'll find some local spots that serve food.

If you're heading south, you might want to know about **Green View Restaurant,** Cargill Creek (tel. 809/329-5097). In a pleasant and cozy white house beside the main highway, this establishment is inextricably tied up with the warmhearted personality of its owner, Elias Bain. Its only drawback is that meals must be ordered in advance by phone, since it opens only when it's assured of business. Many of your fellow diners will be American oceanographers from the island's sea exploration base. Fixed-price dinners cost from $12 each, plus tip, with ingredients to be mutually agreed upon before your arrival. Typical dinners might include seafood, cracked conch, grouper cutlets, crayfish, and chicken. Meals are served any time you want them between 9 a.m. and 9:30 p.m.

Or if you're heading north, try to make it to Nicholl's Town in time for lunch. There, **Eva's Picaroon** (tel. 809/329-2607) is the most welcoming restaurant in town. Contained in a low-slung building a few steps from the beach, it's the undisputed domain of one of Andros's wisest and best-recommended chefs, Mrs. Eva Henfield. You order your meals at a rectangular bar near the entrance, then proceed into an airy dining room with multipatterned curtains, a pseudo-vaulted ceiling, and windows on three sides. There really isn't much of a printed menu: only the dishes Mrs. Henfield has ingredients for at the moment. My most recent meal consisted of an overflowing platter of chicken and barbecued ribs, a mound of coleslaw, bread, butter, and Hawaiian punch. All this, plus a preliminary bowl of vegetable soup, cost $10 per person. The establishment is open daily except Sunday from 7 a.m. to 9 p.m.

Mrs. Henfield also rents out a quartet of well-scrubbed and decent rooms from her private home about four blocks away. Each has a table fan, a shared bath, and access to a communal kitchen for the preparation of meals. Single or double occupancy throughout the year costs $40 per person. For information about the rooms, call Mrs. Henfield.

Dorothy's Palm Tree Restaurant, Swamp Street (tel. 809/329-2373), also in Nicholl's Town, is an alternative choice. Amid a simple modern decor of tiles and exposed wood, you can enjoy the ambience created by the owners, Joniah Walkes and his wife, Dorothy. Breakfast here costs from $5; lunch or dinner, from $10 per person. The establishment is open every Monday through Saturday from 8 a.m. to 10 p.m. and on Sunday from 8 a.m. to 6 p.m. Your meal is likely to include such dishes as bean soup, steamed conch, steamed pork chops, the catch of the day, peas 'n' rice, and coleslaw.

If you're on the trail of the bonefishermen who hang out at Lowe Sound, you'll find good local dishes at a very typical place, the **Big Josh Seafood Restaurant and Lounge** (tel. 809/329-2517), which, like the above recommendations, keeps those long hours from 7 a.m. to 2 a.m. daily except Sunday. In air conditioning, you can drop in for breakfast, ordering corned beef and grits or ham and eggs. Later you might try their conch chowder for lunch or one of their main dishes, such as Bahamian lobster, boiled fish, pork chops, grouper, fried Bahamian chicken, or tasty steaks, each accompanied by johnnycake. Meals cost from $12. Mixed drinks, beer, and a limited selection of wine are also sold. Incidentally, Big Josh is Joshua Bootle, one of the finest bonefishing guides on the island. His wife, Malvese, does the cooking, and she's a charmer.

THE SPORTING LIFE: Golfers and tennis pros should go elsewhere, but those who want some of the best bonefishing and scuba-diving in The Bahamas flock to Andros. I'll survey where to find the best of local sports for those who want to abandon the beach for a while.

Fishing

As widely touted, Andros is called the "Bonefish Capital of the World." The actual capital is Lowe Sound Settlement, a tiny hamlet with only one road. It lies four miles north of Nicholl's Town. Fishermen go here to hire bonefish guides.

Regardless of what area you're staying in—North Andros, Central Andros, or South Andros—someone at your hotel can arrange for you to go fishing.

One of the best places is **Charlie's Haven** at Behring Point (tel. 809/328-

2178), already recommended as a rustic hotel. Bonefishing trips are arranged for $100 for a half day, $180 for a full day. Deep-sea fishing is also available.

Fishing is also arranged at **Small Hope Bay Lodge** (tel. 809/368-2014) at Andros Town. A guide will take you to where there is superb bonefishing, and tackle and bait are provided. A half day costs $90, and a full day goes for $175. If you want to go fishing on the North Bight, you must add $60 for transportation.

Scuba and Snorkeling

As mentioned several times, scuba-divers and snorkelers are attracted to Andros because of the barrier reef, which lies on the eastern shore along the Tongue of the Ocean. Blue holes, coral gardens, drop-offs, wall and reef diving, and wrecks make it even more enticing. The best dive operations are previewed below.

Small Hope Bay Lodge, P.O. Box N-1131 in Nassau (tel. 809/326-2014, 305/463-9130 in Florida, or toll free 800/223-6961), at Fresh Creek, Andros Town, lies a short distance from the barrier reef, with its still-unexplored caves and ledges. A staff of trained dive instructors at the lodge caters to levels of expertise from beginners to experienced divers, the staff having various credentials including certification from many of the world's professional diving organizations. Snorkeling expeditions can be arranged as well as scuba outings, and the staff even claims to be able to teach novices to dive even if they can't swim, beginning with the steps off the establishment's docks. The visibility of the water exceeds 100 feet on most days, with temperatures ranging from 72° to 84° Fahrenheit.

Without hotel accommodations, half-day excursions to the reef, with snorkeling gear included, cost $10; with scuba gear, $25. Scuba instruction is free. Night dives cost $30 per person and require a minimum of six participants. To stay at the hotel here for five nights and six days, all inclusive (meals, tips, taxes, airport transfers, and the like), costs $575 per person.

All guests are allowed access to the beachside hot whirlpool as well as to all facilities of the hotel, such as use of Sunfish, windsurfers, and bicycles free.

Neal Watson, an American holder of two world dive records who made his reputation in Bimini and now runs the dive activities at Chub Cay Club in the Berry Islands (see the preceding section of this chapter), has a branch of his operation called **Andros Undersea Adventures,** Andros Beach Hotel and Villas (tel. 809/329-2582), at Nicholl's Town. It takes advantage of the proximity to the Andros Barrier Reef, offering a complete dive package with a full array of options for interested participants. Simple rentals of the equipment you need can be arranged if you're qualified, although many guests prefer the complete package, with transportation included. A handful of experienced instructors and guides will show you sections of the barrier reef and the Tongue of the Ocean.

When not included in the price of a package, single-tank dives cost $35, two-tank dives go for $50, and three-tankers cost $60. Night dives, minimum of four or more persons, are $40 per person. All equipment is included. Half-day snorkeling trips cost $25 per person. Prices per packages, which include hotel accommodations, vary with the number of days a visitor wants to spend. The cost includes round-trip air fare from Fort Lauderdale or Nassau, land transfers, three meals a day, taxes, tips, and double occupancy. Three days and two nights, which includes seven dives, cost $395. Similar packages cover eight days, seven nights, and 22 dives, for a charge of $895. Single occupancy on any package requires an additional $35 per day.

For additional information, write to Andros Undersea Adventures, P.O. Box 21766, Fort Lauderdale, FL 33335. In Florida or Canada, call 305/763-2188. Outside of Florida, call 800/327-8150 toll free in the U.S.

CHAPTER XII

THE ABACOS

□ □ □

1. WALKER'S CAY
2. GREEN TURTLE CAY (NEW PLYMOUTH)
3. TREASURE CAY
4. MARSH HARBOUR
5. GREAT GUANA CAY
6. MAN-O-WAR CAY
7. ELBOW CAY (HOPE TOWN)
8. LITTLE HARBOUR

The northernmost of the Bahamas—called "the top of The Bahamas"—the Abacos form a boomerang-shaped mini-archipelago, 130 miles long, consisting of both Great Abaco and Little Abaco as well as a sprinkling of cays (pronounced keys).

Ponce de León landed here in 1513, looking for the Fountain of Youth. Visitors, many of them retired Americans, still arrive searching, if not for eternal youth, at least for a pleasant way of life that has disappeared from much of the world.

Fishermen find some of the finest offshore fishing in The Bahamas, and yachtsmen call this "the world's most beautiful cruising grounds" (an appellation also used to describe the Exumas—I'll give them a tie). In the interior are wild boar, and, I am told, wild ponies, although I've never seen the latter.

The location, at least of the Abaco airports, is 200 miles east of Miami and 75 miles north of Nassau.

The Abacos are the leading and most visited attraction in The Bahamas, after Nassau, Paradise Island, and Freeport/Lucaya. The weather is about 10° Fahrenheit warmer than in southern Florida, but if you visit in January or February, don't expect every day will be beach weather. Remember, Miami and Fort Lauderdale, even Key West, can get chilly at times. When winter squalls hit, temperatures can drop to the high 40s in severe cases. Spring in the Abacos, however, is one of the most glorious and balmy seasons in all the islands. In summer it gets very hot around noon, but if you do as the islanders do and find a shady spot, the trade winds will cool you off.

Once the waters around Abaco swarmed with Robert Louis Stevenson–type pirates and treasure ships. It is estimated that 500 to 600 Spanish galleons—many treasure laden—went to their watery graves in and around the reefs of

Abaco. To this day, an occasional old silver coin or a doubloon is found along the beaches, particularly after a storm.

Many of the Bahamians who live in Abaco are descendants of Loyalists who left New England or the Carolinas during the American Revolution. An Elizabethan accent still exists in their speech. They founded towns like New Plymouth and Hope Town that are reminiscent of New England fishing villages. Many of these early settlers were shipbuilders, and they naturally brought that skill with them. To this day many Abaconians claim that the finest island boats are those built with Abaco pine by the Man-O-War Cay artisans. Abaco is still the boatbuilding center of The Bahamas, and it is also rather grandly acclaimed as "the finest sailing capital" in the world.

Other early settlers were farmers who, when they found that they could not make a living in that line—the soil wasn't fertile enough—turned to wrecking (the business of salvaging ships that were wrecked or foundered on the reefs). Since there wasn't a lighthouse in the Abacos until 1836, many vessels crashed on the shoals and rocks, and salvagers legally claimed the cargoes, at the same time saving the lives of crews and passengers when possible. However, this enterprise became so profitable that some unscrupulous wreckers deliberately misled ships to their doom and became rich from the spoils.

Most of the pockets of "Tories"—descendants of the British Loyalists—still live on Elbow Cay, Green Turtle Cay, and Man-O-War Cay. From a sightseeing point of view, these are the main islands of the Abacos to visit, having more interest, in my opinion, than "mainland" Abaco. The first-timer will likely head for Treasure Cay, Marsh Harbour, even Walker's Cay or Green Turtle, but repeat visitors learn more esoteric destinations.

Regular tourists now visit the Abacos because of the first-rate resorts. However, for many years it was a preferred cruising ground for the yachting set who like to sail in what they call "the Sea of Abaco," perhaps the finest cruising waters not only in The Bahamas but also in the Caribbean. Yachting people know of such quaintly named places as Little Pigeon Cay, Tea Table Cay, and Umbrella Cay.

As to accommodations, you can expect special resorts, offering a combination of tropical rusticity and sporting elegance. These are places where ocean-going yachts anchor and celebrities, even U.S. presidents (retired), escape. You may encounter an industrialist on the tennis court, a foreign head of state by the pool, a movie star by the bar, or a princess strolling along the beach. Or you may beachcomb for hours, encountering no one at all.

You have a choice of first-class resorts, cottage colonies for self-sufficient types, and a scattering of guesthouses.

Fishing, swimming, and boating—especially boating—are the top sports on the Abacos. There are also diving, golf, and tennis. If you're a boating type, the favorite pastime is to rent a small boat, pack a picnic (or have it done for you), and head for one of the cays just big enough for two.

Excellent marine facilities, with guides, charter parties, and boat rentals are available on Great Guana Cay, Green Turtle Cay, Hope Town, Marsh Harbour, Treasure Cay, and Walker's Cay. Sunfish, Sailfish, Hobie Cats, and Morgan bareboats are available. In fact, Marsh Harbour is the bareboat charter center of the northern Bahamas.

Anglers from all over the world come to test their skill against the blue marlin, kingfish, dolphin, yellowfin tuna, sailfish, wahoo, amberjack, and grouper. Fishing tournaments abound at Walker's Cay. There are plenty of Boston Whalers for bottom fishing and Makos for reef fishing and trolling. Many cruisers for deep-sea fishing can be rented.

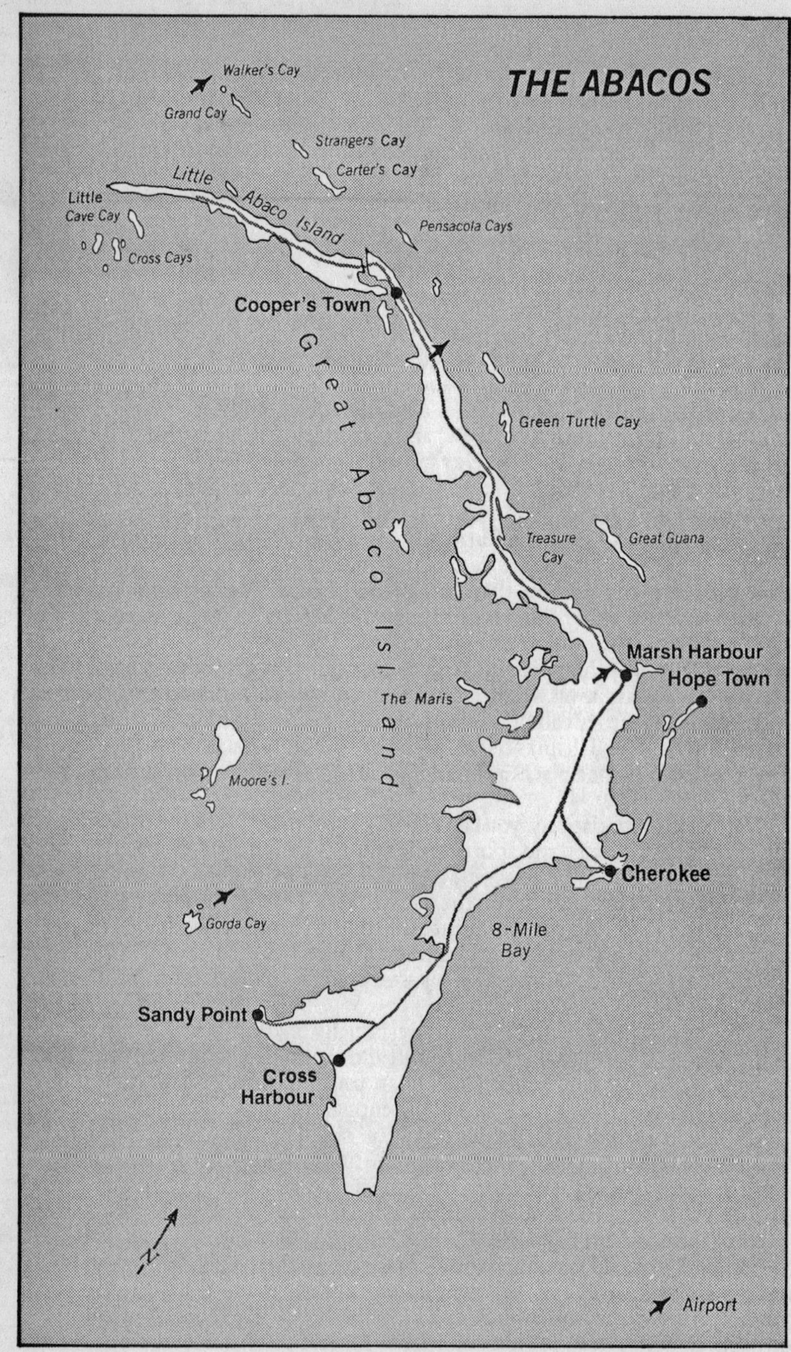
THE ABACOS
Walker's Cay
Grand Cay
Strangers Cay
Carter's Cay
Little Abaco Island
Little Cave Cay
Cross Cays
Pensacola Cays
Cooper's Town
Great Abaco Island
Green Turtle Cay
Treasure Cay
Great Guana
Marsh Harbour
Hope Town
The Maris
Moore's I.
Cherokee
Gorda Cay
8-Mile Bay
Sandy Point
Cross Harbour
N
Airport

Scuba-divers can dive to the depths with UNEXSO (Underwater Explorers Society) and discover Abaco's caverns, inland "blue holes," coral reefs and gardens, along with marine preserves, and wrecks. Night dives are featured. Top-rated dive centers can be found at Marsh Harbour, Hope Town, Treasure Cay, and Walker's Cay, all offering NAUI/PADI instructors and a full line of equipment sales, rentals, and air-fills.

GETTING THERE: Three airports service the Abacos: Marsh Harbour (the major one), Treasure Cay, and Walker's Cay. The official points of entry are Marsh Harbour, Treasure Cay, Walker's Cay, and Green Turtle Cay (New Plymouth). Green Turtle Cay doesn't have an airstrip, but many people of the yachting set clear Customs and Immigration there.

Many visitors arrive from Nassau or Miami on **Bahamasair.** Flight schedules change frequently in The Bahamas, but you can usually get a daily flight out of Nassau, going first to Marsh Harbour, then on to Treasure Cay. If you're in Miami, you can usually get a morning flight to Marsh Harbour. There is also service from Miami on to Treasure Cay.

There are several smaller carriers that also service the area from the Florida mainland.

Aero Coach also flies in (see "Flying to The Bahamas," Chapter VI), with trips to both Marsh Harbour and Treasure Cay in the Abacos among its 70 scheduled daily flights to The Bahamas. Flights are from West Palm Beach, Fort Lauderdale, and Miami. For information and reservations, call 305/359-1600 in Fort Lauderdale, or 800/827-0010 toll free.

Piedmont/Henson (tel. toll free 800/251-5720) flies from Fort Lauderdale to Treasure Cay and Marsh Harbour, with a return flight to the Florida city.

By Mailboat

The mailboat M/V *Deborah I K II* leaves from Potter's Cay Dock in Nassau, going to Cherokee Sound, Green Turtle Cay, Hope Town, and Marsh Harbour. It departs on Wednesday, and the trip to the Abacos takes seven hours. The return is on Monday.

In addition, M/V *Champion II* also heads out from Potter's Cay Dock in Nassau on Thursday, calling first at Sandy Point, then More's Island, and Bullock's Harbour before returning to Nassau on Saturday.

For details of sailings and costs, passengers should get in touch with the dockmaster at Potter's Cay Dock in Nassau (tel. 809/323-1064). One-way fares range from \$20 to \$30 per person.

GETTING AROUND: Unmetered **taxis,** often shared with other passengers, meet all arriving planes. They will take you to your hotel if it's on "mainland" Abaco; otherwise, they will deposit you at a dock where you can hop aboard a **water taxi** to one of the neighboring offshore islands like Green Turtle Cay or Elbow Cay.

It's also possible to make arrangements for a **taxi tour** of Great Abaco or Little Abaco. These, however, are expensive. You don't really see that much either. It's much better to go sightseeing in one of the Loyalist settlements, such as New Plymouth. That you can do on foot.

If you want to risk the potholed roads of Abaco, you can rent a car, usually for \$50 a day. Try **H & L Car Rentals,** Don MacKay Boulevard, P.O. Box 490, Marsh Harbour (tel. 809/367-2840).

Mostly, you'll probably use **Albury's Ferry Service** (tel. 809/367-2306). Its departures from Marsh Harbour coincide with incoming and outgoing flights. It provides ferry connections to Elbow Cay (Hope Town) and Man-O-

War Cay, a 20-minute trip to each destination. The round-trip fare is $12 if you return the same day. The boats run from Hope Town and from Man-O-War Cay to Marsh Harbour at 8 a.m. and 1:30 p.m. daily, making the run from Marsh Harbour to the two island ports at 10:30 a.m. and 4 p.m. For car-ferry service to Green Turtle Cay, refer to the writeup on that cay below.

We'll begin our exploration of the Abacos with the northernmost point, Walker's Cay, then descend in a southerly route.

1. WALKER'S CAY

This is the northernmost and outermost of the Abaco chain of islands, and one of the smallest, lying at the edge of the Bahama Bank. The cay produces its own fresh water and electricity. Coral reefs surrounding this island drop off to depths of some 1,000 feet. It's known around the world as one of the best deep-sea fishing resorts, and has been featured on the ABC-TV network's "American Sportsman" on several occasions. It is usually mentioned as being "The Top of The Bahamas."

Ponce de León is said to have stopped here in 1513 looking for fresh water. That was just six days before he discovered Florida. From the 17th century, this was a place known to pirates who stored their booty here. It became a bastion for blockade runners during the American Civil War, and later it was a hideout for rum-runners in the days of U.S. Prohibition.

To reach it, Walker's Cay Hotel and Marina operates its own plane service, part of Walker's Cay Airline, operating out of Walker's Cay Jet Center in Fort Lauderdale. The airline makes 45-minute flights daily to the island.

Walker's Cay Hotel and Marina, Walker's Cay, Abaco, The Bahamas (tel. 305/522-1469 in Fort Lauderdale, or toll free 800/327-3714, 800/432-2092 in Florida) has the largest full-service, privately owned marina in the Abacos, and each year they run what has become the largest deep-sea fishing tournament in The Bahamas. It is often a favorite rendezvous point for major firms and was named as one of the ten best getaways in the world by *Travel and Leisure, Life Styles of the Rich and Famous,* and *Playboy.*

The hotel has 71 air-conditioned and attractively furnished villas and bedrooms, each with a view of the ocean from your own private terrace. In either a single or double, EP rates range from $135 to $165 daily. "The season," incidentally, is from mid-March to May 31. *In the off-season, from June 1 through the middle of February, rates drop to $110 to $145 per day, either single or double occupancy.* If you're planning a winter visit, ask a travel agent (or else call directly) to see if the resort will still be offering its "Not for Everyone Package." Its most recent one (good through the winter until the end of February) includes three days and two nights with round-trip air fare from Fort Lauderdale or West Palm Beach for $285 per person. Of course, the villas and ocean-view suites are more expensive. For breakfast and dinner, add another $29.50 per person daily.

The food is good, with an assortment of American and Bahamian specialties. The chef bakes his own bread and pastries, and there is also an excellent wine selection. Bahamian lobster and conch fritters are invariably featured, along with fresh fish. The Deep Jigger lounge evokes the early Bahamas of Hemingway, and the Marlin Room and dining terrace overlook the sea. In season, guests can dance to disco music in the Lobster Trap Lounge, at Marina North Dock. There are two all-weather tennis courts, and the resort offers every kind of water sport from scuba to ski, along with freshwater and saltwater swimming. Some of the finest offshore fishing in The Bahamas is just five minutes from the 75-slip marina (many world records have been set here).

To write for a reservation, address your letter to Walker's Cay Hotel and Marina, 700 S.W. 34th St., Fort Lauderdale, FL 33315.

2. GREEN TURTLE CAY (NEW PLYMOUTH)

Three miles off the east coast of Great Abaco, Green Turtle Cay is the jewel of the archipelago, a little island with an uneven coastline, deep bays, sounds, and good beaches, one of the best stretching for 3,600 feet. There are green forests, gentle hills, and secluded inlets. The island is 3½ miles long and half a mile across, and lies some 170 miles due east of Palm Beach, Florida.

Water depths seldom exceed 15 to 20 feet inside the string of cays that trace the outer edge of the Bahama Bank. It is the reefs outside the cays that provide the abundance of underwater flora and fauna that delights snorkelers and fishermen. The coral gardens that make up an inner and an outer reef teem with colorful sea life, and shelling on the beaches and offshore sandbars is considered among the finest in The Bahamas.

If you have a boat, you can explore such deserted islands as Fiddle Cay to the north and No Name Cay and Pelican Cay to the south of Green Turtle Cay.

New Plymouth, at the southern tip of the cay, is an 18th-century settlement that has the flavor of a New England sailing port back in the days when such towns were filled with boatbuilders and fishermen. Much of the masonry of the original town was made from lime produced from conch shells, broken up, burned, and sifted for cement. Records say that the alkali content was so high that it would burn the hands of the masons who used it.

Clapboard houses with gingerbread trim line the narrow streets of the little town, which once had a population of 1,800 people, now shrunk to 400. Green Turtle Cay became known for the skill of its shipbuilders, although the industry, like many others in the area, failed when total emancipation of the slaves came in The Bahamas in 1838. Today the streets lie somnolent in the sun most of the time, except when a festival is under way or when people are going to church on Sunday.

Parliament is the village's main street, and you can walk its entire length in only ten minutes, perhaps acknowledged only by the clucking of a few hens. Many of the houses have front porches, usually occupied in the evening, as people take the breezes and watch their small world go by. The people here are friendly but not outgoing, having lived for generations far from the madding crowd.

The settlers of New Plymouth were Loyalists who found their way here from other parts of the Abacos shortly before the end of the 18th century, with some "new" blood thrown in when émigrés from Eleuthera moved to Marsh Harbour and other Abaconian settlements. The people today are mostly named Curry, Lowe, Russell, Roberts, and especially Sawyer. Because they all came from the same rootstock—English, Welsh, and Scottish—and because of a long history of intermarriage, many of the faces are amazingly similar: deeply tanned, often freckled skin, blue eyes, and red or blond hair. Most of them, even in these sun-worshipping days, wear broad-brimmed hats to protect themselves from the sun.

One morning I spent an hour with a life-long resident. The next morning encountering what I took to be the same man on the ferryboat, I resumed our conversation, only to learn I was talking to a different man entirely. "No relation," he said, until chided by a woman passenger, which elicited from him, "Well, I think my mother's cousin did marry. . . ."

The insularity of these people has also caused their speech patterns to retain many facets of those their forebears brought from the mother country, with even a smattering of Cockney to flavor it. Many drop their initial letter *H,* using it instead at the beginning of words that start with vowels. You may hear someone ordering "'am" and with it some "heggs." Also, the letter *V* is often pronounced as *W,* and vice versa.

Many of the inhabitants of New Plymouth today are engaged in turtling, lobstering, shark fishing, and sponging. New Plymouth is a sister city to Key West, Florida, and if you have ever visited there, you'll see startling similarities between the American people of "conch" descent and the Abaconians, even to their wrecking history, fishing industries, and appearance.

A big event in the day-to-day life of the people of New Plymouth is the arrival at the Government Dock of the mailboat from Nassau. People gather there also whenever the ferryboat is arriving or leaving, just to keep tabs on what's going on.

There is no auto traffic in New Plymouth except for a few service vehicles—but who needs a car? You can walk all the way around the village in a fairly brief stroll.

New Plymouth celebrated its bicentennial in 1984 by opening a **Memorial Sculpture Garden** in the center of town. A monument honors American Loyalists and also some of their notable descendants, including Albert Lowe, a pioneer boatbuilder and historian.

A MUSEUM OF CHARACTER: No visitor to New Plymouth should miss seeing the **Albert Lowe Museum** (tel. 409/365-4089) on Parliament Street where the one-block King Street up from the dock comes to a dead end. This museum, more than anything else I've seen in The Bahamas, gives a view of the rawboned and sometimes difficult history of the Family Islands. You could easily spend a couple of hours reading the fine print of the dozens of photographs that show the hardship and the valor of the citizens who changed industries as often as the economic circumstances of their era dictated.

There's a garden in the back of the beautifully restored Loyalist home, where Ivy Roberts, the caretaker, will give you a guided tour of the stone kitchen, which occupants of the house used as a shelter when a hurricane devastated much of New Plymouth in 1932. Inside the house a narrow stairway leads to a trio of bedrooms that reveal simplicity as the keynote of 18th-century life on Green Turtle Cay.

A plaque in the memorabilia-packed parlor of the house proudly declares: "The museum is dedicated to those Loyalists who crossed the Gulf Stream to settle among the islands of The Bahamas, particularly those who settled on or near the islands of Abaco, and their descendants." Amid Victorian settees, irreplaceable photographs, and island artifacts, you'll see a number of handsome ship models, the work of Albert Lowe, for whom the museum was named.

Also displayed are paintings by Alton Lowe, son of the former boatbuilder who keeps his craft alive by making the models and for whom the museum is named.

Alton Lowe founded the museum. Cherub-faced and red-haired, Alton, who now resides in Miami most of the time, has for some time been one of the best-known painters in The Bahamas. His works hang in collections all over the world. The Bahamian government asked him to paint a landscape, which it then presented to Prince Charles and Lady Diana as a wedding present.

Many of Alton Lowe's paintings have been used as the background for Bahamian postage stamps, blowups of which are displayed in the museum. Whoever guides you on your tour might open the basement of the house for you as well. Here you'll see some of Alton Lowe's work, as well as that of other local painters, for sale.

The entrance fee for this unusual museum is $3. Hours are flexible, usually from 9:30 to 11:30 a.m. and 1 to 3 p.m. Monday through Saturday.

GETTING THERE: Most guests fly to Treasure Cay Airport where a taxi will take them to the ferry dock for departures to Green Turtle Cay (New Plymouth).

At the dock, you may have to wait a while for the ferry or else have one called for you. It's about a ten-minute ride to Green Turtle Cay from the dock. The ferry will take you to the Green Turtle Club, if you're staying there, or to New Plymouth. This land and sea transfer costs $10 per person.

PRACTICAL FACTS: There's no crime in New Plymouth, unless you import it yourself. There is a little jail made of stone, which makes visitors chuckle: the doors have fallen off. No one can remember when, if ever, it held a prisoner.

Banks: Service is limited. **Barclay's Bank PLC** operates a branch (tel. 809/365-4144), open only from 10 a.m. to 1 p.m. every Thursday.

Churches: The people of New Plymouth, for the most part, are deeply religious. With such a small population, they manage to support five churches. The Anglican church is the oldest, dating from 1786.

Medical care: If you need medical attention on Green Turtle Cay, there is a clinic (tel. 809/365-4222), run by a nurse.

Post office: Green Turtle Cay's post office (tel. 809/365-4242) is entered through a pink door. It has the only public telephone on the island.

Shopping: In New Plymouth, there are several gift shops, and well-stocked grocery stores feature freshly baked Bahamian bread.

WHERE TO STAY: One of my favorite getaway places in the Family Islands is the **Green Turtle Club,** Green Turtle Cay, Abaco, The Bahamas (tel. 809/367-2572). This is where such celebrities as Christopher Reeve, Tanya Tucker, Kenny Rogers, and former President Jimmy Carter have gone for a retreat from the pressures of daily life. The resort was built on a half-moon-shaped beach off which yachts of all sizes ride at anchor. The flag-festooned bar is the social center of the resort, which was originally built as a boathouse. Today its ambience is very much that of a clubhouse, lodge, and country club, capped with heavy rafters and flanked on one side by a panoramic veranda and on the other by a pine-covered dining room.

The Green Turtle Yacht Club has its base here. It's associated with the Birdham Yacht Club, one of the oldest in England, and with the Palm Beach Yacht Club. Members have their own villas right on the water, often with private docks, although temporary guests will be lodged in exceptionally spacious bungalows set on the side of the hill. There are no locked doors on this tree-dotted estate. Also, the only telephone is the one in the main office, where the polite staff can organize a full array of sporting as well as sightseeing excursions.

Single or double occupancy of regular rooms cost from $135 daily in winter, *the tariffs lowered to $110 in summer.* Poolside suites for two cost $150 daily in winter, *dropping to $110 in summer.* To rent a villa in winter, two persons pay $375 daily, *but only $264 in summer.* At Christmas, prices go up slightly. Each additional adult in a room pays $18 per day, and children up to age 12 share free. MAP is an additional $36 for adults, $25 for children.

There's an unmistakably British note here: in the evening, meals that begin with before-dinner cocktails beside a roaring fire in the bar (in chilly weather only, of course), as well as in the courteous staff who offer assistance yet don't intrude on anyone's tranquility. Some guests choose to walk the several miles into New Plymouth as part of their daily exercise regimes, although if you prefer a boat ride, someone from the hotel will arrange for you to go on one of the several daily trips. The waters around the resort are shallow enough that landlubbers can spot schools of fish and sometimes even a green turtle paddling along above the sandbanks. Nature has blessed the resort with enough visual splendor to more than make up for its relative isolation. There's a swimming pool dug into one of the flower-dotted hillsides in case swimmers don't want to bathe in the turquoise waters off the hotel's beach.

To get here, most guests arrive at the Treasure Cay airport, then take a taxi (there are usually plenty there) to the ferry dock. From there, a water taxi will take you to the club.

Bluff House Club & Marina, Green Turtle Cay, Abaco, The Bahamas (tel. 809/365-4247, 305/443-3821, or toll free 800/327-0787), is managed by an English-born brother-and-sister team, Martin Havill and Barbara Bartley. The main building has octagonal walls of paneling or glass, slow-whirling tropical fans, wicker furnishings, and polished wooden floors. The dining room has a pitched, beamed ceiling. A wide wooden deck surrounds the swimming pool, sheltered by palms and with a view of the ocean.

Bluff House has 40 pine-forested, oceanfront acres rising from a sandy beach. The kitchen uses local conch, kingfish, grouper, snapper, and lobster (the latter in dozens of dishes). The wine is complimentary at the candlelit dinners served here.

The 32-unit hotel was featured in the Fletcher Knebel novel *Night of Camp David.* The club offers ocean or hillside villas as well as hotel rooms, complete seclusion, and views. Favored units are spacious "treehouse villas," with private redwood porches or balconies. Wide glass doors welcome the glowing bushes. Inside, the decor has floral bedcovers and tropical furniture. In winter, single or double occupancy costs $85 daily in a one-bedroom suite, $100 in a split-level suite, and $110 in a one-bedroom villa. Low season rates exist for only part of the summer. Certain holiday weeks, such as July 4, Memorial Day, and Labor Day, are considered high season. *However, for the rest of the off-season, rates are reduced by $10 daily per room.* MAP can be arranged for another $28 per person daily.

A guide will take you diving for conch, spearing native lobster, or fishing for yellowtail, and your catch will be used for a shore lunch. Many facilities are available, including tennis courts, a marina, boats for hire, free boat rides to the village, and water-sports equipment. The hotel is closed mid-August to mid-October.

New Plymouth Inn, New Plymouth, Abaco, Green Turtle Cay, The Bahamas (tel. 809/365-4161, or 305/665-5309 in Florida), is a restored New England–Bahamian-style inn, which stands next door to the former home of Neville Chamberlain, the prime minister of Great Britain on the eve of World War II. It has colonial charm, a Loyalist history, cloistral gardens, and a patio pool, and it's in the heart of New Plymouth village. It was one of the few buildings in town to survive the 1932 hurricane. The inn is run by Wally Davies, an expert diver and swimmer. He has turned New Plymouth Inn into a charming oasis, refurbishing the 150-year-old building with taste and care.

The inn has wide, open verandas, intricate cut-out wooden trim, and an indoor A-frame dining room. The comfortable hammock on the front porch is constantly fought over. The light and airy rooms are kept spotlessly clean, and each has a private bath and shower. Many of the same guests have come back every year since the inn opened in 1974. Year-round rates, with breakfast and dinner included, are $100 daily in a double, $60 in a single. The inn is closed in September and October.

Out on the veranda, you can smell night-blooming jasmine mixing with fresh baked island bread. Island candlelit dinners of fresh native lobster, snapper, conch, and vintage wines are served. Also roasts, steaks, chops, and imported beer in frosty steins are part of the menu. The bar and lounge, which overlook the garden's small, freshwater swimming pool, are the social center of the establishment. If you plan to dine at the Captain's Table, as the restaurant is called, you'll have to make a reservation. Breakfast is daily 8 to 9 a.m., lunch from noon to 1 p.m., and dinner at 7:30 p.m. sharp. The Sunday brunch, from 11:30 a.m. to 1 p.m., is the most popular on the island, costing only $7 per person. Former President Richard Nixon has dined here.

Cottage Rentals

Sea Star Beach Cottages, Green Turtle Cay, Abaco, The Bahamas (tel. 809/365-4178), is a bungalow colony set on 19 acres, between Black Sound Harbour on one side and Gilliam Bay Beach on the ocean side. A variety of tropical trees and flowers abound in the colony—coconut palms, citrus, bananas, hibiscus, bougainvillea, gumbo-limbo, and casuarina.

Life at Sea Star is simple—you get up at dawn, walk right down to the beach for your morning swim, then go back to a breakfast of homemade bread and tropical fruit. All cottages are on the ocean side (best swimming there), and come completely equipped for housekeeping. They are frame buildings, basic, with few frills. Each cottage has a bath or shower, a weekly supply of linens, stove, refrigerator, and, important, 24-hour electricity. The cottages are only half a mile by footpath to New Plymouth. Boat rentals are available. The cottages cost from $500 per week.

Deck House lies on the leeward side of the island at the entrance to White Sound. Rented as a complex, it can house up to six people. In other words it takes three couples "with privacy." It consists of two bedrooms and two baths, plus a small guesthouse suitable for two. There is a living room, plus a kitchen. Linens and all utensils are provided. Out back is a sundeck. The owner, Dorothy Lang, prefers bookings from Saturday noon to Saturday noon. Incidentally, a maid comes in Saturday to put things in order. The charge for four guests is $650 weekly, year-round. If two more guests join the party, the charge is only $250 extra for the week. As an added bonus, Mrs. Lang includes a 30-horsepower Malibu, a Butterfly, and the use of a Sunfish at no additional charge. For information and more details, write or call Mrs. Lang at 535 Hickory Hill Lane, Cincinnati, OH 42215 (tel. 513/821-9417).

WHERE TO EAT: The hotels previously recommended have the best food on the island. But if, for a change of pace, you'd like to escape for either lunch or dinner, I recommend the following small dining rooms in New Plymouth.

Laura's Kitchen (tel. 809/365-4287) is set on the main street of town, across from the Lowe Museum. This family-owned operation occupies a well-converted white-sided Bahamian cottage. Owner Laura Sawyer serves breakfast, lunch, and dinner within a decor which might best be described as pleasant, cozy, and homey. Open seven days a week, the restaurant serves food from 8 a.m. to 2 p.m. and 5:30 to 9 p.m. Chicken is the specialty, and meals cost from $8.

Rooster's Rest Pub and Restaurant (tel. 809/365-4066) serves good Bahamian food, including lobster, conch, and fresh fish. Lunch costs from $9, and dinner, from $15 for a complete meal. The restaurant is open daily from 10:30 a.m. to 10 p.m. It's wise to call for reservations for dinner. The establishment lies just beyond the edge of town, at the far side of a hill that conceals it from most sections of Parliament Street.

Sea View Restaurant, Crown Street (tel. Green Turtle Cay 5111). Shortly after her marriage to locally born Alphonso, Betty McIntosh set up this restaurant in a green cinderblock building not far from the sea. Today, she serves Nassau-inspired meals to loyal clients, some of whom return every day. The establishment is spacious, airy, and unashamedly simple. It's open daily except Sunday from 10 a.m. to 10 p.m., and is easy to find because about a dozen signs posted all over town point to it. Dinner reservations are preferred, although at lunchtime no advance notice is needed. Lunch menus, costing from $6, include conch fritters, conch chowder, conch burgers, conch snacks (actually a platter of cracked conch), and tuna sandwiches. At dinner, conch chowder, peas 'n' rice, and potato salad or coleslaw are served as part of the full meal, each of which costs from $14. Main dishes, listed on a blackboard, include fish, chicken, Bahamian lobster, and pork chops. The restaurant is open all year. There's a well-stocked bar if you want to stop by just for a drink.

Plymouth Rock Restaurant, Parliament Street (tel. 809/365-4234). It's difficult not to see this Bahamian lunch-only restaurant and liquor store, as it lies on the main street of town at Long Dock. Its cozy air-conditioned dining room is accentuated by lots of local chatter. The Bethell family offers homemade pies and cakes from a 100-year-old glass display case. Bahamian conch chowder and homemade soups are daily fare. Lunch starts at $8 and is served from noon to 2 p.m. The menu changes daily and may feature lobster, conch, grouper, and beef. Beer, wine, and mixed drinks accompany your food. Try a Goombay Smash or their own Calypso Cooler.

THE FAMILY ISLANDS' MOST FAMOUS BAR: Everybody goes to **Miss Emily's Blue Bee Bar,** Victoria Street (tel. 809/365-4181), and it's likely to have the liveliest party in the Family Islands going on in its unpretentious confines any time of the day or night. Despite its simplicity, this family-run bar is one of the most famous places east of Miami. When I was last there, an energetic party was developing just before lunch, as a yachtswoman from West Virginia was rehearsing the frug she'd learned in college, to the enthusiastic applause of her comrades. This and more are likely to be part of the scene at this hallowed bar where the walls and furniture are virtually indestructible. The walls near the bar area are covered with the business cards of the clientele, who have included Glen Campbell, Jimmy Buffet, and the late Lillian Carter.

The Goombay Smash, the specialty here, has been called "Abaco's answer to atomic fission," and its recipe includes secret proportions of coconut rum, "dirty" rum, apricot brandy, and pineapple juice. The world's record for drinking these concoctions is set at 23, but the valiant toper had to be carried out in a wheelbarrow. The bar is open every day (except Sunday) at 10 a.m., remaining open till late. No food is served here other than the sugar content of these tasty, habit-forming drinks, each of which costs $3.50. Jerry Hulse once wrote: "Miss Emily, bless her, gives her customers the impression they've discovered El Morocco, or maybe another Copacabana. It's neither of those, of course. The Blue Bee is really rather tacky, but with loads of atmosphere."

The owner (she's really Mrs. Emily Cooper) is filled with humor and anecdotes. Failing health makes it impossible for her always to be on duty at the bar, but she has taught her daughter, Violet Smith, how to make the secret recipe, which seems to please customers. Although Miss Emily has a fine soprano voice, she used to sing only at St. Peter's Anglican Church. Tips at the bar go into Miss Emily's cigar box for St. Peter's, one of the church's best sources of revenue.

THE SPORTING LIFE: The previously recommended Bluff House Club & Marina (tel. 809/365-4247), is the place to go for **scuba** facilities. A one-tank dive costs $35, including all equipment. A **snorkeling** lesson and trip costs $75. The hotel also has access to a 29-foot "sportsfish" boat, with all equipment included. A half-day rental of this vessel costs $130 or a full day $250. **Bonefishing** (which is on a smaller boat) is $100 per trip for two persons. Each trip takes about four hours, and the schedule depends completely on the tide. Bonefish are said to be, pound for pound, the strongest, most "fighting" fish in The Bahamas.

If you want to go **deep-sea fishing,** the men to see are the Sawyer family, two brothers and a father. Referrals are usually made through the Green Turtle Club or else you can call directly at 809/365-4173. A full day of fishing costs about $200.

REGATTA WEEK: Some critics have hailed the yearly Regatta Week as the "premier annual yachting event in the Abacos." Every year, it's held sometime between Independence Day in the United States and Independence Day of The Bahamas (July 4 and July 10). The events include sailboats and their crews from around the world, who compete in races that are divided into many categories. Some of the corporate sponsors in past years have been Shell Oil of The Bahamas, Barclays Bank, and the Green Turtle Club, which usually accommodates many of the participants.

Another event that draws visitors is the **Green Turtle Club Fishing Tournament,** held sometime in May. In 1984 the winner hooked a 500-pound blue marlin that was so heavy the competing participants from other boats generously came aboard the winning craft to bring the fish in.

AFTER DARK: An out-of-the-way nightspot, **Rooster's Rest Pub and Restaurant** (tel. 809/365-4066), recommended separately as an eating place, attracts a crowd, including both yachting people and locals, who gather here every Friday and Saturday night. "The Gully Roosters" perform on weekends, "the best time to go," according to New Plymouth residents. Beer costs $3 per bottle. The place is open daily from 10:30 a.m. to 10 p.m. on quiet nights, later when there's activity. Not visible from most of Parliament Street, the pub-restaurant is at the far side of a hill beyond the edge of town.

3. TREASURE CAY

Treasure Cay, called Lovel's Island in records as far back as the 1780s, was once separated from the mainland of Abaco by Carleton Creek. Over the years, however, landfill operations have joined the two, although Treasure Cay retains the name. It now contains one of the most popular and elaborate resorts in the Family Islands. On the east coast of Great Abaco, it boasts not only 3½ miles of private sandy beach but also one of the finest marinas in the Commonwealth, with complete docking and charter facilities.

In the publicity advertising this cay, a story has been printed about a German submarine commander, Paul Schmidt, who in World War II emerged from the sea to enjoy a little bit of Bahamian air before going back to Europe. Apparently he was so taken with the place that he vowed one day to return when the war was over and build a retirement home here. In 1968 he fulfilled that long-ago commitment to himself.

Much of today's Treasure Cay owes its look to Capt. Leonard Thompson, a former Royal Canadian Air Force pilot from Marsh Harbour, and Dumas Milner, the biggest Chevrolet dealer in the United States. In 1962 the two launched a development here, digging seven miles of canals through the mangroves.

Before the opening of the tourist complex the cay was virtually unsettled, so the resort has become the "city," providing its thousands of visitors with all the supplies they need, including medical goods, grocery store items (liquor, naturally), and even bank services. The real estate office peddles the condos, and the builders predict that they will reach a capacity one day of 5,000 guests. What is hoped is that many visitors will like Treasure Cay so much that they'll buy into it.

FOOD AND LODGING: The foundation for this sun-drenched resort, **Treasure Islands Club & Cruise,** P.O. Box TC-4183, Abaco, The Bahamas (tel. 809/367-2847, or toll free 800/327-1584 in the U.S., 800/432-8257 in Florida), was laid in 1962, when Dumas Milner helped pay for digging the seven miles of canals through mangrove forests. Today the area enjoys an ambience more like a country club than a hotel. Lodgings are in the 96-room Harbour House, with private porches or terraces built along the marina. The yachting crowd gathers here for sundowners at the Tipsy Seagull lounge. The resort is one of the most publicized, advertised, and frequented in the Family Islands. It has its share of celebrities too, beginning with George C. Scott, who filmed the movie *The Day of the Dolphin* here.

Visitors who prefer to come by boat to Treasure Cay will be able to dock at one of the 150 berths at the marina, which can accommodate vessels up to 100 feet long. They can even plug their TV sets into the cable TV hookup. The resort has a golf course (see below), tennis courts, and a beautiful stretch of white sand beach. Fronting the swimming pool is the main dining facility, the Abaco Room, where you're offered a tempting menu with such choices as fresh grouper, snapper, spicy conch salad, and Bahamian lobster. Huge poolside buffets are set up several nights a week. In addition, the glass-enclosed Spinnaker Restaurant overlooking the marina offers good food and a piano bar on its upper level.

The various time-share buildings scattered around this resort are attractively planned with an abundance of tropical planting and a *House and Garden* look. Interiors are handsomely styled, often in tropical bamboo and rattan. The accommodations include large, air-conditioned hotel rooms and suites. The hotel is all inclusive, one price covering not only the cost of the room but three meals a day, drinks, service, and sports facilities. In winter, the rate is $165 per person per day, based on double occupancy. A single pays $190. For an upgrade to a suite, the cost is another $25 per person per night. *In off-season, singles rent for $178 daily and doubles for $150 per person.* For reservations and information, write to 2301 South Federal Hwy., Fort Lauderdale, FL 33316 (tel. 305/525-7711).

SPORTS AT TREASURE CAY MARINA: Full service facilities for a variety of water sports are offered at the Treasure Cay Marina (tel. 809/367-2570). **Fishing boats** with experienced skippers will guide anglers to tuna, marlin, wahoo, dolphin, barracuda, grouper, yellowtail, and snapper. Treasure Cay's own bonefish flats are just a short cruise from the marina. A full day of bonefishing costs $175; a half day $120. A sport-fishing boat costs $285 for a half day, $395 for a full day.

In addition, sailboat, Hobie Cat, and windsurfing board rentals can be arranged, as well as rental of snorkeling gear and bicycles. The marina has showers, fish-cleaning facilities, 24-hour weekday laundry service, and water and electricity hookups.

The **Treasure Cay Golf Club,** P.O. Box TC-4183 (tel. 809/367-2590), offers 6,985 yards of fairways and was designed by Dick Wilson. Hotel guests at Treasure Cay play free; visitors are charged greens fees of $20 for 18 holes, $15 for 9 holes.

CARLETON: The first settlement in the Abacos was a village that no longer exists—Carleton—to the north and a little east of Treasure Cay (then called Lovel's Island). It was separated from the cay by Carleton Creek as that rivulet flowed to join the sea. The little town was abandoned some 200 years ago and largely forgotten until 1979, when the site of the settlement was discovered and artifacts found by archeological excavation. In a bicentennial ceremony in 1983, a point of land near the site was designated **Carleton Point** and a bronze plaque placed there describing Carleton's brief history.

Loyalist refugees, fleeing the United States in 1783 following the formation of the new country and the withdrawal of British troops from the former colonies, migrated to The Bahamas, some settling in Abaco, which was uninhabited at the time. Their aim was grandiose—they thought they could establish a colony that would be prosperous enough to replace British commerce with Virginia, Boston, New York, and Baltimore, and Abaco would become a new agricultural/mercantile empire within the protection and privileged access provided by the British Crown.

Carleton, named for Sir Guy Carleton, who had been British commander-in-chief in New York, did not fulfill the dreams of the colonists. They staked out claims to land, but they learned, as had other settlers in other parts of The Bahamas, that this was not farming country. They built ships, but could not produce cargoes for them. The town initially had a population of 600 people, but civil strife and a devastating hurricane added to their woes, and soon some two-thirds of the settlers moved 18 miles to the southeast to found Marsh Harbour. Others moved to Cocoa Plum Creek and elsewhere in Abaco, and some left The Bahamas. By 1800 Carleton had ceased to exist.

The Loyalists remaining in the Abacos were joined by migrants from Harbour Island on Eleuthera, who taught them to fish and even how to farm the rough acreage, and this union formed the nucleus from which today's Abaconians descended.

4. MARSH HARBOUR

The largest town in the Abacos, Marsh Harbour on Great Abaco Island is the third largest in The Bahamas. The first settlers were a group of Loyalists who were among those who tried to start a town called Carleton near Treasure Cay (see above). The Abaconians who live here are usually shy but gracious.

Marsh Harbour is also a shipbuilding center, but tourism accounts for most of its revenues. The commercial center of Abaco, the town has a shopping center and various other facilities not found in many Family Islands settlements. You'll even spot the green turrets of a "castle" here, which was designed and constructed by Evans Cottrell, who wrote *Out Island Doctor*.

The shoreline provides one of the finest anchorages in the Family Islands, which is probably what lured the first settlers here 200 years ago. There are good water-taxi connections, making this a center for exploring some of the offshore cays, including Man-O-War and Elbow Cay. Its international airport serves not only the resorts at Marsh Harbour but those at Elbow Key (Hope Town).

I prefer to treat Marsh Harbour more as a refueling depot than a sightseeing attraction, as there are far more colorful towns in Abaco and its offshore cays. However, because of its location—roughly in the center of the island—you may want to use it as a base, since it has a number of good inns. Several places will rent you a bike if you want to pedal around the town, getting to know it.

PRACTICAL FACTS: I have gathered a few pieces of information that may help to make your visit to Marsh Harbour more enjoyable.

Banks: If you're going to be in the Abacos for an extended vacation, Marsh Harbour can serve your banking needs in an emergency. Some cays have banks that operate only three hours a week. In Marsh Harbour, try **Barclays Bank,** on Don MacKay Boulevard (tel. 809/367-2152).

Car rentals: In Marsh Harbour, there's **Veronica's Car Rental,** P.O. Box 463 (tel. 809/367-2725). They charge $90 per day for Jeeps, $60 per day for other cars.

Drugstore: For your pharmaceutical needs, go to **Lowe's Pharmacy,** Lowe's Shopping Centre, P.O. Box 503 (tel. 809/367-2667).

Hair care: Women or men who want to get their hair done should drive up to Treasure Cay. There, they will be taken care of at the **Looking Glass Beauty Salon** (tel. 809/367-2570).

Immigration: The office of Bahamas Immigration is at the airport (tel. 809/367-2675).

Medical care: The best medical clinic in the Abacos is in Marsh Harbour, the **Great Abaco Clinic,** Steede Bonnet Road (tel. 809/365-2510).

Police: To call the police, dial 809/367-2560.

Post office: Marsh Harbour's post office (tel. 809/367-2571) is on Don MacKay Boulevard.

Shopping: If you'd like to shop for gifts or souvenirs, about the best place is the **Loyalist Shoppe,** P.O. Box 445, Don MacKay Boulevard (tel. 809/367-2701), which has leather goods from England and Italy, pottery, crystal, bone china, periodicals, cosmetics, souvenirs, cameras, and nautical gift items.

WHERE TO STAY: At the southeast corner of the harbor, **Conch Inn Resort,** P.O. Box 434, Marsh Harbour, Abaco, The Bahamas (tel. 809/367-2800), is a small colony, painted yellow. Etched into the coast is a 60-slip marina where visiting yachtspeople like to tie in for fuel, ice, water, and use of the laundromat. There is a main building with individual rooms and baths, plus some independent efficiency units and two-bedroom cottages, all air-conditioned. Private patios are on the ocean side. The bungalows are in white, with ceiling fans, casual but attractive deckside furniture, and kitchens with pass-through counters. Rates are the same all year—singles or doubles cost $75 per day. Efficiencies rent for $85, and a two-bedroom cottage is $125 for four guests per day.

Around the marina is the restaurant dock (dinghies welcome), plus the Conch Inn Restaurant, the Conch Crawl Bar (a dockside bar and grill), and the 14-room inn. Adjacent to the marina is an open-air swimming pool with lounge chairs for sunning. Boaters like to moor here and rent a bungalow or one of the pleasantly furnished rooms in the inn. Furnishings are "nautical-Bahamian" style. Rentals of an 18-foot powerboat and Hobie Cats are available. The location is three miles from the Marsh Harbour airport.

Great Abaco Beach Hotel, P.O. Box 511, Marsh Harbour, Abaco, The Bahamas (tel. 809/367-2158), is folksy and very island oriented. Created by a former pilot who served with Canadian forces in World War II, it is now run by Peter Sweeney and Jack Albury. You can rent one of five air-conditioned villas, with two bedrooms and two baths along with a kitchen and both a living and a dining area. Other units are a series of 20 air-conditioned and spacious bedrooms, each with a terrace overlooking a private beach. Year-round rates are $250 per night for one of the two-bedroom villas, suitable for four guests. A standard bedroom costs two persons $150 a night. The rooms are decorated in a tropical motif. The hotel has a beach bar and a restaurant, Penelope's, which serves both Bahamian and American food. The hotel lies four miles from Marsh Harbour airport. You take a taxi from the airport to the hotel, where cars and bicycles can be rented. Special events with native music are often on the bill of fare.

Abaco Towns by the Sea, P.O. Box 486, Marsh Harbour, Abaco, The Bahamas (tel. 809/367-2221), is a pleasant time-share resort complex set on sandy soil on a rolling terrain of rises and valleys. There's a small crescent of beach looking out over the Sea of Abaco, as well as a free-form swimming pool, tennis courts, and a cluster of white-stucco villas grouped in a flowering landscape. You'll be able to identify bougainvillea, coconut, hibiscus, and banana trees scattered over a property that is considered deluxe for the area.

Each of the accommodations contains two bedrooms, a living room, a kitchen, and two baths. Winter charges for four to six persons are $900 weekly, $160 daily in sea-view units; $775 weekly, $150 daily in accommodations with a garden and pool view. *In summer, sea-view units for four to six cost $800 per week, while the daily rate is $140. Those with a pool and garden view cost $775 per week or $130 per day, each housing four to six guests.* Visitors have the opportunity to purchase time shares or to rent for a single sojourn. There's a snackbar on the premises, and other restaurants, each under a different management, are within walking distance. You can rent a bicycle to pedal into town.

The Lofty Fig Villas, P.O. Box 437, Marsh Harbour, Abaco, The Bahamas (tel. 809/367-2681), is a bungalow colony across from the Conch Inn, overlooking the harbor. It is spread around a free-form swimming pool, which is the social center. White lounge chairs are set on a wide sun terrace, and flowering tropical trees and shrubbery surround the pool and bungalows. There is a poolside gazebo and barbecue. Each of the six air-conditioned bungalows is fully furnished for housekeeping and contains one full double and one single bed. Interiors are smartly decorated with colors of the sea contrasted with bone-white walls and furniture. Sliding glass doors lead to a covered terrace. Maid service is provided Monday to Saturday. Meals are prepared in a fully equipped contemporary kitchen, with a pass-through window to the large, screened-in patio. It's just a seven-minute walk to the supermarket, three miles to the airport. All year, villas are rented either as doubles or singles and cost $70 per day, with an additional person paying $10 per day. Rental cars, scooters, bikes, and boats are available, and deep-sea fishing charters can be arranged.

DINING IN LOCAL RESTAURANTS: There are more than half a dozen local restaurants serving both American and Bahamian dishes in and around Marsh Harbour. If you've been in The Bahamas for very long, the fare will be familiar to you: conch chowder, conch salad, conch fritters, along with grouper and Bahamian lobster. But, first, you have a Goombay Smash for your sundowner (everybody, seemingly, makes his or her own version).

Conch Inn/Conch Crawl (tel. 809/367-2800). Both of these restaurants are the best in their neighborhood during their respective operating hours. The Conch Inn Restaurant occupies its own white-sided waterfront building a few steps from the hotel which gives it its name. It's without equal as the most popular, lighthearted, and fun restaurant in Marsh Harbour. Drinks are served at sofas near the dining room, and a separate bar does a respectable business of its own. Dinner is nightly except Monday from 7 to 10:30. As you look out over the nearby marina, you'll dine on such specialties as lobster bisque, conch chowder, seafood platters, butterfly shrimp, lamb chops, sirloin steak, crayfish tails, and banana-nutcake pie. Full meals cost from $20 each.

Breakfast and lunch are equally appealing, but in a different building amid a different ambience. Set within the Conch Crawl, adjacent to the reception area of the Conch Inn, it, too, looks out over the marina. You dine on canvas-backed director's chairs amid pinewood planking and round cedarwood tables with just about every boat owner in the neighborhood. The establishment opens for a thriving business every morning at 8 a.m. Breakfast costs from $7, with generous portions of hearty and well-prepared favorites. The Conch Crawl closes only for a brief rest from 11 a.m. to noon, before opening for lunch business until 4 p.m. Lunches, costing from $12, include two-fisted drinks and such Bahamian dishes as Out Island grouper, Abaco lobster salad, conchburgers, sandwiches, salads, and such special luncheon plates as chopped smothered steak. No dinner is ever served at the Conch Crawl, since the party invariably moves to the Conch Inn Restaurant for before-dinner drinks.

Wally's (tel. 809/367-2074) competes with the Conch Crawl as one of the island's happiest luncheon stopovers. It occupies a well-maintained pink villa behind a lawn dotted with begonias across the street from the water. There's an outdoor terrace covered with terracotta tiles, a boutique, and an indoor bar and dining area filled with Haitian paintings. Lunch is daily from 11:30 a.m. to 3 p.m., costing from $12. The bar, however, stays open until 5:30 p.m. The special drinks are daiquiris, Bahama Mamas, and Goombay Smashes, which most visitors accompany with conchburgers, beefburgers, grouper Nantua style, a selection of sandwiches, and such homemade desserts as guava-filled chocolate cake. The only dinner served is on Monday, promptly at 7 p.m. It costs from $20 and is anticipated by local residents as a kind of weekly ritual of fine dining. The owner, Wally Smith, personally greets each and every visitor at the door. Reservations are required for the dinner.

Mother Merle's Fishnet, P.O. Box 476, Dundas Town (tel. 809/367-2770). More substantial, and far more elaborate than you might have suspected, this restaurant sits about 1½ miles from the main marinas and harbors of Marsh Harbour. Dundas Town was created as a settlement by the government in the postwar years. Mother Merle for many years has been known as one of the best local cooks. Behind an unpretentious façade is a pair of raftered rooms dimly lit with flickering candles. You can drink in the "This Is It" lounge before heading in for dinner. Full meals cost from $15 each and include barbecued chicken, cracked conch, grouper, fresh lobster, conch chowder, and game fish when it's available. Hot johnnycake accompanies most meals, or peas 'n' rice with hot sauce. For dessert, try one of her key lime pies or her coconut ice cream. Dinner is nightly except Wednesday from 6 to 11, and a reservation might be a good idea.

On the other hand, many locals will direct you to **Cynthia's Kitchen,** P.O. Box 580 (tel. 809/367-2268), right in town. Here you can have breakfast, lunch, and dinner, served from 8:30 a.m. to 10 p.m. daily. Native dishes, and good ones, are served in this simple, basic place. Cracked conch and conch chowder are traditionally featured, and you might get Bahamian lobster on occasion, perhaps grouper, even a burger. You can also order a seafood platter, in which the emphasis is on the local catches. Cynthia also does curried goat or chicken, and peas 'n' rice. You can finish off with coconut and pineapple pie. Meals here cost $15 and up, although you can have a much less expensive breakfast.

The Bilge/The Jib (tel. 809/367-2033) lies across the harbor from the main concentration of buildings at Marsh Harbour, so getting here involves a taxi ride. By far the most popular section of this two-story place is the Bilge Bar, near the water's edge on the ground floor. Its only food service is during lunch in high season, when an array of sandwiches and salads appear from 11 a.m. to 3 p.m. Lunches cost from $7 each. The Bilge is better known, however, as the preferred drinking arena of local residents and boat owners, who prefer the loud humor and friendly jostling of this bar.

A somewhat less patronized restaurant, The Jib, is on the second floor. Climb an external staircase to reach its rope-entwined posts, high rafters, and darkly finished paneling. Warm-weather diners prefer the wrap around veranda. Meals are offered only at dinner, daily except Tuesday from 6:30 to 10 p.m., costing $18 to $35. They include black-bean soup, grouper fingers, ham and asparagus rolls, glazed chicken, cracked conch, "reef and beef," lobster salad, and several preparations of fish and lobster. A battered Abaco Island sailing dinghy is suspended from the ceiling.

THE SPORTING LIFE: All the hotelkeepers at Marsh Harbour can help fix you up with the right people to take care of your sporting requirements. For variety, you can also take the ferry over to Hope Town and avail yourself of the facilities offered there.

Water Sports

If you're interested in water sports, your best bet is to go to the **Conch Inn** (tel. 809/367-2800), a previously recommended hotel. There you can rent jet-skis at $35 per hour, Hobie Cats at $20 per hour, and aquabikes at $8 per hour. They have other offerings as well.

Scuba- and skindiving are offered by **Dive Abaco,** P.O. Box 555 (tel. 809/367-2014). You sail with Capt. Skeet LaChance to unspoiled undersea gardens and blue holes. You can rent equipment and take a resort course in scuba-diving, costing $60 for a one-tank dive, $75 for two tanks. A regular diving trip for experienced divers costs $35 for a one-tank dive, $50 for a two-tanker. The tank and weights are included in the prices for the dives. Snorkeling trips cost $25. Dive Abaco trips are offered seven days a week, weather permitting, at 9:30 a.m. and 2:30 p.m.

Boat Charters

If you've got a good track record as a sailor, even of small boats, you can charter a yacht in Abaco big enough for the entire family, with just yourself as skipper to sail to all those places you've heard about. **Bahamas Yachting Services (BYS)** is the operator of the largest charter fleet in The Bahamas, based in Marsh Harbour. A bareboat charter is likely to cost you less than a comparable land-based vacation in the Family Islands or in Florida. Of course, you can cook your own meals in the fully equipped galley, one on every boat, complete with icebox (on larger boats, refrigerator and deep-freeze). You can barbecue your steak and fish on a hibachi fixed to the stern rail. You can go where you like, subject to BYS instructions to keep out of shoal waters and staying, with one exception, within the line of the outer cays. Most of the time you cruise in waters 6 to 18 feet deep, the bottom clearly visible.

When you board your boat, you'll find her cleaned, fueled, watered, provisioned, inspected, and ready to sail. BYS will give you and your crew a complete familiarization briefing on everything on board from bow to stern—anchors, rigging, sails, engine, radio, lights, navigational aids, galley, stove, cooking equipment, marine toilets, shower, storage spaces, and the outboard dinghy towed astern of every boat. Before you actually sail, they'll give you a chart briefing, warning you of the few dangerous areas, how to "read" the water, and how best to make the Whale Cay ocean passage that takes you to the northern section of Abaco Sound.

Bareboat charters are usually in the range of $1,195 to $2,495 per week, depending on the vessel. For more information, or reservations, write BYS, 2 Prospect Park, 3347 NW 55th St., Fort Lauderdale, FL 33309, or phone 800/327-2276 toll free in the U.S. and Canada. In Florida, call collect at 305/484-5246.

Tennis

Two hard-surface courts are available at the **Great Abaco Beach Hotel,** P.O. Box 419 (tel. 809/367-2158).

5. GREAT GUANA CAY

Longest of the Abaco cays, Great Guana, on the east side of the chain, stretches seven miles from tip to tip, lying between Green Turtle Cay and Man-O-War Cay. The cay has a seven-mile-long beach, which some consider unsurpassed in The Bahamas. The reef fishing is superb, and bonefish are plentiful in the shallow bays.

The settlement stretches along the beach at the head of the palm-fringed Kidd's Cove, named after the pirate; and the ruins of an old sisal mill near the western end of the island make for an interesting detour. The island has about 150 residents, most of them descendants of Loyalists who left Virginia and the

Carolinas to settle in this remote place, often called "the last spot of land before Africa."

Like similar settlements in New Plymouth and Man-O-War Cay, their houses resemble old New England. Over the years the traditional pursuit of the islanders has been in the boatbuilding and carpentry industry. They are also farmers and fishermen. It won't take you long to explore the village, as it has only two small stores, a one-room schoolhouse, and an Anglican church—and that's about it.

On the cay, small boats are available to charter for a half day or a full day (or a month, for that matter). For example, a 23-foot sailboat, fully equipped for living and cruising, is available for charter, and deep-sea fishing trips can be arranged.

For transportation to the cay, refer to the "Getting Around" section at the beginning of this chapter. If you'd like to stay on the island, check in Marsh Harbour for the status of Guana Beach Resort, the only hotel. It was closed at presstime.

6. MAN-O-WAR CAY

Visiting here is like going back in time. Man-O-War Cay shares a cultural link with New Plymouth on Green Turtle Cay, but perhaps the people here have not advanced quite so far into later 20th-century lifestyles. The island has some lovely beaches, and many visitors come here to enjoy them—but it's best to leave your more daring swimwear for other shores and look in the back of your closet for some old conservative thing.

Some find the people here puritanical in outlook. They are deeply religious, and there is no crime—unless you bring it with you. Also, you'll find no Miss Emily's Bar here, as you do in New Plymouth. Alcoholic beverages aren't sold, although you can bring your own supply.

Like New Plymouth, Man-O-War is a Loyalist village, with indications of a New England background. The pastel clapboard houses, built by ships' carpenters and trimmed in gingerbread, are set off by freshly painted white picket fences intertwined with bougainvillea.

The people here are basically shy, but they welcome outsiders to their remote, isolated island. They are proud of their heritage, and many, especially the oldtimers, have known plenty of hard times. They are similar to (and related to many of) the "conchs" of Key West, a tough, insular people who have exhibited a proud independence of spirit for many years.

Television has come to the island, and many of the older folk will tell you it's changed their lives, but they won't necessarily say whether that's to the good or bad.

If you look through the tiny listing for this cay in the phone book, you'll see that the Albury name predominates. On this famed boatbuilding capital of The Bahamas, Albury long ago became a famous name in that business. You can still see descendants of the early Alburys at work at a boatyard on the harbor. Albury shipbuilders still make Man-O-War runabouts, so often seen sailing in the waters of The Bahamas.

Tourism has really only begun on Man-O-War Cay. Because of the lack of hotels, many visitors come over just for the day, often in groups from Marsh Harbour.

To reach Man-O-War Cay, you must cross the water from Marsh Harbour. The water taxi leaves from a dock near the Great Abaco Beach Hotel there. The round-trip fare is $12 per person, and the ride takes about 45 minutes. For more specifics, refer to the "Getting Around" section at the beginning of this chapter. Except for a few service vehicles, the island is free of cars. But if you want to explore—and don't want to walk—ask around and see if one of the locals will rent you a golf cart.

WHERE TO EAT: A favorite of mine is **Dock & Dine** (tel. 809/365-6013). Simple, well scrubbed, and respectable, this restaurant is filled with high ceiling beams and a decor the early Puritans might have approved of. It occupies a sea-green building near Albury's Marina. Lunch is served daily from 11 a.m. to 2:30 p.m., costing from $10, and dinner is offered from 5 to 7:30 p.m. except on Sunday, for about $15. If you want dinner, you must phone in advance for a reservation (by 5 p.m.). Menu items include fried crayfish platters, pork chops, steak, fresh fish, conch fritters, cracked conch, milkshakes, and coconut pie.

Bite Site (tel. 809/365-6051). Other than two solitary chairs backed up against display racks, there's no place to sit in this tiny establishment. That doesn't prevent it from enjoying one of the most devoted clienteles on the island, many of whom buy take-out food for consumption at wooden picnic tables near the wharves in front. It sits behind a sea-green and white clapboard house at the edge of the marina. You order food at the countertop from an employee who might have spent her morning baking a tempting array of pastries.

The place is known far and wide for its milkshakes (ever had rum raisin?) which at $2 will appease your craving for ice cream for months. You can also order hamburgers, cheeseburgers, conchburgers, black-eyed peas, and such baked goods as coconut pie, pumpkin pie, apple pie, and doughnuts. A hamburger costs $2.75; a steaming mug of conch chowder, $3. Every Monday, Tuesday, and Thursday the place is open from 9 a.m. to 4:30 p.m. with an additional opening from 8:30 to 9 p.m. for ice cream sales. Every Wednesday, Friday, and Saturday it's open without interruption from 9 a.m. to 9 p.m. It's always closed on Sunday.

WHERE TO SHOP: Perhaps the most unusual store and studio on the island is **Uncle Norman Albury's Sail Loft** (no phone). It occupies a century-old clapboard house which members of the Albury family have painted a soothing shade of avocado green. Part of the floor space is devoted to the manufacture (and the other half to the display) of an inventory of brightly colored canvas garments and accessories. The cloth that is universally used—eight-ounce cotton duck—once served as sailcloth for the community's boats. When synthetic sails came into vogue, four generations of Albury women put the cloth and their talents to use. Don't stop without chatting with the Albury matrons, who say they got into the business "because we wanted to be bag ladies."

Joe's Studio (tel. 809/365-6082). Its inventory of island-related odds and ends makes this an appealing stopover. My favorite item for sale here are the half-rib models of local sailing dinghies crafted from mahogany and mounted in half profile on a board. They're a substantial but durable souvenir of your visit. Other items include glass fishing bobs, T-shirts, Bahamian cookbooks, watercolors, pen and ink drawings, and carved letter openers.

7. ELBOW CAY (HOPE TOWN)

Elbow Cay, noted for its many lovely beaches that attract hundreds of visitors to its shores, is connected by a regular 20-minute, $12 round-trip ferry or water-taxi service to Abaco at Marsh Harbour. The cay's largest settlement is Hope Town, a little village with a candy-striped, 120-foot lighthouse, the most photographed attraction in the Family Islands. The kerosene-powered light is still in service.

You can climb to the top of the lighthouse for a sweeping view of the surrounding land and water. From the time construction on this beacon first began in 1838, it came under a great deal of harassment from the wreckers of Abaco, who lived on salvaged cargo from wrecked and foundered ships. Seeing an end to their means of livelihood, they did much to sabotage the light in the early days.

Hope Town, often called a "time-warp" hamlet, like other offshore cays of Abaco, was settled by Loyalists who left the new United States and came to The Bahamas to remain subjects of the British Crown, spreading out from the now long-vanished settlement of Carleton near Treasure Cay. The town will evoke thoughts of old Cape Cod, or, closer to home, of New Plymouth on Green Turtle Cay. Like them, it has clapboard saltbox cottages weathered to a silver gray or painted in pastel colors, with white picket fences setting them off. The buildings may remind you of New England, but this palm-fringed island has a definite South Seas flavor.

Over the years Hope Town has attracted many famous visitors, some of whom, such as Dr. George Gallup, the pollster, liked it so much that they built "homes away from home" here.

The island is almost free of vehicular traffic. In exploring Hope Town, you can take one of two roads: "Up Along" or "Down Along," the latter running along the water.

Malone seems to be the most popular name here. The founding mother of the town back circa 1783 (perhaps 1775) was Wyannie Malone, who came here as a widow with four children. Her descendants are still a big part of the population of 500 full-time residents. A **museum** is dedicated to Wyannie's memory, containing exhibits tracing the rich history of the cay. It's open from 10 a.m. to noon. Adults pay $1; children, 50¢.

PRACTICAL FACTS: If you're in need of a pharmacy, try the **Clear View Drug Store** (tel. Hope Town 217).

There is also a local **post office** (tel. Hope Town 214), but expect mail sent from here to take a long time reaching its destination. The location is at the head of the upper public dock.

WHERE TO STAY: By anyone's standards, the **Abaco Inn,** Hope Town, Elbow Cay, Abaco, The Bahamas (tel. 809/367-2666) is the most sophisticated and desirable resort on Abaco. It nestles on a ridge of sandy soil on the narrowest section of Elbow Cay, about 1½ miles south of Hope Town. As you stand on the ridge, you'll find yourself on a strategically important land bridge between the crashing surf of the jagged eastern coast and the sheltered waters of White Sound and the Sea of Abaco to the west. The establishment's clusters of shingle-sided buildings were once part of a private club, the Fin & Tonic. But informal "barefoot elegance" and welcoming enthusiasm now prevail. Dynamic Ruth Maury, assisted by a team of polite and gracious helpers, is your host when she's there. The resort's social center and headquarters is in a modern and rambling clubhouse that looks a lot like a beach house in northern California. There's an open fireplace set into a stone wall, heavy beams, pinewood paneling, comfortable sofas, and the most appealing bar on the island. Its modernity is relieved with an antique airplane propeller.

Accommodations are scattered between the palms and sea grapes of the sandy terrain. Each has a hammock placed conveniently nearby for quiet afternoons of reading or sleeping. Each has a ceiling fan, private bath, and air conditioning, along with a comfortably unpretentious decor of white wooden walls and conservative furniture. When you tire of your cabin with its carefully maintained privacy, you can dream of faraway places from a perch in the cedar-capped gazebo which sits between the saltwater pool and the rocky tidal flats of the Atlantic.

In winter, oceanside rooms rent for $109 daily in a single and $115 in a double. Five harborside units cost $89 daily in a single and $95 in a double. *In summer, each category of rooms is reduced by $20 a day.* MAP can be arranged for another $29 per person daily. The inn is closed every year from early September to mid-November.

WHERE TO DINE: The best food is served at the **Abaco Inn** (tel. 809/367-2666). It's in the clubhouse of the previously recommended hotel within view of the crashing surf of the Atlantic and a weathered gazebo looking out to sea. Lunch is offered daily from noon to 2 p.m., costing $12 each. Dave Fiore, the skilled chef, prepares such dishes as conch chowder, lobster salad, pasta primavera, and salads with delectable homemade dressings laced with tarragon and other herbs. Dinner is served in a single seating at 7:30 p.m. every evening, costing $20 per person. The chef prepares a changing menu of seafood and meats, each expertly seasoned and well prepared. Typical offerings are likely to include guava soufflé, zucchini nut bread, coconut soup, crayfish quiche, duck á l'orange, and chocolate peppermint mousse. The inn will send a mini-van to collect you from other parts of the island if you phone them in advance of your intentions. It's closed from early September to mid-November.

Harbour's Edge (no phone). One of the town's most popular restaurants is set on piers above the water, in a clapboard house. A bar is found near the entrance, with an adjacent waterside deck for watching the passage of boats. There's also a tile-floored dining room, where the crackle of a VHF radio is always audible. Since the establishment has no phone, boat owners and local residents reserve tables on the short-wave radio, Channel 16. The bar is open daily except Tuesday in summer from 9 a.m. until very late at night. Lunch is served daily from 11:30 a.m. to 2 p.m., costing $12. The bill of fare includes conch fritters, conch chowder, hamburgers, sandwiches, and conch platters. Dinners, costing from $20 each and served from 6 to 8:30 p.m., include plain, simple, yet well-prepared food such as pan-fried pork chops, grouper filet, New York strip, and fried chicken.

SHOPPING NOTES: Of course, no one comes to Hope Town just to shop, but once you're here you might want to buy a souvenir or gift at **Native Touches** (no phone). Several of the items sold here are handcrafted.

Ebb Tide Gift Shop (no phone) is the best-stocked gift shop in town. It's found in a white clapboard house with yellow trim, one block from the harbor. Inside, an employee sells Androsia batiks, jewelry, T-shirts, fabric by the yard, engravings, maps, baby-size quilts, and suntan lotion.

Also, at **Kemp's Straw Market** you can find some gift items made by local residents.

THE SPORTING LIFE: The best dive operation is **Dave Gale's Island Marina** (tel. 809/376-2822). Gale, a NAUI instructor, takes guests to coral reefs and wrecks, among other attractions. One dive site includes the *Adirondack,* a Civil War gunboat that is covered by 10 to 25 feet of water. It sank on the barrier reef in the summer of 1862. Scuba-diving trips are arranged for two to five people, costing $35 per diver for a half-day trip. All equipment and instruction is included. Snorkeling, at $25 per person for half a day, also includes free use of equipment.

A windsurfer costs $30 per day, and the same amount also rents a Sunfish. A 13-foot Boston Whaler, 25 horsepower, rents for $40 per day; a 17-footer, 70 horsepower, goes for $60 per day. If you prefer, you can rent an Aquasport, 19 feet and 115 horsepower, for $70 per day.

Boat excursions, costing from $20 to $50 per person, will take you to the boatbuilding settlement on Man-O-War Cay, to sculptor Randolph Johnston's bronze foundry in Little Harbour (see below), to the abandoned remains of Wilson City, and to many uninhabited cays and deserted beaches where you can go shelling, beachcombing, exploring, and picnicking. Charter boats are available for bonefishing, reef fishing, and deep-sea fishing. Bonefish, grouper, snapper, wahoo, yellowtail, dolphin, kingfish, and others are abundant in the waters around, and local Bahamian guides can show you where they are. You may prefer to go with a guide, or you can rent a boat and try your own skill.

Boat rentals are offered by **Sea Horse Marine** (tel. 809/366-0091), on the waterfront of Hope Town Harbour. Boston Whalers can be had at $40 per day for the 13-footer for one or two days, $35 per day for three to six days, and $30 per day for seven or more days. The 17-footer rents on the same daily schedule for $60, $50, and $45. Larger boats include a 22-foot center-console vessel, with prices ranging upward accordingly. The top prices (for the 22-footer) are $85 per day, $75 per day, and $70 per day, depending on the time involved. Bimini tops cost extra.

8. LITTLE HARBOUR

In the gift and souvenir shops of Abaco you'll see a remarkable book, *Artist on His Island,* detailing the true-life adventures of Randolph and Margot Johnston, who lived a Swiss Family Robinson–type adventure with their three sons. Arriving on this southerly point of the Abacos aboard their old Bahamian schooner, the *Langosta,* they lived in one of the natural caves on the island until they eventually erected a thatched dwelling for themselves.

That was some time ago—in 1951. Now the Johnstons have achieved international fame as artists and sculptors while still living on their own Little Harbour island, a cay shaped like a circle, with a white sand beach running along most of it.

If you ask at your hotel in Marsh Harbour, chances are that an arrangement can be made for you to visit the island, which is serviced by Albury's Ferry. This is the southernmost stop of the ferry line. Since the island is private property, you are asked to treat it as if it's someone's home you're visiting—as indeed it is.

On the island is a foundry in which Mr. Johnston casts his bronze sculptures, many of which are in prestigious galleries today, using an old "lost-wax" method. Mrs. Johnston creates porcelain figurines of island life, its birds, fish, boats, and fishermen. She also works in glazed metals. They welcome visitors at their studio from 10 to 11 a.m. and 2 to 3 p.m. daily. It's also possible to purchase their art, which comes in a wide price range.

CHAPTER XIII

ELEUTHERA, HARBOUR ISLAND, AND SPANISH WELLS

□ □ □

The most developed of the Family Islands, sickle-shaped Eleuthera was settled in 1648, the first permanent settlement in The Bahamas. It is considered the seat of the first, true democracy in the western hemisphere. In search of religious freedom, the Eleutherian Adventurers came here from Bermuda, finding and colonizing the long, narrow island that still carries their name (Greek for freedom). The locals call it "Cigatoo."

What these adventurers found was an island 100 miles long and a bowshot wide (an average of two miles), lying on the eastern flank of The Bahamas. There, after a long journey from the Iberian peninsula, Atlantic rollers crash ashore. These rollers wash up on an island of white and pink sandy beaches edged by casuarina trees, high, rolling green hills, sea-to-sea views, dramatic cliffs, sheltered coves, old villages of pastel-washed cottages, and exclusive resorts built around excellent harbors.

Eleuthera begins 70 miles east of Nassau, and can be reached by a 30-minute air flight. It encompasses about 200 square miles. The island is known for its ocean holes that swirl salt water into land-locked rock formations.

The population today is estimated at 10,000, a medley of farmers, shopkeepers, and fishermen, and many of course engaged in tourism serving the 20 or so resorts. Eleuthera has come a long way since it was first described by its mid-17th-century colonists as "Ye barren rock." Roads run along the coastline today, but if you engage in any extensive touring, you'll find some of them adequately paved while many others are devastating to cars.

Long before the first English colonists arrived Eleuthera was inhabited by Lucayan Indians. However, around the mid-16th century Spaniards came this way, capturing the peaceable people and shipping them out to the Caribbean as slaves.

Pirates plied the waters off Eleuthera and its adjacent islands, but after the removal of the Lucayans there were no inhabitants here for a century, until Captain William Sayle led the Eleutherian Adventurers here from Bermuda to start a new life. The founding party consisted of about 70 people. They had a rough time of it. Dangerous reefs on the north coast of the island caused their ship and cargo to be lost. Trapped, they had to live off the land as best they could, initially inhabiting a cave (for a description, see "The Current," below).

They were not adept at earning a living in this new environment, and many of them nearly starved, but they nevertheless drew up their own constitution, promising justice for all. Help came from Virginia colonists, who, despite being short of supplies themselves, sent food to the little band of adventurers.

Life on Eleuthera proved too much for many of the founding party, however. Many, including Captain Sayle, later returned to Bermuda. But reinforcements were on the way, both from Bermuda and from England, some bringing slaves with them. A permanent settlement had been founded. Freed slaves also came to this island and established settlements. The next wave of settlers were fleeing Loyalists leaving the new United States in order to continue living under the British Crown. These settled principally in two offshore cays, Harbour Island and Spanish Wells.

Eleuthera is considered "the birthplace of The Bahamas," a sort of Bahamian Plymouth Rock.

The island once had a flourishing farm industry, especially in pineapples, although tomatoes and oranges were also exported. Several dairy and poultry farms were also started. One major plantation still exists today—run by the government. After many eventual failures in various industries, most of the people of Eleuthera are turning to tourism as their major hope for the future.

Eleuthera rivals Abaco in its lure for the foreign visitor. Along with Abaco, it has the largest concentration of resort hotels outside of Nassau/Paradise Island and Freeport/Lucaya. Some of the more famous resorts, such as Cotton Bay Beach and Windermere Island, charge super-expensive prices. However, for those willing to book a no-frills type of accommodation, I've included several self-sufficient housekeeping cottages and some low-cost guesthouses. In some of these places you'll have plumbing that "sometimes has a problem," and furnishings that may have seen better days (or never had a better day when new). But the warmth and hospitality of the local people often make up for inconveniences likely to be encountered. At any rate, these places provide the only low-cost way of vacationing here.

Of the nine destinations recommended in this chapter, Harbour Island gets my vote as the number one choice. Here you'll find a wide range of accommodations. Dunmore Town on Harbour Island was the original capital of The Bahamas, and is the island's oldest and most charming settlement. Many visitors who have traveled all over The Bahamas consider Harbour Island the most beautiful in the archipelago.

Spanish Wells is another small island just off the north end of Eleuthera. Spanish galleons put sailors ashore to fill the ships' casks with fresh water after long sea voyages—hence the present-day name of the island. The men of Spanish Wells are said to be the best seamen in The Bahamas.

Fishing and diving in the waters around Eleuthera are top-notch. There are facilities for the fishermen, the scuba-diver, and the yachting set. The islands offer a wide choice of coral gardens, reefs, dropoffs, wrecks, and drift dives. As divers know, wrecks often form the best dive sites. Eleuthera has several, including a submerged freight train wrecked during a storm off North Eleuthera while being barged to Cuba.

Fishermen come to Eleuthera for bottom, bone, and deep-sea fishing, testing their skill against the dolphin, the wahoo, the blue or white marlin, the Allison tuna, and the amberjack. Charter boats are available at Powell Point, Rock Sound, Spanish Wells, and Harbour Island.

Sunfish, sailboats, and Boston whalers for reef fishing can also be rented.

GETTING THERE: Eleuthera has three main airports. North Eleuthera Airport, obviously, serves the north along with the two major offshore cays, Harbour Island and Spanish Wells. Governor's Harbour Airport serves the center of the island, and Rock Sound Airport handles traffic to South Eleuthera. Make sure, when booking a flight, that you arrive at the right airport. Otherwise, your experience might resemble that of one visitor who flew into Rock Sound Airport only to face a $100 ride and a water-taxi trip before reaching his final destination of Harbour Island in the north.

Air Flights

Bahamasair offers daily flights between Nassau and the three airports, North Eleuthera, Governor's Harbour, and Rock Sound. Bahamasair also flies in from Miami daily.

In addition, several commuter airlines, with regularly scheduled service, fly from the Florida mainland with either nonstop or one-stop service. Many private flights use the North Eleuthera Airport, with its 4,500-foot paved runway. It is an official Bahamian port of entry, and a Customs and Immigration official is on hand.

Flying from Miami and Fort Lauderdale to Harbour Island and back is **R.S.V.P. Air,** 1685 West Commercial Blvd., Hangar 42, Fort Lauderdale, FL 33309 (tel. 809/333-2325, or toll free 800/822-RSVP, 800/235-RSVP in Florida).

Aero Coach (tel. 809/367-2294 in Abaco, or toll free 800/327-0010, 800/432-5034 in Florida) has flights to Governor's Harbour, Rock Sound, and North Eleuthera and back to Miami and Fort Lauderdale several times a day.

Piedmont/Henson (tel. toll free 800/251-5720) flies between Fort Lauderdale and North Eleuthera, Governor's Island, Rock Sound, and Nassau.

Mailboats

Several mailboats from Nassau, leaving from Potter's Cay Dock, visit Eleuthera, but their schedules are subject to change because of weather conditions. For more details of sailings, consult the dockmaster at Potter's Cay Dock in Nassau (tel. 809/323-1064).

The M/V *Current Pride* goes from Nassau to Current Island, serving Lower and Upper Bogue. It departs Nassau at 7 a.m. Thursday, returning on Tuesday.

The M/V *Bahamas Daybreak II* leaves Nassau, heading for North Eleuthera, Spanish Wells, and Harbour Island. Departures are on Thursday at 6 a.m. from Nassau, with a return on Monday.

The M/V *Harley and Charlie* leaves Nassau on Monday (returning on Tuesday), heading for Central Eleuthera: Hatchet Bay and Governor's Harbour, and the same vessel goes from Nassau to South Eleuthera: Davis Harbour and Rock Sound. It departs Nassau on Tuesday, returning on Thursday.

1. ROCK SOUND

In South Eleuthera, Rock Sound is a small, tree-shaded village, the principal center of the island and its most exclusive enclave. To the south of Tarpum Bay, it opens onto Exuma Sound. The town is at least two centuries old, and it has many old-fashioned homes with picket fences out front. Once it was notorious for the wreckers who lured ships ashore with false beacons. In those days it was known as "Wreck Sound."

The largest settlement in Eleuthera, Rock Sound is serviced by an airport. It is also the commercial heart of the southern area, with a modern shopping center. Many residents who live in South Eleuthera come here to stock up on supplies.

Arthur Vining Davis, the Florida millionaire, and Juan Trippe, developer of Pan American Airlines, did much to publicize Rock Sound. A lot of famous people have visited here, including the Mountbattens, and more recently the Prince and Princess of Wales, as well as titans of industry and an occasional movie star.

The Ocean Hole to the east is about 1¼ miles from the heart of the town. This is a saltwater lake that eventually links to the sea. You can walk right down to the edge of the water. This is one of the most attractive spots on Eleuthera. The "hole" is said to be bottomless. Many tropical fish can be seen here; they seem to like to be photographed—but only if you feed them first.

PRACTICAL FACTS: A few pointers may help you enjoy your visit to Rock Sound even more than you may expect.

Car rentals: Ask at your hotel for what's available. No national car-rental agencies operate here. **Dingle Motor Service,** King's Highway (tel. 809/334-2031), might rent you a vehicle.

Church: Rock Sound has an Anglican church, near the water.

Medical care: A doctor and four resident nurses form the staff of the **Rock Sound Medical Clinic** (tel. 809/334-2226).

Police: Telephone 809/334-2244 to call the police.

Shopping: If you're looking for gifts and souvenirs, try **Goombay Gifts,** Market Place King, P.O. Box 21 (tel. 809/334-2191). Buy liquor at **Sturrup's Liquor Store,** Queen's Highway, Market Place (tel. 809/334-2219).

WHERE TO STAY: One of the most prestigious and luxurious beach, golf, and tennis resorts in The Bahamas is **Cotton Bay Club,** P.O. Box 28, Rock Sound, Eleuthera, The Bahamas (tel. 809/334-6101). Once a private club built by Juan Trippe, founder of Pan Am, Cotton Bay, while still having memberships, was opened to nonmembers in 1975. The oceanside resort is on a two-mile stretch of white sandy beach with acres of landscaped grounds. It once advertised itself as "Where Who's Who in America Goes Barefoot in The Bahamas." All public rooms have tropical furnishings. The main cocktail lounge is built with a peaked circular roof, and has furnishings of rattan. Drinks are served around an overscale pool with a fringe of palm trees. Dinner at Cotton Bay is served outside on the pool terrace. Menus are American and continental cuisine, spiced with Bahamian specialties.

Life is quiet and leisurely at this aristocrat of Bahamian resorts. Most units, 77 in all, overlook the ocean. All accommodations are air-conditioned, and living rooms are available in some. All rates are quoted on the MAP. In winter, they range from $255 to $305 daily in a single, from $300 to $350 in a double. *In summer, singles on the MAP pay $165 to $185 daily, with doubles charged $205 to $225.*

The resort contains a Robert Trent Jones–designed 18-hole golf course, a championship layout with ocean holes, and four championship tennis courts. Deep-sea and bonefishing trips are available at Davis Harbour Marina. Cotton Bay is at Powell Point, 12 miles from Rock Sound Airport.

Edwina's Place, P.O. Box 30, Rock Sound, Eleuthera, The Bahamas (tel. 809/334-2094), is Bahamian owned—"Edwina Burrows' place"—just one mile from Rock Sound Airport. Its utter simplicity is balanced with enthusiastic hospitality. Set directly on the water, the rooms are clean and furnished plainly. There is a restaurant on the premises (see below). All village facilities are within walking distance of the motel, and if you want to go farther afield, Mrs. Burrows says that if you'll put some gas in her old car, "you can take off," but you'll be charged for the privilege. Most of the guests live in their swimsuits, so the dress is decidedly casual. In winter, a single rents for $42 per day, *and this is lowered to $37 per day in summer.* Two people pay $60 per day in winter, *only $45 per day in summer.* Tennis, snorkeling, scuba-diving, deep-sea fishing, and boating can be arranged by the management.

In an area of high-priced and often snobbish resorts, she is a welcome breath of air, not only for her low prices but because of her good nature and personality.

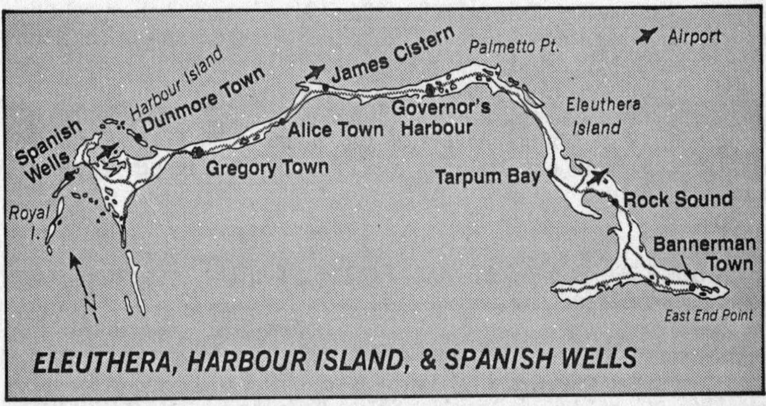

ELEUTHERA, HARBOUR ISLAND, & SPANISH WELLS

WHERE TO DINE: Many guests staying at other hotels enjoy the food served at **Cotton Bay Club** (tel. 809/334-6101), one of the most prestigious hotels in The Bahamas. If you call for a reservation, the maître d' will be happy to welcome you for a meal. Breakfast is served daily from 7:30 to 10 a.m., costing $8 per person. Lunch, from $15, is served from 12:30 to 2:30 p.m., and dinner is a jacket-and-tie, relatively formal affair nightly from 7 to 9 p.m. Costing from $35 per person without drinks, dinner is served near a screen of palms and bougainvillea in a curved and modern dining room stretching between the sea and a freshwater pool, or you can have it on an open-air terrace. It includes a changing array of specialties such as pan-fried grouper, sautéed filet of veal Oscar, grilled pork chops with sauce Robert, Hungarian beef goulash, and broiled lobster tail with melted butter followed by such desserts as lemon pie. The big nights to come here are Wednesday for the buffet (when it becomes "just Bahamian") and Saturday for barbecue night ("how do you like your steak?").

At **Edwina's Place** (tel. 809/334-2094), you "haven't tasted anything yet till you've tried my conch fritters or my conch chowder." That's Edwina Burrows talking, the hospitable owner of this simple little roadside restaurant and adjoining motel (see above). One diner noted, "I get the best food in Eleuthera here." A hard-working, devout Christian woman, Mrs. Burrows will prepare you cracked conch or perhaps a baked fish based on the catch of the day. She takes time with her vegetables too. I've enjoyed her five-bean salad, and her stuffed tomatoes are delicious. "Whenever possible, I use vegetables right from my own little cabbage patch," she confides. Prices of a main course include appetizers. You can also drop in for breakfast from 7 a.m. Figure on spending $12 with tip for lunch, which can be simple fare, such as fish sandwiches. Top off the meal with her coconut pie, or try her rum cake or guava duff. You'll probably spend about $18 for dinner, everything included. Try to go for dinner before 8 p.m.

THE SPORTING LIFE: Many visitors come to South Eleuthera just for the golf at the Cotton Bay Club, but there is a full sports program.

Golf

The **Cotton Bay Club** (tel. 809/334-6101) has an 18-hole, par 72 golf course—one of the most famous in The Bahamas—that was designed by Robert Trent Jones. Its 7,068 yards are almost surrounded by the ocean. Greens fees are $20 for 18 holes. A caddy costs $10 for 18 holes, and electric carts cost $20 for 18 holes. There is a lounge, as well as a snackbar and a drinking bar in the clubhouse, along with showers and lockers. The clubhouse also has a complete pro shop. The course lies some ten miles from Rock Sound and is open daily from 8 a.m. to 5:30 p.m.

Tennis

Cotton Bay Club (tel. 809/334-6101) has four Har-Tru surfaced courts that are complimentary for guests.

Fishing

Cotton Bay Club (tel. 809/334-6101) can make arrangements for guests to go on deep-sea fishing excursions. With all equipment included, a half-day tour costs $250, a full-day voyage going for $450.

Anyone interested in bonefishing can get in touch with **Alfred McKinney** at Deep Creek (tel. 809/334-6180). He charges $70 for a half day of fishing, or $90 for a full day.

2. WINDERMERE ISLAND

Windermere is a very tiny island, connected by a bridge to "mainland" Eleuthera. It is midway between the settlements of Governor's Harbour and Rock Sound.

This island couldn't be more discreet. "We like to keep it quiet around here," one of the staff at the famed Windermere Island Club recently told me. But, regrettably for this deluxe and snobbish citadel, that isn't always possible. When Prince Charles first took his Princess Di here, she was photographed in her swimming suit, even though pregnant, and the picture gained wide notoriety, much to the horror of the club.

Prince Charles himself had first heard of the club long ago, through his great-uncle, Earl Mountbatten of Burma, who was assassinated in 1979 while sailing off Ireland. He was one of the island's more frequent visitors and one of its major enthusiasts.

Aristocrats on both sides of the Atlantic, not only the Mountbattens, but the Astors and the Biddles, have flocked to this club, along with royalty, an occasional visiting head of state, and tycoons of industry.

The club reportedly has some 700 members, and, naturally, these guests are given preference when it comes to renting a room. But the general public is invited as well—that is, those who can afford it. It's one of the most expensive retreats in The Bahamas.

Even if you can't afford its hotel tariffs, you may want to consider dining there. Of course, you must make a reservation and show up in your finery (that is, a jacket and tie for men and, preferably, a long gown for women).

The island has its own charm, especially Savannah Sound, which has lovely sheltered beaches and facilities for waterskiing, sailboating, snorkeling, and skindiving. There are also excellent beaches for shelling. Frequent picnics are arranged at West Beach on Savannah Sound, and there is good bonefishing, with some catches more than ten pounds.

ACCOMMODATIONS: The ideal place for persons seeking a tranquil haven is **Windermere Island Club,** P.O. Box 25, Rock Sound, Eleuthera, The Bahamas (tel. 809/332-2538, or toll free 800/237-1236 in the U.S., 800/451-2253 in Canada; for New York City, see below). Operated by the prestigious chain that runs the Venice Simplon-Orient Express, this gracious and isolated resort is for those who crave unspoiled seclusion. It occupies the sun-flooded southern end of Windermere Island, a snake-shaped formation lying off the eastern coast of Eleuthera. Accommodations sit in a large garden of soft fir trees and palms, directly on one of the most beautiful beaches in The Bahamas.

Capped with a brass replica of a pineapple—the symbol of hospitality—the central building is octagonal, with a second-floor sitting room whose pine beams soar into a single point high above the modern white furniture. A beautiful swimming pool, shaped like an angular interpretation of a pineapple, opens onto a protected terrace. Tall coconut trees, illuminated at night, sway at the edge of the sunbathing area, whose white garden chairs serve double duty for fair-weather breakfasts and buffet lunches. Windermere Island Club is equipped with six all-weather tennis courts with a resident professional. Twice weekly an Eleutheran band plays for dancing. The main living room of the club is overscale and airy, with ring-around 360° windows and a paperback library. The resort's dining facilities are reviewed separately.

The club has 21 rooms, 10 suites, and 10 apartments, each with a private patio or balcony overlooking the sea. Both suites and guest rooms are on the beach, overlooking the Atlantic, its rolling surf, and its sunrises. Suites contain a living room, bedroom, dressing room, kitchenette, and veranda. There are beachfront choices of private apartments, each with two bedrooms, two baths, a full kitchen, a large living room, and a veranda. (These are available all year; however, the club is closed in September and October.) There are also a dozen two- to five-bedroom privately owned homes available for rent year-round. Most accommodations, regardless of their size, have private verandas ringed with neo-Victorian gingerbread and wooden ceilings covered with planks of pickled cedar.

In the guest rooms, winter prices are $290 daily in a single and $350 in a double, with one-bedroom suites renting for $460 single and $520 double, all AP tariffs. The hotel is closed from June to November but quotes *shoulder season rates (that is, spring and fall) of $185 daily in a single and $245 in a double, with one-bedroom suites, either single or double occupancy, going for $350.*

On either side of the clubhouse are two-bedroom apartments, each with a spacious living room, tiny kitchen, and ocean view. Private villas are set in the midst of palms and pines.

For reservations and information, write or call Venice Simplon-Orient Express Hotels, 1 World Trade Center, New York, NY 10048 (tel. 212/839-0222).

DINING AT THE CLUB: Even if you're staying elsewhere, you can visit the glamorous dining room of the **Windermere Island Club** (tel. 809/332-2538). Lunch is a fixed-price buffet laden with a smörgåsbord of warm and cold dishes, elegantly prepared and served by a polite and impeccably uniformed staff from 12:30 to 2 p.m. It costs $15 per person and is offered daily. Sunday brunch, from noon to 2 p.m., goes for $20 per person, plus service. On Tuesday and Saturday, its location moves to West Beach, where a barbecue buffet is presented.

Dinner, from 7:30 to 8:30 p.m., requires an advance reservation and proper attire. Fixed-price meals cost from $35 per person, not including drinks, and are supervised by Rodney Pinder, one of the most capable maître d's in The Bahamas. Don't overlook the possibility of a before-dinner drink in the nearby bar. No meals are served in September and October when the hotel shuts down. Jackets are required for men after 6 p.m.

WINDERMERE'S WORLD OF SPORTS: Guests can enjoy a number of activities from bonefishing to windsurfing. The dockmaster at West Beach is well qualified to guide and advise about bonefishing, or perhaps you'd like to go deep-sea fishing for white marlin, dolphin, grouper, wahoo, Allison tuna, and amberjack, just a few of the big fish found in these waters. A half-day trip costs $300; a full day, $450.

Scuba-diving and snorkeling are also available; equipment for club guests and members is issued from the shed adjacent to the tennis pro's shop. The resort's glass-bottom dinghy is also available free for use of guests. Sunfish and windsurfers, available from the dockmaster on the West Beach, can be used by guests. The Windermere Island Club has its own speedboat, based at the dockmaster's office. It can be used to go waterskiing.

West Beach, a good place for sunning and swimming (great for children), is about a ten-minute walk from the hotel, although the club bus will transport you there and back if necessary. Beer and soft drinks are available. The beach is on Savannah Sound, the body of calm, protected water separating Windermere from the main island of Eleuthera.

Six all-weather tennis courts are near the main Windermere complex. Signup for play or instruction is at the tennis pro shop, where the head pro has international teaching and tournament experience and is available for private lessons.

3. TARPUM BAY

If you're looking for an inexpensive holiday on high-priced Eleuthera, forget Windermere Island or Cotton Bay and head here. A waterfront village, some nine miles north of the super-expensive citadels of fine living at Rock Sound, it has a number of guesthouses that take in economy-minded tourists. This tiny settlement with its many pastel-washed houses is a favorite of artists who have established a small colony here.

It was once flourishing as a pineapple export center. That's when many of the present clapboard homes with their gingerbread trim were constructed. Nowadays an air of nostalgia pervades this old community. It's also good for fishing.

Flanders' Art Studio, P.O. Box 29 (tel. 809/334-4187), is the clapboard domain of Mal Flanders, an American expatriate who found a new lease on life—and inspiration for his art—at the southern end of the hamlet. His renditions of island life and tropical village scenes are painted on either driftwood or canvas. One of his better-known series showed different interpretations of the Miami Dolphins during their winning Superbowl series of 1972, and his paintings now hang in many prominent homes. In Key West in the 1950s, he turned his creative efforts to painting, mostly of island scenes and fishing or shrimp boats. He came to Tarpum Bay in 1973, fell in love with the place, and has been here ever since. He says he hopes his colorful paintings "are an expression of my love for The Bahamas and the Bahamian people."

Honors as the community's artistic patriarch are given to a Scottish-Irish sculptor and painter who since 1957 has occupied an oceanfront house on the northern edge of the hamlet. Bearded, psychic, and gracious, **Peter MacMillan-Hughes** has sold paintings to an impressive array of patrons, one of whom was Lord Mountbatten. He imagines himself a Neptune among the mermaids in Bahamian waters. Eccentric, yes, but fascinating. His pen-and-ink tinted maps, drawings of birds, and hand-lettered poems and histories are displayed in many prominent homes. Some of the canvases glow with the reflected light of Bahamian moonscapes and are sought after by art dealers as far away as London. Often clad in purple ("a difficult color to paint with, but very high in spiritual power"), he built with his own hands the tower of the limestone castle that rises from the center of town, a short walk from his studio. Soft-spoken, talented, and accessible, Mr. MacMillan-Hughes might in his own person be the single most interesting tourist attraction at Tarpum Bay. Visitors are welcome to show up at his door.

One of the local clubs has a fascinating name: "Dark End of the Street Club." The location is about seven miles from Rock Sound Airport.

FOOD AND LODGING: A ten-room motel, **Hilton's Haven Motel and Restaurant,** Tarpum Bay, Eleuthera, The Bahamas (tel. 809/334-4231), is in a modern Bahamian two-story structure with covered verandas. Comfortably furnished apartments, each with its private sun patio and bath, are rented. The units come with either air conditioning or ceiling fans. What makes this place special is Mary Hilton herself, everybody's "Bahama Mama." In fact, as a professional nurse, she has delivered some 2,000 of Eleuthera's finest citizens. Her brother is T. Langton Hilton, solicitor-general of the Commonwealth until his retirement in 1980. "Hilton is our God-given name," she says. "We never met Conrad." She invites you to "come and stay long enough to get to know us." If you arrive hot and thirsty, she'll tell the woman who works for her, "go and get me a fresh lime off the tree. We'll make these people something cold to drink." To provide a retirement income for herself, she started Hilton's Haven "when it was just a pond. I had it filled in and started to build."

The main tavern-style dining room, with a library in the corner, provides well-cooked food; the cuisine puts its emphasis on freshly caught fish. You can order grouper cutlets with peas 'n' rice, steamed conch, and an occasional lobster. There is also a well-stocked bar. Lunches, costing from $8, are served from 12:30 to 2:30 p.m., and dinners, from $12, are offered from 6:30 to 8 p.m.

Mainly retired, Mrs. Hilton is still a registered nurse, and medical facilities are always available. If you're handicapped in any way, you've come to the right place. She'll take good care of you. Life is casual and informal at Hilton's, and you can have privacy and relaxation. *In summer, singles on the EP pay only $35, and a double goes for $40.* In winter, rates go up slightly: singles pay from $40, and doubles cost from $45. For breakfast and dinner, add another $16 per person daily. Each additional person in a room is charged $8. Children under 12 need pay only $5.

Cartwright's Ocean View Cottages, Tarpum Bay, Eleuthera, The Bahamas (tel. 809/334-4215), is a cluster of two- and three-bedroom cottages right by the sea, with fishing, snorkeling, and swimming at your door. This is one of the few places where you can sit on your patio and watch the sunset. The cottages are fully furnished, with bedding, towels, utensils, stove, refrigerator, and pots and pans. Maid service is also provided. Year-round, a large three-bedroom cottage suitable for six people goes for $150 per day. In winter, the rate is $55 a day in a single, $70 in a double, and $90 in a room for four persons. *In summer, the charge is $50 a day for singles, $65 for doubles, and $85 for four guests.* The establishment is within walking distance of local stores and restaurants. The owners, Iris and Hervis Cartwright, are helpful. Hervis operates an informal taxi business and will meet you at Rock Sound Airport seven miles away.

At **Ethel's Cottages,** Tarpum Bay, Eleuthera, The Bahamas (tel. 809/334-4030), Mrs. Ethel Knowles offers beachfront accommodations, each cottage containing a kitchen, a bath, and a living and dining room. They're about seven miles from Rock Sound Airport and within walking distance of stores and restaurants. The cottages rent for $50 per day in a double. This rate applies both summer and winter. If you want your own car, Mrs. Knowles will rent you one for about $50 per day. She also runs a taxi service if you need transportation but don't want to drive.

4. GOVERNOR'S HARBOUR

After passing through Tarpum Bay, the next destination is Governor's Harbour, which, at some 300 years old, is the island's oldest settlement. This is believed to have been the landing place of the Eleutherian Adventurers. It's the largest settlement in Eleuthera after Rock Sound, lying about midway along the 100-mile island, wrapped around a curving bay. It has an airport where Bahamasair comes in on both morning and evening flights from Nassau.

The town today has a population of about 750, with some bloodlines going back to the original settlers, the Eleutherian Adventurers, and to the Loyalists who followed some 135 years later. Many old homes—waiting for "discovery"—can still be seen, showing the wear and tear of decades. A quiet nostalgia prevails amid such vegetation as bougainvillea and casuarina trees.

Leaving Queen's Highway you can take a small bridge to Cupid's Cay (I don't know how it got that romantic name). The bridge is thought to be about a century and a half old, although there don't seem to be any records as to its construction. As you're exploring, you'll come upon one of the most interesting buildings in the area, an old Anglican church with its tombstone-studded graveyard.

The long-ago opening of the Club Med brought renewed vitality to the once-sleepy village. Tourism has unquestionably altered sleepy Governor's Harbour.

PRACTICAL FACTS: If you're staying outside the town in one of the housekeeping colonies, you may find much-needed services and supplies in Governor's Harbour or at nearby Palmetto Point.

Bank: Governor's Harbour has a branch of **Barclays Bank International,** Queen's Highway, P.O. Box 22 (tel. 809/332-2300).

Car rental: If you need a car, try **Asa-Rent-a-Car Service,** Palmetto Shores, P.O. Box 131 (tel. 809/332-2305). The cost is $50 for one day.

Hair care: Women can get their hair done at **Ann's Beauty Salon,** South Palmetto Point, P.O. Box 35 (tel. 809/332-2342). She also offers manicures and pedicures.

Medical care: On Queen's Highway are both the government clinic (tel. 809/332-2001) and the dentist's office (tel. 809/332-2704).

Police: To telephone the police, call 809/332-2111.

Post office: Governor's Harbour has a post office on Haynes Avenue (tel. 809/332-2060).

Taxis: If you need a cab, call **Cecil Cooper Taxi Service,** P.O. Box 101 (tel. 809/332-2575).

Shopping: For gifts or souvenirs, try **Norma's Gift Shop** (tel. 809/332-2002), which sells batik dresses, blouses, skirts, beachwear, swimwear, and men's shirts, as well as jewelry. Some of the clothing is handmade on the premises.

Nearby is yet another place to shop, **Brenda's Gift Store,** Haynes Avenue (tel. 809/332-2089). This two-room store occupies a clapboard-sided building a few steps away from the only traffic light in Eleuthera. Inside is a large inventory of T-shirts, sundresses, bathing suits, and such Bahamian souvenirs as conch jewelry.

WHERE TO STAY: Along the uncluttered beach of fine sand and vegetation, **Club Méditerranée,** P.O. Box 80, French Leaves, Governor's Harbour, Eleuthera, The Bahamas (tel. 212/750-1670 in New York, or toll free 800/CLUB-MED), is a cluster of pastel-colored, twin-bedded bungalows built in two- and three-story colonies. The village seems to be at the world's end. All the rooms are air-conditioned and handsomely furnished with Philippine mahogany furniture and private baths. The social life revolves around a restaurant-bar-dance floor complex built in a free-flowing Bahamian style. In front of this complex, facing the garden, is a large free-form swimming pool, usually filled with bikini-clad guests. Heavy emphasis is on social life—day-long picnics, nightly entertainment, a disco, and taped classical music concerts at sunset.

Accommodation is based on double occupancy only. Three full meals a day, including free unlimited wine at lunch and dinner, are offered, as are all sports activities and equipment, also qualified instruction. The Governor's Harbour resort is a family club, providing total supervision for children. Land-based rates are the highest at Christmas week, $1,200 per person weekly. In winter, prices are from $820 to $1,000 weekly, *lowered off-season to $660 per person weekly.* These tariffs are all inclusive.

The club's scuba program is geared to certified divers as well as beginners. Experienced divers discover the Bahamian "blue holes." Those just taking up the sport go through a series of four lessons before their first deep dive. All equipment and instruction are freely provided. At its underwater photo lab, the club provides cameras and you provide the film. Same-day processing is available for a small charge. This is a unique way to build a library of underwater vacation memories. Waterskiing, snorkeling, sailing, bicycling, tennis (eight courts, two lit for night play), picnics, aerobics, and jogging on the pink-sand beach are ways most members spend their days.

Cigatoo Inn, P.O. Box 86, Governor's Harbour, Eleuthera, The Bahamas (tel. 809/332-2343), set on a hillside, is a motel-like cluster built around a small swimming pool with a terrace. Cigatoo, which is the Arawak name for Eleuthera, is one of the best and most reasonably priced inns (both for accommodations and food) in the Governor's Harbour area. You pass between two rows of Christmas palms to reach the hotel. Set on grounds planted with such tropical foliage as hibiscus, the inn rents 26 streamlined, functional bedrooms, each air conditioned with double beds and private baths and patios overlooking the distant sea or the hotel's pool. The beach is about a five-minute walk away.

The most expensive accommodations are the oceanview suites, and the least expensive are the standard rooms with patio views. Depending on your room assignment, *summer rates range from $48 to $90 daily in a single, going up to $55 to $90 in a double.* In winter, prices increase to $58 to $116 daily in a single and $70 to $116 in a double. The hotel's restaurant, one of the best in the area, serves a combination of Bahamian and American dishes, costing from $18. If you're exploring Governor's Harbour for the day, you can drop in seven days a week from 11:30 a.m. to 2 p.m. and 7 to 9 p.m. for a good-tasting meal. The inn also has a tennis court and a bar serving such drinks as piña coladas and Goombay Smashes. Local entertainment is often provided.

Wykee's World Resort, P.O. Box 176, Governor's Harbour, Eleuthera, The Bahamas (tel. 809/332-2701), run by Chuck and Lee Weiche, is a snug and cozy retreat on a private estate. Lying three miles north of Governor's Harbour, along Queen's Highway, the resort was once owned by a former prime minister of The Bahamas, Sir Roland Symonette. It is set in a landscape of coconut palms and tropical plants. Six well-equipped stone-built villas, each one different, are rented all year, with names such as Bougainvillea House or Jasmine House. The least expensive is the Allamanda House with one bedroom, one bath, a kitchen, a living and dining room, and a screened-in porch. *Two guests pay only $60 per night in summer,* rising to $75 in winter. *The two-bedroom Oleander House, which will sleep four, costs $120 per night in summer,* rising to $150 in winter. *Families may want to consider the four-bedroom Coconut Palm House, ideal for eight guests, which costs $160 per night in summer,* going up to $200 in winter. Minimum rental is one week unless other arrangements are made. The estate has a saltwater pool and beaches are near at hand. No more than 30 guests at one time are ever at the hotel. Some villas offer views of the ocean; all have ceiling fans. Laundry facilities are available, and such sports as snorkeling, fishing, windsurfing, and tennis can be arranged.

NATIVE FOOD: In and around Governor's Harbour and Palmetto Point are found some of the best local restaurants in the Family Islands of The Bahamas. They include the following:

La Rastic Restaurant, on the highway to Palmetto Point (tel. 809/332-2164), is owned by Rodney Pinder, the polite maître d' at the exclusive Windermere Club. His wife, Sharon Pinder, runs the place. In the back is his mother-in-law, Vangie Culmer, one of the best native cooks in Eleuthera. Opened in 1985, this is a pleasant place for either a light meal or a full dinner. Lunches cost from $8, dinners run $20 and up, and service is from 8:30 a.m. to 9 p.m. Monday to Saturday, on Sunday from 9 a.m. to 9 p.m. The fare includes such sturdy dishes as barbecued chicken or spareribs, and boiled or stewed fish. You might begin with conch chowder, then go on to a grilled T-bone steak or broiled lobster tail. Finish off your meal with one of the good-tasting rich pastries, perhaps lemon pie.

Ronnie's Sunset Inn Restaurant and Bar, on the highway, P.O. Box 21 (tel. 809/332-2232). Airy, very clean, and flooded with sunlight, this popular bar and restaurant is one of the best known on the island. Since it was established in 1985 by Mark Thompson, wedding receptions have been held on its patio, and hundreds of workers have left their lunchboxes to be filled in the tile kitchen. Don't overlook the possibility of a drink in the lower-level Sloop Bar where nautical implements line the intimate spaces. If you're looking for a skillfully seasoned meal, the street-level dining rooms serve them with style beneath a raftered ceiling with a glassed-in view of the sea. The chef prepares breakfast and lunch from 8 a.m. to 2 p.m. Lunches cost $7 and up and are served daily except Sunday. You can order stewed fish, omelets, johnnycakes, sheep's tongue souse, fresh conch salad, conch chowder, crayfish salad, pork chops, or grouper cutlet. Dinners are served nightly from 6 to 10 and are more elaborate, costing from $25. Typical fare includes pork chops, cracked conch, strip steak, chicken dishes, and changing daily specials. Dinner is from 6 to 10 p.m. daily except Sunday. The bar closes at 2 a.m.

Coyaba (tel. 809/332-2668) is at Governor's Harbour, between the airport and the center of town. It occupies a veranda-fronted modern building north of town. Guests can also eat in the big-windowed dining room. It is open daily except Monday from 11 a.m. to "until." You get typical Bahamian fare here, including crayfish, cracked conch, grilled chicken, and broiled grouper, along with pizza. Lunches cost from $15, with dinners going for around $25. Ann and Clyde Bethel occasionally present entertainment on Sunday afternoon.

5. PALMETTO POINT

On the opposite side of the highway is North Palmetto Point, a charming little workaday hamlet where visitors rarely venture (although you can get a meal there). Far from the much-traveled tourist routes, little hamlets like this are laid back and for the visitor who is seeking an escapist retreat.

Directly south of Governor's Harbour, on the western coast of Eleuthera, lies the beach-fronting South Palmetto Point, which has some inexpensive housekeeping units for those interested.

SELF-SUFFICIENT UNITS: The creation of a local builder, **Palmetto Shores Vacation Villas,** P.O. Box 131, Governor's Harbour, Eleuthera, The Bahamas (tel. 809/332-2305), is a good choice for a housekeeping holiday. Asa Bethel rents out waterside vacation villas, suitable for two to six guests. Units are built in Bahamian style, with wraparound balconies. Best of all, they open directly onto your private beach. Furnishings are simple but reasonably comfortable, maid service is included, and the villas lie within walking distance of local shops and tennis courts. In winter, a villa with one bed, a living room, and kitchen costs two people a total of $80 daily. A three-bedroom villa, suitable for up to six guests, rents for $190 per day. *In summer, two people are housed in the one-bedroom villa for $60 to $70 per day, the cost going up to $95 to $180 in a three-bedroom villa for four guests.* Deep-sea fishing and waterskiing are available. Free Sunflower sailboats are also provided. You can rent a flipper, mask, and snorkel. For confirmed reservations, call Asa Bethel.

WHERE TO EAT: Even if you have a kitchen in your bungalow, at some point you'll want to head for a meal at **Mate & Jenny's,** P.O. Box 25, South Palmetto Point (tel. 809/332-2504), a simple, concrete building right off the main highway. It's a pizza restaurant with a jukebox and pool table along with a dartboard. It's also one of the most popular gathering places on the island, and the cook is known for conch pizza. It opens daily at 10 a.m., staying open "until the last customer leaves." Light meals, including snacks and sandwiches, are regularly featured; however, full-course meals, costing from $15, require a reservation. The Bethel family will prepare pan-fried grouper, cracked conch, or whatever. On Sunday it doesn't open until 6:30 p.m.

If you're an adventurer, and in the vicinity of North Palmetto Point, a good place to remember is **Muriel's Home Made Bread, Restaurant, and Grocery** (tel. 809/332-2583). Eleuthera-born Muriel Cooper's operation is open daily except Sunday, from 9 a.m. to 10 p.m. She operates a bakery, take-out food emporium, and a grocery store. Her establishment is contained in a simple house half filled with the canned goods of her grocery. Her rich and moist pineapple or coconut cake is some of the best you'll find in the Family Islands. A limited cooked-food menu includes full dinners beginning at $8. Your choice includes chicken with chips, cracked conch with chips, conch chowder, and conch fritters. A dining room, decorated with family memorabilia, is available for clients who want to consume their food on location. If you want a meal more elaborate than the ones cited, you'll have to stop by in the morning to announce your arrival time and menu preference.

6. HATCHET BAY

North of Governor's Harbour, Hatchet Bay was once known for its plantation that raised prize Angus cattle. But that operation now produces poultry and dairy products. The unused chicken parts are thrown to devouring fish at "Shark Hole."

FOOD AND LODGING: Two miles south of Alice Town, the **Rainbow Inn,** P.O. Box 53, Governor's Harbour, Eleuthera, The Bahamas (tel. 809/332-2690), is an isolated collection of cedar-sided bungalows, each designed in the shape of an octagon. The bar and restaurant has a high beamed ceiling, stone trim, and the kind of thick-topped bar where guests down a brace of daiquiris or piña coladas. Each of the tables in the adjacent dining room was crafted of wood salvaged from some kind of wrecked boat. The menu for the evening meal is posted near the bar every day, costing from $25 per person.

There's a sandy beach a few steps away, plus a tennis court, as well as a dozen simple but comfortable accommodations. Each is air-conditioned and has a private bath, lots of exposed wood, and a ceiling fan. Most of the units also contain kitchenettes. In winter, a studio apartment with a full kitchen costs $75 daily in a single, $110 in a double. A one-bedroom apartment with kitchen, suitable for one to five people, is priced at $110 daily. A two-bedroom apartment for up to seven goes for $130. *In summer, studio apartments with kitchen cost $70 daily in a single, $75 in a double. One-bedroom apartments with kitchen rent for $80 for one to five people and two-bedroom apartments, suitable between one and seven guests, are $115 per day.* For MAP in any season, add $25 per person.

At the hamlet of James Cistern, **Lucky's Wagon Wheel** (tel. 809/332-2131) is noted for its Bahamian food. You might choose chicken, grouper, or conch for your main dinner dish, served with peas 'n' rice, potato salad, and vegetables or coleslaw. The charge for these dinners is from $10. If you prefer the lobster, steak, or beef menu, costing $18, you get the same side dishes as with the regular dinner, but with the addition of tossed salad. Fresh Bahamian bread and conch chowder are also available. Lunches from noon to 2 p.m., when a smaller selection is offered, cost from $6.

On Sunday night, the owner-manager, Monica Bethel occasionally offers entertainment. From 7 p.m., join the party, sipping tropical drinks such as a Goombay Smash, rum punch, piña colada, and fruit punch. The staff will also serve beer, wine, or soda. The place is open seven days a week until midnight or later.

7. GREGORY TOWN

On the ribbon of road that continues north, Gregory Town stands in the center of Eleuthera, against a backdrop of hills, which breaks the usual flat monotony of the landscape. A village of clapboard cottages, it was once famed for growing pineapples. It still grows them, but not as it used to. However, the local people make a good rum out of the fruit. You can visit the Gregory Town Plantation and Distillery where pineapple rum is still produced. You're allowed to sample it, and surely you'll want to take a bottle home with you.

Dedicated surfers have come here from as far away as California and even Australia to test their skills on "the second-best wave in the world." (The best is in Hawaiian waters.)

An increasingly popular activity here is spelunking (exploring and studying caves). South of the town there are several caverns worth visiting, the largest of which is called simply **"The Cave."** It has a big fig tree out front, which the people of Gregory Town claim was planted long ago by area pirates who wanted to conceal this cave where they had hidden treasure.

Local guides (you have to ask around in Gregory Town) will take explorers through this cave. The bats living inside are considered harmless, even though you know they must resent the intrusion of tourists with their flashlights. At one point the drop is so steep—about 12 feet—that you have to use a ladder to climb down. Eventually you reach a cavern studded with stalactites and stalagmites. At this point the reason you hired a guide will become obvious, as you're faced with a maze of passageways leading off through the rocky underground recesses. The cave comes to an abrupt end at the edge of a cliff, where the thundering sea is some 90 feet below.

After leaving Gregory Town and driving north, you come to the famed **Glass Windows,** chief sight of Eleuthera. This is the narrowest point of Eleuthera. Once a natural rock arch bridged the land, but it is gone, replaced by a man-made bridge. As you drive across it, you can see the contrast between the deep blue of the ocean and the emerald green of the shoal waters of the sound. The rocks rise to a height of 70 feet. Often, as ships in the Atlantic are being tossed about, the crew has looked across the narrow point to see a ship resting quietly on the other side. Hence the name: Glass Windows.

WHERE TO STAY: A stylish complex of self-catering villas, **Oleander Gardens Beach Hotel and Villas,** P.O. Box 5165, Gregory Town, Eleuthera, The Bahamas (tel. 809/333-2058), is one of the best places for establishing a "beachhead" on mainland Eleuthera. Eight units are available to rent, and they're scattered amid privately owned neighboring villas on either side of a private road. The complex looks like a version of private suburban houses, with their own gardens, each within walking distance of a rocky peninsula jutting into the sea near a sandy beach. A beachfront bar and snack restaurant, tennis court, and facilities for renting sailboats and windsurfers lie within the resort's 40 acres. If you're driving along the coastal highway, consider a luncheon stopover here anytime from 12:30 to 2 p.m. daily. Meals, costing from $12, consist of such concoctions as fried potato skins with a special dip, pepper steak, seafood platter, and other fresh fish.

Stucco covered, with private kitchens and a lot of space, the apartments are ideal for independent vacationers who want to cook within their units. In winter, singles cost $75 daily; doubles, $100. *In summer, singles rent for $70 daily; doubles,* $85. A third person can live in any double room for $30 in winter, $25 *in summer.* In any season, MAP can be arranged for another $25 per person daily. The location is on a scrub-covered landscape about two miles south of the Glass Window Bridge and about 15 miles from the North Eleuthera Airport.

Pineapple Cove, P.O. Box 1548, Gregory Town, Eleuthera, The Bahamas (no phone at presstime; however, write P.O. Box 2007, Woburn, MA 01888—tel. 617/935-5555 or call toll free at 800/327-0787). This is an up and coming resort opening onto its own private beach. George and Ann Mullin acquired what had been the old Arawak Cove Club in the 1970s. From a vandalized and rundown site, they re-created a new resort, lying about 1½ miles north of Gregory Town and two miles south of the Glass Window. Set on 28 acres of grounds, which are still planted in part with pineapple, the resort cluster consists of 32 units scattered about the property. Each has air conditioning and ceiling fans and is comfortably furnished and reasonably spacious, decorated with pastel fabrics and colors and rattan furniture. Each also has a private bath and porch. In winter singles rent for $80 daily, with doubles costing $90 and triples $100. *In summer prices are $70 daily in a single, $80 in a double, and $90 in a triple.* MAP is another $30 per person, and children under 12 stay free. Paths lead along coral coves and cliffs, offering beautiful views.

WHERE TO DINE: You'll receive a warm welcome at **Pineapple Cove,** P.O. Box 1548, Gregory Town (no phone at presstime), lying a mile and a half north of Gregory Town. In a large, spacious dining room, decorated in a tropical style, you'll enjoy a daily changing menu of Bahamian and American dishes. You might begin with the inevitable conch chowder, then go on to such fare as a ribeye steak, sautéed grouper, or baked chicken. Occasionally they also offer baked ham. Lunch is from noon to 2 p.m. daily, costing from $6 to $8, and dinner is served from 6 to 10 p.m. for $21. The owners and managers invite you to come early and enjoy watching the sunset from their patio which surrounds a swimming pool. They don't promise, but hold out the possibility of your seeing the famous "green flash" written about by Ernest Hemingway. They also offer occasional entertainment.

While in Gregory Town, you can follow your nose. A tantalizing aroma of freshly baked goods draws you toward **Thompson's Bakery** at Green Hill (tel. 809/332-2269). There, on a tiny hill in a pint-size building with a wooden sign, Daisy Thompson has been turning out what is considered the best baked goods in Eleuthera, and she's been at it for almost a quarter of a century. Not only do the locals come to her for their dinner rolls and buns, but visitors flock here as well, buying her coconut tarts and pies (all with frothy toppings)—Mother rarely made exotic guava and sapodilla cakes like Daisy does, with help from her sister, Monica. These women begin at five o'clock every morning. They also make doughnuts, which are covered with coconut before serving. Daisy uses much of the fresh tropical fruit that grows on Eleuthera, this flavor giving her baked goods a unique taste for most foreigners. As Gregory Town is noted for its fresh, sweet pineapples, Daisy makes one of the best pineapple tarts I've ever had. So drop off and pick up a bag of goodies to take with you. They also sell medium-size pizzas for $4.50 each. The bakery is open daily except Sunday from 8:30 a.m. to 6 p.m.

8. THE CURRENT

At a settlement called The Current, in North Eleuthera, some houses are built on low piles. The inhabitants are believed to have descended from a tribe of North American Indians. A narrow strait separates the village from Current Island, where most of the men make their living from the sea and the women spend their days plaiting straw goods.

The **"Boiling Hole"** is in a shallow bank in front of the Current Club. It boils at changing tides.

This is a small community where the people often welcome visitors. There are no crowds and no artificial attractions. Everything focuses on the sea, which is a source of pleasure for the visiting tourists but a way to sustain life for the local people.

From The Current, you can explore some interesting sights in North Eleuthera, including **Preacher's Cave.** This is where the Eleutherian Adventurers found shelter in the mid-17th century when they were shipwrecked with no provisions. However, if you want to be driven there, know that your taxi driver may balk. The road is treacherous on his expensive tires. If you do reach it, you'll find a cave that has been compared to an amphitheater. The very devout Eleutherian Adventurers held religious services inside these caves, which are penetrated by holes in the roof, allowing light to intrude. The cave is not too far from the airport, in a northeasterly direction.

COTTAGES FOR RENT: A good place for families is **Sandcastle Cottages,** The Current, Eleuthera, The Bahamas (no phone number; call Nassau and ask for Current, Eleuthera), a housekeeping-cottage complex set amid coconut palms at the edge of the sea. The private beach is furnished with chaises longues and wooden parasols whose sun barriers consist of matted blankets of woven palm fronds. The white sands are perfect for building (what else?) sandcastles, although many guests choose simply to gaze into the azure depths of the expansive waters, which come close to the accommodations. The beach is safe for children, as you can wade for long distances before reaching the deep water. Many families choose this place for its relaxed seclusion. One-bedroom cottages sleeping four people cost about $50 in winter, *$36 in summer.* Two-bedroom accommodations, sleeping up to six people, rent for $65 in winter, *$50 in summer.* There's a village store where you can purchase supplies to use in your built-in kitchen.

Sea Raider, The Current, Eleuthera, The Bahamas (tel. 809/333-2290). Its handful of simple but pleasant accommodations are contained in a stone-fronted motel-like building partially concealed with hibiscus. Each enjoys a glassed-in view of the sea and a private patio just a few steps from the water. Provisions are available if you're interested in preparing your own meals. The food is primarily from the sea, and fresh fruits are plentiful and varied. In winter, oceanfront singles or doubles with kitchenette rent for $45 a day, a one-bedroom studio with kitchenette, either single or double, costing $70 and a mini-efficiency with bath and kitchenette going for $40 for two. *In summer, based on either single or double occupancy, oceanfront accommodations with kitchenette cost only $35 per day, a one-bedroom studio with kitchenette going for $53, and a mini-efficiency with bath and kitchenette, also priced at $35.* Guests are allowed the use of a tennis court nestled amid an orange grove nearby. Bikes are available for rent, as is snorkeling equipment. Tariffs include daily maid service. For reservations and information, contact 922 North Broadway, Rochester, MN 55904 (tel. 507/288-4009).

9. HARBOUR ISLAND

One of the oldest settlements in The Bahamas, founded before the United States was a nation, Harbour Island lies off the northern end of Eleuthera, some 200 miles from Miami. It is three miles long and a half a mile wide. By plane, it's only 1½ hours from Fort Lauderdale or Miami and a 30-minute flight from Nassau. To get here, you take a flight to the North Eleuthera airstrip, from which it's a one-mile ride to the ferry dock, costing $2 per person. The final lap is the two-mile ferry ride direct to Harbour Island, at a cost of $3 per person. Most people don't need transportation on the island. They walk to where they're going or else take a golf cart.

Affectionately called "Briland," Harbour Island is studded with good resorts and is famous for its spectacular pink-sand beach, which runs the whole length of the island on its eastern side. The beach is protected from the ocean breakers by an outlying coral reef, which makes for some of the safest bathing in The Bahamas. Except for unseasonably cold days, you can swim and enjoy water sports year-round. The climate averages 72° Fahrenheit in winter, 77° in spring and fall, and 82° in summer. Occasionally they have cool evenings with a low of around 65° from November to February.

Harbour Island's historic old **Dunmore Town,** with its pastel clapboard houses, often with whitewashed picket fences, was once the capital of The Bahamas. It's one of the oldest settlements in the archipelago, and even today remains one of the most colorful villages in the Family Islands. It evokes thoughts of waterfront vacation spots in the Carolinas.

The town was settled by English religious dissidents who came here in the 17th century. They were joined about 135 years later by Loyalists coming from the new United States, where they had become unpopular during the American Revolution for their support of British sovereignty. Dunmore Town was named for Lord Dunmore, an 18th-century royal governor of The Bahamas.

Titus Hole, a cave with an open mouth that looks out onto the sheltered harbor, is said to have been the first jail on Harbour Island. Also worth seeing is the **Loyalists Cottage,** dating back to 1790. Vestiges of colonial architecture can be seen in other old houses that were built during the latter part of the 19th century.

For years most of the breadwinners of Harbour Island were engaged in farming and boatbuilding, along with fishing and sponge diving. Farming is still done today on the main body of Eleuthera on land given to the Brilanders by Andrew Devereaux, a colonel in the British army, back in 1783. The Civil War in the United States brought an economic boom, with the Brilanders prospering on running the blockade the Union had placed on shipping to and from the Confederate states.

By 1880 Dunmore Town had become the second most important town of The Bahamas. It was not only a port of entry, it also had a major shipyard turning out vessels as large as four-masted schooners, as well as a trio of sugar mills—and it produced rum. It eventually fell on bad days, but with the coming of Prohibition to the United States, another boom era came to Dunmore Town. There was a market for its rum on the U.S. mainland, and rum-running became a major source of income.

The Brilanders suffered a great financial setback with the repeal of the Prohibition amendment, and then came the Great Depression and World War II, neither event helping matters much for Harbour Island. Finally, tourism has again brought prosperity.

Don't come here expecting much nightlife. However, various resorts schedule live entertainment on different evenings, and there are a few local clubs that come and go. Just ask around to find out what's happening. Most of the resorts are an easy walk from one another.

If you consider a **vehicle** a necessity even on such a small island, you can rent a golf cart or a Moke at Johnson's, P.O. Box 64 (tel. 809/333-2376). Mokes (a cross between a Jeep and a golf cart) cost $40 per day. It's wise to reserve well in advance.

WHERE TO STAY: Every major inn or resort at Harbour Island has its own repeat following. Many are quite good, and each has unique qualities. But, as the saying goes, that's why they print menus.

For my bill of fare, it's the **Coral Sands,** P.O. Box 23, Harbour Island, The Bahamas (tel. 809/333-2350), the beachfront lair of two remarkable people, Brett and Sharon King. Theirs is a self-contained all-purpose resort built on 14 hilly and tree-covered acres overlooking a beach of pink sand and lying within walking distance of the center of Dunmore Town, across from Pink Sands, another leading resort.

Brett King had an adventurous life before coming to Harbour Island. A wartime flyer and veteran of 134 combat missions in Europe and Africa, and winner of many medals for his bravery and daring, he later became an actor. He worked with such stars as Bette Davis, John Wayne, and Robert Mitchum and dated, among others, Elizabeth Taylor. He came to Harbour Island to complete plans for the resort which had been envisioned by his father before his death. Brett stayed and the rest of the story is now part of Harbour Island lore.

Since their opening in 1968, the world has come to their door. Sharon functions as a gracious hostess running between phone calls and welcoming guests into her hotel as if it were her own private party, which at times it becomes. California born and bred (a self-styled "valley girl"), Sharon is known for her style and vivacity. She's also very active in the community of Harbour Island.

Guests are welcomed into a choice of 33 rooms, each refurbished in a Caribbean motif. Many guests prefer their two-room, two-bath cottage and kitchen (set back from the beach), *which rents for $115 for two persons daily in fall and spring* rising to $150 in winter. In the main building, you can rent a single for $115 daily in winter, going up to $130 in a double. However, *off-season rates fall to $85 daily in a single and $95 in a double, a remarkable bargain.* The suites, which have oceanview patios, sleep a total of four persons and are ideal for families. In winter, two persons can occupy one of these suites for $150 daily, *the cost dropping to $115 in off-season.* MAP is available for another $33 per person daily.

The food is one of the reasons for staying here. It's like good home cooking, with a selection of American, Bahamian, and international dishes. For example, if you take lunch at the Beach Bar Sun Deck, order a bowl (not a cup) of some of the best-tasting conch chowder in the islands, served with a slice of freshly made coconut bread. You might follow with a toasted lobster sandwich that other hotels have imitated it's so good. Dinner might be preceded by one of the potent rum drinks in the Yellow Bird Bar. The meal might begin with conch fritters and go on to a fresh Bahamian fish such as grouper prepared in a number of ways. Outsiders who call for a reservation can order dinner from 7 to 8 p.m. at a cost of $26 per person. Entertainment is often provided in their nightclub in the park where you can dance under the stars.

The resort is very sports oriented, offering a tournament-class tennis court which can be lit for night games. All water sports, including boats and gear, can be arranged, as well as sailboats, rowboats, surfriders, and snorkeling equipment. The Kings provide beach umbrellas, chaise longues, and cabañeros among other equipment, and will have their staff pack a picnic lunch should you desire to explore some uninhabited islands nearby.

Fronting on both beach and harbor, **Romora Bay Club,** P.O. Box 146, Harbour Island, The Bahamas (tel. 809/333-2325), owned by Bill and Nancy Steigleder, is an intimate resort of 30 well-furnished bedrooms, villas, suites, and housekeeping units. Created from a former private estate, the T-shaped main house is the center of social activities. The club stands in a decades-old semitropical garden with tall, bearing coconut palms, filmy pine trees, and beds of flowering shrubbery.

The air-conditioned accommodations assure more privacy than most, and a harbor is only yards away where you can swim in vodka-clear waters. Each unit is comfortably furnished, containing private bath and private patios or balconies. Rooms are classified as standard, superior, and deluxe, each carrying a different price tag. In winter, doubles go for $115 to $155. A third person sharing pays another $21. For breakfast and dinner, add $30 per person daily. Suites and housekeeping units cost $99 to $125 daily for singles, $125 to $195 for two persons. *Summer rates for rooms are $115 to $115 double, with suites and housekeeping accommodations costing $60 single, $110 to $160 for two persons.*

Buffet luncheons are served at the waterfront patio and bar. Home-cooking is a feature, with continental, Bahamian, and American cuisine served. The homemade breads and pastries are superb. All flights are met at the airport by taxis for the one-mile drive to the ferry dock. There's a two-mile ferry ride direct to the club's private dock. Picnic trips, including an "X-rated one for honeymooners," is offered to a nearby uninhabited island. Couples are shown some low bushes just right for hanging up their bathing suits. They tell the captain when they'll be ready to be picked up, and after that they're strictly on their own. The club is closed from mid-September until the first of November.

For reservations write or call the Romora Bay Club, P.O. Box 7026, Boca Raton, FL 33431 (tel. toll free 800/327-8286, or 305/760-4535 in Florida).

Pink Sands, P.O. Box 87, Harbour Island, The Bahamas (tel. 809/333-2030), is an elite retreat on an 18-acre beachfront estate, functioning somewhat like a private club but open to the general public. By now, it's become a Harbour Island legend, having been founded by Allen Malcolm, a Connecticut yankee. In 1988, he sold the resort to, among others, Wally and Robbie Bregman, formerly of the Cormorant Club in St. Croix. They appointed New York-born Duncan and Joanie Burns as their on-site managers. Lots of paint and modern touches have given Pink Sands a new look, as it launches itself into the 1990s. Much of the old crowd is long, long gone, but new friends are made every year.

The innovative team wants to keep the best of the old but also initiate changes. Rooms are let on a full AP basis, but, as an added extra, afternoon tea plus all the drinks you can consume before 5 p.m. are included as well. The social center of the resort lies between a pair of fireplaces (one stone and traditional, the other a witch's cap iron fireplace in the center of the dining room, with smoke funneled up through a pipe in the ceiling).

Access to the grounds is restricted during the day but open to the public after 5 p.m. (see my dining recommendation below). Touches of whimsy at Pink Sands combine with touches of elegance. As you lie on the beach, you can raise a flag attached to the top, which will signal a beachfront waiter to come and take your order. Morning croissants and coffee are delivered to your door in a woven basket each morning before the formal breakfast service.

The resort, at presstime, contains 49 bedrooms within 27 coral and stucco cottages, with either one, two, or three bedrooms. Rooms are large and airy with tropical furnishings. Each has a dressing room, a bath, a private patio, and a refrigerator. The cost of living in one of the cottages for two persons per day is $275 garden view, $300 ocean view, and $325 ocean front. Singles receive a daily discount of $75. Again, this includes all meals.

The clientele at Pink Sands has been described as "socially secure." The centerpiece of the beachfront is a deck cantilevered over sands, capped with parasols and beach tables. The colony has its own fleet of several types of small sailboats and boats with outboard motors for exploring. Scuba-diving, snorkeling, and waterskiing are available. The resort places a big emphasis on tennis, and there are three professional courts available.

For reservations and information, contact First Hotels and Resorts, Inc. at 116 Radio Circle, Mt. Kisco, NY 10549 or call toll free at 800/235-3505 outside New York State. The resort shuts down from mid-April to Thanksgiving.

Valentine's Yacht Club & Inn, P.O. Box 1, Harbour Island, The Bahamas (tel. 809/333-2142), is a low-slung, rustic-modern, and comfortable place near the sea and a marina complex. You register in the wood-paneled main building. In back, in view of the dining room, there's a swimming pool where first-time divers may have just finished their introductory lessons. There's also a hot tub/Jacuzzi. Simple accommodations sit bungalow-style, each with its own private veranda, in a somewhat hilly flowering garden. In winter, singles cost $95 to $115 daily, depending on the location, and doubles go for $105 to $125. For MAP, add $28 per adult, $14 per child under 12. *In summer, MAP, charges are*

$75 daily in a single, $75 in a double. The place is closed in September and October.

The Bahamian cuisine served is usually preceded by drinks in the comfortably intimate wood- and brass-trimmed bar. The walls are covered with photographs of boats that have berthed in the marina just across the road. Dinner is served by candlelight at tables where artificial gold coins sparkle beneath laminated surfaces and hanging ships' lanterns, each an antique, cast an intimate glow. Either before or after dinner, you might enjoy one or two of the bartender's almost hallucinogenic Goombay Smashes. The bar area often provides live entertainment, becoming one of the social centers of town.

If you plan to arrive by yacht you'll be in good company, since the likes of Barbara Mandrell and Mick Jagger have also moored their vessels here. It's a full-service marina with everything you could need for your yacht, including a "yacht-sitting" service, which makes this dock one of the focal points of the marine activities on Harbour Island. For more information on the Dive Shop, which offers everything a scuba or snorkeling aficionado could want, see "The Sporting Life," below.

Dunmore Beach Club, P.O. Box 122, Harbour Island, The Bahamas (tel. 809/333-2200), is an elegant oasis, a colony of cottages placed in a tropical setting of trees and shrubbery on well-manicured grounds. The Bahamian-style, air-conditioned bungalows are an attractive combination of traditional furnishings and tropical accessories. The club leans toward the old-world style of innkeeping and takes only 28 guests. Excellent Bahamian and international meals are served in a dining room with a high-pitched, beamed ceiling; shutter doors, windows with views, modern oil paintings on the walls, and pots of tropical plants add to the charm. Breakfast is served in a garden terrace under pine trees with a clear view of the beach. Year-round, two people can stay here for about $225 daily, including three meals a day. Dinner is served at one sitting at 8 p.m., when men are requested to wear coats and ties in winter. Nonresidents can call for reservations, paying $30 per person.

Runaway Hill Club, P.O. Box 31, Harbour Island, The Bahamas (tel. 809/333-2150), is a small, intimate hotel overlooking the pink sands of Briland's beach. The resort, built in 1947 as a private home, was later sold to two sisters from New Zealand who ran it as a small inn. After they sold the property, the hotel remained closed for several years. In 1983 a group of Brilanders renovated the property and opened it to the public. The hotel has seven acres of beachfront and a huge lawn, separated from Colebrook Street by a wall. The mansion's original English colonial dormers are still prominent, as are the four stately palms set into the circular area in the center of the driveway. In winter, a crackling fire is sometimes built in the hearth near the entrance.

Each bedroom is different, giving the impression of lodging in a private home, as this used to be. There are eight accommodations in the two buildings that the hotel occupies. *Tariffs in summer are $80 daily for singles, $95 for a double room.* Winter rates are $100 daily for single rooms, $115 for doubles. MAP is $30 additional per person per day in winter. Dinners are served on the breeze-filled rear porch looking over the freshwater swimming pool, which is set into a steep hillside and surrounded by plants, midway between the main building and the pink sweep of the sandy beach. The dining room accepts paying nonresidents who want to drop in for dinner. Fishing trips and water sports can be arranged at the front desk. Roger and Carol Becht are the capable managers here. The club is usually closed in September and October.

Ocean View Club, P.O. Box 134, Harbour Island, The Bahamas (tel. 809/333-2276), offers one of the best values on the island. It's lodged on an oceanside ledge, where flowers and vines spill over the retaining walls. The view from the terrace is of palms, pine trees, and the sweeping expanse of the sea. The nine-room hotel is a low-lying masonry structure shielded by hedges and vines, opposite a schoolteacher's house in an isolated position away from the main part of town. Inside, it opens into an elegant and spacious living room paneled with whitewashed (or pickled) pecky cypress, rows of paperback books, and a stone-trimmed fireplace. An adjacent music room contains a bar and a collection of old-fashioned musical instruments fastened to the wall. Pip and Glen Simmons, the owners, offer a handful of well-ventilated and large rooms filled with simple but comfortable accoutrements. The cost year-round is $100 per person for MAP. Meals emerge from a clean and modern kitchen at the far end of the living room.

WHERE TO DINE: Known for its well-prepared food, **Runaway Hill Club** (tel. 809/333-2150) has a dining room enjoying a sweeping view over the sandy slope stretching down the beach. Inside, in a green-and-white decor accented with polished wood and nautical accessories, you can enjoy evening meals costing from $30 per person, plus service and drinks. The restaurant is contained in a hotel, previously recommended, but outside guests are welcome for the single-service meal beginning at 8 p.m. every night of the week. The kitchen prepares such specialties as marinated London broil, suprême of chicken piccata, spaghetti with conch, crabmeat soup with scotch, spicy lobster bisque, and many versions of local fish. Dessert might be a local favorite, French chocolate pie with a meringue crust and walnuts. Reservations are important.

Pink Sands, P.O. Box 87 (tel. 809/333-2030) is closed to the public until 5 p.m. but is open thereafter to those who call for a reservation for dinner. You can go by early and have a predinner drink, enjoying the physical plant and the amenities of the largest of the hotels on this New England–like island. For residents of the hotel, dinner is included in the daily AP rates. However, non-residents can order a fixed price meal for $40 per person served nightly from 7:30 to 9. You might have, for example, "grouper paradise" (with crabmeat, asparagus, and a dill-flavored mousseline sauce) or else seafood lasagne. The chef likes to emphasize creative Caribbean specialties, so the menu is forever changing. Bahamian and international dishes are featured, and fresh produce is used whenever possible. Service is polite, even a bit formal. In all, it's a low-key but elegant choice for dining.

Valentine's Yacht Club & Inn, (tel. 809/333-2142). Don't even think of a meal here without stopping first for a drink in the warmly masculine bar beforehand. Surrounded with nautical accessories, burnished paneling, and photos of ships that have moored in the nearby marina, you can while away the pre-dinner hours with denizens of the island's boating crowd. Breakfast runs from $6, and it's served from 8:30 to 9:30 a.m. daily. Lunch, at $8, is from noon to 2 p.m., and a set dinner, at $24, is served promptly every night at 7:30. When the main bar closes at 9 p.m., you can walk out to the more raucous bar on the marina (known as the Reach Bar) which remains open till 11 on most nights. The fare in the dining room includes steamed pork chops, steak or grouper cutlets, asparagus soup (or some other freshly made soup), baked stuffed grouper, roast leg of lamb, and sandwiches and salads during the day. Both the restaurant and the hotel are closed from early September to mid-November.

Angela's Starfish Restaurant (tel. 809/333-2253) is one of the simplest and also one of the most popular eating places in Harbour Island. Residents as well as visitors literally plan their Sunday around an evening meal here, although it's equally crowded on other nights. Run by Bahamians, Angela and Vincent Johnson, the house sits on a hill above the channel in a residential section somewhat removed from the center of town. Angela can often be seen in the kitchen baking, assisted by her hard-working daughter, Sally Grant. The kitchen is a turquoise-colored house, where the dishes are prepared for serving in the dining area.

Cracked conch and an array of seafood are specialties, and chicken pot pie and pork chops are frequently ordered. You can dine on the palm-dotted lawn with its simple tables and folding chairs, although there's an unpretentious dining room inside near the cramped kitchen for chilly weather. Nonetheless, some of the best local food is offered here. It can get quite festive at night, after the candles are lit and the crowd gets jovial. You should call ahead for a reservation. Full dinners, served on tables where conch shells are usually the centerpiece, cost $20. Lunch costs from $8, and breakfast, from $5. The establishment is open daily without a break, beginning at 9 a.m. The last dinner order is taken at 8:30 p.m.

THE SPORTING LIFE: The two main sporting centers are the Romora Bay Club and Valentine's Yacht Club, the activities of which are previewed below.

Romora Bay Club (tel. 809/333-2325) is fully geared for a wide array of water sports. The sandy bottom of the sheltered bathing precincts off the hotel (previewed above) serves as the learning area for the introductory scuba lessons. An introductory lesson followed by a half-day dive trip costs $30, with equipment included. Guided scuba trips cost $25 per tank in daytime, $30 for night dives.

Those who prefer snorkeling can join a half-day expedition for $12.50 per person. Experienced divers can rent any piece of scuba equipment they need. Bill Steigleder, the owner of the hotel, is an experienced diver. He is assisted by two PADI instructors. The Romora Bay Club offers dive packages that make combined MAP, housing, and diving less expensive.

Valentine's Dive Center, P.O. Box 1 (tel. 809/133-2309), has a full range of dive activities. The dive center is in a wooden building near the entrance to Valentine's marina. Free lessons in snorkeling and scuba-diving for beginners are given daily at 9:30 a.m. Snorkeling from a boat costs $20 for a half-day tour. A full certification course for scuba is taught for $350. Single-tank dives, at 9:30 a.m. and 1:30 p.m. daily, cost $30, and night dives (four divers minimum) for $40 per person. Underwater cameras, with film included, rent for $15 for a half day, $25 for a full day.

In addition to the dive operation, Valentine's will rent boats to qualified sailors. Day sailers cost $25 per hour, $75 for half a day. If you're not that ambitious, perhaps you'd like a Hobie Cat for $15 per hour. Windsurfers cost $10 per hour.

A final word: The guides here will point out the wreck of the *Caenarvon,* a steel freighter that sank long ago. There's even the rusted hulk of a 19th-century locomotive, which divers can see in the clear waters around Harbour Island. Visibility ranges from 80 to 150 feet on good days. The diving around this part of The Bahamas is considered among the most diversified in the region, including reefs, deep Atlantic coast slopes, shallow garden reefs, and ocean currents that permit "drift waves," which are usually reserved for experienced divers only.

THE WATERING HOLE: One of the most pleasant spots on the island for a drink, the **Pink Sands Lounge,** Bay Street (tel. 809/333-2031), is a place reeking of New England but with a tropical twist. The lounge is directly opposite Government Dock. The expansive veranda in front is likely to be filled with chattering locals who socialize here during parades and regattas, although Sunday afternoon is also a popular meeting time. The roughly finished interior shows the thick posts and beams of the old house. You can enjoy a tropical drink or a two-fisted pick-me-up seated in one of the bentwood or rattan chairs scattered throughout the pair of inside rooms. The bar is usually open daily from 11 a.m. to 9 p.m.

10. SPANISH WELLS

Called a "quiet corner of The Bahamas," Spanish Wells is a colorful cluster of houses on St. George's Cay, half a mile off the coast of northwest Eleuthera. It is characterized by its sparkling bays and white beaches, sleepy lagoons, and a fine fishing and skindiving colony. To reach the island, you can fly to the airstrip on North Eleuthera, from which taxis will deliver you to the ferry dock. Regardless of the time of day you arrive, a ferry boat will either be waiting for passengers or about to arrive to deposit a load. A memorable skipper of one of them is Caleb Sawyer, who runs a well-maintained speedboat, the *Mollie Crab* (tel. 809/333-4254), and charges $3 per person each way for the crossing to Spanish Wells. The ferries depart whenever passengers show up.

The Eleutherian Adventurers were the first people to inhabit St. George's Cay after the Spanish had exterminated the original residents, the Arawak (Lucayan) Indians. However, it was prominent on the charts of Spanish navigators as the final landfall for galleons heading home from the New World laden with plunder. The Spaniards early on sank a well here from which to replenish their potable water before setting off across the Atlantic. Hence the name "Spanish Wells." Ponce de León noted this stopover, where he was able to get water, if not the youth-giving liquid for which he was searching.

After the American Revolution, Loyalists joined the descendants of the Eluetherian Adventurers in Spanish Wells. Some of these, particularly those from southern plantations in America, did not stay long on St. George's Cay, however, as the Spanish Wellsians were adamantly opposed to slavery. Since slaves had been brought by the new wave of immigrants hoping to start island plantations, they were forced to move on to other parts of The Bahamas with their black bondsmen. The people of Spanish Wells still have strong religious beliefs, and there's a bounty of churches on the island.

The towheaded, blue-eyed people of this little town number fewer than 1,500 souls. More than half the people on the island are named Pinder. As the saying goes, "We was Pinders before we married, and we're Pinders now." The names Albury, Higgs, Sawyer, and Sweeting are also prominent. The islanders' patois blends old English with the accents of others who have settled on the island over the centuries. For years they have been known as good seamen and spongers, and some of them are farmers. Because of the infertile soil on St. George's Cay, however, they have to do their planting on "mainland" Eleuthera.

Over the centuries the Spanish Wellsians have tried their hand at many economic ventures, from growing cotton and pineapples for export to shipbuilding, lumbering, and fishing. Of these, fishing and some agriculture have been lasting moneymakers, joined today by tourism.

You can walk or bicycle through the village, looking at the houses, some more than 200 years old, which have New England saltbox styling but bright tropical coloring. You can see handmade quilts in many colors, following patterns handed down from generations of English ancestors. No one locks doors here or removes ignition keys from cars.

There are those who suggest that the island doesn't offer much to do, but this is disputed by those who just want to snorkel, scuba-dive, fish, sunbathe, read, and watch the sun set. You'll also have a choice of tennis, sailing, volleyball, shuffleboard, and windsurfing.

WHERE TO STAY: The premier resort of the island is **Spanish Wells Beach Resorts,** P.O. Box 31, Spanish Wells, The Bahamas (tel. 809/333-4371), which has come under new management. The new owners have big plans for the development of their two properties which are in different locations on the island. They have wisely appointed Sheila Glinton as managing director. She brings to the hotel operation her years of experience with Resorts International on Paradise Island and her time spent in promoting Bahamian tourism in New York. She was also born on Spanish Wells and is well versed in island lore and its people. As a thoughtful touch, she gives all guests a complimentary basket of island-grown fruit as they check in. Long popular as a dive center (see below), the resort is now building a broader base of tourism.

The most desirable branch of the hotel is the best located (close to the center of town). Set beside a good beach, it consists of 21 comfortable prefabricated bedrooms and seven tidy cottages. It was built in the early 1960s and during its lifetime has undergone many name changes. It not only offers the best rooms, but the finest dining facilities on the island (see below). This pleasant enclave lies behind a grove of palms. At low tide, you can walk in waist-deep water for long distances without reaching a dropoff—a fact that makes its 800 feet of beachfront ideal for children.

Most of the accommodations are named after local geographic features (such as Ignamally's Rock, which many local residents will point out), and most, but not all, are air conditioned. Each unit has a wall of sliding glass opening onto a view of the beach and sea. In winter singles rent for $75 to $85 daily, with doubles costing $90 to $100. The most expensive units, either single or double occupancy, begin at $132 daily. *In summer, single units cost from $65 to $75 daily, with doubles priced from $78 to $88. The most expensive units rent for $122 daily, either single or double occupancy.*

The other branch of the hotel sits on a sloping section of sandy land, away from the center of the village above a waterway separating Spanish Wells from Russell Island. It offers 14 well-scrubbed rooms with ceiling fans, private baths, and balconies. In winter singles rent for $65 daily, with doubles paying $78. The most expensive units, either single or double occupancy, cost $132 daily. *In summer prices are lowered to $57 daily in a single and $65 in a double, with the most expensive accommodations costing $122, either single or double occupancy.* This section of the resort is closer to the dive operation.

Spanish Wells Yacht Haven, P.O. Box 35, Spanish Wells, The Bahamas (tel. 809/333-4255), is one of the newest and most modern marinas in the islands. Now owned by the Nassau Yacht Club, these comfortable docks also rent apartments and rooms for the boating crowd or any other visitors to Spanish Wells. First, the array of marine facilities includes a self-service laundry, hot and cold showers, ice, a swimming pool, and a lounge and restaurant recommended separately. You can also get your fill of Texaco marine fuels and lubricants. Should you not want all that, you'll find two apartments and three singles for rent. *The rate in summer in a single is $65 daily,* going up to $75 in winter. *Doubles begin at $85 daily in summer,* rising to $95 in winter. Each additional person occupying a bed in one of the apartments is charged another $10 nightly.

WHERE TO DINE: The most gracious restaurant on an island not overloaded with choices is **Spanish Wells Beach Resort** (tel. 809/333-4371), housed in the social center of this previously recommended hotel beneath a sloping ceiling of varnished pine. The place is air conditioned, and spinning ceiling fans stir the air as you relax on comfortable chairs. Service is polite. An old wood-sided skiff is transformed into a decorative accent at one end of the room. The restaurant is open seven days a week from 7:30 to 9:30 a.m. for breakfast, from noon to 3 p.m. for lunch, and from 6:30 to 9 p.m. for dinner. Breakfast costs from $6; lunch, from $12; and dinner, from $20. The bill of fare is likely to include locally caught lobster, breaded or pan-fried grouper, cracked conch, pork chops, steaks, and a selection of international dishes.

Spanish Wells Yacht Haven, P.O. Box 35 (tel. 809/333-4255), is owned by the Nassau Yacht Club. Its facilities and rooms have been previously recommended, but it's also one of the finest places to dine on the island. Visitors mingle with the yachting crowd from around the world in the lounge and restaurant which is decorated with a few nautical artifacts overlooking the marina. Naturally, the emphasis is on seafood here, including lobster "right out of the water and into the pot." You can on occasion get a perfectly done shark steak, along with such Bahamian fish as grouper. Conch is prepared in a number of ways as well, including in a tasty chowder. Meals cost from $15 to $25. Service is daily, except Monday, from 8 to 10 a.m. for breakfast, from noon to 2 p.m. for lunch, and from 6:30 to 9:30 p.m. for dinner.

Walton's Langosta (tel. 809/333-4147), set on the port and painted a vivid shade of ultra-purple, is the first building most visitors see as they approach by ferryboat. The establishment's orange Formica countertops and horseshoe-shaped bar seem designed to spotlight one of the town's most vocal and colorful citizens, Walton Pinder. Many of the establishment's fish and lobster selections are caught by Mr. Pinder, and are flavorfully prepared in a well-scrubbed kitchen which guests are welcome to inspect personally.

Full meals are served daily from 9 a.m. to 4 p.m. After a two-hour break, dinner service lasts from 6 to 10 p.m. Breakfast costs from $5; lunch, from $6; and a full dinner, from $18. The very fresh conch salad, marinated in island lemon and vinegar, is a specialty. Other dishes include red snapper, chicken, several different preparations of lobster, grouper cutlets, fish sandwiches (including one made with conch), and the inevitable conch chowder.

Roddy's Place (tel. 809/333-4219) stands along the waterfront on the way to Spanish Wells Yacht Haven. It is known for its home cooking and native foods. Open daily from 9 a.m. to 10 p.m., it is also a social center of the town, with its game machines and pool tables. Painted in vivid Caribbean colors, it offers the usual array of sandwiches and hamburgers. But you can also order some good local dishes (not available every day), including a fresh lobster salad. Cracked conch is invariably offered, as is conch chowder. A crayfish salad might be prepared or a barbecued or baked chicken. Lunches cost from $8, with dinners priced at $15 and up.

A DIVE CENTER AND BOATING PICNICS: Although it offers an array of extra activities, the main devotion of the **Spanish Wells Dive Center,** Spanish Wells Beach Resort (tel. 809/333-4371), is to diving. It's under the capable and experienced directorship of Robert (Desi) Stephens. It maintains a duet of flat-topped boats which make expeditions to some of the most beautiful reefs in the region. Its headquarters and information center is in this previously recommended resort. However, its boats moor on the opposite side of the island in a channel between Spanish Wells and Russell Island. For beginners, a resort course with an introductory lecture costs $65. A two-tank dive goes for $50, and NAUI certification costs from $325.

If you're interested in above-water activities, the center offers beach picnics from a flat-topped boat that goes to an array of sandy islands. Perhaps the most alluring of all, an X-rated picnic called Adam and Eve is arranged on special request. The Dive Center provides transportation to an uninhabited island, a hammock, a picnic lunch, and then privacy. Guests are requested not to divulge the location to anyone (so future picnics can continue in uninterrupted solitude). The cost of the picnic is $35 per couple.

CHAPTER XIV

THE EXUMAS

□ □ □

A spiny, sandy chain of islands, the Exumas, which begin just 35 miles southeast of Nassau, stretch more than 100 miles from Beacon Cay in the north to Hog Cay and Sandy Cay in the south. These islands have not been developed like Abaco and Eleuthera, but they have much to offer, with gin-clear waters on the west around the Great Bahama Bank and the 5,000-foot-deep Exuma Sound on the east, plus uninhabited cays ideal for picnics, rolling hills, ruins of once-great plantations, and coral formations of great beauty. Although it's crossed by the Tropic of Cancer, the island has average temperatures ranging from the mid-70s to the mid-80s.

On most maps this chain is designated as the "Exuma Cays," but only two of the main islands—Great Exuma and Little Exuma—bear the name. A single-lane bridge connects those two cays, where the major communities are concentrated.

The Exumas, scattered over an ocean area of 90 square miles, are favorites with sailors and yachtsmen, considered some of the finest cruising grounds in both The Bahamas and the Caribbean. The annual regatta in April in Elizabeth Harbour has attracted such notables as Prince Philip and ex-King Constantine of Greece. The Exumas are often referred to by yachting people as "where you go when you die if you've been good."

The history of the Exumas, whatever it was, is not much documented before the latter part of the 18th century. It is assumed that the island chain was inhabited by Lucayan Indians, at least until the Spaniards wiped them out. Columbus didn't set foot on this chain of islands. However, from the northern tip of Long Island, he is believed to have seen Little Exuma, naming whatever was in the area "Yumey." At least, that's how the island chain appears on a 1500 map of the New World.

By the late 17th century Great Exuma had become a major producer of salt, and permanent settlers began to arrive. The sailing vessels of the salt merchants were constantly harassed by pirates, but some families from Nassau must have looked on this as the lesser of two evils. On New Providence they were subjected to the terrorism inflicted by both the pirates and the Spanish, and in the latter part of the 17th century and the first of the 18th they fled to the relative peace of the Exumas (they still do!).

Some Loyalist families, fleeing the newly established United States of America after British defeat, came to the Exuma Cays in 1783, but nothing like the number that came to settle in Harbour Island, New Plymouth, and Spanish Wells.

In the 18th century cotton and salt were "king" on the Exumas. English plantation owners brought in many slaves to work the fields, and many of today's Exumians are direct descendants of those early bond servants, who were mostly of African origin. The "king" did not stay long on the throne. Insects went for the cotton, and salt lands such as those of Turks and Caicos proved much too competitive for those of the Exumas, so that these pursuits were eventually abandoned.

Most of the white owners went back to where they came from, but the slaves, having no such option, stayed on, subsisting by working the land abandoned by their former owners and taking the names of those owners as their own. A look through the George Town directory turns up such names as Bethel, Ferguson, and especially Rolle, the same as those of the long-gone whites.

At one time Lord John Rolle held much of the Exumas under a grant from the British Crown, giving him hundreds of acres. He is reported to have owned nearly 400 slaves who worked this acreage, but Lord Rolle never set foot on his potentially rich plantation. Stories vary as to what happened to the slaves—whether they were, as some claim, freed by Lord Rolle and given the land by him, or whether, upon being released from bondage by the United Kingdom Emancipation Act in 1834, they just took over the land, with or without Rolle's approval. Whichever, descendants of those same slaves are important Exumians today.

These are among the friendliest islands in The Bahamas, the people warmhearted and not (yet) spoiled by tourism. They seem genuinely delighted to receive and welcome visitors to their shores. They grow a lot of their own food, including cassava, onions, cabbages, and pigeon peas on the acres their ancestors worked as slaves. Many fruits grow on the cays, including guavas, mangoes, and avocadoes. You can watch these fruits being loaded at Government Wharf in George Town for shipment to Nassau. The sponge industry is being revived locally, as the product of the sea is found in shallow waters and creeks to the south side of the Exumas.

This is considered one of the prettiest island chains in The Bahamas. Some even liken its beauty to that of Polynesia. In the Exumas, shades of jade, aquamarine, and amethyst in deeper waters turn to transparent opal near sandy shores: the water and the land appear almost inseparable. Sailors and their crews like to stake out their own private beaches and tropical hideaways, and several vacation retreats have been built by wealthy Europeans, Canadians, and Americans.

Most of my resort recommendations are in and around pretty, pink George Town, on Great Exuma, the capital of the Exumas. A community of some 900 residents, it was once considered a possible site for the capital of The Bahamas because of its excellent Elizabeth Harbour (see below).

A GARDEN SPOT: Under the protection of The Bahamas National Trust, **Exuma National Land and Sea Park,** begins at Conch Cut in the south and extends northward to Wax Cay Cut, encompassing Halls Pond Cay, Warderick

Wells, Shroud Cay, Hawksbill Cay, Cistern Cay, and Bell Island, as well as numerous other small, uninhabited islands. It lies to the northwest of Staniel Cay. The park is some 22 miles long, and much of it is a sea garden with reefs, some only three to ten feet beneath the water's surface. The park is reached only by chartered boat, and is very expensive to visit.

This is an area of natural beauty, which can be enjoyed by beachcombers, skindivers, and the yachting crowd, but it's unlawful to remove any plant, marine, or bird life, except for specific limited catches of certain fish. The park's rules differ from the fishing regulations for the rest of The Bahamas, permitting catches of six spiny lobster (in season), 12 conchs, one hogfish, one rockfish, one grouper, and one muttonfish. Catches must be made by hand, with hook and line, or with a Hawaiian sling. Apply to the park warden, who lives in the area, for information.

Many birdwatchers visit the park, looking for the red-legged thrush, the nighthawk, even the long-tailed "Tropic Bird," plus many, many more winged creatures.

This was once the home of the Bahamian iguana, which is now found only on Allan's Cays, a tiny island group just north of Highborne Cay. The government is taking belated steps to protect this creature, which is found nowhere else in the world. If a person kills or captures an iguana, the penalty on conviction is a fine of as much as $300 and/or imprisonment for a term as long as six months.

GETTING THERE: The most popular way to visit the Exumas is to fly there aboard a **Bahamasair** plane from Nassau to George Town. There is daily service.

Exuma has some private airstrips, but its major commercial airport is at George Town, the capital. (For flights to the private airstrip at Staniel Cay, refer to Section 4 of this chapter.)

Aero Coach offers flights between George Town and the Florida gateways of Miami and Fort Lauderdale. For tickets and reservation information call 205/359-1600 in Fort Landerdale, or toll free 800/327-0010. The number to call in the Exumas is 809/336-2186.

By Mailboat

Several mailboats leave from Potter's Cay Dock in Nassau, stopping at various points along the Exumas.

The M/V *Grand Master* goes from Nassau to George Town. Departures are on Tuesday at 1 p.m. It returns to Nassau on Friday. The one-way fare is $25.

Since hours and sailing schedules are subject to change because of various weather conditions, it's best to check with the dockmaster at Potter's Cay Dock in Nassau (tel. 809/323-1064).

GETTING AROUND: After your arrival at the airport in George Town, chances are you'll meet Kermit Rolle. He's known by everybody. You can stop in at his **Kermit Airport Lounge,** P.O. Box 78 (tel. 809/336-2002), which is just across from the airport. Having the same name as Lord Rolle, Kermit knows just as much about the Exumas as anyone else (maybe more). You learn that Kermit runs things up in Rolleville (more about this later). You'd be lucky if Kermit is free, and you can negotiate a deal with him to take you in his car for a tour of the Exumas. He's filled with local lore.

If your hotel is in George Town, it will cost about $12 to get there in a taxi from the airport. Rides often are shared.

It's also possible to rent a car during your stay. Try **Exuma Transport,** P.O. Box 19 in George Town (tel. 809/336-2101). They have cars to rent for $55 per day or $275 per week. A $200 deposit is required.

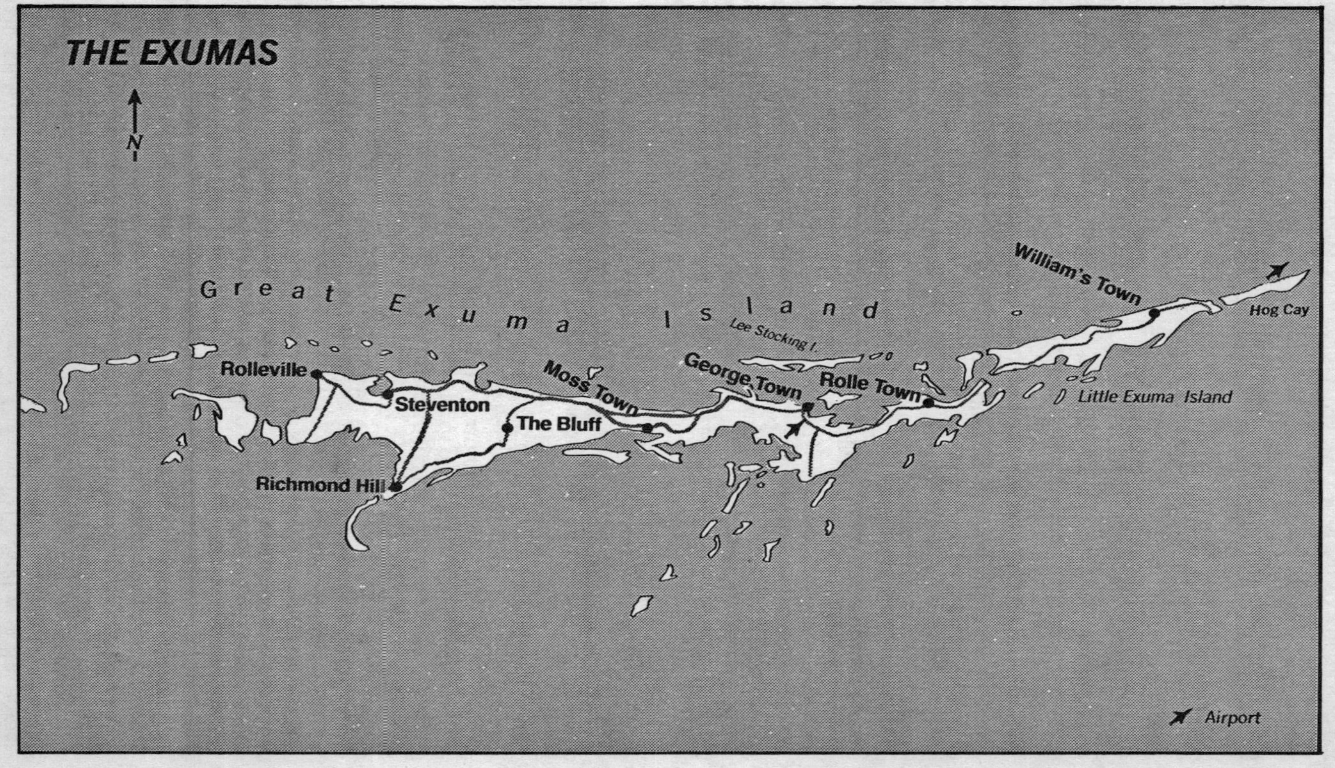
THE EXUMAS
N
Great Exuma Island
Rolleville
Steventon
The Bluff
Richmond Hill
Moss Town
George Town
Lee Stocking I.
Rolle Town
William's Town
Hog Cay
Little Exuma Island
Airport

At the same place, you can ask about renting a scooter for $25 a day. Some adventurous visitors make use of them on Exuma's roads. But, be warned, there have been accidents because of the potholed and dangerous conditions of many of the roads on the island chain.

A TRAVELER'S ADVISORY: Throughout the Exumas, you'll see islands with "no trespassing" signs posted. In some cases this is meant with a vengeance. In the early 1980s, at least on one island, you could have been killed if you had gone ashore!

On a long ago summer day, the boat containing my party sailed by Cistern Cay. Back then, we were told that Robert Vesco owns part of that island. "He likes to keep it *very, very private* here," our guide cautioned, heading for friendlier shores. (Vesco, of course, is the financier much wanted by the U.S. government.) Even though the fugitive is long gone, people around here still like to keep it quiet.

Perhaps the most bizarre "out islands" episode in all The Bahamas centers around Norman's Cay, one of the northernmost islands in the Exumas, 44 nautical miles southeast of New Providence Island. At one time when I stayed at the hotel there, Norman's Cay Club, this was a South Sea island–type outpost. Reportedly it was once the retirement home of the pirate, Norman.

This was always a very special cay. It isn't flat, since parts rise to 50 feet above sea level. It is heavily wooded with lignum vitae, royal poinciana, palmetto, tamarind, and casuarina, and it used to be considered a birdwatcher's paradise. Snorkeling and scuba-diving on the coral heads were among the best in the Exumas, with vertical dropoffs, black coral forests, spectacular cuts, and wrecks. The location is adjacent to the Exuma National Land and Sea Park.

In the old days you might have run into Ted Kennedy, Walter Cronkite, or William F. Buckley, Jr., enjoying the pleasures of Norman's Cay. The remote outpost enjoyed great popularity with a Harvard/Boston clique.

However, the situation in the '80s changed drastically when a German-Colombian, Carlos Lehder (pronounced Leader) Rivas (his mother's name), purchased most of the island. The story of his purchase of Norman's Cay was mentioned in the 1985 *Newsweek* article "Empire of Evil," documenting the horrors of cocaine smuggling. In a short time after Lehder's purchase of the property, the Colombian flag was flying over Norman's Cay, and many of the wintering wealthy fled in horror from the island when they returned to find their homes broken into and "trashed."

Norman's Cay, experts have stated, became the major distribution point for drug export to the U.S. Millions of dollars worth of cocaine was flown from Colombia and deposited in hangars at Norman's Cay before being smuggled into the United States. It is estimated that some 30 pilots crashed attempting to fly in their illegal cargoes. You can still see the wreckage of a C-46 that went down in the bay.

When an undersecretary of state arrived from Washington and landed on the island, he was ordered off at gunpoint by a Colombian commando. He left, but when he returned to the U.S. capital, he launched a major protest. Apparently, strong, hard pressure was applied by the U.S. government on the Bahamian government to "clean up the act" at Norman's Cay.

In recent months, major changes have come. Lehder fled Norman's Cay for further adventures in Colombia where he was captured and extradited to the U.S. (he was later tried, convicted, and imprisoned). The Bahamian police now have the island under surveillance. It is believed that huge amounts of money and cocaine are still stashed on this island.

Norman's Cay may one day realize its tourist potential again, but it is still in private hands and is strictly off-limits, unless you've been personally invited to visit by one of the owners. If you arrive in a boating party, you should seek special permission before going ashore.

I'm reporting on these developments because the wide publicity the cay has received has left the impression with many tourists that the island has been reopened for visits without an invitation. It hasn't! Stay away until further notice.

PRACTICAL FACTS: Much factual information regarding George Town and the Exumas is also applicable to the rest of The Bahamas and appears under the ABCs in Chapter VII. The data presented here are aimed at helping you on matters more specifically pertinent to this area.

Banks: In George Town, a branch of the **Bank of Nova Scotia,** P.O. Box 14, Queen's Highway (tel. 809/336-2651), is open from 9 a.m. to 3 p.m. Monday to Thursday, from 9 a.m. to 1 p.m. and 3 to 5 p.m. Friday.

Churches: If you're a Protestant churchgoer, you'll be warmly welcomed at **St. John's Baptist Church,** P.O. Box 12, Queen's Highway (tel. 809/336-2682).

Customs: The Bahamian Customs office (tel. 809/336-2071) is at the George Town Airport.

Docking: If you come to the Exumas aboard your own boat, **Exuma Docking Services,** P.O. Box 19 (tel. 809/336-2578), has slips for 40 boats, with water and electricity hookups. There's a restaurant on the premises, and you can replenish your liquor stock from the store here. Also they have a laundromat, fuel dock, land-based fuel pumps, and a store selling supplies for boats and people.

Dry cleaning: To get dry cleaning done, go to **Exuma Cleaners,** P.O. Box 96, Queen's Highway, George Town (tel. 809/336-2038).

Hair care: For attention to your hair, try **Exuma Beauty and Barber Fashion,** P.O. Box 14, Queen's Highway, George Town (tel. 809/336-2682).

Medical care: The government-operated medical clinic can be reached by phone (tel. 809/336-2-88).

Police: To call the police, dial 809/336-2666, but only for an emergency or special services.

1. GEORGE TOWN

The Tropic of Cancer runs directly through George Town, the capital and principal settlement of the Exumas, located on the island of Great Exuma. Some 900 people live in this tranquil seaport village, opening onto a 15-mile-long harbor. George Town, part in the tropics and part in the temperate zone, is a favorite port of call for the yachting crowd. Its one road runs parallel to the shoreline of the harbor. Flights from Nassau, Miami, and Fort Lauderdale come into nearby George Town Airport.

Sometimes the streets of George Town are nearly deserted, except when the mailboat from Nassau arrives at Government Wharf, bringing everybody out. If you've rented a housekeeping unit on the Exumas, you can come here to buy fresh fish when the fishermen come in with their catch.

If you need to stock up on supplies, George Town is the place, as it has more stores and services than any other place in the Exumas. There are dive centers, marinas, and markets, as well as a doctor and a clinic.

There isn't much to see here in the way of architecture except the confectionary pink and white **Government Building,** which was "inspired" by the Government House architecture in Nassau. Under an old ficus tree in the center of town there's a straw market where you can talk to the friendly Exumian women and perhaps purchase some of their handcrafts.

George Town has a colorful history, despite the fact that it appears so sleepy today (there's so little traffic, there is no need for a traffic light). Pirates used its deep-water harbor in the 17th century, and then what was called the "plantation aristocracy," mainly from Virginia and the Carolinas, settled here in the 18th century. In the next 100 years **Elizabeth Harbour,** the focal point of the town, became a refitting base for British men-of-war vessels, and the U.S. Navy used the port again during World War II.

The greatest attraction is not George Town but **Stocking Island,** which lies in Elizabeth Harbour. It faces the town across the bay, less than a mile away. This is a long, thin barrier island with some of the finest white sandy beaches in The Bahamas. Snorkelers and scuba-divers come here to explore the blue holes, and it is also ringed with undersea caves and coral gardens. Boat trips leave from Elizabeth Harbour heading for Stocking Island at 10 a.m. and 1 p.m. daily. The cost is $5 per person one way. However, guests of Peace and Plenty are transported free.

Mystery Cave is a famous dive site, tunneling for more than 400 feet under the hilly, seven-mile-long island with its palm-studded beaches.

If you'd like to go shelling, walk the beach that runs along the Atlantic side. You can order sandwiches and drinks at the beach club on the island, which is run by Peace and Plenty (see below). Stocking Island used to be a private enclave for guests at Peace and Plenty, but now it is used by all visitors. They reach the island on high-speed Boston Whaler runabouts (ask at your hotel desk for departure times). The boats leave from Government Wharf in George Town.

Lake Victoria covers about two acres in the heart of George Town. Landlocked, it has a narrow exit to the harbor and functions as a diving and boating headquarters.

One of the offshore sights in Elizabeth Harbour is **Crab Cay,** which can be reached by boat. This is believed to have been a rest camp for British seamen in the 18th century.

WHERE TO STAY: In the heart of George Town, **Peace and Plenty,** P.O. Box 55, George Town, Great Exuma, The Bahamas (tel. 809/336-2551), is an attractive and historic waterside inn. Once it was a sponge warehouse and later the home of a prominent family before it was converted into a hotel in the late 1940s, making it the oldest in the Exumas. It was named for a vessel that brought Loyalists from the Carolinas to the Exumas. The hotel is run by the most famous manager in the Exumas, Charles Pfleuger, who once worked for Pan American Airlines. He managed the hotel once in the late 1960s and early '70s and has now returned. Since his arrival, Peace and Plenty is the finest "ship" in town. The two-story structures of the pink-and-white hotel have dormers and balconies. Rooms have air conditioning. There are 32 units, all tastefully furnished and air-conditioned. All rates are on the EP. In winter, singles or doubles peak at $94 to $98. *In summer, charges are $70 to $76 for singles or doubles.*

The grounds are planted with palms, crotons, and bougainvillea. It fronts on Elizabeth Harbour, which makes it a favorite of the visiting yachting set. The hotel faces Stocking Island and maintains a private beach club there, offering food and bar service as well as miles of sandy dunes. A free boat makes the run to Stocking Island for hotel guests. There is a small freshwater pool on the patio of the hotel. Drinks are served at the hotel in one of two cocktail lounges. One of these lounges was built in the original kitchen of an old slave market. It's filled with nautical gear, including lanterns, rudders, and anchors. Food consists of continental, Bahamian, and American specialties. Dining is both indoor and outdoor. Calypso music is played on the terrace. Drinks are also served around the free-form swimming pool.

Scuba equipment is available for rent, and an instructor takes out diving and snorkeling parties, and arranges deep-sea fishing trips. Bonefishing is especially popular in the area. Self-drive cars, motorcycles, and boats can be arranged.

Out Island Inn Village, P.O. Box 49, George Town, Great Exuma, The Bahamas (tel. 809/336-2171), is an informal "barefoot elegant" resort hotel, the largest on this small island. It's built on a point of land overlooking a natural harbor. The walls of this colony were erected by hand from the old stone fences that once laced Great Exuma. The resort is complete unto itself, with a freshwater swimming pool. In a cheerful, stylized fashion, 88 air-conditioned bedrooms offer plenty of room for living and relaxing. Like its sister hotel, the Pieces of Eight (see below), the inn-village lies on the harbor at the western edge of George Town. Beachfront units are always more desirable than oceanview rooms. Rates include hotel accommodation, tax and gratuity, three meals daily, unlimited drinks, tennis, bicycles, Sunfish sailboats, windsurfing, use of snorkel gear, and a boat trip to Stocking Island with lunch. AP rates in winter are $120 per person, dropping in summer to $100 per person daily. Children up to 5 years of age can stay free with their parents, but kids from 6 to 12 are charged $58 per day. The single rate, also AP, is $145 year-round.

Built on its own peninsula out into the bay, the Out Island Restaurant is recommended separately. The hotel has a cocktail lounge, and the Reef Bar is the place for live music, dancing, and relaxing in the evening. Ferry service is provided twice a day to Stocking Island, just across the bay from the hotels. The village also offers two all-weather tennis courts and a complete dive shop. The staff will arrange guides and boats for deep-sea fishing (the bonefishing, in particular, is renowned).

Pieces of Eight Hotel, P.O. Box 49, George Town, Great Exuma, The Bahamas (tel. 809/336-2600), on a hill overlooking Stocking Island and Elizabeth Harbour at the western end of George Town, is built around a pool and deck. Each of the 32 rooms has an individual balcony and bright island decor. Rates year-round are $73 daily, EP, for one or two people. The food in the Pieces of Eight dining room is quite good, featuring Oriental dishes as well as U.S. steaks. In the Pirate's Den bar you can sip exotic island drinks as you look out over the pool and the harbor. The hotel has a complete dive center, offering daily diving and snorkeling trips.

Two Turtles Inn, P.O. Box 51, George Town, Great Exuma, The Bahamas (tel. 809/336-2545), is a pleasant resort in miniature run by Valerie R. Noyes. The colony consists of 14 rooms with ceiling fans. Built of native stonework and tropical hardwoods, the inn overlooks Elizabeth Harbour and a small local park. On the ground floor is an old-fashioned-style bar and restaurant, vaguely reminiscent of 18th-century pirate days. Some of the accommodations have a self-catering provision installed. One of its chief assets is its meals—good Bahamian dishes as well as fresh seafood dishes. Transportation is available by boat, costing $5 per person, to a private beach on Stocking Island. Entertainment is often arranged in the courtyard. Winter rates, in effect from mid-December to May 1, are $68 to $78 per day in a single or double. *Summer rates are $48 to $55 per day in a single or double.* Tennis, sailing, boating, snorkeling, and scuba-diving and equipment are available.

Efficiencies, Apartments, and Villas

One of the newest resorts in The Bahamas is set on a 300-acre stretch of virgin scrub outside George Town. Its developers have created a hotel, the Flamingo Bay Hotel and Villas (a time-sharing unit), the Flamingo Bay Club, as well as a collection of private houses, each of which is for sale. More are contemplated. Each of these facilities shares access to sports instructors who organize scuba or snorkeling expeditions.

Flamingo Bay Club, P.O. Box 23, George Town, Great Exuma, The Bahamas (tel. 809/336-2661), is surrounded on three sides by a saltwater cove. This is really a vast estate, set on 1,300 scenically spectacular acres just a half mile from

George Town, overlooking Elizabeth Harbour. It is such a desirable spot that the entire main building is normally reserved for government officials at the time of the annual Family Island Regatta. Flamingo Bay is an ambitious development, the creation of a Canadian multimillionaire, Robert Hart. He quit school at 14 to make his way in the world and succeeded brilliantly, not only in publishing but in other fields as well. He conceived this time-share development just a step across the Tropic of Cancer.

The main house, which is a pocket of posh, is decorated somewhat like a private home, with occasional antiques and Caribbean rattan furniture in pastel-hued motifs. Guests who phone for a reservation can come here to dine on the excellent cuisine in cozy, intimate surroundings. At a single kitchen in the main building, guests share the facilities and can cook their own dinners if they wish.

Each accommodation in the main building is actually a suite that can house two to four guests. They are stylishly furnished along contemporary lines, and contain air conditioning and a full bath. Or else one can rent well-furnished, two-bedroom accommodations, with full bath and kitchenette. Prospective visitors can also rent unsold portions of time-share units. However, since the resort is still developing, it is hard to predict what might be available at any given time, so you'll have to call first. In winter, six guests can enjoy a two-bedroom unit for $250 a night, a standard room housing two to four persons costing only $85 nightly. *In summer, prices are lowered, the two-bedroom unit which can sleep six renting for $150 daily, and a standard room in the main house, sleeping two to four guests, going for $65.*

There are tennis courts, a private dock and beach picnic areas, and the fishing and diving are world renowned. At the beachfront you can go in the buff if you wish to display your charms. Such sports can be arranged as scuba diving, snorkeling, boating, waterskiing, windsurfing, and sailing.

Regatta Point, P.O. Box 6, George Town, Great Exuma, The Bahamas (tel. 809/336-2206), lies on a small cay just across the causeway from George Town. The cay used to be known as Kidd Cay, named after the notorious pirate. Overlooking Elizabeth Harbour, the present complex consists of five efficiency apartments. This little colony hums with action at the time of the Regatta. Your hostess, Nancy Bottomley, does much to ease your adjustment into the slow-paced life of the Exumas. An American, she discovered this palm grove cay—really bush country—in 1963, opening the little colony of efficiencies in 1965. She even had to build the causeway herself. Each of the pleasantly furnished units has its own kitchen. The daily rate for two people is $90 in winter, *lowered to $60 in summer.* There is a two-bedroom apartment available, suitable for up to four people, which costs $116 per day in winter, *the price dropping to $78 per day in summer.*

There is a little beach for the use of guests, and Mrs. Bottomley will help with arrangements for water sports and outings. One guest liked the place so much he stayed for seven years. Trade winds keep the place fairly cool. Those guests who don't want to cook for themselves can take dinner out in George Town. They have a choice of the already-recommended hotels in town or else at one of the native restaurants. Grocery stores are fairly well stocked if you want to do it yourself, however.

WHERE TO DINE: In general, the best places to take meals in George Town are the main hotels, previewed above, although there are exceptions.

Peace and Plenty Hotel, P.O. Box 55 (tel. 809/336-2551), has one of the finest island dining rooms, real good home cooking and enough of it so that no one leaves unsatisfied. Who knows who might be seated at the next table? In days of yore, it might have been King Constantine of Greece, maybe Jack Nicklaus, or even Prince Philip. Today it's likely to be a banker from Nassau or perhaps a visiting yachting couple from Newport, Rhode Island. The inn, the oldest in the Exumas, attracts a cosmopolitan crowd. It's best to precede your meal with a drink in the old bar which was once a slave kitchen.

Your host, Charles Pfleuger, welcomes guests for dinner who sign up by 5 p.m. Meals are served nightly from 6:30 to 9:30. Bahamian and American dishes are offered, with dinners costing from $15 to $30, depending on what you order. You might begin with French onion soup, then follow with short ribs or oven-broiled chicken. You sit under ceiling fans, looking out over the harbor, at a table right off the hotel's Yellow Bird Lounge. Windows on three sides and candlelight make it particularly nice in the evening.

But you can also visit for lunch daily from noon to 2:30 p.m., costing $8. You have a selection of such dishes as homemade soups, followed by, perhaps, a burger, a chef's salad, or deep-fried grouper. You can also visit for breakfast from 7:30 to 10:30 a.m., even if you're not a guest of the hotel. For $5 you're given a selection of such dishes as French toast or scrambled eggs and sausage. But if you want to go truly Bahamian, you'll order the breakfast of boiled fish and grits.

Pieces of Eight Restaurant, P.O. Box 49 (tel. 809/336-2600), in this previously recommended hotel, brings exotic flavors to wake up the taste buds of George Town. The restaurant, decorated somewhat like a modern cafeteria, overlooks the swimming pool. You can arrive early for a drink in the half-moon-shaped Pirate's Den Bar. Lunch is served daily from noon to 3 p.m. and dinner from 6:30 to 9 p.m. Lunches cost from $8, with dinners priced at $17 and up, depending on what you order. An Oriental chef delights the palates of diners, often Germans, with such fare as wonton soup, followed by such main dishes as shrimp tempura, Exuma pineapple chicken, or sweet and sour grouper. He also does many variations of fried rice, including the most delectable one prepared with fresh Bahamian lobster. The most elegant main course is also prepared with lobster which is served Cantonese style with a black bean and garlic sauce. At lunch you can visit to sample the chef's steamed chicken or fried conch.

Sam's Place (tel. 809/336-2579). If Bogie were alive today, he'd surely head for this second-floor restaurant and bar overlooking the harbor in George Town. It's one of the newest (opened in 1987) but also one of the best restaurants in Great Exuma, already popular with the yachting set. The decorating has been called Bahamian laid-back. You can visit daily from 7 a.m. to 10 p.m. Sam Gray, the owner, offers breakfasts from $8, catching the early boating crowd going on a cruise of the yachting capital of The Bahamas. Lunches also cost from $8 and are likely to include everything from freshly made fish chowder to spaghetti with meat sauce. You'll also be able to order an array of sandwiches throughout the day. The dinner menu changes daily, but likely main courses include Exuma lobster tail, roast top round beef, grilled lamb chops, or pan-fried grouper. Of course, you can always get native conch salad. Dinners cost from $20, and the talk here is one of everybody's dream—that of owning a private utopia, one of those uninhabited cays still remaining in the Exuma chain.

Out Island Inn Restaurant, P.O. Box 49 (tel. 809/336-2171), offers not only Bahamian dishes but continental specialties as well on its menu. Not only do you get a fine cuisine in their large, grange-like dining room, but you're surrounded by water views in three directions, as the restaurant is set on a concrete pier jutting out into the harbor. If it's too windy at an outside table, you can retreat to one of the tables placed under weathered rafters inside. You might come early and order one of the tropical drinks in the bar (ever had gin and coconut water?). European visitors are especially fond of this place. Perhaps they find much of the bill of fare familiar. You might begin with, perhaps, a freshly made minestrone, then follow with one of the good-tasting pasta dishes such as fettuccine with lobster sauce or cannelloni parmigiana. You can also order salads such as hearts of palm or hearts of artichoke. Main courses are likely to include sirloin steak any style or veal French-style (sautéed with lemon juice and butter). For dessert, it's apple pie and ice cream. Meals cost from $25 for dinner and $10 for lunch, and food is served daily from noon to 3 p.m. and 7 to 10 p.m.

Two Turtles Inn, P.O. Box 51 (tel. 809/336-2545), run by Valerie R. Noyes, is one of the most popular drinking and dining establishments in George Town. Its Friday night barbecue is an island event. The price depends on your main course selection. That is, pork ribs go for $7.50, but a barbecued steak will cost $10. The busy little inn, recommended previously, stands across from the Exuma straw market. Activity overflows onto a central patio with redwood tables. The barbecue is from 6 to 10 p.m., but otherwise dining hours are from 5:30 to 9 p.m. when regular meals cost from $15 and are likely to include such dishes as cracked conch, strip steak, or pan-fried grouper. Lunches, costing from $8, are served from noon to 3 p.m. daily. Both Bahamian and American food are served.

WHERE TO SHOP: Unless you're one of the islanders who resides permanently in Great Exuma, chances are you won't visit George Town just to shop. However, there are a few places where you can purchase souvenirs and gifts.

The Sandpiper, P.O. Box 20, George Town (tel. 809/336-2609), stands across from Peace and Plenty next to Minns Watersports. Its main draw is its original serigraphs by Diane Minns, but it also offers a good selection of Bahamian arts and crafts, along with such items as Bahamian straw baskets (or other handcrafted works), sponges, ceramics, silkscreen fabrics, Seiko cameras, and post cards.

Peace and Plenty Boutique, P.O. Box 55, George Town (tel. 809/336-2551), stands next to the Sandpiper and across the street from this previously recommended inn which owns it. Its main draw is its selection of Androsia batiks for women. Androsia cloth is also sold at $10 per yard (a yard measures 43 inches wide). You can also find the usual practical items such as film and suntan oil.

Perhaps the most popular store in town is **Exuma Liquor and Gifts,** Queen's Highway (tel. 809/336-2101).

BRANCHING OUT FROM GEORGE TOWN: Queen's Highway runs across Great Exuma, and you may want to travel it, in either a taxi or a rented car, to take in the sights in and around George Town, which is still referred to as "the slave route."

Two villages, Rolleville and Rolle Town, each named after Lord Rolle, are still inhabited by descendants of his freed slaves. It is claimed that his will left them the land. This land is not sold but is passed along from one generation to the next.

Rolleville is to the north of George Town. As you travel along the highway, you'll see ruins of plantations. This land is called "generation estates," and the major ones are Steventon, Mount Thompson, and Ramsey. You pass such settlements as Mosstown (which has working farms), Ramsey, The Forest, Farmer's Hill, and Roker's Point. Steventon is the next settlement before you reach Rolleville.

At Rolleville, the traditional luncheon stopover is at **Kermit's Hilltop Restaurant & Tavern,** P.O. Box 78 (tel. 809/336-6038). I've already introduced Kermit Rolle in the "Getting Around" section. He not only has a taxi service, but operates the airport lounge in George Town. This is the most popular place in town, and it serves fresh fish like conch and grouper. Occasionally, it'll offer Bahamian lobster or turtle steak. Meals cost from $12. The place is situated so that you'll have a good view. Sometimes a local group will come in and entertain on weekends. You should call in advance to let him know you're coming. As for hours, he simply promises "good food all day." That usually means from 10 a.m. to 10 p.m. Monday to Saturday, from noon to 10 p.m. Sunday. Many locals come here just to play the game machines.

At Rolleville, the largest of the plantation estates, you will have driven for about 28 miles. There are several beautiful beaches along the way, especially the one at Tarr Bay and Jimmie Hill.

On the way back, if you didn't have lunch at Kermit's place in Rolleville, you might stop in at **Central Highway Inn** (no phone), a roadside tavern, run by Iva Bowe (Bowe, along with Rolle, is one of the most popular names on the island). The location is along Queen's Highway some 6½ miles northwest of George Town. Mrs. Bowe is known locally for her cracked conch. The conch is marinated in lime, pounded to make it tender, and then fried with her own special seasonings. Her food is good Bahamian cookery, and meals cost from $10. Hours are from 10 a.m. to 10 p.m. daily.

Some visitors may also want to head south of George Town, passing Flamingo Bay and **Pirate's Point.** In the 18th century Captain Kidd is said to have anchored at Kidd Cay (you can stay here at the Regatta Point, recommended previously).

Flamingo Bay, the site of a hotel and villa development, begins just half a mile from George Town. It's a favorite rendezvous of the yachting set and bonefishermen.

On the road to Little Exuma, you come to the hamlet of **Rolle Town,** which is another of the generation estates that was once, like Rolleville in the north, owned by Lord Rolle and is filled with what are called his "descendants" today. A sleepy town, Rolle Town has some houses about a century old. In an abandoned field, where goats frolic, you can visit the Rolle Town Tombs, burial ground of the McKay family who died young. Captain Alexander McKay, a Scot, came to Great Exuma in 1789, as he'd been granted 400 acres for a plantation. His wife joined him in 1791, and they had an infant child. However, tragedy struck, and Anne McKay died in 1792, as did her child. She was only 26. Perhaps grief stricken, her husband died the following year. Their story is one of the romantic legends of the island.

The village claims a famous daughter, Esther Rolle, the actress. Her parents were born here, but they came to the United States before she was born.

The road goes on to Little Exuma, coming up.

TOURS: Christine Rolle (there's that name again) is the one to show you Great and Little Exuma with her **Island Tours,** P.O. Box 55, George Town (tel. 809/336-4016). She offers two jaunts, each costing $10 and leaving at 10 a.m. and 2 p.m. daily. The first takes you north along Queen's Highway all the way to Barretarre, including native dishes for lunch, and the second takes you from George Town to Little Exuma, calling on the Shark Lady. If something ails you, Christine Rolle has a cure "from the bush," and she'll explain the medicinal properties of local plants and herbs. You'll take lunch at a local restaurant.

2. LITTLE EXUMA

This is a faraway retreat, the southernmost of the Exuma Cays. It has a subtropical climate, despite being actually in the tropics. The island, about 12 square miles in area, is connected to Great Exuma by a 200-yard-long bridge. It's about a ten-mile trip from the George Town Airport.

Little Exuma has beaches of dazzling white sand. In some places, sea life is visible from about 60 feet down in the gin-clear waters.

Less than a mile offshore is **Pigeon Cay,** which is uninhabited. Visitors often go here for the day and are later picked up by a boat that takes them back to Little Exuma. You can go snorkeling and visit the remains of a wreck, some 200 years old, right offshore in about six feet of water.

On one of the highest hills of Little Exuma are the remains of an old pirate fort. Several cannons are located near it, but documentation is lacking as to when it was built or by whom. Pirates didn't leave too much data lying around.

Coming from Great Exuma, the first community you reach on Little Exuma is called **Ferry,** so named because the two islands were linked by a ferry service before the bridge was put in. See if you can visit a private chapel of an Irish family, the Fitzgeralds, erected generations ago.

When you come onto Little Exuma, you might ask a local to direct you to the cottage of Gloria Patience, "the most unforgettable character of the Exumas." Her house, called Tara, lies on the left side of the road after you come over the bridge. She is famous and much publicized as **"The Shark Woman."** Now in her 70s, she earns her living collecting sharks' teeth, which she sells to jewelers. Called "the Annie Oakley of the Family Islands," this barefoot septuagenarian has some tall fish stories to tell, and she's told them to such people as Peter Benchley, author of *Jaws.* She's also appeared on television with Jacques Cousteau. She discounts some modern theories that sharks are kindly souls with a bad press. Take it from the woman who's bagged at least 1,800 of them single-handedly, "they're vicious." The biggest deadly choppers, she claims, are found in the jaws of the female hammerhead. She sells the flesh of her prey to restaurants, although she says she doesn't eat shark meat herself. Her home is like a museum, and you can come here on a shopping expedition, not only for shark teeth, but for all the flea market stuff and more valuable pieces she's collected over the years. She's a remarkable woman, living in a house split by the Tropic of Cancer.

Along the way, you can take in **Pretty Molly Bay,** site of the now-shuttered Sand Dollar Beach Club. "Pretty Molly" was a slave who committed suicide by walking into the water one night. The natives claim that her ghost can still be seen stalking the beach every night.

Many visitors come to Little Exuma to visit the **Hermitage,** a plantation constructed by Loyalist settlers. It is the last surviving home of the many that once stood in the Exumas. It was originally built by the Kendall family, who came to Little Exuma in 1784, establishing their plantation at **Williamstown** and, with their slaves, setting about growing cotton. However, they encountered so many difficulties in having the cotton shipped to Nassau that in 1806 they advertised the plantation for sale. The ad promised "970 acres more or less," along with "160 hands" (referring to the slaves). Chances are you'll be approached by a local guide who, for a fee, will show you around. Ask to be shown several old tombs in the area.

Also at Williamstown (look for the marker on the seaside), you can visit the remains of the **Great Salt Pond.**

Finally, the explorer who has to "see everything" can sometimes get a local to take him or her over to **Hog Cay,** the end of the line for the Exumas. This is really just a spit of land, and there are no glorious beaches here. As such, it's visited mainly by those who like to add obscure islets to their chain of exploration.

Hog Cay is in private hands, and it is farmed. The owner seems friendly to visitors. His house lies in the center of the island. There is also an old lookout tower with a five-foot cannon at its base. At one time this stood guard for ships coming and going into Elizabeth Harbour.

WHERE TO EAT: The "hot spot" of the island is **Gordy's Palace,** P.O. Box 72 (no phone), at Grays Ville. It's certainly no palace, and if you drop in here on a sleepy afternoon you might think only the weather is hot. You might, in fact, interrupt a poker game. Nevertheless, things get lively around here, especially on Friday and Saturday disco nights. The place is popular mainly with locals, although it gets an occasional visit from a member of the U.S. military stationed in the area. It is open daily, serving food from 9 a.m. to 10:30 p.m. You get typical island fare here, including grouper fingers, conch fritters, or cracked conch, served in modest surroundings. Meals cost from $12 and up. You can also visit just to drink and soak up the laid-back Little Exuma atmosphere. Beer costs $2.

3. BARRATERRE

For years linked only to the world by boat connections, Barraterre during the 1980s became connected to "mainland" Great Exuma by a road link. The area is now open for development, but no one here expects that to happen soon. The place is no more than a sleepy hamlet, and everybody seemingly is named McKenzie. As you're heading north, instead of continuing to "end of the line" Rolleville, turn left in the direction of Stuart Manor. You pass through Alexander and keep going until you reach the end of another road, and there lies little Barraterre, asleep in the sun. For the boating crowd, it is the gateway to the Brigantine Cays which stretch like a necklace to the northwest.

Here you'll see how the "life of the cays" is lived, with the biggest event being the arrival of the mailboat which is a vital link to the outside world. No one, not even one of the McKenzies, is absolutely certain how the place got its name. Perhaps it came from the French, *bar terre,* or land obstruction.

The Barraterrians live in a hilly community, with vividly painted houses (many in decay).

WHERE TO EAT: Virtually your only choice is a happy one. **Fisherman's Inn** (tel. 809/336-5017), is the social center of town, presided over by Mr. and Mrs. Norman Lloyd. The place has a large dance floor, where reggae and calypso music often fills the night. It is especially active during those homecoming parties when Barraterrians return, often in August, from either Nassau or the United States with their newfound ways. Everybody seems to have a good time. The kitchen promises that "fish eaters make better lovers," and, in this nautical atmosphere, they'll give you an opportunity to test that. Conch is queen here, and you can order her in fritters, cracked or scorched, even steamed. You can also ask for grouper fingers and fried chicken. No one will look askance if you want only a hot dog. The place is open daily from 8 a.m. "until the last person leaves." If you'd like, you can also play a game of pool.

4. STANIEL CAY

Staniel Cay lies at the southern end of the little Pipe Creek archipelago 80 miles southeast of Nassau, which is part of the Exuma Cays. This is an eight-mile chain of uninhabited islets, sandy beaches, coral reefs, and bonefish flats. There are many places for snug anchorages, making this a favorite yachting stopover in the mid-Exumas. Staniel Cay, known for years as "Stanyard," has no golf course or tennis courts, but it's the perfect island for "The Great Escape." It was described by one yachting visitor as lying "in a sea of virtual wilderness."

An annual bonefishing festival is sponsored here on July 10, during the celebration of Bahamian Independence Day.

Before the coming of the airplane, it took days to reach the island from Miami or Nassau, but now it has a 3,000-foot paved airstrip. Some of the vacation homes on Staniel Cay today are owned by pilots. A telecommunications center links the island with both The Bahamas and the U.S.

The easiest way to get here is on a flight departing from Fort Lauderdale International Airport. **TransMar International** flies in (call toll free at 800/327-3011). In Florida, information or brochures can be obtained by writing TransMar International, 4250 S.W. 11th Terr., Fort Lauderdale, FL 33315 (tel. 305/467-6850).

There are about 100 Bahamians living on this island, and there's a local straw market where you can buy handcrafts, hats, and handbags. The little cay was settled in the mid-18th century. Its oldest building is a 200-year-old shell.

Just off Staniel Cay is the *Thunderball* grotto where some sections of the famous James Bond movie were filmed. Divers can explore this grotto, but removal of anything but yourself is forbidden, as it is under the protection of The Bahamas National Trust. At low water, it's possible to swim in, and a blow hole in the roof illuminates the cave. Tropical fish can be seen in their natural habitat. Another James Bond flick, *Never Say Never Again,* was also partially filmed at this grotto, as, more recently, was *Splash.*

FOOD AND LODGING: A getaway haven, the **Staniel Cay Yacht Club,** Staniel Cay, The Exumas, The Bahamas (tel. 809/355-2024; 305/522-3814 in Florida, or toll free 800/635-6366), has a complete marina and can take 12 to 15 boats at its docks. Many yachts returning from the Caribbean put in here, their crews enjoying visits to the clubhouse, where burgees and other nautical paraphernalia hang from the rafters of the palm-thatched ceiling. This is a very informal resort, and the talk in the bar is likely to be of fishing or flying. The club serves good-tasting American and Bahamian cuisine—chowders and seafood buffet style. A desalinization plant provides fresh water. The club boasts a cottage sleeping six and a landlocked houseboat. It also has four cottages for couples. Balconies overlook the water. The guesthouse has a screened-in porch set in a stand of casuarina trees. All units have private baths and hot-water showers. On the full-board plan all year, two people in a cottage pay from $175 per day. A single costs $110. Bob Chamberlain oversees everything.

Anglers can bonefish at Staniel Cay, where the "flats" are home to this game fish. Several native fishing guides are available with boat and gear. Guests staying here for three days can use little sailboats, runabouts, and windsurfers free. Boston Whalers and small sailboats are for rent, and scuba gear is also available (see "The Sporting Life," below).

Happy People Marina, Staniel Cay, The Exumas, The Bahamas (tel. 809/355-2008), near the Staniel Cay Yacht Club, is operated by an Exumian, Kenneth Rolle (one of the many descendants of slaves who once belonged to Lord Rolle). His mother was the famous Ma Blanche, who had a mailboat named for her. He offers motel-like rooms on the water, as well as a restaurant and bar, a swimming pool, and a private beach. There are also marina and dockage facilities and a seawall made of whole conch shells. You can rent bareboats at the marina to explore dozens of little cays in the Pipe Creek archipelago. A casual atmosphere prevails here. The 12 comfortable rooms rent for $60 daily in a single or double. Meals cost from $20 up. A local band plays at Happy People's "nightclub," the Royal Entertainer Lounge, around the corner from the hotel.

5. SAMPSON CAY

In the heart of what has been called "the most beautiful cruising waters in the world," Sampson Cay is tiny and has a certain charm. It lies directly northwest of Staniel Cay and just to the southeast of the Exuma Cays Land and Sea Park. It has a full-service marina and some accommodations (see below), as well as a small dive operation. Along with Staniel Cay, Sampson Cay has the only marina in the Central Exumas. To fly to it, you must go to Staniel Cay, unless you arrive on your own boat, as do most visitors. Local guides take out sportsfishermen for the day, and this can be arranged at the club. Sampson Cay lies 67 nautical miles southeast of Nassau, and is considered one of the safest anchorages in the Exumas and a natural "hurricane hole." The cay lies near the end of Pipe Creek which has been called "a tropical Shangri-La."

Accommodations are available at **Sampson Cay Colony,** Sampson Cay, The Exumas, The Bahamas (tel. 809/355-2034). You can also call or write P.O. Box SS-6247, Nassau, The Bahamas (tel. 809/325-8864). Your hosts are Rosie and Marcus Mitchell. Mr. Mitchell is well known in these parts, as he operates his own private seaplane and an overseas salvage operation. Known for handling all sorts of emergencies, he works for The Bahamas Air and Sea Rescue headquarters. This non-profit organization, affectionately known by the acronym BASRA, comes to the rescue of any parties who need help while sailing on Bahamian seas. The Mitchells will also sell visiting boaters provisions in their commissary.

They offer three units for rent. A beach villa with air conditioning and a kitchenette costs $95 per day, single or double occupancy. Guests who do not want to cook usually opt for the two-story, two-bedroom tower villa with bath but no air conditioning. This tower is the best-known artificial landmark on Sampson Cay. It sleeps four people and costs $85 a day. All prices are year-round.

The clubhouse has a bar and lounge, and the yachting crowd often stops in here for dinner at the nautically decorated clubhouse. But reservations are needed (the radio contact is Channel 16 VHF). The restaurant charges $18 per person for an evening meal, which is served at a single seating every night at 7:30. Wednesday is barbecue night when most of the island (it's small) shows up for a bargain price of $9 per person. Arrangements can be made for visitors to explore the *Thunderball* Grotto at Staniel Cay. A 13-foot Boston Whaler can be rented for $45 per half day. There's also a complete dive shop, charging around $50 per person for a one-tank dive.

6. THE SPORTING LIFE

The action in the Exumas is, naturally, mainly water oriented, with fishing, scuba-diving, snorkeling, and boating activities leading the list. However, you can also play tennis, windsurf, waterski—whatever.

The cruising grounds around the Exumas are perhaps the finest to be found in the western hemisphere, if not in the world, for both sail- and powerboats. If you don't come in your own craft, you can rent one here, from a simple little daysailer to a fishing runabout, with or without a guide.

Snorkeling and scuba-diving opportunities draw aficionados from around the world to the Exuma National Land and Sea Park, a vast underwater preserve, and to the exotic limestone and coral reefs, blue holes, dropoffs, caves, and night dives. Dive centers in George Town and Staniel Cay provide air fills and diving equipment.

Fishing is top-grade here, the "flats" on the west side of Great Exuma being famous for bonefishing. You can find (if you're lucky) blue marlin on both sides of Exuma Sound, as well as sailfish, wahoo, and white marlin, plus numerous others.

IN GEORGE TOWN: If you'd like to go **scuba-diving,** the people to see are the **Exuma Divers,** P.O. Box 110 (tel. 809/336-2710). Wendle McGregor, who comes from Andros, is a PADI instructor. The dive center is behind the Peace and Plenty boutique, right off Queen's Highway. A dive costs from $34, $56 including instruction for the inexperienced diver. Experienced divers are taken on night dives at $41 per person. Divers can explore blue holes and Mystery Cave under Stocking Island, as well as the coral gardens.

Snorkeling trips with rental equipment cost $19 per person.

Minns Water Sports, P.O. Box 20 (tel. 809/336-2604), opposite Government Building in George Town, is the best place for boat rentals. You can rent a MWS boat and spend the day snorkeling, sailing, or just beachcombing. You can even take a picnic lunch along. Outboard motor boats, including a 15-foot Boston whaler, costs $53 a day. You can also rent windsurfers for $20 per day, along with snorkeling equipment such as mask and fins for $4 a day. Its office hours are Monday to Friday from 9 a.m. to 5 p.m.; Saturday from 9 a.m. to noon, and Sunday from 9 to 10 a.m. only.

If you want to go **fishing, Exuma Divers** (see above) offers deep-sea trips costing $184 for half a day, $292 for a full day for two to four people. Still fishing, for two to five people, costs $109 per half day.

Many men come to the Exumas just to go **bonefishing.** If so, the best arrangements can be made at **Peace and Plenty,** P.O. Box 55 (tel. 809/336-2551), where you can go out for a half day for $70 per person.

Tennis anyone? The best on the island is at Out Island Inn, P.O. Box 49 (tel. 809/336-2171), which has two professional courts. Nonguests of the hotel can reserve court space, but they are charged $10 per hour for the privilege.

FAMILY ISLAND REGATTA: The April Family Island Regatta, which draws a yachting crowd from all over the world, takes place in broad Elizabeth Harbour. It's a rollicking week of fun, song, and serious racing when the island sloops go all out to win. It's said that some determined skippers bring along extra crewmen to serve as live ballast on windward tacks, then drop them over the side to lighten the ship for the downwind run to the finish. Command post for the regatta is the Flamingo Bay Club. The event, a tradition since 1954, comes at the end of the crayfish season. The George Town regatta is considered the most popular of all the traditional sloop races held in the archipelago.

AT STANIEL CAY: Want to go boating? The **Staniel Cay Yacht Club** (tel. 809/355-2011) has Boston Whalers and small sailboats for rent. Scuba gear is also available.

The **Happy People Marina** (tel. 809/355-2008) also arranges sport-fishing trips with local guides.

Snorkeling trips can be arranged through both the yacht club and the marina.

7. AFTER DARK

Many of the island's inns, such as the just-reviewed **Peace and Plenty** and **Two Turtles Inn** have nights when special events are staged (check when you arrive).

But the **Flamingo Bay Club,** P.O. Box 23, George Town (tel. 809/336-2661), has something going on almost every night at its beachfront bar. One night, as for example, might be devoted to reggae, another to junkanoo and a fashion show. Perhaps it will be a barbecue or a dance contest. Maybe management will stage the Gong Show or a souse and johnnycake night. Who knows? You'll have to ask when you get there. The club is open nightly from 9 "until." Disco admission is usually $3.

CHAPTER XV

THE SOUTHERN BAHAMAS

□ □ □

This cluster of islands on the southern fringe of The Bahamas might be called the "undeveloped islands." That they are—in fact, some of them are proud to proclaim that "we are as we were when Columbus first landed here."

But their history hasn't been that uneventful. In the 18th century Loyalists from the Carolinas and Virginia came here, settling into many of the islands and bringing in slave labor. For about 20 years they had thriving cotton plantations until a blight struck and killed the industry. A second, and perhaps more devasting "blight" from the planters' point of view, was the freeing of the slaves in 1834. The Loyalists moved on to more fertile ground, in many cases leaving behind the emancipated blacks who were left with only the name of their former master. Many people in the southern Bahamas have had to eke out a living as best they can.

With some notable exceptions, such as Rum Cay and Long Island, tourism developers have stayed clear of these islands, although their potential is enormous, as most of them have excellent beaches, good fishing, and fine dive sites.

If you consider visiting any of these islands, be forewarned that transportation will be a major problem. Also, except for two or three resorts, accommodations are severely limited. For these and other reasons, people who have yachts have been the primary visitors up to now.

Many changes may be in the wind for the southern Bahamas. But if you want to see things "the way they used to be," as they say in those Jamaica ads, go not to Jamaica but to Mayaguana Island. That's *really* how things used to be in The Bahamas.

1. CAT ISLAND

The sixth-largest island in The Bahamas, fishhook-shaped Cat Island is some 48 miles long and 1 to 4 miles wide, comprising some 150 square miles of land area about 130 miles southeast of Nassau and 325 miles southeast of Miami. This is not—repeat *not*—Cat *Cay*. The cay is a little private island near Bimini. The location of Cat Island—named after the pirate, Catt—is near the Tropic of Cancer, and its climate is one of the finest in The Bahamas, with temperatures in the high 60s during the short winters, rising to the mid 80s in summer, with trade winds making the place more comfortable. Some 2,000 souls call it home.

With its virgin beaches, Cat Island is considered one of the most beautiful islands in The Bahamas, and it is visited by so few people it could be called "undiscovered." Even though it has remained relatively unknown by mainstream tourism, many local historians claim that it was Cat Island that first saw Columbus. The great explorer himself was believed by some to have been first welcomed here by the peaceful Arawak Indians.

Cat Island remains mysterious to some even now. It's known as a stronghold of such romantic practices as *obeah* and of miraculously healing bush medicines. Its history has been colorful. Regardless of whether or not Columbus stopped off here, the island has been a parade of adventurers, slaves, buccaneers, farmers, and visionaries of many nationalities.

There's an interesting Arawak Indian cave at Columbus Point on the southern tip of the island. In addition, you can see the ruins of many once-flourishing plantations. Some old stone mounds are nearly 200 years old. Early planters, many of them Loyalists, marked their plantation boundaries with these mounds.

You can hike along the natural paths through native villages, past exotic plants. Finally, you reach the peak of **Mount Alvernia,** the highest point in The Bahamas at 206 feet above sea level, and are rewarded with a splendid view. The mount is capped by the Hermitage, a religious retreat built entirely by hand by the late Father Jerome, the former "father confessor" of the island, who was once a muleskinner in Canada. Curiously, the building was scaled to fit his short stature (he was a very, very short man). An Anglican who switched, this Roman Catholic "hermit priest" became a legend on Cat Island. He died in 1956 at the age of 80, but his memory is kept very much alive here, and he's known even among young people born long after his death.

With about 2,000 residents, Cat Island lies between Eleuthera and Long Island, belonging to the eastern part of The Bahamas. An airport near **The Bight,** the most beautiful village on the island, is open, and Bahamasair flies to **Arthurs Town** in the north, the major town and the boyhood home of the actor Sidney Poitier. He has many relatives still living on the island, including one or two amazing look-alikes I recently spotted.

A straight asphalt road (in terrible shape) leads from the north to the south of the island. Along the way you can select your own beach, and chances are you'll have complete privacy. These beaches also offer an array of water sports, and visitors can go swimming or snorkeling at several places. The island's north side is considered wild, untamed shoreline. Diving lessons are possible for the novice, and the experienced will find boating and diving among the reasons to go to Cat Island.

The boating activities reach their peak at the **Annual Three-Day Regatta,** usually conducted at the end of July. That's when Cat Island receives its biggest collection of visitors, and its inns prove inadequate to receive them.

On the southern tip of the island is the **Deveaux Mansion,** built by Colonel Andrew Deveaux of the fledgling U.S. Navy, who recaptured Nassau from the Spanish in 1783 Its heyday was during the island's short-lived cotton boom.

Yet another mansion, **Armbrister Plantation,** lies in ruins near Port Howe, which is the very southern tip of Cat Island.

GETTING THERE: A commercial flight on **Bahamasair** leaves Nassau for Arthurs Town on Monday and Thursday, but that could change so check locally.

Cat Island is also serviced by **mailboats.** The M/V *North Cat Island Special* leaves Potter's Cay Dock heading for Bennett's Harbour and Arthurs Town weekly, leaving on Tuesday. It returns to Nassau on Thursday.

For details of sailing and costs, passengers should get in touch with the dockmaster at Potter's Cay in Nassau (tel. 809/323-1064).

FOOD AND LODGING: On Fernandez Bay, **Fernandez Bay Village,** Cat Island, The Bahamas (no phone) is a place where you can enjoy the same water and sun activities as at big resorts but without the hassle of crowds and constant coming and going. It has been in the Armbrister family since 1870. It's a place where seclusion is a part of the charm, and yet, if you wish, you can get acquainted with other guests of like interests. Right on the beautiful white-sand beach of the bay, nestled among the casuarina trees, are seven full housekeeping villas, each sleeping up to six people, and two double-occupancy cottages, built of stone, driftwood, and glass. Full maid service is provided. Rates in the villas for up to four people year-round are $115 daily in a one-bedroom unit, $125 in two-bedroom accommodations, and $145 in three-bedroom villas, all equipped for vacationers to do their own cooking. The two cottages (no cooking facilities) rent for $135 daily for two persons on MAP. There's a surcharge of $2 per person per day for 24-hour electricity. The resort has a beach bar, a restaurant, video movies, and an ice machine. Its restaurant is considered one of the best in the Family Islands, as fresh supplies are flown in directly from Florida. A general store allows you to stock your villa's kitchen.

Fernandez Bay Village guests have free use of Zuma sailboats and bicycles. Snorkeling and waterskiing are also on the agenda. Guests can rent vans for $15 per hour to drive into the hills. You can picnic on deserted beaches around the island, then dine on authentic island cuisine at the resort's restaurant, after which on many nights a blazing bonfire on the beach is the focal point for guests to listen to island music. For reservations and information, write to P.O. Box 2126, Fort Lauderdale, FL 33303 (tel. 305/764-6945). The resort will supply air transportation from Nassau on request, with flights to New Bight Airport nearby. Your hosts are Frances Armbrister (often called "Mrs. A"), who worked in pictures in Hollywood before coming here in 1938. She is aided by her son, Tony, who flies a plane, and his wife, Pam.

Hotel Greenwood Inn, Port Howe, Cat Island, The Bahamas (no phone), is a group of modern buildings on the ocean side with a private sandy beach. There are 32 beds in spacious double rooms, all equipped with full bath and shower. All rooms have their own terrace, and each apartment has a view of the ocean. The hotel is open all year. There is an all-purpose bar and a dining room. The staff meets each Bahamasair flight when it arrives. Make time for some comfortable chats with fellow guests before jumping into the swimming pool. Tariffs year-round are $60 per day in a single, $110 in a double, including two meals a day. Children four to twelve sharing a room with their parents pay only half the rate. The inn has a 40-foot motorboat for diving excursions. Its Tabaluga Diving Base has complete equipment for 20 divers at a time.

Bridge Inn, The Bight, Cat Island, The Bahamas (tel. 809/354-5013), is a family-run hotel on this Family Island. Allan Russell, who manages it all with the able assistance of a group of family members, offers 12 rooms with room service, a full bar, and a restaurant serving Bahamian and international cuisine. The inn offers babysitting services so that parents can play tennis or go diving, windsurfing, jogging, bicycling, fishing, or just sightseeing with the knowledge that their youngsters are being carefully tended and are having fun too. Year-round, guests pay $40 per person daily, AP, based on double occupancy. AP singles cost $70 daily. There are packages for longer stays. Native jam sessions (rake and scrape) are easily arranged for your entertainment. As Allan Russell points out, you'll learn that life can be "No problem, mon, on Cat Island."

2. SAN SALVADOR

This may be where the New World began. Christopher Columbus, it has for some years been believed, made his first footprints in the western hemisphere here, although this has recently been strongly disputed. The easternmost island in the Bahamian archipelago, San Salvador lies 200 miles east-southeast of Nassau. It is some 60 square miles in area, much of which is occupied by water. There are said to be 28 land-locked lakes on the island, the largest of which is 12 miles long and serves as the principal route of transportation for most of the island's 1,200 population. A 40-mile road circles the perimeter of San Salvador.

The tiny island keeps a lonely vigil in the Atlantic. The Dixon Hill Lighthouse at South West Point can be seen for 90 miles. The last lighthouse of its type in The Bahamas, it rises about 165 feet; the light is a hand-operated beacon fueled by kerosene. It was built in the 1850s. The highest point on the island is Mount Kerr at 138 feet.

Back in 1492 a small group of peaceful Lucayan (Arawak) Indians went about their business of living on a little island they called Guanahani, which they and their forebears had called home for at least 500 years. It is this island that is believed to have been the first landfall for Columbus and his fleet who were looking for a route to the riches of the Orient. It is said that the discoverer knelt and prayed—and claimed the land for Spain.

Unfortunately, the event was not so propitious for the reportedly handsome, near-naked Indians. Columbus later wrote to Queen Isabella about what ideal captives they would make—perfect servants, in other words. It wasn't long before the Spanish Conquistadors cleared the island—as well as most of The Bahamas—of Lucayans, sending them into slavery and early death in the mines of Hispaniola (Haiti) to feed the Spanish lust for gold from the New World.

No lasting marker was placed by Columbus on the sandy, sun-drenched island he had found, resulting in much study and discussion during the last century or so as to just where he really did land. Turks and Caicos said it was on one of their cays, and some students claimed that it was on Cat Island.

During the days of the buccaneers, an Englishman and pirate captain, George Watling, took over the island as his own and built a mansion to serve as his safe haven (see the preview of Watling's Castle, below). This was in the 17th century, and the island was listed on maps for about 250 years as Watling's (or Watling) Island.

In 1926 the Bahamian legislature formally changed the name of the island to San Salvador, feeling that enough evidence had been brought forth to support the belief that this was the site of the landing of Columbus. Finally, in 1983 artifacts of European origin (beads, buckles, and metal spikes) were found on this island together with a shard of Spanish pottery along with Arawak pottery and beads. It is unlikely that the actual date of these artifacts can be pinned down, although they are probably from about 1490 to 1560. However, the beads and buckles fit the description of goods recorded in Columbus's log as having been traded by his crewmen for Indian objects.

It was in 1986 that *National Geographic* magazine published a meticulously researched article by its senior associate editor, Joseph Judge, with a companion piece by former chief of the magazine's foreign editorial staff, Luis Marden, setting forth the belief that Samana Cay, some 65 miles to the southeast of the present San Salvador, was Guanahani, where Columbus first landed in the New World and whose name he declared to be San Salvador. The question may never be absolutely resolved, but there will doubtless be years and years of controversy about it.

At any rate, if a preponderance of monuments is anything to go by, this is the San Salvador found and named by the historic explorer. Three of them are on land, and they certainly can't all mark the spot where Columbus first came ashore, but Long Bay, marked by the **Cross Monument,** is deemed the most likely spot. The *Chicago Herald* installed a monument to the explorer in the 1890s, but it is not probable—indeed, it's almost impossible—that any landing was made at that site. It opens onto reefs along the eastern shore, surely a dangerous place for a landing.

The **Olympic Games Memorial** to Columbus was erected in 1968 to commemorate the games in Mexico. At the time, runners carrying an Olympic torch circled the island before coming to rest at the monument and lighting the torch there, which was then taken to Mexico on a warship for the games. A fourth marker is underwater, supposedly where Columbus dropped anchor.

Watling's Castle, also known as Sandy Point Estate, has substantial ruins which are about 85 feet above sea level and some 2½ miles from the "Great Lake," on the southwestern tip of the island. Local "experts" will tell you all about the castle and its history. Only problem is, each "expert" I listened to—three in all, at different times—had a conflicting story about the place. Ask around and perhaps you'll get yet another version.

In the early part of the 19th century some Loyalist families moved from the newly established United States to this island, hoping to get rich on farmland tended by slave labor. That dream ended when the United Kingdom Emancipation Act of 1834 freed the slaves. The plantation owners, having been compensated for their bond servants' value, moved on, but the former slaves stayed behind.

A relic of those times, **Farquharson's Plantation,** is the best-known ruin on the island. People locally call it "Blackbeard's Castle," but it's a remnant of slavery days, not of the time of pirates. You can see the foundation of a great house, a kitchen, and what is believed to have been a punishment cell.

San Salvador is one of the most unspoiled of the Bahamian Family Islands—not that much changed since Columbus landed. It has wooded hills, the lakes, and white sandy beaches. Its people are hospitable. Some still practice *obeah* and bush medicine.

The island's capital, **Cockburn** (pronounced Coburn) **Town,** is a harbor village, which also has an airstrip. It takes its name from George Cockburn, who is said to have been the first royal governor of The Bahamas who cared enough about this remote island to visit it. That was back in 1823.

Look for the town's giant, landmark almond tree. Whatever is happening at San Salvador generally takes place here, especially the Columbus Day parade held every October 12. The island will probably be in for a tremendous influx of visitors in the not-too-distant future, when the 500th anniversary of the landing of Columbus is celebrated in 1992.

The **New World Museum** in Cockburn Town has relics dating back to Indian times, but you'll have to ask until you find someone with a key if you want to go inside.

If you head south of the town for three miles, you'll see the Cross Monument and the Olympic Monuments to Columbus.

Among the settlements on San Salvador are Sugar Loaf, Pigeon Creek, Old Place (don't you like that name?), Holiday Track, Fortune Hill, and the one with the largest population, United Estates, a village in the northwest corner near the

Dixon Hill Lighthouse. The U.S. Coast Guard has a station at the northern tip of the island.

Bonefishermen are attracted to Pigeon Creek, and some record catches have been chalked up there. San Salvador is mainly visited by the boating set who can live aboard their craft, but if you're visiting for the day, you'll find one or two local cafés. They all serve seafood.

GETTING THERE: This can be a real problem, made all the more so by the scarcity of accommodations on San Salvador and the long time you'll have to wait before being able to get off the island. Nevertheless, history buffs still flock here every year.

Bahamasair has four direct weekly flights, on Sunday, Tuesday, Friday, and Saturday, to San Salvador (check flight schedules).

In addition, a mailboat, the M/V *Maxine,* leaves Potter's Cay Dock in Nassau, heading to Cat Island, Rum Cay, and San Salvador. It departs Nassau weekly on Tuesday, returning to Nassau on Saturday. For details about sailing, contact the dockmaster at Potter's Cay Dock in Nassau (tel. 809/323-1064). The one-way fare is $30.

FOOD AND LODGING: San Salvador's only resort, Riding Rock Inn, San Salvador, The Bahamas (tel. 809/332-2631), lying to the north of Cockburn Town, close to the airport, is good for diving vacations. The inn has a total of 24 comfortably furnished, air-conditioned bedrooms and is fairly simple, basic living. Certified divers appreciate the week-long dive packages, including full board, three dives a day, transfers within the island, and accommodations based on double occupancy. In winter the weekly cost is $899 per dive, *lowered in summer to $699.* Single divers must pay $1,152 per week in winter or *$869 in summer.* The non-dive package includes all of the above except for the dives. Double occupancy costs $649 per person weekly in winter but *only $479 in summer,* and singles pay $902 weekly in winter *or $649 in summer.* Regular EP rates, winter or summer in either single or double occupancy, are $96 per day.

The inn is on a private sandy beach and has a freshwater pool and a tennis court. Car rentals can be arranged, as can flights from Fort Lauderdale. Dive boats make daily reef trips. Fresh seafood, of course, is featured on the menu.

3. RUM CAY

"Rum Cay?" you ask. "Where on earth is Rum Cay?" (That's pronounced *key,* of course.) Even many Bahamians have never heard of it. Midway between San Salvador and Long Island, this is a cay that time forgot.

That wasn't always so. The very name conjures up images of swashbucklers and rum-runners, and it was doubtless at least a port of call for those doughty seafarers, as it was for ships taking on supplies of salt, fresh water, or food before crossing the Atlantic or going south to Latin America. The cay's name is supposed to have derived from the wrecking of a rum-laden sailing ship upon its shores.

Like many other Bahamian islands, this one for a while attracted Loyalists fleeing the former 13 colonies of Great Britain on the North American mainland. They were drawn here by the hope of establishing themselves as farmers and plantation overlords, but even those brave and homeless immigrants abandoned the island as unproductive.

Salt mines were the mainstay of the island's economy before they were wiped out by hurricanes at the turn of the century. After that, most of the inhabitants migrated to Nassau, so that by the 1970s the population of Rum Cay stood at "80 souls."

The well-known underwater cinematographer Stan Waterman visited here and described Rum Cay as "the unspoiled diving jewel of The Bahamas." For that reason, a diving club was opened here in 1983.

To reach the island, guests fly to Rock Sound on South Eleuthera, two hours from Fort Lauderdale, where they are cleared by Customs. By prearrangement only, you are then flown to Rum Cay's runway, 4,000 feet of crushed coral, at Port Nelson, the island's capital. The cost of a round-trip Saturday to Saturday flight is $250 per person. This, incidentally, is where most of the island's present 100 inhabitants live.

There have been statements in some printed matter that Rum Cay was the island where Columbus landed next after finding and naming San Salvador. He dubbed that second island Santa María de la Concepción. However, many students of history and navigation believe that the second stop was at the island today called Conception, which lies in a northwesterly direction from Rum Cay and about the same distance northeast of Long Island. You'll have to go there in a private boat.

Both of these views as to the second island on which Columbus landed are disputed by Joseph Judge in the 1986 *National Geographic* article (see under "San Salvador," above). He holds that, based on modern computer science and knowledge of the ocean bottom and currents, the island the discoverer named Santa María de la Concepción has to be Crooked Island.

Conception is not inhabited, and it is under the protection of The Bahamas National Trust, which preserves it as a sea and land park. It's a sanctuary for migratory birds. The most esoteric of divers find excellent dive sites here, and the rapidly diminishing green turtle uses its beaches as egg-laying sites. Park rules are strict about littering or removing animal or plant life.

Rum Cay Club is a remote divers' hideaway (for information, call toll free 800/334-6869, or 305/467-8355 collect in Florida, or write to P.O. Box 22396, Fort Lauderdale, FL 33335). It was the creation of David Melville, an American businessman from Boston, Massachusetts. He first visited the island in 1977 after hearing of the spectacular diving possibilities here, moving here in 1979 to begin the development of a sport diving club, which has now broadened its services to appeal to rod-and-reel fishing, boating, and beachcombing enthusiasts, as well as to vacationers seeking nothing more than a relaxed escape to a small, relatively uninhabited island. The club is built on a bluff overlooking the ocean, with only a dozen rooms. The club's facilities are modern and styled in an island manner, with large rooms, overhead fans, and candlelit dinners with complimentary wine. *Scuba Times* praised the cuisine as comparable favorably to that of a posh New York restaurant. In addition to a hot tub, video movies, video games, a library, bicycles, Aqua cats, and windsurfers, the club also offers a well-equipped scuba and snorkeling operation and a complete E-6 photo and film-processing lab with a three-hour developing service.

Rum Cay offers the diver some of the best over- and underwater sights to be found in this part of the world. Miles of deserted, sandy white beaches and inland hiking paths lead to colonial plantation ruins and a cave with pre-Columbian Indian wall paintings. A spectacular diving wall lies only ten minutes from the club by dive boat. Also, excellent snorkeling is available around the coral heads near the beach in front of the hotel.

In winter, one week AP (seven nights, eight days) costs $599 per person. The daily AP rate is $109 per person. *In summer, one week AP costs $483 per person or $101 per day.* To these prices, you can add dive packages: six dives cost $100, 11 dives go for $175, and 17 cost $250. A resort course for uncertified divers is $75, and a certification course costs $350. Melville is most interested in keeping his operation small, so as not to "ruin something like Rum Cay."

4. LONG ISLAND

Having nothing to do with that 100-mile land mass at the southern tip of New York state (unless, perhaps, to be visited by residents of the northern place), the Long Island of The Bahamas was the third island to which Columbus sailed during his first voyage of discovery, a point on which everybody seems to agree. The Lucayan (Arawak) Indians who lived there at the time (having come from South America via Cuba) called their island Yuma, but Columbus renamed it Fernandina, in honor of King Ferdinand, and claimed it for Spain.

The Tropic of Cancer runs through this long, thin sliver of land, 400 square miles in area, lying 150 miles south of Nassau. It stretches for some 60 miles running from north to south, and averages 1½ miles wide. It's only 3 miles wide at its broadest point.

Only recently emerged as a tourist resort, Long Island is characterized by high cliffs in the north, wide, shallow sand beaches, historic plantation ruins, Indian caves, and Spanish churches. It is also the site of the salt works of the Diamond Crystal Company. The island's present population is some 3,500 people. Offshore are famed diving sites, such as the Arawak "green" hole, a "bottomless" blue hole of stunning magnitude.

There are two airstrips here, connected by a bad road. The Stella Maris strip is in the north, and the other, called Deadman's Cay, is in the south, north of Clarence Town. **Bahamasair** wings in four times a week from Nassau, connecting the two airports.

Mailboats service Clarence Town weekly, with service to Deadman's Cay and Stella Maris once a week or every other week. The boats leave from Potter's Cay Dock in Nassau. The M/V *Nay Dean* sails from Nassau on Monday, returning on Friday, and makes stops at the Exumas as well as other cays and Long Island. For information on sailing, days and times, and costs, get in touch with the dockmaster, Potter's Cay Dock, Nassau (tel. 809/323-1064).

Loyalist plantation owners came here in the 18th century from the Carolinas and Virginia, bringing with them their slaves and their allegiance to the British Crown. There was a brief cotton boom, but when the slaves were freed in 1834 the owners abandoned the plantations and left the island. Inhabited by the former slaves, Long Island slumbered for years, until its rediscovery in the 1960s by German resort developers.

In June, the sailors of Long Island participate in the big event of the year, the **Long Island Regatta.** They've been gathering since 1967 at Salt Pond for this annual event, which lasts for four days. In addition to the highly competitive sailboat races, Long Island takes on a festive air with calypso music and reggae and lots of drinking and partying. Many expatriate Long Islanders come home at this time, usually from Nassau, New York, or Miami, to enjoy not only the regatta but rake and scrape music (accordion playing).

THE SIGHTS: Most of the inhabitants live at the unattractively named **Deadman's Cay.** Other settlements have colorful and somewhat more pleasant names: Roses, Newfound Harbour, Indian Head Point, Burnt Ground. Cape Santa Maria, generally believed to be the place where Columbus landed and from which he looked on, but did not visit, the Exumas, is at the northern tip of the island. My favorite place name, however, is Hard Bargain. No one seems to know how this hamlet came to be called that.

Try to visit **Clarence Town** in the south, along the eastern coastline. It was here that the stubby little priest, Father Jerome, who became known as the "father confessor" of the islands, built two churches before his death in 1956—one, **St. Paul's,** an Anglican house of worship and the other, **St. Peter's,** a Roman

Catholic church. The "hermit" of Cat Island, where you can visit his Hermitage, was interested in Gothic architecture, and he must also have been of a somewhat ecumenical bent, as he started his ministry as an Anglican but embraced Roman Catholicism along the way.

The days when local plantation owners figured their wealth in black slaves and white cotton are recalled in some of the ruins you can visit. **Dunmore's Plantation** ruins stand on a hill with the sea on three sides. There are six gateposts (four outer and two inner ones), as well as a house with two fireplaces and drawings of ships on the wall. At the base of the ruins is evidence that a millwheel was once used. It was part of the estate of Lord Dunmore, for whom Dunmore Town on Harbour Island was named.

At the village of Grays stand **Gray's Plantation** ruins, where you'll see the remnants of at least three houses, one with two chimneys. One is very large, and one seems to have been a one-story structure with a cellar.

Adderley's Plantation originally occupied all the land now known as Stella Maris. The ruins of this cotton plantation's buildings consist of three structures that are partially intact but roofless.

Two underground sites that can be visited are **Dunmore's Caves** and **Deadman's Cay Cave.** You'll need to hire a local guide if you wish to visit these attractions. Dunmore's Caves are believed to have been inhabited by Lucayans and later to have served as a hideaway for buccaneers. The cave at Deadman's Cay, one of two that lead to the ocean, has never been fully explored. There are two Indian drawings on the cavern wall in the one you can visit. It also has stalagmites and stalactites.

FOOD AND LODGING: On the Atlantic, overlooking the coastline, the **Stella Maris Inn,** P.O. Box 105, Long Island, The Bahamas (tel. 809/336-2106 locally or 305/467-0466 for the Florida booking office), has 60 rooms. Courtesy transportation is provided to a three-mile beach reserve. Accommodations vary widely—rooms, studios, apartments, and cottages consisting of one to three bedrooms. Rentals are all in individual buildings, including cottages and bungalows, set around the clubhouse and a trio of hotel pools.

Each accommodation has its own air conditioning, walk-in closets, and fully equipped bath. Some bungalows are 100 feet from the water; others are directly on its edge. Winter rates, on the EP, are from $86 daily in a double, from $70 in a single. A one-bedroom cottage for two rents for $106 daily, and a one-bedroom townhouse for two costs $106 also. *In summer, the rates drop to $76 daily for double occupancy, from $60 in a single. A one-bedroom cottage for two costs $96 daily, a one-bedroom town house for two costing from $96 also.* Two-bedroom villas for two cost $180 in winter, *$160 in summer.* The inn serves a Bahamian cuisine, as well as continental specialties. Dress here is informal, and much of the action is free.

There are two hard tennis courts, and the inn provides rum punch parties, cave parties, barbecue dinners, Saturday dinners, and dancing. Water sports are excellent here. Divers and snorkelers have a wide choice of coral head, reef, and dropoff diving, along the protected west coast of this island and at the north and all along the east coast, around Conception Island and Rum Cay. Bottom and reef fishing are also offered. There are three good bonefish bays close by. Other sports include waterskiing. You can rent boats. Windsurfing and sailing on 12-foot Scorpions and Sunfish are free to hotel guests.

At Salt Pond, **Thompson Bay Inn,** P.O. Box 30123, Stella Maris, Long Island, The Bahamas (tel. Deadman's Cay), is a modest, nine-room inn. Rising two floors, it was constructed of stone. Other than the Stella Maris Inn, it is the most popular gathering place on the island, with its bar, lounge, dance hall, and restaurant, serving such Bahamian dishes as conch, grouper, and peas 'n' rice. Dinners cost $12. Rooms are simply furnished, and the inn's four baths are shared. Year-round, EP singles rent for $40 daily, a double going for $50. The location at Salt Pond is 12 miles south of Stella Maris.

5. ACKLINS AND CROOKED ISLANDS

These little tropical islands far to the southeast of Nassau comprise an undiscovered Bahamian frontier outpost. Columbus came this way looking for gold, and later Crooked Island, Acklins, and their surrounding cays were retreats of pirates who attacked vessels in the Crooked Island Passage, the narrow waterway separating the two islands. Columbus sailed through this passage. Today a well-known landmark, the **Crooked Island Passage Light,** built in 1876, guides ships to a safe voyage through the slot. A barrier reef begins near the lighthouse, stretching down off Acklins Island for about 25 miles to the southeast.

These are twin-sister islands, which, although separate, are usually mentioned as a unit because of their proximity to one another. The northern one, Crooked Island, is 70 square miles in area, lying 223 miles from Nassau. Acklins, to the south, occupies 120 square miles and is 260 miles from the Bahamian capital, which is to the northwest.

In his controversial article in *National Geographic* in 1986, Joseph Judge identifies Crooked Island as the site of Columbus's second island landing, the one he named Santa María de la Concepción.

It is estimated that by the end of the 18th century there were more than three dozen working plantations on these islands, begun by Loyalists fleeing mainland North America in the wake of the Revolutionary War. At the peak plantation period, there could have been as many as 1,200 slaves laboring in the cotton fields (which were later wiped out by a blight).

There is a government-owned ferry service connecting the two islands, operating from 9 a.m. to 4 p.m. It links Lovely Bay on Acklins with Browns on Crooked Island. The one-way fare is $4. Both these islands have magnificent white sandy beaches, and good fishing and scuba-diving are possible. Both islands are inhabited mainly by fishermen and farmers.

Crooked Island opens onto the Windward Passage, the dividing point between the Caribbean Sea and The Bahamas. Whatever else he may have named it, it is said that when Columbus landed at what is now **Pittstown Point,** he called it Fragrant Island because of the aroma of its many herbs. One scent was cascarilla bark, used in a native liqueur, which is exported. For the best view of the island, go to Colonel Hill, if you didn't happen to land at the Crooked Island Airport there when you arrived.

Guarding the north end of this island is the **Marine Farm,** an old British fortification that saw action in the War of 1812. It looks out over Crooked Island Passage and can be visited (ask your hotel to make arrangements for you).

Fortune Island, south of Albert Town, lies off the coast of Crooked Island. Based on the research done for the article in *National Geographic* mentioned above, Fortune Island (sometimes confusingly called Long Cay) is the one Columbus chose to name Isabella, in honor of his queen. Once it had a thriving salt and sponge industry, now long gone. Albert Town, classified as a ghost town, officially isn't. There are some hardy souls still living there. **Fortune Hill** on Fortune Island is the local landmark, visible from 12 miles away at sea. This small island got its name from the custom of hundreds of Bahamians who went there in the two decades before World War I. They'd wait to be picked up by oceangoing freighters, which would take them as laborers to Central America—hence, they came here to "seek their fortune."

On Crooked Island is **Hope Great House,** which, with its orchards and gardens, dates from the time of George V in England. At the southern end of

Acklins lies **Castle Island,** a low and sandy bit of land where today an 1867 lighthouse stands. Pirates used it as a hideaway, sailing forth to attack ships in the nearby passage.

Acklins Island has many interestingly named hamlets—Rocky Point, Binnacle Hill, Salina Point, Delectable Bay, Golden Grove, Goodwill, Hard Hill, Snug Corner, and Lovely Bay. Some Crooked Island sites have more ominous names, such as Gun Point and Cripple Hill.

If you're coming to these islands, take care of all your banking needs before you arrive, as there is no banking service on either Crooked Island or Acklins. However, there are two government-operated clinics.

GETTING THERE: An airport lies at Colonel Hill on Crooked Island, and there's another airstrip at Spring Point, Acklins. If you should arrive on one island and intend to go to the other, you can use the ferry. **Bahamasair** has two flights a week to Crooked and Acklins Islands, with returns to Nassau scheduled on the same day.

There is also mailboat service about the M/V *Windward Express.* It leaves Potter's Cay Dock in Nassau, heading for Acklins, Crooked Island, Long Cay, and Mayaguana each week. Check on days of sailing and costs with the dockmaster at Potter's Cay Dock in Nassau (tel. 809/323-1064).

Once you arrive at Crooked Island, there is taxi service available.

FOOD AND LODGING ON CROOKED ISLAND: Lying right on the waterfront, **T & S Guest House,** Cabbage Hill, Crooked Island, The Bahamas (tel. 809/133-62096), stands a ten-minute walk from the airport. E. A. Thompson, the manager, will welcome you and offer island hospitality in one of his ten bedrooms, which rent for $30 in a single, rising to $40 in a double. Children under 11 can stay free with their parents. Facilities include TV and laundry, and Mr. Thompson will explain local life, including how to spend the day on the best beach, two miles away. You can prepare your own meals in some of the units, or else enjoy good Bahamian seafood, simply cooked, at the inn itself. Boating and skindiving can also be arranged. If you fall in love with the place, you can also ask about building lots that are available on the beachfront strip.

6. MAYAGUANA ISLAND

"Sleepy Mayaguana" it might be called. It seems to float adrift in the tropical sun, at the remote extremities of the southeastern "edge" of The Bahamas. It occupies 110 square miles and has a population of about 500. It's a long, long way from the powers at Nassau, who rarely visit here.

Standing in the Windward Passage, Mayaguana is just northwest of Turks and Caicos, coming up in the next part. It's separated from the British Crown Colony by the Caicos Passage. Around the time of the American Civil War, inhabitants of Turks Island began to settle in Mayaguana, which before then had dozed undisturbed for centuries.

Acklins and Crooked Islands, just visited, lie across the Mayaguana Passage. This island is only 6 miles across at its widest point, and about 24 miles long. It has most enticing beaches, but you'll rarely see a tourist on them, except sometimes an occasional German. (How do they know about Mayaguana in Frankfurt?) A few tourism developers have flown in to check out the island, but so far no activity has come about.

Mayaguana has hardwood forests, and because of its remote location, the U.S. has opened a missile-tracking station here.

Its southern location makes it ideal in winter, and if you seek it out as a place to retreat from cold weather, no one will ever find you. Summers are scorching hot, however.

Getting to Mayaguana presents a problem. **Bahamasair** flies in here to a little airstrip, but only the most adventurous of travelers seek the place out. A plane wings in from Nassau only on Tuesday and Saturday.

Some of the yachting crowd on their way to the Caribbean stop here, and in winter they may wish this was their location sometimes when they're sitting around a roaring fire in a tavern in the Abacos, waiting for the chill to dissipate. But when they stop by, it's usually just for a quick look and then on their way. This is not a port of entry.

You could take the **mailboat** out of Nassau. The M/V *Windward Express,* going also to Crooked Island, Acklins, and Fortune Island (Long Cay), makes a stop at Mayaguana. For information on the days and times of departure from Nassau and return, check with the dockmaster at Potter's Cay Dock in Nassau (tel. 809/323-1064).

If you should find yourself on the island, ask to be shown to a little café and guesthouse belonging to **Doris and Cap Brown** (no phone). They'll feed you some locally caught seafood and, maybe, put you up for the night. They're at Abraham's Bay, the biggest and most populated place on the island.

7. INAGUA

The most southerly and third-largest island of The Bahamas, Great Inagua, some 40 miles long and 20 miles wide, is a flat land that is home to 1,150 people. It lies 325 miles southeast of Nassau. Henri Christophe, the self-proclaimed Haitian king, is supposed to have had a summer palace built for himself here in the very early part of the 19th century, but no traces seem to be in evidence today. This island is much closer to Haiti than it is to the Bahamian capital.

Long before the coming of Christophe, in 1687, a Captain Phipps discovered 26 tons of Spanish treasure from sunken galleons off these shores.

This is not only the site of the Morton Salt Crystal Factory, here since 1800, but it is also one of the largest nesting grounds for flamingos in the western hemisphere. The National Trust of The Bahamas protects the area around **Lake Windsor** where the birds breed, and the population is said to number 50,000. Besides the pink flamingo, the Bahamian national bird, you can also see roseate spoonbills and other birdlife here.

Flamingos used to inhabit all of The Bahamas, but the bird is nearly extinct in many places, and the reserve can only be visited with a guide. Before going to Inagua, serious birdwatchers should get in touch with Trust Office in Nassau, P.O. Box N-4105 (tel. 809/322-8333).

Green turtles are raised here too, at **Union Park.** They are then released into the ocean to make their way as best they can, as they too are an endangered species. The vast windward island, almost within sight of Cuba, is also inhabited by wild hogs, horses, and donkeys.

The settlement of **Matthew Town** is the chief hamlet of the island, but it's not of any great sightseeing interest. Other sites have interesting names, such as Doghead Point, Lantern Head, Conch Shell Point, and Mutton Fish Point, with Devil's Point making one wonder what happened there to give rise to the name. There's an 1870 lighthouse at Matthew Town.

Bahamasair wings into Matthew Town via Mayaguana twice a week, returning on the same day.

Little Inagua has no population. It's just a little speck of land off the northeast coast of Great Inagua, about 30 square miles in area. It has much birdlife, including West Indian tree ducks, and wild goats and donkeys live there.

FOOD AND LODGING: Of the guesthouses on this remote island, I prefer **Main House,** Matthew Town, Inagua, The Bahamas (tel. Matthew Town 4267). Owned by Morton Bahamas Ltd., the salt people, this place is for the willing recluse or the devotee of flamingos, which abound on the island. Only eight bedrooms are rented, and the furnishings are modest. The rates, in effect all year, are $25 per day in a single room, $40 per day in a double, and $55 in a triple, all these tariffs on the EP. The dining room is simply furnished, and the cook prepares good meals with an emphasis on locally caught fish. Life is casual and decidedly informal.

Ford's Inagua Inn, Inagua, The Bahamas (tel. Matthew Town 4277), is built of concrete blocks, lying about a mile from the airport and always hosting birdwatchers every year. Leon Ford is proud of his island and likes to share it with you. He opens (usually) the last week in July, closing the first week in April. In summer and winter, he charges $35 per day for his simply furnished rooms, suitable for either a single or double. You can get good Bahamian seafood from his kitchen.

8. RAGGED ISLAND AND JUMENTO CAYS

This, the most remote territory recommended in this guidebook, might come under the classification of "far-away places with strange-sounding names." The area is visited by very few tourists, except for a few stray people who come in on yachts.

The thing that's truly memorable here is the sunset, which daily, except in the rare times when clouds obscure the sky and the horizon, bursts forth in some of the most spectacular golds, purples, reds, and oranges, sometimes with a green flash, to be seen in The Bahamas, reflected in the gin-clear waters.

This island group, a mini-archipelago, begins with Jumento Cays off the west point of Long Island, running in a half-moon shape for some 100 miles down to Ragged Island, with Little Ragged Island as the southernmost bit of land at the bottom of the crescent. They comprise the southeastern limit of the Great Bahama Bank.

Ragged Island and its string of uninhabited cays could be called the backwater of The Bahamas, since most of them are so tiny and so unimportant they don't often appear on maps. However, visitors who return from this area talk of the remarkable beauty of the little pieces of land and coral of these cays.

Sailing in this area in bad weather is considered dangerous because of the unrelenting winds. Otherwise the cays would probably be better known among the boating crowd. In summer it's usually a good place to cruise the waters.

Like nearly all the islands considered in this chapter, Ragged Island knew greater prosperity when hundreds of inhabitants worked its salt flats. Today Duncan Town, the little hamlet still standing on the island, evokes a far-away memory. Some of its people are hard-working and weather-beaten, and many have a difficult time making a living. Nassau seems to have forgotten this outpost of the nation.

Visitors are so rare that anybody's arrival is treated as an event, and the townspeople are eager to help in any way they can. There's a 3,000-foot paved airstrip here, but it's only accessible for private planes to land on, so it's not much used.

Some of the little cays, from Jumento Cay around the semicircle toward Ragged Island, with names I like are No Bush Cay, Dead Cay, Sisters, Nurse Cay, Double-Breasted Cay (my favorite name), and Hog Cay. There's a Raccoon Cay and a Raccoon Cut. A light tower stands on Flamingo Cay.

A mailboat, the M/V *Captain Moxey,* leaves Potter's Cay Dock in Nassau on Thursday en route to Ragged Island. It returns on Sunday. For details about costs and sailing, contact the dockmaster at Potter's Cay Dock, Nassau (tel. 809/323-1064).

Regrettably, there are no hotel facilities for tourists.

PART THREE

TURKS AND CAICOS

CHAPTER XVI

TURKS AND CAICOS

□ □ □

1. GRAND TURK
2. SALT CAY
3. NORTH CAICOS
4. MIDDLE CAICOS
5. SOUTH CAICOS
6. PROVIDENCIALES
7. PINE CAY

A recent discovery of sun-seeking vacationers, Turks and Caicos have long been called "the forgotten islands," but there is now talk of a "second Bahamas" in the making. Although they are actually a part of the Bahamian archipelago, they are under a separate government and are tucked away to the east of the southernmost islands of The Bahamas. They are directly north of Haiti and the Dominican Republic, at the crossroads of the Caribbean and the Americas. *Le Figaro* once quoted a developer, and I concur, that "these islands will be the only place left where the jet set, tired of Florida and The Bahamas, will be able to take refuge. They already are!"

The Turks take their name from a local cactus with a scarlet blossom, which resembles the Turkish fez. The word *caicos* is probably derived from the word *cayos,* Spanish for cays or small islands.

The Arawak Indians first settled the Turks and Caicos Islands, and in time Ponce de León sighted the little chain in 1512, although there are those who believe that Columbus landed here, not at San Salvador (Watling Island) or Samana Cay in The Bahamas. It was not far to the south, in the waters off the north coast of Hispaniola (the part that is now Haiti), that the *Santa Maria,* the flagship of the discovery fleet of Columbus, sank on Christmas night, 1492.

Pirates marauding on ships on the Spanish Main learned of the hidden coves of Turks and Caicos, from which they ventured out to plunder Spanish galleons sailing out of Cuba and Haiti. This nest of cutthroats was called "Brothers of the Coast," multiracial pirates. The most famous of these was Rackam the Red, an Englishman.

After the Arawaks were removed to their doom in the mines of Hispaniola, the islands had no permanent inhabitants until 1678. In that year the Bermudians, who had built ships and were searching for goods to trade with the American colonies, established the salt-raking industry. The Spanish drove the Bermudians away in 1710, but they soon returned and thereafter repelled attacks by both Spain and France. Their ranks were augmented during and after the American Revolution by Loyalists fleeing America, bringing with them the slaves who had worked their plantations, adding to the island population of bond servants of African ancestry.

Bermuda finally lost out in Turks and Caicos in 1799, when representation in the Bahamian assembly was given to the little island neighbors to the southeast. This attachment to The Bahamas ended in 1848. The people of Turks and Caicos petitioned to withdraw from the assembly that met in Nassau. They said the Bahamian government had paid no attention to them except to send collectors of the salt tax, and that they saw the mailboat only four times each year.

The islands were allowed to break their ties with their northern relatives and to have their own president and council, supervised as a separate colony by the governor of Jamaica. After a quarter of a century, however, they were annexed by Jamaica as a dependency. It was not until 1962, when Jamaica became independent, that the little group of islands became a separate British Crown Colony.

Turks and Caicos are mainly self-governing today, having a governor selected by Queen Elizabeth, who is her representative in island affairs and appoints the chief minister. He or she, in turn, appoints minor ministers.

The Caicos Passage separates Turks and Caicos from The Bahamas, some 30 miles away. Turks is separated from Caicos by a 22-mile deep-water channel. The entire land mass of Turks and Caicos consists of only 193 square miles. With a population of 7,000 citizens—mostly black or mulatto—who live on six of the colony's islands and cays, everybody could have about a mile of private beach.

Of the Turks Islands, Grand Turk and Salt Cay are regularly inhabited. Northwest of the Turks, the Caicos group includes six principal islands, of which South Caicos and North Caicos are the most important. Coming into the limelight is Providenciales, a little island just west and north of North Caicos, which is rapidly being "discovered" and developed for tourism.

Grand Turk and Salt Cay on Turks Island and Cockburn Harbour on South Caicos are ports of entry.

Many of the islanders today work in the salt-raking industry; others are engaged in the export of lobsters (crayfish) and conch, as well as conch shells.

The mean temperature in these islands is 82° Fahrenheit, dropping to 77° at night, but the cooling breezes of the prevailing trade winds prevent the climate from being oppressive, a fact that vacationers are learning and taking advantage of. Perhaps the first VIP to recognize the attractions of these islands for a holiday retreat was Haiti's self-proclaimed King Henri Christophe, who is rumored to have made excursions to South Caicos in the early 19th century.

The Turks and Caicos Islands are a coral-reef paradise, shut off from the world, free of pollution and crowds. Even with increasing development as a tourist mecca under way, the beauty and tranquility of this little island chain is sure to be still in existence for the foreseeable future.

GETTING THERE: Miami is the gateway for most North American flights headed for Turks and Caicos. Your most economical passage will depend on whatever major carrier is offering reduced passage to that city on the day of your intended departure.

In Miami, **Pan American** is the only carrier flying from the U.S. mainland to Turks and Caicos. Flights depart every Sunday, Tuesday, and Friday from Grand Turk, returning immediately to Miami after a 1½ hour transit. Flights go from Miami to Provo every Monday, Tuesday, Thursday, and Saturday, returning immediately after landing there. If you want to be in Provo on a day when Pan Am flies only to Grand Turk, or vice versa, you must connect on TCNA (see below).

Bahamasair flies from Nassau to South Caicos.

GETTING AROUND: This can be a problem. There is almost no ferry service among the islands. Car-rental agencies are few and far between, and most visitors don't use this means of transport. Each of the islands has taxi drivers with just-adequate vehicles. They will carry you to and from your hotel and the airfields. They'll also deposit you on an isolated beach and return at a predetermined time to pick you up.

Of all the colony's islands, a car on Providenciales might be the most useful, because of its size and the far-flung nature of its hotel and restaurant locations. There are some local outfits, but advance reservations with them are practically impossible. The only national car-rental agency with a franchise in Provo is **Budget Rent-a-Car,** Butterfield Square (tel. 809/946-4214). A Mazda 323, with automatic transmission, rents for $210 a week, with unlimited mileage. This contract requires a seven-day advance booking and that drivers be at least 25 years of age. Collision damage costs $73.50 per week, and the holder of such a policy is freed of financial responsibility in case of an accident. If you don't buy it, you are responsible for all damages to the car. A slightly bigger vehicle, a Ford Tempo or a Mazda 626, costs $252 per week. For reservations and information in the United States, call toll free 800/527-0700.

Taxis are found at the three airports at Providenciales, South Caicos, and Grand Turk. They'll quote you a fixed price to the various hotels. Don't be surprised if your ride is shared (the government is trying to save fuel).

If you wish to visit the outlying islands, and if you don't own or rent your own boat, you can travel by **Turk and Caicos National Airlines** (TCNA), the inter-island plane service which has frequent flights to the **Out Islands.** Some flights, for example, take only three minutes. The local airline is ideal for island hopping, as it provides a twice-daily scheduled air-taxi service to all the inhabited islands as well as charter services. However, make sure you've nailed down a reservation at the airport.

PRACTICAL FACTS: The inns of Turks and Caicos are small and personally run, very casual, and island entertainment is most often impromptu. The islands have no TV, no daily papers, but there is a radio station. Most visitors are interested in skin- and scuba-diving, fishing, sailing, and boating. Divers still dream of finding that legendary chest of gold hidden in the coral reefs or underwater caverns. *Note:* These islands are recommended only to those readers who dare to venture off the beaten track.

Churches: The islanders are deeply religious, and details of church services are available from your hotel.

Clothing: Generally, dress on these islands is informal. Light cotton clothing is the most comfortable. Jackets or ties are not required in the evening for men in bars or dining rooms. A light sweater is advisable for breezy evenings.

Crime: Although crime is minimal in the islands, petty theft does take place, so protect your valuables, money, and cameras. Don't leave luggage or parcels in an unattended car. Beaches are vulnerable to thievery, so don't take chances.

Currency: The U.S. dollar is the coin of the realm here.

Customs: On arriving, you may bring in one quart of liquor, 200 cigarettes, 50 cigars, or eight ounces of tobacco duty free. There is no restriction on cameras, film, sports equipment, or personal items provided they aren't for resale. *Absolutely no spearguns are allowed,* and the import of firearms without a permit is

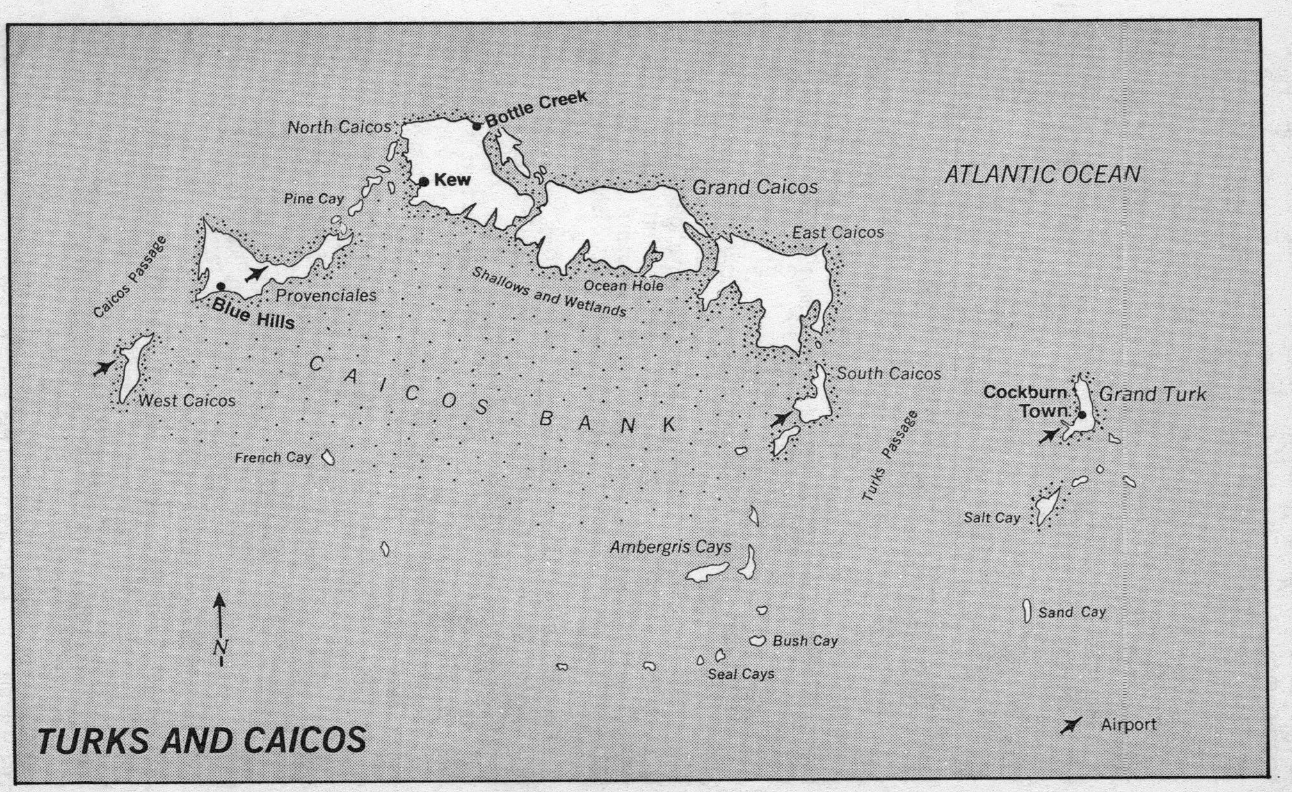
North Caicos
Bottle Creek
Kew
Pine Cay
Grand Caicos
ATLANTIC OCEAN
East Caicos
Caicos Passage
Provenciales
Blue Hills
Shallows and Wetlands
Ocean Hole
West Caicos
C A I C O S B A N K
South Caicos
Cockburn Town
Grand Turk
French Cay
Turks Passage
Salt Cay
Ambergris Cays
Sand Cay
Bush Cay
Seal Cays
N
Airport
TURKS AND CAICOS

also prohibited. Illegal drugs imported bring heavy fines and lengthy terms of imprisonment.

Each U.S. citizen is eligible for a $100 duty-free exemption if he or she has been out of the country for at least 48 hours and if a period of 31 days has elapsed since that privilege was last exercised. This allowance may include a quart of liquor. In addition, you can mail home a number of gifts to friends and relatives amounting to $10 or less per day and not to include more than four ounces of liquor or one ounce of perfume.

Documents: Proof of citizenship is required to enter Turks and Caicos—either a passport, birth certificate, or voter registration card. A driver's license is not considered valid. All visitors must hold a round-trip ticket and may stay for up to 30 days. One 30-day extension is normally granted.

Electricity: The electric current on Turks and Caicos is 110 volts, 60 cycles, AC.

Food: The specialties are whelk soup, conch chowder and fritters, lobster, and special types of fresh fish.

Information: A new facility, the **Turks and Caicos Sales and Information Office,** Grand Turk, is open from 8 a.m. to 4 p.m. Monday to Friday. The U.S. public relations and marketing representative for the **Turks and Caicos Tourist Board, Medhurst & Associates,** is located at 1208 Washington Drive, Centerport, NY 11721 (tel. 516/673-0150).

Language: The official language is English.

Medical care: Should you become ill, the islands are served by three medical practitioners and a qualified nursing staff. There is a 20-bed hospital on Grand Turk with X-ray facilities, an operating theater, and a pathology laboratory, and there are clinics on South Caicos, Middle Caicos, and North Caicos. All the islands are served by one dentist. Anyone critically ill is transferred to Grand Turk for hospital treatment or evacuated to Nassau, Miami, or Jamaica for specialist treatment.

Post office: The General Post Office is on Grand Turk, and there are suboffices on South Caicos, Salt Cay, Providenciales, Kew, Bottle Creek, and Middle Caicos. They are open from 8 a.m. to 4:30 p.m. Monday to Thursday, from 7 a.m. to 1:30 p.m. on Friday. The post office telephone number is 809/946-2300, ext. 35.

Shopping: You can purchase native straw and shell work, sponges, and rate conch pearls here and there on the islands.

Stamps: Collectors consider the stamps of Turks and Caicos as valuable, and there is a philatelic bureau that operates separately from the post office to take care of the demand. It is the **Turks & Caicos Islands Philatelic Bureau,** P.O. Box 121, Grand Turk, Turks Islands.

Taxes: There is a departure tax of $10, payable when you leave the islands. Also, the government collects a 7% occupancy tax, applicable to all hotels, guesthouses, and restaurants in the 40-island chain.

Telecommunications: It's not too difficult to keep in touch with the outside world—if you really want to. **Cable & Wireless Ltd.** provides a modern diversified international service via submarine cable and an earth station. There are automatic exchanges on Grand Turk, South Caicos, and Providenciales. Incoming direct dialing is available from the U.S., the U.K., and most countries in the world. Outgoing direct dialing is being introduced. The Telex service is fully automatic, operating 24 hours a day. The international-operator telephone service is available 24 hours a day and the telegraph service from 8 a.m. to 5 p.m. Monday to Friday from the company's main office on Front Street, Cockburn Town, Grand Turk.

Time: The islands have the same time as Miami, Florida; that is, they are in the Eastern Time Zone.

Water: Remember that water is precious on Turks and Caicos. Try to conserve it.

1. GRAND TURK

The most important of the island chain, Grand Turk (Cockburn Town), with its Government House, is the capital of Turks and Caicos. Cockburn (pronounced Coburn) Town is also the financial and business hub. The largest concentration of population in the colony is here, 3,500 people.

Cockburn Town may remind you of New Plymouth on Green Turtle Cay, but there's more bustle here because of the larger number of inhabitants. The harbor road is called Front Street, as is the one in Hamilton, the capital of Bermuda.

Grand Turk is rather barren, and it's windswept. There is little vegetation, so don't come here expecting to find a lush tropical island.

Once this was the teeming headquarters of a thriving salt industry. Today there are those who want to restore the economy of the colony by making Grand Turk an offshore banking center like the Cayman Islands, but that may be difficult. There are many problems to face with both Great Britain and the U.S. government.

Grand Turk was in the limelight in 1962, when John Glenn, the first American astronaut to orbit the earth, alit in the ocean about 40 miles offshore and was brought in by helicopter to the U.S. Air Force Base here, to be welcomed by Vice-President Lyndon Johnson.

Chances are, if you come here for your vacation, you'll land at Grand Turk. You'll find Governor's Beach, near—you guessed it—the governor's residence. It's the best for swimming. At least, if you are going on to another of the islands, take time to tour the town's historic section, particularly Duke and Front Streets. Here, three-story houses built of wood and limestone stand along the waterfront.

WHERE TO STAY: In many ways, **Island Reef,** PMB 10, Grand Turk, Turks and Caicos, B.W.I. (tel. 809/946-2055, or 817/778-3547 in Temple, Texas), is the most desirable hotel on the island, occupying a stretch of beachfront on the eastern coast. As you negotiate the steep access road that winds down to it, a sweeping view of the sea seems to surround the property in an azure frame. Pleasantly isolated, this is the domain of Texas-born entrepreneurs Tom and Shirley Strasburger. Stretched end to end along the beachfront, and interconnected with a sunny boardwalk, the 21 accommodations each contain a fully equipped kitchenette and a design like that of a comfortably furnished studio apartment. Each was prefabricated in the U.S., then constructed on the site the Strasburgers selected as one of the most attractive.

Each unit contains air conditioning and has maid service and a view of the water. Year-round rates in efficiency apartments run $100 daily for one person. Each additional occupant up to a maximum of four pays $20 per day. A one-bedroom apartment occupied by one person costs $150 per day, with each additional occupant up to a maximum of six paying $20 per person. Taxes and service are extra. Guests can use a small freshwater pool and play on a tennis court. Food is served in a cabaña restaurant whose thatch roof is supported by vertical beams. The 12-acre complex is self-sufficient, as it contains its own desalinization plant, generator, and irrigation system.

Turks Head Inn, P.O. Box 58, Grand Turk, Turks and Caicos, B.W.I (tel.

809/946-2466), is an adaptation of a century-old building constructed by a Bermudian shipwright. It is the principality's oldest pub. Typically, there is a two-level covered veranda with an ornate cut-out balustrade. The inn, owned by H.R. Russell, is placed in an old garden with towering trees and a shady terrace with outdoor tables. A thatch-roofed addition shelters outdoor diners. An indoor dining room has about as simple a decor as you'll find anywhere. Raffish and tropical, the establishment enjoys popularity with divers, writers, local eccentrics, and the occasional contessa who happens to be barefooting her way through the islands. The well-flavored food is served informally, in copious portions. Specialties are recited by a waitress and, depending on the mood of the chef, might include baked grouper, steak, lobster, or steak and lobster on the same platter. Full dinners cost from $20; lunches, from $12; and breakfasts (an island event beginning daily at 8 a.m. and lasting till 3 p.m.), $6. In winter, dinner is offered on Tuesday and Thursday from 6 to 9 p.m. However, when business is good, and there are more visitors to Grand Turk, the evening meal is presented more frequently, including a sometimes-offered prime rib special banquet.

In addition to the restaurant, the inn maintains 11 very simple accommodations. A few contain four-poster beds with canopies. One even has a waterbed. Year-round rates are $30 daily in a single, $50 in a double.

Hotel Kittina, P.O. Box 42, Grand Turk, Turks and Caicos, B.W.1. (tel. 809/946-2232, or 305/667-0966 in Coconut Grove, Fla.), is an island inn whose owners, Tina and Kitt Fenimore, are credited with giving tourism on Grand Turk its initial boost. Their hotel straddles two sides of the main street leading through the center of town. The older section is a low-slung building covered with trailing vines and bougainvillea. It contains a bar and restaurant. The Sandpiper Restaurant is one of the best known on the island, offering a combination of American and local dishes with an emphasis on freshly caught seafood such as lobster and red snapper. The conch chowder is invariably good. Watch for special buffets.

Across the street rise the modern two-story town houses containing the newer accommodations. Each of these has a ceiling crafted from varnished pine, carpeting, a kitchen, a veranda with a view of the sea, air conditioning, and ceiling fans. The units on the upper floors benefit from high ceilings and more space. *In summer, rooms in the older section cost two people from $65 to $75 daily, with newer units renting for $105 to $115. A two-bedroom suite, suitable for four persons, is priced at $190 daily.* In winter, accommodations in the older section cost two people $85 to $95 daily, rising to $120 to $140 in the newer section. A two-bedroom suite for four guests costs $220 daily.

You can snorkel or swim near the white sands of the hotel's beach. If you're sailing, be sure to ask one of the Fenimore's sons for instructions on the best places to moor your sailboat.

Salt Raker Inn, P.O. Box 1, Duke Street, Grand Turk, Turks and Caicos, B.W.1. (tel. 809/946-2260). Consciously informal, it occupies a clapboard house which was originally built in 1810 by a Bermudian shipwright. Its English colonial style is visible in its wraparound veranda, where guests can rock in chairs overlooking the ocean and a garden filled with bougainvillea. The main house, set close to the road paralleling the sea, contains a wide front hallway, a guest library, and the establishment's office. The owners charge year-round rates of $35 to $98 daily in a double, $35 to $78 in a single, depending on the accommodation and size. Each of the rooms has a private bath and a ceiling fan, and some offer air conditioning as well. The two large upstairs suites have a veranda overlooking the sea. The downstairs accommodation has a large screened porch. Several other units are in two motel units spread end to end on either side of the garden.

Meals at the Salt Raker are simple but well prepared and served beneath a fiberglass canopy in the rear garden. Full dinners, offered from 6:30 to 9 p.m. daily, cost from $20, including such specialties as an award-winning version of barbecued spareribs junkanoo, three different preparations of grouper, and steaks. Lunches, from noon to 6:30 p.m., cost from $8. The owners state, "We're not the Hilton, nor is Grand Turk Hawaii, but we do have a large number of return guests who enjoy our intimacy, and the friendly, informal atmosphere."

WHERE TO DINE: With its West Indian accents and its clientele of English colonials and American boatmen, **Papillon's Rendez-Vous** (tel. 809/946-2088) lies between the seashore and the main road running out of town. It's sheltered behind a screen of pinewood lattices and flowering vines. To enjoy the atmosphere, you should order a drink amid the antiques of the nautical bar before your meal. Full dinners cost from $20. Service is every evening except Sunday from 6 to 9:30 and reservations are important. Food items are likely to include lobster, escargots, rib-eye steak, baked snapper, pepper steak, and the fresh catch of the day. The restaurant is closed in September.

"Xs" (tel. 809/946-2775) is owned by a Frenchman, Xavier Tonneau, although it is decorated a bit like an English pub, with plates on the walls, mahogany paneling, framed prints, and lots of cozy warmth. It is open daily from noon to 3 a.m., serving both as a pub and a restaurant throughout its long business day. Specialties include some continental dishes along with island fare such as soups, pâtés, escargot, conch salad, and conch fritters. Main courses feature the catch of the day, lobster, and steak. Full meals cost from $20 per person, but could go as high as $32. The establishment lies in the center of town.

The Pepper Pot (tel. 809/946-2083). Guests dine on battered plastic tables amid crêpe-paper streamers and the kind of decor that might have adorned a 1930s dance at a junior high school prom. Despite its drawbacks, diners retain a happy memory of this place. It's the domain of a hard-working member of the island's Anglican church, Philistina Louise (Peanuts) Butterfield. Born in North Caicos, she has attracted an ardent array of fans. Her conch fritters, carefully frozen and packaged, accompany diners back to the U.S. where they've been served at receptions on Fifth Avenue.

To dine here, you must phone in the evening of the day before your arrival. Any taxi driver in town will conduct you to the clean but simple cement-sided house and pick you up at a prearranged time at the end of your meal. The menu depends on whatever Peanuts produced that day. It's likely to be lobster with all the fixings. Full meals cost from $25 and are served only at dinner at a time mutually agreed upon.

DIVE OPERATIONS: On Duke Street, **Omega Diving Services** (tel. 809/946-2232) occupies a clapboard West Indian house a few steps from the reception area of the Kittina Hotel, with which it is associated. Some of the operations equipment, including a flat-top dive boat, was originally part of a scientific underwater research venture. The safety-conscious divemasters and instructors offer a morning two-tank dive for $55 and a one-tank afternoon dive for $35. Full PADI registration, with all equipment and boat fees included, goes for $350, requiring between three and seven days. Most divers combine underwater excursions with hotel packages at the previously recommended Kittina Hotel. Accommodations arranged in this way are usually less expensive.

2. SALT CAY

Just nine miles from Grand Turk, this sparsely settled cay is named for its salt ponds, a once-flourishing industry that may be revived. The cay has a land mass of 3½ square miles, with a beautiful beach bordering the north coast. The island is most often reached by boat or by air, a five-minute flight from Grand Turk.

You can walk down to the salinas and see the windmills that once powered the salt business, and you can stroll past the 150-year-old "White House," built by a Bermudian salt raker. In addition, you can visit the ruins of an old whaling station and learn how fearless seamen caught whales in the early 19th century. It's also possible to drop in at the local school, where the children are likely to greet you with island calypso songs.

Essentially, Salt Cay is peaceful, quiet, and colorful—the perfect relaxation spot to get away from it all.

FOOD AND LODGING: A homey place, **Mount Pleasant Guest House,** Salt Cay, Turks and Caicos, B.W.I. (tel. 809/946-2485), owned by James N. Morgan, is a remote outpost offering simple accommodations. Year-round, tariffs are $75 daily in a double, $50 in a single, on the full-board plan. Tax and service are extra.

Bethel manages the guesthouse, and her skill with the local cuisine, particularly native dishes and seafood, is known all over the island. This is one of the friendliest little oases you're likely to encounter between Bermuda and Venezuela. The guesthouse is ideal for a relaxing holiday with an excellent beach on the north coast about a 20-minute walk from the front door. The water is crystal clear, with coral heads running close to the beach, which makes it ideal for snorkeling. Guests are reminded to bring their own snorkeling gear.

3. NORTH CAICOS

This island is strictly for people who want to get away from something. If you're seeking deserted soft white sand beaches and crystal clear water, then this is the place. No one dresses up here, so leave your jacket and tie at home. It contains miles and miles of sandy beaches and is surrounded by a sea teeming with fish—an ideal place for snorkelers. Experienced guides can take you fishing for snapper, barracuda, or bonefish. Beach picnics, boating excursions, and fish cookouts on deserted cays are easily arranged. You can snorkel on a barrier reef or tour the island by taxi. A resort in the making, North Caicos is slated for development.

The local airline runs connecting flights to the island's terminal. If you disembark at Providenciales, the airline takes only six minutes to fly you to North Caicos.

For a day's adventure, you can take a car-ferry over to Middle Caicos (see below).

FOOD AND LODGING: A good choice is **Pelican Beach Hotel,** North Caicos, Turks and Caicos, B.W.I. (tel. 809/946-4290), the culmination of a dream of Clifford Gardiner, a native of North Caicos who has always believed in its future possibilities. He operated Gardiner Flying Service, but he always wanted to get into the hotel business, so he opened this attractive, modern, eight-room facility in 1975. In winter, rooms cost $110 daily in a single, $150 in a double, on MAP. *In summer, MAP is $75 daily in a single, $100 in a double.* In 1984 Mr. Gardiner won acclaim from the then chief minister who came here to voice praise to the hotelier for his "blood, sweat, and tears" in getting the hotel launched. The hotel also offers skindiving and snorkeling trips. You can snorkel for a half day for $17; a full day, for $25 (with a native lunch cooked on the beach, $30). Mask, fins, and snorkel are included in the prices. Waterskiing and fishing trips cost $50 per hour, with crew and equipment.

For reservations, call 305/577-0133 in Miami.

Ocean Beach Hotel, North Caicos, Turks and Caicos, B.W.I. (tel. 809/946-4290), sits on a fine beach, and its accommodations lie within a U-shaped motel-like building composed of cedarwood and local stone. There are 10 comfortable units, permutations of which can create up to 16 accommodations. Year-round EP rates are from $89 to $110 daily in a single and from $100 to $120 in a double. A two-bedroom suite costs $170 daily for up to four occupants. This is a family-owned and -operated establishment, managed by Karen L. Preikschat, who has studied at Humber College, Toronto, and at Cornell University. From November to April the place is in full hotel operation. From May to October, units are self-contained and the restaurant and bar are closed.

For reservations, get in touch with Preikschat, P.O. Box 1152, Station B, Burlington, Ontario, Canada L7P 3S9 (tel. 416/336-2876); or Robert Reid Associates, Inc. (tel. toll free 800/223-6510).

4. MIDDLE CAICOS

Towering limestone cliffs protruding into the sea along the north coast, scalloped with secluded beaches, give Middle Caicos the most dramatic coastline of the islands. Conch Barr offers cathedral-size **caves** once used by the Lucayans, as attested by artifacts of the Indians found within. In the 1880s these caves were the site of a thriving guano export industry. Nearby, wild cotton plants are descended from the days when Loyalists from the southern colonies in the new United States came in the 18th century to try their hand at establishing plantations.

Middle Caicos men were some of the most expert boatbuilders in the islands, making their vessels from pine from the middle island's pine groves. The boats were used by fishermen working the waters around many of the cays, and gathering conchs for shipment to Haiti.

Most visitors come to Middle Caicos on a tour just for the day for a visit to the caves. Ask at your hotel if any will be going during your stay.

Accommodations on Middle Caicos can be found only in private homes, if you want to stay over.

5. SOUTH CAICOS

Some of the finest diving and snorkeling in The Bahamas or in this Crown Colony are found here, and there are numerous secluded coves around the island. The coral reefs are spectacular. Long Beach is a beachcomber's paradise. One visitor wrote, "This is like escaping to another era." There are always locals available to take you sailing, boating, or fishing for a small fee.

Some 600 miles southeast of Miami, South Caicos has a 6,500-foot paved and lit jetport where passengers disembark heading for Cockburn Harbour. The island may appear nearly deserted, although there are 1,400 permanent residents and what one local described as "about 65 vehicles and a few wild horses and donkeys in the bush."

FOOD AND LODGING: A two-story, motel-like structure, **Harbour View Hotel,** South Caicos, Turks and Caicos, B.W.I. (tel. 809/946-3251), is set on sandy terrain between the harbor and the town. From the upper veranda, visitors can look over the rocky coastline or the scattered bungalows of the town. Accommodations are exceptionally simple, with double beds and couches clustered in walls of painted concrete. The hotel charges $25 to $0 daily in a single, $35 to $55 in a double, EP.

The Lightbourne Restaurant in the hotel is a casual place, where you can enjoy island cooking from 6 a.m. to 9 p.m. daily. A special buffet dinner is often served on weekends. There is entertainment at the bar and nightclub on Friday and Saturday. The bar opens at 11 a.m. and closes when the customers decide to leave.

6. PROVIDENCIALES

Affectionately known as "Provo," this is an unspoiled island with splendid beaches. Don't expect supper clubs, casinos, or television, and certainly there are no traffic jams. What you get instead is an island of peaceful rolling hills, clear, clear water, white beaches, a natural deep harbor, flowering cactus, and a barrier reef attracting swimmers, divers, and boaters. The roads may not be paved, but you'll still find some stores and two full-service banks. The island is served by an airport capable of handling wide-body jets and has good marina and diving facilities. The opening of Club Med has brought dozens of new visitors, and the place isn't as sleepy as it used to be.

Caicos Conch Farm (call Marco Travel at 809/946-4393 for an appointment to visit it). On an isolated section of the island, in a region surrounded with scrub and sand, this establishment is a pioneer in the commercially viable production of conch. Tours are offered of its breeding basins every Tuesday and Thursday at 3:30 p.m. For tours of the hatchery and laboratory, along with a visit to the gift shop, adults pay $6; children, $3. There's an annex for the enhanced production of algae as well. Rare conch pearls, shell jewelry, and conch T-shirts are for sale.

WHERE TO STAY: Groundbreaking on a new luxury resort hotel, **Ramada Turquoise Reef Resort Hotel & Casino** occurred in 1988. This is slated to be a three-story, 230-room beachfront hotel and casino, estimated to cost $27 million and occupying 15½ acres of prime land in the center of Grace Bay on the north shore of Providenciales. Check its status with a travel agent before booking a hotel on Provo.

Club Med–"Turkoise," Providenciales, Turks and Caicos, B.W.I. (tel. 809/964-4491, 212/977-2100 in New York City, or toll free 800/CLUB-MED), lies on a 70-acre tract of land near Grace Bay, ten miles from the airport. This link in the Club Med chain was erected near a bleached-white sweep of sand for a total cost of $27 million. An irrigation system keeps the arid landscape green. Whether or not you like communal-style vacations, Club Med makes holiday-making easy. This particular branch opened in 1984, and it was conceived as "the most upscale" of all the club villages in the western hemisphere. The village-style cluster of two- and three-story accommodations are painted a pastel pink and capped with cedar shingles imported from Sweden. All meals and most sports are included in the weekly package rates. Drinks are paid for with beads from a necklace. Scuba-diving is included on a space-available basis. Other group activities, part of the package, include windsurfing, sailing, waterskiing, and arts and crafts. There are two Jacuzzis on the property, along with eight tennis courts, four of which are lit for night games. A disco keeps residents active if they wish, from 11:30 p.m. to 3 a.m. nightly.

The resort contains 600 beds, each twin size. Meals are shared at long tables, where the house wine is served in pitchers. Club Med prices its vacations by the week on a per-person basis. In winter, the charge for a seven-night stay, all-inclusive stay ranges from $880 to $1,300 per person. *From May 6 to December 6, charges are lowered to $850 per person weekly all inclusive.* These tariffs include services within the resort, but the cost of transfers is paid by Club Med only for those clients who opt for air fare as part of their land package arrangements. First-time visitors pay a $30 initiation fee to Club Med. After that, there's an annual membership fee of $50 per year for adults and $20 for each child under 12.

Third Turtle Inn, Providenciales, Turks and Caicos, B.W.I. (tel. 809/946-

4230). Imaginative and unusual, this is the most oddly located, and perhaps the most alluring, hotel on the island. Unless you arrive by boat (and many guests do), you leave your car in a sandy parking lot, then trek across a timber-and-plank catwalk above the tidal pools of a sheltered inlet. Built of redwood and natural rugged stone, it seems to blend in tastefully with the hillside on which it sits. The 13 living accommodations are scattered across the crest of a 20-foot cliff rising above the sea. Each is spacious and sunny, with redwood ceilings, terracotta floors, comfortably durable furniture, and verandas. Units contain a private bathroom and a border of oleander, bougainvillea, and cactus. The hotel is closed from mid-August to mid-November. Otherwise, it charges winter rates of $120 daily in a single, rising to $150 in a double and $180 in a triple. *In summer, prices are lowered to $75 daily in a single or $90 in a double and $115 in a triple.* The helpful manager since 1979 has been Gale Anspach.

The social center of the hotel sits on the piers that surround it on three sides. Colonies of ducks paddle beneath, eating table scraps. Built in 1968, the hotel boasts the most famous bar on the island, the Seven Dwarfs. The adjacent restaurant serves seafood specialties and juicy steaks which are grilled within the smoke-stained walls of a miniature grotto, a few feet from the clusters of outdoor tables.

Island Princess Hotel, Providenciales, Turks and Caicos, B.W.I. (tel. 809/946-4260). In 1979 an enterprising American engineer returned after years of building roads and dams in Iran to an island he vaguely remembered from a brief stopover many years before. Today the well-designed domain of Cal Piper includes 80 pleasant rooms, a popular bar, and a sunny dining room with a view of the sea. The hotel sits on some of the best beachfront in Provo. Built of local stone and designed in a zigzagging labyrinth of two-story annexes, the property contains acreage devoted only to gardens, plus a water-sports kiosk where visitors can rent sailboats and snorkeling equipment, or depart with divemasters on scuba expeditions. The hotel has amply proportioned sheets of glass, which are angled for the best views of the sea and the sands of the beach.

It offers an open-handed welcome, often to Canadian tour groups. Each of its comfortable bedrooms has a ceiling fan, a patio or balcony, wall-to-wall carpeting, a private bath, and big windows. All year, singles cost $65 daily; doubles, $80. Reasonably priced dive packages are available, allowing divers to take advantage of the hotel's location at the edge of "The Walls," which drops 6,000 feet into unchartered waters a short distance offshore. Meals are served in an airy dining room. The chef prepares concoctions of island seafood and international specialties. If you catch a conch or lobster during your explorations in the water, it can be prepared for your dinner.

Mariner Inn, Sapodilla Point, Providenciales, Turks and Caicos, B.W.I. (tel. 809/946-4488). Uncluttered simplicity is the byword and motto of this informal hotel whose principal decor is derived from the sweeping sea vistas around it. The only object interrupting the panorama is a Shell Oil unloading dock, a concrete-and-steel giant jutting into the sea at the bottom of the slope supporting the hotel. Even the dock, however, has a form of isolated grandeur about it. Its owners have worked hard to turn the locale into an oasis of flowering plants. These grow around the bases of the villas containing the accommodations. The social center is the sundeck, where palms and parasols protect the planking of the boardwalks which give residents access to it.

Accommodations are basic, unfussy places, with ceiling fans, bathrooms, and modern lines. *In summer, singles or doubles cost from $65 daily, with triples renting at $75.* However, prices go up in winter to $90 to $95 daily in a single or double and $105 in a triple. However, if the season is slow, this place might be closed for several months at a time. Always check before heading there.

Erebus Inn, Turtle Cove, Providenciales, Turks and Caicos, B.W.I. (tel. 809/946-4240), occupies an arid hillside above Turtle Cove on the northern shore of the island. Its ten studio apartments face the marina at the bottom of the hill. Additional accommodations are in a long and narrow stone-sided annex whose breeze-filled central hallway evokes an enlarged version of an old Bahamian house. Ringing both sections of the hotel are dry-weather plants such as cactus and carefully watered vines such as bougainvillea. In the older section, lying closer to the seacoast, guests pay year-round rates of $75 daily in a single, $85 in a double, and $95 for two in a bungalow. Newer rooms, higher up on the hillside, cost $115 to $135 for two people, depending on their exposure. The social center is the big-windowed Spinnaker Bar, whose perimeter offers a view of the marina and the gulf. There is also an open-air terrace ringed with walls of chiseled stone. The establishment is closed every year from the end of August until the beginning of October.

WHERE TO DINE: Sheltered by a low-slung hipped roof and lined with louvered shutters, **Banana Boat Restaurant,** Turtle Cove (no phone) is the best, most popular, and most attractive independent restaurant on the island. It was established in 1981. Since then there's hardly been a yachtsman on the island who hasn't enjoyed at least one of the establishment's island meals and potent drinks. Menu items include a blend of island dishes coupled with foods such as baked chicken with dressing, New York strip steak, cracked conch, lobster or tuna salads, and a cracked conch sandwich. Half-pound burgers are always a favorite. A choice perch is on the timber-and-plank veranda jutting on piers above the waters of Turtle Cove. Full meals cost from $12, unless your bar tab makes it higher. The establishment welcomes newcomers every Monday through Saturday from 11 a.m. to midnight. On Sunday, an $8 barbecue special of ribs, chicken, coleslaw, potato salad, and dessert is served from 11 a.m. to 10 p.m.

Henry's Roadrunner Restaurant, Blue Hills (tel. 809/946-4216). Intensely local and unpretentious, this island restaurant occupies a blue-sided cottage in a ramshackle but respectable neighborhood called Blue Hills. At any hour it's open you're likely to find two dozen or so of owner Henry Williams's friends playing cards, watching a blaring TV, and drinking away the heat. Established in 1975, it's a center of the island's black community. The restaurant is open daily from 8 a.m. until "late at night." The fish served is often caught by Henry himself, and it's usually the freshest on the island: red snapper, grouper, lobster, and conch. Breakfast costs from $5; a fixed-price lunch, $6; and a set dinner, $15.

THE SPORTING LIFE: On Providenciales, **Provo Turtle Divers Ltd.** (tel. 809/946-4332), with headquarters adjacent to the Third Turtle, directly in front of Erebus Inn on the water, is a dive operation offering a personalized service. Dive experts have considered Provo "one of the finest sites for diving in the world," as a barrier reef runs the full length of the island's 17-mile north coast. At Northwest Point there is a vertical dropoff to 6,000 feet.

There are scuba tanks for rent, plus ample backpacks and weight belts. Snorkel equipment is also available, plus 12 full sets of diving gear. A single dive costs $35, the tariff rising to $50 for a double dive. A boat guide costs $275 a day. Provo Turtle is a PADI training facility, with full instruction and resort courses.

Provo Aquatic Centre, Ltd. (tel. 809/946-4455), at Sapodilla Bay on the leeward side of Provo, offers various water sports. Day sails to deserted beaches and islands can be made on a 35-foot sloop. Snorkel gear, lunch, and drinks are included in the price of $35 per person. Dive 'n' sail trips, with backpack, weight belt, tank, lunch, and drinks, go for $40 per person. Snorkeling trips, with gear and instruction, are $15 per person. Waterskiing, at $30 per half hour, and windsurfer sailboards, at $15 per hour, are also offered. Qualified and licensed instruction is given in scuba-diving, sailing, snorkeling, swimming, and underwater photography.

7. PINE CAY

This exclusive territory, a private island in the West Indies, is owned and managed by members of the Meridian Club, who rightly praise its beaches, among the finest in this guide.

Pine Cay is one of a chain of islets connecting Providenciales and North Caicos. Two miles long and 800 acres in land area, it is a small residential community, with large areas set aside for a park. It has its own 3,900-foot airstrip with scheduled local air service, as well as dock and harbor facilities. No cars are allowed, and transportation is by golf cart or bicycle. There is just enough fresh water, and the cay has its own generating plant.

Once a private club, Pine Cay still has members who join the public guests for swimming, sunning, and shelling along the 2½-mile white sand beach. Snorkeling and diving are possible in an unspoiled barrier reef. Explorers look for Arawak Indian and British colonial remains. There is also a wide range of birds and plants.

To reach it, you fly to Miami and then take a Pan Am flight lasting 1½ hours to Providenciales. There, an air taxi can be arranged to meet you for the 10-minute flight to Pine Cay.

FOOD AND LODGING: A place with an eye on the future, **The Meridian Club,** Pine Cay, Turks and Caicos, B.W.I. (no phone), is part of an ambitious development that may eventually be the core of a residential country-club complex with many houses. However, that's a long way off. Facilities at the environmentally sensitive resort include the main clubhouse facing the beach and a freshwater pool. The club, often patronized by members of the Social Register, has a delightful dining room, a comfortable library, and an intimate bar with a panoramic terrace for sunset cocktails.

Two dozen vacation cottages are offered, with bed and sitting areas, dressing rooms, private showers, and terraces facing the beach. In winter, double occupancy is from $450 to $500 daily, whereas *off-season rates range from $300 to $350 daily.* For single occupancy, deduct $60 per person daily. The high standard of cuisine is complemented by the extensive use of local produce, especially lobster, conch, and snapper.

Boats, snorkel and dive gear, tennis racquets and balls, and fishing tackle are available, as are fishing guides and experienced boatmen.

For reservations and information, contact the Meridian Club, c/o Resorts Management, Inc., 201½ E. 29th St., New York, NY 10016 (tel. 212/696-4566, or toll free 800/225-4255).

Index

GENERAL

BERMUDA

THE BAHAMAS

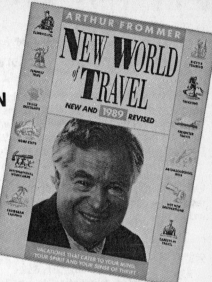

NOW, SAVE MONEY ON ALL YOUR TRAVELS!
Join Frommer's™ Dollarwise® Travel Club

Saving money while traveling is never a simple matter, which is why, over 27 years ago, the **Dollarwise Travel Club** was formed. Actually, the idea came from readers of the Frommer publications who felt that such an organization could bring financial benefits, continuing travel information, and a sense of community to economy-minded travelers all over the world.

In keeping with the money-saving concept, the annual membership fee is low—$18 (U.S. residents) or $20 U.S. (Canadian, Mexican, and foreign residents)—and is immediately exceeded by the value of your benefits which include:

1. The latest edition of any TWO of the books listed on the following pages.

2. A copy of any Frommer City Guide.

3. An annual subscription to an 8-page quarterly newspaper *The Dollarwise Traveler* which keeps you up-to-date on fastbreaking developments in good-value travel in all parts of the world—bringing you the kind of information you'd have to pay over $35 a year to obtain elsewhere. This consumer-conscious publication also includes the following columns:

Hospitality Exchange—members all over the world who are willing to provide hospitality to other members as they pass through their home cities.

Share-a-Trip—requests from members for travel companions who can share costs and help avoid the burdensome single supplement.

Readers Ask . . . Readers Reply—travel questions from members to which other members reply with authentic firsthand information.

4. Your personal membership card which entitles you to purchase through the club all Frommer publications for a third to a half off their regular retail prices during the term of your membership.

So why not join this hardy band of international Dollarwise travelers now and participate in its exchange of information and hospitality? Simply send $18 (U.S. residents) or $20 U.S. (Canadian, Mexican, and other foreign residents) along with your name and address to: Frommer's Dollarwise Travel Club, Inc., Gulf + Western Building, One Gulf + Western Plaza, New York, NY 10023. Remember to specify which *two* of the books in section (1) and which *one* in section (2) above you wish to receive in your initial package of member's benefits. Or tear out the next page, check off your choices, and send the page to us with your membership fee.

TURN PAGE FOR ADDITONAL BOOKS AND ORDER FORM.